Mix Martial Arts

A Comprehensive Guide to Boxing, Brazilian Jiu-Jitsu, Muay Thai, Wrestling, Karate, Taekwondo, Kung Fu, Judo, Sambo, and Capoeira for MMA Mastery

Table of Contents

Part 1: Boxing

What the Best Boxers Know about Training, Footwork, and Combinations That You Don't

CLINT SHARP

Boxing

WHAT THE BEST BOXERS KNOW
ABOUT TRAINING, FOOTWORK, AND
COMBINATIONS THAT YOU DON'T

Introduction

Have you ever been amazed by professional boxers' speed, agility, and technique? What do they know about training, footwork, and combinations that you don't?

From hours of intense training and years of experience in the ring, these elite athletes have developed skills giving them a competitive edge. By learning from the best boxers, you, too, can develop these skills and take your boxing to the next level. This guide will walk you through the fundamentals of boxing, from footwork and stances to punches, defense tips, and pro combinations, to get you started on your journey to becoming an expert boxer.

From the ancient Greek Olympiad to today's pay-per-view extravaganzas, the history of boxing is a thrilling tale spanning centuries. This sport has seen legendary fighters, fierce rivalries, and momentous moments that have gone down in history. A walk through the annals of boxing history reveals how this brutal sport has evolved, from bare-knuckle brawls in the 1800s to the invention of boxing gloves, which made the sport less deadly. Boxing is constantly changing. It's a sport demanding discipline, skill, and endurance from its practitioners, striving to outwit opponents and deliver the perfect knockout blow.

With such a rich history, it's no wonder boxing continues to captivate audiences worldwide, even today. This easy-to-understand guide provides an overview of the origins of boxing. Once you understand the context, you can move on to the techniques and strategies used by modern-day boxers. You'll explore important topics, such as stances, guards, punches, combinations, defense tips, and heavy bag training. You learn about common mistakes to avoid as you embark on your boxing journey. Additionally, you'll pick up helpful sparring secrets from the pros and discover how to execute those pro combinations that make successful champions in the ring.

While the sport of boxing is a serious business, you don't need to take it too seriously. Even beginners can have a great time learning the basics and developing skills in this incredibly rewarding sport. All it needs is dedication, hard work, and the right resources. If you're ready to take the plunge and enter the world of boxing, lace up your gloves and get ready for an exhilarating journey that will keep you on the edge of your seat. This guide is an excellent starting point providing everything you need to start. So, what are you waiting for? Let's get ready to rumble.

Chapter 1: The Beginning

Have you ever cheered on boxers in the ring and wondered where the sport originated? Believe it or not, boxing has a rich history that dates back centuries. In the early days, boxing matches were brutal and lacked any regulation. Boxers fought with bare knuckles, with no rules, leading to gruesome injuries. However, new laws were enacted to protect fighters from serious harm as the sport grew in popularity.

Throughout the years, boxing has evolved into the exciting and dynamic sport people know and love today. So, let's lace up your gloves and step back in time to learn more about the origins of boxing. This chapter provides a brief overview of the history and evolution of boxing, starting with its ancient roots. It highlights some of the most iconic boxers in history and their lasting legacies. By the end of the chapter, you'll better understand why boxing has become such a trendy sport.

The Fascinating Origins of Boxing: Unraveling Its Ancient Roots

Boxing has evolved in various ways over thousands of years, leading to different styles enthusiasts still practice. From gladiators in Ancient Rome to bare-knuckle fights in the 19th century, boxing has a fascinating history. This section examines the charming story of how this sport originated and its many transformations throughout history.

Ancient Egypt and Greece

Ancient Greek boxers depicted on a vase. [1]

The rich history of this fantastic sport has its roots in the ancient civilizations of Egypt, Greece, and Rome. The Greeks practiced boxing as early as the 7th century BC. It quickly became one of the most popular sports in their culture, with athletes competing in local and national competitions. The sport was steeped in mythical symbolism and was an allegory for the hero's journey. Ancient Egyptian art depicts bare-knuckle fighting contests, one of the earliest boxing forms. These fights were brutal and often ended in death, as there were no rules, gloves, or weight classes. Instead, the fighters wrapped their hands in cloth or leather, leading to the development of the first boxing gloves.

Roman Boxing

When it was introduced to the Roman Empire, boxing transformed from a sport for entertainment to a means of protection - mercenaries and soldiers engaged in fistfights to keep in shape and test their fighting abilities. As Roman influence expanded, so did boxing, and it became a regular feature in their athletic competitions, known as the gladiatorial games. These games brought together the bravest and strongest fighters from across the empire, with large crowds gathering to witness this dangerous and deadly sport.

Earliest Evidence

The earliest evidence of boxing comes from ancient Sumeria, around 3000 BC, where people wrapped their hands in leather strips for protection. At first, it was a simple form of combat, but the sport became more structured and refined through its evolution. In ancient Greece, boxing became popular during the Olympic Games in 688 BC, one of the most prestigious events. The boxers wore leather gloves with metal or lead studs to inflict more damage on their opponents. The matches were brutal, often ending with serious injuries or death.

Transformation of the Sport

In the early 18th century, boxing transformed England. The sport became more organized with the Rules of Boxing in 1743, which established weight classes, banned biting and gouging, and standardized gloves. The first recognized heavyweight champion was the English bare-knuckle boxer James Figg, who dominated the sport in the early 1700s. He established a boxing school training young fighters who later became champions.

Recent Developments

The first modern boxing match occurred in 1867 between John Sholto Douglas, the Marquis of Queensbury, and John Graham Chambers, the founder of the Amateur Athletics Club. The match followed the Marquis of Queensbury's rules, which included a three-minute round, gloves, and a ten-second count for knocked-down fighters. These rules revolutionized the sport and made boxing more accessible to the masses.

Modern Day

Boxing continued to evolve throughout the ages and reached its modern form during England's 18th and 19th centuries. The English added further innovations, such as rounds, weight classes, and the traditional Queensberry rules still used today. In addition, boxing became more organized and was no longer confined to a particular style or social structure. From its humble beginnings as a brutal sport, boxing has come a long way and is one of the world's most beloved sports.

Many famous fighters emerged throughout the 20th century, such as Muhammad Ali, Joe Frazier, and George Foreman. These fighters brought new skills, strategies, and techniques to the sport, making it more entertaining and popular worldwide. However, the emergence of Floyd Mayweather Jr. – considered one of the best fighters of all time – forever changed the boxing world. His record-breaking winnings and undefeated streak made him a legend.

Boxing has come a long way since its humble beginnings. From a primitive form of combat to a sophisticated sport with strict rules and regulations, it has dominated the sports arena worldwide. The first boxers paved the way for modern-day champions who have brought fame, glory, and entertainment to the sport. Boxing continues to evolve, and the world can look forward to more exciting matches and legendary fighters in the future.

Boxing in the Common Era: A Legacy of Greatness

From the first fights in ancient Greece to the present day, boxing has always been a physical and mental test of strength, endurance, and skill. The Common Era of boxing produced some of the greatest athletes and most unforgettable moments in sports history. From the golden age of Muhammad Ali and his rivalry with Joe Frazier to the recent triumphs of Floyd Mayweather Jr. and Manny Pacquiao, boxing remains a source of inspiration and awe for millions of fans worldwide.

The Common Era of boxing, known as the *modern era*, started in 1910, when the first heavyweight champion, Jack Johnson, was dethroned by Jim Jeffries in a racist and controversial bout. This era saw the rise of iconic fighters, such as Joe Louis, Rocky Marciano, Sugar Ray Robinson, and Muhammad Ali, who dominated their divisions and transcended the sport through their charisma, courage, and social impact.

Joe Louis, known as the Brown Bomber, reigned as heavyweight champion for a record-breaking 12 years and became a hero to Black and White fans for his sportsmanship and patriotism. Rocky Marciano, the only undefeated heavyweight champion in history, was a relentless and powerful fighter who retired at the peak of his career to preserve his legacy. Sugar Ray Robinson, considered by many experts the greatest pound-for-pound boxer of all time, dazzled his opponents and fans with his speed, technique, and showmanship.

Muhammad Ali, born Cassius Clay, was a boxing legend, cultural icon, and political activist. He won three heavyweight titles and fought some of history's most epic and controversial matches, including his 1964 upset of Sonny Liston, his 1971 defeat of Joe Frazier in the Fight of the Century, and his 1974 Rumble in the Jungle (in Zaire, Africa) against George Foreman. Ali's charisma, humor, and eloquence made him a beloved figure worldwide, and his stand against the Vietnam War and his advocacy for civil rights inspired millions of people.

The common era of boxing saw the emergence of many other great champions and rivalries, such as Julio Cesar Chavez, Mike Tyson, Oscar De La Hoya, Roy Jones Jr., Lennox Lewis, Evander Holyfield, Bernard Hopkins, and Manny Pacquiao. These fighters showcased different styles, personalities, and legacies, but all shared a passion for the sport and a desire to push themselves to the limit.

Today, boxing continues to evolve and adapt to new challenges and opportunities. The rise of MMA, digital media growth, and the pandemic have affected how the sport is watched and consumed, but the core values and excitement of boxing remain intact. The current champions and prospects, such as Canelo Alvarez, Anthony Joshua, Terence Crawford, Gennady Golovkin, Ryan Garcia, and Teofimo Lopez, are carrying on the legacy of greatness that boxing has fostered for over a century.

Boxing in the present era is not just a sport but a testament to human resilience, creativity, and excellence. The fighters who have graced the ring in this era have set the bar high for future generations and inspired fans to dream big and fight hard. So, whether you are a casual viewer or a diehard fan, boxing offers something for everyone who loves a good challenge, a good story, and great shows.

The following section dives deep into the fighters' stories that made this era so special. So, come, it's time to get ringside.

Muhammad Ali

Muhammad Ali is one of the greatest boxers ever – and for good reason. He won the world heavyweight champion title three times and was known for his unique fighting style, wit, and charisma. Ali was a lightning-fast fighter who "floated like a butterfly and stung like a bee." In addition, he was a civil rights activist who stood up for his beliefs regardless of the consequences. Ali retired in 1981 but remained iconic in sports and society until he passed away in 2016.

To this day, Muhammad Ali is still considered one of the greatest of all time. [2]

Early Life and Boxing Career

Muhammad Ali was born on January 17, 1942, in Louisville, Kentucky. He first stepped into the ring at the age of 12 and quickly realized his talent. Ali won numerous titles as an amateur boxer and went on to win the Olympic gold medal in 1960. He joined the professional ranks shortly afterward and became a heavyweight world champion at 22. Ali was the first boxer to win the heavyweight title three times.

Personality and Activism

Muhammad Ali was more than just a boxer. He was a charismatic personality with a natural gift for speaking. He was quick-witted, charming, and always ready with a good joke. But Ali was also a political and social activist, standing up for his beliefs even when it wasn't fashionable. For example, in the 1960s, he refused to be drafted into the army to fight in the Vietnam War, citing his religious beliefs and opposition. This decision cost him three years of his boxing career, but he never wavered in his views.

Ali's Philanthropy

Besides being a great athlete and activist, Muhammad Ali was a philanthropist. He was involved in numerous charitable organizations and causes, including the Make-A-Wish Foundation and the Special Olympics. He established the Muhammad Ali Center, a museum and cultural center in his hometown, Louisville, Kentucky, dedicated to promoting respect, understanding, and tolerance. Ali truly believed in giving back to his community and using his fame and influence for good.

Ali's Legacy

Muhammad Ali's legacy is of excellence, courage, and social responsibility. He was a trailblazer in the world of sports, paving the way for other African American athletes to succeed. His political and social activism inspired a generation, standing up for his beliefs even when difficult. He gave back to his community in countless ways, leaving a lasting impact on the world. Muhammad Ali's name will forever be associated with greatness, and his legacy will continue to inspire everyone for generations.

Muhammad Ali was a larger-than-life figure who left an indelible mark on the world. He was a talented athlete, a political and social activist, and a philanthropist. But most importantly, he was a great human who inspired everyone to be their best selves. Muhammad Ali's legacy and achievements will continue to be celebrated and remembered for generations, reminding people of the power of one person to make a difference.

Mike Tyson

Mike Tyson was one of the most aggressive and dominant fighters in the sport's history. He became the youngest heavyweight boxing champion at the age of 20 and held the title for three years. Tyson was known for his impressive footwork, devastating punches, and intimidating aura. He had a controversial career faced with personal struggles, but Tyson remains a popular and influential figure in the sport.

Mike Tyson became the youngest heavyweight champion at 20. [3]

Career

Mike Tyson's boxing career began in his teenage years. He made his professional debut in 1985 and quickly dominated his opponents. Tyson's style was hard-hitting and aggressive, which earned him numerous victories. He won his first twenty fights by knockouts, putting him in the spotlight as an upcoming superstar. Tyson won his first world title in 1986 by defeating Trevor Berbick and became the youngest heavyweight champion in the sport's history.

Notable Victories

Tyson's style and success in the ring continued cementing his legacy as one of the greatest boxers of all time. He was feared for his power and agility and went on to win more world titles throughout his career. Tyson's notable victories include his knockout of Larry Holmes, his victory over Michael Spinks, and his fight against Frank Bruno, where he won the WBC championship. Tyson retired from professional boxing in 2005 with 50 wins, six losses, and two no-contests. His power and dedication to the sport made him an icon and role model for boxers worldwide. Tyson's legacy in boxing is undeniable – and regarded as one of the greatest boxers in history.

Tyson's Personality

Tyson's impact extends beyond the boxing ring. His personality and charisma made him a pop culture icon. He has appeared in numerous movies, TV shows, and music videos. In addition, Tyson's memoir, "Undisputed Truth," tells his life story and gives audiences a better understanding of the man behind the gloves. Mike Tyson's legacy and achievements as a boxer have inspired many. His strength, resilience, and dedication to the sport have made him a legend. Tyson's career might have been marred with controversies, but his determination to overcome them made him a role model for boxers worldwide. He will always be remembered as one of the greatest boxers ever, and his impact on the sport of boxing will never be forgotten.

Floyd Mayweather Jr.

Floyd Mayweather Jr., known as "Money," is a retired American boxer who needs no introduction. He is considered one of the greatest boxers of all time, with unparalleled achievements in the sport. Floyd Mayweather Jr. made a name for himself with his unbeatable fighting style, an impressive record of wins, and a lavish lifestyle outside the ring. In addition, Mayweather Jr.'s talent and dedication have earned him worldwide recognition, and he is hailed by many as the best defensive boxer of all time. Let's delve into his legacy and achievements as a boxer and understand what made him the undefeated champion.

Background and Career

Mayweather Jr. was born in Grand Rapids, Michigan, on February 24, 1977. He began training at an early age, inspired by his family's boxing background. His father, uncles, and grandfather were all fighters, and they instilled discipline, hard work, and determination in him. Mayweather Jr.'s professional boxing career began in 1996 when he won his first pro-fight against Roberto Apodaca. He went on to win many more titles, including the WBC super featherweight title, WBC lightweight title, WBA (Super) light middleweight title, WBC light middleweight title, WBA (Super) welterweight title, WBC welterweight title, WBA (Super) light welterweight title, IBF welterweight title, and the WBO welterweight title.

Notable Victories

Mayweather Jr. is known for his famous bout with Manny Pacquiao in 2015, dubbed the "Fight of the Century." Mayweather Jr. won the fight via unanimous decision, retaining his undefeated record. Mayweather Jr.'s defensive fighting style sets him apart from other boxers. He has never been knocked out or knocked down, emphasizing his ability to avoid punches and maintain control in the ring. His technique has inspired many young boxers, and his dedication to training is commendable. Apart from his achievements in the ring, Mayweather Jr. is known for his lavish lifestyle. He often flaunts his wealth, fancy cars, private jets, and expensive watches. His fans love him for his flamboyant personality and confidence inside and outside the ring.

Floyd Mayweather Jr.'s legacy as a boxer will always remain unparalleled. His unbeatable record, impressive title collection, and defensive fighting style make him one of the greatest boxers ever. He has inspired many young boxers with his dedication to training and perfecting his craft. His lavish lifestyle outside the ring has made him a celebrity. Floyd Mayweather Jr.'s legacy as a boxer will continue to inspire and awe people for generations.

Other Notable Boxers

Apart from Ali and Tyson, many other legendary boxers have been during the Common Era, including Sugar Ray Leonard, Julio Cesar Chavez, Oscar De La Hoya, and Manny Pacquiao. These men brought their unique style and personality to the ring and built legacies impacting generations. They have left their mark on boxing, sports, and society, inspiring people worldwide to embrace the sport, pursue their dreams, and overcome adversities. Their achievements and contributions continue to be celebrated and studied in various ways, from books and documentaries to films and art. They have set new standards for the sport, and their legacies inspire future boxers and athletes to chase greatness.

Boxing is still one of the most loved and watched sports worldwide. Today, many talented boxers are dedicated to the sport and building their legacies. The impact of Ali, Tyson, and other notable boxers of the Common Era continues as younger fighters strive to emulate their style and success. The sport would not be the same without these great men, whose legacies will continue to inspire and entertain people worldwide.

Boxing is a timeless art, and future generations of fighters will continue learning from the achievements of the greats who came before them.

This chapter covered the origins of boxing, the transformation of the sport during the Common Era, and some of the most notable boxers from this time. From Muhammad Ali to Floyd Mayweather, Jr., these men uniquely shaped the sport and left an indelible mark on boxing, society, and the world. The legacies of these greats continue to inspire and entertain people of all ages, and their achievements will be studied, celebrated, and emulated for years to come.

Chapter 2: Getting Started with Boxing I: Rules and Fighting Styles

Do you want to get into boxing but need help figuring out where to start? Then, it's time to gear up and learn the rules and fighting styles.

Boxing is an exercise and an exhilarating sport to watch and participate in. There are a variety of fighting styles to choose from, each with unique techniques and strategies. However, before stepping into the ring, it's critical to understand the basic rules of boxing, proper fighting stances, and how to throw punches and defend yourself.

This chapter covers the general rules of boxing, the Queensberry Code of Rules for Boxing, and various fighting styles. From swarmers and counterpunchers to sluggers and out-boxers, it provides a detailed description of each type so you can discover which one suits you best. The love of boxing can be shared with friends, family, or strangers. So, let's get into the nitty-gritty of boxing and explore some basic boxing rules.

General Rules of Boxing: Everything You Need to Know

Boxing is a sport admired by millions of people around the world. '

Boxing is one of the most popular sports worldwide, with millions of fans enjoying the excitement and thrill of every match. However, correctly understanding the rules and regulations is essential to enjoy the game and appreciate the art of boxing. Here are the general rules – essential to know before you start watching or participating in this sport.

Objective

The primary objective of a boxing match is to win by either knockout or points, depending on the form of the sport. A knockout victory requires knocking out the opponent so that they cannot return to the fight by the count of 10, or a referee stops the match because the boxer is in danger of serious injury or harm (technical knockout). In contrast, a victory by points is when a fighter lands more successful punches on the opponent within the duration of the match.

Scoring

Scoring in boxing is based on the number of successful punches landed throughout the match. In addition, judges evaluate and score each boxer on their ability to land punches on the opponent's body or head. The punch must land with the front part of the hand's closed glove, and only punches landed above the waist are considered. Punches below the waist are considered fouls unless the boxer's head is lowered to that level.

Fouls

Boxing has strict rules regarding a foul. Common fouls include holding, hitting below the belt, hitting the back of the head, and headbutting. Boxers are not allowed to use their elbows or other parts of their body to hit the opponent. Furthermore, boxers must not bite, spit, or intentionally cause harm to their opponent.

The Tone of Voice

A boxer must maintain a respectful tone and conduct when boxing. Disrespectful behavior like taunting an opponent or using abusive language is considered unprofessional and is potentially dangerous. Boxers must follow the referee's instructions and stop fighting when instructed. Failure to do so can lead to disqualification.

Protective Gear

Protective gear is essential for amateur and professional boxers. The most important protective equipment is a mouthguard that protects the teeth and gums from damage. Boxers are advised to wear hand wraps and gloves to protect the hands and wrists from fractures during impact. Moreover, boxing headgear protects the head and face from cuts and bruises. Boxers who compete professionally typically only wear gloves and a mouthguard, but amateur boxers usually wear more protective gear.

The Queensberry Code of Rules for Boxing: A Brief History

Boxing is a sport that has been around since the ancient Greeks, but it was in the mid-19th century that a standard set of rules was established. The Queensberry Code of Rules for Boxing was introduced in 1867, heralding a new era of boxing emphasizing safety, fair play, and sportsmanship. Let's explore the origins of the Queensberry Code, its key features, and its impact on the sport of boxing.

Origins of the Queensberry Code

Before the establishment of the Queensberry Code, boxing was a brutal and often deadly sport. Fight organizers often pitted men of vastly different sizes against each other, leading to injuries and death. The rules were minimal, and fights would continue until one fighter was incapacitated. Eventually, it led to a public outcry and calls for reform. In 1865, John Sholto Douglas, the 9th Marquess of Queensberry, wrote a letter to the Sporting Life newspaper calling for a standard set of rules governing the sport of boxing. Two years later, the Queensberry Code was published, ushering in a new era of fair play and safety in boxing.

Key Features of the Queensberry Code

The Queensberry Code established several new rules still used in boxing today. Firstly, it mandated using gloves to reduce injuries and deaths in the sport. It established the length of rounds (three minutes), the number of rounds (up to 15), and the duration of breaks between rounds (one minute). The Code introduced the concept of "down and out" – if a fighter was knocked to the ground and could not get up within 10 seconds, the fight was over. In addition, the Queensberry Code prohibited grappling, wrestling, and other forms of "foul" play.

The Impact of the Queensberry Code

The Queensberry Code had an immediate and profound impact on boxing. It made boxing safer for fighters and more palatable to audiences, increasing its popularity. The Code gave rise to a new breed of professional boxers trained in boxing rather than relying on brute strength. In addition, it established the framework for modern boxing matches, including weight classes, rankings, and championship bouts. Today, the Queensberry Code remains the basis for boxing rules in most countries worldwide.

The Queensberry Code of Rules for Boxing was a landmark moment in the sport's history. It transformed boxing from a brutal and often deadly spectacle into a sport emphasizing skill, sportsmanship, and fair play. The Code established a standard set of rules and set the stage for modern boxing as we now know it. Thanks to the vision of John Sholto Douglas, the 9th Marquess of Queensberry, boxing is a safer and more respected sport.

Different Fighting Styles

Boxing is a sport requiring precision, strength, and agility. With so many different fighting styles, each boxer brings a unique approach to the ring, from the flashy footwork of Muhammad Ali to the devastating uppercuts of Mike Tyson. The diversity of boxing styles allows for an exciting match every time. Whether a boxer prefers the defensive tactics of counterpunching or the relentless offense of swarming, the beauty of this sport lies in the creativity and adaptability of each fighter. So, who will come out on top in the ring? The answer lies in the fighters' unique combination of strategy and athleticism.

The Swarmer Style: The Art of Pressure Fighting in Boxing

Each boxing style has its unique charm. The Swarmer Style is about non-stop aggression and pressure. Swarmers are well-known for their relentless approach and constant pressure. They spend most of their time on the inside, throwing hard punches and combinations. Let's delve deeper into the Swarmer style, explore its history, and explain how it works.

Origins

The Swarmer boxing style emerged in the early 20th century and was popularized by boxers like Rocky Marciano and Joe Frazier. The style is characterized by the boxer's ability to get inside their opponent's guard and throw quick, powerful punches from close range. In addition, swarmers are known for their high stamina and intense pressure on their opponents. They apply constant and unrelenting pressure to wear their opponents down.

Basics

Swarmer boxers are usually shorter but have a powerful physique and high endurance. Their strategy is to get inside their opponent's guard and throw multiple punches quickly. They aim to keep their opponents on the back foot, pressing forward and throwing combinations. This style is excellent for boxers with strong chins and can absorb punches because they typically get hit quite often.

Attributes

One critical attribute of a Swarmer boxer is their footwork. They must be fast and agile on their feet to get inside their opponent's guard and throw punches. Swarmers are adept at slipping punches and weaving their way inside their opponent's guard. However, they need excellent reflexes and a sense of distance to land effective punches.

In Popular Culture

The Swarmer style has been significantly used by boxers like Mike Tyson, known for his relentless attacks, quick combinations, and ferocious punching power. Tyson used this style to win the heavyweight championship at the age of 20, making him the youngest heavyweight champion in history. Other notable boxers who used the

Swarmer style include Joe Frazier, Roberto Duran, and Julio Cesar Chavez.

The Swarmer style is an exciting and effective way of fighting in boxing. Its style requires high endurance, excellent footwork, and relentless pressure on the opponent. Swarmers are known for their ability to get inside their opponent's guard and throw powerful punches in quick succession.

Unleashing the Strength of the Out-Boxer Boxing Style

Boxing is a combat sport requiring discipline, focus, speed, and strategy to win. One of the most compelling boxing styles is the out-boxer technique. This style emphasizes long-range punches, mobility, and footwork to outmaneuver the opponent. Here's a brief overview of the out-boxer boxing style, how it works, and why it is an excellent strategy for a boxer's arsenal.

The out-boxer style is often called the "hit and don't get hit" style of boxing. The primary goal is to maintain a safe range away from the opponent, utilizing a lot of footwork and mobility while focusing on long-range punches. This technique requires quick reflexes, accurate timing, and excellent hand-eye coordination, which is essential for any successful boxer.

A boxer must be familiar with the different punches and combinations to use the out-boxer technique effectively. The jab is a standard punch used for offense and defense. It effectively keeps opponents at a distance while setting up other punches. The cross, hook, and uppercut are punches used in the out-boxer style. These punches create angles, disrupt an opponent's balance, and create openings for counterattacks.

Footwork is an integral part of the out-boxer fighting style. Fighters must be mobile and efficient at moving in and out of range while maintaining proper balance and technique. The out-boxer footwork combines pivoting, circling, and lateral movement, allowing them to outmaneuver their opponents quickly and efficiently. Defense is significant in the out-boxer style, focusing on defense before offense. They use their footwork to circle and evade their opponents' punches and rely on their boxing stance, head movement, and combination of blocks, slips, and parries to avoid getting hit while setting up counterattacks.

One challenge of the out-boxer style is it requires exceptional stamina. Boxers must move quickly for an extended time, throw long-range punches, and maintain their accuracy, timing, and speed. They must have the patience to wait for the right moment to strike, using superior movement to create opportunities for landing decisive blows. The out-boxer style is an excellent boxing strategy, offering a unique blend of speed, accuracy, and mobility. It is an intelligent technique allowing the boxer to control the pace of the fight while keeping your opponent at a safe distance. However, mastering this style requires discipline, focus, consistent training, and developing specific skills and techniques.

Aspiring boxers can learn more about and master the out-boxer style by observing and emulating successful out-boxer fighters and working with experienced coaches who understand the nuances of this fighting style. If you aspire to become a successful boxer, consider incorporating the out-boxer style into your repertoire, and be prepared to unleash your strength and precision in the ring.

What's the Slugger Boxing Style, and Why Should You Try It?

Boxing gives you a full-body workout while honing your coordination and overall athleticism. However, with so many different boxing styles, finding the one that suits you best might take a lot of work - enter the Slugger Boxing Style. This boxing form combines power and aggression, so if you like getting up close and personal, this could be the perfect boxing style for you. But first, let's dive into what makes the Slugger Boxing Style so unique.

Heavy on Power

The Slugger Boxing Style is known to be heavy on power and strong blows. It means slugging is about delivering hard punches and dealing with heavy blows instead of relying on quick movements and agility like other boxing styles. The Slugger Boxing Style is perfect for those with a natural aptitude for strength and durable power.

Focused on Close-Range Combat

Another critical element of this boxing style is its focus on close-range combat. You must be comfortable in the pocket, throwing and taking punches in tight quarter circumstances to be successful in slugging. So, if you like to get in and fight dirty, the Slugger Boxing Style might be for you.

Suitable for Taller Boxers

Finding a boxing style that suits you can be challenging if you are over six feet tall. Many boxing techniques rely on agility and speed, which can be tougher to execute for taller boxers. However, the Slugger Boxing Style is perfect for a taller fighter because it emphasizes strength and power, which aligns well with boxers with a more extended reach.

Requires Proper Defense

While slugging emphasizes offense and hard-hitting blows, developing solid defense skills is crucial. Since you are constantly in your pocket, you must protect yourself from incoming punches from your opponent. Without proper defense, you open yourself up to body blows, reducing stamina, affecting your breathing, and weakening your guard. Therefore, practice your defense techniques and continuously improve them to protect yourself from vigorous attacks.

Promotes Discipline and Focus

Every boxing style requires hard work and dedication. Slugger Boxing is no exception, as it demands a lot of practice and focus, but the payoff is immense. By focusing on moves and techniques that lean into body strength and power, slugging provides discipline translating into other aspects of life. Regular practice and persistence will teach you to stay focused and overcome obstacles inside and outside the ring.

The Slugger Boxing Style is a unique boxing style that could be the perfect fit for anyone who wants to emphasize their physical power and close combat skills. This boxing technique provides a dynamic yet challenging physical way of improving your agility skills, strength, and endurance. The Slugger Boxing Style demands dedication and hard work, but the physical benefits and discipline are immense. If you're considering exploring different boxing styles, the Slugger Boxing Style is an excellent option to enhance your overall training.

Unleashing the Counterpunch: Why This Boxing Style Is Worth Learning

One technique in boxing that can give you an edge over your opponent is the counterpunch. This boxing style uses your opponent's aggressive moves and turns them into opportunities for an effective counterattack. While mastering a boxing style takes time and effort, this style is worth learning; this section explores why.

The Element of Surprise

Counterpunching is taking advantage of your opponent's expectations. One moment, they think they have the upper hand. The next, they're stunned by the effectiveness of your counterpunch. It puts you in control and can shake your opponent's confidence, making them hesitant to attack again.

The Importance of Defense

As any boxer knows, defense is as critical as offense. In counterpunching, defense is front and center. You'll focus on slipping, weaving, and blocking your opponent's attacks to create openings you can exploit with a counterpunch.

Strategic Thinking

Counterpunching requires a lot of strategy and timing. You must read your opponent's moves, anticipate their attacks, and know when to strike to maximize your counterpunch's effectiveness. This skill improves your boxing and helps you become a more strategic thinker.

Versatility

One of the most significant benefits of mastering counterpunching is its versatility. This technique can be used against various opponents, from aggressive brawlers to more calculated boxers, making it a valuable skill in your back pocket. The key is to practice, hone your skills, and stay sharp to gain an edge in the ring.

Building Confidence

Last, learning counterpunching can do wonders for your confidence in the ring. As you become more familiar with the technique, you develop better control during fights, leading to bold and confident moves, ultimately leading to better performance and victories. The confidence level of mastering this technique is hard to overstate and well worth the effort.

Counterpunching is a challenging technique to learn, but the benefits are numerous. From keeping your opponent guessing and improving your defense to building strategic thinking, versatility, and confidence, it's no wonder many boxers consider it an essential tool in their arsenal. So, consider adding this technique to your repertoire the next time you train and watch as your boxing skills and confidence grow.

Mixed Martial Arts (MMA)

Mixed Martial Arts (MMA) is a blend of various martial arts styles that focuses on striking and grappling techniques. While MMA fighters predominantly use elbows, knees, and kicks to score points or knock out their opponents, boxing is an essential aspect of the sport. Boxing-style striking highlights the importance of precise footwork, head movement, and powerful punches. Let's explore the significance of boxing in MMA and discover how MMA fighters use it to dominate their opponents in the cage.

Mixed martial arts is a blend of different styles of fighting. [5]

Footwork and Head Movement

Boxing is all about footwork and head movement; the same applies to MMA. An MMA fighter must avoid takedowns and strikes while moving around the cage. Proper footwork allows the fighter to get in and out of range, maintain the appropriate distance, and adjust his striking angles in real-time. The head movement involves the defender moving his head to avoid a strike while simultaneously throwing a counterpunch. This technique is essential for boxers and can be integrated into MMA.

Judging Punches and Combinations

Boxing entails judging the punches thrown by the opponent and anticipating which one is coming next. Reading the opponent is incredibly important, whether via facial expressions, body language, or how he moves. A boxer must learn to throw combinations to set up his opponent and score a knockout punch. MMA fighters utilize these techniques to anticipate their opponent's moves and launch an effective counterattack.

Power Punches and Defense

A power punch is a punch with knockout power or the ability to inflict significant damage to the opponent. Power punches can be thrown from different angles and aim to put the rival down or create an opening for a follow-up strike. MMA fighters use power punches and incorporate them into ground-and-pound techniques when they take an opponent down. Similarly, boxing-style defense is an integral part of MMA. Fighters use shoulder rolls, parrying, and slipping to avoid shots and counterattacks as their opponents expose themselves.

Footwork and Cage Control

Boxing footwork emphasizes maintaining control over the ring, creating angles, and positioning for an attack or defense. In MMA, the fighter must use cage control, meaning they must stay off the cage against a wrestler or BJJ (Brazilian Jiu-Jitsu) fighter while positioning themselves to throw effective strikes. Effective footwork and cage control can make all the difference between losing and winning a match.

Conditioning and Fight IQ

Boxing in MMA requires significant conditioning, mental preparation, and fighting IQ. Fighters must be conditioned to throw punches at high intensity for several rounds while having the endurance to grapple in the later rounds. Fight IQ involves a high combat awareness level enabling a fighter to adapt to the pace of a match, stay composed, and execute strategies based on the opponent's skills. To be a top-tier MMA boxer with a fight IQ, you must box regularly, focus on conditioning, study your opponent, and learn new techniques.

Whether it's footwork, head movement, power punches, defense, or even fight IQ, boxing can give MMA fighters the advantage to dominate and win their battles. Furthermore, properly learning and utilizing these techniques significantly improves fighters' chances of winning a match. Therefore, aspiring MMA fighters should incorporate boxing into their training regimen to elevate their game, increase their chances of succeeding, and ultimately become champions.

Boxing is a sport not for the faint of heart. It aims to knock out or score more points than your opponent by landing punches. However, many rules and regulations must be followed to ensure a fair fight. No boxer would deliberately choose to be penalized for fouls.

The Queensberry Code of Rules for Boxing is the standard for all boxing matches. Beyond the rules are different fighting styles boxers adopt. Some are swarmers - always on the offensive, while others are out-boxers who prefer to fight from a distance. Some sluggers go for the knockout punch, and counterpunchers wait to strike. Due to the rise of Mixed Martial Arts (MMA), boxing has taken on a new dimension. With so many styles and rules, boxing will always keep you on your toes.

Chapter 3: Getting Started with Boxing II: Gear and Physical Conditioning

Are you ready to start your boxing journey? If you're serious about becoming a boxer, you must invest in high-quality gear and equipment. From gloves and clothing to hand wraps and fitness equipment, your gear is pivotal in ensuring you stay safe and perform your best. Whether you're looking for breathable fabrics or padding, choosing the right apparel can significantly affect your comfort and performance. Starting with the right gear and equipment is essential if you're ready to train like a professional boxer.

This chapter discusses various boxing apparel and equipment types, including hand wraps and gloves. It looks at fitness techniques to condition your body for the match. The chapter concludes with expert boxers' tips on physical training. Remember, the best boxing gear and fitness techniques will only be effective if you have the proper diet. By the end of this chapter, you should understand the intricacies of boxing better.

The Ultimate Guide to Boxing Gear, Clothing, and Equipment

If you're passionate about boxing, you know that the right gear can make all the difference to your training and performance. However, choosing your equipment and clothing can be overwhelming with so many options available. This section explores everything you need for a successful and safe boxing routine, from gloves to mouthguards and apparel to equipment.

Gloves

Boxing gloves. [6]

A good pair of gloves is essential to any boxer. Gloves come in a range of weights, typically from 8 to 20 ounces. The correct weight depends on your weight and skill level. If you're a beginner, starting with a lighter glove is better. Pay attention to the fit and closure, lace-up, or Velcro when choosing gloves. Leather gloves are more durable, but hybrid gloves with nylon and synthetic leather are lighter.

Hand Wraps

Hand wraps protect your hands, wrists, and knuckles. [7]

Hand wraps are as essential as gloves. They protect your hands, wrists, and knuckles from injury. Wraps come in various lengths, but a 180-inch wrap is the most common. Wrapping your hands helps maintain a good grip on your gloves. The basic technique is to start by covering your wrist, knuckles, and fingers.

Mouthguards

Mouthguards help protect your teeth. [8]

Protecting your teeth is paramount in boxing. A mouthguard is a cheap and effective gear that can save you from oral and, in severe cases, brain injury. Mouthguards come in two basic types and can be customized to fit your teeth comfortably. It must be thick enough to absorb the impact of a punch.

Apparel

Proper clothing is not only essential for appearance but also critical for comfort and safety. Boxing shorts are typically loose-fitting and reach mid-thigh for maximum mobility. A good training shoe supporting your ankles is an essential piece of equipment. Last, wear a cotton shirt or vest with a sports bra (for females) for comfort.

Boxing Equipment

Last but not least is the boxing equipment. Various equipment, including speed, heavy, and double-end bags, are available. Always ensure the kit fits your physical ability. You'll get the best results from your training when you practice with the right equipment.

The Art and Science of Wrapping Your Hands for Boxing

If you're serious about boxing, you know the importance of protecting your hands during training and competitions. Proper hand wrapping provides valuable support and protection for your wrists, knuckles, and fingers. It improves your punching power and reduces the risk of injury. This section discusses the art and science of wrapping your hands for boxing.

Choose the Right Type of Hand Wraps

Various hand wraps are available on the market, from standard cotton wraps to gel wraps with added cushioning. The wrap you choose depends on your preference and needs. Cotton wraps are the most common and affordable option. However, a gel wrap could be more suitable if you require extra padding.

Prepare Your Wraps Properly

Before you start wrapping, ensure your wraps are clean and dry. Any moisture or sweat can cause irritation and discomfort during training or competition. Also, roll the wraps up tightly and store them in a sealable bag to keep them from getting tangled and to maintain their elasticity. If you're using a gel wrap, shake it before applying.

Wrapping Technique

There is no one-size-fits-all technique for wrapping your hands. There are many methods, but it's up to you to find what works best for your hand size and shape. Here's a general guide for the most common technique:

1. Start with the loop around your thumb
2. Wrap your wrist several times, creating a base for your knuckles
3. Wrap your knuckles several times, crossing the wraps over the back of your hand
4. Cover the thumb and continue wrapping down to your wrist, securing the wrap with Velcro or tape

Common Mistakes to Avoid

A few common mistakes people make when wrapping their hands can reduce the wrap's effectiveness or cause discomfort and injury. These include the following:

1. Wrapping too tightly and restricting blood flow and movement
2. Not covering the thumb, thus leaving it vulnerable
3. Covering over the knuckles too loosely or too tightly, making them weak or reducing mobility

Maintaining Your Wraps

After your training or competition, remove your wraps gently and thoroughly clean and air-dry them. Sweat and bacteria can build up, causing odor and irritation. Also, replace your wraps immediately if they have lost elasticity or show wear and tear. A loose wrap won't provide your hands with the necessary protection and support.

Hand wrapping might seem like a minor detail, but it can significantly affect your boxing performance and safety. Therefore, it's essential to choose the right wrap, prepare them properly, and use proper wrapping techniques to ensure maximum support, comfort, and protection. In addition, remember to avoid common mistakes and maintain your wraps to prolong their lifespan and effectiveness. By following these tips, you can ensure your hands are protected and empowered to deliver knockout punches in the ring.

Best Clothing and Gloves for Boxing

Whether you're new to boxing or have been practicing for a while, having the proper clothing and gloves is critical in enhancing performance and protecting yourself from injury. With endless options, figuring out the best investment items can be challenging. This section delves into the best clothing and gloves for boxing.

Boxing Gloves

Boxing gloves are the most critical gear in the sport. They protect your hands and wrists from injury while delivering powerful punches. The glove you choose should be based on your goals and experience level. Ideally, beginners should choose a lighter pair of gloves ranging between 10-14 ounces, whereas professionals can go for heavier gloves of 16-20 ounces. EverLast, Cleto Reyes, Winning, and Rival manufacture the best gloves.

Boxing Shoes

Boxing shoes can help you perform better. [9]

Boxing shoes should be lightweight, supportive, and stable when you move around the ring. Look for shoes with a rubber sole to help you pivot better and a high ankle providing ample support and preventing your ankles from rolling. Adidas, Title, and Ringside are top brands to check out when shopping for boxing shoes.

Boxing Shorts

Boxing shorts don't have to be expensive, but they should be comfortable and allow free movement. Avoid cotton shorts as they absorb too much sweat and become heavy. Instead, opt for nylon or polyester with split side seams to enhance flexibility. Some recommended top brands include RDX, Venum, and Hayabusa.

Boxing Headgear

If you want to spar, you must wear protective headgear. Headgear offers extra protection, reducing the risk of cuts and brain injuries. Your headgear should fit snugly and have adequate padding to absorb impacts. Some popular brands known for producing top-quality headgear include Title, Ringside, and Winning.

Boxing gear is an essential investment to improve your boxing skills. The right gear enhances your performance and keeps you safe from injury. Boxing gloves, shoes, shorts, hand wraps, and headgear are the most critical items in your gear bag. Consider investing in high-quality gear from trusted brands, and you'll take one step closer to becoming a pro.

Fitness for Boxers: Train Your Body and Mind to Become a Champion

Boxing is one of the most popular sports in the world and a great way to stay fit and healthy. Much effort and dedication go into becoming a successful boxer. It's not only about hitting hard but about technique, speed, agility, and endurance. This section discusses all things related to fitness for boxers.

Can Anyone Start Training as a Boxer?

The answer is a big YES. Anyone passionate about boxing and dedication can start learning and training as a boxer. No matter your age or body type, boxing is for everyone. However, it's crucial to know that boxing is an intense sport requiring focus and discipline. So, if you are willing to put in the hard work and sweat, there's no reason you can't become a great boxer.

Training Your Body to Box

Boxing is an intense sport demanding a lot from your body, so proper preparation is essential. Cardiovascular exercises are a fundamental aspect of boxing, so include running, jumping rope, and cycling in your workout routine. In addition, strength training exercises like push-ups, pull-ups, and squats are a must for building strong arms, legs, and core.

Diet and Its Role in Boxing

A healthy and balanced diet is equally vital for boxers to perform at their best. Fighters need a lot of energy to keep up with rigorous training and matches. Eating a protein-rich diet, carbohydrates, and healthy fats is best. Include chicken, fish, whole grains, vegetables, and fruit. Staying hydrated throughout the day is crucial, as dehydration can affect your performance negatively.

Mental Health and Boxing

Boxing requires immense focus and mental strength. A boxer's mental state will affect their performance, so working on your mental health is essential. Practice meditation, yoga, or visualization to stay calm and focused during your fights. Furthermore, setting achievable goals and celebrating your achievements is important.

General Strength Training

Strength training is no longer just for bodybuilders or weightlifters. It has become an indispensable part of any fitness routine, and everyone, regardless of age or gender, can benefit. As experts in strength training, boxers have many valuable insights to share. Their training regimes are about improving their boxing abilities and overall strength and conditioning. This section covers some of the best-talented boxers' general strength training tips.

Don't Skip the Warm-Up

Before an intense workout, it is essential to do a proper warm-up. Boxers recommend starting with light aerobic exercises to get your blood flowing. Some of their favorite warm-up exercises include jumping jacks, jogging, skipping rope, and shadowboxing. These exercises help to increase the heart rate, warm up the muscles, and reduce the risk of injury.

Focus on Compound Exercises

The best way to build overall strength is by focusing on compound exercises. These exercises involve multiple muscle groups simultaneously. Examples of compound exercises include squats, lunges, deadlifts, bench presses, and pull-ups. These movements help develop strength and stability, benefiting your boxing techniques and overall physical health.

Incorporate Plyometric Exercises

Plyometric exercises involve jumping and explosive movements to develop explosive power. Boxers often include plyometric exercises to improve speed, agility, and coordination. Plyometric exercises include box jumps, burpees, jump squats, clap push-ups, and more.

Take Rest Days

It's essential to avoid overtraining, and expert boxers recommend rest days between workouts to allow the muscle fibers to regenerate and repair. Rest is as important as exercise for building strength, so schedule enough rest time into your routine. Aim for two to three days of rest a week. Focus on strength training exercises for the remaining days.

Be Consistent

Consistency is the key to achieving strength training goals. It's not about working out every day for a week and giving up the next. Instead, it's about maintaining and sticking to a consistent routine for long-term results. The boxers recommend aiming for at least three to four strength training sessions a week and gradually increasing the weights over time.

Incorporating strength training into your fitness routines helps you build stronger muscles, increases endurance, and improves your overall physical health. In strength training, listening to and learning from experts like boxers can help you create a more effective workout routine. Remember to incorporate warm-up exercises, focus on compound exercises, include plyometric exercises, take rest days, and consistently train. By following these tips, you can achieve your strength training goals and improve your overall health.

Core Exercises to Improve Punching Power

Whether you are a professional boxer or enjoy practicing martial arts, a solid core is essential for delivering powerful punches. Core strength refers to the abdominals, back, and hip muscles that all work together to stabilize your body and transfer force from the ground up through your fists. This section explores five practical core exercises to help improve your punching power, taking your game to the next level.

Plank

Planks are excellent for building core strength by engaging your entire midsection, including abs, back, and hips. The basic plank involves holding a push-up position for as long as possible, keeping your body straight and parallel to the ground. To add an extra challenge, perform plank variations, like side planks, leg lifts, or walking planks. Incorporating planks into your workout routine, you develop excellent stability and control, allowing you to throw more powerful punches with less effort.

Russian Twist

The Russian Twist is an excellent exercise to target your obliques, the muscles on the sides of your waist. To perform this exercise:

1. Sit on the ground with your feet flat on the floor and your knees bent.
2. Hold a weight or medicine ball with both hands and twist your torso to the right, touching the weight to the ground.
3. Turn to the left and repeat the movement. This exercise develops rotational power in your torso, which is essential for generating force in your punches.

Russian twist.

Dead Bug

The Dead Bug exercise targets your lower abs and helps improve your core muscle stability. To perform this exercise:

1. Lie on your back with your arms and legs extended toward the ceiling.
2. Lower your right arm and left leg until they hover just above the ground, then return to the starting position and repeat on the opposite side.
3. Keep your lower back pressed into the ground to prevent arching and maintain proper form as you perform this exercise.

Dead bug.

Medicine Ball Slam

Medicine ball slams are a fantastic way to develop explosive power in your punches by training your body to transfer force quickly. To perform this exercise, stand with your feet shoulder-width apart and hold a medicine ball overhead. Slam the ball onto the ground as hard as possible, then catch it on the rebound and repeat. This exercise will help you improve your speed and power, so you can deliver lightning-fast punches that pack a punch.

Medicine ball slam.

Bicycle Crunches

Bicycle crunches are a classic core exercise targeting your abs and obliques, developing rotational power in your torso. To perform this exercise:

1. Lie on your back with your hands behind your head and your knees bent.

2. Lift your shoulder blades off the ground and bring your right elbow toward your left knee while extending your right leg straight.

3. Switch sides and repeat.

Performing many reps of bicycle crunches develops endurance and core strength, which are essential for boxing.

Bicycle crunches. [10]

Improving your punching power requires a combination of training and technique, but strengthening your core through targeted exercises makes a substantial difference. Incorporate these five core exercises into your workout routine, and you'll see noticeable improvements in your stability, power, and speed. Remember to focus on proper form and gradually increase the exercises' intensity over time for the best results. You will take your punching power to the next level and dominate in the ring with dedication and consistency.

Interval Training and Other Options to Improve as a Boxer

Are you a boxer looking for ways to improve your skills? Or maybe you're just starting and want to know how to improve? Whatever your situation, this section introduces you to interval training and other options to improve as a boxer. These tips will refine your skills, build endurance, and achieve your goals in the ring.

Interval Training

Interval training is great for building endurance and increasing fitness levels. This training involves alternating periods of intense exercise with rest periods. For example, you could sprint for 30 seconds and then rest for 30 seconds. This cycle could be repeated for a set time or a certain number of reps. Interval training is practical because it pushes your body to work harder, burning more calories and building stamina. Incorporate interval training into your workout routine for optimal benefits.

Shadow Boxing

Shadowboxing is another effective way to improve as a boxer. This training technique involves practicing your moves without an opponent. It can be done anywhere and is a great way to work on footwork, punches, and combinations. Focus on perfecting your form and technique and speed up your movements as you become more comfortable. Shadowboxing can be a warm-up or a standalone exercise to improve your skills.

Sparring

Sparring is an essential component of boxing training. It allows you to practice your moves in a realistic setting and to learn from your mistakes. Sparring is done with a partner or a coach and is excellent for improving reaction time and agility. Wear proper safety gear and start slowly to avoid injury. Then, as you become more experienced, gradually increase your sparring session's intensity.

Cardiovascular Conditioning

Cardiovascular conditioning is crucial for any athlete, especially boxers. It improves endurance and increases the high work rate during fights. Incorporate cardiovascular training into your routine by running, swimming, cycling, or using a cardio machine at the gym. Aim for at least 30 minutes of cardiovascular exercise daily or longer if you're preparing for a fight.

Invest in quality gloves, hand wraps, and a mouthguard to protect you from injury and confidence in the ring. Once you have your gear, it's time to focus on your physical conditioning. Boxing requires strength, endurance, and agility, so incorporate cardio, strength training, and flexibility exercises into your routine. Remember, working on your footwork and balance is imperative. With the right gear and physical preparation, you'll be ready to step into the ring and unleash your inner boxer.

Chapter 4: Stances, Guards, and Footwork

Boxing is an incredible sport requiring physical strength, mental agility, and quick reflexes. One of the most important aspects of boxing is your stance, which determines the effectiveness of your movements and punches. A strong and stable stance is critical to getting the upper hand in any match. Guards are equally essential to protect yourself from incoming punches and to set up offensive strikes. But don't forget the footwork. Proper footwork allows you to move around the ring confidently and dodge incoming blows.

These components together make for an exciting and dynamic fight, and mastering these skills can bring you one step closer to becoming a champion. This chapter provides essential stances, guards, and footwork techniques to help you get started. Training your body, mind, and spirit is necessary to becoming a well-rounded boxer. Take the tips from the experts mentioned in this chapter to heart, and you will be well on your way to improving your skills and taking your boxing game to the next level.

Getting in Position: Understanding Different Boxing Stances

One of the first things you learn when training for boxing is the importance of your stance. How you position your feet, hands, and body makes all the difference to the success of your punches and the effectiveness of your defense. This section tackles the basics of the most common boxing stances and gives tips on switching between them seamlessly.

The orthodox stance is considered the normal boxing stance.

The Orthodox Stance[11]

The orthodox stance is the most common in boxing. It's so well known that it's often called the "normal" stance. In a traditional stance, your left side faces forward, and your left foot is ahead of your right. Your left hand is held to protect your face, while your right hand is held close to your chin to set up powerful punches. This stance provides a good combination of offense and defense, so many beginner boxers start here. Remember, always keep your left elbow tucked close to your body in an orthodox stance.

The Southpaw Stance

The Southpaw stance is less common but is still essential in boxing. In this stance, your right side faces forward, and your right foot is ahead of your left. Your left hand is held close to your face while your right hand is extended to deliver jabs and hooks. Southpaws can be challenging to fight because their stance is unfamiliar to most boxers, and their punches come from unexpected angles. This stance requires more skill and practice to master. However, once you're comfortable, the Southpaw stance can be great for surprising your opponents.

The Southpaw stance is less common in boxing.

Switching Stances

The ability to switch stances quickly is necessary for boxers.

Boxers must have the ability to switch stances quickly and effectively. This skill can be a powerful weapon when fighting against opponents more comfortable fighting from a particular stance. To switch stances, step forward or backward with your back foot, pivot your front foot, and rotate your hips. Keep your guard up throughout the transition to protect yourself from counterpunches. Practice switching stances regularly to ensure you are comfortable and confident with the orthodox and southpaw stances.

Stance Adjustments

A boxer's stance must be adjusted depending on the situation. For example, if you're fighting a taller opponent, lowering your stance to get under their punches and delivering powerful shots to their body is beneficial. Alternatively, raising your stance is more effective for keeping them at a distance if you're fighting a shorter opponent. Therefore, pay attention to your opponent's stance and adjust yours to gain the upper hand.

Benefits of Proper Stance

A proper boxing stance can deliver powerful, precise punches while keeping you safe from your opponent's strikes. The correct posture improves your balance and footwork, allowing you to move quickly and efficiently in the ring. When you're in the right position, you have a much more effective defense and can set up powerful combinations to knock out even the toughest opponents.

Your stance is the foundation of your boxing technique, and it's essential to master it early in your training. By understanding the different stances, practicing switching between them, and adjusting for various situations, you'll be well on your way to becoming a formidable fighter. Remember, a proper boxing stance isn't just about looking good in the ring; it's about delivering powerful punches while avoiding your opponent's strikes. With time, practice, and dedication, you can become a skilled boxer with an impressive command of the different stances. So, get in position and let those punches fly!

Getting Defensive: Guards and Blocking Techniques

The High Guard

In most sports, defense is as important as offense. After all, even the best teams can't win if they don't stop the opposition. It is especially true in combat sports like boxing and martial arts, where the ability to defend is essential. One of the most critical aspects of defense is using guards and blocking techniques. This section explores three standard methods; the high guard, the low guard, and slip and roll. You'll better understand how to defend yourself against your opponents.

The high guard can be beneficial to defend your face.

The first technique is the high guard. It is one of the most common techniques in combat sports, particularly boxing. Raise both hands before your face to do a high guard. Your palms should face inward, and your fingers tightly clenched. Your elbows should be close to your rib cage to protect your body. With a high guard, you can deflect many punches, especially those aimed at your head. The downside of a high guard is it can be challenging to counterpunch effectively, so it's best used in a defensive position.

The Low Guard

Another technique is the low guard. This technique is beneficial when you're defending your body. Lower your hands and bring them closer to your body for a low guard. Your palms should face outward, and your fingers relaxed. Bend your knees slightly to make it harder for your opponent to land a punch to your stomach. With a low guard, you can better defend your body, but you are more vulnerable to punches aimed at your head, so keeping your head moving is essential.

The low guard can be beneficial when defending your body.

Slip and Roll

The slip-and-roll technique will leave your opponent vulnerable. [12]

Last is the slip-and-roll technique. This technique involves moving your body out of your opponent's punches. Move your head to one side and pivot on your front foot to make a slip; it causes your opponent's punch to miss you completely. To do a roll, you must lean to one side, bend your knees, and pivot on your back foot. Again, this will cause your opponent's punch to graze past you. Slip and roll are fantastic techniques for a counterpunch, as they leave your opponent vulnerable and off balance.

These three standard guards and blocking techniques are for defending yourself in combat sports. Each method has strengths and weaknesses, so it's essential to practice and use them strategically, depending on the situation. With enough practice, you will anticipate your opponent's moves and defend yourself effectively. Remember, defense is as important as offense, and the best defense is a good offense. So, keep practicing, keep learning, and you'll be an unbeatable opponent in no time.

Mastering Footwork Techniques: Tips and Drills

Boxing is a great physical workout and art form. One of the most critical aspects of this art form is footwork. Footwork is essential since it provides balance and power to a boxer's strikes, allowing them to move around the ring with speed and agility. This section delves into the essential footwork techniques every fighter should know. Included are tips and tricks to improve your footwork immediately. Last, here are some drills to help you master these techniques.

Step and Slide

This technique can help you efficiently move away from your opponent.

Footwork is about positioning yourself correctly to throw punches while quickly and efficiently moving out of harm's way. One of the most basic footwork techniques is the "step and slide." This technique involves stepping with your lead foot toward your opponent, sliding your back foot forward, and placing it next to your lead foot. This moves your body forward with your lead foot while maintaining balance. Not stepping too far or close to your opponent is important, or you'll risk losing balance or opening up to counterpunches.

Pivot

Pivots can help you control the direction of your body.

This technique can control the direction of your body while throwing a punch or moving around the ring. A pivot is a movement of the front foot, turning it to the side so that your body turns while maintaining balance. When pivoting, it's vital to keep your back foot anchored or to move it only slightly so you don't lose balance. Pivoting quickly and efficiently improves your maneuverability, allowing you to avoid your opponent's punches or get closer to throwing a punch.

Lateral Movement

Lateral movement is another critical aspect of footwork in boxing. A great way to practice lateral movement is a ladder drill. A ladder drill is placing a ladder flat on the ground and moving up and down it, keeping your feet inside each rung. This drill improves quickness and agility, which are essential when evading punches or moving around the ring.

Footwork Drills

In addition to practicing moving forward, backward, and laterally, specific footwork drills will improve your footwork. One drill is the Slalom Drill - set up cones in a zigzag formation and practice shuffling through them from side to side. Another drill is the Jump Rope Drill - jump over a rope while keeping your feet together, alternating between jumping forward and backward. Also, the Balance Pad Drill - stand on a balance pad and practice different footwork techniques while maintaining balance.

Incorporating speed and double-end bags into your training routine improves footwork. These bags simulate an opponent's movements, and by hitting them, you practice footwork techniques improving your reaction time. Footwork is essential in boxing because it provides balance and power to your strikes, allowing you to move around the ring with speed and agility. By incorporating these drills and techniques into your training routine, you'll master your footwork skills in no time.

Mastering footwork techniques is crucial to be successful in boxing. The proper footwork can help you avoid punches, move in and out of range, and deliver powerful strikes. Using these methods and incorporating drills into your training routine improves your footwork skills to become a more effective boxer. Remember, footwork is the foundation of boxing, so practice often and refine your skills.

Knockout Tips from Boxing Experts

Whether you're a beginner or a seasoned pro, boxing is an intense and rewarding workout. However, you must know more than just the basics to truly excel at this popular martial art. Below is a compilation of some of the best tips from boxing experts to improve your skills and reach your full potential in the ring. From staying balanced to developing mental toughness, you are covered.

Staying Balanced: Maintaining balance is crucial to throwing powerful punches and evading your opponent's attacks. Boxing experts recommend keeping your feet shoulder-width apart and slightly angled, with your weight evenly distributed. In addition, slightly bending your knees and engaging your core improves balance and mobility in the ring.

Maintaining Focus: Boxing requires intense concentration and focus, as even the slightest distraction can cost you the fight. Experts suggest practicing mindfulness and visualization techniques to help you stay focused and present in the moment. Additionally, practicing proper breathing techniques keeps your mind and body calm under pressure, which is essential for success in the ring.

Reacting Quickly: In boxing, speed is everything. One of the best ways to improve your reaction time is by training with a speed bag, a small punching bag that rebounds quickly after each punch. You will develop hand-eye coordination and reaction time by hitting it consistently and promptly.

Using Your Opponent's Movement: The best boxers know how to use their opponent's movements to their advantage. For instance, if your opponent moves to your right, you can pivot on your left foot and throw a powerful left hook. You can gain an edge in the ring by studying your opponent's style and reacting appropriately.

Blending Stances and Guards: While most boxers have a traditional stance, boxing experts suggest blending different stances and guards to keep your opponent guessing. For instance, switch between a square stance, the classic boxing stance, and a staggered stance, giving you more power and versatility in your punches. Changing your guard protects different areas of your body and throws your opponent off their game.

Developing Strength, Power, and Agility: Boxing is a physical sport and requires strength, power, and agility to succeed. To develop these skills, boxing experts suggest doing exercises like squats, burpees, and pushups. Additionally, they recommend running sprints or using an elliptical machine to improve endurance in the ring.

Working On Hand-Eye Coordination: Hand-eye coordination is a crucial skill for any boxer and can be improved through practice. To sharpen your technique, boxing experts suggest throwing drills with medicine balls or shadowboxing in front of a mirror. Additionally, they recommend working on hand-eye coordination by playing sports like tennis or basketball.

Practicing Mental Toughness: Boxing is a mental game as much as a physical one. To achieve success in the ring, boxing experts suggest developing your mental toughness by visualizing yourself winning, setting achievable goals, and pushing yourself to be your best. Additionally, they recommend visualizing every punch you throw and establishing a positive mindset before each fight.

Improving Speed and Cardiovascular Endurance: You must throw fast, powerful punches and move quickly to reach your maximum potential in the ring. To improve your speed and cardiovascular endurance, boxing experts suggest interval training or short-distance running sprints. Additionally, they recommend focusing on exercises targeting the legs to increase your overall power and mobility in the ring.

Taking Care Of Your Body: Boxing is a physically demanding sport, and taking care of your body after each fight is essential. Boxing experts recommend gently stretching your muscles, getting plenty of sleep, eating healthy meals, and cooling down with light exercise or yoga. Additionally, they suggest using ice packs on sore areas and drinking plenty of water to stay hydrated.

Training with a Partner or Instructor: Boxing is a complex sport, so it's essential to have someone to guide and help you develop your technique. To ensure you get the most out of training, boxing experts suggest working with an experienced partner or instructor. You will receive feedback on your technique and practice different combinations in a safe environment.

Analyzing Your Fights and Performance: You must know your weaknesses and strengths to become a better boxer. After each fight, boxing experts suggest watching footage of the match and analyzing your performance. You will identify areas needing improvement and develop strategies for future conflicts. Additionally, they recommend getting feedback from coaches or instructors on your technique so you can make the necessary adjustments.

Properly Wrapping Your Hands: Correctly wrapping your hands is an essential skill for any boxer and helps prevent injury in the ring. To wrap your hands properly, boxing experts suggest placing four-to-six inches of gauze around each hand. Then, add a layer of athletic tape above that. Finally, secure the ends with adhesive tape so the wrap is snug and secure.

Eating a Balanced Diet and Staying Hydrated: Eating a balanced diet and staying hydrated is critical to performing at your best in the ring. To fuel your training, boxing experts suggest eating plenty of lean proteins, whole grains, and fruits and vegetables. Additionally, they recommend drinking plenty of water throughout the day to keep your body hydrated and functioning optimally.

Getting Enough Rest: Rest and recovery are essential for any athlete, especially boxers. To ensure you get enough rest, boxing experts recommend aiming for eight hours of sleep each night. They suggest short breaks throughout the day to avoid fatigue and burnout.

Taking Time to Recover after Training Sessions: Boxing is a physically demanding sport, and giving your body time for proper recovery after each training session is essential. To help speed up the recovery process, boxing experts suggest taking an ice bath after each workout and using compression garments to reduce swelling and soreness. Additionally, they recommend taking a few days off each week to give your body an extra chance to rest and recover.

Staying Positive: A positive attitude can make all the difference in success in the ring. To stay motivated and focused on training, boxing experts suggest setting realistic goals and celebrating each milestone. Additionally, they recommend surrounding yourself with positive people who support and encourage you in your journey.

Learning from The Best: Learning from the best is essential to become a better boxer. Boxing experts suggest watching footage of world-class fighters and studying their techniques. Additionally, they recommend reading books and articles written by experienced boxers to gain insight into the sport's strategies and tactics.

Practicing Visualization Techniques: Mental strength is as important as physical strength in boxing. To help enhance your mental game, boxing experts suggest practicing visualization techniques. For instance, picture yourself in a fight and visualize the moves you must make to succeed. Additionally, they recommend setting aside time each day to practice visualization techniques and build mental toughness.

Finishing Strong: To finish strong in a fight, boxing experts suggest saving energy for the final rounds. They suggest staying focused on your goals and visualizing success to stay motivated until the end. Additionally, they recommend taking deep breaths to help you remain calm and energized in the final moments of a match.

Feet Shoulder-Width Apart: To improve your performance, start by focusing on the position of your feet. Ensure they are shoulder-width apart. Next, stand straight and hold your hands near your head. This stance lets you move around the ring quickly, maintain balance, and deliver powerful punches.

Move Your Rear Foot: To strike a blow, you must transfer your weight from the rear foot to the front foot. Keep your feet balanced and stable to maintain stability while moving by distributing your weight evenly between your feet.

Keep Your Feet Parallel and Your Hips Forward: When standing in the boxing stance, keep your feet parallel to each other. Your feet should be pointing straight ahead rather than angled inward or outward. Also, keep your hips forward to maintain body alignment and balance.

Maintain A Low Center Of Gravity: To have a solid boxing stance, you must keep the center of gravity low by bending your knees slightly. It helps maintain your balance, making moving around the ring easier and avoiding being knocked down by an opponent's punch.

Keep Your Hands Up: Your hands are your primary weapon in boxing. Keep them near your face and chin to prevent your opponent from landing a knockout punch. Keep your elbow close to your body and your lead hand slightly away to create an opening quickly.

Relax Your Shoulders: Tension in your shoulders can restrict your movement, making it much harder to dodge your opponent's punches. Ensure your shoulders are relaxed to execute roundhouse punches and hooks.

Keep Your Head Moving: When in the ring, you must keep moving your head to avoid punches by moving your head up, down, and to the sides. However, ensure your chin is tucked into your chest to prevent it from getting hit.

Stay Light on Your Feet: Stay light on your feet to keep your reaction time sharp. It means bouncing up and down and moving your feet quickly to be ready to throw a punch or dodge an oncoming blow.

Use Your Angles: Use angles to gain an advantage over your opponent. For example, an opening can be created by moving your feet at a diagonal angle instead of perfectly forward.

Practice Your Stance: Finally, practice is essential in boxing. You must practice maintaining and changing your stance to give your muscles the memory to maintain a proper posture, making it easier to adopt the perfect stance during your boxing matches.

Boxing can be thrilling and challenging, but with these tips from boxing experts, you can take your skills to the next level. From improving your balance and hand-eye coordination to developing mental toughness and staying hydrated, there are countless ways to boost your performance in the ring. Whether you're a beginner or a seasoned pro, the key is to stay focused and disciplined and never stop learning and growing as a boxer. Remember, practice makes perfect.

Stay dedicated and commit to honing your skills each day. You can reach your boxing goals with hard work, perseverance, and dedication. It's essential to take the necessary steps to prevent injury, stay hydrated and fueled, get enough rest, and practice visualization techniques to ensure you remain healthy in the ring and maximize your performance. Incorporating these basic boxing techniques, you'll be on your way to becoming a better boxer and champion.

Chapter 5: Punches and Counterpunches

"Float like a butterfly, sting like a bee." - Muhammad Ali

Boxing is not just about throwing punches. It is an intricate dance involving many strategies, footwork, and, most importantly, punches and counterpunches. These are essential elements that make boxing the sport it is today. In the ring, it's not only about the strength of your punches. It's about using your opponent's movements to land the perfect counterpunch. A successful boxer knows how to anticipate their opponent's next move and react accordingly. It's like a game of chess, where you must always be one step ahead of your opponent.

Punches and counterpunches are the building blocks of boxing, and mastering them will take you one step closer to becoming a great boxer. This chapter is divided into sections, each focusing on a particular punch or counterpunch. It explains the purpose of each punch and counterattack, the mechanics behind them, common mistakes to avoid, and drills to help you improve. After reading this chapter, you'll be well on your way to becoming a master of the ring.

Introduction to Boxing Punches: The Basics and Safety Tips

Boxing punches are a fundamental skill that must be mastered for a successful match. However, it is not about throwing hard punches and defeating your opponent. Boxing punches involve a lot of technique and safety. Therefore, it's essential to know the basics of boxing punches and their purpose, the techniques involved, and safety tips to reduce your risk of injury.

Purpose of Punches

Boxing punches aim to score points or knock out your opponent. Scoring points is a technical way of winning a boxing match. A boxer must throw the right punches accurately and effectively to score points. However, a knockout is the most popular way a fighter wins a game. To knock out your opponent, you must deliver a powerful punch that can cause the opponent to fall or lose consciousness. Knockouts don't only come from power punches. They can come from repeated punches that fatigue the opponent and leave him vulnerable.

Safety Tips for Punching

Boxing punches can be dangerous if not done correctly. Therefore, safety should always come first when practicing boxing punches. Here are some tips to help keep you safe while practicing:

1. Always wear the required safety gear, such as gloves, headgear, mouthguard, elbow pads, and knee pads, to minimize the risk of injury.
2. Warm up before starting any punches to prevent muscle injuries. Stretch before and after a workout to keep your muscles relaxed.
3. During practice, always have a trainer supervise your punching form to ensure safety and prevent bad habits.
4. Always take your time, and don't overdo it by rushing. Take breaks between punches and listen to your body.

Basic Punch Mechanics

The basic punch mechanics in boxing include the jab, cross, uppercut, and hook. Understanding basic punching techniques is integral to developing your skills and avoiding injuries. The jab is a quick straight punch delivered with the lead hand. The cross is a straight punch delivered with the rear hand. The uppercut is a punch delivered to your opponent's chin from below by bending the legs and the trunk. Last, the hook is a sideways punch by bending the arm at an obtuse angle and hitting the opponent's side of the face with the knuckles.

Punch mechanics use proper punch alignment, stance, and footwork. Proper punch alignment consists of the correct posture for maximum power and accuracy. Boxing stance means standing with the feet shoulder-width apart with one foot slightly ahead of the other. As for footwork, it is using your feet not only to move but also to generate power.

Learning the basics of boxing punches and their purpose is crucial in becoming a great boxer. It includes understanding the safety tips for executing punches, basic punch mechanics, and maintaining the correct posture and alignment. By practicing and perfecting these basic skills, you can become a better boxer, reducing the risk of injury. Always keep safety in mind and listen to your body while training. Developing your boxing punch skill requires patience, dedication, and practice.

Mastering the Jab: A Guide for Beginners

The jab is one of the most basic punches to master. It might seem like a simple punch, but a well-executed jab can make all the difference to the outcome of a fight. A quick and effective jab can keep your opponent at bay, set up other punches, and, most importantly, score points. This section reviews everything you need to know about the jab, including its definition, purpose, execution, common mistakes to avoid, and training drills to improve your technique.

A jab can make all the difference in a fight. [18]

Definition and Purpose of a Jab

The jab is a quick, straight punch thrown with the lead hand in boxing. Its primary purpose is to keep your opponent at bay, allowing you to create distance and set up other punches. The jab effectively scores points and disrupts your opponent's rhythm. It's the most common punch in boxing, with numerous variations, including the double jab, the triple jab, and the jab to the body.

Step-By-Step Set Up and Execution of the Jab

To execute a jab correctly, follow these steps:

1. Start with your feet shoulder-width apart, your knees slightly bent, and your weight evenly distributed.
2. Your lead hand should be held at chin level, with your elbow tucked in and your wrist straight.

3. When you're ready to jab, step forward with your lead foot and extend your arm straight out, turning your wrist slightly as you do so.

4. Your shoulder and hips should rotate slightly to generate power but don't overextend your arm or lean forward.

5. Once your jab lands, quickly retract your arm back to your chin, avoiding unnecessary movements.

6. Keep your non-lead hand up to protect your face, and stay light on your feet, ready to move or throw another punch.

Common Mistakes to Avoid

Here are some common mistakes to avoid when executing a jab:

1. Extending your arm too far can leave you vulnerable and decrease power. Keep your arm straight but not fully developed, and practice retracting it quickly to avoid this mistake.

2. Reaching with your jab takes away power and exposes you to counterpunches. Instead, step forward into the punch while keeping your chin tucked down.

3. Not stepping forward enough when you jab can result in a weak or ineffective punch. Instead, quickly step forward with your lead foot before throwing your jab.

4. Telegraphing your jab by positioning your body or hand before throwing it is a common mistake. Refrain from allowing your opponent to anticipate your movement and prepare a defense.

Training Drills to Improve Your Jab

The jab is the most important punch in boxing and should be the focus of your training drills. A good jab will set up your other punches and help you control the fight. Here are some exercises to improve your jab technique:

Wall Jab Drill: Stand a few feet away from a wall and practice throwing jabs at it. Focus on the set-up and execution of the punch, ensuring to avoid common mistakes. Visualize an opponent and practice your techniques without actually hitting anything.

Shadowboxing: Shadowboxing will help you get comfortable with throwing jabs and other punches without the pressure of a real opponent.

Speed Bag: Working on your speed and accuracy on the speed bag is a great way to practice throwing jabs quickly and accurately.

1-2-3 Drill: Throw a jab, then follow it with a right hand. Finish with a left hook to the body. Repeat this drill for 3 minutes, rest for 1 minute, and repeat three times.

Double-end bag drill: Throw a jab at the top, then quickly move to the bottom of the bag and throw another jab. Repeat this for 30 seconds, rest for 30 seconds, and repeat three times.

Focus Mitt Drill: Have a partner hold a focus mitt or punching pad in front of their face and throw jabs at it while moving around them. Repeat this for 3 minutes, rest for 1 minute, and repeat three times.

Partner Drill: Sparring with a partner can help you apply what you've learned in an actual fighting situation. Start slow, focus on technique, and gradually increase the intensity as you improve.

Mastering the Cross in Boxing: A Step-By-Step Guide

A cross is one of the most effective punches in boxing. [14]

Boxing may look effortless when you watch professionals in the ring, but executing each move requires a lot of hard work, skill, and strength. A cross is one of the most effective punches in boxing and can change the game in seconds. Therefore, it's an essential technique every boxer should master to become a formidable opponent in the ring. This section looks closely at the definition, purpose, execution, common mistakes, and training drills to improve your cross in boxing.

Definition and Purpose of a Cross

A cross, also known as a straight, is a power punch thrown from your rear hand, usually your right hand if you're right-handed or vice versa if you're left-handed. The purpose of the cross is to create distance between you and your opponent while simultaneously delivering a powerful punch to their head or body. In addition, the cross often sets up other punches, like a hook or an uppercut.

Step-By-Step Set Up and Execution of the Cross

To execute a cross, follow these steps:

1. Position your feet shoulder-width apart with your left foot slightly forward and the right foot slightly back.

2. Next, keep your fists raised, elbows tucked close to your body, and your chin down to protect yourself from counterattacks.

3. From this position, use your hips, core, and shoulder to rotate your body as you straighten your back arm to extend your punch toward your target.

4. Remember to twist your wrist so that your knuckles are vertical when making contact with your opponent.

5. Last, recover by quickly returning your backhand to its original position, close to your face.

Common Mistakes to Avoid

Many people throw their cross without a set-up. However, a successful cross requires more than just a powerful punch. It must be timed correctly and using your entire body. Here are other common mistakes to avoid:

1. **Not Practicing with the Correct Weight:** The cross is a powerful punch, and if you're not used to throwing it with the proper weight, you won't generate the same power when in a fight. Use a heavy bag that can take the punishment and that you're comfortable throwing your punches with the proper weight.

2. **Not Keeping Your Guard Up:** Remember to keep your chin down, tuck in your elbows when throwing the cross, and be prepared for a counterpunch.

3. **Throwing Wild Punches:** This mistake will quickly get you knocked out in a fight. Instead, keep your punches tight and controlled, and only throw them when you have an opening.

4. **Not Following through with Your Punches:** Extend your arm fully, snap your wrists when you throw the punch, and follow through with your entire body.

5. **Not Staying Balanced:** Keep your feet planted firmly on the ground when you throw it. Additionally, keep your body loose and relaxed so you can quickly shift your weight from one foot to the other.

Training Drills to Improve Your Cross

Like any boxing technique, mastering the cross requires consistent practice. To improve your cross, here are some training drills to practice:

1. **Jab-Cross-Slip Drill:** Stand in your boxing stance with your left hand in front of you and your right hand at your chin. Jab with your left hand, then immediately cross with your right. As you cross, slip to the side so that you are no longer in front of your opponent to avoid getting hit by their counterpunch. Repeat this drill for 30 seconds.

2. **Jab-Jab-Cross Drill:** In the same position as the first drill, with your left hand out and your right hand at your chin. Jab twice with your left hand, then cross with your right. As you cross, step forward to be in front of your opponent. This way, you can land your punch and set up a follow-up attack. Repeat this drill for 30 seconds.

3. **Jab-Cross-Hook Drill:** In the same position as the first two drills, with your left hand out and your right hand at your chin. Jab with your left hand, then immediately cross with your right. As you cross, throw a hook with your left hand. You will catch your opponent off guard and land a powerful punch. Repeat this drill for 30 seconds.

The Art of the Hook: Improve Your Boxing Skills

A hook is a punching technique used to hit opponents from the side. [15]

A hook is a powerful punch combined with speed, accuracy, and technique. Whether you are a novice or a seasoned boxer, it is a great tool to have in your arsenal. This section discusses the definition and purpose of a hook, a step-by-step guide on how to set up and execute a hook, common mistakes to avoid, and training drills to improve your hook.

Definition and Purpose of a Hook

A hook is a punching technique in boxing to hit an opponent from the side, either to the head or body. It is an effective punch requiring excellent timing and coordination. The hook aims to deliver a decisive blow while maintaining control and accuracy. A properly executed hook can differentiate between winning and losing a fight.

Step-By-Step Set Up and Execution of the Hook

Successfully executing a hook requires patience and practice. Here is a step-by-step guide on how to set up and execute the hook:

1. Stand in a boxing stance facing your opponent.
2. Shift your weight to your back foot while keeping your elbow close to your body.

3. Pivot on the ball of your foot and turn your hip towards your opponent while swinging your arm in a circular motion.

4. Aim for your target's temple, cheek, or ribs, and land the punch with the knuckles of your middle and index fingers.

5. Always keep your other arm up to protect yourself, and be prepared for counterattacks.

Common Mistakes to Avoid

While a hook is a powerful and effective punch, it is essential to avoid inevitable common mistakes:

1. **Not Turning Your Body Enough:** You must turn your whole body and hip during the punch to generate maximum power.

2. **Not Keeping the Elbow Close to Your Body:** It decreases the power of your punch and makes it easier for your opponent to block or counter.

3. **Not Pivoting on the Ball of Your Foot:** You must pivot on the ball of your foot to generate enough power for the punch to land effectively.

4. **Not Aiming for the Correct Target:** You must aim for your target's temple, cheek, or ribs to land the punch with maximum power.

5. **Hitting Too High or Too Low:** Always aim for the correct target to ensure maximum power and accuracy.

6. **Leaving Yourself Vulnerable to Counterattacks:** Always keep your other arm up to protect yourself from counterattacks.

Training Drills to Improve Your Hook

You can do several drills to improve the accuracy and power of your hook. Here are a few examples:

1. **Jump Rope:** Jumping rope is a great way to improve footwork and coordination. Focus on moving quickly and smoothly while jumping rope; it will help you develop the footwork necessary to throw accurate and powerful hooks.

2. **Punching Mitts:** Punching mitts are a great way to improve accuracy and power with your punches. Focus on throwing accurate and powerful punches while working with punching mitts; it will help transfer those skills into the ring.

3. **Reflex Ball:** A reflex ball is an excellent tool for developing hand-eye coordination. Focus on hitting the ball as quickly as possible; it will help transfer those skills into the ring.

4. **Heavy Bag:** One of the best ways to improve your hooks is to practice on a heavy bag. A heavy bag helps you develop power and accuracy with your hooks. You should focus on throwing your hooks with evil intent to knock your opponent out.

5. **Shadowboxing:** Shadowboxing is a great way to work on your technique without having an opponent present. It would be best if you focused on throwing accurate and powerful punches. Shadowboxing helps you develop the muscle memory to throw real and powerful hooks in the ring.

A hook is a technique that takes time and practice to master. Incorporating the hook into your training improves your overall boxing skills and gives you an edge in the ring. Remember to focus on your technique, aim for the right target, and always protect yourself. With these tips and training drills, you will be on your way to throwing powerful hooks like a professional boxer. Keep practicing, and never give up on your boxing journey.

How to Master the Uppercut Punch

An uppercut can deliver a knockout blow. [16]

The uppercut punch is a powerful tool to add to your boxing arsenal. This punch is designed to deliver a knockout blow and is handy during a fight. However, correctly delivering an uppercut punch takes great skill and practice. This section guides you through the definition, purpose, and execution of the uppercut punch. Also provided are tips on avoiding common mistakes and training drills to improve your uppercut.

Definition and Purpose of an Uppercut

The uppercut punch is a short punch thrown upward toward the opponent's chin or torso. The uppercut delivers a knockout blow by taking advantage of the opponent's guard. Most boxers use the uppercut when the opponent is leaning forward or trying to make a move. This punch is very effective when the opponent attempts to close in on you.

Step-By-Step Set Up and Execution of the Uppercut

Here's how to properly execute the uppercut punch:

1. Stand in your boxing stance with your feet shoulder-width apart and your chin down.

2. Shift your weight to your back foot and pivot on the ball of that foot. It gives you power and leverage for the punch.
3. Keeping your elbow close to your body, throw the punch up with the knuckles of your middle and index fingers.
4. Aim for the opponent's chin or solar plexus and put your body into it.
5. Return to your stance after throwing the punch and immediately be prepared for a counterattack.

Common Mistakes to Avoid

Out of all the punches, the uppercut is often one of the most misused or over-applied. Here are some common mistakes to avoid:

1. **Rushing:** Take your time, and don't rush the punch. Ensure you set up the punch correctly before executing it.
2. **Reaching:** Wait to reach for your opponent with the punch. Keep it close to your body, and pivot on the ball of your foot for power and leverage.
3. **Lowering The Guard:** Always keep your chin down and your guard up. An exposed chin could be a potential target for a counterpunch.
4. **Not Loading:** Load up the punch by shifting your weight to your back foot before throwing it.
5. **Dropping Your Elbow:** Keep your elbow close to your body as you throw the punch. It increases the power of the punch and avoids getting countered.

Training Drills to Improve Your Uppercut

To perfect your uppercut punch, incorporate the following training drills into your routine:

1. **Fist Movements:** Practice moving your fist from the guard to the uppercut position and back again. Keep your hand close to your body as you move it.
2. **Sparring Partner:** Find a partner and practice throwing the uppercut on focus pads or heavy bags. The goal is to set up and execute the punch properly.
3. **Shadow Boxing:** Practice throwing the uppercut in front of a mirror or without one. Focus on setting up correctly and throwing the punch with proper form and power.
4. **Practice Standalone Uppercuts:** Do the uppercut punch independently and pay attention to details. Focus on your form, power, and timing. The more attention you pay to the elements, the better your uppercut will become.
5. **Follow Up with Combinations:** Combine uppercuts with other punches after perfecting the form. It helps you learn to use the punch with different shots.

How to Perfect Your Counterpunches in Boxing

Counterpunches can help you deflect your opponent's punches. [17]

The great boxer Muhammad Ali was known for his swift footwork and powerful counterpunching. In a sport like boxing, anticipating and countering your opponent's moves can give you a significant advantage. Counterpunch is a strategic move to deflect and counter your opponent's punches while conserving your energy and maximizing your chances of landing a punch. This section discusses the definition and purpose of a counterpunch, step-by-step set-up and execution, common mistakes to avoid, and training drills to improve your counterpunching skills.

Definition and Purpose of a Counterpunch

Counterpunch is a punch thrown after dodging an incoming punch from your opponent. The counterpunch aims to exploit your opponent's mistakes by catching them off guard and generating power. It allows the counterpuncher to take control of the round convincingly. Effective counterpunching is all about timing and precision.

Step-By-Step Set-Up and Execution of the Counterpunch

Remember, the counterpunch should be used sparingly. Here are the basic steps for setting up and executing a counterattack:

1.   Step out of the way of your opponent's punch as you lean slightly to one side and put your chin down; this puts you in a position to throw a counterpunch.

2. Bring your guard back up and your fist forward as you pivot on the ball of your foot.

3. Use power and speed to land your punch while keeping your elbows close to your body and chin down.

4. Return to the guard position when the counterpunch is thrown.

When an incoming punch is thrown, move your upper body, head, and feet away from the incoming punch. If the incoming punch is a jab, use a slip and slide to the outside of the jab and deliver a counterpunch to the head. For incoming hooks, pivot your feet, move your hips, and throw a counterpunch to the face or body. For incoming uppercuts, lean back to one side and throw a counterpunch to the head or body.

Common Mistakes to Avoid

When attempting a counterpunch, avoid the following common mistakes:

1. **Being Too Slow:** Remember to time your counter punch just right. Waiting too long to throw your punch gives your opponent time to recover and launch another punch.

2. **Not Keeping The Balance:** Keep your balance by keeping your feet, knees, and hips aligned; this helps you move quickly and throw a powerful counterpunch.

3. **Not Anticipating The Opponent's Move:** Always look for the signs of an incoming punch and anticipate your opponent's next move.

4. **Not Maintaining Proper Form**: Keep your elbows in, chin down, and guard up to help you move quickly and maintain balance.

Training Drills to Improve Your Counterpunching Skills

The following are some training drills to help improve your counterpunching skills:

1. Double Slip Drill: This drill involves slipping two jabs before throwing a counterpunch.

2. Jab/Cross Drill: This drill involves slipping a jab and counters with a cross punch.

3. Hook/Uppercut Drill: This drill involves slipping a hook and countering with an uppercut punch.

4. Shadowboxing Drill: This drill involves shadowboxing and working on your timing

5. Double Uppercut Drill: This drill involves slipping two uppercuts before throwing a counterpunch.

Regularly practicing these drills improves your timing, power, and accuracy and helps you to achieve an effective counterpunch. In addition, with these tips and tricks, you can maximize your chances of landing a powerful punch.

This chapter provided an overview of the various punches and counterpunches in boxing and some training drills to improve your skills. From jabs and crosses to hooks and uppercuts, you've learned the basics of throwing each punch and how to effectively time and execute a counterpunch. With practice and dedication, you can produce an effective counterpunch, taking advantage of your opponent's mistakes and increasing your chances of winning the round. Good luck.

Chapter 6: Defense Tips and Techniques

While throwing punches is the flashy side of the sport, the art of defense is as important. A good defense can help you avoid getting hit and conserve energy for when it counts. Skilled boxers can slip punches, weave through opponents, and use footwork to dodge incoming attacks. It's not easy, but the result is well worth it. A successful defense can give you the edge to come out of a brutal battle victorious.

This chapter focuses on defensive boxing tips and techniques. It instructs how to block and deflect various punches, defend your head, use the proper footwork, bob, weave, slip, clinch, roll, parry, and pivot. These critical elements of defensive boxing put you in a prime position to win. The fight is won or lost in the details; mastering these skills can make all the difference.

Defensive Blocking

Defensive blocking can be used for an offensive strategy.

Boxing can be an exhilarating sport, but it is dangerous. A well-timed punch can abruptly end a match, so fighters must master the art of defense. Defensive blocking is as vital as an excellent offensive strategy. This section discusses two essential boxing techniques, deflecting punches and protecting your head. Whether a seasoned professional or a novice, these techniques will keep you safe and extend your fighting career.

Deflecting Punches

Deflecting punches is a crucial defensive blocking technique every fighter should master. It involves using your hand or forearm to redirect the opponent's punch, making it miss its target. When done correctly, deflecting punches can disrupt the opponent's rhythm, waste their energy, and create an opening for a counterattack. Here are some tips for perfecting this technique:

1. **Maintain a Relaxed Stance:** Fighting with a tense stance tires you out quickly. Instead, keep your body relaxed, maintain a low center of gravity, and stay light on your feet. If you remain alert, your reflexes will be quicker, allowing

you to sense better and redirect incoming punches.

2. **Use the Forearm:** A firm forearm is an excellent tool for deflecting punches. Keep your arms in a guard position and use the forearm to brush away any incoming hook or jab. The forearm should be angled to absorb the punch's force and redirect it away from your head or body.

3. **Keep Your Eyes on Your Opponent's Shoulders:** The torso initiates all the punches. Keeping your eyes fixed on your opponent's shoulders, you predict the direction of the punch and prepare accordingly. When you see the shoulder tense, you know a punch is coming, and use the appropriate defensive blocking technique to avoid it.

4. **Use a Deflection Technique:** Depending on the punch's angle and direction, you can use several deflection techniques. The most common is the parry, block, and slap. If the punch comes from high, use a parry to deflect it. If the punch is coming from low, then use a block. If the punch is coming from an angle, use a slap to deflect it.

Protecting Your Head

Protecting your head is the most vital defensive blocking technique in boxing. A blow to the head can lead to a knockout, brain damage, or death. Here are some tips for protecting your head:

1. **Keep Your Guard Up:** Keep your hands close to your face and your elbows tucked in. This stance shields your head from punches. The ideal guard position is with your chin down, elbows in, and fists up around the face.

2. **Keep the Ideal Distance:** An excellent way to protect your head is by keeping the proper distance between you and your opponent. If you are too far away, it will be hard to land punches. If you are too close, your opponent will have a clear shot at your head. Therefore, the ideal distance is just outside the range of your opponent's punches.

3. **Practice Head Movement:** Good head movement involves ducking, slipping, and bobbing. Practice these techniques to become more elusive and avoid being hit. In addition, it's essential to keep your head moving so that the opponent cannot predict where you'll move and set up their punch accordingly.

4. **Know When to Clinch:** If your opponent's punches are too fast or too strong, then clinch. Clinching is holding your opponent in a close embrace to stop them from hitting you. Grabbing the opponent's arms and holding them close to your body prevents them from throwing punches.

Footwork Basics of Boxing: Moving Around the Ring with Speed and Precision

Footwork is one of the most critical aspects of the sport. Proper footwork allows boxers to move quickly and efficiently around the ring, throwing effective punches while avoiding their opponents' attacks. This section looks closely at some basic footwork techniques boxers use when moving around the ring. It covers everything from basic stance and balance to shifting weight and adjusting foot position for different punches. Whether you are a seasoned pro or a beginner, mastering these basics is essential for success in the ring.

Getting into Stance

Before moving around the ring, you must get into the proper stance. It means standing with your feet shoulder-width apart, with your toes pointed slightly outward. Your knees should be slightly bent, and your weight should be evenly distributed on both feet. You can adjust your stance from here depending on your opponent's position and movements.

Professional boxers often adjust their stances to be more aggressive or defensive, depending on the situation. For example, if your opponent throws a lot of jabs, you might take a more defensive stance with your hands up and your chin tucked down. On the other hand, if you intend to throw a combination, you may adjust your stance to be slightly broader and more aggressive.

Moving around the Ring

Once you're in the proper stance, it's time to start moving. You can move forward, backward, and side to side by taking small, quick steps. Stay light on your feet and keep your knees bent to maintain balance and stability. Take short steps with your lead foot, using your back foot to propel yourself forward as needed. When moving backward, reverse this motion, taking small steps with your back foot and using your lead foot to push off. Lateral movement involves taking small steps to the side to avoid your opponent's punches or to get into a better position for your punches.

Balancing and Shifting Weight

As you move around the ring, you must maintain proper balance and shift your weight effectively. It involves keeping your weight centered over your feet and shifting it from foot to foot. For example, when throwing a punch with your lead hand, you turn your weight slightly to your lead foot while anchoring your back foot for stability. The same principle applies when throwing punches with your backhand. You shift your weight to the opposite side and use your lead foot for balance.

Adjusting Foot Position for Different Punches

Different punches require different foot positioning. For example, when throwing a jab, your lead foot should step forward slightly, giving you more reach for your punch. Your lead foot should pivot outward for a hook, allowing you to twist your body and generate more power behind your punch. Finally, for an uppercut, get close to your opponent, stepping forward with your lead foot to get in range.

Practicing Footwork

Like any skill, footwork requires practice to master. Spend time working on your footwork in the gym, focusing on moving quickly and efficiently around the ring. Practice different punches and foot positioning, getting comfortable with each movement and transition. You will throw more effective punches and easily avoid your opponent's attacks as you improve your footwork. Here are some drills to get you started:

1. **Shadowboxing:** Practice your footwork and punches on the heavy bag, focusing on speed, power, and accuracy.
2. **Reaction Drills:** Have a partner throw punches at varying speeds and angles. Practice shifting your weight, adjusting foot positioning, and dodging or blocking the punches.
3. **Speed Drills:** Time how fast you can move around the ring, practicing footwork drills at various speeds.
4. **Slip Drills:** Have your partner throw jabs and crosses at you, and practice slipping the punches or dodging to the side.

Head Movement Techniques

Boxing is not just about throwing punches but also knowing how to avoid them. Therefore, head movement techniques in boxing are essential if you want to be a good boxer. These techniques can help you avoid punches, counterattack, and move confidently in the ring. This section discusses in detail these techniques and how to master them.

1. **Bobbing:** Bobbing is a technique that moves the head up and down while keeping the feet rooted to the ground. It is an excellent technique to avoid hooks and overhand punches. To perform this technique, keep your knees slightly bent, and move your head up and down fluidly. Keep your hands up to defend yourself against jabs and straights. Practice bobbing by having a partner throw punches at you while you bob and weave to avoid them.

2. **Weaving:** Weaving is a technique of moving your head from side to side while bending your knees. It is an effective technique to avoid straight punches. To perform this technique, move your head to the left and right while keeping your hands up to defend against hooks. You can practice weaving by having a partner throw straight punches at you while you weave to avoid them.

3. **Slipping:** Slipping is a technique of moving the head to the side to avoid a punch. It is an excellent technique for avoiding jabs and straights. To perform this technique, move your head to the left or the right while bending your knees. Practice slipping by having a partner throw jabs and straights at you while you slip to avoid them.

4. **Rolling:** Rolling is a technique of moving your head in a circular motion to avoid punches. It is an effective technique for preventing hooks and overhand punches. To perform this technique, move your head in a circular motion while keeping your hands up to defend against jabs and straights. Practice rolling by having a partner throw hooks and overhand punches at you while you move to avoid them.

5. **Parrying:** Parrying is a technique using your hands to deflect a punch. It is an excellent technique for avoiding jabs and straights. To perform this technique, use your front hand to deflect a jab or straight by pushing it to the side. Practice parrying by having a partner throw jabs and straights at you while you dodge to deflect them.

6. **Pivoting:** Pivoting is a technique that involves turning your body to avoid a punch. It is an effective technique for preventing hooks and overhand punches. To perform this technique, pivot on your front foot to turn your body to the left or the right. Keep your hands up to defend against jabs and straights. Practice shifting by having a partner throw hooks and overhand punches at you while you pivot to avoid them.

Mastering head movement techniques in boxing is essential to be a good boxer. These techniques can help you avoid punches and counterattack effectively. Bobbing, weaving, slipping, rolling, dodging, and pivoting are essential techniques every aspiring boxer should master. Practice these techniques regularly with a partner to improve your skills and your confidence in the ring. Remember to keep your hands up at all times, stay calm, and move with fluidity and grace.

Clinching for Defense: How to Use Your Arms and Control Distance

Clinching is a valuable defensive tool.

In boxing, sometimes you need to use your entire body to defend yourself, including your arms and clinching skills. A clinch is when you grab your opponent's body to control their movement and reduce potential damage. Clinching can be a valuable defensive tool. This section explores two critical aspects of clinching, using your arms for defense and controlling distance in the clinch.

Using Your Arms for Defense

Your arms are a crucial component to successful clinching. When your opponent is attacking, use your arms to protect your head and body. For example, keep your elbows in and your hands up around your face. If your opponent tries to hit you, your head and body are protected.

When in the clinch, your arms should grab your opponent's body. Keep your elbows in tight and press your body into theirs. You can control their movements and restrict the space they have to move around you. Use your arms to block your opponent's knees, which can be very effective against fighters who try to knee you in the clinch.

Another excellent use for your arms is creating space when needed. For example, if you are in a tight clinch, and your opponent controls your movement, use your arms to push them away. It creates distance between you and your opponent, giving you room to move and defend yourself.

Controlling Distance in the Clinch

Controlling distance is a fundamental aspect of clinching. You must know how to get close to your opponent and stay there without giving them too much space to move around you. The key is taking small steps and making minor adjustments to your stance and body position. When first entering the clinch, take small steps toward your opponent. Get your head and body close to theirs, and wrap your arms around their body. Once you control their movement, take small steps backward or sideways to maintain your position.

If your opponent tries to move away from you, use your arms to pull them back. Keep your elbows tight to your body and use your chest and shoulders to press into theirs. You will control their movement and keep them close. Sometimes your opponent will push you back or move away from you. In these situations, be patient, and make minor adjustments to your stance and body position. Keep your arms up, ready to defend, and wait for the right opportunity to strike.

Clinching can be a very effective defensive tool when used correctly. Using your arms for defense and controlling distance in the clinch are two critical aspects of successful clinching. Practice these skills with a partner to improve your technique and control. Remember to keep your elbows tight and use your chest and shoulders to control your opponent's movements. Clinching can become a valuable component of your fighting repertoire with some practice.

Essential Boxing Defense Tips from Pro Fighters

Whether a beginner or an experienced boxer, defense is essential to your training regimen. Proper defense can minimize the damage inflicted by an opponent's punches and tire them out. Some of the best boxing defense tips from pro fighters you can incorporate into your training are listed below.

1. **Keep Your Hands Up:** One of the most basic and essential aspects of boxing defense is to keep your hands up in front of your face. Your hands should be positioned to cover your nose and chin while providing enough room to see your opponent's punches. This defensive technique blocks punches coming directly at you and from an angle.

2. **Stay Alert and Keep Your Eyes Open:** While fighting, you must maintain your focus and stay alert. Watch your opponent closely and look for signs of an attack. This way, you can plan your moves based on your opponent's. Keeping your eyes open is an essential skill you must develop.

3. **Boxing Stance:** A solid boxing stance can help you defend yourself better during fights. Keep your feet shoulder-width apart, your left foot forward (if you're right-handed), your knees slightly bent, and your hands up to protect your face. Use your left hand to block your opponent's jab and your right hand for power punches. Last, keep your elbows close to your ribs to make it harder for your opponent to hit your body.

4. **Counterattack:** The best defense is a good offense. When you see an opening, take full advantage of it. Throw a counter punch and keep your opponent backtracking, relieving the pressure on you and helping you gain momentum. When you get the opportunity to counterattack, be quick and aggressive.

5. **Partner Drills:** Practice with your partner to learn to defend yourself. Do partner drills and learn to block their punches and land your punches. Practicing with a partner develops timing and reflexes. In a real fight, you must anticipate your opponent's moves and get your punches in before they do. Getting hands-on experience with a partner will develop this skill.

6. **Focus on Timing:** Timing is an essential skill for boxing defense. You must time your blocks and counterpunches perfectly to avoid getting hit. Focus on developing your timing and reflexes by doing live drills with a partner. Remember, you can only sometimes rely on your guard to protect you. You must be alert and time your blocks correctly to defend yourself effectively.

7. **Look Out for Opponent's Combinations:** Paying attention to your opponent's combinations is essential. If you notice them throwing a variety of punches, be prepared to block them all. Learn to defend against combinations by doing drills with a partner and to ensure you stay alert during your fights. Learn to anticipate your opponent's moves and react quickly.

Defense is vital for your boxing performance. Developing a good defense to avoid taking unnecessary hits is crucial. This chapter covered defensive blocking, deflecting punches, bobbing and weaving, slipping, clinching, rolling, and parrying. It shared some of the best boxing defense tips from pro fighters to incorporate into your training regime. Remember to keep your hands up, stay alert, and keep your eyes open. Always move your head, focus on your footwork, be ready to counterattack, and practice partner drills. These tips will improve your defense and lead you to success.

Chapter 7: 13 Pro Combinations You Didn't Know

The art of boxing is not only about throwing punches. It's combining them the most strategically. The right combination of punches can differentiate between victory and defeat. A well-executed combination involves precision, accuracy, and timing. It's like a choreographed dance where each step must be taken with total focus and determination. Combining punches can be challenging, especially when facing a skilled opponent, but it's a thing of beauty once mastered.

Mastering combinations should be high on your priority list to have a shot at becoming a boxing champion. This chapter teaches the basics, intermediate, advanced combos, and some finishing moves to help you gain the upper hand in a fight. In addition, it contains step-by-step instructions on each combination so you can practice and hone your skills until they become second nature. After all, practice makes perfect.

Basic Boxing Combinations to Boost Your Skills

Every boxer is familiar with the importance of mastering the basics. Basic boxing combinations are the bread and butter of boxing that help you gain the upper hand in the ring. You must work on your technique and form to execute the perfect punch, block, and counterattack. This section guides you through the essential combinations to take your boxing skills to the next level.

Jab and Cross Combination

JAB   CROSS

Jab and cross combination

This is one of the most common and effective boxing combinations. Start with a quick and sharp jab to your opponent's face, followed by a powerful cross punch with your dominant hand. Keep your guard up after the cross punch to avoid retaliation from your opponent. Practice this combination with a speed or heavy bag to improve your timing and coordination.

Hook and Uppercut Combination

The hook and uppercut combination is a great way to surprise your opponent. Start with a quick hook punch with your dominant hand to your opponent's head or body, followed by an uppercut with your other hand to catch them off guard. Keep your body balanced and grounded during the combination to avoid getting knocked out. Practice this combination on a heavy bag to improve your stamina and power.

Overhand Right Combo

Right overhand combination. [18]

The right overhand combination is a powerful punch that can knock your opponent down. Start with a jab to set up your punch, then throw a right overhand punch with your dominant hand directly to your opponent's head. This combination must be executed using the proper technique to avoid telegraphing your move. The key to this combination is to turn your hips and follow through with your shoulder during the punch.

One-Two-Three Combo

JAB   CROSS   HOOK

One-Two-Three Combo

The One-Two-Three combination is a staple in a boxer's arsenal. Start with a jab, followed by a cross punch, and finish with a hook punch to your opponent's head or body. Pivot your foot during the hook punch to add more power to your punch. This combination is perfect for taking down your opponent with a quick and powerful sequence of punches.

Mastering Intermediate Boxing Moves

Intermediate moves are critical for boxers to improve their performance in the ring. These moves involve combinations of punches requiring speed, agility, accuracy, and power. This section reveals three intermediate boxing moves to help you gain an edge over your opponent. Practicing these moves regularly on a heavy and speed bag to perfect your technique will make you unstoppable in the ring.

Left Hook and Overhand Right Combo

The left hook and right overhand combo is a powerful combination that can leave your opponent disoriented and off-balance. Start by throwing a left hook to the head or body, followed by a right overhand punch. Ensure you pivot your left foot as you throw the left hook. This movement helps increase the power of your punch by transferring your weight to the front foot. The right overhand should come as a surprise to your opponent, throwing them off balance. Remember to follow through with the strike to maximize the impact.

Lead Uppercut and Rear Uppercut Combination

LEAD UPPERCUT   REAR UPPERCUT

Lead and rear uppercut combination

A lead and rear uppercut combination is an effective inside-fighting move closing the distance with your opponent. Start by throwing a lead uppercut punch with your left hand and follow up with a rear uppercut with your right hand. The lead uppercut should focus on landing on the chin, while the rear uppercut should aim for the solar plexus or liver. Practice this combination with a speed or heavy bag to increase your accuracy and speed.

Double Hook and Uppercut Combo

The double hook and uppercut combo is a flashy and effective technique to confuse your opponent. Start by throwing a left hook to the body or head, follow it up with a right hook to the body or head, and end it with a left uppercut. Pivot your feet and rotate through the hips as you deliver the punches. The hooks should be aimed at the ribs or the temple, while the uppercut should aim at the chin. Practice this combo by imagining your opponent's movement and adjusting your punches accordingly.

Advanced Combos

Boxing combos are tricky to master, but they can take your game to the next level once you get the hang of it. The right combos can help you set the pace, create openings, and stun your opponents with quick power strikes. So, to advance your boxing game, it's time to work on advanced boxing combos. This section shares some of the most effective combos to elevate your game and keep your opponents on their toes.

Lead Right Hook and Rear Left Hook Combo

This combo starts with a lead right hook

The lead right hook and rear left hook combo is a powerful combination to close the distance and overwhelm your opponent. Start with a jab, create an opening, and follow it up with a lead right hook. Then, as your opponent's guard drops to defend against the lead hook, follow up with a rear left hook that can deliver a knockout. This combo requires good footwork and timing, so practicing it with a sparring partner is better.

Lead Right Uppercut and Rear Left Hook Combo

The lead right uppercut and rear left hook combo is another effective combination to catch your opponent off-guard. Start with a quick jab followed by a lead right uppercut. The uppercut should connect with your opponent's chin, leaving them stunned and open for a rear left hook. The left hook is a devastating punch that can knock your opponent out, so ensure you have good balance and stance before you attempt it.

Four-Punch Combination

The four-punch combination is worth trying for a more complex combo. This combo starts with a lead left hook, followed by a jab, a lead hook, and a cross. The first punch should create an opening for the jab, which sets up the lead hook. The final punch, the cross, delivers the knockout power shot that can end the fight. This combo requires good coordination and timing, so practicing it slowly and gradually adding speed is better.

Lead Right Straight and Rear Left Uppercut Combo

Start this combo with a right straight punch

The lead right straight and rear left uppercut combo is a variation of the previous combos and can be performed differently. Start with a lead right straight followed by a rear left uppercut. Then, the uppercut can be delivered to your opponent's chin or body, depending on their guard. This combo can be performed with different variations, including a left hook, a right hook, or a body shot.

Double Jab and Right Cross Combo

The double jab and right cross combo is a classic combination to control the fight's pace. Start with two quick jabs creating an opening for a powerful right cross. The double jab keeps your opponent on their toes and sets up your power shots. This combo requires good accuracy and speed, so practice your jabs and crosses before attempting it.

Knockout Techniques: Master These Finishing Moves

It's no secret that knockout punches can be the difference between winning and losing a fight. But, as a boxer, mastering finishing moves can give you the upper hand in ending the battle in your favor. This section looks at some of the most effective finishing moves in your arsenal.

Lead Left Hook and Rear Right Hook Combo

One of the most popular finishing moves in boxing is the lead left hook and rear right hook combo. This technique starts with a left-lead hook and a rear right hook to throw your opponent off balance and muddle their defense. The key to executing this combo is ensuring both punches are thrown with quick, fluid movements. Make sure to land your punches with precision and power to ensure a successful knockout.

Lead Left Uppercut, Rear Right Cross, and Lead Right Uppercut Combo

Another effective finishing move is the lead left uppercut, rear right cross, and lead right uppercut combo. This combination leads with a left uppercut, followed by a rear right cross, and finishing with a lead right uppercut. This combo is highly effective in close combat situations, as it allows you to land powerful punches even when your opponent has their guard up. Again, to ensure maximum impact, the key to executing this combo is maintaining good footwork and speed.

Six-Punch Combination

The six-punch combination is a powerful and complex finishing move involving six punches thrown quickly. This technique can be executed in several variations. The most common is a combination of two jabs, crosses, and hooks. This finishing move requires excellent timing and precision, so focusing on your technique and speed is essential when practicing. The six-punch combination is effective in wearing down your opponent and finding an opening for a knockout punch.

Body Shots

Body shots target the liver and solar plexus.

While many finishing moves focus on targeting your opponent's head, body shots can also be highly effective in securing a knockout. This technique targets your opponent's midsection, specifically their liver. A well-placed body shot can effectively weaken your opponent and set them up for a knockout punch to the head. To execute a successful body shot, aim for your opponent's midsection, and use your body weight to generate power and force behind your punch.

Feints and Fakes

Feints can distract your opponent

Last, another effective finishing move technique is using feints and fakes to distract and confuse your opponent. This technique pretends to throw a punch in one direction before throwing a knockout punch in another. It is a highly effective way to catch your opponent off guard and land a successful knockout punch. However, it's essential to be cautious when using this technique, as it requires a high skill level and can be risky.

Tips for Finding the Best Boxing Combinations

Boxing is a fascinating and challenging sport requiring much skill and endurance. One of the most important aspects of boxing is learning to use combinations effectively to gain an advantage over your opponent. Good boxing combinations require physical strength, strategic planning, and swift execution. This section provides excellent tips for finding the best boxing combinations to improve your boxing skills and dominate the ring.

Develop a Strong Foundation

Before practicing complicated boxing combinations, you must build a solid foundation that includes basic techniques like jabs, crosses, hooks, and uppercuts. These moves, when executed correctly, can devastate your opponent. Start with the basics and practice until you can perform these moves perfectly. Then, gradually move on to more complex combinations. Your initial combinations should be basic enough that you can execute them without thinking and become second nature.

Study Professional Boxing Matches

Watching professional boxing matches provides excellent opportunities to observe and learn from the best. When you watch these matches, take note of the combinations your favorite boxers use and try to recreate them during your training sessions. Feel free to pause the videos and practice the moves slowly to gain a clear understanding of how to execute them with precision.

Practice with a Partner

Practicing with a partner can help you improve your techniques. [19]

Practicing with a partner is a great way to improve your boxing techniques. Find someone willing to collaborate on your training sessions and create various combinations. Start by throwing basic punches and gradually add more intricate moves once you feel more confident. Working with a partner helps improve your timing, accuracy, and speed.

Practicing with a partner is a great way to improve your boxing techniques. Find someone willing to collaborate on your training sessions and create various combinations. Start by throwing basic punches and gradually add more intricate moves once you feel more confident. Working with a partner helps improve your timing, accuracy, and speed.

Develop Your Style

A good boxer has a unique style. It takes time to develop your boxing style, but experimenting with different combinations and techniques creates a personal style that matches your physical abilities. Trying different combinations will help you to find the right moves that work for you in the ring. Of course, the best way to find your style is to practice, so spend enough time mastering the basics and learning new combinations.

Practice against Different Opponents

Once you've developed a few combinations, it's time to test them out against different opponents. You will understand the strengths and weaknesses of your technique and make necessary adjustments. Working with other opponents sharpens your reflexes, giving you an edge in the ring. The more opponents you practice against, the higher your chances of success.

Consistency Is Key

Consistency is vital to developing boxing skills. You must practice regularly to get the most out of your training sessions. Consistency helps build muscle memory, which is significant in executing complex techniques. A big part of success in the ring comes down to practice and repetition. Consistency will improve your boxing skills and give you the confidence to succeed in the ring.

Keep Your Combinations Simple

Keeping your combinations simple but effective is the key to success in the ring. You don't need a lot of fancy moves to win a fight; all you need is one or two powerful punches that will land and impact your opponent. So, keep it simple and stick with the basics. It's far more effective than executing complex combinations that might not work. A few well-executed punches can go a long way and make all the difference in the ring.

Mastering boxing combinations takes time, dedication, and patience. Remember to start with the basics and gradually move to more complicated moves. Watching professional boxing matches, working with a partner, and developing your style are ways to improve your boxing skills. Consistency is critical, and practice makes perfect. Stay focused, keep working hard, and you'll execute impressive combinations in no time.

Boxing is not only about throwing punches but also executing them precisely and accurately. Mastering the basic boxing combinations can help you become a skilled fighter. It's essential to start with the basics, work on your form and technique, and graduate to more complex combinations. Find a good boxing coach to guide you through these combinations and improve your skills. Remember, practice makes perfect, so keep training and pushing yourself to become your best boxer.

Chapter 8: Peek-A-Boo: Sparring Secrets of Pro Boxers

Boxing is an intense sport demanding physical fitness and mental agility. Pro boxers are known for their skill and technique, but what are their secrets regarding sparring?

The key to winning the match is not just brute strength but strategy and quick thinking. With thorough preparation and a determined attitude, anyone can learn the sparring secrets of pro boxers and become a champion. This chapter will start you on the path of sparring success.

This chapter explores the basics of sparring, discusses the right time to start sparring with an opponent, breaks down the technical aspects of sparring, and provides expert-level tips from the pros. From Mike Tyson's infamous "peek-a-boo" style to head movement and footwork, you'll be well prepared to take on your first match. Then, on your way to the sparring party, explore everything about sparring.

The Basics of Sparring

Sparring can help you improve your skills. [20]

Sparring is a standard part of almost every combat sport and a great way to improve your skills. Whether learning martial arts or practicing kickboxing, sparring is essential to becoming a better fighter. This section covers sparring basics, providing everything you need to know to get started, from the benefits of sparring to the techniques.

Why You Should Spar

Sparring is integral to martial arts training because it exposes you to real-life situations. It allows you to practice your techniques against an opponent and learn to react in different situations. Additionally, sparring helps you improve your reflexes, timing, footwork, and endurance. With these benefits, sparring is essential to becoming a skilled fighter.

The Different Types of Sparring

Sparring can be broken down into different types, like hard, light, or technical. Hard sparring is the most intense form, where opponents fight at full power. In contrast, light sparring is less severe, with fighters only using 30%-60% of their strength. Finally, technical sparring focuses more on technique, where fighters practice specific moves and counters.

Tips for Beginners

Sparring can be intimidating, especially if facing someone more experienced than you. However, you can turn sparring into a valuable learning experience if you have the right mindset. Firstly, approach every sparring session with an open mind, ready to learn and improve. Secondly, always wear the proper safety gear, such as headgear, gloves, and shin guards. Last, don't hesitate to ask your coach or sparring partner for feedback after each session to help you identify areas you need to improve and track your progress.

The Right Time to Start Sparring

Are you an aspiring boxer waiting for the right time to start sparring? Sparring is essential to boxing training, preparing a fighter for real-life situations. However, it can be challenging to determine when it is the right time to start sparring. This section provides insight into when it is appropriate to start sparring and its benefits.

Getting the Basics Right

Before sparring, ensure you have learned and mastered the fundamental boxing techniques. For example, it would be best to have sound footwork, balance, and head movement to effectively evade your opponent's punches. Also, ensure you are comfortable with the stance and that your punches are accurate and robust. With a good grasp of these fundamentals, you can protect yourself and avoid getting injured during sparring.

Build Up Your Fitness Levels

It is imperative to have adequate fitness before sparring. Sparring is an intensive form of training requiring you to move continuously for a few rounds. It can be physically and mentally exhausting, and you must build your endurance to cope with the sparring demands. Therefore, start with some cardiovascular exercises to improve your cardiovascular fitness, such as jogging, skipping, or cycling.

Confidence Is Key

Having confidence before sparring is beneficial. Remember, you will face an opponent trying to hit you. Therefore, being confident with your techniques and mentally tough is essential. Your coach can mentally prepare you to deal with the stress and anxiety of sparring. Moreover, a little self-confidence will make you enjoy sparring and bring out your best.

Spar with Similar Ability Levels

As a beginner, sparring with boxers with similar abilities is essential. In addition, sparring with someone with more experience will help you because they can teach you a lot. However, sparring with someone above your skill level can be risky and intimidating, affecting your confidence. Therefore, spar with someone at your own level and slowly progress to a more challenging opponent.

Learn from Sparring

Last, sparring is an opportunity to learn from mistakes and improve your technique. Closely watch your opponent's moves and learn to counter them. Try different combinations and methods and test them out during sparring. Your coach will give feedback on your performance and suggest improvement areas.

Sparring is an essential part of boxing training but requires preparation and timing. Ensure you have learned the fundamentals, built your fitness, developed confidence, spar with similar-ability boxers, and learned from sparring. Remember, with good preparation, sparring becomes an enjoyable and beneficial part of your training, which will help you achieve your boxing goals.

Technical Aspects of Sparring

Sparring sharpens your techniques, improves confidence, and hones your reflexes. The technical aspects of sparring make it effective. Knowing the details, from your stance to your gaze, body movement, and technique, can help you become a better boxer. Let's delve into the technical considerations of sparring.

Stance

The stance you take when sparring is crucial. The correct stance provides a good balance, essential for maintaining stability while sparring. The stance helps you move in and out of range efficiently while keeping your guard up. A good stance includes keeping your feet shoulder-width apart, your head and shoulders relaxed, and your knees slightly bent.

Footwork

Footwork helps you move around quickly and effectively to dodge and evade attacks while setting up your own. A good footwork technique includes:

1. Keeping your weight on the balls of your feet.
2. Shifting your weight from one foot to another.
3. Using small and quick steps to move around.

Striking Techniques

Striking is the primary technique in sparring, and mastering the striking methods can make a huge difference in your ability to spar. An excellent striking technique includes proper form, timing, and accuracy. Focus on controlling your punches, kicks, and other strikes. Your striking techniques should be faster and more complex than your opponent's to keep them on their toes.

Defense Techniques

Defense is an essential aspect of sparring, helping you to avoid getting hit by your opponent. There are various defense techniques, including blocking, dodging, and parrying. A good defense involves:

1. Keeping your hands up.
2. Blocking with your arms and legs.
3. Using your footwork to move out of range.

Like with striking, keeping your defense tight and under control is vital. When sparring, you should always be ready to defend yourself.

Counters and Combination Techniques

Counterattacks and combination techniques help you gain the upper hand in sparring. Combining different methods, such as punches and kicks, can throw your opponent off balance, and counterattacks can strategically counteract your opponent's movements. A good counterattack and combination technique involves timing your attacks efficiently and using various techniques to keep your opponent guessing.

Sparring has many critical technical aspects to consider for improving your skill level. Your stance, footwork, striking and defense techniques, and ability to use counterattacks are all essential to become an effective sparring partner. By developing these technical aspects, you will become a better boxer, gain more confidence, and get the most out of your training.

Expert Tips to Improve Your Sparring Game

Anyone who has sparred knows it's not merely about throwing punches. You must be strategic and learn to move correctly to win a sparring match. Here are a few expert tips to help you improve your sparring game and get ahead of your opponents. From peek-a-boo style to timing and distance control, these tips will help you become a better and more effective fighter.

Peek-a-Boo Style

One of the most popular and effective styles in boxing is the peek-a-boo style. A high guard and a bobbing and weaving motion characterize this style. Keeping your arms up high protects your face while weaving in and out, making it difficult for your opponent to hit you. To practice the peek-a-boo style, you should focus on keeping your chin down, with your elbows tucked in and your upper body relaxed. You can practice weaving while throwing punches to keep your opponent guessing and creating openings for counterattacks.

Head Movement and Footwork

Another critical aspect of sparring is head movement and footwork. Learning to move your head and feet in unison helps you dodge your opponent's punches and create openings for your attacks. Keep your feet shoulder-width apart and your weight evenly distributed, ready to move in any direction. Moving your head side-to-side helps you avoid punches; pivoting on your back foot helps you move quickly to the side and escape danger.

Timing and Distance Control

Timing and distance control are vital to any sparring session. Controlling the distance between you and your opponent is crucial. Anticipate your opponent's moves by analyzing his movements and patterns to improve your timing. Practice reacting quickly to his movements by shadowboxing or practicing with a partner.

For distance control, you should get in and out of range quickly while keeping your opponent at the end of your punch. Use footwork to move in and out of range, and learn to throw a punch while moving. The more control you have over the distance, the more effective you'll be in sparring.

Mental Preparation

Sparring is not only about physical strength and technique but also about mental preparation. Going into a sparring session with a clear and focused mindset helps you stay calm and make better decisions. Learn to breathe deeply and focus on the task. Don't let your emotions take over, but instead, use them to fuel your movements and keep you driven.

Consistent Training

Practicing consistently is vital to becoming a better fighter and gaining the confidence to master a discipline. Find a sparring partner you can trust and work with them regularly. Also, pay attention to your technique, focus on proper form, and get feedback from your coach. The more you practice, the better boxer you will become.

Honing Reflexes

Reflexes are essential to successful sparring. As a boxer, you need to have offensive and defensive reactions. The more reflexive you are, the better fighter you will become. You can hone your reflexes by practicing drills involving quick reactions to punches or movements from your opponent. Look at sparring as a way to practice and test your limits in a safe environment. It is not about winning or losing but learning and developing as a boxer.

Ready, Set, Spar! Preparing for Your First Sparring Match

Stepping into the ring for your first sparring match can be intimidating. You're facing an opponent who's actively trying to strike you. It can be nerve-wracking. But with the proper preparation, you can confidently approach your first sparring match. Whether it's your first time or your hundredth, practice is critical. Here are some tips and guidelines to help you prepare for your first sparring match.

Training

Training is the foundation of any successful sparring match. So, before stepping into the ring, ensure you regularly engage in exercises that build your endurance, strength, agility, and balance. Your training should include shadowboxing, bag work, and partner drills. All of which will help you hone your technique and reaction time.

Safety Gear

Safety should be the top priority. Invest in high-quality safety gear to protect your head, mouth, and hands. If you're doing kickboxing, you should also have protective equipment for your shins and feet. Keep your gear clean and in good condition, and replace it when necessary.

Know the Rules

Different martial arts have specific rules for sparring matches, so ensure you know what to expect before entering the ring. For example, familiarize yourself with the points system, the match duration, and the strikes allowed. You should also know what protective gear to wear; this knowledge will help you have a safe and enjoyable sparring experience.

Be Mindful of Your Opponent

Your opponent is your best teacher, so pay attention to how they move in the ring and learn from their techniques. Respect your opponent's physical and emotional boundaries, and always show courtesy. Use the sparring match as an opportunity to build a relationship with your opponent, as they can give you valuable feedback and constructive criticism.

Focus on Footwork

Footwork is often overlooked in training but is crucial for a successful sparring match. Your footwork will help you avoid incoming strikes, keep your balance, and set up counterattacks. So, include footwork drills in your training routine, and practice moving in and out of range.

Master Your Punches

Your punches are your most potent weapons in the ring. You must practice throwing different punches with proper form. Pay attention to your technique and power. You want to ensure you can deliver accurate, powerful punches while controlling your body movements. Test your jabs, crosses, hooks, and uppercuts in sparring matches to see how they work against opponents.

Pick Your Opponents Wisely

When you're sparring, it's essential to find a suitable partner. You need someone who can challenge you and help push your skills to the next level. Working with someone with similar experience may be best if you're a beginner. If you're more experienced, find someone who can challenge you and help you refine your techniques. However, ask your coach for advice if you need help deciding who to choose.

Carry Yourself Confidently

Your mindset is as important as your physical preparation for a sparring match. Before stepping into the ring, focus on positive thoughts and visualize your success. Carry yourself confidently and remember why you're doing this in the first place. Have fun, stay relaxed, and trust in your training and instincts.

Visualize Success

Visualization is a powerful tool for athletes and can help you prepare for the rigors of your first sparring match. Spend time visualizing yourself successfully executing your techniques, dodging your opponent's attacks, and coming out on top. Stay positive, believe in yourself, and remember that sparring is as much a mental challenge as a physical one.

Sparring can be a challenging and rewarding experience, and it's natural to feel nervous before your first match. But with the right mindset and preparation, you can confidently approach your sparring match. Focus on your training, invest in safety gear, familiarize yourself with the rules, prioritize your footwork, and stay positive. By following these tips, you'll be well on your way to success in the ring. Happy sparring.

Chapter 9: Hacking the Heavy Bag

It's no secret that boxing is an intense workout challenging physical and mental resilience. But have you ever tried hacking the heavy bag to take your fitness game to the next level? This workout hack will push you to unleash every ounce of strength you possess. High-intensity training entails throwing punches and kicks on the heavy bag rhythmically and continuously. This workout challenges many muscles, forcing you to engage your core, legs, arms, and shoulders.

When you get the moves right, you'll feel like a champ as you punch and kick your way through the bag, leaving everything out on the mat. This chapter enlightens you about the benefits of training with a heavy bag, what materials you need to get started, and drills to help you perfect your technique. So, grab your gloves, put on your game face, and begin hacking that bag. It's time to unleash the power within.

Punch Your Way to Fitness: Benefits of Training with a Heavy Bag

Besides being a means of self-defense, boxing training provides an exceptional full-body workout. A heavy boxing bag for exercise is a great way to get fit, build strength and endurance, and improve overall coordination and balance. So, if you want to level up your fitness routine, let's dive into the benefits of training with a heavy boxing bag.

A heavy bag can help you improve coordination and balance. [21]

Total-Body Workout

Bag boxing is a great way to shed off those extra pounds and work toward building a lean and toned physique. Punching, kicking, and dodging movements engage your entire body and activate multiple muscle groups. In addition, throwing high-intensity combinations forces your body to exert a lot of energy and burn calories. Throw various punches and movements, and remember to keep your core engaged throughout the exercise to get the most out of your workout.

Improved Cardiovascular Endurance

Boxing bag training is excellent for improving your cardiovascular endurance. The continuous movement of your body while engaging in different punching combinations adds a significant challenge to your heart and lungs. The increased heart rate during training helps build better endurance, stamina, and cardiovascular health. Gradually increasing the intensity and incorporating high-intensity interval training (HIIT) into your workout routine helps you achieve optimal fitness.

Increased Strength and Power

The weight of the boxing bag ranges from 70-100 pounds, meaning you engage your upper and lower body muscles and work toward developing stronger punches, kicks, and overall strength. In addition, the resistance training aspect of bag boxing helps you build muscle and increase your general power. This training can be especially beneficial for athletes like wrestlers and football players, as it improves their power, speed, and explosiveness.

Improved Footwork and Balance

Your footwork and balance are crucial in boxing. Without proper footwork and balance, you risk losing control of your punches, leaving yourself vulnerable to attacks. By training with a heavy boxing bag, you learn various footwork techniques, improve your balance, and better understand how to shift your weight during boxing combinations. In addition, incorporating shadowboxing and lateral movements into your workout improves your overall footwork and balance.

Better Accuracy and Timing

Bag boxing allows you to work on your accuracy by throwing punches and aiming for specific points on the bag. This training improves your timing and reaction by mimicking sparring conditions. Throwing quick and precise combinations improves hand-eye coordination, making it easier to respond quickly to punches.

Warm-Up Exercises

Boxing is one of the most intense and physically demanding workouts. It requires strength and endurance, along with proper technique and form. Therefore, before you start training with a heavy boxing bag, you must do warm-up exercises to get your body ready for the rigors of the workout. This section discusses the benefits of pre-workout warm-up exercises and explores five activities to prepare your body for an intense boxing workout.

Jumping Jacks

Jumping Jacks are a classic warm-up exercise, and for a good reason – they are an efficient way to get your heart rate up and blood flowing throughout your body. Start with your feet together and your arms at your sides. Then jump, spreading your legs apart while raising your arms out to the side until your hands meet above your head. Return to the starting position and repeat. Do this for about a minute or until your heart rate is up.

High Knees

High Knees are another warm-up exercise to increase your heart rate and blood circulation. Stand with your feet hip-width apart. Then, raise your right leg, driving your knee toward your chest. As you lower your right leg, lift your left leg similarly, alternating legs quickly while standing in place. Do this for about a minute or until you feel warmed up.

Arm Circles

Arm circles prepare your upper body for the workout. Stand with your feet shoulder-width apart with your arms straight out at your sides, parallel to the floor. Make small circles with your arms and gradually increase the size of the circles until you are making large circles with your entire arm. After completing a set in one direction, reverse the direction and repeat. Do this for about 30 seconds in each direction.

Leg Swings

Leg Swings are an excellent warm-up exercise. Stand next to a wall or pole to maintain your balance. Then swing your right leg forward and backward as far as it comfortably goes while keeping your upper body still. After completing a set with one leg, repeat with the other leg. Do this for about ten swings on each leg.

Dynamic Stretches

Dynamic stretches involve movement with controlled momentum and improve flexibility and range of motion. Start with a lunge and transition to a hamstring stretch by straightening your front leg while leaning forward. Then return to the lunge position and transition to a quad stretch by bending your back leg while bringing your heel towards your buttocks. Repeat this movement for 5-10 reps before switching legs.

Training with a heavy boxing bag is highly beneficial for your overall fitness, but it also puts a lot of stress on your body if you don't do it right. Adding these warm-up exercises to your boxing routine reduces the risk of injury and increases your performance. Always warm up before a workout and make it a regular part of your routine to ensure you get the most out of your training.

Basic Heavy Bag Drills: The Building Blocks of Boxing

Boxing is not only about punching hard and knocking out your opponent–it's a skill requiring discipline and consistent training. One of the best ways to improve your boxing skills is by incorporating regular heavy bag drills into your routine. Heavy bag drills help boxers of all skill levels build endurance, improve technique, and increase strength. This section discusses basic heavy bag drills every fighter should learn to master.

Jabs and Crosses

The jab is a basic punch in boxing. It's efficient and sets up other punches. To execute a basic jab-heavy bag drill, do the following:

1. Start by standing in front of the bag with your feet shoulder-width apart and your dominant foot slightly behind the other.
2. Place your lead hand near the bag, and extend your arm, making a quick, snappy punch.
3. After the jab, step back and follow it up with a cross to the bag.

The cross is a straight punch with your dominant hand to follow the jab. Jab-cross combination heavy bag drills are great for warming up and perfecting techniques.

Uppercuts and Hooks

Uppercuts and hooks are punches meant to be thrown at close range. First, stand close to the bag with your knees slightly bent to execute an uppercut-heavy bag drill. Then, bend your arm and use your body weight to throw the punch upward toward the bag. On the other hand, hooks use your body's rotational power to throw a punch from the side toward the bag. Hook-heavy bag drills are perfect for working on body mechanics. Practice on both sides to ensure you have equal strength in both arms.

Body Combinations

Body combinations are a vital pillar of boxing training. These combos work the entire body and get the boxer moving around the bag. Body combination-heavy bag drills include movements like body jabs, body hooks, and body crosses, targeting the opponent's torso. Mix and match these combinations to create endless exercises to improve your boxing technique.

Footwork Drills

Footwork drills improve your foot speed, agility, and balance. An excellent footwork drill for beginners is the "Step and Pivot." Stand in your basic boxing stance, take a small step with your lead foot, then pivot on the ball of your foot to turn your body. Repeat the drill by following up with a punch or a combination. This drill helps with stability and balance.

Fill the Bag Drills

"Fill the bag" drills are when you use the entire upper and lower body to hit the bag as hard as possible. Begin a fill-the-bag exercise with a round of combination punches. Follow it up with a series of aggressive jabs, crosses, uppercuts, and hooks. This drill builds confidence and is a great way to push yourself to keep your energy levels up.

Get Your Sweat On: A Guide to Heavy Bag Drills

Not only is it a great way to relieve stress and release pent-up frustrations, but training with a heavy bag is also a fantastic way to improve your physical health. Professional boxers and MMA fighters use the serious bag workout to improve their strength, power, and endurance. But don't let that intimidate you. Here are simple drills to follow for a great heavy bag workout:

Rounds 1-3: Basic Punches

The first three rounds of your workout should focus on perfecting the basics: jabs, crosses, and hooks. These three punches allow you to establish a rhythm, getting a feel for the bag and the impact you're generating. Next, focus on a proper technique. For example, move from the hips, twist your shoulders, and imagine your target in front of you. This works your upper body and core muscles. Each round should be 1-2 minutes, and you must maintain a steady pace. Consider taking a 30-to-60-second rest between rounds.

Round 4: Fill the Bag

Now it's time to let out some of that pent-up frustration. For this round, focus on hitting the bag with as much rage and power as possible. As you strike the bag, pick up the pace and throw the combination you've just worked on. Keep this up for a complete round of two minutes, then rest for 30 seconds. Repeat this for two to three rounds, keeping up that intensity.

Round 5: Footwork Drills

The fifth round is all about footwork. Play some of your favorite tunes and circle the bag with different combinations of step-by-step movements. You can shuffle around the bag in different directions. For instance, start by stepping left, then as you move around the bag entirely, start with the combination moving to the right. Again, you get a significant drill in improving your footwork and core strength while burning calories.

Rounds 6-8: Body Combinations

Use these three rounds to focus on hitting the bag with combinations using your upper and lower body. Body combinations should be the primary focus of this round. Remember, the power comes from your hips. So, keep moving them and switch between throwing punches from both sides of the body. Each round should last two minutes, with a minute rest in between. These rounds work your entire body, not only the arms.

Rounds 9-15: Jabs, Crosses, and Hooks

In the last few rounds, focus on short bursts of high-intensity action, with short rest periods between rounds. Perform a series of jabs, crosses, and hooks on the heavy bags, maintaining that rhythm you worked on during the first three rounds. Add power to each combination and feel the impact of every punch. Repeat these rounds one, two, or three times, taking a 30-second rest between each round.

Cool Down Exercises after a Heavy Bag Workout

If you've ever taken a kickboxing or boxing class, you know how intense a heavy-bag workout can be. The punching, kicking, and footwork require much energy and exertion. After an intense workout, it's essential to take a few minutes to cool down and properly stretch your muscles. This section discusses practical cool-down exercises to avoid injury and recover from your heavy bag workout.

Calf Stretches

Calves are one of the areas that can become stiff and sore after a heavy bag workout. To properly stretch them out, stand facing a wall about an arm's length away. Place your palms on the wall and step with one foot back, keeping it flat on the ground. Lean into the wall until you feel a stretch in the calf of the back leg. Hold the stretch for 15-30 seconds, then switch legs. Repeat this stretch a few times on both sides.

Quadriceps Stretches

The quadriceps, or front thigh muscles, also work heavily during a heavy bag workout. First, stand with your feet hip-distance apart and bend one knee, bringing your heel towards your glutes. Next, grasp your ankle and gently pull it toward your glutes, feeling a stretch in your quadriceps. Hold the stretch for 15-30 seconds, then switch legs. Repeat this stretch on both sides a few times.

Glute Stretches

The glutes, or butt muscles, are frequently used during a heavy bag workout. To stretch them out, do the following:

1. Lie on your back with your knees bent and feet flat on the ground.
2. Cross your left ankle over your right knee, grab your right thigh, and gently pull your leg towards your chest. You should feel a stretch in your left glute.
3. Hold the stretch for 15-30 seconds, then switch legs.
4. Repeat this stretch a few times on both sides.

Neck and Shoulder Stretches

Carrying tension in the neck and shoulders is common, especially after a heavy bag workout. Sit or stand straight and slowly roll your head from side to side, bringing your ear toward your shoulder to release this tension. Take your time; don't force the stretch. Next, shrug your shoulders toward your ears, hold for a few seconds, then release. Repeat these stretches a few times.

Yoga Poses

Yoga poses are excellent for stretching your entire body and promoting relaxation after a heavy bag workout. Beneficial poses include downward-facing dog, child's pose, and cat-cow pose. As you move through these poses, focus on your breath and release muscle tension.

Taking a few minutes to cool down and stretch after a heavy-bag workout significantly affects how you feel the next day. Incorporating calf stretches, quadriceps stretches, glute stretches, neck and shoulder stretches, and yoga poses into your post-workout routine can prevent injury and promote muscle recovery. Always listen to your body, and don't push yourself too hard when stretching.

A heavy bag workout is excellent for working your entire body and relieving stress. While the training might seem intimidating, now that you know what to do, it's easier than ever to get started. Follow the guidelines above, and soon enough, you'll be an expert. Remember, the key to the heavy bag workout is to focus on technique and power, so take time to perfect your form and keep pushing yourself. You will soon see results and power punches.

Chapter 10: Twenty Common Mistakes to Avoid (Rookie or Not)

Boxing is daunting, especially with the high stakes of fighting against an opponent and the pressure to win. As with any skill, mistakes are bound to happen, whether a seasoned pro or a beginner. However, errors can be turned into opportunities for growth and improvement. The key is learning from them, adjusting your technique, and pushing forward. So, whether you've accidentally dropped your guard or thrown a wild punch, don't be too hard on yourself. Instead, please take it as a chance to improve and keep slugging it out in the ring.

This chapter examines some of the most common mistakes beginner and even advanced boxers make, why they're wrong, and how to avoid or correct them. Everything from incorrect breathing to not taking breaks is covered. These are issues you want to avoid if you're serious about being a better boxer. The best fighters learn from their mistakes and continually strive to improve.

Common Mistakes Beginner Boxers Make

It takes a lot of effort and time to master the required skills and boxing techniques. However, as a beginner, you must avoid common mistakes that could harm your training and progress. This section explains common mistakes beginner boxers make, why they are wrong, and how to avoid and correct them.

Not Warming Up Properly

Warming up is essential in any workout, including boxing. However, some beginner boxers don't give it the attention it deserves. A proper warm-up prepares your body and mind for the intense training ahead and prevents injuries. Skipping the warm-up can lead to muscle strains and soreness, delaying your progress or even ending your career.

A warm-up is necessary for any sport. [22]

Spend 10-15 minutes warming up before you start training to avoid this mistake. A good warm-up should include cardiovascular exercises (jumping jacks or jump rope), joint mobilization exercises (leg swings or arm circles), and dynamic stretching exercises (such as lunges or squats). Also, cool down and stretch after your training session to help your body recover and prevent soreness.

Not Using the Proper Technique

Having the proper technique is crucial in boxing. With the wrong approach, you risk injuring yourself or your opponent. Unfortunately, many beginner boxers neglect to focus on the proper technique because they think it's unimportant. Yet, it is the foundation of everything you do in boxing. Learn the appropriate technique for each punch to avoid this mistake. First, work on the basics, like footwork, stance, and head movement, before moving on to advanced techniques. Next, practice each punch, focusing on the correct form and movement. Also, consider hiring a coach or a mentor to guide you through the technical aspects of boxing.

Not Eating the Right Foods

Boxing requires a lot of energy and stamina, so you must fuel your body correctly. However, some beginner boxers don't pay enough attention to their nutrition, thinking it's unnecessary. Wrong. Eating the right foods will significantly impact your performance and progress.

To avoid this mistake, do the following:

1. Ensure a balanced and healthy diet, including carbohydrates, proteins, and fats.
2. In addition, eat plenty of fruits and vegetables, which provide essential vitamins and minerals.
3. Avoid eating junk and processed food, which can harm your body and negatively affect your performance.
4. Drink enough water to keep your body hydrated.

Not Anticipating Your Opponent's Movements

In boxing, you must anticipate your opponent's movements to counter them. Unfortunately, many beginner boxers don't consider this, leaving them vulnerable to attack. However, most opponents are experienced, so they may sense your lack of preparation and take advantage.

To avoid this mistake, do the following:

1. Stay on your toes and pay attention to your opponent's body language.
2. Learn to read their movements to predict what they will do next.
3. Practice counter-punching drills with a partner to help you develop good reflexes and anticipation skills.

Not Following the 3-Second Rule

The 3-second rule is a classic boxing strategy that's been around for many years. It states that you should take 3 seconds to think and plan your next move after a punch has been thrown. It is important because it allows you to assess the situation, develop a strategy, and carry it out. Unfortunately, some beginner boxers don't follow this rule, leading to hasty and ill-advised moves.

To avoid this mistake, do the following:

1. Take a few seconds to think before you act.
2. Focus on your breathing and clear your head.
3. Analyze the situation and decide.

Practicing this rule in drills with a partner would be best to help you develop a better sense of timing.

Not Working on Footwork

Footwork is essential to being a successful boxer. Unfortunately, many beginners neglect this aspect of their training and suffer the consequences. Good footwork enables fighters to move efficiently around the ring, avoid punches, and land their own. Therefore, beginner boxers should focus on developing footwork drills into their training routine to improve their agility, coordination, and balance.

Not Focusing on Defense

Defense is equally as important as offense in boxing. Unfortunately, many beginners only focus on landing punches instead of their security, leaving them vulnerable to their opponent's attacks. Good defense allows a boxer to block, slip, duck, or weave to avoid punches and counterattack effectively. Beginner boxers should incorporate defensive drills into their training routine to hone these skills, including practicing blocking punches, slipping, and moving their head.

Incorrect Breathing

Boxers need to learn to breathe correctly during training and fights. Many beginners do not control their breathing, causing them to lose energy and oxygen supply to their muscles, resulting in exhaustion and poor performance. Boxers must learn to breathe deeply and regulate their breathing during training to improve their stamina and endurance.

Not Focusing on Strength and Conditioning

Boxing requires a high level of strength and conditioning to be successful. Unfortunately, many beginners focus more on boxing drills and neglect their overall strength and conditioning. Building and maintaining power and conditioning through weight training, cardio exercises, and other conditioning drills will make any boxer more effective in the ring. Combining strength and conditioning exercises improves performance and takes your boxing to the next level.

Not Stretching Enough

Stretching before training is essential for preventing injuries and increasing flexibility and range of motion. Sadly, some beginner boxers skip stretching or do it minimally. Not stretching enough can lead to muscle strains and tears, significantly impacting the training's progress. Schedule sufficient time for stretching before each training session to avoid this mistake. Start with simple stretches, like neck rotations, arm circles, and trunk twists. Then, gradually work up to more advanced stretches, like splits, back bends, and hip openers.

Not Staying Hydrated

Boxing is a high-intensity workout making you sweat profusely, leading to dehydration if you don't replenish lost fluids. Not staying hydrated leads to tiredness, dizziness, and cramping. In addition, it significantly affects your stamina and performance during training. Drink plenty of fluids before, during, and after training sessions to avoid this mistake. Keep a bottle of water nearby and sip regularly to stay hydrated. *Avoid sugary drinks or drinks with caffeine, as they can lead to dehydration.*

Over-Relying on Upper Body Strength

Boxing is not solely about upper body strength. Your lower body, core, and coordination are significant and dictate how you box. Unfortunately, many beginners make the mistake of focusing too much on upper body strength, leading to muscle imbalances, poor form, and fatigue. Incorporate lower body and core exercises into your workout routine to avoid this mistake. Examples of lower-body exercises include squats, lunges, and jumping rope. Core exercises can consist of planks, Russian twists, and sit-ups.

Poor Footwork

Boxing is a sport requiring excellent footwork. However, beginners don't pay more attention to the importance of footwork, leading to several mistakes, including improper balance, poor movement, and susceptibility to injuries. To avoid this mistake, focus on improving your footwork by practicing footwork drills, like shadowboxing, ladder drills, and pivots. In addition, work on your reaction time and coordination by doing exercises like jump squats, hurdle jumps, and burpees.

Training too Hard

While it is essential to train hard, overtraining can lead to burnout, injury, and fatigue. Beginners often make the mistake of training too hard or too frequently, leading to a lack of progress in the long run. Establish a regular training schedule and include rest days to avoid this mistake. Work on gradually increasing the intensity of your workouts while listening to your body and not pushing yourself to exhaustion.

Not Working on Punch Speed

One of the common mistakes beginner boxers make is not working on their punch speed. Your punch speed is crucial in boxing; neglecting it can cost you the fight. Include speed drills in your training routine to avoid this mistake. Practice shadowboxing, speed bag drills, and double-end bag drills to improve your punch speed. Another way to improve your punch speed is to work on your footwork. Proper footwork enables you to move quickly and punch faster. Learn the proper boxing stance and footwork to improve your speed.

Not Keeping Balance

Beginner boxers often overlook the importance of balance in boxing. Keeping your balance is crucial. It allows you to move quickly and dodge punches. Not keeping balance makes you an easy target for your opponent. Practice balance exercises specific to boxing to avoid this mistake. Practice moving around the ring, shifting your weight, and pivoting on your feet. Regularly practicing these exercises will help you to maintain your balance during your fights.

Not Relaxing During Rounds

One of the common mistakes beginner boxers make is not relaxing during rounds. Boxing requires a lot of energy, and you must conserve it during games. Tensing up drains your energy and tires you quickly. Practice breathing exercises during your training sessions to avoid this mistake. For example, take deep breaths and exhale slowly to relax your muscles. Also, focus on your technique instead of the outcome to conserve your energy and stay relaxed during your rounds.

Lack of Mental Strength

One of the biggest mistakes beginner boxers make is underestimating the importance of mental strength. Boxing is a mentally demanding sport, and your ability to stay focused and determined is as important as your physical skills. When you don't have mental strength, you might struggle to push yourself in training and shrink in the face of pressure during a fight. Working on your mental strength is essential. Set achievable goals, visualize success, and stay positive and focused during training to avoid this mistake. You can also work with a coach or sports psychologist to help you develop mental toughness.

Not Having a Good Workout Routine

Another mistake beginner boxers make is not maintaining a consistent and well-rounded workout routine. Fighters need strength, endurance, and agility, but you'll be disadvantaged in the ring if you only focus on one area. Developing a comprehensive workout routine that includes strength training, cardio, and agility drills is important to avoid this mistake. It's essential to vary your workouts to prevent hitting a plateau. Working with a personal trainer or coach can help you create a customized workout plan that caters to your specific needs and goals.

Not Taking Breaks

Many beginner boxers fall victim to overtraining. They think the more training they do, the faster they'll improve. However, overtraining can lead to injuries, burnout, and plateauing. Taking regular breaks and rest days is crucial to avoid this mistake. Rest allows your muscles to recover and repair, reducing the risk of injury and preventing burnout. Listening to your body and accordingly adjusting your training schedule is important. If you feel exhausted or sore, take an extra day off to recover.

Boxing is an intense sport requiring discipline, focus, and hard work. As a beginner, it is essential to avoid these common mistakes to prevent injuries and make consistent progress. Taking the time to stretch, staying hydrated, focusing on whole-body strength and footwork, and finding a balance between hard work and rest are crucial to becoming a successful boxer.

Overall, becoming a successful boxer takes more than just punching hard. It is imperative to be mentally tough, have a comprehensive workout routine, and take regular breaks. By working on your punch speed, keeping your balance, and relaxing during your rounds, you'll improve your boxing skills and avoid making costly mistakes. Remember, success in boxing is a journey, and the path to success often requires patience and persistence. Follow these tips, and you'll be well on your way to becoming a successful boxer.

Conclusion

Boxing is an intense and captivating sport that has been around for centuries. From its humble beginnings to the spectacular world championships we see today, boxing has captivated audiences with its skill, speed, and power. In this ultimate boxing guide, you explored everything about getting started with boxing, from the basics of the sport to advanced techniques and drills. This easy-to-understand guide explored how the sport evolved and gained international popularity from ancient Greece to today. It touched on the different modern boxing styles, from amateur to professional leagues, and the various weight classes and rules that apply.

Boxing is a great way to stay fit, improve coordination, and release steam. But if you want to step into the ring, you must know the most basic rules and regulations of boxing. Firstly, you need a sturdy pair of boxing gloves to protect your hands from injury and to pack a punch. A heavy bag is another essential piece of equipment for practicing jabs, hooks, and uppercuts. Hand wraps help support your wrist and prevent injury, and a mouthguard is crucial for protecting your teeth and jaw. Finally, comfortable and durable boxing shoes provide the necessary support and traction in the ring. With this essential equipment in your kit, you are ready to start throwing punches like a pro.

You must understand the importance of your stance, guard, and footwork to be a successful boxer. These three elements are the boxing technique's foundation and can make or break your performance in the ring. Mastering the right stance helps you maintain balance and stability, while a solid guard protects you from your opponent's punches. Footwork is essential to keep you on your feet, ready to move in any direction.

This guide focused on the different punches and counterpunches in boxing, illustrating the jab, the straight, the hook, the uppercut, and how to throw them correctly. It covered some of the most effective counterpunches used to gain an advantage in the ring. However, you will always need a solid defense to become a successful boxer, regardless of how good your offense is. This book discussed the most effective defense techniques in boxing. In addition, it discussed the importance of distance control, how to slip and block punches, and using your guard to avoid getting hit.

This ultimate boxing guide has given you an excellent overview of the sport and everything you need to get started with boxing. From the sport's history to the Peek-A-Boo technique, it explored a wide range of topics and provided valuable insight and tips. Remember, boxing is a highly skilled and demanding sport requiring plenty of dedication, discipline, and training to master. So, whether you are a newbie or an experienced pro, use this guide as a foundation to build your skills and become the best boxer you can be.

Part 2: Brazilian Jiu-Jitsu

A Comprehensive Guide to BJJ Grappling Basics for Beginners and a Comparison with Japanese Jujitsu

CLINT SHARP

Brazilian Jiu-Jitsu

A COMPREHENSIVE GUIDE TO BJJ
GRAPPLING BASICS FOR BEGINNERS AND
A COMPARISON WITH JAPANESE JUJITSU

Introduction

Are you interested in learning about Brazilian Jiu-Jitsu? Also referred to as the gentle art, BJJ (Brazilian Jiu-Jitsu) became prominent during the early '90s when Royce Gracie, a Jiu-Jitsu expert, won three times (first, second, and fourth rankings, respectively) in the Ultimate Fighting Championships.

Gracie's opponents were much larger and underwent extensive training in other styles and techniques like wrestling, karate, Muay Thai, and boxing, but he was still able to defeat them. His success was why Jiu-Jitsu became a popular MMA style, where the main focus is on ground fighting.

BJJ is a martial art technique that gives even weaker and smaller participants the chance to defend themselves successfully against stronger and larger attackers. It focuses on ground fighting, grappling, and applying joint locks and chokeholds to defeat opponents. It also involves punches, throws, and kicks.

The key is leverage, enabling even someone small to learn and master the technique.

The good news is that anyone can learn and master Brazilian Jiu-Jitsu. All it takes is to access the right material and training that tackles every important detail and how to do it. The material in this book is written with the reader in mind, focusing more on detailing the actions and techniques you can do to perform this martial art.

The most important aspect of Jiu-Jitsu is grappling, and you can efficiently master it with this book as your guide. What's great about this reading material is that it is written so you can easily understand concepts, techniques, forms, and any other important aspects of BJJ quickly. It makes use of simple terms for you to grasp easily.

After reading, expect to know most, if not all, of what you need to know about BJJ and begin your journey towards becoming a Master. Putting the knowledge you gained here into practice, you will enjoy the rewarding benefits of practicing BJJ, including better balance and coordination, self-discipline, confidence, and mental focus.

I highly advise pairing up this material with relevant Brazilian Jiu-Jitsu videos so you can gain a more active visual input. In this way, it will be easier to follow the techniques and instructions in this book.

Chapter 1: What Is Brazilian Jiu-Jitsu?

Brazilian Jiu-Jitsu, otherwise referred to as BJJ, is a form of martial arts with techniques that focus more on grappling. This grappling-based martial art also emphasizes the use of leverage and techniques that can force opponents to submit through chokes and joint locks. It is widely recognized as a highly effective method of unarmed combat, which continues to rise in popularity since it is constantly represented in global combat sports organizations like the UFC.

A Brief History of BJJ

The roots of Brazilian Jiu-Jitsu can be traced to Japanese Kodokan Judo, a martial art adapted originally from Jigoro Kano's Japanese Jujutsu. Since Judo was classified as a martial art, it consisted of the throwing strategies from Jujutsu together with the groundwork. The ground focus was limited, making it relative to BJJ's revolution.

In 1904, one of the top experts of Judo groundwork, Mitsuyo Maeda, traveled from Japan to different places around the world to teach Judo. His teachings mainly emphasized ground fighting techniques. Maeda reached Brazil in 1914, where he also started teaching and tried to build a Japanese community.

Carlos Gracie, one of Maeda's students in Brazil, studied under him for about five years. Gracie passed the techniques he learned from Maeda onto his four brothers, and in 1925 they opened the first Jiu-Jitsu academy in Brazil.

Gracie's brother, Helio, had poor health and small stature. As a smaller person, he was encouraged to pay more attention to using the techniques Maeda taught. He started working on and adapting even the most basic techniques and concepts of Judo by integrating leverage. His adaptation increased the possibility of even smaller opponents to fight – and beating larger ones.

He also started to experiment with Judo's basic techniques to modify and improve them. It led to the evolution and development of Gracie Jiu-Jitsu, more popularly recognized as Brazilian Jiu-Jitsu, a more effective yet gentle version of the art.

Also, at the time when Judo evolved, there were a few changes in the rules, reducing the emphasis on groundwork and focusing more on throws. This also limited the use of legal joint locks. During this time, BJJ started to emerge as a different sport from Judo. In BJJ, participants are permitted every takedown from Judo.

Aside from that, Helio Gracie put a lot of emphasis on full-contact fighting when practicing BJJ, including strikes and increasing the sport's practicality as a form of self-defense. These rules caused BJJ to keep on evolving as a distinctive and unique fighting system in Brazil.

This further led to no-holds-barred competitions where BJJ participants competed with other martial art disciplines in fights that had no rules. Due to these competitions, the effectiveness of BJJ as a unique fighting system became widely recognized.

In 1972, Carley Gracie left for the US and started teaching BJJ there, and Rorion Gracie followed him in 1978. As Brazilian Jiu-Jitsu became more and more popular in the US, Rorion Gracie, among others, founded the Ultimate Fighting Championship.

During the early stages of UFC, Royce Gracie showed how powerful BJJ was by beating martial artists who were prominent in many other disciplines. The effectiveness and power of BJJ were also demonstrated to a wider audience in the first UFC event made available in pay-per-view.

Significant Highlights in BJJ History

- **1925** - Academia Gracie de Jiu-Jitsu, the first school for practicing the sport, was opened by Master Carlos Gracie.
- **The 1990s** - Brazilian Jiu-Jitsu started gaining recognition in the US. It was also during the '90s that Royce Gracie scored a win against a strong opponent who practiced another form of martial arts. He earned that title during the Ultimate Fighting Championship (UFC).
- **1994** - the founding of IBJJF (International Brazilian Jiu-Jitsu Federation). The goal of this organization is to regulate and govern the sport's competitions.

Core Concepts and Aspects of Brazilian Jiu-Jitsu

Brazilian Jiu-Jitsu's core and fundamental concepts involve bringing any fight to the ground. It is all about the use of pins when attacking opponents and performing attacks through a submission.

Every time you are at the bottom, you should set a goal of creating space by shrimping and bridging and creating distance through wedges and frames. This is also possible by using leverage to flip your opponent over, providing an opportunity to be in a more dominant position.

Note: the core concepts and fundamentals of Jiu-Jitsu have to be applied in every concept, technique, and position of this sport. While this sport continues to adopt new methods and techniques, the fundamentals of the sport that serve as their underlying basics remain unchanged.

Therefore, you must constantly remind yourself that the primary focus of BJJ is to beat opponents by bringing them to the ground, as this form of martial art is all about ground grappling. BJJ requires you to take your opponent to the ground as it is the only way to take away his power and the chaos caused by fighting while in a standing position.

Bottom and top positions are considered the core of BJJ since these are the only available options while opponents are both on the ground. Learning to change to more dominant positions and escape dominant positions to beat opponents and survive is necessary.

While practicing BJJ, you will encounter new and modern techniques; some may be shelved. The core concepts, however, will stay, proving that they are indeed fundamental. Several techniques applied in BJJ will demonstrate how these fundamentals operate.

For instance, the scissor sweep demonstrates how important grips, leverage, off-balancing, and creating space are when sweeping or knocking the opponent over.

Understanding the 4-Step System

When learning and understanding Brazilian Jiu-Jitsu's basic rules and concepts, familiarizing yourself with the 4-step system vocalized by John Danaher will help. This 4-step system involves taking opponents to the ground, passing the legs, working your way through the pins' hierarchy, then attacking using a submission technique.

Implementing this system requires a total of three positions – standing, ground bottom, and ground top. The first step involves taking the opponent to the ground, and the goal is to stay away from the natural volatility of fighting while in a standing position.

The advantage of bringing the fight down to ground level is that it eliminates the power your opponent may create using his arms and legs. You can then pass the legs, which is crucial in getting rid of the dangers imposed by your opponent. Use your legs to kick, sweeping you over to get into a bottom-ground position.

After passing the legs, your goal is to achieve and maintain a dominant position. Your focus is on knee-on-belly, back mount, mount, and side control positions, as they are considered the core. Since they are the top core positions, it helps you obtain that ability to keep your opponent under control.

Moreover, it enables you to strike, set up, and implement a submission technique with only minimal risk. It is like being in a chess match where you need to be one move ahead in order to gain an advantage over your opponent.

Hand-to-Hand Combat Ranges

Hand-to-hand combat, which is also crucial in Brazilian Jiu-Jitsu, has three major ranges or categories.

Standing Position and Free Movement

Most matches or fights start in the standing position. If the fighter throws kicks and punches, it is called the striking range. Many striking arts, like boxing and kickboxing, usually spend much of their time in this range. Most grappling arts also begin matches and fights from a standing position, though it often quickly goes to the clinch, the second range.

Clinch

The clinch range is when the fighters grab and hold each other in a standing position. Since both fighters are still standing, it is also referred to as standing grappling. Other martial arts which specialize in clinch or standing grappling are Greco-Roman wrestling, sambo, Muay Thai kickboxing, and Judo.

The clinch's main goal is to stop or soften punches, set up throws and takedowns, establish strikes from the clinch, and block takedowns until one fighter breaks away. The ultimate goal will always depend on the situation and the current position of the combatant.

Ground Fighting

The third range is ground fighting, which occurs when one of the two fighters no longer stands. While several forms of martial arts perceive being on the ground as a failure, Brazilian Jiu-Jitsu will train you to bring your fight there deliberately. Ground fighting is what you should specialize in when practicing Brazilian Jiu-Jitsu. It's also essential to focus on training in other grappling arts, such as wrestling, Judo, and sambo, which also require you to spend a considerable chunk of your time fighting on the ground.

Why Does BJJ Focus on Ground Fighting and Grappling?

Fights and matches that last longer than usual will most likely move through the clinch, and it is from this range that fighters take the match to the ground. In most cases, being on the ground results from an intentional takedown, schoolyard tackle, or losing your balance, such as while tripping or getting rocked due to a strong punch.

One crucial fact to remember is that the Gracies earned an excellent reputation by sticking to the premise of the participant preventing themselves from being knocked out while standing. Their goal was to control their opponent once they were already on the ground. They were trained to use a few crude takedowns, leading to ground fighting, that put them in a position to take full advantage of their opponents' inexperience and unfamiliarity with this specific range.

When practicing BJJ, remember that the sport does not have a lot of resets to standing, making it different from other forms of martial art. Additionally, you will not win outright through pinning, unlike in Judo or wrestling.

With that in mind, BJJ fighters have to stay biased toward ground fighting as it is the specific area where most matches lead and remain on the ground if you continue to let the match flow naturally.

Positional Dominance Hierarchy

Another of the most fundamental concepts and theories to know about Brazilian Jiu-Jitsu is positional hierarchy or dominance. This concept involves specific positions that produce better or worse results, so it is crucial to be aware of them and know what to do whenever you encounter them.

Knowing positional dominance or hierarchy will give you a clear understanding of what occurs within the fight on the ground, helping you to protect yourself and possibly helping you win the fight. If you are on the dominant or top side, the traditional hierarchy will be:

- Rear mount
- Mount
- Knee-on-belly
- Side control
- Turtle
- Half, open, then closed guard

If you get into the bad or bottom side of the above-mentioned positions, expect this traditional hierarchy to flip, too, meaning the worst out of the mentioned positions will be on top, followed by the lesser ones working down to the different poses.

To beat your opponent successfully, you must maintain a dominant position as much as possible. You will know you're in a dominant position if you can easily maintain it instead of escaping it. A dominant position is also one that provides you with leverage and mechanical advantage. It keeps you safe from submissions and strikes, giving you plenty of opportunities to end the match through submissions or strikes against your opponent.

During a BJJ match or fight, you score points as you progress and move through various dominant positions while on the ground. Here's a view of BJJ's scoring system based on dominant positions.

- Rear mount = 4 points
- Passing the guard = 3 points
- Mount = 4 points
- Takedown from standing = 2 points
- Knee-on-belly = 2 points
- Sweep from guard = 2 points

Position before Submission

Brazilian Jiu-Jitsu also operates on its traditional mantra, which is "position before submission." This means that a secure and safe positional hierarchy is more significant than submission.

For instance, it would not be wise to make your opponent submit if you are still in a bad position or within his guard. It is also not advisable to fall or jump into arm bars that are vulnerable to failing, putting you at risk of being underneath him.

As you gain more experience and skills in the sport, you can adjust your mantra because improvements in your skills will make you more confident and secure in your potential escapes and defenses.

In other words, despite having failed submission attempts, the skills you have learned from training and experience help you recover confidently and try another more effective position. However, beginners must stick to the mantra, as it requires focus on position before submission – which is the basis of BJJ.

Benefits of Learning BJJ

Now that you know about BJJ's core concepts and fundamentals, it is time to learn more about the benefits you can attain from learning this ancient martial art. In this section, you will learn more about the benefits of learning Brazilian Jiu-Jitsu and what it can do for you.

A Form of Self-Defense

By practicing Brazilian Jiu-Jitsu, you will learn moves that will prove useful whenever you are in a situation where you need to protect yourself, particularly in a physical confrontation. As a proven self-defense system, BJJ will train you to defend yourself whenever you are attacked, and you will know exactly how to take your attacker to the ground, control him, and prevent him from hurting you.

Better Physical Fitness

Undeniably, Brazilian Jiu-Jitsu is a great form of exercise. Each sparring round, otherwise known as a roll, lasts for around 5 minutes but includes various low and high-intensity movements with only minimal rest. BJJ is indeed a fantastic workout requiring anaerobic and aerobic endurance. Spending half an hour of hard rolling helps you burn around 500 calories.

Good for Your Mental Health

Another incredible benefit of Brazilian Jiu-Jitsu is that it can improve your mental health. It is even an effective stress reliever, which can boost your mood. Every time you roll on your mat to practice Jiu-Jitsu, you get the chance to disconnect yourself from the world and the surrounding worries.

Brazilian Jiu-Jitsu even helps you live in the present, which is beneficial for building your self-esteem and creating a positive self-image. Since it is suitable for mental health, it can help you avoid depression and anxiety.

Builds Discipline

The mental and physical challenges you will likely encounter when practicing BJJ will build and foster discipline. For instance, the requirement to attend classes every week without fail already develops discipline. You also have to be disciplined when dealing with losses during sparring, which is essential in attaining growth.

Improves Problem-Solving Skills and Creative Thinking

Your problem-solving and creative thinking skills will be put to the test when you practice Brazilian Jiu-Jitsu, which is why many also refer to this sport as a game of human chess. You must constantly adapt to various body types, techniques, and styles in this martial art.

Expect your brain to be trained to think creatively and calmly, even when under stress and pressure. It also trains your brain to overcome and handle complex problems. Your ability to adapt and think fast will also be honed as you will encounter different challenges each time you practice the sport.

Going out of your comfort zone is possible if you constantly practice BJJ. This sport will challenge you to grow and learn something new constantly. You will be trained to conquer your fears and pursue things that you thought were previously impossible. BJJ martial art is, therefore, valuable for your personal growth.

Chapter 2: Tips That Everybody Doing BJJ Should Know

As you will probably have learned by now, Brazilian Jiu-Jitsu is about martial art based on the ground, which incorporates different chokes and joint locks to beat an opponent. Anyone who has experience with Judo or wrestling will immediately realize that Jiu-Jitsu requires a unique and different challenge.

Before putting your opponent into submission, it is important to take your opponent to the mat. Once on the ground, you will use your Judo skills and take advantage of various takedown techniques and throws. While on your feet, BJJ requires spending most of your time doing throws, wrestling techniques, and trips.

Standing is also vital in BJJ, but it focuses more on the importance of ground fighting. The ultimate objective of this strategy is adapting a dominant position with effective scrambles and implementing a wide range of finishing techniques.

Similar to other martial arts, BJJ firmly bases its principles on tradition, respect, and honor. Therefore, beginners need to leave any overconfident and egoistic nature at home when attending classes.

Also, note that the only acceptable means to overcome your struggles in Brazilian Jiu-Jitsu is to practice humility. Be humble and listen intently to what your coaches teach, and you may also want to seek advice from your more experienced and skilled teammates.

Preparing for Your First Brazilian Jiu-Jitsu Class

The key for beginners to be able to overcome the initial training difficulties in Brazilian Jiu-Jitsu is to be fully prepared for the first session. Anyone serious about learning and mastering BJJ may experience unpleasant sweaty hands and some butterflies in their stomach, especially if they are still unsure of what to expect when they walk through the doors of their chosen academy for the first time.

Many Brazilian Jiu-Jitsu schools allow new and potential students to watch a class first. You can meet an instructor, giving you the chance to ask some questions before you begin training. Some schools even provide a trial class, allowing aspiring BJJ students to decide whether they really want to push ahead with the actual classes and training.

What Should You Wear?

As a beginner, you do not have to invest in a BJJ Gi during your trial class or the first session. A t-shirt or rash guard and a pair of board shorts will be okay. However, ensure that you don't wear clothing with pockets, baggy fabrics, or belt loops, as they may put you in danger, especially if they catch your toes and fingers.

Wearing a pair of flip-flops instead of shoes is also advisable, as no shoes are worn on the mat. If, after a trial session, you decide to go ahead with BJJ, purchasing a Gi must be a priority and should be worn to all classes.

The traditional BJJ uniform needs a belt to keep the jacket in place. The belt is also used for some defensive or offensive positions, which you'll learn as you train. Belts also represent your rank as a Brazilian Jiu-Jitsu martial artist. You'll also need grappling shorts, which don't slide easily and give you much-needed flexibility on the ground. A rash guard is always a good idea as it can absorb moisture and keep your body cool during training sessions and actual matches. You'll definitely have to get a mouth guard despite BJJ not having kicks or punches, but it's worn for safety in case you fall head-first or an accident happens during training.

You might want to get groin protectors as that area is highly exposed in BJJ and could suffer an injury. Headgear or ear protectors are used to protect the head and ears. The head is pulled during games, which could lead to serious ear injuries; in particular, cauliflower ear is a common BJJ injury. As a beginner, it's recommended that you get knee pads and braces as you'll likely fall and may land on your knees.

Hygiene

Proper hygiene is also a must before setting foot into your first class. Ensure that your toenails and fingernails are properly groomed. If your hair is long, style it into a bun or a ponytail during the class. Take out any piercings and remove any jewelry to avoid injuries. Generally speaking, you need to keep clean because no one really wants to train with an untidy partner. You need to ensure you're the kind of person people want to train with. Ensure your uniform is always clean and your breath is fresh to avoid alienating training partners and making the experience bad for others.

What to Expect During the First Class?

Since it is your first time attending the BJJ class, it is advisable to arrive at class early. If possible, go to the school or academy 5 to 10 minutes ahead of your scheduled class. This way, you will have time to introduce yourself to your instructor. If you have not visited the school yet, you may use those extra minutes to check out what is available.

Also, note that you may be required to sign an indemnity form before taking your first or trial class. Before the class starts, dress appropriately for the training and do some stretching to prepare your body.

Each training session will also start with a lineup, so expect this during your first time attending the class. Note that this lineup is not the classic or traditional one often implemented in kickboxing classes. In BJJ, groups are split based on experience levels and belts. Since you are still a beginner who may not have either, you will line up at the end, where the beginners' group is situated.

Warm-Up Sessions

Your first BJJ class will teach you the importance of warming up. The warm-up session is similar to the ones implemented in other sports. However, if you don't consider conditioning as your strength or forte, avoid rushing it. It would benefit you to keep your energy level for what comes next.

Also, note that since you are still a beginner, there is a possibility that you will spend more of your time watching and observing your instructor as they demonstrate basic BJJ techniques and the logic behind each one. During this initial stage, you will most likely learn the following ground positions:

- Ground (open, closed, and half-guard positions)
- Full and back mounts
- Side control

Some instructors will let you do light warm-ups, while others begin their classes with heavy-duty conditioning. Some classes also begin with a warm-up that is done in groups, like push-ups and running laps. Expect these group warm-ups to be followed by solo drills, such as backward and forward break-falls and shrimping.

Some moves may be very new to you, but don't fret. Watch and observe what others are doing and copy them. Your goal is to learn ways to fall to the ground safely. Also, as a beginner, be lenient with yourself. Do not be too harsh on yourself if you have a hard time doing the exercises and training correctly at first.

Remember that no one can get everything right on their first day. It requires much practice. With discipline and perseverance, you will eventually receive a higher belt. Your instructor will teach you how to correctly do the BJJ moves and techniques.

What to Look for in a BJJ Instructor

Finding the right BJJ instructor is one of the most important steps on your Black Belt journey. Without the right teacher, you could easily get frustrated or seriously injure yourself. A good instructor will push you to improve, and you'll want to, but at the same time, they won't be so overbearing and obnoxious that you wouldn't enjoy the experience. At the end of the day, hard and challenging as the sport may be, you should enjoy yourself and have a good time with your BJJ classes. Here's what you need to look for in a BJJ instructor.

Knowledge and Abilities: The first thing you want in your BJJ instructor is technical knowledge. They don't need to be a world champion or anything, just someone who has practiced the sport long enough to know what they're doing. You need to remember that champions don't necessarily make for good coaches. In fact, in many cases, they don't. You need a Brazilian Jiu-Jitsu coach who has the necessary knowledge about the fundamentals of the sport and the specifics of the techniques. The instructor's current knowledge isn't the only thing to keep in mind, but also, how willing are they to learn and grow? The last thing that you need is a rigid teacher who is unwilling to learn, let alone teach, new moves.

The question is, how do you know if your teacher has good technical knowledge and abilities? Try a class or two with them and observe how they do things. If your teacher just does moves quickly without taking the time to explain the details of every move and why they did it like that, chances are their technical knowledge isn't very good, and they don't have much to teach you. A knowledgeable instructor will let you know how everything is done and how you can replicate those moves. They will take the time to explain the tiniest details and answer any question you might have.

Level of Care: The last thing that you need is a BJJ instructor who doesn't even pay attention to what you're doing in the class. It can be common to find the head coach just walking around the school, watching students go about their techniques, making a remark here or there. This is not a good approach to learning Jiu-Jitsu. You need hands-on experience, a coach who will step into the ring and help you learn and grow, not sit on the sidelines checking their social media. Your BJJ instructor needs to be active and involved in your training. It's also a sign of respect for the sport and you; respect always has and always will be a cornerstone of martial arts.

You're paying a lot of money for your classes, so the head coach should also be the one training you. Make sure they're not pawning you off to some inexperienced instructor still learning the ropes. Moreover, the level of care you get in the school is shown in their teaching style. Is there a fixed curriculum, or are they just doing things without a proper course to follow? You need to have a plan with end goals to monitor and assess your progress. Winging it is not the way to go regarding martial arts. A fixed plan followed with all new students ensures that you deal with professionals who know what they're doing.

Communication Skills: A good teacher is a good communicator, whether with sciences or martial arts. Teaching BJJ doesn't just require physical skills but also verbal ones. How good is your instructor at delivering their point and explaining their intended meaning? Are they clear in their instructions? An instructor may have all the technical knowledge and experience in the world, but if they can't effectively deliver that information, they are not benefitting their students. The instructor's body language makes a difference, too. How approachable are they? Do they feel like the kind of person you can approach with questions and concerns? You don't really want to be training with a confrontational BJJ instructor who is not open to questions. You also don't want to be taught by someone who doesn't like what they're doing and can't wait to get the classes over.

This brings us to patience, the quality you need the most in your BJJ instructor. Getting better in this sport takes a long time, and you will struggle at first to learn new moves and understand new techniques. You need a patient instructor who will give you the space you need to learn. Many instructors seem to forget how scary it can be to begin something new, especially martial arts, and they can show frustration at their students' inability to grasp the terms and the moves. This naturally reflects on your own feelings as a student, and you begin to feel their frustration. If you find that your instructor is impatient from the get-go, you need to find another. A patient instructor can help you learn and give you a safe space to do so. Their patience also affects higher-belt students, who will be just as patient as their teacher with lower-belt novices. This creates a healthy environment for students of all belts to grow and learn together without being rushed. It also creates a powerful bond between you and your instructor, which is very hard to break.

Conduct: A good BJJ instructor carries themselves outside of the ring just as well as inside. You need to find a qualified instructor who is also a decent person. As you'll explore in this book, Brazilian Jiu-Jitsu -- like many martial arts -- is about humbling yourself and letting go of your ego. It's about being honorable and kind. This is why the coach's behavior outside the ring is just as important. You don't want to be taught by someone who happens to be an abuser or a bully who uses his martial arts knowledge to terrorize the weak. You might think the separation between their teaching abilities and conduct is possible - but it isn't - and before you know it, you might turn into them and misuse your newly learned abilities.

Make sure you read online about a coach and see what other former students say about their behavior. If some former students or parents say that the instructor is abusive or a bully, stay away from them. If you can't find much about the coach online, take a few classes with them and see if the school's culture and the instructor's attitude suit you before deciding to continue or find another.

First Few BJJ Techniques

After warming up, your instructor may partner you with someone. Also, similar to other beginners in their first lesson, you may have to stay at the side of the mat to observe and practice basic BJJ techniques. But, there will be instances when you will be combined with the class.

Some schools let you practice BJJ based on their beginner curriculum, while others require you to learn the techniques taught on the day you first attend the class. A few basic techniques you will most likely learn during your first BJJ class are the scissor sweep, mount escape, side control and escape, and guard pass.

If you are included in the primary class, inform your partner that it is your first lesson. Your partner will then know to take things slowly, guide you, and inform you accordingly.

After your first class, reflect on your overall experience to decide whether you should push through with the training. If you choose to continue, discuss membership fees and availability of classes; also, you'll need to obtain a Gi. You can buy your BJJ Gi from most instructors and legit online and martial arts stores.

Essential Tips for Brazilian Jiu-Jitsu Beginners

Since you have decided to go through with the training, you have to arm yourself with valuable tips other than those you learned during your first class. Guiding yourself with additional useful tips will lessen the somewhat intimidating feeling of learning the art of Brazilian Jiu-Jitsu.

Commit to Training Consistently

Obviously, consistent training is vital to succeeding in mastering Brazilian Jiu-Jitsu. While there is no guarantee that you will participate in each training session, especially if there are emergencies, you still have to stick to a consistent approach in training. It is the key to developing your skills while keeping up with developments within the class.

For example, if your instructor teaches a specific technique, position, or move for at least a week and you only take part in the class towards the end, it will be harder to put together the entirety of the session.

So, commit to practice and repetition, and you will notice a significant improvement in your entire performance.

Train at least twice or three times every week and, if possible, take on additional training, too - staying after class for additional roles, attending open mats, and working on solo drills once you are at home. You may also want to coordinate with your team members so you can roll even during those times when the gym is not open. Extra practice will be enough for you to notice steady progress in your Brazilian Jiu-Jitsu performance.

Ask Questions

As a beginner, you will have many questions regarding the practice of Brazilian Jiu-Jitsu. Do not hesitate or be afraid to ask whatever question is on your mind during classes. If you don't raise your questions, you may have a difficult time mastering this new activity.

Luckily, most senior members, coaches, or instructors will always be around to answer your questions and concerns about BJJ. You may have to wait for the Q&A portion, which often happens at the end of every class or training to raise your concerns.

Also, make it a point to pick up hints from others with more experience after each training session. Your classmates will be more than willing to offer what they know about this sport, and you can ask them to give you honest opinions regarding your performance.

This way, you will know your mistakes and the specific areas you should improve. All these details play a crucial role in your performance and will certainly help your progress.

Arrive Early

Another crucial tip for Brazilian Jiu-Jitsu beginners is to get to class as early as possible, or at least 10 minutes before your scheduled class. It gives you sufficient time to change, loosen up and step onto your mat for a quick warm-up session.

If, for some reason, you run late for a session, let your instructor or coach know about your arrival. A quick apology for your tardiness is a must, and get onto the mat without delay. Regardless of what you do, avoid slipping onto your mat unnoticed because this may disrupt the entire class's training.

Keep Your Fingernails and Toenails Short

You must keep your fingernails and toenails short when attending Brazilian Jiu-Jitsu classes to ensure no injuries from you or your training partners during sparring or drilling. This is not an exaggeration, as long fingernails and toenails can cause damage during each of your BJJ sessions, and some even have scars as proof of the damage caused by long nails.

Moreover, your fingernails are home to plenty of bacteria, which may cause cuts to become infected. So, make it a point to ensure your nails are trimmed prior to attending class. It is also good hygiene.

Master Fundamental Movements First

It's imperative as a beginner to avoid attempting complex movements before you ever master the fundamentals. As a White Belt holder (a new Brazilian Jiu-Jitsu student), you must focus on learning and mastering the fundamentals to prepare you for more complex actions later. You should initially focus on some fundamental movements: shrimping, bridging, sweeping, and getting up.

- **Bridging** - Lie on your back and raise both your knees, keeping your legs at a 90-degree bend, forming the shape of a bridge by raising your hips.
- **Shrimping** - This movement is about mobility even when you are on your back, requiring you to use your hips and shoulders as if they are feet to move around conveniently.
- **Sweeping** - In this BJJ move, you use both your feet to take out your opponent's legs and base. The result of this movement is enforcing a better ground position to increase your chance of winning.
- **Getting Up** - Of course, this involves moving to a standing position. However, it is important to stick to a technical stand-up, as the most vital aspect is ensuring you never compromise your head.

Shrimping and bridging are two of the most vital movements connecting all other moves and techniques together. It is also crucial to perfect bridging before learning and understanding the basics of escaping a bad and unwanted position. Moreover, you must develop shrimping on both sides and improve your ability to get up and complete a sweep before you can finally try more advanced and complex submissions and positions. By honing your skills in these fundamentals and connecting them smoothly, you will significantly mark your advancement as a beginner (white belt holder).

Relax When Rolling

Another essential tip for Brazilian Jiu-Jitsu beginners is to let go of nervousness, anxiety, and tension during your first roll. The first time you have to conduct rolling is also your first chance to put everything you have practiced and learned into action.

Remember, you are still in the initial stage of your journey, so your understanding and knowledge about this position may be limited. But, it is not a reason to feel nervous and tense during your first attempt at rolling. Let go of these emotions by accepting that you are still a beginner, as all you can do right now is go with the flow.

You may also want to take this chance to try new things - making mistakes and taking some risks. Learn how to relax your body before making this move, and remain comfortable throughout, as this is the key to multiple rolls and speeding up your learning process.

Train for Strength and Endurance

Integrate some strength and endurance training into your routines. You need these skills to perform Brazilian Jiu-Jitsu moves more effectively and easily. There is no need to turn yourself into a powerlifter or long-distance runner. You merely have to train for strength and endurance to get into the best shape for BJJ and avoid injuries.

Do Not Bring Your Ego to Your BJJ Classes

It would be best for you to leave your ego at home. If your goal for training is to prove that you are good at something, then maybe you should stop now. Remember, as a beginner, you will only evolve in this martial art form if you train with humility and without your egotistical personality. You will achieve better results if you train while keeping your mind open.

Here are some points to remember during training so that you can continue practicing with humility and an open mind:

- You can never expect to learn everything, especially if you are only starting.

- Avoid hurting yourself by patting as many times as needed.
- Avoid forcing a position if your partner says he does not want to. For instance, if he does not like to palm, avoid forcing him to do it. You can't benefit from it, and it may only hurt your partner.
- Do not beat yourself up when you make mistakes. Allow yourself these mistakes every now and then, and learn more from your mistakes.
- Receive every piece of advice about BJJ with an open mind.

Never let your ego exist during your training. Otherwise, you may bruise it, causing you to stop training. To succeed in BJJ, humility is a must, and you must keep your head down and commit to training hard.

Speaking of humility, make it your goal to become a better version of yourself rather than others when it comes to BJJ training. The philosophy behind martial arts, in general, isn't about surpassing others but yourself. This isn't just a lesson in humility but a way to keep steady progress without suffering setbacks and frustration. The surest way to hinder your own progress is to compare yourself to others. We all have our different journeys, and yours is special and unique. Looking at what others are doing and comparing yourself will only bring you down. The people you're comparing yourself to might have freer schedules to practice or are natural athletes. The competition you put yourself in with them is pointless and won't work in your favor, so don't start one in the first place.

Your soul goal should be to work on your own skills and improve, regardless of other people's progress. Discipline yourself to focus on your own progress. Rather than ask if you could defeat your classmate, ask if you can beat yourself from a few weeks ago. This will help you stop worrying about whether or not your classmates are better. It doesn't matter; the only thing that matters is your own progress.

Patience and Persistence

They're your only hope if you want to get better at BJJ. This type of martial arts is an art form; like any other art form, it takes time to master. This isn't about natural talent or skills. It's about who can persist and endure the grueling training process to get better with each passing day. The thing about martial arts is they build a powerful work ethic because every inch of progress you make is hard-earned through tears, sweat, and probably blood. This makes the whole journey very satisfying, but you just need to be patient and trust the process.

BJJ has a very high dropout rate because many beginners feel frustrated when they start training. It looks and feels hard, and, normally, you would feel this is something you'll never be able to do well. You can spend months training and still feel like you're not going anywhere, which is also normal. However, this is not the case. You are getting better, and there is progress. You just can't see it. Those who plow through the negative emotions and frustration will, though. One day sparring with your classmate, you will feel stronger and more confident, and you'll win. Becoming skilled in Brazilian Jiu-Jitsu takes years, and it's not something that will happen after a couple of months of training.

It helps along this journey if you set short and long-term goals. Yes, you need to progress at your own pace, but that doesn't mean you shouldn't have long-term goals and hopes. You shouldn't aspire to get the Blue Belt but the Black Belt. It might seem far now, but the more you work and put in the hours, the closer this goal becomes.

Tap Out

One of the most important lessons you must remember as you train to become a BJJ martial artist is that there is no shame in tapping out. This isn't to say that you should surrender easily or quit whenever it gets tough, but it's important to learn when you've lost and tap out. This is a very common mistake for many beginners who are simply unwilling to tap out. While a fighting spirit is commendable in BJJ and something you should keep, not knowing when to tap out can lead to serious injuries and complicate your journey before it even starts.

Remember that the goal of training is to get better and improve. You have nothing to prove to anyone. It's not about winning or losing at this point in your BJJ journey. You have to train yourself to forego the traditional notions of winning and losing because they serve you no good. When you tap out, there's always something to learn. Don't think of it as a loss but rather as a learning opportunity. As you get better, you will learn the necessary techniques to help you get out of chokes and submission attempts, but until then, stay safe and learn when it is time to tap out.

Common Beginner Mistakes in Brazilian Jiu-Jitsu

You can make the most of your BJJ classes if you are aware of common mistakes. This section discusses common BJJ beginner mistakes.

Not Learning Appropriate Grip

Grappling against an opponent requires you to get a hold of them. Many beginners are unaware of the significance of correctly making a proper handgrip, and it is something you must master if you want to succeed in BJJ. There are three vital components for an effective grip which are hand strength, the exact place where you should grip, and efficient gripping.

Hand strength is essential in Jiu-Jitsu, so it is necessary to properly train the muscles in both hands to improve hand strength. A few exercises are meant to make your hands stronger, including kettlebell swings, rope pulls, rope climbs, using claw-hold weights and pinch-hold weights.

It is also crucial to learn how to do an efficient grip because no matter how excellent your hand strength is, an inefficient grip will still cause your forearms to weaken, resulting in the loss of your grip. Among the handgrips you need to master as a beginner, include the following:

- **Pistol Grip** - Grab onto the BJJ Gi using your pinky closest to your opponent's wrist. Ensure that you are grabbing a lot of the material. The grip is the same as when you hold the handle of a pistol.
- **C-Grip** - Use four fingers and curl your thumb inward, similar to when forming the letter C, to grab your opponent, usually at the arm or wrist.
- **Spider Grip** - In this grip, you have to use four fingers, curling inwards to grab your opponent's GI sleeve.
- **Monkey Grip** - Grab using the topmost parts of the joints of your four fingers.

Another vital element to gripping is the exact spot where you should grip in order to obtain the best leverage.

If you have no idea about the exact places where you should grip, you will be unable to gain leverage regardless of how secure you think your grip is. To give you an idea, the perfect spots to grip include the pants, cuffs, lapels, and the ends of the collar sleeve.

Not Focusing on the Basics

Some beginners in Brazilian Jiu-Jitsu are so excited to move on to more complex and advanced techniques that they neglect the importance of honing their basic skills. As a white belt, you may also be tempted to learn everything at once. However, do your best to avoid making this common mistake.

Make it a point to perfect the basic moves in Jiu-Jitsu and be patient along the process. You will eventually reward yourself with a much better experience when you move on to more complex techniques.

- **Side Control Escape** – This famous move allows you to effectively move your hips starting from the bottom, and it is also the most basic move you can perform for a great escape.
- **Triangle Choke** – This signature move is for submission. It is a basic move that you have to master as you will have to use it when dealing with an opponent who is bigger than you.
- **Scissor Sweep** – This is another basic move you should master, as every sweep technique is based on this sweep. Using the scissor sweep will cause your opponent to lose his balance to your advantage. It would be best to use the scissor sweep together with other basic moves for the best results.
- **Cross Collar Choke** – This grip serves as your starting point before you do any sweep or attack.
- **Americana Lock** – This basic move refers to a common lock used when grappling an opponent. Performed correctly, you can take complete control of your opponent's arm.
- **Hip Bump Sweep** – Master this sweep technique as you will use it once your opponent is already down on his knees.

Never ignore the importance of learning these basic moves, and you can become one of the best Brazilian Jiu-Jitsu masters.

Neglecting the Importance of Self-Defense

Never overlook the importance of learning a few self-defense techniques. Some beginners make this mistake and consequently cannot get out of a simple choke because they do not know basic self-defense.

Instead of neglecting self-defense, continuously go over the essentials you learned at the start of your training. Once you have mastered them, you will know how to rehash them and turn them into a defense tactic.

Holding onto a Submission or Position for Too Long

One of the things you will learn when practicing Brazilian Jiu-Jitsu for the first time is the perfect time to let go when you're in a position that does not work for you.

As a BJJ beginner, you should master how to move to the cross choke after posing for the mount for too long – when the opponent already knows how to protect himself. The faster you master the art of recognizing when to let go, the faster you will improve your Brazilian Jiu-Jitsu skills.

Not Knowing Your Physical Limits

If you are serious about mastering Brazilian Jiu-Jitsu, then learn how to train wisely. In their attempt to learn and master this martial art quickly, some beginners force themselves to train twice a day, six days a week. Ultimately, this is not wise and may only cause burnout.

Once you reach a burned-out stage, you may feel the need to stop training for a while, defeating your purpose of mastering it. Instead of burning yourself out, stick to the average training frequency of twice or three times every week. Keep in mind that BJJ is not a sprint, so learn slowly but surely.

Probably the most important of all the tips that Brazilian Jiu-Jitsu beginners must know is to have fun. Trust the entire process, and do not forget to enjoy the entire experience. Avoid holding a completion after three taps. If you are in doubt whether your partner tapped, just let go. It would be much better for you to be cautious than to have to deal with discomfort.

Trust your coaches, instructors, and partners, too. You will make the environment where you are training look and feel safer, resulting in a much more enjoyable and fun experience learning this martial art.

Chapter 3: The Basics of Grappling in BJJ: How Not to Get Bullied in a Fight

In One-on-one combat, grappling involves seizing or gripping an opponent at a close range as a means of getting a significant physical edge or advantage. Fighters do this by imposing a solid position. Grappling encompasses many disciplines – among them are those followed by Brazilian Jiu-Jitsu participants.

The term grappling involves techniques used in many combat sports, particularly martial arts and Brazilian Jiu-Jitsu. Successful grappling means that you effectively apply counters and maneuvers to your opponent, giving you a better position and physical advantage.

It also covers techniques designed to force your opponents to submit. However, remember that grappling will never involve using weapons, and you should never strike your opponent when applying the grappling technique.

Importance of Grappling in BJJ

Brazilian Jiu-Jitsu's main focus will always be on ground grappling. You must master grappling techniques as it is the key to taking your opponents down to the ground and forcing submissions through triangle choke techniques.

Ground grappling includes all grappling styles and techniques that you apply when you are no longer standing. The most important part of implementing this technique is proper positioning. You must be in a dominant position, which is often characterized as on top of your opponent.

In this dominant position, you have plenty of options on what you can do next. You may attempt to escape by standing up, striking your opponent, performing a submission hold, or obtaining a hold-down or pin with the end goal of exhausting and controlling your opponent. Meanwhile, expect the bottom grappler to focus more on how to escape and improve his position. In this case, they may use a reversal or sweep.

Mastering grappling techniques should be one of your ultimate goals when learning and mastering Brazilian Jiu-Jitsu to control your opponents and defeat them. Many martial artists even make it a point to learn a few submission techniques and counters to ensure that they can integrate a ground element into their usual, traditional training.

It would be best to practice and hone your knowledge and skills about grappling under the supervision of a martial arts instructor. That way, you can avoid injuries and ensure that you learn and master the correct techniques.

Grappling Classifications

Grappling is an effective means to improve your endurance and strength to prevent being bullied by your attacker. It involves the use of various muscle groups and maximizes their efficiency. Aside from muscle-building, grappling techniques also offer cardiovascular benefits while boosting your mental focus. These are all vital skills required in intense BJJ physical training.

The good thing about grappling is that you can also use it in self-defense. By mastering grappling techniques, you can use one or two to protect yourself from attackers successfully. There are limitless possibilities and variations in grappling to reach a takedown and seize and control your opponent. Also, take note of the following classifications of Brazilian Jiu-Jitsu:

- **Clinching** - Also called clinch work, this grappling classification occurs when both fighters are on their feet using a wide range of clinch holds directed to the opponent's upper body. Clinching is often used as a means of setting up or defending against takedowns or throws.

- **Takedown** – A takedown is the effective manipulation of an opponent to bring them to the ground from a standing position. Your goal for the takedown is to get into a dominant position.

- **Throw** – This grappling technique involves lifting the opponent or putting them off-balance, so you can forcefully maneuver them to the ground. The main objective of throws differs from one discipline to another, but the thrower can get into a controlling position, obtain a takedown, or leave them standing.

- **Submission Holds** – There are two types of submission holds – the choke, which potentially requires strangling or suffocating your opponent, and the lock, which requires injuring a joint or any part of the body. If you perform a submission hold and your opponent can no longer escape, expect them to submit by tapping or even verbally indicating their acceptance of defeat. A fighter who refuses or fails to tap out is at risk of incurring a serious injury or becoming unconscious.

- **Sprawling** – This is a defensive grappling technique you can use if your opponent tries to perform a takedown. Shift your legs backward, then spread them out in a single, rapid motion. The correct execution of sprawling results in your opponents landing on their back, giving you complete control.

- **Controlling or Securing Techniques** – One technique that falls under this classification is a pin, which you can do by holding your opponent on the back. The pin forces your opponent into a position where they can no longer attack.

Some competitive grappling styles consider the successful execution of a pin as an immediate victory. Other styles consider it a dominant position that awards the athlete several points.

Aside from the pin, there are other controlling and securing techniques, like holding your opponent face down or on all fours, preventing them from attacking or escaping. All these techniques, when successfully performed, lead to a submission hold.

- **Escape** – This grappling classification is when you maneuver yourself out of a dangerous or inferior position. For example, when the grappler, who is beneath an opponent, controls movements sideways to guard or successfully returns to a standing position considered neutral. Also, when the grappler escapes from a submission attempt and returns to a position, that lowers the submission hold risk.

- **Turnover** – The turnover is used to control your opponent, particularly when they are on all fours, prepare for a pin, or get into a dominant position. You will score valuable points with a turnover.

- **Sweep or Reversal** – This grappling technique is when a grappler maneuvers the position beneath their opponent while on the ground. The goal of the sweep or reversal is to obtain a top position.

Grappling Styles and Techniques

Apart from the major classifications of grappling already mentioned, some other styles and techniques are also perfectly suitable for Brazilian Jiu-Jitsu.

Leg Trip

This method requires you to use your leg to force your opponent off balance and bring them to the ground. This technique is further subdivided into two - the single and the double leg trip.

The single-leg takedown - grab one leg of your opponent using both your hands. The goal here is to bring your opponent to the ground by pulling the lower part of the leg using your shoulder.

Single leg takedowns also come in several types; the ankle lift, which requires you to pick up the leg by the ankle, and the high crotch, which requires you to pull up your opponent's leg by the crotch area. Using either technique, you can attack the leg across or away from the body.

The Double-Leg Takedown

Grab the legs of your opponent using both arms. Keep your chest closer to your opponent's leg, and force them to the ground, which is the ultimate goal of grappling.

Other skills to force your opponent to the ground include slamming, pulling the legs, and pushing them forward using your shoulders.

Ankle Pinch Takedown

This style is perhaps one of the best techniques adopted by Brazilian Jiu-Jitsu. Push the head of your opponent over one knee. Your goal is to immobilize your opponent's leg. Complete the ankle pinch takedown by stepping inward and blocking the targeted foot before grabbing the ankle. Then lift your opponent's foot, causing them to fall.

Triangle Choke

This is an iconic and popular BJJ submission hold. Many fighters use the triangle choke from the guard. However, it is a very versatile technique that can be done in many ways.

Use your legs to trap your opponent's neck and one arm.

The pressure of your thigh across your opponent's neck disrupts blood flow. It is a very effective technique as the opponent will most likely tap out, signifying their acceptance of defeat.

Rear Naked Choke

This is another popular submission hold used by grapplers in BJJ. Exert pressure on your opponent's head's blood circulation, making them uncomfortable and prone to unconsciousness unless they tap out.

This technique also usually follows a back mount, which requires you to wrap your arm around the neck of your opponents. Use your opposite arm to grab or take hold of your opponent's biceps. Apply pressure to the designated area using the strength and force of your biceps.

Using your free hand, put pressure on the back of your opponent's head, deepening the choke.

Guard

Trap your opponent between your legs. You can open or lock this position using your ankles. The guard is designed to force your opponent to break the stronghold of their posture, tiring them out. You can also consider the guard a defense strategy requiring strikes.

Closed Guard

The closed guard is a crucial concept in grappling with many variations. Expect the closed guard to be one of the first guards you will learn as a white belt or BJJ beginner.

Lock your opponent between your legs by crossing your feet behind their back. A significant advantage of the closed guard is that you have the opportunity for submission or sweep simultaneously.

Note there is no one superior technique with guards as it depends on the situation. Aside from the closed guard, the other variations are half guard, X guard, butterfly, and open guard.

Technical Mount

The mount is another powerful position for those wanting to make the most out of grappling. However, it's essential to understand everything about this move and position so you can maximize its full advantage.

While some find it overrated, it is an extremely important move you can use once you reach more advanced BJJ levels. It is a useful counter technique allowing you to maintain a reasonable and excellent position for an attack.

Importance of Stretching and Flexibility

Undeniably, Brazilian Jiu-Jitsu is a sport that is physically and mentally demanding. Grappling alone has many techniques, variations, and positions that require you to move various parts of your body unconventionally. It is the primary reason you must learn more about stretching and flexibility, as both have crucial roles in improving your grappling technique performance.

Stretching and flexibility help you stay healthy while keeping you free of injuries as you continue with your training. Moreover, including stretching in your BJJ training assures you of a balanced and long-term program.

Depending on your game plan and your unique grappling style, your flexibility level will either be lower or higher than that of your opponent. Understanding your flexibility level enables you to control and force your opponent to submit.

You must be familiar with the different stretching techniques to succeed in BJJ. These techniques will improve your flexibility, leading you to better performance.

Active Stretching

Active stretching techniques refer to exercises that allow you to move your joints actively using various motions. It is ideal to do active stretching as part of your warm-up exercises before BJJ class or conditioning. You can also use active stretching as a component of an independent mobility routine, which you perform separately from other training, like in the morning after your rest day or when you wake up.

Some warm-up exercises designed explicitly for BJJ, like shrimping and bridges, can be classified as active stretching, provided you do them while consciously exerting effort in executing a full range of movement.

Passive Stretching

Stretching techniques and exercises are considered passive if they involve moving your joints to their flexibility tolerance. Hold the specific position when you experience mild discomfort for at least 20 seconds. It encompasses external assistance, like a BJJ belt, as a means of stretching your hamstrings.

Just like the active stretches, you can also do the passive ones independently at the end of mobility routines. Perform the passive stretches after your BJJ training, preferably within five to ten minutes after the session, as it is also when you have an elevated body temperature.

Passive stretching performed *after* your workout also helps improve your flexibility or range of motion, provided it's done consistently.

What Muscle Groups and Joints Should You Stretch Regularly?

Now that you are familiar with stretching and its importance in boosting your flexibility, it is important to know what specific muscle groups and joints to stretch to improve your BJJ performance. Regularly stretching the right muscle groups and joints improves your strength, which can make you even more effective in grappling.

Ankles

To master BJJ, you need to improve the mobility and flexibility of your ankles to execute techniques correctly and prevent injuries during training and competitions. Note that tight calf muscles can also cause stiff ankles and may cause limitations in flexing your foot.

Rearward tension in your feet is necessary when executing strong butterfly hooks and proof that you must improve the mobility of your ankles with controlled rotations. If your calf tightens, then you may want to do static calf stretches.

Hips

It is essential for Brazilian Jiu-Jitsu fighters to improve their hip mobility (to prevent injury), and this also helps them to deliver incredible performances. External hip rotations will help you obtain a strong offensive and defensive guard.

Having good hip extension is also helpful whenever you need to escape from a bad position, bridging, completing the submission, or passing guard. Do passive and active stretching techniques that target the glutes, hamstrings, hip rotators, and quads to improve hip mobility.

Upper Back

Also called the T-spine, your upper back must have high flexibility levels to prevent spine and upper back injuries. If you have tight shoulders, lats, and pecs, your upper back likely lacks mobility. BJJ requires many rounded defensive postures, and low flexibility will result in a stiff upper back or T-spine.

Shoulders

Improve the mobility of your shoulders by doing appropriate stretching exercises that target the muscles in this area. With improved shoulder mobility, you can prevent the most common shoulder injuries many grapplers often deal with. Similar to the defensive and rounded posture that triggers stiffness in the T-spine, it also causes immobility or inflexibility to the shoulders.

When and How Often Should You Stretch?

If you want to master grappling, never neglect the importance of stretching consistently. Apart from the muscle groups and joints mentioned, stretch your neck and wrists regularly to improve mobility. It is advisable to perform stretching as frequently as possible, and it is even more important if you have mobility problems. Do your chosen active stretching routines daily as part of your morning rituals.

Focus on passive routines after workouts or before you go to bed. Add a few passive stretching exercises to the active ones, but avoid passive stretching before you do heavy physical activities. It is not highly recommended before strength and conditioning training.

You will notice a significant improvement in your mobility, flexibility, and strength by doing these recommended stretching routines, ultimately executing various grappling techniques without any problems and demonstrating promise as a future dominant BJJ fighter.

Chapter 4: The Law of Action and Reaction

From an outsider's perspective, Brazilian Jiu-Jitsu may get the impression that the entire sport is only about complicated chokeholds and grappling. As a white belt or a beginner with only a few days of training, you may view BJJ in the same way.

You will notice that most moves and techniques require many steps. You feel like effectively mastering and employing them is only possible after many years of practice.

However, as you gain more experience, you gain a deep appreciation of the high level of skill, knowledge, and dedication required to transform yourself into a great BJJ fighter.

Even though you experience difficulties at first, try to grasp everything you're taught during classes. Eventually, you will realize that embracing and understanding the core principles and disciplines of BJJ gives you an edge over others.

Importance of the Principle-based Approach to Learning BJJ

Brazilian Jiu-Jitsu, like other martial arts, relies on its core disciplines and principles. Mastering BJJ is not about mastering each step, technique, or move; it is when you understand its principles and modify them based on various scenarios and opponents.

While still recognizing the principles, theories, and disciplines of BJJ, you can add a few personal touches to demonstrate your own artistry level. It is safe to say that the principle-based approach to mastering BJJ differs a lot from the memory-based one.

Remember, while memorizing each move is essential to learn Brazilian Jiu-Jitsu's basics, it may hinder growth. The reason is that committing certain moves to memory may also indicate that you lack the inherent comprehension of its core principles.

This can be disadvantageous, especially when an unfamiliar move performed by your opponent catches you off-guard. To help with this, beginners (white belts) must work with different partners, as it helps to reimagine various fight scenarios.

It is a fantastic opportunity to put the moves you learned in class into practice in the real world. It also helps you understand the underlying theories that make the movements effective.

Core Principles and Disciplines of BJJ and Other Martial Arts

As mentioned earlier, Brazilian Jiu-Jitsu is a martial art that focuses on grappling and that uses leverage principles. The focus of BJJ is always on positional control, takedowns, submissions, and grappling, and this is an effective means to improve every modality of fitness, like agility, mobility, and core strength.

Mentally, you can liken Brazilian Jiu-Jitsu to a chess game, as tactical thinking is the correct strategy and will contribute to success. When you are on the training ground or in your class, it is important to show that you have a solid grasp of the fundamental principles and disciplines of BJJ. Some of the essential principles and disciplines of BJJ, and other martial arts, are covered in this section.

Zen Stage

The Zen stage is a vital principle that allows fighters to learn and understand Brazilian Jiu-Jitsu. The principles valorize the significance of repetition. Note that repeating a Jiu-Jitsu technique several times over many years may lead to you executing the BJJ technique *without even thinking about it.*

It is even possible for your muscle memory to do the BJJ technique as if on autopilot in the same way as habits are formed. Therefore, you must apply proper repetition to enjoy its varied benefits, including - but not limited to - what's listed here.

- **Perfect the Technique** - This builds a strong base for all moves, no matter how different. You will also gain a solid foundation to improve your strength, the overall quality of execution, and movement sequences.
- **Puts Your Mind at a Phase of Emptiness** - this is needed for more effective execution of your moves and techniques
- **Becomes a Habit** - Drilling a BJJ technique repeatedly and correctly turns it into a habit. Humans are creatures of habit, so what you do repeatedly makes up who you are. So, if you improve your habits, expect to improve your performance when competing.

However, you must be extra careful when repeating a particular technique incorrectly because repeating it too often will develop incorrect and unwanted habits. Work with a good Brazilian Jiu-Jitsu instructor capable of pointing out your mistakes and guiding you toward developing good and healthy habits.

Balance

In the martial arts world, especially in Brazilian Jiu-Jitsu, a core concept is the principle of balance - not too little nor too much. This specific principle is useful in martial arts training in regard to various aspects of your everyday life, your body, and your emotions.

BJJ fighters - and any other martial artist - perceive balance as not moving or acting too slowly or too fast, meaning that you should not be too tentative or too aggressive, or too low, high, right, or left. It's imperative to practice the principle of balance to control your timing and pace. You must learn to rely on your balance if you want to succeed in BJJ and other martial art forms.

Balance also helps filter your mindset while training. By fully understanding the principle of balance, you accept that your training days will not always be good, and you will experience bad days. So, avoid becoming too frustrated or impatient because of your unrealistic expectations that each training day will be good.

Developing this principle is also key to freeing your mind from depending on the outcome of a specific training session. Instead of doing that, focus on the training's practical process and recognize that attaining balance is also needed by accepting both good and bad days.

You can turn your training session into one that balances your body, emotions, and mind and contribute to delivering an excellent physical performance.

Natural Order

To become a successful BJJ fighter, you must have a complete grasp of the principle related to the natural order. This specific process is about understanding the progressive and continuous changes and development, so prepare for them instead of evading them.

Progression in BJJ and other martial arts will always be equal to concentration and time. It requires spending minimal time to achieve similar progress if your focus is on intensity, but you still have to retain the balance. Also, forcing yourself to train too intensely and for an extended period will only lead to overtraining or burnout. In some cases, your body will be incapable of recovering properly from stress.

However, insufficient training and lack of passion in this martial art form may also result in you failing to attain your goals. So, it is crucial to maintain balance and adhere to the natural order.

One sign that you have attained the correct balance in your attitude towards your BJJ training is when you are genuinely happy with the process. You are also aware that regardless of your BJJ and martial arts achievements, they won't matter that much based on the cosmos' scale and the universal scheme of things.

Action and Reaction

The most important aspect of the many principles and disciplines governing any martial art form is the "action and reaction" principle. In other words, "for every action, expect a reaction."

Brazilian Jiu-Jitsu requires minimal effort to attain maximum results. So, using the action and reaction principle is the best way to achieve success in this sport.

As a beginner still in the learning phase of Brazilian Jiu-Jitsu, there is a chance that your focus is frequently on reacting. You defend submissions or try maintaining your balance and are always on the defense. It's okay as you are still a beginner and learning the ins and outs of the sport.

However, once you begin to learn to defend instinctively, expect your game to change. One significant change is that you spend less brainpower on defense and use more on your intention. For instance, if an attacker is on guard while you throw triangles and set yourself up for the kimura, you may be asking what is running through their mind.

Remember, your attacker is not thinking at that moment – they are reacting. They do not think of the moment passing; they are taking defensive/offensive steps.

Now, think about what will happen if you wait just a little longer to determine their moves. The best possible scenario would be that they will pass your guard. The key to getting a good player to submit is keeping them from a moment of thought.

Importance of Action and Reaction Principle

The action and reaction principle will always be vital in BJJ fighters and martial artists because you can use this principle to set up most of your takedowns and throws.

Attempting to control an opponent who is still standing can be more challenging than fighting on the ground. The reason for this is that your opponent can move freely, react instantly, and escape when standing.

To dissect the meaning of the action and reaction principle, think of your opponent who is about to make a move against you – this is an action. The response (reaction) is when you think and act quickly based on that move, like a counter-attack.

Also, by ensuring that you are aware of the possible defensive reactions of your opponent, you will attack appropriately. Understanding your opponent's best defensive response gives you a chance to equip yourself with knowledge and information to gain more leverage or power. With the action and reaction principle, your strategy is to force a reaction from your opponent, take advantage and react immediately to use their energy to add power and leverage to your moves.

When to Act and React?

Once you know that every attack can provoke a reaction, you will also be smart with your attacks. For instance, you can fake an attack to disguise your real intention and use your opponent's reaction as an opening for your successful technique.

You have to be very observant of the clues that will let you act and react appropriately. Always apply this principle, even when you are no longer in the class. You may lose your belt or even be arrested if you harm someone using the BJJ moves and techniques, whether provoked or not. Therefore, anticipating a person's action and reaction is crucial.

In class, you will realize that the skills associated with acting and reacting at the proper times are due to *repetition.* The more training you undergo, the quicker you will execute the practiced techniques and expect your muscle memory to develop.

When competing and pushing your opponent, expect them to push you back instinctively with similar or increased intensity levels that force the action and reaction principle. Likewise, with pulls, if you intend to pull them forward, push them backward first.

Once your opponent reacts by pushing you, pull them. You will draw on their energy and expend just minimal energy when pulling your opponent forward. You will also do this when implementing the art of reversal (more about this topic later) in your fights.

Taking Advantage of the Action and Reaction Principle

There are several ways to apply this principle, especially when planning to lead your opponent into a different position from that which they planned. Do you intend to sweep them to your left? Then stimulating them to move to your right first is a wise move, as it compromises your opponent's balance. Then decide on your next move based on what happens.

Another way of viewing the action and reaction principle is as bait and trap, meaning luring your opponent so they will react or respond in the way you intended. It helps to react quickly to your opponent's moves so you can make the most of this principle.

For example, if they move their body forward with a specific speed, increase their speed further by pulling them in a similar direction. It may result in your opponent losing their balance, which you can use to your advantage.

The deeper and more experienced you become in Brazilian Jiu-Jitsu, the more you realize that a single move or attack is not as effective when inflicted on more skilled and experienced fighters. You must combine various techniques for the best results when applying the action and reaction principle.

The best way to apply the principle is to analyze what went wrong when a technique failed. Analyze and brainstorm the reaction of your opponents and create your Plan B, which will surely arouse your excitement for your next match, especially if you feel they will prepare a defense against your Plan A.

Chapter 5: Defending Against Attacks: The Art of Reversal

One reason many people become interested in Brazilian Jiu-Jitsu is that it is an excellent form of self-defense. Knowledge about this form of martial art is the key for someone to defend themselves against an attack. Apart from the action and reaction principle, Brazilian Jiu-Jitsu will also help you brush up your knowledge on the art of defense and reversal.

The action and reaction principle has a strong connection to the art of self-defense and reversal that's also a vital part of Brazilian Jiu-Jitsu because you must follow the action and reaction principle to establish a strong defense against an attack. Your defense will be based on your opponent's attack.

What Is Reversal?

Brazilian Jiu-Jitsu reversal is when a player in a disadvantageous position or at the bottom succeeds in reversing their position. The successful reversal will result in the player being in an advantageous or top position. It is a great skill that Brazilian Jiu-Jitsu fighters must master because it gives them the chance to skip a few steps when changing positions every time they initiate the reversal.

A typical change results in the player moving through neutral to good positions after finding themselves in a bad one. Depending on your chosen reversal technique, you can go directly to a good position. The art of reversal is the key to protecting yourself from an attack.

Brazilian Jiu-Jitsu and Self-Defense

Self-defense forms a significant part of BJJ. It is based on the original Japanese Jiu-Jitsu when the Samurai fought for survival; it continues to be a practical fighting system today. All moves taught in BJJ are effective self-defense moves, and some of these techniques are specifically designed for that purpose.

So, it is not surprising that most BJJ schools worldwide pay special attention and focus more on self-defense. In modern Jiu-Jitsu self-defense, strikes do not form part of the system. However, learning the basics of moving around, blocking, and using them is still essential.

It is not that essential to learn and master complex jumping attacks and spinning kicks. Instead, it is better to set simpler goals, like getting close to your attacker or opponent, intending to force submission, or taking them down.

Another thing to remember is that around 90 percent of altercations or fights end with fighters on the ground. People without BJJ skills will be unsure of what to do once they are taken down onto the ground. Your knowledge of Brazilian Jiu-Jitsu can change that, especially with grappling, and it encourages your best techniques.

With your BJJ training, you will know precisely how to defend yourself and remain safe whether you are in the top, back, or bottom position. The self-defense you learn in BJJ will train you to build dominance, even when you are placed in a bad position.

Once you can protect yourself and be in a more dominant position, BJJ will give you an option to do something not offered by other forms of martial art – resolving the situation without harming your opponent or causing an injury. Self-defense in BJJ and several other techniques help you to pin someone down while de-escalating the situation.

On the other hand, you are also allowed to use a submission technique designed to hurt your attacker or opponent when necessary. If you prefer, you can perform strikes. Overall, you won't find other forms of martial arts that are as good for self-defense as BJJ, especially with one-on-one fights or altercations.

Why Is BJJ Perfect for Self-Defense?

Constantly remind yourself that the best weapon for self-defense is your ability to stay away from confrontation. If possible, escape from the situation. However, if the situation reaches the point of becoming physical, make the most of your Brazilian Jiu-Jitsu training to get you out of trouble.

What are the specific reasons why BJJ is good for self-defense?

It Improves Your Comfort Level When Fighting

If you have experienced a situation when someone has tried choking you until you become unconscious, you are probably aware of how uncomfortable it is. Your training will make you feel comfortable with the discomfort and sometimes the pain, and you will deal with the situation automatically.

Unlike striking arts, like Muay Thai, which require sparring for only about 20 percent of the training, Brazilian Jiu-Jitsu involves sparring up to almost 100 percent of the training. Rolling in BJJ is close to an actual fight, though it still does not involve kicking and punching.

Whenever you are in a situation where you are required to protect yourself, you will not be shocked or intimidated by the fighter's physical size due to your sparring training. You will not also experience discomfort when you grapple with someone and take them to the ground.

Since you are already comfortable with grappling and fighting, you will not make the mistakes of untrained people or beginners, like turning their backs on the attacker as a means of shielding themselves. This is a natural response to a dangerous situation, but it puts you at a greater risk since you cannot see your opponent and anticipate their possible means of attack.

As someone trained in BJJ, you are more skilled and adept at protecting yourself and understanding your opponent's attacks, so you can easily set up measures to avoid them. You will also be more comfortable fighting and grappling with others, increasing your chance of winning the fight or escaping the situation unharmed.

Ideal for All People Regardless of Size

Knowing Brazilian Jiu-Jitsu will give you a fighting chance against an attacker or in a situation that requires you to defend yourself. The good thing about this form of martial arts is that it is perfect for everyone, regardless of size.

Even if you are small, you can still perform BJJ for self-defense. It will not pose the problems associated with smaller students of other martial arts training, such as their lighter bones and weight that may cause difficulty in inflicting damage on a bigger opponent. With Brazilian Jiu-Jitsu, even smaller individuals have a chance of defeating a bigger opponent.

Also, note that those with smaller physiques can generate limited force against their attackers or opponents. If you are bigger, expect that your hits will have more force because you have that added weight.

BJJ is such an incredible practice for self-defense as it teaches you how to choke and grapple larger and bigger individuals than you, negating the issue associated with the size.

Unlike Muay Thai, boxing, or any other form of martial arts that depends on athleticism, power, and speed, Brazilian Jiu-Jitsu focuses on technique. Smaller fighters can enforce a submission because of gaining confidence in their BJJ self-defense techniques.

A perfect example of the effectiveness of BJJ in dealing with bigger or larger opponents is Royce Gracie and his domination in UFC. In his fights, he was consistent in making his opponents submit regardless of their size. As far as ground technique is concerned, no other form of martial art compares to BJJ.

Helps You Stay in Control in a Fight

Brazilian Jiu-Jitsu is also perfect for self-defense as this form of martial art is highly effective in being able to control your opponent. You can use your BJJ skills to stop your attacker or opponent while ensuring that they do not get hurt or injured.

BJJ practice teaches you how to use leverage and frames to control the body weight of your opponent. Some positions, such as the knee-on-belly position, control an opponent on the ground.

You can also use a shoulder lock pose, which helps you to increase control over an attacker, especially if they are still untrained. If you are dealing with an attacker carrying a weapon, BJJ can't guarantee the highest level of protection, but it is still more advantageous compared to other forms of martial art, like Muay Thai.

Brazilian Jiu-Jitsu is more effective when dealing with situations involving a knife, as it teaches you to control your attacker. Positions like the Omoplata or shoulder lock will enable you to clearly observe your opponent's hand, giving you the edge over the opponent.

You will be at an advantage since you can clearly see what their next actions are. For instance, this gives you sufficient time to respond and stop the attack if they reach for the gun or knife.

Brazilian Jiu-Jitsu Self-Defense Techniques

When using Brazilian Jiu-Jitsu for self-defense, remember that strikes alone are not applicable, and it may be necessary to combine strikes with other BJJ tactics to be effective. However, most schools recommend starting your training without strikes, especially when executing stand-up grappling.

Only add strikes once you obtain a solid and stable grappling base. A second in time can make a significant difference, especially if the fight is fast-paced. That second could make you win or lose, so practice BJJ self-defense using your attacking knowledge.

Closed Guard

Guards in BJJ come in different formats, but for the purpose of self-defense, we will focus on the closed guard because this tactic is what grapplers currently use. It also carries several benefits when used in a self-defense situation.

The BJJ guard refers to how you use your legs when dealing with an adversary, like wrapping your legs around your adversary. You may do this lying on your back or keep the attacker or adversary away from you.

An appropriate use of the closed guard in a self-defense situation is to block punches.

Standing BJJ ArmBar

The standing armbar is an easy yet highly effective self-defense tactic you can learn from BJJ training, and it is also an effective combat submission technique. The standing armbar originated from Japanese Jiu-Jitsu.

It led to the seated version of the armbar that is often used in BJJ. The difference is that Japanese Jiu-Jitsu requires fighters to remain on their feet as there is a greater chance the opponents or fighters are using a weapon, like samurais.

Knee-On-Belly

This technique is vital if you want to be in control of your adversary or opponent. It is ideal in situations where you can grab the top position in a fight. In this position, use the knee-on-belly to move above your adversary easily. One example is when your adversary pulls a weapon, like a knife, from their boot or pocket while you control them through the knee-on-belly. You will have an easier time disengaging, moving away, or escaping from them.

Using a different move or position, such as the mount, may signify to your opponent that you are surrendering. It may also limit your movement, making it hard to disengage.

Cross-Face

This specific position requires you to be on top of your opponent or adversary to control them. Using your arm, go behind the head of your adversary or opponent. Place your shoulder to the side of your opponent's jawline. The pressure brought on by this position will give you control.

The correct execution of this technique and properly applied pressure from your shoulder will cause your opponent to look away and limit their movements. Since your opponent faces away from you, it is hard for them to execute any movements or techniques.

Side Control Escape

Many consider this technique the hardest position to escape from, and it comes in different variations. However, it would be best to learn the basic side control principles and disciplines so you can escape an attack.

Can You Use Brazilian Jiu-Jitsu When There Are Multiple Attackers?

As mentioned earlier, BJJ works perfectly in one-on-one confrontations. But the question is, will its self-defense techniques be effective when dealing with more than one attacker? The answer is no. This fighting system may be unsuitable to use against multiple opponents or on the battlefield.

The basic premise of self-defense is throwing an attacker or adversary to the floor. Speed is also vital in self-defense, and it is in this area where BJJ for self-defense may be at fault.

However, you can easily alter this if you spend time learning Judo throws instead of wrestling takedowns. Your goal would be to master throws capable of leaving your attacker on the ground while you are standing.

If possible, combine this with the other BJJ techniques and disciplines, and you can make the most of self-defense and reversal.

Where Can You Apply BJJ Self-Defense?

The effectiveness of BJJ as self-defense depends on the setting or location where the fight or altercation takes place. For instance, it would be difficult to use BJJ in a fight in a crowded bar; in this case, it would be much better to control your opponent from a standing position.

If the altercation occurs in an open space, such as a parking lot, and the attacker does not have a weapon, then the setting is suitable for BJJ self-defense skills.

You will have a better chance in an open space with takedowns since there are no barriers to control your attacker or assailant. The knee-on-belly is the best position to keep your assailant under control while sharpening your self-defense skills.

Chapter 6: Guards: Why Are They So Important to Know?

The Brazilian Jiu-Jitsu guard is one of the most useful and effective ground grappling positions to know. This position is characterized by a combatant with their back on the ground as they attempt to control their opponent with their legs.

The guard is a favorable position in mastering BJJ because you can attack your opponent using different chokeholds and joint locks from the bottom. On the other hand, the priority of your opponent on the top is to transition to a better and more dominant position. This is a process called passing the guard.

With the proven importance and undeniable benefits of this BJJ position, it is not surprising that it has several types. The type used will depend on your specific grips or points of control. Some Brazilian Jiu-Jitsu guards are ideal for use when you have an opponent in a standing position, and other guards work well when the opponent is kneeling.

When learning about BJJ guard positions, remember that some are perfect for grappling submissions but are harmful when used in MMA (mixed martial arts) tournaments. Other guard positions serve as a great escape or defense when dealing with the opponent's dominant positions.

Overall, the guard will always be a key component of Brazilian Jiu-Jitsu, considering its usefulness when fighting for an offensive position. In this chapter, you will learn more about the BJJ guard position, its different types, guard passing, sweep techniques, drills, and attacks. You will be able to make the most of this vital BJJ element after reading this chapter.

Closed Guard vs. Open Guards – The Differences

Two of the most basic and popular guard positions you will encounter are closed and open guards. Both are popular because they provide players with excellent tools, whether on the top or bottom.

The closed and open guards give you opportunities to sweep, control, and submit your opponent, establishing a strong and solid defensive and offensive grappling game.

Closed Guard

This is how to hold a strong closed guard

It is a basic type of guard that you will learn in your BJJ training. The closed guard is largely used by beginners and high-level competitors in BJJ. It is the founding guard and one of the first few positions you will learn as you begin your training in Brazilian Jiu-Jitsu.

Also called the full guard, the closed guard position occurs when you close your legs around the hips or waist of your opponent, and you must simultaneously grip your opponent's collar or sleeve.

The closed guard perfectly showcases the exact place where you can see the power and strength of guards in BJJ, specifically distance management, meaning you can be in complete control if you dictate the specific range that the grappling exchange takes place and have a free arm to use for attacks.

You also have to focus on successfully pulling through the vital aspects of the closed guard. These are discussed briefly.

- **Leg Position** – Wrap both your legs around the waist of your opponent, and interlock your ankles behind your opponent's back, securing the position. You may have to squeeze both your knees while bringing them simultaneously to your chest. It helps you to pull your opponent towards you, eliminating the space for their appropriate posture.

- **Grip** – Before performing the closed guard, think of the significance of grip placement because where you position your grip will give you the versatility to execute the move successfully.

  However, gripping from a closed guard position in most martial arts and self-defense situations, you will use the double sleeve/wrist grip. This grip allows you to control the arms of your opponent, keeping you safe from any form of attack.

- When you pair this grip with effective postural control, specifically with your legs, you will be in a dominant position to start your attack.
- **Goals** – Determine your goals when doing the guard, too. Like other guard types, your primary goal for the closed guard is to prevent your guard from being passed. Your goal is the only way to ensure that your guard is impenetrable, and that will help you start your attacks.

When making the attacks, it is beneficial to break your opponent's posture first. Note that you will be unable to attain much from an opponent who sits upright while implementing your chosen guard.

The good news is that effectively using your legs and the dual wrist grips help make your job easier. If they have broken posture, you can use sweeps, attacks, and back takes.

Open Guard

This is how to push for an open guard

The open guard differs from the closed guard because it does not require you to close your legs around your opponent's waist or chest. Use the open guard to transition from a half or weak full guard triggered by the opponent's movements.

There are several transitional positions, submissions, and sweeps when doing the BJJ open guard. For instance, you can transition to a butterfly, reverse De La Riva, De La Riva, and spider guards. It differs from the closed guard in a few aspects:

- **Leg Position** - Your legs have specific purposes in an open guard that stay the same no matter what the guard is. In the open guard, one leg will always serve as the hooking leg and is what you will attach to your opponent.
- You will use the other active leg based on what you want to execute, especially for guard retention, submissions, and sweeps. The exact leg positioning or placement will greatly depend on the type of open guard you intend to use.
- **Grips** - The open guard position allows a wide range of grip options. However, remember the underlying principle, which is always diagonal control. Preferably, you must grip a leg and the opposite side arm no matter which guard variation you use.
- **Goals** - An open guard position means that you will have to retain the position first before you can make an attack. Several open guard positions only provide a few attacks as they prioritize more on sweeps and off-balancing.

Other guard positions allow you to do chain sweeps and attacks and can force an opponent to be in a defensive position all the time.

Other BJJ Guard Types and Variations

Apart from the open and closed guards that are popular for BJJ beginners, there are also other types and variations to familiarize yourself with. These guards are useful o master every BJJ position and to win in a fight or attack.

High Guard

Trapping the opponent's shoulder in high guard

Also called the climbing or crooked guard. Maneuver your legs to climb up the opponent to trap one or both of their shoulders. Trapping the shoulders puts your opponent in danger because you can easily execute the armbar, sweep, and triangle attacks.

Compared to other types of guards, especially the rubber guard, the high guard requires only minimal flexibility. There are similarities, though, as they involve using both legs to keep the opponent's posture down. It is a fantastic BJJ guard, as your opponent will have a hard time striking you or passing your guard without providing you an opportunity for submission or sweep.

Deep Half Guard

The Deep Half Guard With triangled legs

In no gi, with one butterfly hook insterted under the opponent's lower leg

This guard position requires rolling beneath your opponent, so you can easily take their weight. Once you are in this position, use your legs to trap your opponent's legs while using both arms to grip around their hips. Swing your legs to take your opponent off balance. The deep half guard offers just a few submissions, but it is still a great position to sweep.

Rubber Guard

The rubber guard is challenging and tough to execute as it requires more flexibility. Execute this position if you are from a high or full guard. In Jiu-Jitsu, the rubber guard could be a variation of the high guard that requires you to use both feet and put them in a high position. This position helps you to control your opponent's neck and ensures that his head stays down. The result is perfect control of your opponent, who will be in a poor BJJ posture.

Spider Guard

The Spider Guard being used against a kneeling opponent (both feet on biceps)

Against a standing opponent, one foot on biceps and the other on the hip

Against a standing opponent using one foot on the bicep and one leg wrapped around the arm

The spider guard is a tough BJJ position that you can use to gain excellent control of your distance in the kneeling or standing opponent. This position can contribute to putting your opponent off balance, giving you opportunities for a few submissions or sweeps, including the arm bar and triangle chokes.

You can also use the spider guard to transition to other BJJ guards, such as the De La Riva. You can execute it as an open guard by gripping the sleeves or wrists of your opponent, and using one foot to control their arms, too.

In most cases, you only have to put one foot against their biceps; otherwise, your leg is at risk of spiraling near their elbow, and your toes are hiding beneath their upper arm.

Butterfly Guard

The Butterfly Guard an underhook and a belt grip

Using a pant leg and lapel cross grip

The Butterfly Guard in no gi using a bearhug grip. Occasionally used in MMA, since it is difficult for the opponent to generate a lot of force in his strikes.

A very difficult position from which to play the Butterfly Guard (referred to as the TK Guard by early UFC commentators.

This dynamic butterfly guard position features several options for sweeps and can be used in no-Gi and Gi grappling. To execute this guard, first, familiarize yourself with the sitting position and how to remain active when trying to get your opponent off-balance.

Many fighters in Brazilian Jiu-Jitsu use this position to initialize leg lock submissions. Some use this position to transition to half guard, single leg X guard, and X guard positions.

Knee Shield or Z-Guard

The Z Guard with the bottom leg hooking and the top knee pushing at the hip

The same position with the top knee pushing in the chest / shoulder area

You can execute this specific guard from the standard half-guard position. Raise one knee to take the weight off your opponent. It creates a skeletal frame, ensuring that you will not be crushed by your opponent when threatened with submissions and sweeps. To defend a submission, attack the far arm, and to enact the sweeps, get the nearside under hook and simultaneously threaten the back.

Octopus Guard

The Octopus Guard in no-gi

In most cases, you get an opening for the octopus guard position when your opponent executes a hip switch after being in a knee shield position. Another way to do the octopus guard is to move your far shoulder behind your opponent's.

Use this specific position to sweep into the mount or reach the back. Otherwise referred to as the reverse half guard, the octopus guard also requires you to base or depend on your elbow to get into the position.

Koala Guard

Koala Guard

You can do the koala guard position as you get into a sitting position against a standing opponent. Latch onto your opponent's leg, similar to how a koala does, while hugging them, leading to a tighter connection. The koala guard is frequently used to transition to other guard positions, and it is also useful whenever you need to attack leg locks, like foot locks, Achilles' locks, and knee bars.

Collar Sleeve Guard

Collar Sleeve Guard

To get into this guard position, use one of your hands to grab your opponent's sleeve, the other hand to grab the collar, and put your leg on the sleeve's bicep that is in your grip.

Place your other leg on your opponent's hip. Alternatively, you can wrap this leg into a hook. Like other sleeve guards, your goal when executing the collar sleeve guard is pushing and pulling your opponent off-balance. You can effectively hit different sweeps and prompt a submission, which is usually the triangle.

Quarter Guard

Quarter Guard

This position is between a mount defense and the half guard. In most cases, the quarter guard provides little for attacks, so it is mainly used as a retention position to stop you from passing your guard.

Most fighters are not fond of the quarter guard because it is categorized as an inferior position. This position depends on keeping the foot of the opponent trapped rather than their knee. Despite that, it is still useful for sweeps when your opponent makes a mistake.

What Is Guard Retention?

Now that you know some of the most useful guards, it is time to understand how you can retain this position. As a BJJ beginner, besides mastering different guard positions, you also have to learn how to retain them.

The goal of mastering guard retention is to avoid being overcome by the opponent's guard passes without getting the chance to retain the position. Act immediately whenever you sense that your opponent is about to pass your guard.

Of course, the first step in handling this dilemma is to remain calm. Facing your opponent is also necessary. Remember that for you to pass the guard, your opponent has to come to your side and get into side control. So, you want to continue rotating your body to ensure that you're facing your opponent all the time.

In doing so, they will be unable to get to the pose that will prompt you to pass the guard. The primary guard retention principle you must always remember is to *face your attacker or opponent.*

Keeping the Head under Control

Do not worry if your opponent is already halfway in his attempt to make you pass your guard, as it is still possible to save and restore your position. The best way to handle this situation is to control your opponent's head by using both hands.

It will prevent your opponent from moving efficiently and prioritizing dealing with your hands, giving you sufficient time to move your body away. Use this time to reset your main position, which is also essential for effective guard retention.

Proper Knee Positioning

Proper knee positioning is also crucial in guard retention. The goal is to ensure that your knees continue to stay together as much as possible, but it does not necessarily mean keeping your knees closed without putting any space in between. The best position for your knees is to keep them very close to your chest. Your opponent would have a hard time making you pass your guard if you managed to keep your knees close to your chest successfully.

However, you must also learn how to pull away from your legs to create an opening for your side-control entry. Guard retention is possible if you make sure that your opponent stays close to you.

Chapter 7: The Art of Takedown

Takedowns are vital to Brazilian Jiu-Jitsu, so all participants must know how to perform them regardless of belts, expertise, and skill levels. In BJJ competitions, the fight starts in a natural standing position, but you will earn valuable points if you land a good takedown. The takedown also defines how the fight will end.

What is even better about having a good drop is that it provides you with an excellent ground position, like side-control and mount positions. It even gives you the opportunity to take the back of your opponent.

Why Learning the Art of Takedown Is Important for BJJ

When grasping the importance of takedowns in BJJ, it is crucial to understand the roots of this form of martial art – one of which is self-defense and extremely significant. Takedowns offer an opportunity for a quick escape when you need to defend yourself or execute your ground fighting skills.

Mastering good takedowns is crucial as it provides you with great defense skills, especially if the situation involves more than one attacker. Almost everyone believes that in street fights, the ground is probably the least favored area.

Yes, your training in Brazilian Jiu-Jitsu has offered you a strong physical edge whenever you get into the ground, but it would be best to avoid it if you are in danger. Your goal would be a quick escape, and your knowledge of takedowns will enable you to achieve that.

Takedowns are also vital in rules that penalize guard pulling and indicate whether you should start the match from a position on top. Moreover, the takedown will serve as a surprise for an attacker or your opponent in competitions.

Never underestimate the importance of takedowns not only in BJJ competitions but also when you are faced with dangerous situations.

Takedown Fundamentals

All combat sports and martial arts, like Brazilian Jiu-Jitsu, consider the ability to take someone down as a vital aspect. Your takedown skill will be valuable self-defense during street fights. With a successful throw or takedown, you weaken your attacker or opponent's position, putting them in a difficult and vulnerable spot to your advantage.

It's imperative first to learn the fundamentals of takedowns so you can successfully pull them off. This section gives the concepts, tips, and exercises to improve your takedowns.

Targeting the Weak Plane

The weak plane is a fundamental aspect of takedown that BJJ beginners must learn and understand. The weak plane refers to the point that forms a triangle using the line you visualize when you connect your two feet. In this line, you will find your center of gravity.

For instance, if an attacker or opponent stands square with their feet parallel on the ground, their weak plane is most likely directly backward or forward. Remember that the weak plane changes constantly, but it will not disappear.

Once you improve your proficiency in performing takedowns, it will be easier for you to automatically feel the exact spot of your opponent's weak plane. You can use it to determine the perfect direction to do the takedown in just a single glance.

Off-Balance Your Opponent

When executing takedowns, learning how to off-balance your attacker or opponent is extremely important; it is extremely difficult to take down your opponent if they have perfect balance. Also called *kuzushi* in Judo, you can off-balance your opponent through drags and snap downs.

You can also do it by pulling their Gi, causing them to step off-balance. The act of off-balancing your opponent works along with targeting the weak plane, and the reason is that you can use this technique to expose the weak plane of your opponent.

The goal is to force your opponent to step in a particular direction allowing easier access to their weak plane. It also helps expose the leg of your opponent, promoting further ease in executing the takedowns.

Other Fundamental Strategies and Concepts

Every grappling style has its own fundamental concept, which improves its level of effectiveness. The following are among the key and fundamental strategies and concepts that will improve your takedown abilities even further:

Takedown Roadmap

It is necessary to improve your ability to chain together the sequences for takedowns and combine them with various clenching setups. In other words, you must build a roadmap with the specific techniques worthwhile to pair up or combine.

Creating a roadmap will also help you with specific clinching positions guaranteed to work for you, depending on your opponent's reaction. Roadmaps contribute to building a strong and solid foundation for moving from all possible takedowns and setups.

Head Position Fighting and Manipulation

Make sure that you also know how to fight for and manipulate the head position of your opponent using your forehead. This action will impede their vision and keep them off balance. Remember, when grappling, the head serves as the fifth limb. You can consider yourself an excellent grappler if you know how to push your opponent by using your head.

Grab and Go

When fighting a larger opponent who is most likely superior in strength, focus on using setup movements allowing you to grab them quickly and disrupt their posture or balance right away. While they are recovering, make openings to use for your preferred takedowns.

Train yourself to perform the movements rapidly, and your opponent will not be able to hold or grab you. If you fail during your first attempt, disengage. Some examples of grab-and-go moves are snap downs and arm drags.

Let Your Opponents Guess Your Next Moves

The repeated use of similar technique combinations and moves is not good BJJ, as your opponent will have an easier time predicting and countering your movements. Make use of your takedown roadmap to avoid this. Ensure that the roadmap is extensive enough to eliminate predictability in your fights. Change your takedown combinations and positional setups frequently and keep your opponent guessing all the time.

Move Opponents to Your Preferred Positions

During your fights, ensure that your tactics will encourage your opponent to move into the position you intended. For example, if you are doing the single leg takedown while engaging in a clinch, move your hands so that they slide forward to gain double bicep control.

If the arm on the side of your lead leg side is pulled, take advantage of your footwork and force your opponent to move with your body instead of utilizing the strength of your arms.

Expect your opponent to step forward to maintain their balance. This step will most likely be on the pulled arm's side, resulting in their lead leg matching yours. It is the perfect time to shoot into a single leg.

Essential Takedowns That BJJ Beginners Must Know

To start mastering the art of takedowns, here are the essential ones for BJJ beginners:

Double Leg

A double-leg takedown is a vital takedown technique that has many BJJ applications. It is challenging to make a list of beginner takedowns without including the double leg. It is the most commonly used takedown in martial arts because the technique is simple and easy to understand.

To execute the double leg takedown successfully, you must first change levels, meaning bringing your head down to the belt-line of your opponent and performing the penetration step. You must grab the legs of your opponent and then drive through.

Practice this technique often, and you will immediately notice an improvement in catching your attackers or opponents off-guard, catching them with this technique when they least expect it. Note that while you can execute the double leg explosively, it is often unnecessary.

It would be much better to slowly start when practicing and build gradually to provide your partner with enough time to break the fall.

Ankle Pick

This takedown is probably the most effective technique adapted by BJJ. The relative simplicity of the ankle pick technique is why it is one of the first taught in BJJ and other martial arts.

To perform the ankle pick takedown, push your opponent's head over one of their legs, immobilizing the leg as it will bear excess weight. While the leg cannot move, complete this takedown technique by stepping in; this is necessary for blocking the target foot before you reach down and grab the ankle.

At this point, raise the opponent's foot leading to the takedown or fall of your opponent. As you may have observed, this technique is not like other takedowns that involve high-amplitude slams and throws. You just have to pluck one foot of your opponent from beneath him, and he will fall safely to the mat.

One advantage of the ankle pick takedown is that the penalty for failure is very low. Also, unlike what is usually involved in conventional wrestling, it is unnecessary to enter beneath your opponent when executing the ankle pick, eliminating the possibility of getting crushed beneath your opponent's weight.

Another reason to train for the ankle pick takedown is that it teaches grapplers to prioritize their takedown strategies during live competitions and rounds without frustration. It is also an incredible technique to learn if you're uncomfortable with your game when in a standing position.

Single Leg Takedown

As a vital technique in wrestling, single-leg takedown is also useful in Brazilian Jiu-Jitsu. This technique is more strength-dependent compared to other takedowns. In Brazilian Jiu-Jitsu, particularly the no-Gi, several sweeps result in single-leg takedowns, so you must learn how to finish a single leg when involved in no-Gi grappling.

Performing the single-leg takedown, first change levels, then hook your left arm around your opponent's right knee while pivoting to your left leg. Lift your opponent's leg from the ground while you connect your hands and maintain closed elbows. Ensure that the topmost part of your head drives to the chest of your opponent, too. Pinch their leg between yours.

Finish this technique with a double-leg takedown. Using your right hand, grab the knee of your opponent's base leg; this will encourage the execution of the double leg. You may also end it up with a foot sweep - sweep out their base leg with one of your feet.

High Crotch

The high crotch is a cross from the single and the double leg takedowns. The high crotch does not need the athleticism required by the double leg. However, you must have a more technical aptitude than the single leg when executing this takedown.

Similar to the single leg takedown, shoot for the lead leg when executing the high crotch. However, your head must be at the outside of the attacker or opponent rather than inside.

Collar Drag

The collar drag is a common takedown that is only applicable in Brazilian Jiu-Jitsu. It is a popular guard sweep you can also execute when standing and is very easy to learn, which is why it forms part of the arsenal of most BJJ participants.

The collar drag is easy to learn as it does not require you to get under your opponent's center of gravity, and it is also not necessary to do a lot of off-balancing. Moreover, the collar drag's motion is similar to pulling a half guard.

To execute the collar drag, give your opponent a cross collar grip using your right hand and let your left foot step outside of your opponent's right foot. Slide one leg between the legs of your opponent and drop your right hip to the floor.

Visualize pulling the half guard. While sliding the right hip and leg, yank the collar of your opponent to the ground. Your knees must end the takedown and drive into your attacker or opponent if needed.

Chapter 8: The Art of Submissions

The art of submission in Brazilian Jiu-Jitsu, also recognized as the Gentle Art, serves as your pinnacle of success when mastering this martial art. Note all BJJ participants will always go after a submission despite the fact that many BJJ tournaments and matches end on points.

As a beginner, you may get overwhelmed with the numerous submissions you have to learn, monitor, and master. Well, don't panic. You only need to learn the basic categories of submissions in BJJ to grasp the fundamental principles and have an easier time submitting your opponent.

How to Make Every BJJ Submission Work

There are many BJJ submissions, so remembering each of them as single tactics and techniques may be difficult. However, once you determine the specific reasons for submissions and familiarize yourself with the categorization system, you can fully understand each and master them easily. Another crucial point is that those specific aspects of ending submissions are considered universal for each terminal Brazilian Jiu-Jitsu move; thus, positioning is an important factor and concept. As you hunt for submissions, positioning most of your body against a single part of your opponent's body is necessary. Using your strong body parts, you will have an easier time attacking your opponent's weaker parts.

Grips are also among the most vital aspects of BJJ submission because you can either make or break your intended submission attempts. Grips contribute a lot to building tension in the specific body parts you intend to attack. You can also use the proper grips to apply torsion to introduce a twisting motion in each submission.

These are a few mechanical principles that serve as the major elements of performing Jiu-Jitsu submissions. However, remind yourself that various submissions also operate using various fundamentals, meaning that you can only monitor all these submissions if you categorize them into a sensible system.

Effective Brazilian Jiu-Jitsu Submission Techniques

This section also gives you an idea of how you can organize the submissions to easily remember them.

Moreover, you will learn how to get several taps. To understand various submissions easily, divide them based on their primary categories, with each category having specific sub-categories regarding tactics and techniques.

Strangles (Chokes)

Chokes or strangles are straightforward and easily understandable, and it involves wrapping something around an opponent's neck and tightening it. There are four strangle techniques to obtain BJJ submissions – three can be used as finishing strangles.

- Air chokes by closing the trachea
- Chest compressions by preventing chest expansion through pressure
- Blood chokes by compressing carotid arteries on both sides of your opponent's neck

It is also possible to do the neck crank, even though this move falls under the spinal locks category. When performing chokes, an important principle to remember is to make sure you plug the hole.

You can't expect any choke to work if space is still left around the opponent's neck. By putting every structural element together, you must plug the hole and increase the chance of a successful choke.

Also, it is crucial to exercise patience when waiting for the choke to take hold. Once you are sure that the choke is set, count to 20, readjust if the opponent still does not tap out, and use a squeeze or do the choke again.

Submissions that fall under the choke or strangle category are discussed next.

Rear-Naked Choke

This vital Brazilian Jiu-Jitsu submission is a must for beginners to learn. The rear-naked choke often operates from back control, especially when your arms surround your opponent's neck. You can reinforce this move by placing the remaining arm in a configuration that resembles figure 4.

Let your elbows stick to your chest and sides. Do this while you are squeezing to ensure that you can plug the hole, ensuring that you obtain adequate torsion and tension, too. This choke is legal in every BJJ belt and is applicable with or without Gi.

Guillotine Choke

Guillotine Choke

Unlike the rear-naked choke, the guillotine choke refers to a submission from the front, frequently from the guard, among other positions. To execute this choke perfectly, ensure that your opponent's head gets under your armpit. Follow this up with the vital chin strap grip.

Completing the guillotine choke depends significantly on the exact variation you decide to use. Also, the choke may work as air or blood choke since there is an element of chest compression in each version.

The guillotine choke produces favorable results whether you use a Gi or not. You can also do it from the guard, standing, half-guard, and mount positions. Also, it has several variations, including the high elbow, power guillotine, ten-finger, low elbow, and arm-in.

Triangle Choke

Triangle Choke

As a vital grappling submission, the triangle choke involves using your opponent's legs and his arm. This specific choke variation originated from Judo, but it is a famous BJJ submission nowadays as it delivers a good performance regardless of the position and with or without a Gi.

You can initiate the triangle choke submission from a closed guard. However, it is versatile to initiate it from other moves, like open guards, back control, half guard, mount, and standing.

Grapefruit or Helio Gracie Choke

Grapefruit or Helio Gracie Choke

Many BJJ practitioners are fond of this BJJ submission as it provides a simple method of choking an opponent out. It's a traditional choke you can do from a mount, positioning the knuckles on both sides of your opponent's neck.

Clench your fists when doing this, and it also helps to put your elbows on the ground to access an excellent position that allows your knuckles to put direct pressure on the artery. It is a quick submission that is effective and painful.

Bow and Arrow Choke

Bow and Arrow Choke

This specific choke is similar to a collar choke initiated from the back control. You can perform it by grabbing your opponent's leg and lapel while keeping the movement in their legs under control.

The name of this submission is derived from the configured two bodies when the choke is executed. You may also initiate the bow and arrow choke from the closed guard, side control, and turtle.

Arm and Shoulder Locks

Another BJJ submission category to familiarize yourself with is the arm and shoulder lock. Most of the submissions that fall in this category involve attacking the arm's joints, including the shoulders, wrist, and elbow, and it is the most commonly used submission today.

Although the arm lock is in various sub-categories, it will greatly depend on whether the target arm is bent or straight aside from attacking the joint. The primary principle that governs all arm locks is the importance of controlling two of the neighboring joints on both sides of your opponent.

Armbar

Armbar

The armbar involves the use of a straight arm while targeting the joints of the elbow. Once you have completed the top or bottom grapple, use your hips to press on your opponent's elbow forcing your opponent to bend in an unwanted and wrong direction.

Your hips and legs have complete control over your opponent's shoulder joints, and your torso and arms also affect their wrist. This specific submission is often set from the guard or mount. However, almost every position provides an armbar entry. This submission is legal for everyone and tends to work well whether you wear a Gi or not.

Straight Armlock

Straight Armlock

This specific submission typically starts from either the bottom or top. If you do it from the guard, it will be called the inverted armlock. The ultimate goal is to use your arms to add pressure on the elbow instead of the hips. Your legs are also expected to control the joint of your opponent's shoulders. Use your head to block the wrist, and use your shoulder to trap the arm.

Kimura

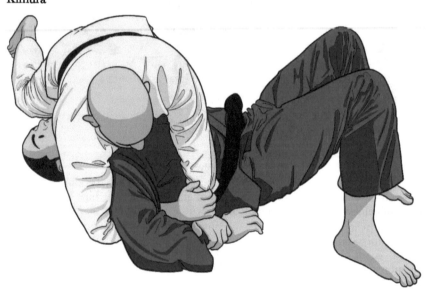

Kimura

This submission falls under the bent armlocks category, which often targets the opponent's shoulder joints. It is a popular form of Jiu-Jitsu submission that many fighters use. Using the figure 4 grip configuration, target your opponent's wrist.

It means that you will control the elbow using leverage and your legs to care for the neck. The Kimura involves a twisting motion with the arms and torso, but the hold can break if not done effectively.

Americana

Americana

The Americana submission serves as a Kimura while also having a bent arm in an opposite direction. This form of submission is exclusive to fighters in top positions, especially if you consider the arm's direction. The Americana will be effective once you get a figure-4 grip on the opponent's wrist.

Make sure to use your elbow to block your opponent's neck allowing the grip to handle the opponent's elbow. Drag the palms back across the mat towards your opponent's hip.

The Americana is possible from the mount, top half guard, and side control. There are no strict restrictions regarding who can make this submission, and the Americana can be used with many other armlocks.

Squirrel Lock

Many consider the squirrel lock as the sneakiest of all armlock submissions in Brazilian Jiu-Jitsu. You can get a tap from this move by using your legs. However, it is quite different as the bottom side control makes it preferable, and the entire submission is very unexpected.

The entire setup needs tinkering and training. However, essentially, you are executing a Kimura since you use your legs to entangle the opponent's far arm and finish from the bottom. You may also wrap up the entire process by rolling over on top.

Neck Crank

Neck Crank

The neck crank falls under the spinal lock category and is a simple form of submission. It is executed by bending your opponent's neck in a specific direction that adds pressure to their spine. This fairly dangerous move may cause a lot of pain, so you have to be extra careful.

The neck crank has different variations – among which are the following:

- **Can Opener** - This is a submission move that has earned a bad reputation. The can opener is executed from the guard's inside. Your goal is to cusp your opponent's head using both hands, similar to the Thai clinch. Bend the neck forward, adding extra pressure by using your hips.

- **From the Mount** - If you initiate the neck crank from the mount, you will realize how easy and simple it is to execute. The process is quite intuitive for many, as it allows you to execute a rare naked choke initiated from the mount.
  - An arm goes around your opponent's head, and while setting the grip, your palm ends on your opponent's forehead. It may involve nasty pressure as you have to let your forearm press on the spine directly.

- **From the Back** - You can also do the neck crank from the back control. When you start from the back, there are plenty of BJJ submissions you can do. Ensure that the forearm goes across the jaw, allowing the opponent's head to turn to one side, and finish by keeping your arms locked in a palm-to-palm grip, preventing pulling.

Hip Lock

The hip lock is also another category of Brazilian Jiu-Jitsu submissions with a couple of variations.

- **Banana Split** - This specific hip lock you can initiate if you are in a turtle position. Trap one leg of your opponent using your legs and arms to trap the other leg and extend away from their legs, contributing to a painful and uncomfortable hip lock.

- **Electric Chair** - This submission form is a groin stretch and a sweep that you can initiate from a half-guard and lockdown position. You can execute this submission if you establish a lockdown. Use your hands to force your opponent off-balance, then grab their leg.

Finish this by keeping the leg on your shoulder. This form of submission will not always work on versatile opponents, meaning there is also a chance to get to your opponent's knees as they maintain the grips for the guard pass initiation.

Foot Lock

The foot lock submission comes in a wide range of variations. The ones you use in BJJ will always include the following.

Straight Ankle Lock

This submission targets the joints in your ankle and your Achilles tendon. Do this as you immobilize your opponent's leg using both your legs and wrap your arm around your opponent's foot.

Hyperextend the foot away and down from the leg; it is possible if you arch the back. This versatile submission is accessible from numerous positions, like the half guard, back control, and leg drag pass.

Kneebar

The kneebar submission efficiently works when done in a specific position. Your goal when doing the kneebar is to sit on your opponent's hips and hug their legs before falling to your side.

This position gives adequate space to triangle your legs and focus on getting into a figure-4 grip on the leg. If performed correctly, it is possible to break your opponent's knee. To execute the break, extend your hips, and twist your shoulders to the ceiling. Note that only Black and Brown Belt fighters are permitted to do the kneebar.

Chapter 9: Combining What You Have Learned: More Advanced Techniques

After learning the basic techniques designed for beginners in Brazilian Jiu-Jitsu, it is time to move on to more advanced techniques, probably to intermediate. When you can master the basic BJJ techniques and proficiently use them in a match, it is time to think about combinations.

One straightforward attack may not be enough, especially when dealing with an expert and experienced opponent. Expert and skilled opponents will immediately detect your intentions before you even get the chance to make a move and put up a defense.

Intermediate and advanced belts are required to create attacks that use various tactical and technical combinations. The action-reaction principle discussed in a previous chapter is vital in attaining success with attack combinations. When you attempt to execute your primary or first attack, your opponent will put up a defense, exposing them to your second attack.

Importance of Learning Combinations

The ultimate secret to becoming a well-rounded fighter in Brazilian Jiu-Jitsu and all martial arts is to learn combinations. Your knowledge of strikes and throw combinations can separate a beginner from a skilled and experienced BJJ fighter.

Newbies in martial arts, especially in Brazilian Jiu-Jitsu, have yet to learn how to throw combinations with any form of structure and fluency. Each tactic and move is still new, making it hard for them to combine multiple tactics while learning and understanding the basics. However, as soon as you gain more experience, you can move to a more advanced level that teaches these combinations.

The ability to do combinations is crucial in all BJJ competitions and training. If you cannot perform any combination, it will be extremely difficult for you to beat a skilled and experienced opponent because skilled fighters will defend themselves from a single strike or takedown you throw.

Integrating feints, tricks, and follow-ups to your attacks, strokes, or throws, can change the intensity of a fight. No matter how experienced and defensive a fighter is, they will still be overwhelmed if you combine various takedowns and punches. An attempt to set up a defense for one attack may lead to the opening of a counterattack.

If you have only learned to throw singular jabs, it will be impossible to hit an experienced striker's head. Your moves will be predictable to your opponent.

A single attack executed alone is useless when used against an experienced opponent and will only be effective when fighting an untrained and inexperienced opponent.

Using Combinations in BJJ

As you have already discovered, Brazilian Jiu-Jitsu is a ground-fighting martial art. This martial art aims to sweep your opponent and force them to submit. It becomes part of the fighter's toolkit when on the floor.

Similar to Judo, Brazilian Jiu-Jitsu also concentrates on the weight distribution of you and your opponent. Any time your opponent positions their arm or leg incorrectly, you can attack them and use your opponent's incorrect position to make them lie on their backs on the mat.

In BJJ, combinations are used similarly to Judo. For instance, you can chain together several attacks to catch your adversary or opponent off-guard and obtain complete control of their back.

Some BJJ skilled fighters can switch from an armbar and a rear-naked choke, or vice versa, ensuring that their opponents cannot guess what attack will come next.

By chaining many attacks together, your opponent will have a hard time finding answers and defenses, and it will be challenging for them to put up a defense that would result in a submission.

So, what are the combinations you can use to become a more well-rounded and skilled BJJ fighter? These combos are among the best answers:

Chaining Combinations

This specific combo can move and transition through several different attacks and deal with various submission escapes and defenses. Start this combination from the knee-on-stomach position, then establish a strong and stable spinning armbar.

Hug the arm of your opponent tightly, ensuring that it is held close to your body, and plant your foot close to the opponent's shoulder. Your opponent might try to come out on top during the transition, so it's important to remain tight.

Turn your body over to position yourself correctly for your next attack, the kimura that you will start from the bottom. Use this technique to flip your opponent over so they will be in an armbar position.

While straightening the arm, your opponent may turn up their thumb in a runaway or hitchhiker to break free from the armbar. Essentially, they will be running around in circles as they try to escape successfully. Allow your opponent to continue while you transition to the Omoplata as you alter your angle and kick your leg through.

Your opponent might posture up, preparing to defend themselves from the Omoplata, switch to the triangle. The goal of this technique is that as soon as you feel you're losing your attacked submission, you should switch to a new submission.

To ensure that you get excellent results from this combo, get a feel of your opponent as they escape your submission. Let them have slight chances for an escape as they serve as your opening for another attack. You will learn the things that work and what doesn't.

Combo That Lets Your Lower Body Flow

This is a relatively short combo designed for the flow drill but can give highly favorable results. It is a great combination to use your opponent does more work than you as they roll. Begin by setting up for the execution of the inverted heel hook. As soon as you start torquing the heel of your opponent, retain your grip as they try circling to escape.

You may be inclined to follow your opponent at this point, which is not a poor tactic if you are one hundred percent sure you can finish the initial attack. However, if they get even just half a step ahead, it would be best to let them escape while you determine your next move.

While they are circling, resist the urge to alter your hip's position, except when you do the kneebar finish. If you have already performed the kneebar, let your partner continue circling or rotating beyond the kneebar. It will serve as your starting point for the simple switch to the 50/50 position that you can use to finish the game with a heel hook.

Guard Passing and Submission Attack Combo

This specific tactic provides you with a means of combining a guard pass or positional advance with a submission. What is great about this combo is that it is designed to bring your game to a whole new level because it's hard to defend a submission attack and guard pass simultaneously.

Your opponent may even have a hard time defending themselves as you perform these moves one after another. As soon as they addressed the first attack, you have already moved into another attack, making it challenging for them to keep up.

For this specific technique, begin by doing a knee-cut guard pass. The key to quickly finishing the pass is to use the under hook often. However, if your opponent still triumphs during the under hook fight, you can back step into a solid kneebar attack.

Wait for your opponent to triangle their legs to defend themselves from the kneebar, then slide to finish the fight with a straight ankle lock submission.

Guard to Triangle Choke

Guard to Triangle Choke

If you are searching for a trendy technique, a triangle choke from any form of the guard is the most viable move. The triangle choke is extremely popular in BJJ as every fighter seems to be using it, from the white to the black belts. The triangle choke is an indispensable technique in MMA and other global competitions for Gi and no-Gi.

To perform this combination, attack your opponent using both your legs and from the bottom. This specific technique is effective, especially if your opponent is larger than you. In this case, you may have a hard time reversing positions and getting yourself on top.

Start from any type of guard and set up the triangle choke differently, but be very sure that you are familiar with the mechanisms of the guard you choose. You must study various ways to exact the guard to perfection.

Also, be careful not to use the triangle choke to attack once your opponent is in a good position and posture. Your chances of winning will drop since an excellent posture is the most reliable position for defense with the triangle choke.

Making the Most Out of BJJ Combinations

Experts and legends in BJJ all agree on how important it is to use sequences and combinations for a participant to experience exponential growth. As soon as you move to the intermediate level and learn the basics look for sequences or tactics that you can proficiently and comfortably execute. Practice them with your training partner regularly.

It is also crucial to find dynamic partners, specifically those that will not defend your attempts for submission but move enough to challenge you to master your combinations. The advantage of this is that it directs you towards a new level of progress.

You must adapt to the sequences and combinations you created based on the effort and movements exerted and executed by your training partner. You will be forced to understand when and how to use other tactics when necessary; this is the key to reinforcing and strengthening your already expanding skillset in Brazilian Jiu-Jitsu.

Chapter 10: Weight Pressure and Energy Control

Pressure is another important aspect and concept to master in Brazilian Jiu-Jitsu. Even during the first stages of your beginner training in BJJ, you will already know that pressure can significantly improve your grappling skills.

Applying pressure in a BJJ practice or fight helps hold the other person down for an extended period, leading to setting up a submission. It is also necessary to apply pressure whenever you need to pass the guard or execute certain moves and positions. Pressure is also required to improve the effectiveness of your submissions from the top.

Types of Pressure in Brazilian Jiu-Jitsu

In Brazilian Jiu-Jitsu, the term "pressure" means more than merely the concept of weight or how heavy an opponent is. In most cases, it revolves around controlled points and the specific manner you can hold these points.

Pressure also enables you to retain control when executing major positions, including mount, back mount, and side control. This pressure comes in three forms.

Weight Distribution

An area in BJJ you must focus on is weight distribution, a vital element or concept of BJJ that's also classified as pressure. Unlike speed and strength that diminishes as you age, your skills in using your weight to your best advantage do not.

It means you must use your weight properly to expend less energy while your opponent is at risk of exerting more. The correct use of your weight will force an opponent in a lower belt to become fatigued faster. On the other hand, if you are fighting against a higher belt, you can use your weight to frustrate them.

Note that when dealing with those with higher belts, you will need more time mastering how to use your weight to your best advantage, but you will eventually grasp it with constant practice.

For example, when you take the top position, quickly eliminate the points of contact your opponent has with the ground. These points of contact include the shoulders, the back of your opponent's head, and elbows.

It may force your opponent to handle your weight on the soft midsection, and pressure applied to this area can greatly affect their breathing. Also, to ensure that you use the weight distribution to your advantage, take note of the following:

- **Weight on Top** - Back mount, side control, guard passing, mount
- **Weight on the Bottom** - Closed guard. It is highly recommended to consistently use both your legs' weight on your opponent's back while ensuring that there are assisting angles.
- **Angling Weight** - A certain angle to your opponent causes you to become heavier because of the discomfort.
- **Shifting Weight** - Lifting hips, dropping hips, rotating

One sign that you are correctly distributing your weight is when there is only minimal holding and squeezing, meaning that you expend minimal energy while your opponent exerts more.

Another way to improve using your weight is to lessen your movement and use more gravity. Your opponent will feel like they are beneath a heavy wet blanket or drowning in cement.

It is crucial to concentrate on your breathing when defending your weight. Aside from that, focus on getting better postural alignments by ensuring that your knees remain beneath your waistline. It helps prevent your weight from crushing a rib or your leg from rotating inward, injuring the knee ligaments.

Pain Compliance Pressure

Pain compliance pressure is often found in catch wrestling, but many also use it in Jiu-Jitsu and regular grappling. It is used as a means to force rapid openings and reactions to achieve submission.

What's great about using the pain compliance pressure is that it can elicit sharp and quick responses from your opponents. Your opponent will respond by panicking, jumping, or even flinching, and these are the responses you are hoping to get from applying this pressure.

However, the pain compliance pressure will not be effective when used against an opponent holding a higher belt or rank because most high-ranked and advanced fighters will have already mastered feeling comfortable in discomfort.

Still, you can enjoy using pain compliance pressure in the following techniques with the right opponent.

- **Sawing** - This technique requires using the elbow to apply pressure to your opponent's pressure points. It could be the front deltoid or the jaw.
- **Shoulder Pressure** - Use the shoulder pressure starting from the side control, and crush your opponent's jaw or execute a choke resulting in a fast response from your opponent.
- **Muffler** - This technique requires restricting the airway. It falls under pain compliance pressure as it can elicit a pain reaction from the opponent.
- **Knee to Belly or Neck** - This technique also belongs to the weight distribution pressure. The knee applies pressure to the opponent's neck or stomach, causing their sharp reactions.

Before using pain compliance pressure, remember that you can't expect it to work with advanced BJJ fighters, so you must prepare before using these pressure tactics. You will become proficient in using pain compliance pressure tactics for fights, tournaments, and self-defense effectively through regular practice.

Panic Pressure

The last type of pressure that you can use in Brazilian Jiu-Jitsu is panic pressure. You will most likely feel this panic pressure if you are in the early stages of your BJJ training. Your panic may be due to worrying that you will land in bad positions all the time, causing you not to breathe properly or think clearly. Worse, you will always be thinking that you are at risk of submission.

However, after much practice and your acquisition of more knowledge and skills, everything becomes less stressful. You will learn to use the panicky feeling to deal with your opponent.

When you advance to a higher level, you can induce panic in a lower belt to win by applying panic pressure when you are in a dominant position. Your goal is to control your opponent so they feel there is no point of escape.

You can start this tactic with position control - having positional control and dominance, preventing any possible means of escape. If your intended submissions are not yet available and your opponent is still full of energy and vitality, stop their means of escape by focusing more on countering their moves. They will become frustrated to the point of panic.

If you suspect your opponent is at this point, do some sub-attempts. Control the position, and threaten them with their leg, neck, or arm to elicit a panic or frustration response. Your opponent will feel they are backed into a corner with no other choice but to submit

Energy Management and Its Importance in BJJ

Out of the many principles that govern Brazilian Jiu-Jitsu, energy management has its level of importance. Many BJJ participants overlook energy management and fail to see its importance in winning fights. Imagine what will happen to you during a fight if you become exhausted first. You will probably lose because you no longer have the energy to continue fighting.

You need to learn how to manage your energy properly because, in BJJ, high stamina is crucial and gives you a superior level of control in a fight. Your goal is never to run out of fuel when you fight. By ensuring that you have excellent energy management skills, you will survive and outlast your opponent.

Following a healthy lifestyle will ensure you properly manage your energy at elevated levels continuously by sticking to a daily workout and training routine. Your goal is to be in the best shape and physical condition to avoid losing your energy quickly.

How to Maintain Maximum Energy during Your Fights?

Here are a few ways to ensure that your energy will be at an all-time high during your fights, boosting your chances of success.

Breathe Properly

In a BJJ fight, proper breathing focuses on pushing the air out via your nose or mouth rather than sucking the air in. Note that inhalation will come naturally on a completed exhalation, meaning that it's unnecessary to suck in the air again.

Another tip for proper breathing is to produce sounds every time you exhale. This way, you hear your exhalation occurring until you eventually become used to it.

The object of this exercise is that you monitor your breathing during the entire BJJ fight. Inhale through your nose and utilize your diaphragm for breathing rather than the upper portion of your lungs.

Develop Proper Mindset

When you've mastered proper breathing and control your breath effectively, you will notice that you easily control your mind. In a BJJ fight, your mindset also contributes to your energy levels. The goal is to stay calm even when dealing with pressure; otherwise, you will be at risk of losing your energy too fast.

One way to keep yourself calm during a fight is to focus on your breathing patterns, like exhaling more for a prolonged period. Also, learn to control your emotions, like excitement, fear, and anxiety. However, regardless of your BJJ level, you will still be at risk of feeling at least one of the above-mentioned emotions.

If you can't control them and use them to your best advantage, you will be at risk of losing your position, not thinking clearly about your next move, and falling into submission. Remember, these emotions come from your mind, so you have to develop the right mindset during your fights.

When in a BJJ match, being in the present moment ensures that your mind stays focused on your goal, and you can make wiser decisions. It will also help you control your emotions and prevent you from losing your energy, causing you to make even just a tiny slip that will compromise your accomplishments in a fight.

Chapter 11: Brazilian Jiu-Jitsu Versus Japanese Jiu-Jitsu

One common misconception of Jiu-Jitsu is that the Brazilian and Japanese variations are the same; it is easy to get confused. However, while there are similarities in history, origin, and techniques, there are also several differences.

This chapter illustrates what Brazilian Jiu-Jitsu and Japanese Jiu-Jitsu have in common – as well as their differences – so you can know the truths behind each misconception. Learning about the individual facts of each also helps you decide which the most suitable type of Jiu-Jitsu is for you.

What They Have in Common

The first similarity between Japanese and Brazilian Jiu-Jitsu is that both disciplines are closely related to Judo. If you are familiar with Kodokan Judo, you will realize that it is a modified variation of the traditional Japanese Jujutsu.

The birth of BJJ resulted from people's knowledge of Kodokan Judo, so it is safe to assume that Japanese Jiu-Jitsu and BJJ have an indirect relationship.

Apart from their indirect relationship as far as origin is concerned, there are similarities in some techniques, namely pins, leg locks, arm locks, chokeholds, and joint manipulations.

Another thing that makes the two so similar is that they are designed for participants regardless of their sizes and physical builds. Both are created to allow smaller participants to fight stronger and larger opponents. The skills and knowledge you can acquire from both martial arts are useful for self-defense, martial combat, and competitions.

The Differences

Brazilian Jiu-Jitsu and Japanese Jiu-Jitsu are also very different in many vital areas.

History

One significant area where the two greatly differ is in their history. Japanese Jiu-Jitsu came first and is even recognized as the oldest form of martial arts with roots that date back from 780AD to 1200AD. In the early 1300s, many used Japanese Jiu-Jitsu as a means to protect themselves from heavily armored and armed opponents on the battlefield.

During Japan's 17th century Edo period, Jujutsu and other forms of hand-to-hand combat became popular. It was also during this time that grappling arts were recognized together as Jujutsu.

In the later parts of the 1800s, Jigoro Kano, a jujutsu practitioner, made some changes in the art and started focusing more on submissions. He named this new art Kodokan Judo and started teaching it in Tokyo's Kodokan Institute. It led to the birth of modern Judo or Japanese Jiu-Jitsu.

BJJ's history is quite different. As discussed in an early chapter, the story of BJJ started after the creation of Judo, specifically when Judo experts started traveling around the world.

Some found themselves in Brazil introducing the art – one of whom was Mitsuyo Maeda, a Judo expert, master, and prizefighter. Maeda traveled around Brazil during the 1910s and 1920s, challenging many in other fighting arts. Eventually, Maeda and Carlos Gracie crossed paths, leading to the birth of Brazilian Jiu-Jitsu.

Rules

BJJ and Japanese Jiu-Jitsu have significant differences in their implemented rules. Japanese Jiu-Jitsu is more relaxed in that it does not hold the strong sports component BJJ has, evidenced by the competitions held worldwide.

As for the actual rules, BJJ competitions start with the two fighters in a standing position. They will attempt to take each other down or directly move to the guard, also called pulling guard. Upon bringing the fight to the ground, they will grapple to get their opponent to submit or get into a more dominant position and earn more points.

The fighter who is successful in making their opponent submit will instantly emerge as the winner. In the event of unsuccessful submission, the points earned by each will decide the winner of the match.

- 2 points for takedowns
- 3 points for a guard pass
- 2 points for knee-on-belly position
- 4 points for mount
- 4 points for back control
- 2 points for sweeps

Several Brazilian Jiu-Jitsu organizations hold competitions for this martial art every year, and each organization may have its own set of rules, but there is a high chance that most of these rules are similar.

Traditional Japanese Jiu-Jitsu does not come with a solid and strong sports competition environment like BJJ. However, you can still find modern offshoots for it, including the JJIF (Jiu-Jitsu International Federation). The competitions held by the JJIF come with three events – the duo, the fighting, and the Ne-Waza.

- **Duo** – Two practitioners have to do self-defense tactics randomly based on what the referee calls. The criteria for judgment would be control, reality, and power, among others.
- **Fighting** – This involves a 3-part competition where strikes are used in the initial stage of the fight. Once one fighter holds onto the other, it puts an end to the use of strikes. At this point, it is no longer permitted to use strikes, and the goal of the fighters is to take each other down.

Upon bringing the fight to the ground, the participants will use strangulations or joint locks to make the other submit. This event is scored on a points system, with the participants earning points based on their techniques throughout the match.

- **Ne-Waza** – The last one is very similar to the match or competition conducted in BJJ. It involves pitting two fighters against each other initially at a standing position, and the match does not allow using strikes.

The participants' goal is to bring their opponent down to the ground and forces them into submission using strangulation or joint lock. Participants will also earn points for dominant positions, throws, and takedowns.

Progression and Belts

BJJ and Japanese Jiu-Jitsu also have differences in the belt levels and how to progress in performance levels. BJJ utilizes a belt system comprised of eight belts.

- White for those still building a foundation
- Blue for technical proficiency
- Purple for game development, experimentation, and submissions

- Brown for conceptual thinking, strengthening of weaknesses, and setting traps
- Black for reflection and teaching and starting anew
- Red and black for seventh-degree black belt
- Red and white for eight-degree black belt
- Red for ninth and tenth-degree black belt

Every belt that falls below the black belt comes with four stripes demonstrating the skill level within a specific belt. The instructor has the authority to grant stripe and belt promotions. Also, note that every school has its own set of rules and policies on how to progress BJJ students.

Some schools may use a grading system for the stripes or belts granted to their students. The grades earned are based on the demonstrated sparring and techniques. Other schools depend entirely on their instructors for decisions regarding progression and promotion. So, you can earn a new belt based on your performance combined with technical knowledge, time or speed, and sparring proficiency.

Japanese Jiu-Jitsu also follows a different belt system, which depends on the school where you attend classes.

- White
- Yellow
- Orange
- Green
- Blue
- Purple
- Brown
- Black

Some schools provide a red belt to beginners before they get the white belt. On the other hand, other schools feature tips in between belts. Most Japanese Jiu-Jitsu school training requires students to participate in the formal grading system to progress to the following belt. The school will determine the specific techniques you must learn.

For instance, schools like the World Ju-jitsu Federation in Ireland require students to learn and display a specific number of tactics, a few Japanese terminologies, and a bit about anatomy.

Uniform

Both forms of martial arts require participants to wear the same uniform known as the Jiu-Jitsu Gi. However, these uniforms still differ in weight. The Gi used in BJJ is usually heavier than those used in karate, and the Japanese Jiu-Jitsu Gi is lighter than the Gi used in karate.

Aside from the clothing (Gi), BJJ students must also wear mouthguards for protection. Japanese Jiu-Jitsu students must wear groin guards to protect themselves from strikes that might inflict harm.

Important Technical and Technique Differences

The main focus of BJJ is grappling and also prioritizes ground fighting. BJJ participants will use strangles, joint locks, and chokes to make their opponents submit. Japanese Jiu-Jitsu focuses on joint manipulation, strikes, blocks, strangulations, chokes, and the throwing of opponents.

BJJ uses takedowns as a means of bringing their opponents down on the ground. Their focus is on establishing dominant positions to control their opponents and make them submit.

One of the most distinctive positions in Brazilian Jiu-Jitsu is the guard. It is an umbrella term covering various positions where participants lie on their buttocks or back with their legs defensively around or in front of their opponents. Many of the prospective techniques in BJJ are used for submitting opponents, moving into positions, and escaping positions.

Japanese Jiu-Jitsu participants gain knowledge by defending themselves from an attacker in various ways. Techniques are taught for submission or strikes to incapacitate attackers. Practicing these techniques will also involve sparring with a partner in different scenarios to block an attacker's initial punches and execute the joint lock. It is quite similar to BJJ as it also focuses on self-defense.

Brazilian and Japanese Jiu-Jitsu – The Pros and Cons

When deciding between Brazilian and Japanese Jiu-Jitsu, it is crucial to understand their pros and cons. You can better decide which of these two incredible martial arts is most suitable for you by deciphering their unique strengths and weaknesses.

BJJ Pros and Cons

One significant advantage of BJJ is that it is more fast-paced and physically demanding than Japanese Jiu-Jitsu. If you want rigorous workouts, BJJ is the right choice. What you learn from this martial art, including groundwork techniques, will make you more adept in competitions and matches.

Your improved skills in BJJ will allow several opportunities to attend competitions and high-level training as a partner and contested situational sparring. BJJ is also excellent for self-defense.

It teaches you how to use specific techniques whenever you're in a self-defense setting. Many fundamental techniques in BJJ, including escapes, back takes, and takedowns, are extremely useful for restraining your opponents or attackers.

However, BJJ also comes with its share of weaknesses. For one, it does not involve striking, which is highly useful in self-defense. BJJ also prioritizes teaching students about fighting on the ground, and in some instances, takedowns are ignored.

Japanese Jiu-Jitsu Pros and Cons

One advantage of Japanese Jiu-Jitsu is that it teaches you a plethora of skills and techniques to use for self-defense. In some instances, the training resembles real-life combat scenarios, but it does not train you to participate in competitions.

Also, your decision to learn Japanese Jiu-Jitsu will introduce you to valuable techniques you can use for fights and attackers, including strikes, throws, and groundwork.

It has its weakness, though. One is that it does not have the sparring training often included in BJJ classes. It also puts more emphasis on participants with low-level training, which is why their movements are calmer and more controlled than those of BJJ.

Aside from these, Japanese Jiu-Jitsu does not provide many opportunities for competitions, so it may not be suitable if you enjoy official matches and competitions.

Chapter 12: Daily BJJ Drills

Do you intend to become one of the greatest experts and masters in the world of Brazilian Jiu-Jitsu? Then just like the others who have already mastered this form of martial art, you must exert effort and spend endless hours practicing. It is not only the effort that brings you closer to your goal of mastering BJJ but your consistency and dedication.

The good news is that everyone can master this martial art, provided you are persistent and dedicated enough. One way to become adept in this field is to do BJJ drills regularly. With the BJJ drills you perform at home, you will internalize those unfamiliar motions.

Committing to a daily training regimen will be like sharpening your sword. Do this every day, and you will improve your body's flexibility, become less rigid, make it possible for your movements to flow smoothly, and execute your movements and techniques without any problem.

Your daily BJJ drills will also make you less prone to injury during a fight. This last chapter, a bonus chapter, educates you on the best daily BJJ drills you can use to begin your daily training and practice, regardless of where you are.

Use them to learn BJJ on your own or combine it with your actual classes to improve your expertise and knowledge further.

What Are BJJ Drills?

BJJ drills refer to a movement or a series of movements mimicking an actual match or sparring round scenario of BJJ. Some of the drills are doable alone, and others require you to do them with a partner. When doing BJJ drills, practice the specific technique to refine even the slightest component of your game. The drills are useful for improving general movement that you can apply in several positions during sparring.

Solo BJJ Drills

As mentioned earlier, solo BJJ drills are those you can do alone. These are a few examples.

Shrimp

A basic BJJ movement that you will learn during training or class is the shrimp. It should form part of your daily BJJ drills, as your mastery of this move can help you escape easily from a bad or unwanted position, such as under a mount or side control.

Plant one leg, then scoot your butt to one side. Use both hands on your other side, promoting ease in executing the movement and producing excellent results. Make this move as part of your warm-up exercises for as long as you want.

Technical Stand-up

This vital BJJ drill is perfect for beginners and is highly recommended to practice every day. Many consider it a safe and effective movement that allows you to get up after getting into a fallen position.

Start by sitting on the ground, bend your knees and place your feet flat on the floor. Tilt to one side, placing your leg and hip onto the floor. Your hand on the same side must also be palm flat on the floor, near your hip, and slightly back.

With the knee still bent, press on your other foot and put your weight on your free hand and your foot on the ground, pushing upward.

Reverse Shrimp

This is a reverse variation of the shrimp. It is a little harder to execute than the typical shrimp, but it has a lot of uses, such as setting yourself free from a north-south position, escaping from an armbar, and closing the gap or distance between you and your opponent.

Lie down on the floor with your legs straightened, and hold both your hands up. Choose a side to roll onto, then crunch down your shoulders based on your waist's direction and pivot using one shoulder.

Using your heels move your body so it faces in the direction of your feet. Extend both legs outward, and roll onto the other side. Repeat the steps.

Bridge to Shrimp

This is a move that you can also do alone, and it is useful if you are dealing with an opponent who has already mounted you. The bridge to shrimp will provide you with an effective means of escape.

The first thing to do is build a bridge by letting your butt go up in the air as you lie down on your back and execute the shrimp motion. It is a fantastic movement that is very effective if you want to improve your ability to escape from a bad or unwanted position.

Granby Roll

The Granby Roll is classified as a wrestling technique, but it is useful in Brazilian Jiu-Jitsu. It is a great technique for escaping inferior and bad positions and defending yourself from attacks. Be prepared to spend time practicing until you perfect it, and once you've mastered the technique, it will be relatively easy performing it.

Note that flexibility is not the ultimate key to performing a Granby roll. It is good mechanics. When you execute this move, avoid rolling on the back of your head or neck.

Begin this movement from your knees. Put one arm between your legs until you notice your shoulder touching the ground. It is important at this step to look away so you will not see your lowered shoulder. Raise yourself slightly to your toes, and this will bring both your knees off the mat.

Then crab walk in a specific direction. Your other shoulder will come close to the mat, and you should be looking at the ceiling between your legs.

Make sure that both your shoulders and feet are on the ground. Continue to crab walk until you go back to your knees.

Sprawls

Sprawls refer to defensive movements in BJJ combats, and you can perform them when countering your opponent's takedown strikes. Based on its name, sprawls require extending your body while aiming to pounce the opponent and dominate them.

Do this technique by first standing erect. Bend slightly and stretch both hands outward. Bring yourself down to the floor until your back is lying flat. Ensure that you let your palms support your entire body weight when doing so. Your legs also have to extend backward.

Keep your right leg straight and bend your left knee. Lift the middle part of your body quickly and squat walk to the right, pivoting your body on your palms. Do the same steps on the other side.

Non-Solo BJJ Drills

Non-solo BJJ drills are done if you do not have a training partner. It would be helpful to have a grappling dummy to perform these drills in the comfort of your home.

Leg Drag

This specific BJJ drill is a lot of fun and exciting at the same time, as it gives you an idea of how to improve your coordination. It is a fundamental move that will always form part of your training and practice in BJJ. Begin the leg drag drill by standing close to your partner or opponent.

Your opponent must lie on the ground with their feet on both sides of your hips. Grab one of their knees and shove it aside, specifically to one side of your body. This is necessary to pass the guard of your opponent. Repeat the steps.

Bridge Drill

This BJJ drill is also fun, though it could also be slightly harmful. Begin by lying by your opponent's side. Hold their legs and throw yourself so that you execute a front flip over the top of their body. Ensure that you land on your back and legs. Make sure you continue holding onto your opponent's legs while making the move. Repeat the steps but this time, do them on the other side.

Tornado Drill

This BJJ drill is similar to the leg drag, and the only difference is that this drill requires pulling the legs of your opponent to the side. Move to your side, then pass the guard of your opponent. Return to your initial position and repeat the same steps on the alternate side.

Conclusion

With discipline, commitment, hard work, and consistency, you will master Brazilian Jiu-Jitsu in no time. You must be prepared to go through all the training that teaches everything you need to know about this martial art.

BJJ is a lot of fun, especially for younger students, and provides many benefits. Rarely will you find a sport like Brazilian Jiu-Jitsu that offers tremendous mental and physical integration during every class and training session. It adds an element of fitness to your daily routine as you train to master this martial art.

Hopefully, this Brazilian Jiu-Jitsu book for beginners has helped jumpstart your journey toward mastering this art. Consult the information provided to improve your knowledge of BJJ and become a well-equipped participant.

Part 3: Muay Thai

A Comprehensive Guide to Thai Boxing Basics for Beginners and a Comparison with Dutch Kickboxing

CLINT SHARP

Muay Thai

A COMPREHENSIVE GUIDE TO THAI BOXING
BASICS FOR BEGINNERS AND A COMPARISON
WITH DUTCH KICKBOXING

Introduction

Thailand's rich cultural history has included physical fitness training like Muay Thai for hundreds of years. Many accounts record it as an essential self-defense technique that Thai warriors frequently employed in various battles. The Chupasart wartime manuscript informs using every part of your body is critical to executing effective techniques when battling an opponent with the full commitment of mind, body, and soul.

Kickboxing aims to prepare your body and improve concentration. Therefore, you must train in a somewhat real-life setting. Muay Thai has proved to be the best striking style available in kickboxing. There are other brilliant techniques, like Dutch Kickboxing, but Muay Thai is much more practical and approachable. When you want to build confidence and get physically fit, this is the best sport to be involved in.

Muay Thai is a sport requiring all eight limbs of your body. It focuses on improving concentration and strength in and out of controlled situations. Several techniques are involved, but as a beginner, focusing on building the foundations of your Muay Thai journey is necessary.

This book exposes the philosophy behind Muay Thai and why it is considered the most practical form of Kickboxing, accepted worldwide, especially in the West.

In this book, you learn practical techniques in Thai Kickboxing - Muay Thai, using elbows, knees, arms, legs, kicks, and punches to attack an opponent and using the same means as a defense against them.

This book is a comprehensive yet simple guide taking the reader on a gradual but practical process to applying every technique listed. It's a hands-on approach, and its easy readability sets it apart from others.

This book teaches you that your mind is crucial in building focus and resilience, keeping your stance, and diving more through practice and consistency.

During most training, you would encounter sparing, rhythms, fundamental movements, kicks, jumping knees, and spinning back elbows. You will learn the basics of each and dive into even more advanced styles like uppercuts, head kicks, and spinning elbows. Initially, you might experience very slow development, but with practice and perseverance, improvement will come.

So, grab this opportunity and keep reading to get to the level you desire and master the skill of Muay Thai.

Chapter 1: Muay Thai Rules and Philosophy

Thai boxing, or Muay Thai, is a combat sport with its roots embedded in Thai culture and history. *Muay* translates to "boxing," so Muay Thai translates to Thai boxing. This martial arts form was developed a few hundred years ago, allowing the boxer to use their entire body as a weapon during close combat.

Muay Thai is a close combat sport. [23]

Although historians infer that Muay Thai originated centuries ago, no historical record of the sport can be found before the 14th century because of the Burmese invasion and looting. Most of the written history at the time was lost after the Burmese looted Ayudhaya, a capital city in Siam (currently Thailand).

Unlike boxing, throwing knees and hitting the opponent using elbow strikes and kicks is the norm. Furthermore, grappling techniques, initiating throws, and clinching are other techniques allowed and widely practiced in Muay Thai. If you're unfamiliar with Muay Thai, you can easily confuse it with MMA or other forms of combat sports, but there are several differences. The most evident difference giving Muay Thai a unique place in martial arts is the eight points of contact,

Other martial art and combat sports typically have two or four points of contact, whereas Muay Thai follows the art of eight limbs. A fighter can use eight points of contact, allowing punches, knee, and elbow strikes.

This combat sport places a lot of emphasis on cultural aspects, including engaging in the Wai Kru Ram Muay, a pre-fight ritual dance done by Muay Thai fighters, and wearing a Mongkon, a traditional headdress, and playing Sarama music throughout the competition.

This chapter focuses on tapping into the origins of Muay Thai with a brief overview of its history. You read about the philosophy behind this martial arts form and the characteristic features that make Muay Thai stand out from other branches of martial arts.

A Brief History

Before exploring the philosophy behind this powerful fighting style, let's take a quick peek at the history of Muay Thai. The traditional Muay Boran, from which today's Muay Thai was born, was a form of Thai martial arts taught to soldiers to defend the Thai kingdom from enemy attacks and invasions. Due to frequent wars with neighbors, the Muay Thai fighting style became embedded in their culture and lifestyle.

Muay Thai Origins

It originated with the Burmese invasion of Ayudhaya. The invaders plundered what they could put their hands on and turned everything else into ashes. The invading troops took people as prisoners of war. Among these prisoners were a significant number of Thai kickboxers who were held mostly in the city of Ungwa.

Later in the early 1700s, the Burmese ruler honored the Buddha's relics by conducting a seven-day-seven-night celebration. During the celebration days, comedy shows, plays, sword-fighting, and Thai boxing matches were arranged where Thai boxers would compete against Burmese fighters.

The story of Nai Khanom Tom marks the origins of this combat sport. During the celebrations, a Burmese nobleman introduced Nai Khanom Tom to the ring to pit his strength against a Burmese boxer. As a norm, Nai Khanom Tom initiated the pre-fight dance, fascinating the crowd. The Burmese fighter was no match for the veteran Muay Thai boxer as Nai Khanom attacked his opponent fiercely and he collapsed on the ground.

However, the knockout of the Burmese fighter was not considered a victory, and the judges decided that the Thai boxer had to face nine more Burmese fighters as the first one was distracted by the traditional pre-fight dance. Hearing this decision, other Thai boxers held as captives volunteered to fight with Nai Khanom Tom, only to uphold Thai boxing's reputation. His last opponent was a veteran boxing teacher that Nai Khanom Tom used to visit. He, too, was defeated in the fight, after which no other Burmese boxer dared to challenge him.

Upon seeing the courageous and skillful fights, the Burmese ruler wished to reward him. The Muay Thai fighter was given a choice of taking money or beautiful girls as wives, and he chose the Burmese girls. The fighter was released from captivity and sent to his hometown, where he spent the rest of his life.

Now that Muay Thai's history and origin have been covered, let's explore more about modern-day Muay Thai, its principles, and related information to educate you on this robust combat sport.

Modern Muay Thai

The modern form of Muay Thai became the norm in the 20th century, especially after the First World War. The fighting ring and codified rules show how heavily it is influenced by British boxing. Other changes were also accepted, such as wearing gloves instead of wrapping ropes around the hands.

The elements of traditional boxing, like padded boxing gloves, three or five-round limits per game, and the implementation of several rules, shape this combat sport. As mentioned, the fighting style is inspired by the traditional martial arts form of Muay Boran, created for hand-to-hand combat.

Implementing rules that set certain thresholds and limits is necessary since several techniques taught in Muay Boran can be deadly for the opponent when executed. For example, hitting your opponent on the joints or their neck is forbidden. Besides having numerous punch variations like uppercuts and jabs, you can also perform throws, sweeps, and clinching in Muay Thai. Due to the many fighting variations allowed in Muay Thai, it has gained the title of an all-rounded combat sport involving several fighting techniques and protocols from different combat sports.

The Principles of Muay Thai

Whether a veteran in the sport or a newbie, you need a lot of persistence, passion, and dedication to improve. Here are some principles that should be understood and incorporated in your training and life to achieve the best outcomes.

Having a Solid Defense

Instead of working endlessly to perfect your offensive strikes and moves, working on your defense for a well-rounded skill is equally crucial. If you don't have a strong defense, you give the opponent more chances to hit you by allowing openings. Keeping your guard up and anticipating your opponent's next move is key here.

Putting in Effort

Making your best effort and showing dedication is necessary if you expect better results. To be good at the sport, putting in your best when training is crucial.

Working on the Technique

Keep a balance between strength and technique training to achieve your optimum level. You might have seen a Muay Thai fighter knocking out their opponent with a single blow. It seems easy to execute at first, but the fighter puts a lot of dedication and time into perfecting these techniques. To master a technique, start with the basics, like learning the correct stance for the technique, openings during a fight you should look for, and practicing the technique numerous times to build muscle memory and quick reflexes.

Do What You Want

There's no compulsion about how to fight as long as the set rules are followed. Since Muay Thai is a physically challenging sport, training consistently and mastering techniques will only be possible when you enjoy what you're doing. This sheer enjoyment can motivate enough to achieve the set goals on time.

Timing and Distance

Besides working on perfecting techniques and learning new moves, having the correct timing and the right distance is essential in fights. If you don't time your hits well or when the distance is not to the mark, the hit won't make an impact and can result in self-injury.

Following a Plan

When training for Muay Thai, ensure you have a feasible plan. Likewise, in a fight, a Muay Thai fighter can anticipate their opponent's moves after fighting for a few minutes and can instantly develop a viable plan. For example, after the first round, the Muay Thai boxer should initiate a plan, like whether they will distract their opponent with a fake kick or would most likely clinch.

Relaxing the Body

Due to excessive physical activity, the body gets exhausted. In training or a fight, avoiding putting too much strain on the body is necessary. Avoid pushing the body to its limits to avoid injury. Besides training and polishing your skills, rest well and eat nutritious, balanced foods instead of fried and processed foods.

Muay Thai Techniques

Muay Thai uses three basic techniques: attacking, defending, and countering. Consistent practice of these techniques is imperative as it will improve how you use that particular technique and build muscle memory. The training starts with working on the stance and movements to control the body during fights.

The legs are held almost two feet apart, the body is erect, and the hands guard the head. Combatants who favor the right hand will keep their left foot forward and their right foot angled 45 degrees outside. Left-handers will position their right foot ahead and their left foot at an angle.

After the stance and movements are practiced, the next step is to learn attack, defense, and counter moves. The most fundamental attacking moves are clinches, punches, kicks, push kicks, and elbow strikes. Defensive maneuvers include leg catches, dodges, redirecting strikes, leaning back, and blocks. Mixing these basic and other advanced techniques and using them at the right time can win a fighter the game.

Beginners are frequently taught the jab-cross-low kick combination during training. The fighter can progress to practice other advanced techniques and combos. Please remember the techniques shared here are basic and have several variations. Without further ado, let's read about common techniques and their variations.

Punching

It's the most common attack technique in every combat sport, including Muay Thai. Punches have hundreds of variations, but this book only sticks to the established punching techniques and variations. The cross punch (straight rear punch), the jab (straight lead punch), the hook, the spinning back fist, the uppercut, and the overhead punch are some typical punch varieties.

These punching styles have varying stances, as it's the movement that gives power to the punch. For example, a normal punch requires moving the feet quickly by shifting the body weight and rotating the hip and shoulders.

Throwing Kicks

Muay Thai boxers can deliver impactful kicks to devastate their enemy using their shins. Most kicks are initiated from the outside while the opposite arm is swung backward. Simultaneously, the hip joint is rotated to generate force and land an effective kick.

Low kicks are thrown at the opponent's legs, medium kicks at the torso, and high kicks at the head. Besides using the typical roundhouse side kick, Muay Thai has numerous kick variations like spinning back kicks, cartwheel kicks, jumping kicks, and axe kicks, to name a few.

Throwing Elbows

Muay Thai fighters are famous for throwing shin kicks and elbows, as these body parts can deliver an effective blow to the opponent. Several variations are used to throw elbows at opponents, like hitting on the head's side, the chin, from the top down, or in the opposite direction. Other variations include the famous flying elbow and the spinning back elbow that can confuse the opponent to lower their guard and deliver a devastating blow. Perfect elbow strikes have the force to deal serious cuts and swiftly knock the opponent to the ground.

Teep Kicks

In Muay Thai, a push kick is called a *teep kick* and is used for defense and offense. These kicks are mostly used when the opponent is charging in and when you want to create distance for your next offense. The opponent's advances are stopped by using the push kick on the lead leg and torso. Some teeps are aimed at the face and intentionally initiated to show dominance. Teeps can be mixed with kick variations to push the opponent further. Adding a teep to a jumping front kick can push the opponent or cause them to lose their stance.

Knee Throws

Knee throws are the most effective weapon in Muay Thai when in close range or the clinching position. These knee throws mostly aim at the torso, ribcage, thighs, and the opponent's head. Jumping knee strikes are often used in this combat sport and can deliver a knockout blow, ending the fight early.

Clinching

Clinching is a Muay Thai grappling technique combining knee and elbow strikes for maximum damage. While clinching might seem simple at first, it can take several years to master the technique. Clinching can be a game-changing move when executed perfectly, making the opponent tap out in no time.

To improve at Muay Thai, learning these basic techniques and continuously practicing building muscle memory is crucial. Most Muay Thai fighters train twice daily, dividing their practice routine into two parts. The routine is mostly followed year-round except Sundays. As Muay Thai is deeply rooted in Thai culture, it's no surprise to see Muay Thai boxers as young as five years old training to be better at combat sports.

As you start building muscle memory by constantly repeating the techniques, building muscle strength and stamina are equally important. Therefore, cardio and weight exercises are incorporated into a Muay Thai boxer's training routine. This striking balance of strength, agility, and quick reflexes improves a Muay Thai fighter. For beginners, it's best to find a teacher or mentor to build a strong foundation of the philosophy, principles, and practices of Muay Thai.

Benefits of Muay Thai

Although Muay Thai is a combat sport, more people are interested in this sport due to a variety of reasons besides competing in the ring. These reasons include practicing for recreational purposes and improving physical and mental health. Let's review the benefits of practicing Muay Thai for better clarity.

Controlling Calories

As mentioned, combat sport involves cardio, strength exercises, and repeatedly practicing techniques. When executed properly, these training sessions burn calories like no other workout. A typical Muay Thai session lasts at least two hours. It includes a cardio warm-up, a few minutes of shadowboxing, repeating defensive and offensive techniques, and performing numerous strength exercises. These sessions can easily burn more than a thousand calories, making them extremely effective in not only making you lose weight but also developing stamina, endurance, strength, and agility.

Increased Mental Health

Besides improving health, these workouts and training sessions boost mental health. Physical exercise, stamina, and endurance training are some effective methods linked to decreased anxiety, stress, and depression. The exercise, sleep, and diet routine a Muay Thai boxer follows is effective enough to keep stress levels in check and provide clarity when brainstorming.

Improved Self-Defense

Learning attack and defense techniques are the main pillars of Muay Thai. Muay Thai training can help someone inflict damage and defend themselves from harm during close combat because the fighting sport evolved from a previous Thai martial arts style that was created primarily for warfare. Self-defense and disarming tactics include employing offensive techniques, including knee strikes, elbow throws, and push kicks.

Mental Strength

Besides improving mental health, the mental strength of a Muay Thai fighter increases drastically, enabling the boxer to channel their emotions, keep worrisome thoughts at bay, and develop mental fortitude. Muay Thai is about being mentally and physically strong enough to endure adverse and uncertain situations with courage, determination, and a winning attitude.

Endorphin Surge

As Muay Thai involves lengthy training sessions followed by a rest phase to relax and replenish energy, the brain during this relaxation period releases endorphins promoting relaxation and comfort, aiding drastically in managing stress.

Social Bonding

A Muay Thai gym provides a sense of comradeship where you find people striving for the same goals and sharing similar passions. The pain you endure during training with your partners at the gym can forge strong bonds and relationships that can go a long way.

Increased Self-Confidence

With training, your physical appearance improves, boosting self-confidence. A physically strong and appealing body gives you the confidence to not worry about your body shape and be what you truly want to be.

Improved Health

The risk of common medical conditions like cardiovascular diseases, high blood pressure, and diabetes can be reduced through adequate Muay Thai training. Since the sport is cardio-intensive, it improves cardiovascular health and reduces blood pressure.

Besides these benefits, Muay Thai is an amazing combat sport for fitness enthusiasts seeking more than hitting the gym and lifting weights. Instead of repeating the same exercises, you can tweak your routine and learn a new technique or combo.

This last section briefly compares Muay Thai with other popular combat sports forms.

Muay Thai vs. Boxing

Traditional boxing allows punches, but in Muay Thai, you can use knees, elbows, kicks, clinching, and other techniques without restrictions. Both combat sports are ideal for self-defense and competing professionally. Still, it all comes down to personal preference of which combat sport to pursue.

MMA vs. Muay Thai

The most evident difference between these two combat sports is that MMA fighters are more efficient in grappling and use several of these techniques to make their opponent tap out. On the other hand, a Muay Thai boxer will be more efficient in landing impactful strikes.

Brazilian Jiu-Jitsu vs. Muay Thai

Muay Thai is a more athletic combat sport. In contrast, Brazilian Jiu-Jitsu (BJJ) is a more ground fighting and grappling martial art form. Muay Thai fighters believe their techniques can knock out a BJJ fighter instantly. On the other hand, BJJ fighters can use advanced grappling techniques to pin the fighter to the ground and force him to submission.

Key Rules in Muay Thai

There might be slight changes in the rules and regulations, but here are the most common rules virtually every Muay Thai organization follows.

- A standard ring should be between 4.9 by 4.9 meters to 7.3 by 7.3 meters. Adequate cushioning material must be applied on the four corner posts and the floor.
- The official minimum age for a Muay Thai fighter to compete professionally is 15 to 18 years, depending on the country.
- Protective gear like gloves, elbow pads, head guards, and even a padded vest are sometimes mandatory.
- The glove size should be six to ten ounces according to the weight category. Some organizations allow MMA gloves with open fingers between four to six ounces.

- Weigh-ins are carried out one day earlier or on the same day of a fight. Fighters are categorized according to their weight division.
- Only Muay Thai shorts are allowed as apparel for male fighters. Some Muay Thai fighters with strong traditional beliefs wear sacred armbands called *prajiad.*
- Each fight is five three-minute rounds with two-minute breaks after each round. For the casual viewer, some TV programs and sports networks cut the game into three rounds of three minutes each.
- The winner is decided via a scoring system if there is no knockout in a match. The Muay Thai boxer that effectively lands more and inflicts more damage is considered the winner. When a player wins a round, ten points are awarded, and the opponent is given a number lower than ten, depending on their performance in the round.
- A referee has the authority to stop the fight in the case of a knockout or when one Muay Thai boxer clearly overpowers their opponent.
- If the combatant is deemed unfit to continue (which could result in other health problems), the on-call doctor can call off the fight.
- Common offenses that result in a fighter's disqualification include headbutts, groin shots, kicking knee joints, and prodding the eyes.
- Spitting or swearing are also prohibited and can result in a penalty.

Muay Thai has a rich and fascinating history carried through generations and styles to become today's intense and rewarding combat sport.

Chapter 2: Starting with Stance

Muay Thai's foundation lies in the Jot Muay, a crucial element for executing fighting techniques effectively. Without a stable stance, it's impossible to develop advanced combat skills.

Over time, varied fighting postures replaced older ones. Now, many centers train their students using a variant of Western boxing guards regarded as standard everywhere among instructors globally. When looking back at heritage practices, it was discovered that most training camps taught distinct techniques based on geographical location – North, Northeastern, South, or Central Thailand.

But in this chapter, you learn the traditional Muay fighting stances, which is the origin of different techniques and variants used today. This chapter covers detailed instructions for practicing each stance using factors like balance, rhythm, and basic footwork. You learn additional tips for mastering these stances and positions, popular mistakes, and avoiding them.

The Significance of Foot Placement in Muay Thai

If you aim to master Siamese fighting culture, honing your foot's accuracy and precision is a must. According to the age-old customs of Muay Thai martial arts, there are three broad classifications for foot positions: 1-point support, 2-point support, and 3-point support systems, including the triangle stance-imaginary vertices where fighters stand.

Advancing through each position is vital to react promptly against your opponent's movements. The triangle stance is the basis for all other techniques within Muay Thai and underpins its philosophy.

Knowledge about foothold techniques is essential for a comprehensive understanding of this discipline. Therefore, adhering strictly to conventional rules becomes vital in attaining success while perfecting footing practices like standing legs apart at shoulder distance recommended by experts.

Balance is everything in Muay Thai, and proper foot placement makes all the difference. Aim to position your feet so the rear foot is higher than the front to master the art of balance. This stance allows for excellent evasions alongside swift, accurate counterstrikes that pack a punch.

The Significance of Arm Positions

You must master adopting optimal stances that create triangular shapes using the body as a guide to excelling in Muay Thai fighting. This technique enables professionals to move effortlessly while maximizing the potential of their limbs as lethal weapons.

Achieving the desired combat posture necessitates proper hand placement and shielding against vulnerabilities like exposing the throat and opening yourself up to danger from opponents.

In close-quarter encounters, when stability takes precedence over movement or flexibility during long-range encounters, defensive measures must prioritize protecting vulnerable areas like the torso and front regions.

Muay Thai technique execution success is mostly dependent on low gravity center tactics. You must maintain slightly bowed knees, slightly crouching shoulders, slightly spread legs, and an upright chest. These crucial elements provide fighters optimal stability and protect their throats from attacks when engaging opponents head-on.

Traditional Muay Thai Fighting Stances

The five common traditional Muay Thai fighting stances are outlined in this section.

1. Muay Chaiya Fighting Stance

Muay Chaiya stance

Efficiency is key in achieving victory through Muay Chaiya's fighting stance, as advised by Grand Master Khet Sriyaphai. This posture is similar to durian fruits protected by thorns inflicting pain on anything that touches it.

Jot Muay Chaiya can hurt an opponent similarly as long as the stance is done correctly. A fighter must divide their body into six quadrants: left lower, right upper, left upper, right middle, left middle, and right lower. Each requires a unique defensive technique tailored to the corresponding attacks.

Arms defend the upper to middle quadrants, while legs shield the lower ones. Defensive maneuvers aim for maximum efficiency by using the shortest path to cover an endangered quadrant, eliminating wasted motion.

2. Muay Korat

Muay Korat stance.

In contrast to Chaiya, the Muay Korat posture represents an offensive approach. Its structure has been thoughtfully designed to maximize attack effectiveness. Implementing this fighting stance requires assertive and aggressive movements using powerful strikes employing both arms and legs.

Fists should be parallel to your chest with one arm stretched outward to cover a large area in front and block any susceptible openings for an opponent's attack. This position allows for quick, fierce counterattacks. The strong defensive character of this stance allows for quick, lethal counterattacks.

The location of the feet creates an aggressive, commanding posture that places most of the body's weight on the front leg. The rear leg offers stability and support, shortening the space between the knees, which must be kept flexed. The stability of the back leg and the closer knee distance enable quick, aggressive footwork.

3. Muay Lopburi

The *Muay Lopburi* fighting stance has a unique hand position with fists turned, palms facing upward, and elbows bent. The hands are lower than the other two stances.

Western bare knuckle boxers' guard inspired this stance to enable swift punches, particularly the upward swing punch popular among Lopburi boxers. The positioning of the feet is critical in this stance allowing for flexibility in attack and defense.

You require quick footwork with legs not too far apart to maintain balance and your center of gravity. While defending, the rear foot should be flat but raised while attacking or moving forward to show versatility.

Muay Lopburi fighting stance

4. Muay Pranakorn

One of the most dynamic postures fighters adopt is known as *Muay Pranakorn*. It borrows specific elements from other styles and combines them to form a well-rounded stance worth mastering.

The most notable aspect of this position is how far apart it keeps each leg, creating ample space between them, standing out immediately upon observation by onlookers or opponents.

While standing firmly, one leg is turned outwards at ninety degrees; the other leg must be centered forward, facing the opponent. The fighter's knees are significantly bent to lower their center of gravity and increase balance.

The benefit of this stance is it makes fighters appear smaller while providing an edge in combat by unsettling their opponents.

Muay Pranakorn fighting stance

Bent at the elbow, the fighter's rear arm offers protection from potential attacks toward the upper body region for added defensive advantage. Its unique formation and defensive capabilities make the Muay Pranakorn stance perfect for launching powerful limb strikes.

Additional Tips for Mastering These Stances

To excel at Muay Thai, you must understand how vital proper positioning is for attacking and defending effectively. If you don't master this skill, sparring sessions might feel more like frustrating exercises than enjoyable ones. Additionally, hitting pads or bags won't produce much force.

Western boxing and Muay Thai combat sports recognize two fighting styles - orthodox or southpaw - depending on whether an athlete uses his left or right hand more often as his primary striking weapon.

The orthodox fighter stands with his left foot forward, relying mostly on his right side to push out powerful punches. Conversely, the southpaw fighter typically stands with his right foot forward, using his left arm for the attack.

Interestingly, some Muay Thai fighters showcase their preferred side by wearing ankle straps. Some choose one strap on the stronger foot, while others might choose an eye-catching anklet contrasting with their shorts' hue at the opposite ankle.

But whether they're southpaws or orthodox athletes, correct body positioning remains crucial if you want maximum power output and success rates.

Here are several essential factors in establishing an unwavering foundation anyone should consider as they enhance their personal approach to achieving top-notch results in Muay Thai.

Elbow, Head, and Hands Positioning

The wrong elbow, head, and hands positions may get you seriously hurt - no matter how cool you might think you look!

To properly position yourself and make your hands hang down naturally, bring both thumbs level with your eyebrows and your palms facing each other.

Achieving optimal results requires careful attention to form, including positioning your elbows slightly farther apart than your hands. But don't force anything; you don't want to feel like you're pushing or pulling any part of your body into an uncomfortable or unnatural position.

Your hands should be touching your forehead, and you should tuck in your chin just enough to safeguard it with both shoulders in case a punch comes flying at you from either side. Don't tilt too much but keep your chin up.

With your stance and bodily alignment in check, it's time to focus on refining footwork techniques for optimal performance.

Footwork

Maintaining proper form is key for a good stance in martial arts training. While it's typically recommended fighters keep their feet slightly apart, at least shoulder width or wider, exceptions like those of fighter Nong O Gaiyanghadao, who varies foot distance throughout fights, cannot be overlooked.

By taking a wider stance during some fights as part of deflections and strikes, he maintains balance under pressure, absorbing incoming kicks better than with the narrower foot placement used during Teep strikes.

For those beginning martial arts, start with a good foundational stance that has your feet more than shoulder width apart while staying steady on your feet with knees bent and flexed. As you become more comfortable in your foundation, experiment with different foot distances to determine what works best while maintaining a solid center of balance.

You should keep your hips directly facing the opponent's and not sideways like a boxer. Always adjust your foot position based on the technique you plan to use for optimal results while keeping good form at all times.

A crucial point to remember is this principle is also true for your hands and arms. Work harmoniously with your footwork and overall game plan to attain peak performance.

Mistakes to Avoid During Stance

The Fighting Stance is a topic ripe for debate within Muay Thai circles concerning what constitutes the best posture and approach in combat. However, critical errors can significantly impair your performance. This section looks closely at some mistakes.

1. Poor Flexibility and Adaptability

Flexibility and adaptability are essential to succeed with a proper fighting stance because there isn't a single universal stance that applies across all situations. It's about adapting to specific circumstances rather than relying on a particular approach or style. Always be ready to strike while protecting vulnerable areas of the body from an opponent's attack.

Depending on the situation, you might stand up straighter for techniques like sidekicks or assume a lower profile with heightened protection for better defense against incoming blows.

What happens when special opportunities present themselves tactically? Sometimes intentionally lowering your guard could lure an unwary opponent right into your counterattack trap.

The bottom line is to stay aware of the context and adapt accordingly with flexibility to changing circumstances. Flexibility is key to being successful in combat. Avoid getting anchored down by a rigid fighting stance. Be ready and willing to modify your tactics based on the scenario.

2. Neglecting the Neck

Neglecting the protection of the neck area when adopting a fighting stance is a prevalent mistake among many martial artists or combat sports practitioners. Getting punched in this vulnerable region can have severe consequences like concussions or death.

Consciously be aware that it must not be overlooked or neglected at any cost. Hence prioritizing its defense becomes imperative while devising or adopting a sub-discipline-related approach like Thai boxing or kickboxing techniques.

A proper fighting stance entails raising the arms while tucking in the chin securely and leaning forward to provide optimal protection for the neck region. However, novices often overlook this aspect while keeping their hands up, which can have detrimental effects.

Therefore, during sparring sessions or training drills, focus primarily on shielding your neck effectively. Once this objective is achieved, other necessary aspects of a complete fighting stance will follow naturally.

3. Not Relaxing

When attempting Thai boxing or kickboxing for the first time, many people struggle to balance tension and relaxation on the mat. It is understandable; making quick moves while staying cool under pressure takes time and practice. So, what's the solution?

One trick is to imagine yourself feeling completely spent after running an arduous marathon. Let yourself sink into complete exhaustion before gradually raising your arms toward your chin, remaining as loose as possible throughout every motion. It might be tough at first, but mastering this level of relaxation is essential for improving your Thai boxing performance.

Whether an experienced fighter or just starting in the world of Thai boxing, perfecting your fighting stance is critical for success. A strong stance enables more efficient executions of attack and defense movements. But it's not only about holding a fixed position.

In reality, fighting stances are adopted during transitional moments between movements requiring flexibility and fluidity to execute properly. Different combat sports have unique rules regarding which strikes are permitted within competition settings. Therefore, diverse stances have been developed to fit specific needs.

By honing your understanding of these techniques and exploring those that work best for your particular style, you'll boost your chances of coming out on top in a contest.

Chapter 3: Chok: Punching Techniques

Even though Muay Thai is known worldwide as the "Art of Eight Limbs," punches are an important aspect of the sport. Punches for this sport were once limited, relying mostly on knees, kicks, clinching, and basic punching techniques.

However, things have changed, and boxing is now fundamental in the sport, putting fighters restricted to their hands at a disadvantage. Numerous Muay Thai stars are recognized for their techniques, expertise, and sudden and rapid punches. Saensak Muangsurin, Veeraphol Sahaprom, and the famous Samart Payakaroon are examples of fighters who succeeded when progressing from Muay Thai to boxing.

The Major Punching Techniques

Muay Thai has been imbued with Western boxing styles, and the development of punching techniques resulted from this combination. Currently, these punching techniques are broken down into 8 major types. The descriptions of the punches below are explained from the view of a typical fighter. If you fight orthodoxly, the punches would be performed with the opposing feet, hands, and limbs.

1. The Jab

The jab is the easiest punch.[24]

The jab is widely used in Muay Thai and boxing, making it the most significant in the sport. It is the easiest punch and very important, unlike in boxing, where it does not assure dominance. As a beginner in Muay Thai, your trainer will certainly dwell on improving the jab. It works for defense and offense. Various combinations can be set up from the jab, helping a fighter maintain distance from the opponent.

Why is jab frequently used? It is the fastest punch to deliver and is usually the punch to throw when within reach of your opponent. A jab is handy for countering an opponent who keeps advancing toward you aggressively. You require strength to throw an excellent jab. When used correctly, it can be a technique to throw your opponent's combination into disarray. Also, jabs can initiate other moves and punches. Your opponent is within reach and open to further attacks once your jab hits.

To counter the jab, you must paw or parry it with the aid of the high hand on the right. Then, you can push your jab up front, with just a little jab step, as it is parried off. Boxers use an effortless act of ducking to safeguard themselves from jabs. Ducking is a movement to get around and disorient your opponent.

How to Throw a Jab

When throwing a jab, launch your shoulders forward when punching to produce a nice snap so that your jaw and shoulder meet. It increases the jab's reach, and your shoulders shield your chin. As you extend your fists, let your knuckles face upwards and your palm downward while your elbow stretches. Don't forget to bend your knees a little during the punch and pop back up after you've delivered your jab. Your balance would be off if your knees were straightened, lessening the power and control in your jab.

Always keep your rear hand close and tight to your face when throwing the jab with your lead hand. If you drop your guard, you are left wide open for the opponent to throw a left hook. Also, remember your stance must be correct to throw a good jab.

2. The Cross

The cross travels farther than a jab. [25]

The cross, known as the straight punch, is a powerful punch launched from the backhand. It is usually used as a punch to knock out the opponent in Muay Thai. Although used regularly, like the jab, it is not regularly used as a punch to set up combinations. It is thrown mostly after a combination or a jab. Unlike the jab, the cross does not immediately connect after throwing it. Also, it travels the farthest.

The cross punch is made with the hand furthest from the opponent. This distance and the potential to add rotational force and weight to the strike make it one of your strongest punches. The cross can ward off your opponents because it is a very strong punch. When a good cross connects with an opponent's chin, it can knock them out or at least stun them.

Jabs can be countered with a cross. The cross is excellent for landing power punches on an opponent's outside and can be launched before or after a low kick. You can combine or add it to normal punch and kick combinations. The trick to throwing a great cross is to begin with a body punch to lower your opponent's guard and create the opening to land your shot.

How to Throw a Cross

The common setup for a cross is to give a hard, fast jab first. The trick is to drive your right toe into the ground while rotating your body as you bend your knees and lean your upper body forward slightly to align with your opponent. Then, throw the punch with your thumbs rotated downward, facing the floor, and following your elbow as it extends. Also, ensure your rear foot is pivoted while throwing a cross; when you do this correctly, your heel will be upwards with your toes on the ground, facing the exact direction your punch is headed. You must do everything in one motion so your body's power goes with the punch. Then, quickly return the hand to avoid a counter.

3. The Hook

A hook is a difficult punch to perfect.[26]

Your opponent's sides can be attacked with the hook. It is delivered with your leading or rear hand. Launching a hook with your leading hand is a great strategy to catch an opponent with good movement, and it is difficult to see if you can lure the opponent into a trap. By the time you have mastered the technique, it can be launched easily and even delivered while jumping.

It is widely known and used in Muay Thai, even though it is the most difficult punch to perfect. A bad-hooking technique can lead to a fractured wrist and even back pain. The hook delivered with the rear hand can often knock out your opponent and is very hard to disguise. It is commonly thrown in close range to your opponent. Still, it leaves you open to counterattacks if the timing is off and launched carelessly. However, it is a good way to end a fight. Before backing up, launch a hook at your opponent's head and finish with a shot to his ribs.

The left hook is regularly used in combinations. Like the cross, a hook is not a long-range shot to reach your opponents. Therefore, it is infrequent for a right-footed fighter to launch a right hook in their basic stance. Suppose you throw a right hook in a right-foot stance; your fist would be inches from your lead hand. It doesn't make right hooks impossible; they are just not as conventional as the left hook.

How to Throw a Hook

Adjust your body weight to your back leg from a correct stance while bending your knees slightly. At the same moment, turn your body with your hips, transferring all the kinetic energy to the punch. Bend your arm at an angle of 90 degrees while placing your elbow just behind your lead hand to land the punch with the elbow of your lead hand bent and your knuckles and closed fist pointing to the ground. The shoulder, elbow, and hand must all be in a line. To boost the punch's force, rotate with your lead foot simultaneously while your right-hand guards your chin for defense.

4. The Uppercut

An uppercut is an attack aimed at the chin.[27]

Those who disagree that the hook is the most powerful blow in Muay Thai usually claim it is the uppercut. The execution method of this punch is similar to the hook, but the angle of attack is aimed at the chin. A tricky punch, the uppercut can incur great damage if it connects. Imagine having a hard smack on your chin; it can throw you off balance and achieve a knockout if the force is powerful enough.

The uppercut can be brutal and devastating during close combat, but connecting your opponent with it from the outside is difficult. It is rarely used as starting or lead punches because it can be detected, blocked, or countered easily. Due to the skill and timing needed to master this shot, it is the hardest blow to land.

If you practice Muay Thai, you should perfect your hook and know that landing this punch leaves you open to elbows and front kicks.

To deliver an uppercut, you must ensure producing an upward motion does not disrupt your defense. First, turn before adjusting your weight to the side where you hit from, before bringing up your looped arm toward the opponent's jaw or chin.

How to Counter an Uppercut

The two common mistakes that open you to uppercuts are not taking the right stance, exposing your chin, and overextending your blows. Being in the proper stance and having your techniques closed helps guard against your opponent's uppercuts. To counter an uppercut, you must launch a jab when your opponent punches. Many fighters move forward before delivering the uppercut, so you must catch them immediately. The step is taken as soon as their head crosses the centerline.

5. The Swing

The swing's movement is similar to the hook. [28]

The swing's movement is almost the same as the hook, but the arm is more extended. The punch is best understood as being more of a swipe. Its capability of reach makes up for its inadequacy in power. A fighter can reach far when they throw the swing delivering an attack to the opponent's side. Like the hook, it is not often launched with the backhand or used as a lead punch. A jab or another strike usually conceals this swing. Also, it is not used in close combat because it is far-reaching.

The swing is not regarded as a punch for a knockout because it lacks power, but it is a good technique to catch your opponent off guard. It's uncommon to deliver a hooked blow from a distance. However, catching opponents when they're off guard is a good attack and makes them nervous. The swing is useful for fighters lacking in height because it helps them close the distance.

You must keep your distance to counter a fighter who swings wildly; if you cannot, try blocking, but not for long. A barehanded blow can easily pass a block. So, quickly step back and rush toward the legs below the knee to take the opponent down.

6. Overhand Punch

The overhand punch is tricky to learn. [29]

The overhand punch is another hook punch, launched from behind and looping over the head. It can knock the opponent out if executed properly with sufficient power. However, this technique is very tricky to learn.

The two disadvantages to this technique are:

- If you fail to hit, your balance will be off, and you will be wide open for counterattacks.
- The blow is not easy to deliver when you are up against left-handed fighters because their head, which is your target, is far away.

This technique works well when fighting taller opponents because it can surprise them and override their defenses. A good combination where to use this punch is after a left-leg onside kick. A suitable way to counter this technique is to tilt backward, launching your punch before your opponent returns to their stance. Raising your left hand upward, like picking up a phone, can block the overhand punch.

How to Throw an Overhand Punch

Suppose the distance between you and your opponent is shrinking, and you see an opening to land an overhand. In that case, it must be done quickly and directed at your opponent's head. You must bend your elbows at an angle between 90-135o, depending on the distance between you and your opponent. Ensure the punch comes above your shoulder and head in a loop motion to guide the strike downward as you lean slightly outside your lead foot. Bending your knees simultaneously as you strike to keep your balance is important.

7. Spinning Back Fist

The spinning back fist is an advanced technique. [30]

This technique is advanced. The motion and movements are unique to other punches mentioned. To counter this technique, duck as your opponent throws it or keep a high guard, rotate your head, and launch a counter hook.

How to Throw a Spinning Back Fist

To throw a spinning back fist, do the following:

- Take a step turning your body. Those who fight conventionally would take a step to the right with their lead.

- Then, raise your right leg, turning around with your left while your right arm is fully extended.
- Hit your opponent using the backside of your hand or the base of your fist.
- The rotating action with the centrifugal force from the spin gives this punch a powerful impact. If this technique is executed properly, it will carry a lot of power and knock out your opponent if it connects.

8. Superman Punch

The superman punch is also known as the flying punch. [31]

This technique is a basic flying overhand punch. Even though people feel it's a spectacular technique, it is not the strongest punch. It can be easily countered because it is quickly detected once launched.

To counter a Superman punch, deflect it or step out of the way.

How to Throw a Superman Punch

To throw a Superman punch:
- You must fake a kick before leaping into the air
- Launch your hand forward in the air, stretching your leg out simultaneously

This technique is suitable against tall opponents because it reduces the distance and gets past their defense. The punch should not be frequently executed because it is very exposed, making it easy to counter.

Practice makes everything perfect; this old saying is never incorrect. Ensure you use these techniques regularly. The Superman and spinning punches might seem cool but do not affect opponents if executed incorrectly. When used by an inexperienced fighter, the counterattacks will be executed easily. Try not to execute these techniques until you are confident in your ability to do them correctly, thus *effectively*.

Chapter 4: Sok: Elbow Techniques

The Muay Sok in Thailand means "elbow fighter." The fighter focuses on being in close range with his opponent in Muay Sok. The aim is to avoid many kicks and catch the opponent off balance to deliver a nice sharp elbow strike. Whoever closes the distance has a better chance to ring off the target and force them to fight in the suitor's range.

What makes this technique so unique is the level of aggression. The Muay Sok fighter uses different elbow strikes to succeed in various positions. There are several elbow strikes, including *sok ping* (spare elbow), *sok tad* (horizontal elbow), *sok ngad* (uppercut elbow), *sok ti* (slashing elbow), and *sok klap* (spinning elbow). These strikes are used differently, i.e., horizontal, diagonal upward and downward, uppercuts, etc.

This chapter exposes you to the different practical ways to apply each technique, creating a defense system from an opponent's attack and making a counterattack. You learn the minor mistakes you will likely encounter as a beginner and how to overcome them.

What separates this kickboxing technique from others is the elbow strikes. These strikes can knock out an opponent at a shorter range and deliver a bladed cut or blow to the target's face. This is the uniqueness of Must Sok, which no other fighting style employs.

How to Use the Elbow Strikes

The elbow is so sharp and hard that it can give a blunt cut to your target's skin if you attack at a close range or ground level. The elbow strike works effectively as a counterattack for an opponent's punch. Due to these multiple benefits, the elbow strike should be implemented as a style for every self-defense mechanism.

In martial arts, just throwing your elbows to hit an opponent's face is not as effective as applying a few other brutal techniques. In Muay Thai boxing, the elbows are used in various ways: horizontal motion, vertical upward motion, vertical downward motion, an uppercut, backward spinning movement, and the flying elbow. The elbow can attack your target's face from the side, and this could cut their brow. The vertical elbows are more efficient in speed, although not as fast as the others.

The elbow strikes are executed in two ways; the single elbow and the follow-up elbow. However, there's a great distinction between both. The single elbow is independent of other strikes, while the follow-up is done with the same arm on the same target. For example, throwing a punch and immediately striking your opponent with an elbow. However, elbows are only used when the distance between opponents is small. Elbows are a good defense against side knees, body kicks, punches, etc.

In Muay Thai boxing, there are nine elbow strikes, including;

● **Sok Tad (Horizontal Elbow)**

The horizontal elbow is the easiest and most popular elbow strike. This elbow strike can be likened to a hook punch. How is that possible? When you strike, turn your hips, and move the feet on the lead side of your body to deliver the blow. Keep your other arm over your face during this strike to protect against counterattacks. The aim of this movement is directed toward the target's chin and lower face. You can use this move to breach the defense of your opponent.

Sok Tad is similar to a hook.

● **Sok Ngad (Uppercut Elbow)**

The uppercut elbow is one of the most striking and fastest elbow strikes in Muay Thai. This strike is quick and lands a sharp blade cut on the target. Using this can weaken your opponent's defense. How is this possible? With the uppercut elbow, you strike your elbow between your opponent's arms aiming directly for their chin. It can result in a clean knockout blow.

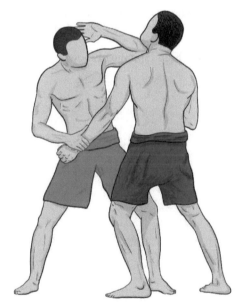

Sok Ngad is one of the fastest strikes in Muay Thai.

- Sok Ti (Slashing Elbow)

Sok Ti can break your opponent's defense.

This elbow movement is thrown in a slicing downward motion. The target point for this strike is the forehead, the cheeks, or directly above your opponent's eyes. This strike is effective in breaking your opponent's defense. Your opponent will put up a defense to block your attack, but you can wear them out if you keep striking with your elbow.

- Sok Klap (Spinning Elbow)

This movement is a classic move in Muay Thai. It takes a level of mastery of the previous techniques to apply this one. This technique requires care as it must be performed with your back turned against your opponent while striking with the other elbow. Do not underestimate this move, as it can effectively land a knockout blow to the target. How do you apply it? Step your feet across your opponent's side and rotate your upper torso. Use the rear elbow to land a blow to the side of the target's face. Ensure to observe your target from the side of your shoulder while executing this strike, and rotate back immediately after you land the strike.

Sok Klap is a classic Muay Thai move.

• Sok Phung (Forward Elbow Thrust)

This elbow movement is often mistaken for the uppercut elbow. The only distinction between both is that the elbow is thrown forward instead of upward in the forward thrust, as in an uppercut. How do you apply it? Step toward your opponent, pushing them with your hip. Set up your elbow like a spear and thrust it into the target.

Sok Phung is similar to the uppercut elbow.

• Sok Ku (Double Elbow)

This is a fantastic movement, and when used properly can make a smart move. It could be a brilliant move to end your opponent. During combat, once you realize an opening where your opponent might be weak or hurt, you can jump high and land both elbows on the top of their head.

Sok Ku can help you eliminate your opponent

• Sok Tong (Downward Elbow)

This strike is often known as the "12-6" strike because the landing of the elbow resembles the clock reading 12-6. This elbow strike isn't commonly used during combat and is banned in some matches. It is applied similarly to Sok Ku. In this technique, you hit your opponent's thigh, catch his kick, and strike it with your elbow.

Sok Tong is not commonly used in combat.

Blocking Elbow Strikes

Muay Thai is kickboxing using several clinching techniques, including blocking. Blocking is a crucial defense mechanism skill requiring you to protect your opponent's strikes with your arms, legs, or dodging. In defense, your arms and hands absorb the defects from your opponent's strike. There are other defensive methods in blocking, such as weaving or slipping.

An elbow strike is one of the most powerful strikes in Muay Thai. These strikes usually aim at the target's face, neck, or body. With this strike, you can cut your opponent, causing them to bleed and get distracted. It requires a precise and careful application to be effective. You use your elbow to block another fighter's kick or punch. You bring down your elbow to shield a side of your body using a good fighting stance. To master the art of self-defense, you must first learn to block punches with the shoulder, arm, or elbow so the force's effect is lessened on those sensitive areas of your body.

Due to the hardness of the elbow, it'll take an experienced fighter to use it effectively to knock out or cause harm to their targets since it is difficult to hit with an elbow. They are more effective in a combined attack with punches or kicks, allowing close-range attacks. Learning to block elbow attacks with your forearms and shoulders is essential. Blocking places you in a good position to counterattack with the same arm as soon as your opponent's elbow touches you.

Common Elbow Mistakes Made and How to Overcome Them

Muay Thai is an art new to the Western world. Elbow strikes aren't practiced often because the elbow strike is a very sharp and dangerous technique that can cause injuries and harm easily. The elbow strike is only allowed when competing under the full Thai or MMA rules. However, this does not mean the elbow strike technique should be discarded but used under careful practice without error. Beginners must know the "do's and don'ts" before venturing into this technique. Below are a few elbow strike mistakes beginners and advanced fighters make and how to strengthen them.

Flaw 1: Over Swinging of the Arm

A common mistake is swinging your arm excessively to hit your opponent. This technique adds little or no advantage to a fighter, giving the strike from the elbow more strain and less impact. The goal is to get close to your target and make your upper body flexible enough to turn and land an elbow strike precisely and directly on the target. So, instead of swinging your arm excessively, allow your upper body to be flexible in turns.

It can be difficult resisting using an elbow, but ensure your upper body can turn and engage, so your elbow can connect with the target.

Flaw 2: Leaving the Chin Unprotected

This is a common mistake when punching. While focusing on reading and targeting your opponent, you might lose focus on yourself and leave your chin unguarded; this takes a great toll when there's a counterattack. When reading your opponent and attacking with a punch, ensure your upper arm is folded over your chin in a scarf-like manner. When your opponent counterattacks, your arm shields your face from getting hit.

It is especially important because elbow strikes are in very close range, making it easy for you to get caught off guard when using one.

Flaw 3: Flaring Up the Elbow

Beginners are majorly affected by this. Elevating your elbow before hitting a target when throwing an elbow makes them aware of your stance before you make it. Your elbow should be up with your stance toward the target before you turn and make contact with the target. This move makes it difficult for your opponent to predict your next move.

Flaw 4: A Hard Blow

You might want to land a hard strike to finish your opponent, but using the elbow would cause greater damage, reducing the effects on your hands. Your hands are fragile and can easily get broken, but an elbow is a strong piece of bone, and with it, you can cause significant harm to the target. The best way to use an elbow is horizontal or vertical whipping.

Flaw 5: Fist Clenching

This mistake is common at all levels, beginner and advanced. You don't throw an elbow with your fist clenched; this is poor performance and creates tension on the forearm muscle, making a fighter produce an awkward elbow swing. How to solve it? Keep your hands and fingers loose or relaxed when throwing an elbow. It creates a fluid movement of the arm and allows free motion of the hands.

Tips and Techniques in Sok

First, you must be familiar with the basic techniques. With consistent practice, these techniques grow to cause real harm to your opponent when applied carefully. Basic techniques include the hook, uppercut, spiking elbow, horizontal elbow, and spinning back elbow.

Elbows can be applied in a close or clinch position regardless of the distance. The most essential aspect is that your strike is strong enough to affect your opponents. Here are tips on how to better use the elbow technique:

- Move your hips explosively toward the opponent: While learning punches and kicks, you should also learn to drive your hips explosively toward the opponent to deliver a close-range elbow shot. In an attempt to strike, dig down from your hip to generate more energy for an elbow strike. Your elbow becomes stronger when you learn to move your hips explosively.

- Stabilize your lower back: The muscles on your lower back, when strengthened, stabilizes your hip rotation, allowing efficient movement of the shoulders. To create power, imagine freely thrusting your shoulders at an opponent with a strong elbow strike.

- Keep your shoulders relaxed and flexible: To transfer the energy your hips generate into your elbow, you must learn to relax your shoulders. The body has worked hard to create the energy, so your shoulders must align to strengthen your elbows.

Muay Sok is a crucial aspect of Thailand kickboxing and uses the elbow to strike an opponent. This aspect of combat is what separates it from all other kickboxing forms. The elbow, one of the hardest parts of the body, is used as a weapon and can only be fired at short range and in clinching. It can be dangerous when used correctly and precisely.

This technique can be applied and countered in various ways. As a beginner in Muay Thai, you must learn the basic techniques, master each level, and then progress to other areas of the game. Relying only on an instructional manual would not have as much effect as hitting the gym and registering under a coach. Most importantly, practice is key to mastery.

Chapter 5: Ti Khao: Knee Techniques

Under ancient Thai rule, the knee technique was a highly regarded, high-scoring move. When properly executed, it can leave your opponents with their faces on the ground. In Muay Thai, the knee gives the most prominent and all-round strike capable of giving you victory in a fight. The anatomical part of the knee responsible for perfectly executing this move is your kneecap (patella). It usually works best and produces the most devastating effect.

You observe your kneecap moving as you sit down with your leg straightened on the floor or while standing straight. But when you bend it against the femur, or as if you're striking a Kungfu pose with your leg lifted at an angle, you will notice the kneecap becomes firm. Ensure your heel is up to your butt when attacking while the other leg's toes point to the ground, then hit with your kneecap. This positioning makes it easy to attack your opponent, and driving this striking point with precision and the force coming from your hip makes the strike more effective.

Muay Thai Knee Techniques

Muay Thai, without a doubt, has the best knee techniques in all martial arts. Below are some with the potential to render an opponent unconscious, break their ribs, trigger paralysis, or leave them seriously injured:

The Straight Knee Technique (Khao Trong)

As a beginner, this is the simplest and the most direct knee technique in Muay Thai. The straight knee can be delivered from within or outside the double collar tie (the clinch) and is mostly aimed at your opponent's midsection, striking below the sternum. While it might seem easy, do not let the simplicity of this striking technique throw you off because, when executed correctly, it causes excruciating pain to your opponent's midsection.

If you can use the upward thrust and momentum when you lock your hands behind your opponent's skull, the strike's impact will be more severe. Every goal-oriented fighter must learn the trick behind this technique.

Khao Trong is the simplest knee technique in Muay Thai.

Here are a few tips when using this technique;

- Move forward while stretching forth a leg.
- Thrust your hips forward to generate force by acquiring momentum.
- Target your opponent's upper abdomen while extending your knee diagonally; this improves your strike's effectiveness.
- You must lean back to increase your force.
- Protect your chin by tucking it into your chest.
- When landing from your hit, your kneeling shin should be vertical.
- Extend the upper part of your elbow forward when hurling from mid-range to defend against counterattacks and maintain balance.

Curved Knee Techniques (Khao Khong)

Khao Khong is effective in close combat.

Another excellent technique for beginners is the curved knee. This knee strike is particularly effective in close quarters, like tight clinches. This attack can be directed at your opponent's sides, specifically their hips, thighs, and ribs. Although this knee technique won't do as much damage to your opponent as others, it can be quite effective at slowing them down and depleting their energy.

Here are a few tips to help you get the better of your opponent using this technique:

- As you bend your knee into the object of attack, twist your hips.
- Move to the opposite side or gently slant your opponent's body.
- Ensure you have a firm footing when locked in the clinch position.
- Step back a bit before releasing your knee to your opponent's side.

Horizontal Knee Technique (Khao Tat)

Khao Tat can be used offensively and defensively.

The horizontal knee technique is a common move among fighters, offensively and defensively. This knee technique can occasionally be a life-saver because it's quite simple to perform with the proper technique. Some fighters transition into a horizontal knee guard once they establish a connection with their opponent.

The horizontal knee is effective when launched from the back and the leading leg. The switch adds to this knee strike's diversity, especially in the clinch, as it can catch an opponent by surprise. Work hard on your balance and learn to establish an advantage over your opponent in the clinch while practicing this strike because, if not done correctly, you risk being swept off your standing leg.

Follow these tips when performing the Khao tat;

- Moving the striking leg upward parallel to the floor.
- Launch yourself forward, bending your shin into the object of your attack.
- Generate power by rotating and turning on the standing leg.

Diagonal Knee Techniques (Khao Chiang)

The diagonal knee is a second short-range strike that works inside and outside the clinch. It is targeted at your opponent's sides, especially the ribs. Its dynamics make it challenging to predict and, if executed well, could be a show-stopper. While coming from an open clinch to deliver the diagonal knee, do this:

- On your front foot, take a slight step back.
- Simultaneously move your striking leg forward.
- Flex your leg just enough so that the portion of your leg from the knee down is pointed at an upward 45-degree angle at the point of contact.

Khao Chiang is a short-range strike.

Flying Knee Technique (Khao Loi)

Although this technique is far from what a beginner should concentrate on, it's okay to have an overview of how it works. To land this strike, you must have considerable technical skills and develop balance and posture. Still, you can do it with enough practice and commitment.

One of the hardest techniques to accomplish against an opponent in Muay Thai is to conceal a flying knee. This strike is quite effective when an opponent is unprepared. You might have witnessed some spectacular flying strike knockouts in MMA. Still, your chances of executing this technique in Muay Thai will most likely be restricted because fighters deliver this knee as a surprise attack against an opponent's attempt to take them down. Nevertheless, here is how to land a flying knee:

Khao Loi is a more advanced technique

1. Ensure your opponent is in your line of sight.
2. While delivering the knee, fire upward, slightly bending your knees before driving up.
3. Twist the lead hip backward, then the opposite.
4. As you reach the top of your jump, extend your knee.
5. Lastly, protect your chin from counterattacks.

Small Knee Technique (Khao Noi)

In the clinch, the little knee is a powerful strike that can be executed. You can reduce your opponent's ability to move by delivering quick, little knees to their thighs. These can stop the opponent's momentum and lessen the force of their kicks and knees. An opponent with the advantage in the clinch might be persuaded to break off by the little knee strike, giving you time to change things up.

Khao Noican reduces your opponent's attacks.

Long Knee Technique (Khao Yao)

Khao Yao is effective from a long distance.

The long knee is the most effective strike from a great distance instead of a short range. It can potentially be an eye-catching spectacle because of the increase in impact with momentum. Your opponent might be unable to counter or defend against your attack, even if they anticipate the strike. Some ideas for the long knee include:

- Step out slightly rather than directly into your opponent
- Lift while twisting from your front foot and pressing your knee into the target
- Be certain your knee connects solidly with your opponent's body
- Pick up the pace when practicing this knee technique since throwing it is easier than drilling it slowly

Mistakes Made When Striking with the Knee

Following are some mistakes beginner fighters make while executing knee techniques.

Straightening Knee: While implementing the knee strike, you must understand that you're not trying to skim a person's body but to destabilize your opponent. Most beginners frequently thrust their knees straight up as if touching their adversary. Remember, you must penetrate through your opponent with your knee attack.

Although it is moving upward, you must attack your opponent's torso while aiming to breach your knees into them. Consider yourself at an angle, attempting to grab your opponent's ribs. In this situation, your kneecap should strike the opponent in the ribcage.

Failure to Achieve Fluid Motion: You must use your knee's strength, distance, and power to the full extent possible to perform a knee strike. You can only create a smooth motion when you mix these three components. Although extending the hips can be challenging for beginners, it is possible with regular practice.

Knee Not Bent: Not bending the knee is a fairly common error by novices. The strike's impact is diminished if the knee isn't bent since it isn't sufficiently solidified. If you do it incorrectly, you also risk suffering a major injury.

Dropping Hands Low: Most beginners make the mistake of positioning one hand low to prepare for a jab after a strike. It's not an excellent habit; you should avoid it whenever possible. Instead, lift both hands at once, defending your jaw from attack.

Launching Lunging from Afar: Beginners believe they can catch their opponent from a distance, like with a training bag. However, they soon discover their reach falls short as it exceeds the one they rehearsed with a bag. As a result, if you attempt to land the knee from the same distance during a fight, you'll fall short.

How to Strengthen and Condition the Knee for Strong Attacks

Although it takes time to build knee strength, you can hasten the process by learning the correct methods and exercises. Here are some guidelines to assist you in pulling it off.

Conditioning

No matter how skilled or gifted you are, it would all amount to nothing if you were not in shape. Sometimes you might be fortunate, but it will not be for long. You must ensure you are in the best condition to have strong knees. Every time you fight, you should be in top physical condition because you can bet your opponent will be.

A battery-operated torch comes to mind when discussing conditioning. When the batteries are juiced up, it becomes brighter; this applies to all fighters equally. Training is essential. Your legs, which you rely on for movement and striking in Muay Thai, will give out if they grow weary. As a beginner fighter, you must be in excellent shape since you depend on your legs. Here's how to improve your conditioning;

- Go for a 10-kilometer long-distance run five or more days a week.
- Do a series of sprints, like five rounds of 100m sprints in a row
- Go for mountain runs
- Do regular stretches and pushups
- Run up or take the stairs regularly.

The Right Team Coach and Coach

You will invariably improve your knee strikes with the correct coach and team. Before taking control of those knees, you must put much effort into your technique. Lifting weights or briefly carrying heavy objects over your head is not equivalent to producing energy in knee strikes.

Your technique must be perfected to produce the most power possible. Every part of a strike can be taken apart by a knowledgeable coach who will concentrate on how you stand, set up, execute, and deliver—practicing with fighters who will share a few suggestions here and there, is also essential.

Drills

Before adding power to your knee strike, you must first comprehend how crucial your stance, hips, feet, legs, and knees are for a great stroke. Each technique, the curved, straight, horizontal, or diagonal knee, must be practiced to develop power. In developing considerable power, the strike's fundamentals should be intuitive.

During the various training sessions, you must practice knee drills. Pick the knee strike you want to master, then spend as much time honing and repeating the drills required. Hitting your knees in sparring, on the bag, the pads, and during shadow boxing will help you develop your balance, positions, penetration, and timing. Your knee's strength can be increased by strengthening its vital parts. You will experience a change in the force you use to enforce the strike, albeit it might take a few weeks. You can get where you're going faster than you think if you pay careful attention to detail and focus appropriately.

How to Best Block a Knee When Fighting

If not correctly countered, Muay Thai knees can fracture the ribs. The following tips will help you defend against your opponent's knees, whether in or out of the clinch.

Extending your arm (jabbing) to your opponent's chest will block your opponent's knee if they are not in the clinch. Your arm should extend farther than your opponent's knee if you lean slightly into it. You should strike the chin as opposed to the chest.

When your opponent raises their leg to throw the knee while you are still engaged in the clinch, you can attempt to knock them off balance. Turn them in the direction of their standing leg. If they throw their right knee, you can turn to the right.

If the opponent shifts their weight beyond their standing leg, you can throw them or respond with your (right knee) knee. It takes some work to master this move because it is difficult to see your opponent's leg when engaged in the clinch. You must practice detecting it by observing how their weight changes.

The best offense is the best defense in Muay Thai. Therefore, as a Muay Thai fighter, it is essential to have effective techniques, understand how to produce power for your techniques, prevent common mistakes, and block your opponent's tactics. As a beginner, you should devote the same amount of effort to learning and practicing these knee techniques since they can truly be handy in emergencies. The best option for mastering the knee technique is a good training partner. You can strengthen each other's defenses and weaknesses, positioning yourself to be the best.

Chapter 6: Te: Kicking Techniques

Strong kicks are a significant part of Muay Thai. Being proficient in various kicking techniques allows you to develop powerful attacks, and they can also be very useful for defense. They help you keep your distance from the opponent, making it harder for them to reach you while still landing powerful blows to all areas of their body. Moreover, if you want to strike the opponent's legs, the most effective approach is to use good kicks.

Here are some of the most useful kicking techniques you should be well versed in and additional information to help you maximize your kicking techniques.

Top Kicking Techniques

These kicking techniques can be used on their own or combined. Depending on the situation and the attack you want to formulate, you can combine two kicks or pair some punches and upper-body moves with these kicks.

1. **Spinning Round Kick – Tae Klap Lang**

Tae Klap Lang is a powerful kick.

This kick is one of the most powerful kicks you can master. When used correctly, it can easily knock out your opponents; if used carelessly, it can be fatal. This kick is primarily used as a defensive strategy, but with the right combinations and setup, it can be part of your offensive strategy.

You will use your rear leg for this kick, creating a spinning motion. Your back faces the opponent, then spin your attacking leg around your body to create momentum. The target is the opponent's upper body, neck, and face.

It is the spinning motion that generates the momentum and what makes round kicks so deadly. For this kick, you should train your legs for flexibility and dexterity and work on hip mobility.

2. Jumping Push Kick – Kradot Teep

Kradot Teep will help you gain an advantage

If you don't have room to spin to create extra force in your kick or want to create more force in a kick while approaching an opponent, the jumping push kick will come in handy.

This kick is like the straight kick, except you use your rear leg to jump off the floor and create more momentum. A popular technique is to lead your opponent with your kicking leg, putting it straight up like you would with a straight kick but then jumping off your rear leg in the middle of the kick to generate extra force.

This kick is great for the upper body and face area. If you are going for the regular straight kick, it only takes a moment to transform it into the jumping push kick.

3. Straight Front Kick – Tae Trong

Tae Trong is similar to the Mae Geri Karate technique.

The straight front kick is commonly used in Karate. In Japanese, it is called *Mae Geri*.

With this kick, you use your toes or the upper part of your foot to attack the opponent instead of the sole of your foot. It is a simple forward kick aimed at the chin or the sides of the face.

4. Downward Roundhouse Kick – Tae Kod

Tae Kod is known as the Brazilian Kick.[32]

This kick is known as the question mark kick or the Brazilian kick. Again, due to the spinning motion required in the roundhouse movement, this kick generates a lot of momentum and can be devastating when used correctly.

The main difference from a traditional roundhouse kick is that your kicking leg has to be picked up higher in the downward roundhouse kick. Essentially, you must position your leg above your target, then angle your leg down onto the target to complete the move. It can be particularly challenging if your opponent is taller than you. Also, you must have excellent hip flexibility for this move as you spin around and push your leg upward.

This is an excellent kick as you nullify the opponent's guard and attack the head, neck, and shoulder area from above rather than from the front, where you would have to penetrate the guard.

5. Diagonal Kick – Tae Chiang

Tae Chiang is a quick kick.

This is a very quick kick using the shin to strike the opponent's body, specifically the ribs. This kick is perfect for close-quarter situations and can be a very painful blow when done right.

Typically, the attacker's leg has a 45-degree angle from the floor and is pushed straight into the opponent's sides.

Tae Khao targets the face, neck, and shoulders

The Muay Thai axe kick is similar to the downward roundhouse kick but without the spinning movement to create momentum. This kick targets the face, neck, and shoulders.

From a standing position, the attacker launches a straight kick slightly above the target area, then drives the heel of the foot down onto the target area. Similar to an axe coming down on its target.

While this is a powerful kick, it opens the attacker to a quick counterattack, so fighters rarely use it.

7. Slapping Foot Thrust – Teep Top

Teep Top is helpful for defense.

In this kick, the knee of the striking leg is bent, and the top of the foot or the entire foot is used to "slap" the opponent. Depending on how high you take your striking leg and whether you twist during this kick, it can be a straight kick to the abdomen, a slap to the ribs, or even a slap to the head.

This kick is a great move in a defensive situation. It helps keep the attacker off you and also unbalance the opponent. However, not much power can be generated from this kick.

8. Straight Foot Jab – Teep Trong

Teep Trong is usually aimed at the abdomen.

This quick, sharp, straight kick can be considered the leg version of a straight jab. For this move, you will lean back slightly and "punch" out in a straight line with your kicking leg. This kick is typically aimed at the abdomen and chest but can also be aimed at the head.

It is a great move for controlling the opponent's distance away from you. It can be used very effectively to push the opponent or unbalance them as they approach an attack. It can also be a good kick to unbalance your opponent before you launch your attack. These are considered blocking or "checking" kicks.

9. Muay Thai Side Kick – Te Tad

Te Tad is slightly different than a normal sidekick.

The sidekick in Muay Thai is slightly different than in other disciplines, such as Taekwondo and Karate. In Muay Thai, there is no chambering of the kicking leg. Rather, the fighter steps in with the standing leg to create momentum and then shoots out the kicking leg from the side of the hip. The aim is to hit the target with the sole of the foot, the side of the sole, or even the heel if the kick is aimed slightly higher at the chin or nose.

In other disciplines, chambering of the leg (pulling the knee into the chest) is used to generate power. However, this slows down the movement and opens the fighter to a counterattack.

10. Muay Thai Roundhouse Kick-Te Tat

The Muay Thai roundhouse kick is the most recognizable in this fighting form. It is also the one kick that differentiates a Muay Thai fighter from other martial artists.

This kick involves striking the shin against the opponent. This kick can be delivered to the opponent's legs, abdomen, head, or arms. It can be delivered from a standing position, or a spin can be incorporated into the move to generate even more power.

When done correctly, it is an extremely powerful and dangerous move. It can cause serious damage and even break tough bones, such as the opponent's shin or thigh bone.

Te Tat differentiates Muay Thai from other martial arts.

Tips for the Roundhouse Kicks

The roundhouse kick is a very flexible and versatile kick to use in nearly any situation or purpose. Knowing how to execute this kick with the utmost precision will help you in countless situations.

Best Posture for Roundhouse Kicks

Before you launch your roundhouse kick, ensure you are in the right position. Firstly, your feet must be shoulder-width apart, with the bulk of your weight on the balls of your feet. You cannot drive power or accuracy into the kick if you aren't balanced when kicking.

The next most important thing to consider is your distance from the target. A good way to check is to throw a quick jab. If you can comfortably land a jab, you are at the right distance since the shin kick or knee kicks will be slightly longer range.

Lastly, you must have the right posture when launching the kick and throughout the movement. If you want to deliver a powerful kick, you must be balanced. Also, consider what the opponent can do in response to the kick; you should be positioned to handle any response.

You must focus on a few things to achieve a successful roundhouse kick. First, keep your weight on the ball of your foot when launching the kick and stay on the ball of your foot throughout the rotation. Ideally, you should spring up from the heel of your foot to the ball of your foot when you step in and launch the kick. This shift drives more power into the kick.

Also, ensure the foot of your pivoting leg is pointed out at a 45-degree angle when kicking. This will do two things; 1. You will have proper balance in the kick and, therefore, more power. 2. You will not be in the centerline of the kick so that you can negotiate a response from the opponent. Also, having your foot out at an angle decreases the distance your leg has to move, increasing the kick's perceived speed and power.

An open hip is an essential component of the roundhouse kick. It allows you to load the kick more effectively, gives better balance, facilitates better energy transfer, and drives momentum from your entire body into the kick. Moreover, it helps with stabilization after the kick, helping you spin back into position faster.

Common Mistakes

As discussed in the "best posture" section, the hip is crucial in the roundhouse kick and is often the one area where people make a mistake. Making this one mistake can lead to numerous problems. Ensuring your hip is open and your feet are in the right position will solve this issue.

Another issue is kicking with the foot; this is very common for people new to Muay Thai. Hitting something with your shin can hurt quite a bit, so it's important to condition your shins. However, during kicking training, you must focus on hitting the target with the center of your shin, where you have the most momentum.

Returning from the kick is another problem. Your leg must come back down to the ground just as fast as it went up with the roundhouse kick. Being slow in this part of the kick will put you in a vulnerable position where you can easily be taken down.

Another issue is timing the kick and having good defense during the kick. Even though it is powerful, the roundhouse kicks must be timed properly for the best results. You don't want to be caught by the opponent or be countered to the point where you are in trouble! Throwing a few punches or checking kicks, double-checking that you are off to one side of the opponent, and having good positioning with your arms to protect your chin will make a massive difference in how securely you land the roundhouse kick without being an easy target for the opponent.

Leg Conditioning

You need strong legs and shins to get proficient in the roundhouse kicks. You can do a few things for this:

The first is the heavy bag. Ideally, do 200 kicks on each leg on the heavy bag three times a week. It doesn't have to be very hard; even a soft bag will do. The idea is to deaden the nerves on the shin. Over time, as the nerves become less responsive to the kicks, they will stop hurting as much since they are no longer sending pain signals to your brain.

Next, do plenty of box jumps and squat jumps to help strengthen the tibia and fibula. Doing 5 sets of 15 of these exercises 2 or 3 times a week will condition your shin bones and prepare them for the heavy stress they face in the ring.

Lastly, you must do plenty of sparring with the shin pads on. Even with shin pads, heavy sparring has a massive impact on your shins. It will work wonders for strengthening and seasoning them to withstand high impact.

Blocking Kicks

To block a roundhouse kick, lift your shin and block in a shin-on-shin fashion. Lift your knee to a roughly 90-degree angle between your shin and thigh. Of course, if you block a kick to the midsection, your knee will be higher up. You can use your shin to block blows to the shins, thighs, and abdomen. You must use your arms for defense against anything coming to your chest or head.

The roundhouse kick is a fantastic kick to use in many situations. However, to make the most of it, you must know how to perform it correctly, avoid common mistakes, and have legs that are properly conditioned for this skill. Good leg training will help you land excellent kicks and give you protection for defending yourself from roundhouse kicks.

Chapter 7: Teep: Foot Techniques

Foot sweeps are important in Muay Thai. Whether sparring or competing at the highest level, having several different foot kicks and foot sweeps at your disposal will put you in a better position in combat.

While the sweep is simple, it can be applied in many ways to unbalance your opponent, disarm them from an attack, or set them up for your attack. Like many other things in Muay Thai, excellent foot technique is about speed and timing. Here is everything to know about the different foot techniques in Muay Thai.

Muay Thai Foot Kicks

Muay Thai foot kicks are important in a fight. They deflect oncoming attacks, unbalance the opponent, and also block or check kicks. These kicks are primarily targeted at the opponent's abdomen, chest, or face. Still, they can also be used on the legs and to defend against kicks. In these quick kicks, the toes, heel, or sole can be used to attack the opponent. These are also called "foot slaps" since they are less powerful than a straight kick or well-positioned punch. However, with speed and accuracy, you can use them to great effect.

There are two main forms of foot kicks, listed below.

1. Straight or Forward Foot Kick (Teep Trong)

From a standing position, the fighter lifts his knee and kicks out forward with his shin to land his foot on the opponent. Typically, this is used for attacking above the waistline. It is an excellent attack at the opponent's abdomen, chest, or face but must be executed quickly. The kick back to the body must be just as fast as the kick out to the opponent. Good hip mobility will also be required to use the teep trong for the face.

2. Sideways Foot Kick (Teep Khang)

Teep Khang is used similarly to when a straight kick is used.

199

This kick is used in the same fashion as the straight kick. The difference is that the fighter is on their side when launching the attack. This way, the fighter's side faces his opponent, the hips are turned to the side and dipped down, facing the floor, and the side of the sole lands on the opponent. Since this move involves rotating the hips, it has a bit more force since momentum from the upper body is transferred into the kick. This kick is slightly more challenging as it requires better hip mobility and balance to be carried out properly. Foot position, hip rotation, and even how the upper body is positioned will influence how well one can balance in a teep khang.

Standing Foot Sweeps

Sweeps are used extensively in Muay Thai and can benefit the fighter. Several versions of sweeps can be employed, depending on the situation. This section covers some of the most basic but also most versatile sweeps you should master.

1. Catch and Sweep

The catch and sweep is a great response to kicks.

The catch and sweep is a great technique used to amazing effect in response to kicks. It is one of those things most opponents will not expect. Usually, a checking kick is used to block kicks. The sweep will block the kick and make it less likely for the opponent to use that kick again since they know it will be viciously countered.

For this sweep, catch the sidekick or roundhouse kick with your arms, nearly hugging the leg as you catch it to minimize impact. Next, lift the opponent's leg slightly and switch your steps. This will unbalance the opponent and make sweeping them off their feet easier. As your opponent tries to hop to regain balance, you can very easily sweep them down to the canvas with a kick to the calf of their pivoting leg.

2. Roundhouse Sweep

A

B

The roundhouse sweep can allow you so exploit your opponent.

This sweep exploits the tendency of most fighters to respond to a kick with a kick. If you throw a roundhouse kick to your opponent, you can be nearly certain they will throw one back.

For this sweep, throw a roundhouse kick to the body to see how your opponent reacts. If you get a kickback from them, throw another one to prime them for the sweep. These initial kicks are to prep the opponent. Putting too much force into them is unnecessary as you risk being caught and countered.

Before the opponent can reply with their second kick, use your rear leg, targeting the ankle area on the opponent's rear leg to kick them off balance while their lead leg is in the air for an attack. Ideally, you want to land your sweep blow while the opponent's attack leg is in the air. This way, you can ensure their weight is on their leg, and the sweep will be effective. Depending on your opponent's height and reach, this might require you to take a small step forward.

3. Rear Sweep

This is a great sweep and quite painful for the opponent since they land completely flat on their body when all their weight is involved. This sweep is best done after a few punches or kicks to be sure your opponent is putting the bulk of their weight on the rear leg.

As you kick the right side of the opponent's body, they will put up their right leg to defend. On the second or third kick, throw a feint kick to the right and move in with your rear leg to sweep the leg they are standing on. For an even better effect, use your opposite hand to move their leg out of the way to get closer and push them back on their pivoting leg so all their weight is on the leg you are about to sweep.

The rear sweep can be painful for your opponent.

---

4. Teep Counter Sweep

The teep counter sweep is a valuable skill

One of the most common attacks you will encounter is the forward teep. Knowing how to counter this attack with a quick and effective sweep is a valuable skill.

The objective is to catch the opponent's leg during a teep, pull them towards you, take out their pivoting leg, and push them down as they fall for greater impact against the canvas.

Ideally, catch their leg in a vice grip cupping the back of their ankle with one hand. Then, jerk them toward you to unbalance them and bring their pivoting leg into range. Next, kick their pivoting leg in the ankle area to execute the sweep and finish with a strong push to the chest or shoulders to speed up the fall and increase impact against the canvas.

5. Low Kick Feint to Sweep

The low kick feint to sweep can help you brock your opponent's attacks.

The objective is to sweep under your opponent's rear thigh to get them on the canvas. Again, you must set up your opponent with a few low kicks or kicks to the ribs to get them in the right position to execute your sweep.

Move in close to your opponent as they lift their leg to defend against what looks like a kick. As their leg is up in the air and all their weight is on the pivoting leg, throw a hard kick to the inner side of their rear thigh to get them to land flat on the floor. Having your hand out in front of you with your chin secured behind your shoulder is also a good approach so you are ready to block any oncoming counters.

If you want to increase the impact, push the opponent as they begin to fall to increase the speed of the fall.

Benefits of Foot Sweeps

Sweeps are commonly used in many martial arts. Each martial art has certain sweeps unique to that particular martial art. Also, many sweeps might be allowed in one martial art but not in other martial arts in a competitive setting.

Having multiple sweeps at your disposal as a Muay Thai athlete would be a good idea. Here are some of the main benefits a sweep provides:

Strike Setup

Sweeps are an excellent way to unbalance your opponent. When learning to sweep, there will be many instances where you don't do a clean sweep, but even then, you will have displaced your opponent. This moment of instability is all you need to launch a full attack and possibly end the match.

If you are using Muay Thai as part of your MMA training, where ground and pound are permitted, then sweeps are a useful technique to get the opponent on the floor. Moreover, when an opponent lands hard on the floor in a sweep, it is tough for them to stabilize and be prepared for the groundwork required to fight on the ground. In both cases, you benefit from the sweep.

Match Pace

A player's rhythm is significant in their match performance, especially if the player can synchronize their moves with footwork and a natural fighting rhythm. You can use the sweeps to disrupt this rhythm effectively. When you sweep an opponent, it takes them a moment to get back up and restart their rhythm. Doing this enough times and with enough force during a match can be devastating for the opponents' rhythm. A lack of rhythm leads to bad timing, causing poor impact and making it harder for them to dodge and defend your attacks.

Sweeps have much more impact than just a plain kick or punch to the body. If you want to tire your opponent, break their confidence, and hurt their body, then sweeps will be more effective than quick kicks and jabs. Moreover, when you add a hard push to a sweep, it is even more dangerous.

Space

Regardless of how seasoned you are, going head-to-head with a strong opponent can be tiring. Sweeps are a great way to earn you a few moments to take a few deep breaths and refresh yourself. If your opponent is constantly on you, it makes it hard to breathe and focus; sweeps will earn you some space to gather yourself. If you're ever in a tight situation, throwing a sweep will help give you some clarity.

Dominance

The mind game, especially your frame of mind, plays a major role in your fight performance. Sweeps are one of those moves that give you confidence while demotivating your opponent. It gives you a moment to think; when you are more confident, you can formulate better plans.

Standing tall above your opponent after a sweep influences your psychology directly and subconsciously. If you feel you cannot land anything on your opponent but then successfully break out a sweep, it can drastically change the situation. Moreover, being on the mat flat on your back in competition chips away at a player's confidence. Falling down and getting back up tires out a fighter – another added benefit of sweeps.

Points

It's not always about hurting your opponent. In a competition setting, the objective is to score points, and sweeps can earn valuable points with the judges. It also shows the judges that you control the situation and have excellent spatial awareness.

Sweeps can stop your opponent from scoring too many easy points with small, quick moves. If you feel a round is getting out of your control, throwing a sweep will help level things for the next few seconds.

Illegal Sweeps

Knowing the illegal sweeps, especially for players coming from other martial arts, is important. Players coming from Taekwondo, Jiu-Jitsu, and Judo have the most problems in this regard. Common sweeps in those sports, such as Ouchi Gari and Ostoro Gari, are illegal in Muay Thai. *All sweeps involving picking up the opponent from the waist or using a limb are also illegal in Muay Thai.*

Knowing sweeps is crucial, but it takes time and practice to perfect the art of implementing a good sweep at the right moment to turn the tables. It takes a lot of practice to anticipate moves and engineer the appropriate sweep for the situation. Further sections explore how to pair sweeps with other moves to create combinations to overcome your opponent.

Chapter 8: Chap Kho: Clinching and Neck Wrestling Techniques

Perhaps the most iconic aspect of Muay Thai, besides the Mangkon, is the clinching and neck wrestling moves fighters use. In Western-style boxing and even some martial arts forms, clinching is not allowed. If two fighters get in a clinch, they are instantly broken up, or the fight is paused. Fighters in other combat sports, especially Western-style boxing, use clinching to defend themselves from oncoming attacks and to get a little break during the fight.

In Muay Thai, clinching is an essential part of the fight. It is one of the most intense and dangerous situations a fighter can be in. With the right skills and approach to clinching, it can be a game-changing skill for a fighter who knows what to do in a game. Fighters who favor the Muay Plam technique are all about clinching, just as Muay Sok is all about elbows; Muay Thai is about kicks. If you want to specialize in Muay Plam, or you merely want to improve your clinching game, this chapter covers everything to know.

Most Common Clinching Techniques

Different clenching techniques can be used to set up your opponent, defend, sweep, kick, knee, or other objectives. Some of the most commonly used and versatile techniques are the following:

1. Double Collar Tie

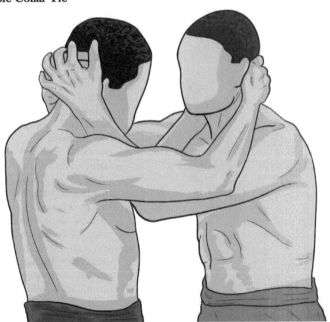

The double collar tie is a common clinching technique.

This technique is one of the most common clinching techniques in Muay Thai. It has been used by many of the best in the sport to amazing effect, including the highly decorated Petchboonchu. This technique is a favorite of knee-style fighters as it allows excellent control over opponents and opens their heads and abdomens to knee attacks.

There are two versions of the double collar tie; around the head or the neck.

If your objective is getting to the head, start by getting your hand through their guard and around the back of their head. Then, take the second hand and follow a similar path so you have both hands behind the opponent's head. From this position, it is very easy to bring the head downward for a blow with the elbow or knee. Also, maneuvering the body is far easier once you have good control of the head. You can easily set up the opponent's body for knee shots to the sternum and abs. In this grip, it's easier to spin the opponent around and move their body if you want to set them up for other attacks.

The other option is to grab the opponent's neck. For this, get your hands around the back of their neck and use a gable grip to clasp your hands together. This particular grip gives you excellent control, making it harder for the opponent to break your grip and allowing you to squeeze their neck. With this grip, it can be quite painful when you close your forearms into the sides of their neck, making this grip effective. You won't have as much control over their body from this position, but it is still an effective clinch in many situations. This will be particularly useful for opponents a bit taller than yourself. Reaching for their head will expose your abdomen, which can be extremely risky. However, by grabbing their neck, you are protecting yourself while also bringing yourself into striking range of the opponent.

2. Single Collar Tie

The single-collar tie is more commonly practiced.

The double-collar tie can certainly lead your opponent into a lot of damage. However, it is relatively easy to defend against and not that difficult to break once you understand how to counter it. The single-collar tie is a more commonly practiced clinch for these reasons.

This technique involves having one hand around the opponent's neck while the other hand is wrapped tightly against the opponent's bicep on the opposite side. With your right hand around the opponent's neck, your left hand should firmly grasp the opponent's right bicep. This way, you have good control over their entire body since there are two places where you can move their weight and unbalance them. Moreover, this clinch is more challenging to break, and while you can't hit the head easily from this position, you still have plenty of opportunity to knee their abdomen and chest and throw them around.

In this position, you can use your left hand (the one on the bicep) to land heavy uppercuts and hooks to the opponent's face. As you gain more experience in this position, you will learn to throw hard elbows using your right hand to the opponent's face and chest.

3. Over-Under Clinch Position

The over-under clinch position is very common in Muay Thai.

The over-under clinch is one of the most common clinch positions in Muay Thai. It is versatile and can be used effectively if you understand how it works.

In this position, you will have one arm coming over your opponent's arm with your hand on their neck while your other arm snakes under their opposite arm. Depending on your reach length, both hands could be on the opponent's neck, or one will reach their shoulder or bicep. In either case, with a good grip, you can do plenty of maneuvers from this position.

You can use your upper arm to pull your opponent down and your lower arm to push them up. If you have a longer reach, you can reach around your opponent and clasp your hands together in a tight hug to gain more control of the situation.

In this clinch, you can use your knees effectively into the opponent's sides or abdomen and are in a good position to deflect oncoming knee attacks. It is easy to push and pull the opponents to unbalance them and even sweep them down onto the mat. However, due to the close range, being proficient in defense in this position takes a lot of practice and fight awareness.

4. Double Underhooks

The double underhook is a common clinch in combat sports.

This is a common clinch in Western wrestling, MMA, Judo, and other combat sports involving ground fighting. In Muay Thai, ground fighting is close to non-existent. However, this clinch can still be used effectively for unbalancing the opponent and gaining control of the situation. Moreover, its close proximity also protects you and acts as a form of defense from knees, albeit your sides will still be exposed, so be ready to react. If you want to carry out sweeps, this is also a great clinch to use for this purpose. This grip gives a good stance to generate power and enough reach to sweep your opponent even when both their feet are on the mat.

To get into this clinch, scoop your hands under the opponent's arms and reach around to their back. Your arms should go down under their arms, through the bottom of their shoulders, and around their back. You can clasp your hands behind their back if you can reach that far. Simultaneously, move your hips forward to nearly touch the opponent's. The closer your hips are to the opponent, the more control you will have since your body weight is significant rather than only your upper body strength.

The tricky thing about this clinch is getting too carried away with shoving your opponent and shuffling around on your feet. Moving too much will move your center off balance, and your opponent can easily use this to their advantage. The objective is to counter the opponent's moves with opposite moves while moving your body weight in the opposite direction.

Once you have mastered the basics, you can use this clinch to bump, lift, and swivel your opponent. For this, your hands must be lower down on their back, around the base of their ribs, from where you can get a tighter lock around them and then pick them up, bump into them, swivel them around, and throw them onto the floor. Managing your opponents' weight from this position makes it easier to sweep in many ways.

Common Mistakes in Clinching

Developing good clinch technique is one part of the clinching game. You must perfect many other aspects of clinching to dominate this style and phase of the fight. Here are some common issues to consider:

Stance – Many fighters walk into the clinch with their regular fight stance; this leads to a weak clinch and exposes you to several attack possibilities. The clinch stance is distinctly different from your regular fight stance. Ensure you don't mix the two and make the change at the right time. How smoothly you can transition into the clinch stance will play a big role in how effective you are in the clinch.

Knee Impact – Getting into the clinch is one thing, but making the most of the clinch boils down to how effectively you can knee your opponent. Initially, your knees will not have much impact, leaving the opponent thinking you are just tapping them with your knees. While you might feel you are driving a lot of force into the knees. It takes practice to deliver a painful knee to the abdomen.

This technique requires much practice on the heavy bag. Practice driving the point of your knee into the opponent. When kneeing the sides, ensure you drive the hard knee bone into the opponent, not just push your knee against their side. With low knee impact, your clinch technique is of little use.

Open Neck – The clinch is all about getting the neck or the head. Many fighters leave their neck completely exposed when going into the clinch, giving their opponent easy access and, consequently, easy access to controlling the clinch. Ensure your defense is up when going into the clinch, making it as hard as possible for your neck or head to be given away. Fight back and resist if you sense that your opponent is going for the neck. You can always break free and go in again, so you get to their neck first.

Wrestle - The clinch is difficult to negotiate, especially when fighting a taller or stronger opponent. However, the objective of the clinch is not to overpower your opponent through your wrestling skills; it is a place to show what you can do with your knees and possibly your elbows and fists. Use the close-quarter situation to inflict damage, not to move your opponent around.

Transition Defense - Fighters will have good defensive posture, but as soon as it is time to clinch, their arms drop, or their head comes up to get into the clinch. This gives the opponent easy access to your body, and a blow from that close can easily be a knockout. You must maintain good defensive posture until the last moment you are about to grab the opponent.

Optimizing the Clinch

Here are a few tips to help you take your clinch game to the next level:

Damage Posture - Once you have your opponent in a clinch, keep them in a forward posture as long as you can. The only way for them to defend against their knees is to regain their upright posture, and the longer you can prevent them from doing so, the longer you can maintain control of the situation and land your blows.

Protect Your Neck - As long as you don't give your head or neck to your opponent, you control the clinch. The harder you make it for them to grab onto you in the clinch, the lower your chances of getting hit or thrown around.

Flexibility - There are multiple ways to attack while in the clinch. If you can't get your knees in, try elbows, punches, throwing your opponent, or anything else that works. Stay aware of the situation and be flexible to different attack options, depending on the circumstances. Land anything you can, as long as it is accurate.

The clinch is something most fighters prefer not to get involved in. However, if you can master the basics of the clinch and understand how to negotiate the situation, you can use it to your advantage. Especially if you are caught up with someone who isn't very good in the clinch, this can be your opportunity to pull the match in your favor.

Chapter 9: Combination Techniques

Muay Thai is a fast-paced sport with room for hard-hitting blows and intricate combinations that will leave the opponent stumbling. As a Muay Thai fighter, you must develop competence in both aspects of the fight. You need laser-sharp accuracy in your kicks, punches, and elbows, and you want them to land hard.

Muay Thai is a fast-paced sport. [33]

You also want to use these in different combinations to gain the upper hand in a match. This chapter looks at some of the best combinations to ensure a win.

Combinations

When using combinations, gauging distance before launching the combination and keeping track of where you are during the combination is vital. Sometimes, you might need to step forward during the combination, like throwing the combination while walking into the opponent. In other cases, it could be the opposite.

Also, be aware of how the opponent responds to the combination. It will not always be possible to land the entire combination, and in some cases, you must have room to add more moves to the combinations.

1. Fake Push Kick – Left Hook – Right Low Kick

1. First, fake a push kick to set up the opponent for this attack. This will give you the space and show you what to expect in the opponent's response to a push kick.

2. Nine out of 10 times, the opponent will raise a leg to defend against the oncoming kick. Here you want to take them by surprise and throw your left hook.

3. After the hook has connected, follow through with a strong kick to the opponent's lead leg or abdomen, depending on what is more easily accessible considering their defense and reaction.

4. If you manage to land all three, it will definitely have your opponent seeing stars. However, the key to this attack is deception. This combination will be

more challenging against fighters familiar with your particular deception style and also with players who pick up deception quickly.

2. Jab – Overhand Right – Liver Kick

1. For this combination, start with a quick jab using your lead hand. This serves two functions. One is to get your opponent facing the direction of the jab. The other is to open them up for the rest of the attack.
2. Follow up the jab with a punch using your rear hand. It will be the punch that really has an impact, as you have a full range of motion to deliver this second punch.
3. In quick succession, deliver your kick (from the leg opposite the punching arm) to their midsection, ideally the liver. When you hit with your second punch, the opponent will raise their hands to defend, giving your kick access to the liver. However, you must be quick to make the most of this opportunity.
4. This combination incorporates hits to the upper and lower body making it hard to defend against, confusing, and also quite painful when done right.

3. Left Knee – Right Elbow – Left Hook

1. This combination starts with the left knee. To make this more effective, you can feint the opponent with a right leg kick to open them up and then step forward to get your left knee into their midsection.
2. Bring your left knee back down as soon as possible and shift your weight to the right, from where you throw your right elbow. You should aim for the temple, nose, jaw, or collarbone with your elbow.
3. Again, switch your weight to the opposite side, and while your opponent has their hands defending the right side, you come in with a swinging left hook.
4. This combination is about attacking from opposite sides with speed, not giving your opponent enough time to set up the necessary defenses. You will need good accuracy in your shots and excellent balance to carry this out properly.
5. If your opponent cannot handle this attack, continue with another elbow from the right and then back to the left knee to restart the loop.

4. Push Kick – Hook – Cross

1. Start with a push kick (teep) to get your opponent a step or two away from you and off balance. The added distance will help you take a step forward, adding momentum to the punch and allowing you to take a full swing.
2. Come in with a strong hook to the side of the head. Ideally, you want to target the temple, but anything on the side of the head will do.
3. Immediately after the hook, center your weight and come straight through the guard with a cross to the nose or chin.
4. For maximum effect, you must be lightning-quick after the teep to capitalize on the imbalance created by the push-kick.

5. Jab – Cross – High Kick

1. Start the attack with a jab. This will inflict some damage, but more importantly, it will distract the opponent.
2. Immediately, come through with a strong cross from the opposite end. Here you must make as much impact as possible.
3. Next, launch the high kick to the face, neck, or collarbone area. Generally, a straight kick will be the quickest option, but if you are exceptionally fast, you could squeeze in a roundhouse kick. In either case, the element of surprise is the highlight of this combination.

6. Jab – Cross – Left Hook – Right Knee

1. Start with a quick jab to see how your opponent reacts and to create some room in the center for your next move.

2. In nearly the same movement as the first jab, release a cross straight through their guard. You want to make the most of the moment when they are distracted by the jab.

3. Again, in quick succession, throw in the left hook while they are recovering from the cross and putting up their gloves in front of their face anticipating another blow but leaving the sides of their face open.

4. Lastly, throw in a strong right knee to the midsection. If you have the opportunity, grab the opponent to ensure they stay in position to receive the knee.

7. Jab-Cross-Switch Kick

1. Here, you use a quick jab to "open up" the attack.

2. As soon as your opponent starts to defend potential hooks, put a cross straight through their guard. You will temporarily unbalance them, making it harder for them to focus on what to defend next.

3. At this point, switch your feet so your lead foot falls back. You want to swing your rear leg out using the momentum you developed from the switch foot technique and aim for the opponent's neck or head. With more room, you will easily swing high and, with a full swinging motion, drive immense force into the kick.

8. Left Elbow – Straight Right – Left Uppercut

1. Getting an elbow on your opponent can be a game-changer. Even if you don't land it with 100% accuracy, it can still do a lot of damage. In this combination, start with a left elbow to the opponent's face, neck, or collarbone.

2. It will be enough to put them off balance as a lot of body weight is behind an elbow. With the opponent unbalanced and their guard out of place from the elbow, you create the opportunity to launch a straight right. Ideally, you should do this with the same arm you landed the elbow with. Do this without pulling your elbow back but driving a straight punch in that small area.

3. By this time, you have opened up a good size cavity. Here you can capitalize on the opportunity and use your left arm again for an uppercut or a blow to the solar plexus.

This in-the-face combination is best suited to fighters comfortable in close-range situations. However, it is an excellent combination for others to practice against the pads or the bag to help with speed. It will improve fluidity in your moves in those tight spaces and make the most of your available space.

9. Push Kick – Cross – Left Hook – Right Knee

1. Again, the evergreen Teep (push kick) will come into play. Start the combination by pushing your opponent back and getting them off balance.

2. Quickly moving forward to catch up with your opponent, follow up with a cross straight into your opponent.

3. A left hook to the side of the head should closely follow the cross,

4. Next, bring the right knee to the opponent's midsection with as much impact as possible. Again, you can grab onto the bicep or the neck to hold your opponent in position while you drive in a knee.

This combination is a comprehensive attack that can yield excellent results, but it takes practice to execute properly. It is a combination requiring a higher degree of coordination and also stamina. Practice this thoroughly until you can execute it flawlessly before using it in a game. You don't want to get caught up in the middle of your combination with a counterattack.

10. Right Cross - Left Uppercut - Right Roundhouse Kick

1. This is another combination that starts with a punch to the face. To make this possible, you must look for the right opening to successfully land a good cross to the opponent's nose, cheek, or chin.

2. A good cross will disorient your opponent, giving you the room to proceed with the next step, a left uppercut. If you can connect this left uppercut to the opponent's chin, it will certainly have them walking around with wobbly legs.

3. The last piece of the puzzle is the roundhouse kick. As you land your uppercut, pivot your weight on your lead foot, shifting the momentum to the other side, where you can launch a heavy roundhouse kick to the opponent's body or head.

The main element of this combination is the roundhouse kick at the end, hopefully leading to a knockout win. However, you must be on point with the punches to get it done right. It is the punches that will put the opponent in the right position to deliver the roundhouse kick easily without the issue of being blocked or countered.

What determines how effective a combination will be is the timing with which you launch it. One strategy is to look for the perfect moment to launch a combination that will last the entire length. The other approach is to attack whenever you see a slight opening and go as far as possible with the combination. You can never be certain how your opponent will react, so it's best to make the most of every chance and inflict as much damage (score as many points) as possible in every burst.

These are some of the best combinations in a Muay Thai faceoff. However, remember, in a competitive environment; there are rules you must stick to. There are other ways of executing these combinations and many ways to make them more lethal – but always stay within the confines of the regulations when competing.

Also, regardless of how good you are at the combinations, you must be proficient in managing your opponent's weight in the ring. The power you develop for these combinations will come from the momentum you get through weight distribution and channeling your weight to the side you attack from. When you can better control your opponent's weight, you can use this to your advantage to create more momentum in your attacks. Practice these combinations on pads and bags, but also during sparring. It will give you the real-fight experience of managing yourself and your opponent.

Chapter 10: Defense Tips and Techniques

Muay Thai is a dangerous martial art with techniques that can be used as a defense in the ring, on the street, and outside. This combat style is known worldwide as the "deadly art of 8 limbs," which uses kicks, knees, elbows, punches, clinch movements, etc. Its origin is as far back as the old South-Asian kickboxing era. As a Muay Thai fighter, it is not enough to learn better ways to strike or attack your opponent; a defensive position is as necessary as an offense.

Muay Thai is a sport that requires you to be able to defend yourself. [34]

This chapter teaches the many ways to block a strike and give a counter-attack in any position, in the ring or the street, and the essential tools to master for a good defense anytime, anywhere.

Muay Thai directs your focus on a simple yet effective strike position, using several limbs to attack or quickly defend against an attack. These are done in a matter of seconds, so as a fighter, you must build short-term focus and speed to have a great advantage in the world of Thailand kickboxing. As you journey through the defense tips and techniques for Muay Thai, get your mind ready to be exposed to the fundamentals, the benefits of good defense techniques, and practical ways to defend and remain dominant in the ring and on the street.

Fundamentals of a Good Defense

Unlike most combat sports, many factors must be considered when participating in Muay Thai. You must learn fundamental skills to build good defense techniques. These techniques might seem difficult to beginners, but remember that even world-class professionals had difficulties when they first trained. So, do not get overwhelmed and discouraged on your journey; follow the tips below to build a good defense in this combat sport:

Having a Tight Guard

In combat, you get all these limb attacks coming from every angle, and they can catch you off guard. Hence, the need to always be guarded. When your guard is tight, it will be hard for your opponent to land punches and strikes on sensitive areas like your face or head. It is also advised that while keeping a tight guard, you should ensure it is flexible enough to protect other body parts. The reason is the flexibility of your guard makes it easy to see or predict your opponent's next move and block or defend the strike. It is an essential skill to be equipped with when using Muay Thai techniques.

Movement of Your Head

Knowing how to move your head and dodge punches is useful when facing head-to-head with an opponent that lands many punches. Unpredictable head movements are not only for boxers, as they can also be applied in a sport like Muay Thai. Head movement is a great way to avoid strikes to the face. Although in Muay Thai, you should know that ducking under punches is a terrible way to defend and prevent them. You will likely get a knee kick in the face if you do. This is not to override the need to dodge punches, just a call to caution not to exaggerate certain head movements to avoid your opponent gaining an advantage.

Balance

In the art of self-defense, balance is a crucial factor that must be deliberated. When your defense style is a firm stand but adventurous, you could get kicked in the face and set off guard. If your legs aren't firm on the ground, you will be thrown off balance, giving your opponent an upper hand. So, how can you imbibe this? Take a stance that keeps you on your feet, even with several shots. Keep the space between your feet wide enough to give good stamina. You won't easily stumble over after you get kicked or punched when you do this.

Calculated Movement

Accuracy is paramount to getting a cool and perfect shot on your opponent. A well-calculated move would stun your opponent and make them double-check their next move. For example, elbows are an important move, but with the right timing and distance, it could knock your opponent out. Elbows and kicks are Muay Thai combat's most dangerous and powerful techniques.

Benefits of Muay Thai Defense

In every combat style outside of Muay Thai, defense and offense are common topics that are never overlooked. Although other combat styles have good defense and offense techniques, none surpasses those in Muay Thai. Thailand kickboxing allows you to blend as many techniques as you can. Due to its practicality and flexibility, and uses of all body limbs, you can learn several techniques while training.

Adding these techniques to your self-defense style, you will never regret it because you will know how to defend yourself in any situation, making this martial art style a great advantage. For example, when you find yourself entangled in a street fight, you must be familiar with ways to quickly overshadow and bypass your attacker.

However, when involved in street fights, it takes much more than self-defense to overcome an attack; there must be counter-attacks to form a balance, and Muay Thai does just that for you.

Why Muay Thai Is Important in and Out of the Ring

Self-defense training doesn't only protect you but also others, too. It keeps you physically and emotionally fit and able to defend yourself while increasing your self-esteem and confidence. Learning self-defense helps you stay in shape and healthy; although these techniques demand a lot from you in strength, training, and focus, it has many benefits. The following are more reasons Muay Thai should be considered important for self-defense:

- **Socializing** – It might be an individual sport, but it does open you up to meeting different trainees and trainers during gym sessions and tournaments. Like in the movie "Rocky Balboa," the trainee had a close call with his coach, which gave him an upper hand in the end.
- **Discipline and Focus** – This form of combat requires much dedication and discipline. It requires that you undergo consistent routines and remain

focused and determined. If you have yet to master the art of determination, you could easily quit, but Muay Thai naturally helps build discipline.

- **Self-Defense** – In Muay Thai, as you learn the ways of attack, you also know the ways of defense. You must ensure they go hand in hand. Whatever you do, avoid confrontation as a beginner, but if life happens, use your defense skills.
- **Respecting Boundaries** – As much as you want to showcase your skills as you grow, you might be in a situation where you suddenly feel like taking dominance. This is a wrong mindset, and Muay Thai teaches that when you fight, you fight to win, not to kill your opponent. So, it ensures you go easy on those elbows or knockouts.
- **It Builds Confidence** – As discussed earlier, Muay Thai gives you a sense of belonging and strengthens your emotional well-being. You no longer feel easily intimidated, so you walk and talk confidently.

Muay Thai on Ring Defense

In Muay Thai, gaining dominance while in the confines of a ring is an important skill you must have. It doesn't come easy because it takes resilience and skillfulness to get there. Even top fighters lose fights occasionally by miscalculating moves or losing an advantage over their opponents. But in the ring, what increases your confidence is that you know your opponent's weakness and how to override their guard and dominate them.

So, how can you become the best ring fighter? Using a good defense system and moving with speed to counter every attack from your opponent shows you'll dominate the ring. Be ready and in a good stance to counter every attack from an opponent with speed. Make it sharp and unpredictable; this position makes you dominate a ring. When all your moves are sharp and unpredictable, your opponent will fall backward while you're up and pushing.

Using Defense and Counters

- **Catching and Sweeping** – This has many advantages when you use it well as a defender. For example, your opponent throws a kick, and you quickly grab the leg and sweep his other foot off the ground. You could use that measure to strike because, at that point, your opponent has been caught off balance. There are many ways to catch kicks, but it takes precision and timing. With Muay Thai, you cannot be short of ideas for practical ways to catch and sweep your opponent off the ground.
- **Blocking and Counter Attacks** – It is good to defend yourself in a fight, but know that winning a match takes more than blocking and self-defense; you must learn to make counter-attacks when least expected.

Muay Thai on Street Fights

Muay Thai has powerful and lethal techniques, making it even more perfect and interesting for a street fight. Landing a few elbows to your opponent's head or face doesn't take much effort to knock and keep them down. The knees can be lethal, especially when used on your opponent's ribs. Elbows are sharp and land more cuts to the body. The knees are strong and cause more internal injuries.

One main reason Muay Thai is very efficient in street fights is the subtle violence it delivers to the body. The main goal is to strike and stop your attacker from advancing toward you by all means. It's an aggressive and direct move leaving a mark at a strike. It is what makes it different from other sports. You must be good with your kicks, punches, elbows, knees, and trips (to sweep off balance) to have a good defense mechanism in Muay. As you become stronger, you will have a greater chance of defending yourself in a street fight.

So, what are the advantages of using Muay Thai in street fights?

It Permits Close Range Technique

With close combat, there is a conservation of energy and distance between fighters. This practice has been the most popular among martial art practitioners. For example, you can clinch your opponent and throw them off balance during street fights. The clinch is a technique essential in Muay Thai. You get to close the distance between you and your opponent and inflict injuries on them with your knees to their sides or head, giving you more control over the fight – and them.

Street Fights Have Many Grabs

Although it will be considered as a foul if you hold or grab your opponent, unless you want to attack them, you should be alert to their attacks. When you are attacked by an opponent, you should maintain a good stance, and be ready to counter attack at any time. You can do any of these – block the punch, blow or kick, and strike them down. You can also maneuver your opponents by grabbing their attacking limb as a means of self-defense.

A Good Defensive Position

Having your shoulders and feet apart in width gives a good, stable defense stance, giving you easy mobility for a fight. You can have more fluid movements, and your reactions are swift and sharp when you move. Use your elbows to guard your body against attacks and counter-attacks. Another good fighting stance is keeping your hands facing upwards and loose, not tight as in a fist. Hold them up, covering your chin to protect your face from unknown strikes.

Whether you're considering engaging in a ring fight or involved in a street fight, using Muay Thai techniques proves best for self-defense. It is fierce and precise, using eight limbs for combat. To engage in any fight, street, or ring, you must build certain fundamental skills: balance, head movement, tight grip, and guarding your face. You can build your defense using calculated moves with these. For every defense, there must be a counter-attack. So, while gauging your opponent's techniques, strengths, and weaknesses, you should plan to dominate by working on your speed and flexibility. Have a good defensive position and learn to use your elbows for short-distance strikes and your knees to take your opponent off balance.

Chapter 11: Spar Like a Master

Sparring represents one of the most vital components of boxing training. It's the closest thing to a real battle. It helps you better understand how to use the skills and strategies you learned in the gym (regarding range and reach, rhythm and time, and different power levels). This chapter guides you through the sparring basics and ensures you know when best to begin. You will learn sparring etiquette, gear, and other relevant tips, making your beginner sparring journey smooth.

Sparring can help you practice the skills you've learned. [35]

Basics of Sparring

Making you and your partner acquainted with the ups and downs of a real battle is the main goal of sparring. It's created to imitate particular events and situations you might encounter in the ring or real life so that you are fully prepared to apply your talents when necessary.

It can be intimidating to spar as a beginner in boxing or kickboxing. The idea of entering the ring and using what you learned against a live subject can make you uneasy. It's a reality you never encountered, and nothing can compare.

However, you will eventually achieve a high level in your training. Your abilities improve, as does your technique. Indeed, sparring is rather intimidating to those uninformed and untrained.

When Does a Beginner Start Sparring?

Many boxers practicing for a few months have frequently pondered when they should begin sparring; this is one of the most commonly asked questions. The response differs from person to person, although sparring should be started after around three to four months of steady, solid training.

It is a good time to begin sparring once you're comfortable with basic Muay Thai moves like footwork, strikes, and blocks.

The fundamentals should be part of your regular workout program. The basic defensive tactical strategies include evading, slipping, countering, and fundamental offensive and defensive combinations. You don't want to rush into a sparring session, so wait until you are sufficiently secure in your skills, at least in theory.

Then, it's time to move on to dueling sessions once you have trained and rehearsed them enough. Your reflexes, timing, and general fighting abilities will then improve.

Asking your coach is another excellent idea to determine if you are prepared to spar. Your coaches can assess your training progress and decide if you have reached the necessary level to test your prowess in the ring against a live opponent. You are certainly ready when your coach thinks you are.

Sparring Gear

The size of your bank account and gym bag is your only restriction when purchasing Muay Thai training equipment. Most beginners can get by with little equipment. Still, after you make a name for yourself, you'll discover that acquiring Muay Thai gear is as fun as engaging in "the practice of eight limbs."

To ensure you are set up correctly, use the following appropriate sparring gear to prevent injuries:

Shin Guards

An important piece of gear for a Muay Thai fighter is the shin guards or shin pads. It protects the shin and foot from strong kicks and blows. They are essential for honing kick-checking reflexes.

Although many sizes and materials are available, the most basic version will work for beginners. Make sure you can move about freely without feeling constrained. Also, ensure they are thick enough to protect you and your companion by offering ample padding.

Ankle Wraps

If you want more support for your ankles, get a pair of ankle wraps. They might not be the first thing you include in your workout bag, but they are equipment your ankles will benefit from.

Sparring Gloves

Your weight index, experience, and fighting style are significant in your selected glove. However, 16-ounce boxing gloves are generally the most preferred option for sparring. You won't strike as hard if you use a 12 or 14-ounce glove because they provide the perfect balance of comfort and protection. Gloves are essential because they safeguard your and your opponent's hands. While gloves are usually available at the gym, getting your own is advisable for acquaintance and personal hygiene.

If you want to try them on, it is best to purchase them in person. The gloves must be properly sized, with adequate wrist support and padding.

Mouth Guard

A quality mouthguard will shield strikes and keep your teeth from breaking or cracking, giving them adequate protection. While you can exert pressure by biting down firmly and keeping your jaw clenched, a mouthguard aids in lowering the risk of concussions or other head injuries. Various mouthguard styles are available, but a boil-and-bite mouthguard is ideal for beginners. Nevertheless, a frequent problem with a boil-and-bite mouthguard is that it occasionally cannot fit properly, hence the reason top athletes wear custom-fitted mouthguards. Although a custom mouthguard is unnecessary for routine training, you could get one for additional safety.

Headgear

Headgear is a smart idea. But don't let it fool you into thinking you're safe. Don't open yourself up to headshots merely because you're wearing headgear. Head traumas do accumulate over time if your gym has a tendency to host intense sparring matches or if you mix Thai boxing with pure boxing. It is sensible to consider donning protective headgear in these circumstances. When selecting the best headgear, you must consider a few things: safety coverage, suitability, visibility, and weight. However, visibility improves with less protection coverage and vice versa.

Like your gloves, the more protection it provides due to denser padding, the heavier the weight, and vice versa. Although a more serious, protective headgear offers superior defense against blows to the head, it can slow down your ability to dodge attacks. The most effective way to prevent head injuries is unquestionably through avoidance. Therefore, the ideal headgear balances sufficient security and high visibility – all within a natural and comfortable fit.

Hand Wraps

Hand wraps shield the 27 small bones in your hands, protecting them (and the soft tissue surrounding them) from harm. Additionally, hand wraps secure your hand so that your fingers and wrists do not move while you punch. Invest in a high-quality pair when purchasing hand wraps because they will serve you longer and provide additional protection. Along with investing in good hand wraps, you must know about proper hand-wrapping techniques.

Groin Guard

Due to the biological and anatomical makeup of men's genitalia (and greater outward positioning), the groin protector is more suitable for men than women. A groin kick is known for shattering many men's sense of self. This soul-crushing torment will leave the strongest men screaming in agony and curled up like a fetus. Keep yourself safe; always wear a groin guard when sparring. It could save your life.

Some practical advice while choosing a groin guard; the family's precious gems should be completely covered by the right groin guard, with no slippage. The guard should be comfy and tightly fitted so that it doesn't move about while you move. Of course, for effective protection against unintentional forceful knocks, the cup must be strong and long-lasting.

Groin guards come in three primary varieties: the jock strap, compression shorts with cups, and Thai steel cups with laces. All have identical goals and different designs. It comes down to personal preference for a good fit and feel when choosing one.

Muay Thai Knee and Elbow Pads

Muay Thai elbow and knee pads are less frequently used during sparring. People with knee injuries or issues or who want more thorough protection typically wear knee pads. Nobody will prevent you from donning knee protectors as an extra measure if you practice Muay Thai for leisure.

The knee pad can minimize the pressure if you strike your sparring partners with knee blows. While elbow strikes are permitted in sparring, elbow pads are worn to lessen damage and safeguard the elbows.

Elbow blows are extremely risky, so most gyms forbid them during sparring. Despite wearing protective gear, elbow blows can be very harmful. As a result, elbow sparring ought to be carried out under professional guidance, and special care must be given when regulating power or pace to prevent bodily harm.

Muay Thai Shorts

Get a pair of Muay Thai shorts because one of the worst things you would want to do is arrive at a Muay Thai gym with basketball shorts. The thighs and groin of Muay Thai shorts are designed with space to strike freely. Perform a couple of kicks while trying on a pair to evaluate if they fit comfortably and provide enough room for kicking.

Comfortable Clothing

Even though most male athletes like to work out only in shorts, ladies must invest in a top that doesn't retain excessive sweat. Veteran martial artists usually advise a sleeveless, form-fitting, and cozy top for women. If you're unsure, get one made expressly for Muay Thai training. Also, procure an ideal pair of workout bras. They have three advantages: they're comfortable, protect your breasts, and are made from ventilated material.

Sparring Etiquette

Below are some sparring etiquettes you must know in Muay Thai:

- Have the required gear
- Keep the contact nice and light; sparring is not a fight
- Always show respect
- Communicate with your sparring partner
- Don't "walk through" punches and kicks

Sparring Tips

The practice of sparring exercises is one of the essential elements for fighters to develop how they fight and gain experience in a real-life combat setting. Muay Thai sparring is intimidating and thrilling for a beginner. Muay Thai sparring assists you in getting ready to apply your abilities correctly when the occasion demands it.

Below are a few sparring beginner tips you should know before you enter the ring with your sparring partner.

Prioritize Your Safety Above All Else

For your first sparring session, the primary and most crucial thing to consider is your safety should always come first. A sparring match must occur in a safe and regulated atmosphere to ensure you and your sparring partner can hone your moves without concern of needless injuries.

Moreover, wearing the correct safety equipment, like headgear, mouthguard, gloves, and protective shin pads, is essential. To increase your training sessions' effectiveness, your coach and other trainers must be on the ground to oversee your sparring sessions.

You Are Not Required to "Win" When Sparring

There is no such thing as "winning" a sparring match. Read that again – and remember it!

There have been numerous sparring sessions, far too often, wherein beginners attempt to kill one another as if it were a title match. This way of thinking causes you to focus excessively on landing powerful blows on your partner while neglecting to hone your technique. Nobody will believe you are a great warrior regardless of whether you did well in one round of sparring.

The trick is to improve. When you spar, you must constantly attempt to do better than what you did previously. Therefore, if this is your first attempt at sparring, you will undoubtedly have a ton of strategies you can practice and perfect. Relax and concentrate mostly on what you can learn from the experience.

Pick an Aspect to Concentrate On

You must decide which areas to improve before your Muay Thai sparring matches. It is crucial since it helps create better-organized training sessions by giving your sparring a specific goal.

Choose a few primary areas to concentrate on throughout your sparring session. For instance, you might use different elbow strikes and combinations in your sparring session if you seek to improve your elbow techniques. Following this process, you polish a particular skill or aspect more effectively.

Ensure Your Coach Approves

Don't be a jerk who enters an unsupervised maiden sparring session. You likely haven't traded blows because your coach thinks you're unprepared. You are not qualified for a sparring match if your coach feels that way.

It is crucial for you and your sparring companions' protection. Many veterans have sparred with folks on their debut sessions, yet they always go crazy, unleashing full-throttle strikes and behaving like it is a brawl. Avoid being *that person.*

Develop a Strategic Plan

Believing that you are playing a game while you spar is useful because, like in any game, developing a winning strategy is essential. The most fundamental principle of Muay Thai is to rack up the most points while preventing your opponent from doing the same. Body kicks get more points in traditional Muay Thai than other techniques like low kicks, knees, and punches. Developing a game plan before your sparring exercise provides a clear path to stick to. Additionally, depending if you operate in defense or attack, you might prefer to select a strategy beforehand.

Have a Wonderful Time

Take things easy and have fun during the process. You should be proud of yourself for having the courage to fight. Always be cordial to your rivals, and enjoy the new bonds you form with your crew of sparring companions.

Muay Thai sparring will help you as a beginner by developing your skills and allowing you to regulate your body.

Chapter 12: Muay Thai vs. Dutch Kickboxing

Now that the basics have been covered, like working on the stance and various offense and defense techniques, let's read about one of the biggest rivalries between two martial art forms. Yes, you read it right. This rivalry is between Muay Thai and Dutch kickboxing - a hot topic for combat sports enthusiasts for several decades.

This chapter compares both fighting styles by listing the key differences between their rules, training, techniques, and relevant information to decide the boxing style that suits you the most.

An Introduction to Dutch Kickboxing

Dutch kickboxing is a combination of Muay Thai and Kyokushin Karate. [36]

Since the history and origins of Muay Thai have already been covered, let's have a brief overview of this equally popular rival of Muay Thai from the history books.

Dutch Kickboxing is a fusion of Muay Thai, Japanese kickboxing, and Kyokushin karate combat styles and originated in the Netherlands. This fighting style has become popular since it originated and has managed to captivate hundreds and thousands of people to choose Dutch kickboxing. One major difference that sets Dutch kickboxing apart is the Kyokushin karate influence. Dutch kickboxing mostly gets its moves, combos, and techniques from Muay Thai and Japanese kickboxing, but their speed and aggression are from Kyokushin. These boxers always take an aggressive stance to keep the pressure on.

Another general reason differentiating the two combat styles is the heavy use of punches and low kicks for finishing moves.

The Dutch kickboxing style was developed by local karatekas who traveled to Japan to learn Japanese kickboxing and Kyokushin karate. These Dutch boxers returned home to teach these styles, and over time, a mix of these Japanese fighting techniques and Muay Thai gave birth to Dutch kickboxing.

Key Differences

Dutch Kickboxing Training Protocols

The training protocols and drilling techniques in Dutch kickboxing and Muay Thai vary greatly. Dutch kickboxing drills are different in pad work, as there's no need for coaches to hold the pads when drilling. Boxers deliver drills to each other, replacing the pads with boxing gloves.

Dutch sparring is quite popular as training protocols, like without using pads, push the body to its limits, improving results in physical strength and cardiovascular health.

Strengths of Dutch Kickboxing Drills
- Training becomes consistent when you drill with a partner
- Countering moves and using footwork for a better stance are improved
- It provides a step-wise mechanism where you can add new and complex drills as you progress

Drawbacks of Dutch Kickboxing Drills
- Although you can perform drills, there's little to no room for learning new moves or improving existing ones because many fighters are not coaches and can't correct the other person when they make a mistake.
- Using force is limited when striking during drilling because there are no pads to withstand forceful impacts.
- You repeat the same drills as opposed to drilling under the supervision of a coach.
- You won't receive instant feedback from the coach or know the correct moves to make.

Muay Thai Training Protocols
Using forearm and belly pads is required during Muay Thai training. During Muay Thai drilling, most fighters have an experienced partner or a coach holding the pads. These training partners also wear shin and instep protectors to throw kicks during drilling to improve reflexes further.

One significant difference to mention in Muay Thai and Dutch kickboxing training is related to a technique known as clinching. You'll only see clinching and its training in a Muay Thai gym because all other combat sports have restricted or excluded this technique.

Strengths of Muay Thai Drilling
- You get massive chances of improving your techniques and combos as the coach will be there to correct your techniques.
- Since coaches are trained to improve the fighter's skills, it gives the fighter a window of opportunity to experiment with different tempos, rhythms, and ranges to polish their skills.
- You won't worry about the impact and can unleash your full power when training.
- The training session won't be limited to punches only. You can try every technique with ease.

Drawbacks of Muay Thai Training
- Not every pad holder can take the impact of strikes when training. If the pad holder is not doing their job effectively, it lowers the fighter's chances of polishing their skills.
- Poor pad handling can make the fighter develop ineffective or wrong techniques.

While drilling in Dutch kickboxing is all about repeating combinations or drilling for a specific set of rounds, Muay Thai maintains a more laidback approach with no specific drilling sets or repeating the same exercises. Furthermore, under the supervision of a coach, developing new skills and refining existing skills becomes much easier.

Pad Usage
Using pads for training pad work is mostly seen in Muay Thai than in Dutch Kickboxing, mainly because most Dutch kickboxing gyms avoid incorporating them during training sessions. However, it doesn't mean these pads are banned or cannot be

used; it's merely a matter of preference. In contrast, many gyms and Dutch Kickboxing coaches regularly use these training pads while training their fighters.

Before moving further, addressing another misconception is necessary. Many people believe you only use punches and low kicks in Dutch kickboxing. However, that's only partially true. You can use your knees and elbows and throw a few high kicks like Muay Thai. If you're still confused and might think that if all the moves are in both fighting styles, then what makes them different?

The answer is the fighter's attitude or stance in both combat styles. For example, a Muay Thai fighter will throw a bunch of moves and use techniques strategically to weaken their opponent. In contrast, a Dutch kickboxer always maintains an aggressive stance and focuses on the volume of strikes. The most volume can only be delivered through punches -the main difference between these robust combat sports forms.

The Differences in Techniques

This section compares techniques to know their differences and better understand the reasons that set these two combat styles apart.

Punching

Using punches is similar to Western boxing, but Dutch kickboxing has a few added variations, like the Superman punch or the back fist. Instead of working on a variety of punches, Dutch kickboxing is more about maintaining an aggressive stance and delivering impactful strikes while moving forward.

On the other hand, Muay Thai fighters use a different approach to using punches. Rather than delivering a high volume of punches at a fast pace, Muay Thai fighters use a combination of techniques for effective results. For example, they might throw a left jab and immediately clinch the opponent to pin them to the ground or use a mix of knee strikes and punches to create an opening for the next strike.

In a nutshell, a Dutch kickboxer will focus on their pace and the volume of attacks, but a Muay Thai fighter will always incorporate different techniques together and execute them strategically for the desired outcomes.

Kicking

If you are not a boxer, it might be difficult to understand the differences in the kicking style. While you will find identical techniques in both fighting styles, the way and the frequency with which they are executed varies. For example, in a Dutch kickboxing match, the emphasis is on delivering a high volume of punches and low kicks. However, Muay Thai has more room for different kicking techniques instead of relying on only a few.

Knee Strikes

Using knee swings and targeting the legs with knees can only be seen in Muay Thai. However, using knee strikes to the face is common in Dutch kickboxing. When executed properly, this lethal strike can knock out the opponent within a few seconds.

(Likewise, Muay Thai boxers use lethal elbow strikes to knock out opponents.)

Stance

The stance Dutch kickboxers take is more squared and dynamic. They always place their feet close, so their stance allows heavy striking and quick movements. Without maintaining a firm stance, they cannot use their upper body effectively and throw punches to potentially knock out the enemy. When making a guarding stance, the head and face are the main areas a Dutch kickboxer is focused on to protect.

In contrast, Muay Thai boxers focus on a stance for being prepared for action, but in a slightly relaxed manner. Their feet are placed wider and are angled, making it easier to use kicking techniques, maintain balance, and improve mobility. The guarding position in Muay Thai is focused on protecting the midsection and lower body instead of only the face. This guarding position in Muay Thai enables boxers to counter incoming strikes using various counter techniques and to minimize the impact these strikes have on the body.

Striking Techniques

When striking in Dutch kickboxing, the main emphasis is throwing powerful punches and adding low kicks. This combination is quite popular and is even elevated by some enthusiasts to an art form. The delivered strikes are lightning-fast and transition from punches to low kicks and back again in the blink of an eye. The punches are aimed at the face or an opening on the upper body, and low kicks are aimed at the legs.

On the contrary, Muay Thai incorporates a massive combination of moves stemming from the art of eight limbs. The mix of jabs, kicks, elbow strikes, and grapples can break the opponent's spirits and turn the tides. Whether the opponent is in short or long range, there are moves and endless offensive and defensive combinations to use against the opponent.

Clinching

Clinching in Muay Thai makes it different from Dutch kickboxing, as many Muay Thai fighters mix clinching with elbow, knee, and forearm strikes to target different body areas. Unlike Muay Thai, Dutch kickboxing clinching is only done occasionally, like when the opponent is too near for an attempt to look for openings to strike. Clinching is also done to land a few strikes and create distance.

As mentioned, clinching is one of the core techniques used in Muay Thai and more than in other combat sports. These fighters put endless hours into training and perfecting the techniques to win fights. In Muay Thai, boxers are always on the lookout for an opening to initiate a grapple, use several clinching techniques, and find opportunities to land strikes that can make their opponent lose their balance or other techniques like sweeps and knee strikes.

Fighting Style

Dutch kickboxing's fighting style is kept aggressive by throwing a series of powerful punches and low kicks. This approach maintains pressure on the opponent. With each strike, a Dutch kickboxer moves forward to overpower the opponent and control the duel's pace, rhythm, and tempo.

On the other side of the picture, Muay Thai boxers are trained to endure impactful strikes and blows, sustain damage, and constantly seek the opponent's weaknesses. Maintaining this attitude and deciphering the weak points allows these boxers to plan their next move effectively. Effective countermoves and hitting hard at the right time make a Muay Thai fighter different than their rival combat sport, Dutch kickboxing.

Training Emphasis

Although we have already explained some differences in training, let's take a deeper dive. The training in Dutch kickboxing focuses on developing strength and stamina to primarily maintain an aggressive stance and deliver one powerful strike after another to assert dominance in the game. Their drills are high-intensity and aimed at improving physical strength and agility.

While Dutch kickboxers work on a specific skill set, Muay Thai boxers maintain a holistic approach striving to balance techniques, strength, agility, and fluidity. Furthermore, Muay Thai boxers spend most of their training session improving their clinching techniques. Their approach is well-rounded, and they are always ready to face varying situations in the ring.

Fighting Distance

Dutch kickboxing favors a medium to long-range fighting distance between opponents. In contrast, Muay Thai can fight at long, medium, and close ranges without issue. Close combat in Muay Thai can result in a knockout as the boxer can land their clinching moves and throw knee strikes for a knockout. A Dutch kickboxer might not be comfortable switching the fighting distance like a Muay Thai boxer who can change their stance and execute a new set of moves in the blink of an eye.

Defensive Techniques

The counter moves a Dutch kickboxer aims to evade the strikes and minimize their impact. While defending, the boxer promptly changes their foot placement and posture and simultaneously throws offensive strikes whenever a window of opportunity opens.

Like the offensive moves, Muay Thai has a massive range of defensive techniques and combinations to counter virtually every incoming strike. Blocking the attacks, parries, and redirecting the attack are common defensive techniques. Clinching is also a defensive tool effectively used to limit the number of attacks and reduce their impact.

Fighting Culture

Although both combat sports forms have several differences, a clear difference is their fighting culture. While Dutch kickboxing is a hybrid combat style mainly influenced by other professional martial arts and combat sport forms and is competitive, Muay Thai has deep roots in the region's culture and traditions. A Dutch kickboxer will maintain a professional, organized, and structured approach in training. In contrast, pre-fight dances, post-fight ceremonial events, and paying homage to their ancestors and teachers are expressions Muay Thai fighters exhibit the most.

Scoring System

Some evident differences are in the scoring systems. In a Dutch kickboxing match, landing clean strikes on target areas will score points. Similarly, knocking out the opponent impacts the final score. While Muay Thai awards a similar score for knockouts and clean strikes, an additional emphasis is put on the strikes made during clinching. Defending effectively and asserting dominance throughout the game are other factors affecting the final score.

Finalizing Your Pick

Before choosing any combat style, it's crucial to understand the following factors to decide the fighting style that suits you best.

Training Environment

The environment in which you train will define the learning outcomes. Working out in a training environment resonating with your inner self provides a sense of relaxation, and acting as a sanctuary will make you step up your game to the next level. Regardless of the combat sport you select, the gym or training institute you enroll in must have a supportive community, a learning atmosphere, and coaches with enough experience to unlock your true potential. Along the way, you'll forge unbreakable relationships with other members and share the same passion to push you forward whenever you feel low.

Personal Goals

Take time off and dwell in your inner self to understand your preference. For example, if you are spiritual and ready to embark on a cultural journey connecting deeply to your training, then Muay Thai would be a feasible choice. On the contrary, Dutch kickboxing might be the answer if you want to maintain a more professional training-based approach and develop self-confidence. Nevertheless, exploring your personal goals and preferences will guide you to the combat style aligning best with your aspirations.

Fighting Style

Picture both combat styles in your mind and evaluate whether you will be comfortable with close-range combat, clinching, and delivering impactful strikes. Or would you like to take the pressure up a notch and prefer delivering constant strikes to the opponent? Choose the fighting style that resonates with you the most so it becomes easier to train, learn, and master these combat styles.

Physical Demands

Although both are physically demanding sports activities, being physically fit is crucial if you want to opt for training. Furthermore, the physical demands of both styles vary slightly. For example, Muay Thai requires a balance of strength and endurance. In contrast, Dutch kickboxing focuses more on being agile to deliver consistent strikes. Watching a few matches of both fighting styles will make it easier to decide.

In a nutshell, the choice between Muay Thai and Dutch kickboxing should always be influenced by a person's preferences and goals. If you want to experience the cultural connection and are fine with balancing striking, clinching, defense, and strength activities, Muay Thai is an excellent choice. However, Dutch kickboxing is the perfect sport if you are fast-paced and want to keep asserting your dominance over the opponent while constantly landing strikes.

Taking Trial Sessions

The best way you can learn a combat sport is through hands-on experience. Several gyms and clubs offer trial sessions which are mostly free or have a nominal fee. Whichever martial arts discipline you choose, you'll face challenges while training, but it will benefit improving your basic fighting skills.

Attending a few trial classes, you will grasp the basic movements, techniques, and related moves to better judge if you are physically and mentally capable of training and competing in combat sports. Since most gyms want new members to join, they occasionally offer fee waivers and discounts, saving you much more money than purchasing a membership for regular days.

Cost of the Program

Most gyms and combat sports clubs have paid membership plans of varying amounts and services. Evaluating every cost related to your training should be calculated beforehand. For example, consider the training fee, the cost of the gear, and other related fees so you know how much money to put aside for these training sessions.

It's always tempting to pick a gym or a training class that costs the least, but you won't get your value for money in most situations. It's better to commit to a gym by evaluating their services and knowing you will learn the combat sport to compete or just to indulge in a physically fun activity while learning self-defense. Finding the answers to these questions will make your choice more solid, suiting you best.

Nonetheless, never compromise on the quality of training and the instructor's experience in the relevant combat sport. The better the training quality and coaching, the better the results in learning the martial arts form. Therefore, having a reputable training environment with the required facilities is imperative if you want to improve your game.

Chapter 13: Daily Training Drills

Are you looking to sharpen your daily routine? Or do you want to mix up your fitness regime? Whatever your daily fitness regimen goals, this comprehensive chapter has what it takes.

In this last chapter, you will discover many ways to build a daily Muay Thai workout plan catered specifically toward beginners (within the confines of your dwelling place or a local fitness center). From tried and tested routines to proven effective training techniques, expect nothing less from this packed chapter.

Working on Your Stretching, Mobility, and Hip Rotation

When most people reflect on their first day of Muay Thai training, they realize that focusing on hip rotation, flexibility, posture, and mobility would have made them better fighters. Properly executing hip rotation is essential since it determines how much power you can put into your kicks and knee strikes. Surprisingly, anyone can practice these exercises with minimal resources anywhere.

Stretching, flexibility, and mobility are necessary for Muay Thai.[87]

Good Hip Rotation

Consider if someone broke into your home: would you swing a baseball bat vertically or use your hips to generate full force? In Muay Thai, kicking correctly depends on proper hip rotation. An inexperienced fighter attempting upward motion kicks could lead to unintended effects like self-injury instead of effectively striking the intended opponent.

Similarly, when executing a roundhouse kick in Muay Thai, always keep the following in mind:

- Extend your lead leg's heel beyond your toes while rotating it 180 degrees in line with the kick direction
- To execute a more effective kick, focus on directing your force upward instead of downward
- Additionally, swiftly swing your arm, using the same one as your kicking leg, while propelling your shoulder forward

The key to accurately performing this technique is activating your lateral gluteal muscles while rotating your hip; you will feel a specific sensation telling you when you've got it right. While unconventional in Muay Thai, mastering proper hip rotation is crucial for efficient kicks. This exercise should be part of your daily routine to enhance hip flexibility.

1. Start by placing one foot on an elevated surface like a sofa and the other foot on tiptoes as you would do preparing to kick.
2. Rotate the elevated foot while engaging your arms and repeat this sequence 25 times before switching legs and repeating it 100 times on each leg.
3. Aim for a minimum of 100 repetitions daily on both legs and even up to 300 reps per leg if you have tight hips, as they do in Thailand.

Mobility

If you live a sedentary lifestyle in the Western world, your hips are likely tight. This impacts your athletic performance when executing kicks, particularly in sports like Muay Thai boxing.

Luckily, there are ways you can regain hip mobility independently. Maintaining proper hip rotation is essential for professional athletes and minimizing injuries during physical activities like soccer games.

Research on injury prevention among professional athletes who incorporated muscle-mobility exercises into their training regime has shown impressive outcomes. Practicing alone provides an excellent opportunity to improve movement quality patterns.

One excellent video clip shared by Don Heatrick provided beneficial advice aimed at assisting Muay Thai practitioners in unlocking their hip joints. The routines highlighted therein have proven remarkably successful in enhancing kicking techniques, regardless of form.

You can significantly improve your hip flexibility by following the instructions outlined in this section and carrying out all three daily exercise routines using materials like foam rollers, lacrosse balls, and resistant bands (available at affordable prices on Amazon).

1. Releasing Your Hips

- To start, place a foam roller just above your knees before gradually moving it up along your thighs, which aids in breaking down muscle tissue more effectively.
- If tight spots arise while doing this exercise, gently move your leg from left to right, targeting troubled tissues while flexing the hip joint muscles.
- Ignore IT (iliotibial) bands located midway since they are prone to injury if rolled on directly.

2. Opening Your Hips

1. Secure one end of a resistance band tightly onto solid structures like squat racks or TV stands.
2. Step into the band with it placed high behind the gluteal muscles so there's significant tension pulling at your hips.
3. Initiate the movement by squeezing the glutes tightly and tilting the pelvis forward, propelling the hip joint in front of the knee.
4. Do not over-arch your back while prioritizing mobility at the hips. Specifically, switching up stances helps you practice from different angles.
5. Set aside 1-2 minutes for continuous repetitions on each side before moving on.

3. Anchoring Your Hips

Stabilizing the hips takes more than just following any old workout routine; it takes effort, precision, and technique.

- The best way to get started is to find a solid platform, a bench, or a chair that matches up perfectly with where your foot needs support.
- Once you've located this footing, ensure when positioning yourself on it, one hip sits lower than or lines up exactly at knee level; this ensures proper alignment throughout the execution.
- Furthermore, keep good posture during every step: chest upright and chin pointing downward.

- By exerting force from underfoot while simultaneously engaging the glute muscles (feel free to savor the gentle stretch), you'll be effectively stabilizing your hips in no time.
- Lastly, incorporate weights into the mix and aim for three sets of ten reps per leg to test your limits.

Do you want to take your Muay Thai performance to another level? Then do these exercises; they'll enhance your overall well-being and have powerful effects on muscle length, joint alignment, neuromuscular control, and pivotal components in optimizing range of motion for improved fighting ability.

Ensure you integrate these exercises into a robust warm-up routine with dynamic moves to ensure correct kick execution while decreasing the risk of harm from bad movement patterns.

The release and opening of the hips can happen any time during the day as an active rest technique between weightlifting sessions or partake in designated recovery days while addressing postural issues and decreasing muscle discomfort.

Investing in high-quality gear is paramount to attaining the maximum benefits of these Muay Thai exercises and maintaining good posture.

However, today's technological advancements like smartphones and computers have led to poor posture, resulting in future health complications. But fret not. The various routines outlined above aid in releasing tension from the hips and stabilizing them.

Stretching

In Muay Thai, where precision matters greatly, taking time out for stretching greatly enhances your overall performance. Once you have warmed up appropriately with mobility exercises, focus on lengthening your muscles through stretching.

Regular stretching results in better flexibility, translating into improved agility when performing strikes or kicks that need maneuverability from your body. Moreover, going through an extensive stretch regime before training or competitions aids in injury prevention by creating greater elasticity in muscles.

1. Warm Up

Don't skip warming up before starting any stretching exercises because you don't want to risk muscle strains or pulls. Begin with some easy aerobic activities like jogging or jumping jacks for 5-10 minutes to get your blood flowing and muscles prepped for stretching.

2. Dynamic Stretches

Dynamic stretches are great as warm-ups and as movements simulating what you do during training or competitions. They improve blood circulation, expand the range of motion, and condition the muscles. Dynamic stretches include leg swings, arm circles, and torso twists. To carry out dynamic stretches, do the following:

1. Stand next to a wall or other stable structure and swing one leg back and forth while keeping balance; repeat 10-15 times per leg.
2. Continue with arms extended sideways from your shoulder, making small clockwise circular motions, gradually increasing size until you feel stretched enough.
3. Keep things fresh by alternating the direction of your twists; switch to counterclockwise after a few rotations.
4. Stand with feet shoulder-width apart and place your hands on the hips before making torso twists – rotating the upper body from left to right and back again.

3. Static Stretches

Static stretches are a good option targeting several key muscle groups to improve flexibility during stretching sessions. These exercises require you to hold positions for roughly 15-30 seconds, which helps loosen tightness in those areas.

After completing warm-ups or exercises, do your best to focus on performing proper techniques and holding positions as long as possible. A static stretch should focus on muscle groups like the hamstring, quadriceps, chest, shoulder, hip flexor, triceps, and groin.

- The hamstring stretch is one method that entails sitting down on a flat surface with one leg extended straight while bending the other before leaning forward slightly, reaching toward the toes with your back straight.
- Quadriceps stretching is another beneficial technique for improving flexibility by pulling corresponding heels (opposite side) toward the buttocks without curving your back while remaining balanced and standing tall.
- When targeting the chest muscles, use doorways by placing the forearm against the frame before leaning forward gently for an effective stretch.
- Incorporating shoulder and hip flexor stretching could be beneficial. Extend your arms across your body or kneel with one knee on flat ground while extending the opposite leg ahead for better results.
- Are you seeking to ease pent-up tension in those hip flexor muscles? Simply maintain a proper standing posture and thrust forward from the hips for a couple of rounds, each time swapping back and forth between the left and right side until you detect pleasant stretching sensations.
- For your triceps region, raise one arm high above your head, and bring it back toward the scruff of your neck before slightly tugging at the elbow with the opposite hand for added intensity until you sense beneficial pulling sensations. Repeat this procedure on the other arm.
- You can also address the groin area by sitting down with feet touching each other and the knees extending outwards. While keeping a firm grasp on both feet with your hands, pull inward using elbows against knees to maximize stretch across this region.

4. Proprioceptive Neuromuscular Facilitation

If you're searching for more challenging stretching techniques requiring interaction, give PNF (proprioceptive neuromuscular facilitation) stretching a try. This unique approach combines strategic muscle contractions with relaxation periods to increase flexibility and expand the range of motion in various body parts.

To get started, try this uncomplicated PNF stretch focusing on the hamstrings:

1. Begin by laying on your back with one leg lifted in the air
2. Position yourself so that you can easily reach your ankle with one hand while extending the arm outwards to meet your partner's grasp with their other hand.
3. Now engage in an intense push-pull routine where you push against their grip toward them, using every bit of effort for 6-10 seconds before finally relaxing.
4. Your partner will continue guiding your leg forward and gently pushing it into greater extension at each progressive round lasting 20-30 seconds.
5. Test each leg until both are equally stretched out.

5. Foam Rolling Stretching

Foam rolling is an effective method to relieve muscle tension and enhance flexibility in different parts of the body through self-myofascial release. For this technique to work wonders on tightness issues, you need a foam roller to target the specific muscles requiring attention.

- To alleviate tightness in quadriceps muscles along the front upper part of the thighs, lie face down with a foam roller under the thighs. Maneuver the roller from your hip area to just above the kneecaps; stop at tender points along this path.
- Similarly, targeting the hamstrings requires seating upright using a foam roller under both thighs. Glide it smoothly upward from your glutes toward your knees, putting even pressure on sore areas encountered during this process.
- If the calf muscles are causing trouble, sit on the ground with the legs straight, using slow rolling movements to slowly work upward along each section.
- Relief of upper-back pains can be achieved by lying flat on your back and placing a cylindrical foam roller under your shoulder blades. Move the foam roller up and down your spine gently.
- Ensure to stop and stay still whenever you come across tender areas.

Daily Shadowboxing Regimen

Every Muay Thai training routine requires a strong foundation for exceptional performance, something shadowboxing can deliver thanks to its multiple advantages, like refining techniques, intricate footwork patterns, and enhancing distance control capabilities.

Below are some priceless tips to derive maximum gain from daily shadowboxing drills:

- Always begin by warming up sufficiently before diving into practice sessions, a routine aimed at preparing muscles appropriately for upcoming intense workouts.
- Utilize dynamic stretching alongside joint rotations, finishing with light cardio exercises like skipping rope or jumping jacks. This activates the muscles early and reduces the likelihood of muscle sprains or strains during subsequent workouts.
- You should choose a spacious area allowing unrestricted mobility without the risk of hazardous elements or barriers. With ample room, you can confidently perform defensive techniques and execute a wide range of striking moves with maximum precision and impact.
- To maximize the effectiveness of shadowboxing during training, it is advisable to mentally visualize an opponent standing in front of you before starting each session. Visualize their movements, anticipate their strikes, and imagine yourself immersed in intense combat scenarios for a more focused approach.
- Perfect your stance and guard position by assuming a balanced position allowing easy transition between offensive and defensive modes. Always keep your feet shoulder-width apart with the lead foot slightly turned outward.
- Ensure you have a raised guard posture covering the face; tuck your chin down while keeping both elbows close to the body sides for added protection.
- During shadow boxing sessions, incorporate various striking techniques starting from basic moves like jabs, crosses, hooks, and uppercuts using proper techniques before advancing slowly to more difficult ones like elbows, knees, or kicks.
- Always maintain fluid motion without sacrificing precision and power.

- To improve your Muay Thai boxing defense tactics, refine your ability to block or evade incoming strikes by incorporating methods like slipping, ducking, weaving, or parrying while keeping a sturdy guard position on the move. With the power of visualization, imagine going up against different opponents' attacking styles while practicing swift ways of dodging them with quick reflexes through repetition.
- Timing is crucial in accurately landing power hits during fights. Hence, it would be wise to regularly include shadowboxing techniques in training routines to visualize your rival's movements before delivering well-timed counter-strikes

Cardio

This section outlines key exercises and techniques below to help you incorporate cardio into daily Muay Thai training:

- Before starting a workout program, determine what you want from adding more cardio to boost endurance or improve cardiovascular fitness.
- Warming up is necessary to prepare properly before an intense cardio session. Engage in dynamic stretching movements like arm circles, torso twists, or leg swings, which loosen up muscles, boost blood flow, lower the risk of injury, and increase performance levels.
- Ensure correct form throughout to enhance performance in future matches. Engaging in kick and punch pad workouts with a training buddy or coach can greatly improve your cardio endurance while refining your striking techniques. Using the pads, you encounter resistance mimicking the intensity of a genuine fight, urging you to exert maximum effort.
- Running has always been popular for boosting cardiovascular fitness. It enhances leg muscle strength and improves stamina and endurance levels remarkably.
- Consider incorporating steady-state runs, hill sprints, or interval runs into your regimen to add variety to running sessions.
- Circuit training might be a perfect choice for an all-encompassing full-body workout that blends strength exercises with cardio intervals (like push-ups, squats, burpees, and kettlebell swings). Progress through each exercise promptly without breaks in between for maximum benefit.
- Bag work sessions at high intensity are another excellent addition to your training program. They encourage explosive strikes while combining techniques and swift movements and improving cardio-respiratory endurance by challenging you to maintain a rapid pace throughout each round.
- Whether recovering from intense workouts or just wanting to rest your joints from high-impact activities, swimming laps, or engaging in water-based interval training can help enhance cardiovascular function while protecting vulnerable areas.

This last chapter provided multiple alternatives for establishing an effective daily Muay Thai training program suitable for every environment. Committing yourself to these exercises over time will enable advancement and proficiency in techniques and physical endurance. Last, please do not neglect the utmost importance of safety; always be vigilant and seek expert advice if in doubt. Remember, enjoy yourself in every aspect of mastering this incredible martial art.

Conclusion

Thailand's kickboxing has a centuries-long history and is now an art accepted worldwide. This combat form requires using your eight limbs, and as a beginner, you will make striking moves with kicks, elbows, punches, and your knees.

These are weapons a Muay Thai fighter uses, making it stand out from other combat sports. Centuries ago, Muay Thai fights were often brutal; today, it has been modified, making it a safer competitive sport with referees recording scores and prioritizing safety.

Although Muay Thai is a modern-age sport, it doesn't make it safe for everyone. Still, you can learn the foundations of this combat sport and become a professional fighter with proper learning and coaching. The combat sport might seem dangerous to a beginner who views it through an outdoor lens, but with Muay Thai, there are better ways to learn the techniques, making it as friendly as other sports.

One great benefit of Muay Thai is it brings out an inner warrior within you. It keeps you physically and emotionally fit while exposing you to real-life attack scenarios during training. It is an excellent way to learn self-defense and teaches you how to remain calm when faced with real-life opponents. With Muay Thai, you can confidently enter the ring or fight. While you train, you build stamina and stance, enhancing your concentration skills.

Now that you've been exposed to these practical tips and techniques on Muay Thai, you should put everything into practice. This guide is written so that it leads you through every technique simply and understandably. So, take those steps, hit the gym, train under a coach, set a routine, and ensure you're accountable to someone.

You might burn out in the first few months of training, but that's fine; it's part of the process. Don't give up. While you train, you must practice each technique you learn with other trainees; start cautiously and use protective equipment for sensitive areas.

Muay Thai is one of the most practical and fierce martial art forms. Good luck on your journey to mastering it!

Part 4: Wrestling

The Ultimate Guide for Beginners Wanting to Learn Wrestling Techniques for Self-Defense, Physical Prowess, or Competition

CLINT SHARP

Wrestling

THE ULTIMATE GUIDE FOR BEGINNERS
WANTING TO LEARN WRESTLING
TECHNIQUES FOR SELF-DEFENSE,
PHYSICAL PROWESS, OR COMPETITION

Introduction

Are you looking for a way to take your fitness and sports skills to the next level? Then, wrestling could be the perfect choice. Its combination of strength, agility, and technique can provide an incredibly challenging workout while building skills to help you in other areas.

Wrestling is not merely a sport but a life-changing experience. It challenges individuals to push their limits physically and mentally, teaching discipline, perseverance, teamwork, and resilience. Wrestlers learn to navigate adversity, overcome setbacks, and find creative solutions to problems on and off the mat. This guide takes you through the basics of wrestling, from rules and skills to posture and balance to successful training techniques.

Beyond the competition, wrestling builds camaraderie and brotherhood like no other. It's a community of individuals united by their love of the sport and a shared pursuit of excellence. Wrestling isn't only about winning or losing; it's about the journey and the lessons learned along the way. You'll learn about penetration, lifting, attack and counterattack, reversal techniques, escape techniques, pinning combinations, and more. You'll learn about training at home and coaching youth wrestlers.

Wrestling teaches invaluable life skills and character qualities to carry throughout life. From discipline and perseverance to humility and leadership, wrestling instills valuable traits, making the participants better individuals. The bond between teammates is unbreakable, and the adrenaline rush of competing on the mat is unlike anything else. Wrestling challenges people physically and mentally, pushing the limits and helping them discover their true potential. This book explores all these aspects and more.

Navigating it can be overwhelming if you're new to the wrestling world. The sport's intensity, the seemingly endless rules and regulations, and the sheer physicality can be intimidating. But don't let that deter you because once you dive in, the rewards are endless. A sense of discipline and harmony permeates every aspect of wrestling, from training to competition. In addition, the personal growth and confidence you gain from pushing yourself to your limits are invaluable. The road is sometimes challenging, but the payoff is worth it. So, step onto the mat because the wrestling world is waiting for you with open arms and endless opportunities.

By the end of this practical and concise guide, you'll have a thorough understanding of the sport and all it entails. With an eye for detail and commitment to excellence, wrestling will make you a better athlete and person. From learning the basics to finding success at the highest levels, this guide has you covered. The world of wrestling is vast and incredibly rewarding. So, what are you waiting for? Take the plunge and let this book guide you on your journey.

Chapter 1: Why Should I Choose Wrestling?

Wrestling might be your new obsession if you're looking for a sport to physically and mentally challenge you. Not only does it require incredible strength and endurance, but it also demands mental toughness and strategic thinking. Wrestling is a great test of character. It teaches you to push through pain and adversity, never giving up when the going gets tough. Moreover, the skills you learn on the mat apply to all areas of your life. As a result, you gain confidence and discipline, which carry over into your relationships, academic pursuits, and career.

If you want to become a better version of yourself while having fun and making lifelong friends, choose wrestling. This chapter explores the origins, philosophy, and benefits of wrestling. It discusses how it compares to other martial arts and which techniques can be used for self-defense training. The chapter ends with advice for parents considering enrolling their children in wrestling. By the end, you should thoroughly understand wrestling and why it's so popular.

Introduction to Wrestling

Wrestling is a sport where you try to pin your opponent to a mat. [38]

Wrestling is one of the oldest and most popular sports in the world. It is a combat sport where two competitors aim to pin their opponent to the mat or force them out of the wrestling ring. Wrestling requires physical strength, agility, and strategic thinking. In addition, it's a sport that has evolved over centuries from its origins in ancient civilizations to modern-day Olympic competitions. This section explores the history of wrestling, its origins, and the philosophy behind this sport.

Origins

Wrestling has been around for over 15,000 years. It is believed to have originated in ancient civilizations such as Greece, Egypt, and Rome. Wrestling was popular in the earliest Olympic Games in Greece, where it was one of the five events in the pentathlon. In the Middle Ages, wrestling was a popular sport in Europe, with evidence of organized competitions in France, Germany, and England. Wrestling was also used as a means of self-defense and to prepare for hand-to-hand combat.

History

In the United States, wrestling became popular in the early 20th century with the formation of the Amateur Athletic Union (AAU) and the National Collegiate Athletic Association (NCAA). Collegiate wrestling became popular in universities, and high schools introduced it to their athletic programs. Professional wrestling emerged in the United States as entertainment, with staged matches and storylines.

In the latter half of the 20th century, wrestling became an international sport when the International Federation of Associated Wrestling Styles (FILA) formed and the inclusion of wrestling in the modern Olympic Games. Wrestling continues to be a popular sport worldwide, with millions participating and watching wrestling matches yearly.

Philosophy

Wrestling is more than just a physical sport. It's a mental and spiritual discipline. Wrestlers train their bodies to be strong and agile, developing a strong work ethic, perseverance, and mental toughness. Wrestling teaches skills such as focus, discipline, and self-control, which can be applied to other areas of your life. Wrestling also emphasizes respect for oneself and the opponent. In wrestling matches, competitors shake hands before and after the game, and sportsmanship is highly valued. Wrestling teaches humility and the importance of hard work and dedication.

From its origins in ancient civilizations to the modern-day Olympic Games, wrestling has evolved over the centuries. Wrestling is a mental and spiritual discipline teaching valuable life skills, such as self-control, discipline, and respect for self and the opponent. Whether you are a wrestler or a sports fan, wrestling offers a unique and rewarding experience.

Benefits of Wrestling

When people think of wrestling, they often picture two athletes grappling and throwing each other to the mat. While this is undoubtedly a big part of the sport, wrestling goes much deeper than that. Wrestling is a full-body workout requiring strength, agility, and endurance. It's a mental challenge promoting discipline, sportsmanship, and personal growth. This section explores the many benefits of wrestling and why it's more than just a sport.

- **Physical Strength and Endurance:** Wrestling is a physically demanding sport requiring strength and endurance. It engages every major muscle group, from the arms and shoulders to the legs and core. Wrestlers must have cardiovascular endurance to sustain their efforts throughout a match. This intense workout helps wrestlers build muscle, burn fat, and boost fitness.

- **Mental Toughness and Discipline:** Wrestling isn't only about physicality. It's a mental game. Wrestlers must think on their feet, make split-second decisions, and maintain focus throughout a match. It requires mental toughness and discipline, positively impacting all aspects of a wrestler's life.

- **Teamwork and Sportsmanship:** While wrestling might seem like an individual sport, it requires a great deal of teamwork and sportsmanship. Wrestlers often train together and support each other through tough workouts and competitions. They learn to respect their opponents and demonstrate good sportsmanship, even in the heat of a match.

- **Community and Belonging:** Many wrestlers connect with their teammates deeply and develop lifelong friendships. Wrestlers can join clubs, attend events, and participate in philanthropic activities, helping them feel connected to something larger than themselves. As a result, the wrestling community is tight-knit, and many wrestlers feel a strong sense of belonging.

- **Personal Growth and Confidence:** Wrestling can help individuals grow and develop in numerous ways. It teaches resilience, perseverance, and the value of hard work. It promotes self-awareness and self-confidence as a wrestler sets and works toward achieving goals. Wrestling can be a transformative experience helping individuals become their best selves.

The benefits of wrestling go far beyond the physical aspect of the sport. It promotes mental toughness, discipline, and sportsmanship while creating a sense of community and belonging. Wrestling can be an excellent option for individuals looking to grow, build confidence, and strive for their best selves. Whether you're a seasoned athlete or someone just starting, wrestling has something to offer everyone.

Comparing Wrestling with Other Martial Arts

Combat sports have been around for centuries and are enjoyed by people of all ages. As a grappling-based martial art, wrestling is a great way to improve your strength, agility, and coordination while gaining valuable self-defense skills. Numerous other martial arts, like Judo, Karate, Taekwondo, and Boxing, also promote these skills. While all martial arts are effective in their way, each has unique characteristics setting it apart from the others. This section compares wrestling with other martial arts, highlighting the differences and similarities to help you decide which is best.

Wrestling is a great martial art for people who enjoy physical activity and high-intensity workouts. Wrestling involves a lot of grappling and clinching techniques and is considered one of the most challenging contact sports. Wrestling generally focuses more on takedowns, ground grappling, and submission moves than other martial arts like karate or kickboxing. It is an excellent exercise to develop muscle strength, endurance, agility, and balance.

While wrestling is a close-contact martial art, Judo is a slightly less physically demanding and more defensive sport. Judo is a martial art using throws and trips to take down opponents. It is considered one of the best forms of self-defense, especially against larger or stronger opponents. Therefore, Judo is a great martial art for people with a different physical fitness level than that required for wrestling.

Boxing, another famous martial art, is a combat sport using striking techniques like jabs, hooks, and uppercuts. Unlike wrestling and Judo, boxing primarily focuses on punching, fast footwork, and evasion techniques. The sport is widely popular for its cardio and weight loss benefits and improves cognitive function and balance.

Taekwondo, a Korean martial art, is a combat sport emphasizing quick, explosive movements and high kicks. Taekwondo is all about dynamic activities. This art form has proven exceptionally effective in self-defense and has been accepted as a full-contact sport in the Olympics.

Comparing wrestling with other martial arts indicates that each has unique strengths appealing to different people, depending on their interests and physical abilities. Wrestling might be the best choice to improve strength, coordination, and grappling skills. Judo could be the best pick for a less rigorous, defensive approach to martial arts. Boxing and Taekwondo are kickboxing arts to suit individuals who want to rely on striking techniques more than grappling. Choosing the right martial art (for yourself) is best based on your interests, goals, and physical capabilities. Whatever you choose, regular training and hard work will undoubtedly lead you toward self-discipline, mental toughness, and physical achievement.

Including Wrestling in Martial Arts Training

Martial arts have been practiced for centuries and encompass many combat techniques enhancing physical strength, mental agility, and overall well-being. From karate to jiu-jitsu, each martial art style has its unique set of movements, philosophies, and strategies. Wrestling is a popular martial art that has proven itself as a highly effective combat and self-defense form. This sport originated in ancient times and required intense physical effort, discipline, and practice to master. This section explores the benefits of including wrestling in your martial arts training routine and how it can enhance your practice.

Improved Physical Fitness

Wrestling is a demanding sport requiring strength, speed, agility, and endurance. By including wrestling in your martial arts training, you challenge your body in new and demanding ways, significantly improving physical fitness. Wrestling builds core strength, improves balance and coordination, develops explosive power, and increases cardiovascular endurance. These physical attributes are crucial to excelling in martial arts and will benefit overall health and well-being.

One primary reason people practice martial arts is to learn self-defense techniques to protect them from harm in dangerous situations. Wrestling is a technique enhancing your self-defense skills, making you more confident in your ability to defend yourself. In wrestling, you learn to take down your opponent, control their movements, and leverage your body weight to gain the upper hand. These same skills can be used in real-life self-defense situations, making wrestling a practical martial art to learn.

Mental Toughness

In addition to physical fitness, wrestling develops mental toughness, discipline, and focus. The intense physical demands of wrestling require a high level of mental fortitude, staying focused, and the discipline to keep pushing past your limits. These mental attributes are critical to excelling in martial arts. Through wrestling, you will learn to overcome mental barriers, develop a strong mindset, and remain calm and focused under pressure.

Variety in Your Training

Adding wrestling to your martial arts training routine can add variety to your workouts and keep them exciting. Wrestling provides a different form of training than some martial arts, such as striking-based martial arts like karate or Taekwondo. Incorporating wrestling into your training routine challenges your mind and body in new and exciting ways and gives you a more comprehensive martial arts skill set.

Competitive Opportunities

Last – but certainly not least – if you enjoy competitive sports and want to take your martial arts practice to the next level, wrestling can provide many opportunities to compete. Wrestlers have numerous opportunities, from local to national championships, to showcase their skills and compete against other skilled fighters. Including wrestling in your martial arts training could open doors to new experiences and opportunities you might not have had otherwise.

There is no denying that martial arts are a fantastic way to stay physically fit, mentally sharp, and disciplined. Including wrestling in your martial arts training routine amplifies these benefits. You will improve physical fitness and self-defense skills, develop mental toughness, add variety to your training, and open doors to competitive opportunities. So, whether you are a seasoned martial artist or a novice, consider adding wrestling to your martial arts training routine and take your practice to the next level.

How Is Wrestling Practiced?

Wrestling is an ancient sport that has grown in popularity over the years. It is an intense and physically demanding sport requiring skill, agility, and power. But have you ever wondered how wrestlers train to achieve this level of competitiveness and toughness? Wrestling involves rigorous training in various techniques, strategies, and physical conditioning.

Training Locations

Wrestling practice typically occurs in a wrestling room or on a wrestling mat designed for wrestling. The sport requires a specific mat created with high-density foam and vinyl fabric. These mats are critical to ensure the wrestlers are not hurt during training, and they help absorb shock and reduce the risk of injuries. During practice, wrestlers will include strength and conditioning exercises in the gym, which involve weightlifting, conditioning drills, and cardiovascular exercises to increase endurance, agility, and strength.

Intensity

Wrestling practice is intense and physically demanding. Most wrestling teams practice regularly, often for several hours each day. The intensity of exercise increases as wrestlers become more competitive, and training often incorporates high-intensity workouts pushing wrestlers to their limits. Succeeding in wrestling requires dedication and persistence, and a willingness to drive yourself beyond your limits.

Techniques and Strategies

Wrestling is a strategic sport requiring a combination of physical and mental skills. During training, wrestlers learn various techniques enabling them to control their opponents. These techniques include takedowns, escapes, pinning combinations, and top-and-bottom wrestling. Wrestlers should study their opponents, analyze their strengths and weaknesses, and develop strategies to gain the upper hand. To stay on top of their game, successful wrestlers must consistently work on perfecting their technique.

Safety

Safety is paramount in any sport, and wrestling is no exception. During wrestling practice, coaches and athletes take every measure to avoid injuries. It includes proper warm-up routines, stretching exercises, and injury-prevention drills. During wrestling practice, coaches closely monitor athletes to ensure appropriate techniques to prevent injuries. Many wrestling teams require athletes to wear protective gear, including headgear, mouthguards, and knee pads.

Wrestlers undergo rigorous training in various techniques, strategies, and physical conditioning – all geared toward making the athletes more muscular and agile. The intensity during practice can be high, but coaches and athletes prioritize safety measures to avoid injuries. Overall, wrestling practice is a well-organized, well-structured system ensuring wrestlers are at their optimal training level and ready to compete, making it a test of physical and mental strength.

Styles of Wrestling

While wrestling may look like a simple sport at first glance, various styles have unique rules and techniques. This section discusses the different wrestling styles, their origins, and what makes them stand out.

Freestyle Wrestling

Freestyle wrestling is the most common wrestling form worldwide and is a regular Olympic event. This wrestling style originates from Great Britain and emphasizes fast and agile movements over brute force. Wrestlers can hold and catch their opponent's legs and use their arms to perform takedowns like Greco-Romans. The winner is determined by gaining the most points, scored through takedowns, reversals, and exposures.

Greco-Roman Wrestling

Greco-Roman wrestling is another wrestling form dating back to ancient civilizations. Named after its origins in Rome, this wrestling style does not allow below-the-belt attacks, leg holds, or using an opponent's legs. Instead, the focus is on upper body strength and throws using arms and shoulders. Although takedowns are legal, they should be executed while standing. Grip strength, explosive power, and proper leverage techniques are essential in Greco-Roman wrestling.

Folkstyle Wrestling

Folkstyle, or collegiate wrestling, is the style most Americans are familiar with. This wrestling form is popular in high schools and colleges in the United States and Canada, emphasizing takedowns and pinning. In folkstyle wrestling, takedowns are worth two points, while a pin is worth five. A wrestler wins if he pins his opponent's shoulders on the mat or gains the most points in the match.

Sumo Wrestling

Sumo wrestling originates from Japan and combines elements of wrestling and Japanese Shinto belief. Sumo matches are held in a circular ring, where the wrestler's objective is to push their opponent outside the ring or make them touch the ground with any part of their body except their feet. To compete effectively, Sumo wrestlers must maintain a strict diet and training regime to reach the required weight and size.

Beach Wrestling

Beach wrestling, known as sand wrestling, is relatively new compared to other forms. This style usually takes place on a sand surface and requires high levels of explosiveness and agility. In beach wrestling, wrestlers save time clinching and trying to get control. Instead, they immediately try to grip the opponent's legs or perform a throw. The match ends when the wrestler pins the opponent's shoulders to the ground.

Freestyle wrestling, Greco-Roman wrestling, collegiate wrestling, sumo wrestling, and beach wrestling each have specific rules, techniques, and traditions. In addition, each form requires a different set of skills, making every style unique and engaging.

Wrestling as a Sport for Children

Wrestling is a highly competitive and challenging sport requiring immense energy, endurance, and perseverance. In addition, the sport positively impacts physical and mental health, especially for children. This section explores the benefits of wrestling for kids and how to find the right environment.

Benefits to Kids

- **Physical Development:** Wrestling is an intense physical activity incorporating cardiovascular, muscular endurance, and muscular strength. It helps children build lean muscles, improve bone density, and promote flexibility. In addition, wrestling boosts children's cardiovascular health, leading to a healthy weight and an active lifestyle.
- **Discipline and Character Building:** Wrestling is more than physical activity. It teaches kids focus, discipline, and perseverance. Wrestling helps children learn to set goals and work hard toward them. It teaches them essential life skills, such as resilience, courage, and teamwork.
- **Mental Health:** Wrestling positively impacts mental health, especially for children. It boosts self-confidence, self-esteem, and self-awareness. Children who participate in wrestling feel more in control of their bodies and have a better self-image.

Finding the Right Environment

- **Age-Appropriate:** Finding an age-appropriate wrestling program for your kids is essential. Young children should start with basic wrestling techniques, while older kids can learn more complex moves. The program should be tailored to their physical abilities and experience level.

- **Safe Space:** Wrestling requires close contact with other wrestlers, which could increase the risk of injury. Therefore, choosing a wrestling program that focuses on safety and offers protective gear is essential. Additionally, a good wrestling program should have experienced coaches who know how to teach wrestling safely.
- **Cultural Environment:** The environment in which your kids learn and participate is essential. Ensuring the program fosters a positive and supportive culture encouraging values like discipline, sportsmanship, teamwork, and respect is crucial.

Wrestling is an excellent sport for children providing many physical and mental benefits. It teaches skills like discipline, perseverance, and focus, which are essential in life. When choosing a wrestling program for your kids, find one that is age-appropriate, safe, and fosters a positive cultural environment. It's important to nurture future fighters and give kids a chance to experience this sport.

Children aren't the only ones who benefit from wrestling. Adults can improve their physical and mental health, too. Wrestling teaches you to be strong yet humble, to discipline yourself, and stay focused. It is a great way to release steam, gain strength, and practice balance. As with any sport, the best way to enjoy it is in a safe environment with knowledgeable coaches and teachers providing proper instruction. Don't let the intimidation of wrestling keep you from trying it. There are many different levels and styles, so whether you are a novice or have been practicing for years, there is something for everyone. So, grab your gear and join the fight.

Chapter 2: Basic Rules and Skills

Learning the basic rules and skills is crucial to success in wrestling. Whether a beginner or an experienced wrestler, understanding the fundamentals of the sport gives you a competitive edge. From basic moves like takedowns and pins to understanding the scoring system and rules regarding illegal activities, having a solid foundation of knowledge will help you outperform your opponents. Moreover, learning the basics will improve your technique and help prevent injuries on the mat.

This chapter discusses the basic rules and skills of wrestling so you can get off to a strong start in this exciting sport. It covers the fundamental laws of wrestling, basic skills, and techniques you should master. With this knowledge, you'll be well on your way to becoming an experienced and successful wrestler. The following chapters go into greater detail about specific skills and strategies. But, for now, let's look at the basics.

Fundamental Rules of Wrestling

At its core, wrestling is a fight between two athletes governed by rules to ensure fair play and protect the competitors' safety. This section looks at the fundamental laws of wrestling, including the match set-up, scoring system, and disqualifications and penalties. It'll give you a solid understanding of how wrestling works and what it takes to be successful in this thrilling sport.

Match Set-Up

Wrestlers weigh in to determine the class they'll compete in.[39]

Before a wrestling match begins, a few things must happen. First, the wrestlers must weigh in to determine which class they will compete in. Once they have weighed in, the wrestlers are called to the mat and introduced to the audience. Each wrestler takes their position on the mat, with one wrestler in the blue corner and the other in the red corner. Next, the referee signals the start of the match, and the wrestlers will engage in takedowns, reversals, and escapes to score points and win the game.

Scoring System

The scoring system in wrestling is relatively simple. Points are awarded for various maneuvers, such as takedowns, escapes, reversals, and pins. A takedown occurs when one wrestler takes their opponent to the ground and maintains control of them. An escape occurs when a wrestler escapes from under their opponent and breaks free from their grasp. A reversal occurs when a wrestler on the bottom manages to flip their opponent over and gain control. Finally, a pin occurs when one wrestler holds their opponent's shoulders on the mat for a specified period (usually two seconds) to secure the win. Points are also awarded for penalties and disqualifications.

Disqualifications and Penalties

Wrestling is a competitive sport, and sometimes tempers can run high. As a result, several rules govern disqualifications and penalties to ensure the competitors' safety and protect the sport's integrity. For example, wrestlers are not allowed to hit or strike their opponent with any part of their body and are not allowed to bite or pull hair. If a wrestler violates these rules, they can be penalized with a warning, a point deduction, or disqualification, depending on the severity of the offense. These rules are in place to protect the wrestlers and the sport of wrestling.

Weight Classes and Divisions

One of the most fundamental rules of wrestling is weight classes and divisions. Each competition features a weight bracket, and wrestlers must weigh in before each match. The weight classes provide fair competition among athletes with similar sizes, weights, and strengths. If a wrestler is overweight for their bracket, they can be penalized, disqualified, or moved to the next weight class.

Out-of-Bounds

Another essential rule of wrestling is out-of-bounds. The ring is known as the mat in wrestling, typically marked by an outer circle. If a wrestler steps out of bounds, they receive a penalty or forfeit the match. Therefore, staying aware of the mat's edge is vital, and ensuring your body doesn't cross over the line during a game is critical. Additionally, a wrestler must constantly maintain contact with the carpet and cannot purposely push their opponent out of bounds.

Time Limits

Most wrestling matches have a time limit, and understanding how it works is essential. Typically, high school and college-level matches are three periods, each lasting two minutes. If the match ends in a tie, the athletes go overtime and have one minute to win. During the overtime period, the first wrestler to score a point wins.

Scoring

The final essential rule of wrestling is scoring. Following the end of each period, the wrestler with the most points wins the round. If the points tally is tied at the end of the final period, wrestlers go into overtime. Points are awarded for different actions within the ring: 1 point for an escape, 2 points for a takedown, and 3 points for a combination of riding time and a near fall, where a wrestler almost pins their opponent.

The fundamental rules of wrestling ensure fair and safe competition for all participants. Mastering these rules is essential to becoming a successful wrestler. Weight classes, out-of-bounds, time limits, and scoring are vitally important to strategic wrestling. By understanding the match set-up, scoring system, and disqualifications and penalties, you'll tackle your opponents on the mat better and win more matches.

Basic Skills of Wrestling

Wrestling requires a unique combination of strength, agility, and balance. To succeed, you must develop fundamental abilities to overcome your opponent. This section discusses essential skills every wrestler should master to take their performance to the next level.

Balance

One of the most critical skills in wrestling is balance. A good sense of balance in wrestling allows you to maintain your position and keep your opponent from taking control. Good balance starts with proper body alignment and footwork. To improve your balance, work on your stance and positioning regularly. It includes practicing basic moves like the single and double-leg takedowns and challenging yourself with variations of those moves to improve your balance further.

Strength

Wrestling requires a lot of strength. You must apply force to your opponent and maintain your position effectively. Strength training is an essential part of a wrestler's training regime. It includes weight training and other resistance training to build overall strength. Focus on compound exercises, like squats, deadlifts, and bench presses, to develop functional strength. Working on grip strength is essential to help control your opponent and execute your moves more effectively.

Agility

Agility is the ability to move quickly and respond to your opponent's movements, another crucial skill in wrestling. Focus on exercises to improve your quickness and reaction time to develop agility. Agility ladders and cone drills can improve your footwork and reaction time. Plyometric exercises, like box jumps and lateral jumps, can help you develop explosive power and speed.

Mental Toughness

While not a physical skill, mental toughness is a critical attribute every wrestler must cultivate. Wrestling matches are mentally and emotionally strenuous events that test your limits. Developing mental toughness helps you push through the difficulties of a match and keep you motivated when training. To develop mental toughness, stay focused on your goals and visualize succeeding. Always remember that wrestling demands discipline, perseverance, and mental fortitude.

Endurance

Wrestling is an intense sport requiring significant physical endurance. Therefore, wrestlers need consistent cardiovascular training, such as running, biking, or swimming, to build endurance. The training improves your ability to sustain physical activity and last longer during wrestling matches. Additionally, it would be best to focus on developing strength and flexibility to maintain proper posture and movements during wrestling. Building endurance takes time and discipline but is an essential skill that can be the difference between winning and losing.

Mental Toughness

Wrestling puts a lot of pressure on athletes, and it's easy to become overwhelmed by stress and anxiety. Mental toughness helps you stay calm and focused during matches, perform at your highest level, and make better decisions. You can improve your mental toughness by setting realistic goals, working on visualization skills, and using positive self-talk. Learn to control your emotions, especially when things get tough. A wrestler who has honed mental toughness is better equipped to handle challenges that come their way.

Basic Knowledge of Strategy and Tactics

Wrestling matches require strategic planning and execution of moves. Knowing the basic tactics and strategies of wrestling is essential to succeed in the sport. Key strategies include controlling the center of the mat, maintaining balance, and staying aggressive. Knowing different techniques, such as takedowns, escapes, and pins, giving you an edge during matches is crucial. A good wrestler must understand how to anticipate their opponent's moves while avoiding predictable patterns. Work with your coach to develop a solid understanding of various strategies and tactics.

Self-Confidence

Wrestling is a one-on-one sport requiring you to trust your abilities and skills. Self-confidence is vital to winning matches. You must be confident in your physical skills, mental toughness, and knowledge of the sport; it comes with practice and experience. To build self-confidence, focus on your strengths, analyze your weaknesses, and set achievable goals to improve both. It would be best to surround yourself with positive and supportive people who believe in you. Self-confidence helps you overcome adversity, leading to more success on the mat.

Wrestling is a challenging but rewarding sport, and mastering the fundamental skills discussed in this section will help you become a successful wrestler. Endurance, mental toughness, strategy and tactics, and self-confidence are critical aspects of wrestling to enhance your performance and lead you to victory. Remember, wrestling is a sport requiring dedication, hard work, and discipline, but the rewards are plentiful. So, keep working on your skills, stay focused, and always improve.

Tips for Wrestling Beginners

Wrestling is a physically demanding sport of endurance, strength, agility, and technique. It's a sport that challenges physical capabilities and mental toughness. If you are a beginner in the world of wrestling, here are a few things to consider.

- **Work on Your Cardio:** Cardiovascular endurance is essential in wrestling, as the sport requires maintaining high intensity for an extended period. You must train your heart and lungs to efficiently deliver oxygen to your muscles. Some great ways to improve cardio include running, cycling, swimming, and jumping rope. Incorporate cardio into your training regimen; you will last longer in matches.
- **Proper Nutrition:** Proper nutrition is crucial in any sport, and wrestling is no exception. As a wrestler, you must consume a balanced diet of proteins, carbohydrates, and healthy fats. In addition, eat plenty of fruit and vegetables. Avoid sugary and processed foods, which can affect your energy levels and hinder performance.
- **Master the Fundamentals:** Wrestling requires a strong foundation in the fundamentals. Learning the basic stances, shots, and takedowns is best. Spend time drilling these basic moves so that they become second nature. Once you have a firm grip on the fundamentals, you can move on to more advanced techniques.
- **Train with Partners of Different Skill Levels:** Training with partners of different skill levels challenges you substantially. For example, wrestling with someone better than you can hone your techniques while wrestling with someone less skilled refines your moves. You can learn something from everyone, so feel free to step outside your comfort zone and train with different partners.
- **Stay Motivated:** Wrestling can be physically and mentally challenging, so it's essential to stay motivated. Set realistic goals and track your progress. Surround yourself with positive, like-minded individuals who will support and motivate you. Be bold and seek inspiration from top wrestlers, and always remember why you started wrestling in the first place.

Basic Techniques in Wrestling

Whether you're a casual observer or a serious athlete, wrestling is a fun, challenging, and rewarding sport. From the high school mat to the Olympic stage, wrestling demands a perfect blend of strength, speed, and technique. One of the most important things to remember when just starting in wrestling is to master the basics. You don't need fancy moves or intricate leg locks. Instead, focus on simple techniques that can significantly impact the mat. This section discusses some of the most fundamental processes in wrestling.

Stance and Motion

Before you can execute a move – at least *well* – you must master the basic wrestling stance, a balanced and athletic position. Start with your feet shoulder-width apart and your knees slightly bent. Your back must be straight, and your head should be facing forward. Keep your hands up and your elbows in. This position allows you to move quickly without being thrown off balance. Always keep your feet moving, shuffling from side to side, circling your opponent, and changing levels to keep them guessing.

Escapes

Escapes are key to getting out of challenging positions and avoiding being pinned. The most basic escape is the stand-up, pushing off the mat with your hands and rolling onto your feet. From there, you can escape your opponent's grip, return to your feet, and start again. Another good escape is the hip heist, using your hips to create space and twist out of a hold. But, again, remember to keep your movements quick and dynamic and keep your opponent from getting too comfortable on top of you.

Reversals

Reversals are about turning the tables on your opponent, taking what they had, and making it your own. The simplest reversal is the switch. It includes turning into your opponent and rolling them onto their back. This move can be very effective if executed smoothly and quickly. Another classic reversal is the Peterson roll. This move requires more finesse and practice but can be versatile if mastered. Again, it would be best to bait your opponent to overcommit before flipping them over onto their back or exposing their shoulders.

By learning the basics of wrestling, the stance, motion escape, and reversals, you'll quickly develop your skills and become a more confident wrestler. Remember, keep your movements quick and fluid and your chin up. Wrestling is about challenging yourself, pushing your limits, and having fun. Whether a beginner or experienced wrestler, the basics are always the building blocks of success.

Takedowns

Takedowns are essential to wrestling, earning points and giving a wrestler an advantage. The objective is to bring your opponent down to the mat by taking them off their feet. Several takedown approaches include the single leg, double leg, and fireman's carry. Mastering one or two takedown techniques through repetition and practice is essential for success. The method requires studying your opponent's movements and anticipating their next move. Once you have the opponent on the mat, the next step is to initiate a pinning combination.

Pinning Combinations

Pinning combinations are the cornerstones of wrestling. Knowing different techniques to score points is essential once your opponent is on the mat. Various pinning techniques include a cradle, half Nelson, and chicken wing. A good wrestler should have a repertoire of several pinning combinations to surprise their opponent and score essential points. Depending on the situation, pinning techniques can be executed after a takedown or from the standing position. A wrestler's ability to read an opponent and identify their weaknesses is essential to implement these techniques successfully.

Practice

To master the basics of wrestling, you must practice consistently with a positive attitude to enable you to learn from your mistakes. The repetitive drills help perfect your moves and build muscle memory, increasing your technical abilities and efficiency. Watching and learning from other wrestlers and coaches is an excellent way to learn.

Conditioning

Last, conditioning, including strength training and cardio, is essential to building endurance and keeping up with the physical demands of wrestling. Therefore, a good wrestler should have a balanced workout regime, including strength and cardio exercises, to build athletic abilities and resist fatigue.

Leg Riding and Control

Leg riding and control are fundamental techniques in wrestling. The first step is establishing control over an opponent's leg by wrapping your leg around them or hooking your arm under their leg. Once you have control, focus on maintaining pressure and balance. Keep your weight on your opponent to prevent them from escaping. To ride the legs effectively, use ankle and hip control. Keep your opponent's ankle tucked tightly against your body, and use your hip to apply pressure, making it difficult for your opponent to escape or maneuver their body. From here, you can transition to various moves, like a tilt or a turn.

Finishes

Once you've gained control over your opponent, it's time to execute a finish. The most common finishes in wrestling are pins, takedowns, and turns. Each requires different techniques and strategies. To perform a pin, your opponent's shoulders must be on the mat for two seconds. The easiest way to achieve this is to lift your opponent's leg and sweep their torso to the mat. Once your opponent is on their back, hold them down with your body weight and drive your shoulder into their chest.

Takedowns' objectives are to take your opponent to the mat. The key is to use your momentum and leverage to overpower your opponent. One of the most common takedowns is the double-leg takedown. It involves shooting quickly toward your opponent's legs, wrapping your arms around them, and lifting them off the ground. Turns are used to gain points by exposing your opponent's back to the mat, typically done from a top position. Use your weight and hip control to turn your opponent onto their back, then hold them down to secure the points.

Wrestling is a sport demanding physical endurance, mental agility, and mastering basic wrestling techniques. Takedowns and pinning combinations are fundamental skills every wrestler must know. Fundamental techniques help wrestlers establish and maintain a dominant position against their opponents. Refining essential wrestling techniques takes a lot of practice, persistence, and dedication. Building endurance is critical for a wrestler to survive the rigors of the sport, and a balanced workout regime, including strength and cardio exercises, is essential. With a positive attitude and regular practice, mastering these basic techniques will help you become a better wrestler.

Chapter 3: Posture and Balance

Posture and balance are the most critical factors in achieving success on the mat. Maintaining good posture ensures you can generate maximum power and leverage in your moves while preventing injury. Meanwhile, having excellent balance allows you to stay in control of your opponent, preventing them from gaining the upper hand. But mastering these skills is a challenging feat. It takes time, dedication, and a willingness to push yourself to your limits.

With patience and practice, you'll improve every day. This chapter provides an in-depth look at the importance of posture and balance in wrestling and the exercises that develop them. It explores how they positively affect your everyday life. You'll observe the mistakes people often make in posture and balance and how they affect your health, and you'll understand how posture and balance are essential to success in wrestling.

Posture and Balance in Wrestling

Wrestling is an intense and physically demanding sport requiring agility, strength, and skill. Wrestlers must learn to maintain proper posture and balance to excel in this sport. Good posture and balance can mean the difference between winning and losing a match. This section explores the importance of maintaining proper posture and balance in wrestling.

Importance of Good Posture

Posture is critical to the performance of a wrestler. Proper posture helps wrestlers maintain balance, prevent injury, and control their opponents. Wrestlers with good posture can remain in a more advantageous and stable position, giving them a tactical advantage. Wrestlers in good posture are less likely to suffer from injuries like strains and sprains. Also, proper posture ensures wrestlers can generate maximum power and leverage from their moves.

Benefits of Good Balance

Balance is another crucial factor in wrestling. Wrestlers with good balance can move quickly and fluidly, helping them evade the opponent's attacks and launch counter-offensive moves. Good balance allows wrestlers to maintain control when grappling on the mat. Additionally, a wrestler with good balance can use their body position to keep an opponent in place and avoid being pinned. Moreover, a wrestler with good balance is less prone to injury.

Working on Posture and Balance

Wrestlers can improve their posture and balance through targeted exercises. Strengthening the core muscles is critical to creating a solid foundation for good posture and balance. One exercise that targets the core muscles is the plank, which involves holding a push-up position for a specified time. Additionally, lunges can improve balance by strengthening the legs and hips. Resistance band exercises are practical for improving balance. For example, standing on one leg while holding a resistance band can develop balance and stability.

Good posture and balance prevent injuries, maintain control during matches, and create strategic advantages. You can achieve better posture and balance by incorporating exercises to improve your core and lower body strength and by maintaining proper positioning during games. The key is to be consistent and persistent in your training and to make good posture and balance a natural part of your wrestling technique. You will see the benefits and dominate your opponents with time and dedication.

Exercises for Good Posture and Balance

Maintaining good posture and balance during a match requires focus and awareness. Keeping the head up and the shoulders back is vital to maintaining good posture. Additionally, you must constantly be aware of your foot and body position for good balance. This section covers the essential exercises for improving posture and balance, which wrestlers should prioritize in their training routine.

Planks

Planks can be helpful for developing core strength. [40]

Planks are one of the best exercises for developing core strength, which is essential for maintaining good posture and balance. They target all the major muscles in the core, including the abs, obliques, and lower back. To perform a plank, get into a push-up position with your forearms on the ground. Your elbows should be directly under your shoulders. Hold this position for 30 seconds to 1 minute, or as long as you can without losing form.

Mini-Band Walks

Mini-band walks can help improve balance and stability.

Mini-band walks are excellent exercises for improving balance and stability. They target the muscles in your legs and hips that control lateral movement, essential for maintaining a solid base in wrestling. To perform mini-band walks, place a mini-band around your ankles and stand with your feet shoulder-width apart. Then, take small steps to the side, keeping the tension on the band during the entire exercise. Repeat this action taking ten steps in each direction.

Lunges

Lunges can improve posture, balance, and leg strength. [41]

Lunges are excellent for improving posture, balance, and leg strength. They work the muscles in your glutes, hamstrings, and quads – essential for maintaining a stable base in wrestling. For example, step forward with one foot and lower your body until your front knee is bent to a 90-degree angle to perform a lunge. Your back knee should be just above the ground. Repeat with the other leg.

Single-Leg Deadlifts

A   B

Single-leg deadlifts target your hips, hamstrings, and lower back muscles.

Single-leg deadlifts are a challenging exercise targeting your hips, hamstrings, and lower back muscles. They improve balance and stability, which is vital for wrestlers to maintain their balance while taking down opponents. Stand on one foot with a slight bend in your knee to perform a single-leg deadlift. Slowly lower your torso toward the ground while extending your other leg behind you. Keep your back straight and your core engaged. Repeat with the other leg.

Stability Ball Pikes

Stability ball pikes target your core, shoulders, and hip muscles.

Stability ball pikes are an advanced exercise targeting your core, shoulders, and hip muscles. They improve balance and stability, and overall body control. To perform a stability ball pike, start in a push-up position with your feet on a stability ball. Next, push your hips up toward the ceiling while bringing your feet toward your hands. Finally, slowly lower back to the starting position.

Benefits of Good Posture and Balance

Wrestling is one of the most physically demanding sports requiring strength, agility, and coordination. These skills are heavily reliant on posture and balance. As a wrestler, you understand the importance of these two components for performance in the ring. Additionally, good posture and balance are crucial for wrestling because they reduce the risk of injury and enhance overall performance. This section discusses the benefits of good posture and balance in wrestling and how to improve them to take your game to the next level.

Improved Technique

A wrestler's technique is the bread and butter of their game. You must have a proper foundation of posture and balance to execute techniques accurately. Good posture allows you to maintain a stable base while performing offensive or defensive moves. The right balance lets you adjust your weight distribution and movement to anticipate your opponent's next move. By improving your posture and balance, you'll be ready to execute your techniques effectively and react confidently to your opponent's moves.

Reduced Risk of Injury

Wrestling is a high-risk sport, often leading to injuries. Good posture and balance help maintain proper body alignment and reduce the risk of getting hurt. Correct posture keeps your spine in a neutral position, minimizing the strain on your back muscles and reducing the risk of back injuries. Proper balance allows you to distribute your weight evenly, preventing you from landing awkwardly and injuring your joints.

Increased Strength and Endurance

Proper posture and balance are essential for building strength and endurance during training. However, maintaining good posture and balance takes a lot of energy, especially during long wrestling matches. By practicing balance exercises and techniques, you develop core and leg muscles, allowing you to build strength and endurance. Additionally, improved endurance helps you stay focused and alert throughout the match, giving you a competitive edge over your opponent.

Better Movement Coordination

Wrestling involves a lot of quick and seamless movements necessitating coordination between your upper body, lower body, and core muscles. Good posture and balance improve your movement coordination by connecting all your muscles and allowing them to work together smoothly. Improved coordination enables you to move efficiently and quickly, putting less strain on your muscles and reducing fatigue.

Enhanced Mental Focus

Last, good posture and balance can enhance your mental focus. Wrestlers require a lot of mental toughness to excel in the sport. Practicing postures and balance exercises help you focus on your physical movements, clearing your mind of distractions. A focused mind keeps you alert, concentrated, and calm under high-pressure situations.

You must regularly improve your posture and balance to become a successful wrestler. Incorporating posture and balance exercises into your routine can enhance your technique, reduce injury, and develop strength, endurance, movement coordination, and mental focus. A well-rounded wrestling performance requires a strong foundation of proper posture and balance. With dedication and effort, you can unlock your full wrestling potential.

Mistakes People Make in Posture and Balance

Unfortunately, many wrestlers make common mistakes regarding posture and balance, leading to injuries and match losses. Ensuring your body is in the correct position, and your weight is evenly distributed is essential. Taking too wide a stance can impede movement and throw you off balance. Here are a few more common mistakes wrestlers make regarding posture and balance and how to correct them.

Hunching the Shoulders

One of the most common mistakes people make in wrestling is hunching their shoulders - hunching strains the neck and back muscles, leading to chronic pain and injury. Hence, keeping your shoulders down and your back straight when wrestling is essential. This posture prevents unnecessary strain on the shoulders and back muscles and maintains balance.

Leaning Too Far Forward

Leaning too far forward is another common mistake in wrestling and can lead to injury. When wrestlers lean too far ahead, they put a lot of pressure on their knees and are more prone to getting taken down. The best way to prevent this mistake is to maintain a balanced stance. Keep your feet shoulder-width apart and bend your knees slightly to keep your weight centered.

Lifting the Chin

Many wrestlers lift their heads and chin while wrestling, impacting their balance. This posture is more challenging to maintain eye contact with your opponent, making it harder to anticipate their movements. Instead, tuck your chin into your chest, lower your head, and maintain eye contact with your opponent. This sets you up for better balance and control of the fight.

Not Maintaining Strong Core Muscles

Another mistake people make in wrestling is not keeping their core muscles engaged. The core muscles are essential for good balance and proper posture. Wrestlers lose their form and become more susceptible to injury when they don't engage their core muscles. Focus on breathing and engaging your abdominal muscles throughout the match to keep your core muscles activated.

Allowing Overextension in the Legs

During wrestling, overextending your legs is a common mistake fighters make. This posture can make you lose balance and expose you during your opponent's attack. It can lead to injuries to your legs and joints. Instead, focus on keeping your feet hip-width apart and engaging the muscles in your legs to keep your balance. You will maintain better control of the fight and avoid unnecessary damage to your body.

By avoiding these common mistakes, you can perform at your best and reduce the risk of injury. Remember, maintain proper balance, keep your core muscles engaged, and watch your posture, and you'll be on your way to becoming a better wrestler.

Developing Posture and Balance for Wrestling

Good posture and balance allow you to maintain stability and control while executing moves in the ring. Good posture ensures your body is aligned correctly, reducing the risk of injury and increasing overall strength. So, to improve your wrestling game, building a solid posture and balance foundation is a must. Here are tips and exercises to help you achieve good posture and balance.

Practice Good Posture

The first step in developing good posture is to practice daily. For example, consciously stand straight, pull your shoulders back, and keep your head up. It helps build muscle memory to maintain good posture during wrestling matches. Also, practice good posture while sitting, walking, and sleeping. For example, standing or sitting with hunched shoulders or slouching leads to muscle imbalances and poor posture over time. Also, it is best to have a comfortable mattress and pillows that support your back to maintain good posture while you sleep.

Strengthen Your Core

Your core muscles are the foundation for your posture and balance. Strengthening them maintains proper alignment and stability during wrestling matches. Some exercises to improve core muscles are planks, V-ups, and bicycles. These exercises target your abs, lower back, and obliques - vital for maintaining good posture and balance.

Improve Your Balance

Having good balance is critical while wrestling. Luckily, you can do several exercises and drills to improve it. Start with basic balance exercises like standing on one leg or using a balance board. Once you've mastered these, move on to more advanced exercises like single-leg squats, lunge variations, and instability ball exercises. These improve your balance while building leg and core strength.

Work on Your Footwork

Footwork is another crucial aspect of good posture and balance. Quick and precise movements require a solid foundation to build upon, which usually comes from proper footwork. Spend time practicing basic footwork drills like shuffles, ladder drills, and sidestepping. Once you've mastered these, move on to more advanced footwork drills to simulate movements commonly used in wrestling matches.

Focus on Your Breathing

Breathing is often overlooked in posture and balance discussions, but it's a crucial piece of the puzzle. Proper breathing techniques allow you to maintain stability and control while performing moves and increase endurance. Practice breathing deeply and intentionally while working on your posture and balance exercises. Inhaling on the way up and exhaling on the way down benefits balance.

Whether a seasoned wrestler or novice, working on posture and balance is essential to your success in the ring. By practicing these tips and exercises, you can develop a stability and control foundation to execute your moves with greater precision and agility. Remember, work on your posture, core strength, balance, footwork, and breathing, and soon you'll see a noticeable improvement in your wrestling game.

Tips for Maintaining Good Posture and Balance During a Wrestling Match

Maintaining good posture and balance during a match is crucial, as it helps you conserve energy, avoid injuries, and ultimately win the game. You must practice good posture and balance regularly to stay in control and on top of your opponent during a match. Here are tips to help you maintain good posture and balance during a wrestling match.

Engage Your Core

Your core muscles stabilize your body and maintain good posture during a match. Engage your core by pulling your belly button towards your spine and keeping your back straight. It keeps you balanced and avoids getting thrown off balance by your opponent. The key is to keep your core muscles engaged throughout the match by continuously contracting your abdominal muscles.

Keep your Feet Shoulder-Width Apart

Having your feet shoulder-width apart provides a solid base for maintaining balance and helps you resist takedowns. Keeping your weight distributed evenly between both feet is essential to avoid being thrown off balance. If your opponent tries to push you, keep your feet firmly planted on the mat and resist their force. You'll better counter their moves if your feet are stable.

Stay Low

Staying low helps you maintain balance while executing takedowns and reversals. Keep your hips below your opponent's level to gain leverage and increase control. It helps you avoid getting taken down or reversed. If you're on the defensive, stay low and use your core to resist your opponent's force.

Maintain Open Hands

Open hands provide balance and a better grip. If your hands are closed, it's difficult to react quickly to your opponent's moves, and you'll get thrown off balance more quickly. If your opponent gets close enough to grab you, having open hands will give you the flexibility to adjust and counter their moves. Once you get into the habit of keeping your hands open, you can take advantage of opportunities to execute takedowns and reversals.

Bend Your Knees

Slightly bending your knees helps you maintain balance and react quickly to your opponent's moves. It lets you lower your center of gravity, making it more difficult for your opponent to lift you off the ground. The key is to keep your knees slightly bent but still have them straight enough to move quickly. Also, stay low and bend your knees even more when in a defensive position. It will give you more control and gain leverage against your opponent.

Keep Your Head Up

Keeping your head up helps maintain good posture and awareness of your surroundings. It is crucial in wrestling because you can anticipate your opponent's moves and react accordingly. The ideal position is to keep your chin up and your eyes focused forward. It helps you avoid getting taken down or thrown off balance by your opponent.

Practice Yoga

Regularly practicing yoga can improve your balance, flexibility, and posture. Yoga poses focusing on balance, such as Tree Pose and Warrior III, can be particularly useful for wrestling. Even if you only practice a few poses for five minutes daily, it can give you an edge over your opponents. The benefits will be even more significant if you practice regularly and for a more extended period.

Use Your Breath

Your breath is crucial in wrestling as it helps you stay relaxed and focused. Taking deep breaths throughout the match conserves energy and keeps your muscles loose. When you exhale, visualize the movement of your body as if you were executing a move flawlessly; it helps you focus on the task and maintain good balance and posture.

Maintaining good posture and balance during a wrestling match is crucial for success. By engaging your core, keeping your feet shoulder-width apart, bending your knees, keeping your head up, and practicing yoga, you can improve your balance and posture and become a better wrestler. Regularly practice these tips and watch your performance on the mat improve.

Chapter 4: Penetrating, Lifting, and Other Maneuvers

Wrestling is an intricate blend of agility, strength, and strategy. At its core, wrestling involves several moves, including penetrating and lifting, requiring takedowns, pins, and submissions. It's a thrilling experience keeping spectators on the edge of their seats, marveling at the wrestlers' strength, skill, and technique. The sport demands dedication, perseverance, and discipline to master, but it's also an excellent way to get fit and build self-confidence.

Whether you're a fan or a wrestler, there's no denying the thrill of executing a perfect maneuver on the mat. This chapter focuses on some of the most common and valuable maneuvers in wrestling, offering details for each move and cautionary advice to avoid physical harm. It explains the different levels of motion and what is essential to focus on. By the end of this chapter, you'll better understand how to execute these moves and why they are so important.

Penetrating

Penetrating is an essential skill in wrestling, where a wrestler creates a successful offense by breaking through their opponent's defense and gaining control. It requires a combination of technique, strength, and agility. This section discusses three penetrating techniques: push-through, step-around, and rolling. Each technique works differently based on the opponent's body movement, positioning, and timing. So, let's dive into the penetrating world and master the art of dominating the wrestling mat.

Push-Through Technique

The push-through technique is best when an opponent is standing upright.

Push-through is a technique where the wrestler charges forward with speed and aggression. The aim is to overpower the opponent's defense by applying firm pressure on the upper body. Here's how to perform this technique:

- Start with a low stance and your head level with the opponent's chest.

- Next, drive the shoulder into the opponent's chest and push with the lead leg.
- Follow through with the trail leg and get behind the opponent.
- Secure control by locking the hands or grabbing the waist.

The push-through technique is best when the opponent is standing upright or has a weak defensive posture. However, if the opponent anticipates the move, they can counter with a sprawl or a Whizzer.

Step-Around Technique

The step-around technique involves a circular movement to get around the opponent's defense and secure control from the back. It requires good footwork and timing to execute effectively. Here are the steps to perform this technique:

- Start by faking a shot or an attack to force the opponent to react.
- Step to the outside of the opponent's lead leg and circle.
- Keep the head low and wrap the arms around the opponent's waist.
- Finally, secure control from the back and bring the opponent down to the mat.

The step-around technique suits opponents with a solid upper body but weak lower body defense. However, if the opponent sprawls, the wrestler can switch to a single-leg takedown or transition to another technique.

The step-around technique requires good footwork.

Rolling Technique

The rolling technique is best used when an opponent has a strong stance.

The rolling technique is a unique way to penetrate the opponent's defense by using their momentum against them. It involves rolling over the opponent's body and getting control from the side. Here's how to perform this technique:

- Start with a collar tie or a wrist control to manipulate the opponent's movements.
- Drop the weight and roll over the opponent's back by tucking the head and shoulder.
- Flip to the other side and secure control by grabbing the leg or the waist.
- Drive the opponent to the mat or transition to another move.

The rolling technique is best executed when the opponent is expecting a standard attack, or they have a strong stance. However, it requires excellent timing and coordination to execute effectively.

Penetrating is a crucial skill in wrestling, giving a wrestler the upper hand in the match. The push-through, step-around, and rolling techniques are three ways to penetrate the opponent's defense and gain control. Therefore, it's essential to practice these techniques regularly and master the timing, footwork, and positioning. Remember, the key to successful penetrating lies in anticipating the opponent's movements, keeping the pressure on, and maintaining focus and discipline. With dedication and hard work, anyone can master the art of penetrating in wrestling and become a formidable opponent on the mat.

Lifting

Wrestling is a combat sport demanding strength, agility, endurance, and technique. Regarding technique, lifting is essential to the game. Lifting can help you take down your opponent, control the match, and score points. However, lifting is a challenging task and requires proper training and technique. This section discusses the three most effective lifting techniques in wrestling: hip heist, step-over, and rolling split. Also provided are tips to improve your lifting skills and avoid common mistakes.

Hip Heist

The hip heist is the most basic lifting technique in wrestling.

The hip heist is the most basic lifting technique in wrestling and involves using your hips to lift your opponent. To perform a hip heist, you must be in a low stance with your feet shoulder-width apart, hands on your opponent's back, and your head down. Push your hips forward and lift your opponent while turning to the side. It gives you the leverage to take control of the match and score points.

Step-Over

The step-over is effective when your opponent is in a low stance.

The step-over is another effective lifting technique in wrestling, especially when your opponent is in a low stance. To best perform this maneuver, step over your opponent's leg with one foot while grabbing their opposite arm to perform a step-over. Then, lift your opponent's leg in the air with your other hand and step forward with your foot. It will cause your opponent to lose balance, allowing you to take them down.

Rolling Split

The rolling split is an advanced lifting technique.

The rolling split is a more advanced lifting technique in wrestling and requires proper training and strategy. To perform a rolling split, grab your opponent's leg and pull it towards you while rolling onto your back. Then, split your legs and lift your opponent with your legs, causing them to fall onto their back. This technique requires a lot of flexibility and agility, but it can be a game-changer if appropriately executed.

Tips and Mistakes to Avoid

You must focus on your technique, strength, and flexibility to improve your lifting skills in wrestling. It's essential to practice with a partner who can give you feedback and help you improve your technique. However, you should avoid common mistakes, such as lifting with your arms instead of your hips, not using your legs to support your lift, and not keeping your balance.

Lifting is a crucial part of wrestling, and mastering the proper techniques gives you the edge to win matches. The hip heist, step-over, and rolling split are three effective lifting techniques to take down your opponent and score points. However, mastering these techniques requires a proper approach, strength, and flexibility. You can improve your lifting skills and become a better wrestler by practicing with a partner, focusing on your technique, and avoiding common mistakes. So, keep training and honing your skills. Remember, practice makes perfect.

Back-Stepping

One of the most crucial and fundamental techniques in wrestling is back-stepping. The back step move allows wrestlers to gain leverage, control, and score points against their opponents. This section discusses the three back-stepping maneuvers, including the crab walk, step-behind, and reverse rolling, and their applications in wrestling matches. Whether a beginner or an experienced wrestler, this section provides vital insights and strategies to improve your back-stepping skills and dominate on the mat.

Crab Walk

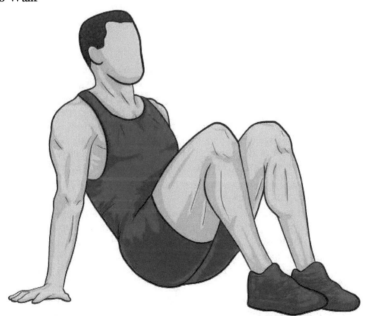

The crab walk allows you to move backward diagonally.

The crab walk is a back-stepping technique where the wrestler moves diagonally backward, stepping their foot across their opponent's foot. The wrestler's body lowers as they do, pressing the chest against their opponent's back. This move is beneficial when the wrestler's opponent is initiating a forward attack, and the wrestler wants to avoid the attack and gain leverage. The crab walk technique is a great defensive tool but can lead to counters, so it must be executed quickly and efficiently.

Step-Behind

The step-behind is another useful back-stepping technique by stepping diagonally backward while simultaneously stepping around the opponent's body. The wrestler places their foot behind their opponent's and controls their opponent's hips. This move is excellent for gaining an advantageous position over the opponent, especially when the opponent is attacking forward. The step-behind move is effective and leaves the opposing wrestler open to many other forms of attack, making it a versatile and effective technique to use in competition.

Reverse Rolling

Reverse-rolling can change the direction of a fight.

Reverse rolling is a back-stepping technique where the wrestler moves their body in a circular motion backward while stepping behind their opponent's leg. The wrestler turns their body so they face their opponent. In this position, they have a clear and dominant position to control their opponent. This technique is useful when the wrestler's opponent tries scoring points by grabbing their leg, allowing them to escape and attack from a position of dominance. When executed correctly, the reverse rolling technique is swift and dynamic for changing the direction of a fight, leaving the opponent vulnerable and lost.

Tips for Back-Stepping Moves

Back-stepping techniques are great tools but must be implemented with caution and precision. Here are some tips to help you improve your back-stepping techniques and make them useful in matches.

- **Practice Regularly:** Regularly performing back-stepping moves with the help of a training partner can help you confidently master the art of back-stepping.
- **Be Agile:** Back-stepping aims to dodge and avoid your opponent's attack, so it's essential to be light on your feet and nimble on your toes.
- **Control Your Opponent's Hips:** One of the most crucial aspects of back-stepping moves is to gain control of your opponent's hips. It helps you dictate the direction of the match and leverage against your opponents.
- **Use Combinations:** Mastering back-stepping moves is part of an excellent wrestler's arsenal. So, it's helpful to integrate this technique into various other methods, such as throws, takedowns, and submissions.

Back-stepping moves are fundamental skills every wrestler should master. The crab walk, step-behind, and reverse rolling moves are versatile techniques helping wrestlers avoid attacks and gain an advantageous position in matches. It's essential to practice and master these moves, along with sprucing up your agility and control. These moves are great techniques to use and integrate with other methods. Remember, a great wrestler requires patience, diligence, and strategy.

Back Arching

One essential skill in wrestling is getting up from the ground as quickly as possible, especially when your opponent is trying to pin you down. Back arching or kipping up is one technique to get up from the ground, but there are others, such as rocking up and springing up. This section explores the different methods of back arching in wrestling and provides tips to master them.

Kipping Up

A kip-up can help you get up quickly.

Kipping up is a widespread technique in wrestling, and many wrestlers use it to get up quickly from the ground. This technique involves rocking your legs to gain momentum and then thrusting your body upward to reach your feet. To perform a kipping up, you must start by lying on your back with your knees bent and your feet flat on the ground. Then, swing your legs toward your chest to generate momentum and kick them straight up while pushing your body off the floor with your arms. To master kipping up, ensure you swing your legs with enough power to generate the necessary momentum to get up. Also, you must push your whole body off the ground, not just your upper body.

Rocking Up

Rocking up is another famous technique wrestlers use to quickly get up from the ground. This technique involves rolling your shoulders off the ground to gain momentum, then bringing your knees under you to stand up. To perform rocking up, start by lying on your back with your knees bent, feet flat on the ground, and your arms by your sides. Then, rock your shoulders forward to create momentum, and bring your knees up while pushing off the floor with your arms. To master rocking up, roll your shoulders far enough to generate momentum. Also, push off the ground with your arms and keep your core tight to control your body's movement.

Springing Up

Springing up is a less common technique in wrestling, but it is an effective way to get up quickly. This technique involves springing off your feet and hands to reach a standing position. To perform springing up, start by lying on your back with your knees bent, feet flat on the ground, and your arms by your sides. Then, push off the ground with your feet and hands in one swift motion, bring your knees up, and stand. To master springing up, push off the ground with significant force, making the motion as fluid as possible.

Back arching is a crucial skill in wrestling, and mastering the different techniques can give you an advantage on the mat. Kipping up, rocking up, and springing up are three effective techniques wrestlers use to get up quickly. To master these techniques, practice the basics of each and focus on your form. Remember to swing your legs with enough power, maintain movement control, and keep your core tight. You can master these techniques and elevate your wrestling game to the next level with dedicated practice.

Different Levels of Motion

Understanding and implementing the various levels of motion is crucial to mastering wrestling. This section discusses the different levels of motion in wrestling, including high, medium, and low energy. By the end, you will better understand how to incorporate these levels of motion into your wrestling techniques.

High Energy

Fast, explosive movements characterize high-energy wrestling; this level of motion requires a lot of stamina and strength. High-energy wrestlers are constantly moving and attacking, rarely giving their opponents a chance to catch their breath – this wrestling style best suits agile athletes who can move quickly and easily. To incorporate high-energy wrestling into your technique, focus on initiating quick and explosive movements, like takedowns and reversals.

Medium Energy

The medium energy level is slower than the high energy level but requires significant energy and effort. In medium-energy wrestling, athletes constantly move but at a slightly slower pace. This level of motion is often used for strategic reasons, like setting up a takedown or waiting for the right moment to strike. Good medium-energy wrestlers can maintain a constant pace throughout the match, conserving energy for later rounds.

Low Energy

Low-energy wrestling is the slowest level of motion and is typically used for defensive strategies. This level of motion requires a lot of patience and skill, as wrestlers must move skillfully and avoid being caught off-guard by their opponent's attacks. Athletes control their opponent's movements while waiting for an opportunity to strike in low-energy wrestling. This level of motion is best suited for wrestlers with strong defensive skills who can maintain their composure even in high-pressure situations.

The different levels of motion in wrestling are crucial in every match. By mastering different levels of motion, wrestlers can strategically expend their energy, stay ahead of their opponents, and ultimately come out on top. Whether you prefer high-energy, medium-energy, or low-energy wrestling, understanding these levels of motion helps you become a more effective athlete. So, the next time you hit the mat, remember to incorporate these levels of motion into your technique and watch your performance soar.

Essential Focus Points

Wrestlers have to be mentally and physically tough to compete and be successful. Therefore, it requires strategy, practice, and discipline to master the techniques and tactics of wrestling. For a wrestler, the focus is critical and starts with understanding essential focus points. This section discusses three crucial focus points in wrestling: the center of gravity, balance, and kinesthetic awareness.

Center of Gravity

One of the most important focus points in wrestling is the center of gravity. Your center of gravity is the point in your body where your weight distribution is equally balanced. Having a low center of gravity is critical in wrestling. The lower you are, the harder it is for your opponent to take you down. Wrestlers must maintain this low center of gravity to stay balanced and prevent their opponents from gaining leverage. Therefore, focus on keeping your hips down and tight to your opponent to maintain an intense center of gravity.

Balance

Balancing your weight distribution is another crucial focus point in wrestling. You must remain balanced to execute moves and defend against your opponents. It requires core strength and ensuring your feet are correctly positioned. If you lose your balance, it will be much easier for your opponent to execute a move against you. Wrestlers work on balance by practicing moves requiring them to shift their body weight and maintain control. Focusing on balance allows you to stay in control during a wrestle.

Kinesthetic Awareness

Last, kinesthetic awareness refers to being conscious of your body's positioning and movement. For example, having control over the position of your body to execute moves to win wrestling matches is crucial. Knowing where your body is in relation to your opponent and the mat requires a specialized sense called kinesthetic awareness. This awareness can be developed through rigorous practice and improved by routinely working on drills and focusing on your opponent's movements.

By recognizing the essential focus points in wrestling, such as the center of gravity, balance, and kinesthetic awareness, wrestlers can position themselves to become better competitors. These three focus points are essential not only to master in wrestling but also in everyday life. Like in wrestling, maintaining a low center of gravity, balanced weight distribution, and awareness of movement allows you to progress and succeed in anything you set for yourself. So, focus, practice, and discipline as much as possible.

This chapter covered penetration, lifting, and other standard moves in wrestling. Knowing how to use these moves properly is essential for success on the mat, and mastering them requires focus, practice, and discipline. Awareness of your body's position and distribution of weight are crucial elements when executing moves. Additionally, you must understand the different levels of motion in wrestling, such as high, medium, and low energy. By mastering these levels of motion, you increase your mobility and agility on the mat, which ultimately helps you become a better wrestler. So, focus on the essentials and watch your performance soar.

Chapter 5: How to Attack and Counterattack

Wrestling is a sport necessitating skill and strategy to emerge as the victor. Wrestlers must be confident in their abilities to attack and counterattack effectively and know how to read their opponent's moves. It's about understanding their weaknesses and taking advantage of opportunities. Whether it's a takedown, pin, or submission, every wrestler has preferred moves they rely on. However, knowing how to counter these moves is crucial to stay ahead of the game.

With practice and determination, wrestlers can master the art of attacking and counterattacking, making them a formidable force on the mat. This chapter outlines some of the most common wrestling techniques to attack and counterattack and tips on avoiding mistakes and minimizing bodily harm. These techniques are significantly advantageous when attempting to gain control over an opponent. By the end of this chapter, you will better understand the different attacks and counterattacks in wrestling.

Unlocking the Power of Headlocks in Wrestling

Headlocks are a popular wrestling move.

Headlocks in wrestling are a popular move known for the effectiveness and ease with which they can be executed. However, not all headlocks are created equal. Some are more effective than others, and some can cause severe injuries if not done correctly. This section discusses the different headlocks, their benefits, and the correct ways to execute them. It provides tips on common mistakes and how to avoid injuries. So, let's dive into the world of headlocks.

Setting Up the Move

The first step in executing a successful headlock is correctly setting it up. It involves creating the correct position to perform the move. The position for a headlock typically starts with both wrestlers standing face to face. The attacking wrestler places their arm over the opponent's head and grabs onto their wrist or the opponent's arm. The wrestler must move their body close to the opponent, with their head tight against the opponent's head or neck. It creates a firm grip and position to execute the move.

Executing the Move

Once you have set up the move correctly, it's time to execute it. The wrestler squeezes their arm tight against the opponent's neck and twists their body to the side to apply pressure and maintain control. This should be done gradually without pulling the opponent too hard, as it could cause injury. The move puts immense pressure on the opponent's neck, making it difficult for them to breathe and escape if executed correctly.

Common Mistakes

One common mistake wrestlers make when attempting a headlock is pulling too hard. It can be potentially dangerous, especially if the opponent is unprepared for the move. Another common mistake is not setting up the move correctly, leading to losing control and a failed attempt. Avoiding being too predictable with this move so your opponent does not easily counter it is essential.

How to Avoid Injury

As with any wrestling move, it is vital to pay close attention to your opponent's body language and only perform moves you have practiced and are comfortable with. If you experience discomfort or resistance during the move, it's crucial to release the hold and try again later. Stretching and warming up is essential before attempting any wrestling move, including headlocks.

Headlocks are a decisive move in wrestling that can effectively control your opponent. It's essential to execute this move correctly, set it up properly, take it slow once you've grabbed the opponent, and avoid common mistakes. As with all wrestling moves, safety is critical. Always pay attention to your opponent's body language and avoid using too much force. With practice, you, too, can become a master of the headlock and a dominant force on the wrestling mat.

Master the Art of Executing Takedowns

Takedowns are necessary in combat sports.

Takedowns are an essential skill in martial arts and combat sports. It is a move that can instantly change the course of a fight and give you the upper hand against opponents. However, executing a takedown is more complex than it seems. It requires combining technique, timing, and strategy. Whether a beginner or an experienced fighter, this section will help you master the art of executing takedowns and avoiding injuries.

Setting Up the Move

Before executing a takedown, you must set it up properly. A takedown can be performed in many ways, from clinching, shooting, or catching the opponent off guard. One popular way to set up a takedown is using fake strikes or feints to draw your opponent's attention and create openings. Many experienced fighters use this technique in stand-up and ground positions. Other ways to set up takedowns include footwork, angles, or creating unbalanced positions to throw your opponent off balance.

Executing the Move

Once you have set up the takedown, it's time to execute it. A successful takedown requires good timing, technique, and speed. Some common takedowns include the double-leg takedown, single-leg takedown, and hip throw. To execute the takedown, you must ensure you're in the proper position and your opponent's weight is shifted in the right direction. Takedowns can be adjusted on the fly, so keeping your options open while executing the move is important.

Common Mistakes

Like other techniques, takedowns come with common mistakes that can harm your fighting performance. One frequent mistake is not setting up the takedown properly, leading to you getting countered or caught in a submission. Rushing the takedown or telegraphing the move can give your opponent enough time to defend and set up their counterattack. Other mistakes include overcommitting (rather than controlling the opponent's center of gravity) and failing to follow through with the takedown.

How to Avoid Injury

Takedowns are powerful and associated with high risk for you and your opponent. To avoid injury, first, ensure you execute a controlled move. Avoid using excessive force or momentum, which can cause serious harm to you or your opponent. Also, wear the proper protective gear, like a mouthguard and headgear. Last, if you're unsure about the appropriate execution of a takedown or are experiencing discomfort, consult a trainer or physician.

Mastering the art of takedowns is a crucial skill for an aspiring fighter. You can significantly improve your chances of winning a fight by setting up the move correctly, executing it with proper timing and technique, and avoiding common mistakes and injury. So, whether a beginner or an experienced fighter, remember these tips and continue practicing perfecting your takedown skills.

Mastering Submission Holds

Submission holds are the most effective way to dominate your opponent. [42]

Have you ever been awed by how technical and precise some moves in professional wrestling are? Submission holds are one of these moves. This technique is one of the most complex and effective ways to dominate your opponent and win a match. However, submission holds can be intimidating, especially for beginners. This section walks you through the basics of submission holds and explores the steps to execute them flawlessly.

Setting Up the Move

Before anything, remember all submission holds start as a result of controlling your opponent's body position. You must put your opponent in a vulnerable position to set up a submission hold. Here's how you do it: you must create openings by being aware of your opponent's stance and looking for signs of weakness. When you notice an opportunity, seize it, and work your moves. If your opponent attempts to counter or resist the move, remain calm but assertive. Keep up the pressure until you execute the move. Setting up a submission hold requires skill, attention, and careful movements.

Executing the Move

After setting up the move, you must execute it efficiently, or you'll lose the match. Practicing submission holds repeatedly is the best way to perform the move flawlessly. Here are some steps to execute a submission hold: First, you must get close to your opponent. This way, you have a better grip to hold them down. Then, lock your grip and wrap your opponent's body parts, like the legs and arms, in your hold. Some submission holds require keeping a tight grip for a few moments, so be patient, focused, and always maintain your grip and balance. Last, ensure your hold is sufficient to force your opponent to tap out.

Common Mistakes

Some wrestlers make mistakes when executing submission holds, causing them to lose matches. Here are a few common errors in submission holds you can quickly correct:

- Not being patient enough to set up the correct position for the move can lead to counterattacks
- Not gripping tightly can lead to losing the hold and the match
- Losing focus controlling your opponent's body leads to them escaping the hold quickly
- Failure to observe balance can topple a wrestler and lead to a lost match

How to Avoid Injury

Injuries are commonplace in wrestling. However, you can reduce the risk of injuries by:

- Always correctly stretch before practice
- Wearing protective gear during training and matches
- Knowing your limits and not overstretching beyond your capabilities
- Seeking medical attention immediately if an injury occurs

Remember, a wrestler's overall health and well-being are essential to executing, winning, and enjoying the sport.

Submission holds are a great way to showcase wrestling techniques and win matches. To set up submission holds, keep an alert mindset, look for openings, and remain focused. Executing submission holds will require practice, patience, balance, and focus. By avoiding the common mistakes wrestlers make during submission holds, you can increase your chances of winning. Last, always take care of your health and well-being and seek medical attention when necessary. With these tips, you can master submission holds and become a successful wrestler.

Escaping Your Way to Victory

One of the most crucial skills in wrestling is the ability to escape. When caught in a hold or moved by your opponent, an escape can change the course of a match or prevent your opponent from scoring. This technique requires strength, flexibility, and quick thinking. This section guides you on recognizing an opponent's move, executing an escape, avoiding common mistakes, and preventing unnecessary injuries.

How to Recognize an Opponent's Move

The first step toward executing an escape is recognizing the hold or move your opponent has on you. It can be challenging since several moves in wrestling require different escapes. An excellent way to identify the move on you is to focus on the body part your opponent uses to hold or control you. For instance, if your opponent has a leg hold on you, try using various leg escapes to free your legs. Closely watching your opponent's movement will help you anticipate their subsequent actions, allowing you to prepare your escape.

Executing the Escape

Once you have identified your opponent's move, you must act fast to escape it. Being calm and level-headed is vital in this situation because you must think quickly. Common escapes include sit-outs, switches, and stand-ups, which require strength, flexibility, and technique. Additionally, practicing these moves beforehand increases your chances of executing a successful escape during a match.

Common Mistakes

One of the most common mistakes wrestlers make while attempting to escape is only partially committing to the move. If you hold back or hesitate, you will lose the upper hand, allowing your opponent to overpower you. Another mistake is relying solely on strength to escape rather than on technique. Using brute force works occasionally, but it will often tire you out faster, leaving you vulnerable to your opponent's next move.

How to Avoid Injury

The risk of getting injured is high in wrestling. Practice proper techniques and warm up before matches to prevent harm and injury. When executing escapes, avoid arching your back or twisting your neck, positions that could predispose you to injury. Last, knowing when to tap out is crucial. Although tapping out is a sign of weakness, saving your body from unnecessary harm is wise.

Escaping in wrestling is not merely a skill helping you to score points but a technique preventing your opponent from scoring. It takes patience, practice, and a keen sense of your opponent's moves. However, it can make all the difference in a match once mastered. Remember, stay focused, commit to the move, and prioritize safety first.

How to Master Reversals in Wrestling

To master reversals, you need to be able to anticipate your opponent's moves.

Wrestling is a highly technical combat sport involving muscle, speed, agility, and strategic thinking. One of the most critical aspects of wrestling is learning to reverse your opponent's move. This technique is essential for self-defense and can be significantly advantageous over your opponent. This section explores the art of reversals in wrestling, including recognizing an opponent's move, executing the reversal, common mistakes, and avoiding injury.

How to Recognize an Opponent's Move

Before executing a successful wrestling reversal, you must recognize your opponent's move. Some standard moves wrestlers make include a double-leg takedown, single-leg takedown, or a high crotch takedown. The key to reversing your opponent's move is analyzing your opponent's position, leverage, and momentum. Learn the various wrestling techniques, drills, and sparring with experienced wrestlers.

Executing the Reversal

Once you recognize your opponent's move, timing the reversal execution is essential. Several reversals in wrestling include sit-out and switch reversal, Granby Roll reversal, hip-heist reversal, and Whizzer-based reversal. To perform a reversal, you must use your strength, speed, and agility to counter your opponent's momentum. Timing and precision are crucial to executing a successful reversal. It takes practice and training to master the art of reversals, so don't get discouraged if you struggle initially.

Common Mistakes

Even experienced wrestlers make mistakes with reversals. One of the common mistakes is forcing a reversal before the right moment. Another mistake is not following through on the reversal, leaving you open for a counterattack. Last, wrestlers might use too much force and injure their opponents, resulting in disqualification. Understanding the rules and regulations of wrestling to avoid penalties or injuries is essential.

How to Avoid Injury

Last, staying safe and avoiding injury when executing a reversal is essential. It involves proper technique, strength training, nutrition, and injury prevention strategies. Before performing a move, stretch and warm up your muscles to prevent sprains and strains. Furthermore, always listen to your body and communicate with your coach if you feel pain or discomfort. Wrestling is a physically demanding sport, and caring for your body to perform at your best is crucial.

Reversals are one of the essential techniques in wrestling, and mastering them can give you a significant advantage over your opponent. To execute a successful turnaround, you must recognize your opponent's move, analyze their position and leverage, and move with precision and timing. Avoid common mistakes like forcing the reversal too early or failing to follow through. Last, stay safe and avoid injury by following proper wrestling techniques, strength training, and injury prevention strategies. You can dominate the wrestling mat with practice and dedication and become a formidable opponent.

Effectively Counter Your Opponent's Move

You need to be able to counter your opponent's moves quickly.

As a wrestler, you aim to pin your opponent or score more points than them. However, you can only achieve these goals by reacting quickly to your opponent's moves and counters. This section discusses how to recognize your opponent's move, execute the counter, common mistakes to avoid, and techniques to prevent injury.

How to Recognize an Opponent's Move

The key to countering your opponent's move is to recognize it early. Therefore, it's crucial to have a good understanding of wrestling basics. Study your opponent's moves closely during the match by observing their positioning and movements. Pay attention to the subtle changes in their stance or body position, as these can indicate what move they are preparing to execute. Some wrestlers are known for their signature moves, so watch videos of their matches to familiarize yourself with their wrestling style. It helps you anticipate and counter their moves and prepare for their technique before the game.

Executing the Counter

Executing the counter requires quick reflexes, precise timing, and technique. Your countermoves depend on your opponent's moves, position, and wrestling style. A standard countermove is a "switch," where you quickly shift your position to reverse the move your opponent just executed. Another technique is a "roll-out," where you use your momentum to roll out of your opponent's hold and control the match. Once you have identified the move your opponent is attempting, execute the counter immediately. Being confident and decisive while performing the counter is essential, as hesitation can give your opponent an advantage.

Common Mistakes

While countering an opponent's move can be exciting and rewarding, it can also result in injury if not executed correctly. Wrestlers' mistakes while countering include poor timing, improper technique, and lack of focus. These mistakes lead to losing control of the match and allowing the opponent to capitalize on the error. To avoid making these mistakes, you must stay focused and patient. Remain in control of the situation and never panic, as this can lead to rushed or improper technique. Instead, take your time to execute the counter with the proper technique and timing.

How to Avoid Injury

Prioritizing your safety while executing counters is essential. Many injuries, such as sprains, fractures, and dislocations, result from countering. To avoid these injuries, you must warm up before the match, use proper technique, and keep your body limber. Another important tip is gradually increasing the practice's intensity to avoid overworking and straining your muscles. If you feel muscle or joint pain or discomfort, immediately stop and seek medical attention.

To become a successful wrestler, you must master the art of attacking and countering your opponent's moves. It includes recognizing your opponent's move, executing the strategy correctly, avoiding common mistakes, and prioritizing safety. This chapter covered tips and techniques to help you develop your skills as a wrestler. Remember, practice makes perfect, so keep practicing and improving your skills until you reach your goals.

Chapter 6: Reversal Techniques

As a wrestler, there's nothing more satisfying than landing in a tricky situation and executing a perfect reversal. You can transform what looked like a surefire defeat into a glorious triumph with the proper techniques. Reversal moves take different forms, from using your opponent's momentum against them to using your strength to flip the situation in your favor. Whatever the tactic, the key is to be confident in your ability to pull it off.

Building your arsenal of reversal techniques is essential to becoming a force to be reckoned with on the mat. So, get ready to enhance your wrestling skills and dominate your opponents. This chapter explores the reversal maneuvers, from basic switching techniques to more advanced offensive counters. It explores strategies for analyzing your opponent and gaining the upper hand.

Switching Maneuvers

Wrestling is about overpowering your opponent and being agile and quick in your movements. One critical factor in wrestling is switching to a favorable position when the opponent has caught you in a compromising position. Switching maneuvers helps wrestlers get out of holds and locks and gain control of the match. This section explores the different switches and their applications.

What Is the Switch?

Switching in wrestling means changing your body position from one hold or move to another. It allows wrestlers to break free from their opponents' grip and gain control. A switch can also be used to counterattack or execute a move. One of the most common switches in wrestling is the "sit out" switch. The move requires the wrestler to sit on their hips while pulling their opponent toward them and shifting their weight. The switcher shifts and takes control from behind as the opponent moves forward.

Reversing from Body Locks

The body lock is a common maneuver where the opponent wraps their arms around the wrestler's waist and shoulders, making it difficult to move. Wrestlers can use the "hip heist" switch to escape from this grip. In this maneuver, the wrestler drops their hips to the ground while pulling the opponent toward them. As the opponent falls forward, the wrestler shifts their weight and gains a favorable position to attack. The hip heist switch can also be used to counterattack.

Reversing from Backbreaker Holds

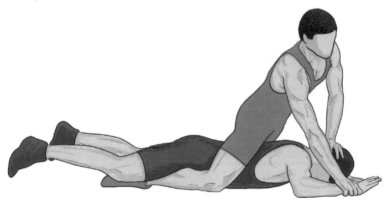

The grapevine switch helps you gain an advantage.

The backbreaker hold is a painful move putting pressure on the wrestler's spine and neck. However, wrestlers can use the "grapevine" switch to escape from this hold. In this maneuver, the wrestler loops their leg around the opponent's leg and twists their body, applying pressure to the opponent's knee and ankle. The grapevine switch is an effective maneuver to escape from the backbreaker hold and take control of the match.

Reversing from Chokeholds

A headlock switch can help you gain control.

The chokehold is a dangerous maneuver restricting the airflow to the wrestler's lungs and brain. Wrestlers can use the "headlock" switch to escape from this hold. In this maneuver, the wrestler wraps their arm around the opponent's neck, bringing their weight down. As a result, the opponent's grip loosens, allowing the wrestler to shift their weight and gain control. The headlock switch is an effective maneuver to escape from chokeholds and take control of the match.

Reversing from Pin Holds

A bridge switch will help you reverse a pin hold.

The pin hold is when the opponent tries to trap the wrestler's shoulders on the mat for a count of three. Wrestlers can use the "bridge" switch to escape from this hold. In this maneuver, the wrestler shifts their weight onto their feet and flips their body onto their shoulders, lifting their opponent's weight off them. The wrestler shifts the weight onto their feet and gains a favorable position to attack. The bridge switch is an effective way to escape from the pin holds and take control of the match.

Switching maneuvers are a critical aspect of wrestling. They can change the outcome of a match and give the wrestler an advantage. Understanding the different switches and their applications helps wrestlers improve their skills and technique.

Transitional Maneuvers

Wrestlers are always looking for ways to outsmart their opponents in a match. The ability to seamlessly transition from one move to another is crucial for a wrestler to gain an advantage over their opponent. Transitional moves are like a bridge between different wrestling techniques that, when executed correctly, can make a significant difference in the outcome of a match.

This section discusses three transitional maneuvers to make you a better wrestler. These moves include the reversal to bridge, the roll-through escape, and the momentum to reverse. Each move requires precision and timing but can be mastered with focused practice.

Reversal to Bridge

The reversal to bridge is a great transitional move to counter an opponent's takedown attempt. Get into a seated position with your opponent on top of you and pin one of your shoulders to the mat. From here, push upward with the shoulder not pinned while simultaneously arching your back to roll your opponent over your body and onto their back.

You can bridge up and attack once your opponent is on the mat. Timing is crucial to execute this move successfully. You should initiate the move as soon as you feel your opponent's grip loosen, even a little. It helps move your head toward the unpinned shoulder to give yourself more leverage.

Roll-Through Escape

A roll-through escape will help you escape a side control.

The roll-through escape is another tremendous transitional move helping you escape your opponent's side control. Create space between you and your opponent. Next, turn onto your side, facing away from your opponent's chest, and pull your knee toward your chest while reaching your opposite hand toward your ankle. Use this momentum to roll onto your back and slide your knee toward your opponent.

Once you are in a more favorable position, you can attack. The key to this move is using your momentum and staying relaxed. The roll should be smooth and flowing, almost like a dance. It's essential to keep your movements fluid and controlled so you don't give your opponent opportunities to capitalize.

Using Momentum to Reverse

The momentum to reverse is a great transitional move to counter an opponent's attack. Get into a defensive position and wait for your opponent's attack. As they come toward you, use their momentum against them by sidestepping and pulling them forward, causing them to lose balance. Then, use your momentum to reverse the position and attack. This move requires excellent timing and awareness. It's crucial to know when your opponent is committed to an attack and to have the reflexes to react quickly. Stay low and relaxed and use your opponent's force against them to gain the upper hand.

Transitional maneuvers are an essential aspect of wrestling, giving you a strategic advantage over your opponent. The three moves discussed in this section, the reversal to bridge, the roll-through escape, and the momentum to reverse, are effective transitional moves helping you become a better wrestler.

Offensive Maneuvers

Whether a beginner or seasoned wrestler, learning offensive maneuvers can give you the edge to dominate your opponents, this section discusses three effective offensive maneuvers wrestlers use to gain an advantage in matches. These maneuvers include using an opponent's momentum against them, performing reversal sweeps and slams, and executing reversal counters.

Using the Opponent's Momentum against Them

The first offensive maneuver is using an opponent's momentum against them. This technique requires paying close attention to your opponent's movements and anticipating their next move. The aim is to use your opponent's energy to your advantage by redirecting it and taking them down. For example, if your opponent charges forward, step aside, grab their arm, and use their momentum to toss them over your shoulder. This move is called a hip toss.

Another move using this technique is the arm drag. Grab your opponent's arm and pull it past you. Then, as they move forward, you step aside and use their momentum to twist their body and take them down.

Reversal Sweeps and Slams

The second offensive maneuver is the reversal sweep and slam. This technique counters your opponent's takedown attempt by quickly transitioning into your takedown. For example, if your opponent goes for a single-leg takedown, you can quickly shift your weight and use a hip toss to take them down. This move requires a lot of speed and balance, but it can be devastating when executed properly. Another move using this technique is the arm drag takedown. In this move, grab your opponent's arm and use their momentum to throw them to the ground.

Reversal Counters

The third offensive maneuver is the reversal counter. This move requires anticipating your opponent's takedown attempt and using it against them. For example, if your opponent goes for a double-leg takedown, sprawl and use their momentum to take them down. This move is called a sprawling counter, one of the most effective moves in wrestling. Another move using this technique is the switch. Start on your back and use your leg to trap your opponent in this move. Then, as they move forward, quickly roll over and take them down.

Offensive maneuvers are essential in wrestling. Using an opponent's momentum against them, performing reversal sweeps and slams, and executing reversal counters are three effective ways to dominate the sport. The key to mastering these maneuvers is to practice them regularly and pay close attention to your opponent's movements. By incorporating these offensive techniques into your wrestling arsenal, you'll be well on your way to becoming a dominant wrestler.

Reversal Strategies

Wrestling, the oldest sport in the world, is more than just a competition of physical strength. It's a game of intelligence and strategy where the best wrestlers always watch their opponent's moves. When in the middle of a match, it's essential to be calm and patient, whether on top or bottom. Reversals can take you from being the underdog to becoming a winner in no time. By developing solid reversal strategies, you can swiftly seize control, leaving your opponent confused and stressed. This section explores the art of reversal in wrestling and three essential techniques to master it.

Mastering the Basics

The first step to mastering the art of reversal is learning the basics. A solid understanding of the fundamental movements and techniques, such as hip heist, Granby Roll, switch, and sit out, are the cornerstones to developing an effective reversal strategy. Practice these basics on a mat daily. Reversals require lightning-fast reaction and timing, and by ensuring these movements become second nature, you will have a winning edge. Moreover, it's essential to work on your grip strength. A firm grip will help you control the opponent throughout the match.

Developing Counterattacks

A counterattack is an offensive move to deflect and redirect the opponent's aggression or attack. Developing these counterattacks is highly effective during a wrestling match. First, familiarize yourself with your opponent's moves, anticipate their next steps, and prepare your counterattack. Counterattacks, like the Peterson and Granby rolls, are examples of effective retaliation moves to learn.

Work on Timing and Execution

Timing is significantly vital in wrestling. The same goes for reversal strategies. The wrestler who can quickly switch from defense to offense will most likely win. When targeting a reversal, excellent timing and execution to make it successful are essential. Be patient, anticipate your opponent's moves, and select the most effective reversal strategy at the right time. Remember, timing is everything.

Developing Mental Toughness

Good wrestlers possess outstanding mental toughness – they don't get affected by their opponent's moves. Instead, they use it to their advantage. As a result, they are calm and composed, even under pressure, and can quickly decide during matches. To develop mental toughness, you must keep practicing and build confidence. Participating in wrestling tournaments and facing tough opponents is a great way to gain experience and build mental strength.

Analyzing Your Opponent

Wrestling demands an assessment of your opponent before a move can be made. Wrestlers must leverage their strengths and exploit their opponent's weaknesses to gain advantage. Therefore, it would be best to learn your opponent's movements, timing, and tendencies to plan your moves correctly. Analyzing your opponent is critical to winning in wrestling. This section explains some essential tips to help you succeed on the mat.

Identifying Weaknesses

The first step to successfully analyzing your opponent is identifying their weaknesses. Every wrestler has their strengths and weaknesses, including your opposition. Take note of how they move, their body type, position, and style. You can tell if they struggle with takedowns, escapes, or pins. Understanding their weaknesses helps you plan strategic maneuvers targeting these vulnerabilities. Then, build your game plan based on your opponent's weaknesses and aim to outsmart them.

Looking for Opportunities

When you identify your opponent's weaknesses, look for opportunities to apply your strengths. Observe your opponent during warm-ups or at the start of the match. Study their footwork and timing to predict their moves and plan countermoves. Understand that opportunities arise anytime during a match, so be alert and ready to adjust your game plan.

Using Defense Tactics

Learning to defend yourself against your opponent's attacks is essential. Protecting yourself is as crucial as executing takedowns. Study your opponent's technique and learn to identify when you are vulnerable. Your opponent will likely take advantage of observed weaknesses, so practice countering their attacks and staying on the offense.

Mustering Stamina

Stamina is essential for wrestlers hoping to win. Your ability to perform at peak levels for the entire game relies heavily on your fitness levels. A lack of endurance and strength will almost immediately ruin your chances of winning. Therefore, keep up your workouts and training routines to sustain your energy and focus for the entire match.

Reversals are essential for a wrestler's game plan; it requires a comprehensive strategy to master. However, with practice, a solid foundation, developing counterattacks, and a great sense of timing and execution, you can outsmart your opponent quickly. Work on perfecting your fundamental movements, study your opponent's moves, familiarize yourself with your counterattack techniques, and build physical and mental toughness. Remember, every second of a match is an opportunity; with the right strategy, you can emerge as the winner.

Chapter 7: Escape Techniques

There's nothing quite like the thrilling intensity of a wrestling match. When locked in a grapple with your opponent, finding a way out is the only thing on your mind. Hence, the importance of escape techniques is paramount. These moves let you break free from your opponent's grip and gain an advantage. As a wrestler, mastering escape techniques is essential to come out on top. The best wrestlers can turn their opponent's momentum against them, using their body weight and leverage to gain the upper hand. But it's not only about raw power. It's about strategy, instincts, and quick reflexes.

With the proper escape techniques, anyone can turn the tables in battle and claim victory. This chapter covers various escape techniques and how to use them effectively. It explores defense techniques and tips on how to increase your escaping efficiency. So, if you're ready to step up your wrestling game, start mastering those escapes and show your opponents whose boss.

Top Position Escapes

Wrestling requires physical prowess, mental fortitude, and a good understanding of techniques. Whether you're a beginner or an advanced wrestler, mastering the various escape techniques to escape a tough spot is crucial. For example, your opponent catches you in a top position through a takedown or a pinning combination. This section looks at the top position escapes to regain control of the match.

Overhook Escape

Overhooks can be difficult to escape. [48]

When your opponent has an overhook, it can be challenging to get away. The best way to escape an overhook is using the "Overhook Wrist Control" technique. First, move your arm under your opponent's arm and grab their wrist, giving you better leverage and control. Use your other arm to press down on their shoulder, twisting them toward the mat. Now, slide your body away and get into a neutral position. This technique helps you break free from your opponent's overhook and return to the game.

Underhook Escape

Underhook escapes are effective in taking down your opponent.

If your opponent has an underhook, you can use a few techniques to escape. One of the most effective escapes is the *Whizzer*. First, grab your opponent's wrist with one hand and their triceps with the other. Now, push their arm up and out while rotating your body away from them, creating enough space for you to get away and gain control of your position. Keep practicing this technique until you can do it effortlessly during a match.

Headlock Escape

Headlocks can quickly lead to a pin.

A headlock is a dangerous position that can quickly lead to a pin. If you're in a headlock, don't panic. Instead, use the "switch" technique to escape. Grab your opponent's elbow with one hand and their opposite wrist with the other. Now, roll toward their trapped arm and use your legs to create space. Once you're out of the headlock, get back on your feet and use your techniques to take control of the match. With enough practice, the switch technique will become second nature.

Bear Hug Escape

A bear hug can be deadly if you don't know how to escape it. To escape the bear hug, first, wrap your arms around your opponent's waist as tightly as possible, preventing them from tightening their grip on you. Now, drop your weight and use your legs to lift your opponent off the mat. Twist your body as you drop down, creating enough space to break free from the bear hug. Once free, take advantage of your opponent's vulnerability to regain control of the match.

Bear hugs can be deadly if you don't escape.

Waist Lock Escapes

A waist lock can be difficult to escape, but it isn't impossible. You can use the "Granby Roll" technique to free yourself. Tuck your head and roll your body to the side of the waist lock. As you do, grab your opponent's ankles, and pull them toward you. It opens their grip on your waist, allowing you to move away and regain control. Once free, use your techniques to take charge of the match.

Being caught in a top position can be daunting, but with these effective wrestling escapes, it is easy to regain control of the match. Mastering these top-position escapes takes practice, but they can become second nature with hard work and dedication. Knowing how to escape your opponent's grips can turn the tide of a wrestling bout in your favor. With these top-position escapes in your arsenal, you'll be well-equipped to handle even the most formidable opponents.

Bottom Position Escapes

Wrestling is a challenging and physical sport demanding high-level skills to dominate an opponent. It combines technique, strength, and endurance, requiring constant training. The bottom position is one of the most challenging positions in wrestling and is difficult to escape from. This section discusses effective bottom-position escapes wrestlers can use to escape from this position.

Granby Roll Escape

Granby rolls can be effective when escaping from the bottom position.

The Granby Roll is one of the most common bottom position escapes in wrestling. It requires speed, flexibility, and coordination. The Granby Roll starts when the wrestler on the bottom position initiates a roll while keeping their opponent's weight off them. Wrestlers should use their hands to keep the weight off as they bridge and roll in the opposite direction. Once the roll is complete, the wrestler must create distance from their opponent. The Granby Roll is an effective escape helping wrestlers transition from the bottom to a neutral position.

Switching Bases Escape

Wrestlers can use the Switching Bases Escape as another effective bottom position escape from their opponent's control. The wrestler creates space between themselves and their opponent. The wrestler in the bottom position should use their lower body to push their opponent's arms to create an opening. Once the wrestler creates this space, they must use their arms to switch their base and get back on their feet. This escape is effective because it allows the wrestler in the bottom position to get out from under their opponent more quickly.

Hip Heists Escape

The Hip Heist is another practical bottom-position escape wrestlers use to escape their opponent's control. The wrestler uses their hips to create space between themselves and their opponent. The wrestler in the bottom position posts their hands on the mat, lifting their hips. Next, the wrestler should shift their weight to one side while kicking their opposite leg backward to create space to escape. The Hip Heist is an effective escape helping wrestlers quickly move from the bottom to a neutral position.

Leg Laces Escape

The Leg Lace is another bottom position escape wrestlers can use to escape their opponent's control. The wrestler creates space between themself and their opponent by lacing or tying their legs together. The wrestler on the bottom puts their hands on the mat and laces their legs together. The wrestler lifts their hips to create space between them and their opponent. Once the wrestler has created the space, they use their arms to switch their base and get back on their feet. The Leg Lace is another effective escape helping wrestlers quickly move from the bottom to a neutral position.

Bridge Escape

The Bridge is the final bottom position escape wrestlers can use to escape their opponent's control. The wrestler creates space between themselves and their opponent by bridging in the opposite direction. The wrestler posts their hands on the mat, arching their back to lift their hips. The wrestler then uses their hands and feet to bridge away from their opponent. Once the wrestler has created the space, they use their arms to switch their base and get back on their feet. The Bridge is just one more effective escape helping wrestlers quickly move from the bottom to a neutral position.

The bottom position is challenging to escape from, requiring skills and training to escape. The Granby Roll, Switching Bases, and Hip Heists are three effective bottom position escapes wrestlers can use to transition from the bottom to a neutral position. These moves require speed, flexibility, and coordination. However, they help wrestlers escape their opponent's control and return to their feet. These escapes take time and practice to perfect, but they are practical tools for wrestlers to win a match once mastered.

Defense Techniques

Wrestling is a sport requiring offensive and defensive skills. While many wrestlers are great at attacking their opponents, wrestling is equally about defending against the opponent's attack. This section discusses defense techniques commonly used in wrestling. These techniques include the Turtle Defense, the Reverse Motion Breakdown, and the Whizzer Counter. Understanding and mastering these techniques are crucial for any wrestler wanting to excel in the sport.

Turtle Defense

The turtle defense makes it difficult for opponents to attack.

The Turtle Defense is a defensive technique wrestlers use when their opponent is about to attack them with a takedown. To execute this technique, the wrestler drops to their knees, placing their hands on the mat, forming a turtle-like position. This position makes it difficult for the opponent to attack with a takedown, as the wrestler is low to the ground, and their head is protected. The Turtle Defense is a simple yet effective technique that could save a wrestler from being taken down by their opponent.

Reverse Motion Breakdown

The reverse motion breakdown prevents opponents from gaining points.

The Reverse Motion Breakdown is a defense technique used by wrestlers when their opponent controls them on the ground. When the wrestler feels their opponent has secured control, they use the Reverse Motion Breakdown to reverse the situation.

To execute this move, the wrestler quickly rolls over onto their stomach and back onto their back, taking their opponent with them. It allows the wrestler to return to the neutral position and prevent their opponent from scoring points.

Whizzer Counter

The Whizzer Counter is a defense technique wrestlers use when their opponent is attempting a single-leg takedown. To execute the Whizzer Counter, the wrestler uses their arm to push their opponent's head down, simultaneously using their opposite arm to wrap around their opponent's body and grab the elbow. This move allows the wrestler to break away from their opponent's grip and gain control of the situation. The Whizzer Counter is an effective technique to defend against a single-leg takedown.

It is essential to have excellent defense skills to become a successful wrestler. The Turtle Defense, Reverse Motion Breakdown, and Whizzer Counter are a few techniques to defend against an opponent's attack. By mastering these techniques and adding them to your arsenal, you significantly increase your chances of protecting against attacks and scoring points. Remember, wrestling necessitates offensive and defensive skills, and a well-rounded wrestler excels in both areas.

How to Increase Escaping Efficiency

Wrestling is a challenging and intense sport, full of grueling physical demands and mental challenges. One of the most crucial skills in wrestling is escaping, the ability to get out from underneath your opponent or avoid being pinned. Developing your escape skills can be the difference between winning and losing a match. This section explores the three main areas to increase your escaping efficiency in wrestling: drilling and repetition, proper body mechanics, and recognizing escape opportunities.

Drilling and Repetition

Focusing on drilling and repetition is the first key to improving your escaping efficiency in wrestling. Escaping is a skill that must be learned and practiced. Coaches should have the wrestlers work on escaping in every practice, using various techniques and scenarios. Wrestlers should also practice independently, taking time to drill specific techniques until they become second nature. The more you practice a particular escaping technique, the more comfortable and confident you become in using it during a match.

Proper Body Mechanics

Focusing on proper body mechanics is the second key to improving your escaping efficiency. Escaping is a complex movement using your whole body. You must use your hips, knees, and shoulders in a coordinated effort to maneuver your body and escape from your opponent. In addition, you must develop a strong core and leg strength to make escaping easier and more efficient. Proper body mechanics include maintaining good posture and balance to help you avoid getting stuck and unable to move.

Recognizing Escape Opportunities

The third key to improving your escaping efficiency is recognizing escape opportunities. Every match differs, so you must identify the right moment to move. It requires wrestling intelligence, reading your opponent, and anticipating their next move. It would be best to focus on developing a set of go-to escape moves while being flexible enough to adapt to your opponent's style. Be patient and keep alert for the right moment to make your move.

In addition to focusing on these three areas, here are a few other tips to improve your escaping efficiency. First, you must maintain your fitness level to stay strong and agile throughout the match. Practicing visualization techniques to help you mentally prepare for escaping scenarios would be best. Finally, don't let your ego get in the way of improving your escape skills. You must be willing to learn new techniques from coaches, teammates, and opponents.

Escaping is a fundamental skill in wrestling, and improving your efficiency in escaping can make all the difference. So, you must focus on drilling and repetition, proper body mechanics, and recognizing escape opportunities. By practicing these three areas and incorporating additional tips, you will become a better wrestler and a more successful competitor. Remember, every match offers a new challenge, and by improving your escape skills, you will be better equipped to face whatever comes your way.

Chapter 8: Pinning Combinations

Wrestling is an art form where strength, technique, and strategy converge to create pinning combinations. As a wrestler, you must clearly understand how to take your opponent down, control them, and ultimately pin them to the mat. It takes practice, discipline, and a fearless attitude to master the art of wrestling, especially with pinning combinations. But once you've learned it, there's nothing more exhilarating than feeling your opponent give in and surrender to your skillful pin.

Wrestling pin combinations will help you become a better wrestler. "

So, let's grab our wrestling gear, hit the mat, and perfect pinning combinations until they come as naturally as breathing. This chapter explains the fundamentals of combining moves to become a proficient wrestler and how to create effective pinning combinations. It covers movements to optimize combinations, strategies to make them effective, beginner combos to practice, and advanced techniques.

Movements to Optimize Combinations

One of the keys to success in wrestling is combining various moves to take down your opponent seamlessly and effectively. Combining various techniques allows wrestlers to gain the upper hand in a match and ultimately emerge victorious. This section explores movements to help wrestlers optimize their combinations, increasing their chances of competition success. It examines combining strikes, locks, and holds and flowing between moves.

Combining Strikes

Strikes are essential components of wrestling to take down your opponent effectively. When combined creatively, they can be a powerful weapon in your arsenal. The key to effectively combining strikes is always to think of your next move. For instance, you can throw an elbow strike, then seamlessly transition into a double-leg takedown to take your opponent down. Another effective technique is combining a straight punch with a leg sweep. This involves throwing a punch, then quickly stepping behind your opponent and sweeping their leg. This move catches them off guard and helps imbalance them enough to take them down.

Combining Locks and Holds

Locks and holds are some of the most influential wrestling techniques. Combined, they can be even more powerful. To combine locks and holds, grip your opponent's wrist, giving you control over their arm. Then, use this hold to lock their arm and simultaneously get behind them, putting you in a highly advantageous position where you can easily take them down. Another effective combination is using a half-nelson to set up a cradle. This technique involves locking up your opponent's arm with a half-nelson, then rolling them onto their back with a cradle. This move requires a lot of practice and skill, but it can be a game-changer in a match.

Flowing between Moves

Finally, one of the most crucial aspects of combining movements in wrestling is flowing between them seamlessly. You must anticipate your opponent's next move and quickly adjust your strategy. For example, suppose you're going for a takedown, and your opponent counters. In that case, you immediately transition into a different move to maintain control. Another critical factor is combining moves complementing each other. For example, you can set up a double-leg takedown with a jab-cross combination. The jab-cross will distract your opponent and create an opening for you to go for the takedown.

Strategies for Effective Combinations

Wrestling is a dynamic and highly technical sport requiring great skill, strength, and endurance. Whether you're a beginner or an experienced wrestler, mastering combination moves is essential to take your game to the next level. You can develop effective combinations in various ways, but it all boils down to three crucial strategies: identifying weaknesses and strengths, capitalizing on your opponent's weaknesses, and developing adaptability. This section delves deeper into these three strategies and provides practical tips to boost your performance to become a more formidable wrestler.

Identifying Weaknesses and Strengths

The first step toward developing effective combinations is identifying your strengths and weaknesses as a wrestler. Analyzing your matches helps you identify areas where you excel and areas for improvement. This knowledge is crucial as it enables you to build on your strengths and overcome weaknesses. Once you know your strengths and weaknesses, you can tailor your training to address these areas. For instance, if you're stronger on your feet than on the mat, you should focus more on your ground game. Similarly, if you lack endurance, work on cardio exercises and drills to build stamina.

Using the Opponent's Weaknesses

The next strategy is focusing on your opponent's weaknesses. As you gain experience, you learn that every wrestler has specific weaknesses which can be exploited. Recognizing these weaknesses, whether a lack of endurance, poor balance, or a susceptibility to certain moves, puts you at a significant advantage. One way to develop this skill is by watching matches and analyzing your opponent's wrestling style. Look at their past performances and see if they struggled in any areas. Then, use this knowledge to develop moves and combinations to effectively exploit these weaknesses and put your opponent on the defensive.

Developing Adaptability

Finally, adaptability is one of the most crucial aspects of developing effective combinations. Wrestling is an unpredictable sport, and you must think on your feet and adjust your strategy as the match progresses. Developing adaptability means assessing the situation and quickly altering your game plan accordingly. One way to build adaptability is to practice and refine your moves constantly. Then, as you get more comfortable with the techniques, experiment with different variations and create new combinations. This method will help you prepare for unexpected situations and give you more tools to work with during a match.

Beginner Combos to Practice

Winning a wrestling match is about being stronger than your opponent and using the proper techniques at the right time. One way to improve your technique is to practice beginner combos. Combos are a series of moves combined to gain an advantage over your opponent. This section discusses some basic combos that beginners should practice to improve their wrestling skills.

Basic Striking Combos

Basic striking combos are essential in wrestling. They use strikes to create openings in your opponent's defense, then capitalize on them with takedowns or throws. Some basic striking combos include the jab-cross, jab-uppercut, and the overhand-right.

- The jab-cross is a standard combo to create distance from your opponent and strike. The jab is a quick, powerful punch aimed at the opponent's face or body. The cross is a straight punch aimed at the opponent's chin or chest. This combo can be used to set up a takedown or a throw.

- The jab-uppercut combo is another basic combo to create openings for takedowns or throws. The jab keeps the opponent at a distance, while the uppercut closes the distance and strikes. The uppercut is a punch aimed at the opponent's chin or body. This combo works best when you get the opponent against the cage or in the corner of the mat.

- The overhand-right combo is a powerful combo to strike with force. The overhand-right is a wide, looping punch aimed at the opponent's chin or cheek. This combo is best used when your opponent is not expecting it and must react quickly. The overhand right can set up a takedown or throw.

Essential Locks and Holds Combos

Locks and holds combos are another vital aspect of wrestling. They use leverage and pressure to control your opponent's body, immobilizing them. Some essential locks and holds combos include the armbar, the kimura, and the rear-naked choke.

- The arm bar is an effective lock to control the opponent's arm. This lock involves grabbing the opponent's arm and wrapping your legs around it. Then, you apply pressure to the opponent's elbow, forcing them to submit or risk a broken arm. You can use this lock when on top of your opponent or at the bottom.

- The kimura is another effective lock to control the opponent's arm. This lock involves grabbing your opponent's wrist and twisting it behind their back. Then, use your other hand to apply pressure to their elbow, forcing them to submit or risk injury. Again, the kimura can be used from the top or bottom position.

- The rear-naked choke is a well-known submission hold controlling the opponent's neck. This hold involves wrapping your arms around the opponent's neck and squeezing until they submit or pass out. This hold is best used when you have the opponent's back.

Beginner Flows

Beginner flows are a combination of striking and grappling techniques flowing from one to the other. These flows help build muscle memory and improve reaction time. Some beginner flows include:

- The jab-takedown flow uses the jab to create an opening for a takedown. For example, you jab the opponent's face, create distance, and shoot for a takedown.

- The jab-cross-shoot flow is a combination of striking and takedown techniques. Start with a jab, throw a cross, and then shoot in for a takedown.
- The double jab-double leg takedown flow combines striking and takedown techniques. Start with two jabs, create distance, and shoot for a double-leg takedown.

Effective Combinations

In wrestling, one of the most critical aspects of the sport is combining moves seamlessly. When done correctly, combining different moves can catch your opponent off guard, putting them on the defensive and ultimately leading to a victory. This section delves into some of the most effective combinations in wrestling.

The Multi-Strike Combination

The Multi-Strike combination is a powerful tool in a wrestler's arsenal. It combines different strikes to create an opening for a takedown or pin. This combination can include punches, kicks, or even headbutts – for instance, some wrestlers like to lead with a punch to the stomach, followed by a kick to the leg or a headbutt to the chest. The idea is to keep your opponent guessing and off-balance, leaving them open to your takedown attempt. When executed correctly, the multi-strike combination can be devastating.

The Lock and Strike Combination

The Lock and Strike combination is another effective way to take down your opponent. This technique involves locking up with your opponent and striking them with a series of blows to create an opening for a takedown or submission hold. This combination includes strikes to the head, gut, or legs. Once your opponent is stunned by the strikes, use the lock to leverage them into a vulnerable position. Many wrestlers use this combination to set up a chokehold or armbar.

The Evasive Combination

The Evasive combination is all about movement. This combination uses quick, evasive movements to avoid your opponent's strikes while setting up your takedown attempt. One typical evasive move is the "slip-and-rip." You slip to the side of your opponent's punch, then strike with a short hook or uppercut. Another standard evasive move is the "duck-under." You duck under your opponent's arm, then go for the takedown. The Evasive combination is excellent for wrestlers who are good at reading their opponent's movements and can react quickly.

Mastering pinning combinations in wrestling is critical in taking down your opponent. By practicing these combinations during training, you will become a formidable opponent on the mat and dominate your opponent in the ring. Remember, wrestling is all about technique and knowing how to use each move to your advantage. So, practice your combinations, learn to read your opponent's movements and reactions, and become the champion wrestler you were born to be.

Advanced Techniques

Wrestling, known for its unique blend of strength, agility, and technique, has evolved into a competitive sport demanding physical and mental skills. As a wrestler, developing advanced techniques is essential for staying ahead of the competition. This section discusses advanced techniques to help you dominate on the mat.

Advanced Combinations for One-on-One Combat

One of the most crucial aspects of wrestling is stringing together different techniques to create a compelling combination. Advanced wrestlers know how to combine various grips, throws, and takedowns fluidly. To elevate your game, you must have a solid understanding of the fundamentals and build on them. For example, a basic shoulder throw can be combined with a leg sweep for a decisive takedown. As you progress, mix up different techniques to surprise your opponent, like a fake shot followed by a single-leg takedown. You can outsmart and outmaneuver your opponent on the mat by mastering advanced combinations.

Grandmaster Combinations for Multiple Opponents

One of the most common challenges a wrestler faces is overcoming multiple opponents simultaneously. Grandmasters have developed techniques to help overcome this challenge. One approach is using the momentum of one opponent against the other. For example, you can use an arm drag on one wrestler to throw them into the path of another. Using peripheral vision and situational awareness is crucial when taking on multiple opponents. Another advanced technique is using a double-leg takedown on one wrestler, then using the momentum to roll into submission on the other. These advanced combinations require precision, timing, and agility but can be game-changers in a tough match.

Combining Strategies and Mental Triggers

Wrestling isn't only about physical techniques. It's also about being innovative and strategic. Elite wrestlers understand how to execute moves and when to use them. Mental triggers give you a significant advantage, like understanding your opponent's weaknesses or capitalizing on their mistakes. Combining different strategies can help keep your opponent off-balance. For example, if you're known for your strong takedown abilities, start with a stand-up the next time, catching your opponent off-guard. You can become a formidable opponent by incorporating mental strategies with technical ones.

Using Feints and Fakes

Feints and fakes can be powerful tools in wrestling. A fake or feint can be as simple as pretending to shoot for a leg takedown to cause the opponent to reach down for a defense opening their arms to counter and throw. Feints can test your opponent's reactions before going in for the actual move. You can create openings in your opponent's defense and put them off balance using feints and fakes.

Advanced wrestling techniques take time and practice to perfect. However, combining different styles, utilizing strategic mental triggers, and incorporating feints and fakes can make it easier to dominate your opponents on the mat. By mastering these techniques, you can anticipate your opponent's moves, create openings, and execute decisive takedowns and throws. Remember, only some strategies or plans will lead to success. Instead, it would be best to experiment with different combinations to find what works best. Then, keep honing your skills and refining your techniques, and you'll be well on your way to becoming an elite wrestler.

Chapter 9: Training at Home

Are you tired of missing out on your wrestling training due to gym closures or scheduling conflicts? Don't let that stop you from achieving your goals. With the right equipment, you can efficiently train at home and maintain strength, technique, and endurance. Whether setting up a mat in your garage, investing in a wrestling dummy, or simply finding creative ways to substitute a partner, there are endless possibilities to keep your training on track.

With dedication and a focused mindset, you can turn your home into a formidable training arena and stay ahead of the competition. This chapter outlines the drills and exercises you can practice alone at home, with and without equipment. Training alone and practicing daily is as important as practicing with an opponent and improving skills and physical condition.

Solo Drills

Wrestlers must be sharp and precise with their techniques, which comes with constant practice. Sometimes, injury or lack of partners or facilities necessitate solo training. Solo drills are essential in helping wrestlers refine and develop their skills while training independently. This section explores some solo drills wrestlers can undertake to improve.

Shadowboxing

Shadowboxing helps with reenacting wrestling techniques. [45]

Shadowboxing is one of the most fundamental solo drills for wrestlers. The technique requires visualization and reenactment of wrestling techniques in the air. It is helpful in refining movements and techniques, mastering balance and coordination, and developing footwork and range. Shadowboxing solo drills are completed devoid of equipment or props. Moreover, the drive behind shadowboxing is to simulate an actual match, and wrestlers must execute their techniques with precision and power, like in actual competition. Wrestlers must focus on their footwork, head movement, stance, and hand positioning when shadowboxing.

Footwork and Movement Drills

Wrestlers need excellent footwork to outpace their opponents, control their range, and maintain balance while executing a technique. Movement drills are essential in developing the flexibility and agility required for wrestling. The exercises help shift weight swiftly from one foot to the other, pivot, and maintain variances in the opponent's movement. Footwork and movement drills include pivoting, shuffling, side-step, jump rope, and more.

Pad Work Drills

Pad work drills are instrumental in developing proper weight distribution, range, and striking techniques. The pads offer resistance and replicate an opponent's body, helping wrestlers develop precision and power in their targeting. One of the most popular pad work drills is the focus mitt drill. Wrestlers focus on attaining a rhythm and flow in their striking techniques to simulate an opponent's movement.

Heavy Bag Drills

Heavy bag drills are essential in building strength, endurance, and explosiveness in wrestlers. In addition, the drills are instrumental in refining targeting and movements in real-life situations. Heavy bag drills involve striking a heavy bag with intensity and precision. Performers use a range of strikes, such as kicks, punches, and knees, to work on form, power, and range. Wrestlers must focus on maintaining proper technique in their strikes, ensuring the safety of their joints.

Partner Drills and Exercises

While solo practice sessions are crucial for personal growth, partner drills and exercises are essential for perfecting wrestling techniques and building problem-solving skills. In addition, they help wrestlers practice specific techniques, improve their timing and awareness, and build endurance to enhance their competitive edge. This section discusses some of the most effective partner drills and exercises for wrestlers. Whether new to wrestling or an experienced grappler, these exercises and drills will help you sharpen your skills and become a formidable opponent.

Sparring

Sparring is a staple in wrestling and is considered one of the best partner drills for grapplers. It lets you apply techniques you learned in practice to a live, competitive situation. With a partner, you can take turns attacking and defending, using all the different methods, like shooting and sprawling. Sparring sessions can be conducted in various formats, but free sparring and live wrestling are two of the most popular. Free sparring allows wrestlers to practice their moves and counters without predetermined actions. In contrast, live wrestling limits the techniques used in the match to give wrestlers the feeling of a more organized wrestling practice.

Partner Pad Work Drills

Partner pad work drills are excellent for practicing and improving the power and accuracy of your strikes and throws. These drills involve working with a partner who holds pads, giving you targets to hit. For instance, the focus mitt drill involves striking moving targets (mitts) held by your partner. This drill allows you to work on your punches, kicks, and other striking techniques while increasing your power and speed. The partner can hold pads and give you targets to throw at to help perfect your throws and takedowns.

Clinching and Grappling Exercises

Clinching and grappling exercises improve positioning, control, and submission techniques. They develop a firm grip and arm strength. Drills like pummeling, where wrestlers clinch and reposition their arms while in a stand-up position, or drilling various takedowns and defenses are some of the best drills for demonstrating these skills. Another exercise to increase your grip strength is the monkey grip drill. This drill is holding a partner's wrist and hand while they pull their arm away. The goal is to secure your grip and maintain a steady stance while your partner attempts to break free.

Conditioning Drills

Although wrestling matches typically last only a few minutes, they require high endurance and stamina. Therefore, conditioning drills are best for wrestlers to build endurance and improve fitness. One drill is the "Suicide Drill." The drill involves running at full speed from one line to another, followed by a reversal of direction to complete the next run. The drill is performed in a "ladder" format, where the distance you run is increased with each repetition. Another effective drill for conditioning is the bear crawl. In this drill, you get on all fours and crawl forward by moving your left hand and right foot simultaneously, then your other hand and foot. The aim is to crawl a specific number of meters or until you're too tired to continue.

Reaction Drills

Reaction drills are essential in all combat sports, especially wrestling. They improve wrestlers' ability to anticipate their opponent's next move while developing punch and response timing. One of the most popular reaction drills in wrestling is the shadow drill. This drill is shadow wrestling with a partner, where they execute a series of moves, and the other wrestler responds with countermoves to improve reflexes and reaction time. This drill also improves footwork, head movement, and overall body control.

At-Home Exercises without Equipment

Wrestling is a sport requiring physical and mental agility and strength. It is entertaining and helps improve an individual's overall health. If you're a wrestler, you know how important it is to maintain body strength. The good news is you can easily do this at home without gym equipment. Here are some at-home wrestling exercises to do without equipment.

Jump Rope

Jumping rope might seem like a simple activity, but it's one of the best exercises to improve agility, coordination, and footwork. It is an effective cardio exercise improving cardiovascular fitness and endurance. Jumping rope consistently for at least 10 minutes can burn up to 100 calories. As a wrestler, jumping rope improves balance and quick footwork, which are essential for taking down your opponent.

Burpees

Burpees are a full-body workout engaging every muscle group. It is a high-intensity interval training (HIIT) improving cardiovascular fitness while building muscles. Burpees are easy-to-do workouts requiring no equipment and can be modified according to your fitness level. It is also an excellent exercise to improve endurance and stamina.

Push-Ups and Sit-Ups

Push-ups and sit-ups are two classic exercises that can be done anywhere. They are affordable and require no equipment. They are essential exercises for wrestlers as they help develop upper body strength, core stability, and balance. Push-ups work on your chest, shoulders, triceps, and upper back, while sit-ups improve abdominal muscles.

Squats and Lunges

Squats and lunges are two critical exercises to build leg muscles. They help improve your balance, flexibility, and mobility. Squats work on your quads, hamstrings, and glutes, while lunges work on your calves, quads, and glutes. Regularly doing squats and lunges can improve agility, endurance, and balance, which are essential for wrestling.

Running, Cycling, or Swimming

Cardiovascular exercise is essential for any fitness routine. Running, cycling, or swimming can improve cardiovascular health while keeping you in excellent physical shape. Running helps burn calories, increases endurance, and builds leg muscles. Cycling is a low-impact exercise that builds quad and hamstring muscles while increasing stamina. Swimming is an excellent low-impact exercise engaging your entire body while improving cardiovascular health.

At-Home Exercises with Equipment

Wrestling is one of the most challenging sports, requiring strength, stamina, and agility. But if you're a wrestling enthusiast, you don't need to hit the gym to maintain a good physique. Instead, you can do it right from the comfort of your home. Here are some of the best at-home wrestling exercises with equipment to help you get in shape, stay healthy, and improve your wrestling game.

Resistance Bands

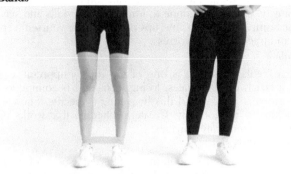

Resistance bands can improve strength and tone the body. [46]

Resistance bands are a great way to improve your strength and tone your body. Wrap the bands around your feet, hold them in your hands, and perform exercises like the standing chest press, bicep curls, tricep extensions, and standing rows. You can use the bands to work on your legs by doing squats, lunges, and leg curls. In addition, you can adjust the intensity of the exercises by using different bands with varying resistance levels, making it an excellent workout for beginners and seasoned wrestlers.

Medicine Balls

Medicine balls are another piece of equipment to help you get into shape. They come in various weights and sizes, so choose a comfortable and suitable one. Hold the ball with both hands and perform exercises like the overhead press, chest pass, side throws, and slams. You can do partner exercises like the Russian twist, wall pass, and sit-ups. These exercises are great for developing core strength, speed, and agility.

Punching Bag or Punch Mitts

Punching is an essential component of wrestling, and a punching bag or punch mitts can be a great way to improve technique and endurance. Hang the bag in your garage, or buy a pair of punch mitts and have a partner hold them up for you. Then, practice your jabs, hooks, crosses, and uppercuts for a great cardio workout and help you tone your arms and upper body.

Kettlebells

Kettlebells are great for full-body workouts with excellent results. They come in various weights, so choose one you are comfortable with. Then, perform exercises like the kettlebell swing, goblet squat, clean and jerk, and Turkish get-up to build strength and improve your overall conditioning. Kettlebells can be challenging, so start with a lower weight and work your way up as you get stronger.

Ankle Weights

Ankle weights help you develop strength and power in your lower body. Wear them during exercises like leg lifts, calf raises, and side leg lifts. Wear them while walking or jogging for a great workout for building endurance. However, be careful not to overdo it, as ankle weights can place too much stress on your joints and lead to injury.

Tips for Training Alone at Home

The current health crisis has presented new challenges for wrestlers who are used to training in a team environment. However, you can continue your passion for the sport. With some creativity, you can continue to improve your skills and stay in shape while training alone at home. Here are some tips on preparing yourself, remaining focused and motivated, and tracking your progress.

Set a Schedule

Maintaining a regular schedule is one of the most important aspects of training alone. Without a coach or teammates, losing focus and becoming less committed to your training sessions is easy. Avoid this by setting a specific time each day for your workout and sticking to it rigorously. Create a schedule that works best for you and allows you to focus on your daily activities.

Choose a Variety of Exercises

Choosing a variety of exercises to improve different aspects of your wrestling game is crucial to developing a well-rounded training program. Start by selecting basic exercises developing strength, speed, and endurance, like push-ups, squats, and sit-ups. Next, add plyometric exercises like box jumps, bound jumps, and jump squats. For power development and bodyweight exercises, include crab walks, burpees, and planks.

Focus on Technique and Form

Wrestling requires exceptional technique and form. To reach your full potential, you must take time to work on your form and ensure your techniques are performed correctly. Although analyzing yourself during training is challenging, you can make significant improvements by watching tutorial videos and carefully breaking down the movements.

Don't Neglect Conditioning

In wrestling, conditioning is everything. It determines whether or not you'll last an entire match and help you win. When training by yourself, it's essential to include conditioning exercises that mimic the intensity and duration of a wrestling match. Activities like running, sprints, hill climbs, and interval training will build a strong foundation.

Track Your Progress

While training alone, tracking your progress is vital to stay motivated and to help you to document your gains. Keep a journal or download a training app to help you gauge your progress and monitor areas for improvement. Knowing your achievements helps you turn challenging training sessions into more positive experiences and pushes you closer to your goals.

Wrestling can be challenging but also the most rewarding. With discipline and dedication, you can improve your skills, continue to train alone, and take your wrestling game to the next level. Setting a schedule, choosing a variety of exercises, focusing on technique and form, not neglecting to condition, tracking your progress, staying motivated, and taking regular breaks encourage progress and keep you inspired through this challenging time. Don't be convinced that training without equipment or alone is inadequate. It could make or break your wrestling career.

Chapter 10: Training and Coaching Youth

Wrestling isn't just a sport. It's a way of life. Teaching youth the art of wrestling takes dedication, patience, and the right coaching strategies. It's not enough to show them the techniques and moves; discipline, resilience, and self-confidence that come with being a wrestler must be instilled in them. As a coach, it's crucial to understand the different learning styles of each wrestler and provide a supportive environment encouraging their strengths and weaknesses.

By investing in developing young wrestlers, you're building outstanding athletes and honorable leaders who will carry the lessons they learned on the mat into every aspect of their lives. This chapter aims to provide coaches and parents with the necessary information to ensure each wrestler is safe, nurtured, and equipped with a fun learning environment to thrive. Remember, with the proper guidance and support, these budding wrestlers will reach their full potential.

Safety and Precautions for Young Wrestlers

Young wrestlers should use protective gear.[47]

Wrestling is a challenging and physically demanding sport. While it might look like a fun game for many kids to play with friends, it is essential to remember that wrestlers are at a heightened risk for injury. As a parent or coach, ensuring wrestlers practice this sport safely, in and outside the ring, is crucial. This section outlines some essential safety precautions for young wrestlers every coach, parent, or athlete should know.

Protective Equipment for Wrestlers

Many young wrestlers jump into the sport without the right protective gear. However, proper gear is essential to keep the wrestlers safe while participating in the sport. The following are crucial protective equipment every young wrestler must have:

- **Headgear:** Headgear is the most crucial protective gear a wrestler can wear. It minimizes and avoids critical head and ear injuries.
- **Wrestling Shoes:** Wrestling shoes protect wrestlers' feet and provide grip on the mat.
- **Mouthguard:** A mouthguard is recommended to protect the teeth and jaws from injuries. A flying headbutt, or an accidental elbow to the mouth, could easily knock a tooth out or cause severe jaw and neck injuries.
- **Knee Pads:** Knee pads are not necessary but highly recommended to protect the knees and prevent scrapes, cuts, or bruises.

Additional Rules for Safety and Fun

Wrestling is not just about physical strength. It's about following rules and techniques. Here are some additional rules and tips to ensure the safety and fun of every young wrestler:

- Always respect the opponent and avoid rough or unsportsmanlike conduct when practicing or competing.
- Avoid mimicking professional techniques seen on TV, as they can be dangerous for young wrestlers.

- Follow weight requirements to avoid competing with someone much larger or heavier than you.
- Hydration is critical. Wrestlers should drink plenty of water and avoid sugary drinks before, during, and after matches.

Learning the Basics of Wrestling

Before young wrestlers take to the ring and compete, they must learn the basics of wrestling. Proper techniques and rules can help prevent injuries. Professional coaches should handle teaching these fundamental techniques. Here are some essential strategies for beginners:

- **Takedowns:** Teach children proper shooting techniques to avoid head and neck injuries.
- **Escape:** This technique can help wrestlers get back on their feet or avoid being pinned.
- **Pinning Combination:** This technique can help wrestlers to dominate in a match and get their opponent onto the mat.

The Importance of Rest and Recovery

Rest is essential for young wrestlers to recover from the physical and mental stress of the sport. Young wrestlers should not be pushed too hard in training, as it can lead to burnout and injuries. Proper rest and recovery help avoid muscle strains and other injuries.

Promoting Respect for the Sport

Teaching young wrestlers the importance of respecting the sport and their opponents is crucial. As a coach or parent, it's your responsibility to ensure your wrestlers understand the importance of respecting the sport and demonstrating good behavior. This section discusses ways to promote respect for the sport in young wrestlers and how to lay the foundation for positive behavior.

Being a Good Coach or Parent

As a coach or parent, it's essential to lead by example. Young wrestlers look up to those around them and mirror their behavior. If you exhibit positive behavior and respect the sport and opponents, you're more likely to inspire the same behavior in your wrestlers. Clarify your expectations and demonstrate them consistently.

Maintaining open communication with your wrestlers is crucial. Encourage them to express their thoughts, concerns, and ideas. By doing so, you let them know their opinions matter, and they can learn from constructive criticism. Ensure you are approachable and supportive, understand what motivates your wrestlers, and provide the necessary support.

Teaching Good Behavior

Wrestlers should be taught the sport's rules and the code of conduct early. Emphasize the values of integrity, humility, and respect for opponents, on and off the mat. They must know they represent themselves and their team, school, and community. Encourage them to strive toward excellence and remind them of the importance of respecting everyone. Inculcate this behavior by rewarding those who show positive behavior.

Teaching them good sportsmanship is another behavioral aspect essential in wrestling and life. Congratulating your opponent, helping them back up, and never gloating are qualities of good sportsmanship. This behavior should be regularly reinforced since it promotes respect toward everyone.

Rewards for Good Conduct

One way to promote respectful behavior is to incentivize positive behavior. Rewarding wrestlers for good behavior promotes a positive environment and helps reinforce the values of respect and integrity. For example, reward them with tokens, badges, certificates, or anything the wrestler finds valuable. This motivation will include better behavior, and others will emulate their behavior to receive recognition.

Wrestling is an individual sport, but it takes a team to be successful. Therefore, create a team atmosphere that instills unity, respect, and mutual support. As everyone feels more united and valued, it could bring a new level of fulfillment and satisfaction to your wrestling journey.

Giving the Kids a Chance to Shine

Wrestling is about physical strength, mental toughness, and strategic thinking. For young wrestlers, it can be a challenging but rewarding experience. For parents and coaches, it can be a chance to mold future champions and instill essential life skills. This section explores how encouraging and supporting participation, creating, and achieving goals, celebrating success, and learning from mistakes can help young wrestlers shine.

Encouraging and Supporting Participation

One of the most important things parents and coaches can do for young wrestlers is to encourage and support their participation. It means attending their matches and providing emotional support, positive feedback, and constructive criticism. Encouragement comes in many forms, such as offering encouragement before a game, praising hard work and improvement, and recognizing a wrestler's achievements. In addition, supporting participation includes ensuring young wrestlers have access to appropriate gear, transportation to matches, and access to coaches and other resources. Finally, parents and coaches can help young wrestlers stay motivated and enjoy the sport by fostering a supportive environment.

Creating Goals and Achieving Them

Setting goals is an essential part of any sport; wrestling is no exception. Goal-setting helps young wrestlers stay focused and motivated, measure their progress, and celebrate their successes. Goals can be short-term or long-term, including milestones like winning a match or achieving a certain fitness level. Coaches and parents can help young wrestlers create achievable goals that are realistic but challenging to help develop their skills and improve performance. By setting and achieving goals, young wrestlers gain confidence in their abilities and develop a growth mindset.

Celebrating Success and Learning from Mistakes

In wrestling, as in life, success and failure are vital learning opportunities. When young wrestlers achieve their goals or win a match, it is essential to celebrate their accomplishments and recognize their hard work and dedication. It can take many forms, such as praising their efforts, giving them rewards, or acknowledging them publicly. Celebrating success helps young wrestlers feel valued and appreciated and motivates them to continue working hard. At the same time, learning from mistakes and setbacks is essential. After a loss or failure, coaches and parents must help young wrestlers identify what went wrong and how they can improve. It can include constructive criticism, practicing specific skills, or finding new ways to approach a challenge.

Creating the Right Environment for Learning

Young wrestlers, especially those just starting, need a safe, positive, and encouraging environment to develop their skills effectively and grow as athletes. This section highlights some essential tips that coaches and parents can use to create the right environment for young wrestlers.

Ensuring the Environment Is Safe and Stress-Free

Safety is the first and most important factor in creating a positive learning environment. Coaches and parents must ensure the wrestling environment is safe for young athletes to practice without risking injury, including maintaining proper equipment, ensuring the wrestling mats are clean and well-maintained, and teaching athletes good techniques to avoid injuries.

Additionally, the environment must be stress-free. Young wrestlers can easily get overwhelmed and discouraged if they feel pressured to perform or fear making mistakes. Instead, coaches and parents should focus on creating an atmosphere of positivity and encouragement where athletes feel comfortable and supported and are not afraid to take risks and try new things.

Encouraging Fun While Learning

Wrestling is a challenging and demanding sport, but it doesn't mean it can't be fun. Coaches and parents should strive to make learning wrestling skills an enjoyable experience by incorporating games, challenges, and other activities to engage young athletes and keep them motivated. For example, coaches can organize wrestling drills and games, allowing wrestlers to practice their skills while having fun. Parents can also get involved by attending matches and cheering for their children, showing them that wrestling is not just about winning but also about having a good time.

Making Wrestling Instruction Enjoyable

It's essential to make wrestling instruction enjoyable and engaging so young wrestlers stay focused and motivated throughout their training. Therefore, coaches should vary their teaching methods and use different techniques to communicate new skills and techniques effectively. For example, coaches can use video demonstrations, group discussions, and one-on-one coaching sessions to teach wrestling skills. They can provide regular feedback and encouragement and create individualized training plans that cater to each athlete's strengths and weaknesses.

Fostering a Growth Mindset

Last (but not least), coaches and parents should foster a growth mindset in young wrestlers. The growth mindset is the belief that skills and abilities can be improved through hard work, dedication, and persistence. It encourages young athletes to embrace challenges and setbacks as opportunities to learn and grow and not to be discouraged by them. Parents and coaches can help develop a growth mindset by praising wrestlers for their effort and progress instead of only their results. They should encourage wrestlers to set realistic and achievable goals and celebrate their achievements.

Creating a positive and productive learning environment is essential for young wrestlers to develop their skills and grow as athletes. Coaches and parents create an environment where young athletes can thrive and reach their full potential by prioritizing safety, encouraging fun, making wrestling instruction enjoyable, and fostering a growth mindset. As coaches and parents, it's your responsibility to provide proper guidance and support and instill the love of the sport in young wrestlers to keep them engaged and motivated for years.

Considerations during Practice and Matches

Wrestling can be an excellent way for children to learn discipline, improve their physical health, and build self-confidence. However, as with any sport, wrestling requires precautions, including proper nutrition, warm-ups, and reminders of rules, which young wrestlers and parents must remember. This section provides parents and young athletes with essential considerations during practice and matches to improve safety and performance.

Proper Nutrition

While most people know nutrition is significant for an athlete, young wrestlers must have a proper diet to ensure they have the energy to compete. A sufficient and healthy diet should offer adequate carbohydrates and proteins for an athlete's growing body, sustaining the demanding training sessions and fast-paced matches. For example, a protein snack and a banana before practice or a game should provide the necessary energy to last the duration. In addition, parents can consult with coaches or nutritionists to ensure their young wrestlers get the proper nutrients.

Warm-Ups and Stretching

Wrestling demands intense physical exertion, and young wrestlers must prepare their muscles correctly before matches or practice sessions start. Therefore, coaches should lead warm-up sessions lasting up to 30 minutes. These sessions should include stretching exercises to prevent muscle injuries, agility drills to improve flexibility and explosiveness, and calisthenics like push-ups and sit-ups to improve strength. In addition, young wrestlers should be instructed on stretching correctly, including slowing down if they feel strained or pain during warm-up exercises.

Reminders for the Referee's Rules

Wrestling matches require referees to ensure all games meet the required regulations and prevent injuries like falls and injury. Therefore, young wrestlers should know the game's rules to keep matches safe and fair. For example, they should understand that grappling moves and certain grips are permitted while holds like headbutting, biting, or poking opponents' eyes are prohibited. In addition, young wrestlers must listen to their coaches and the referee's guidance and behave respectfully toward their opponents, coaches, and referees. They must be taught to deal with both mental and emotional situations, like losing a match or responding to aggressive behavior.

Stress Management

Wrestling is an intensive and challenging sport, often resulting in emotional and mental stress on young wrestlers. This stress can impact their performance during practice and matches. Educating young wrestlers about the importance of stress management techniques, such as deep breathing exercises, yoga, and visualization, helps reduce stress levels and increase their overall performance. In addition, parents can help their young wrestlers recognize their stress triggers and encourage them to practice relaxation exercises to manage their stress.

Wrestling is an exhilarating sport benefitting young athletes' physical and emotional well-being. However, young wrestlers must take the necessary precautions and follow essential considerations to remain safe and perform at their best. Proper nutrition, warm-up sessions, knowledge of the referee's rules, and stress management techniques make all the difference in young wrestlers' success on and off the mat. Therefore, parents, coaches, and young wrestlers must work together to create a safe, healthy, and successful athletic experience.

Chapter 11: Wrestling Success

Wrestling is about the dedication, hard work, and passion that goes into every practice and moment on the mat. Successful wrestlers understand that every move counts and that their mindset and preparation determine their outcome. They have the confidence and determination to face any opponent with a strategic plan and mental toughness to push through fatigue and pain. Wrestling success is earned through continuous training, sacrifice, and a "never-give-up" attitude.

The satisfaction and pride are indescribable when all the hard work pays off and you stand victorious on the mat. This chapter is dedicated to celebrating success stories of wrestlers who have achieved greatness and providing advice to help aspiring athletes achieve their dreams. These stories and tips will leave you feeling inspired and ready to take on any challenge. These wrestlers' successes are a living testament to the power of hard work and perseverance. Let's get started.

The Triumphs of Wrestling Champions

Wrestling is far more than just a sport or entertainment. It involves passion, perseverance, and dedication. Over the years, many wrestlers have crossed boundaries and achieved new milestones. Notably, some wrestlers with inspiring journeys are worth knowing. This section closely examines the success stories of wrestling champions, including John Cena, The Rock, Charlotte Flair, Hulk Hogan, and CM Punk.

John Cena

John Cena is a well-known wrestling icon. [48]

John Cena is a well-known wrestling icon with a vast fan base. He began his career in wrestling with the Ultimate Pro Wrestling (UPW) and then signed with the WWE in 2000. Cena has an impressive WWE record, with 25 championships to his name. His inspiring story lies in his perseverance. Cena had to work through numerous setbacks and injuries but never lost sight of his goal and worked tirelessly to get back in the game. He became one of the greatest wrestlers ever through hard work and dedication.

The Rock

The Rock, aka Dwayne Johnson, has one of the most inspiring stories in professional wrestling. He started his career in wrestling with his father, Rocky Johnson, and later joined the WWE. After years of hard work and dedication, he became one of the greatest WWE champions ever. Even after achieving great success, The Rock continued to push himself further. In addition, he pursued his passion for acting and has starred in several blockbuster movies. The Rock's tenacity and dedication to his craft make him a true inspiration.

Charlotte Flair

The daughter of wrestling legend Ric Flair, Charlotte Flair, has always had big shoes to fill. She started her wrestling career in 2012 and soon got signed with the WWE. Since then, she has won numerous titles and broken several records. Her journey to success is founded on hard work, dedication, and a passion for the sport. Flair continues to work tirelessly, inspiring women wrestlers everywhere to follow their dreams.

Hulk Hogan

Hulk Hogan is a name that echoes throughout the history of wrestling. His dynamic showmanship and in-ring presence made him one of the most recognizable faces in wrestling. Hogan started his career in Tennessee and was soon signed with the WWE. His journey to success is derived from non-stop dedication, hard work, and practice. Despite numerous setbacks, he continued to push forward and became a living legend in wrestling.

CM Punk

CM Punk began his career in wrestling with the Independent Circuit and later joined the WWE. He quickly gained popularity due to his unique personality and wrestling style. Punk became one of the most significant forces in the WWE. However, Punk felt unfulfilled despite his successes and ultimately retired in 2014. Since then, he has inspired wrestlers worldwide to pursue their dreams and push themselves further.

The stories of John Cena, The Rock, Charlotte Flair, Hulk Hogan, and CM Punk embody the fundamental traits of a true champion. Their journeys are inspiring and have set a benchmark for many wrestlers to follow in their footsteps. These wrestling icons have reached the pinnacle of their careers, not once but repeatedly. They remind us that, with hard work and strong determination, we can achieve anything we set our minds to.

Pro Tips from Pros

Pro wrestling is a physically demanding sport requiring strength, agility, and mental toughness. Becoming a pro wrestler takes a lot of hard work and dedication, but with the right approach, you can achieve your goals and take your performance to the next level. This section lists valuable professional wrestling tips to help you become a better wrestler and succeed in this exciting field.

- **Train Hard and Consistently:** The key to success in pro wrestling is to train hard and consistently. Work on your strength, agility, and endurance to become a better wrestler. Ensure you have a well-rounded workout routine, including weightlifting, cardio, and flexibility training. Regularly practicing wrestling techniques to improve your skills and build muscle memory is best.
- **Stay Positive and Believe in Yourself:** Pro wrestlers must have a positive attitude and believe in their abilities. This sport is very challenging, and there will be times when you face setbacks and failures. However, it's essential to stay positive and keep pushing forward. Believe in yourself and your abilities; never give up on your dreams.
- **Use Mentors and Coaches:** Pro wrestling is a team sport, so it's essential to have a support system, including mentors and coaches. Find a mentor who can guide you through the challenges of pro wrestling and advise you on improving your skills. Also, work with a coach who will help you develop a training program tailored to your needs.
- **Take Time to Rest and Recover:** Pro wrestling is a high-impact sport, and it's essential to rest and recover. Ensure you sleep well, eat a healthy diet, and care for your body. You must listen to your body and take breaks when needed; it will prevent injuries and ensure you consistently perform at your best.
- **Stay Focused on Your Goals:** To become a successful pro wrestler, you need clear and focused goals. Whether winning a championship, getting

signed to a major wrestling organization, or simply improving your skills, ensure you have a plan and stay committed. Focus on your strengths, work on your weaknesses, and always strive to be the best wrestler you can be.

Advice for Those Pursuing Pro Wrestling

Professional wrestling is an exciting career. It's no secret that pro wrestlers are some of the most talented athletes in the world. However, to become a successful professional wrestler, every aspiring wrestler must consider certain things. This section discusses some critical advice for those pursuing pro wrestling as a career. Whether you are just starting or have been wrestling for a while, these tips will help you become a successful wrestler.

Get the Proper Training to Succeed

The first and most important piece of advice for anyone pursuing pro wrestling is to get proper training. It's not enough to be athletic or have a good physique. You must have proper training in the art of professional wrestling. Many wrestling schools and trainers exist, so take your time to research the best ones. Look for experienced trainers who have trained successful wrestlers in the past. Getting good training will help you understand the nuances of the wrestling industry and prepare you for everything that comes with it.

Find a Mentor or Coach to Guide You

In addition to getting good training, finding a mentor or coach who can help guide you is essential. It is especially important in the early stages of your career. A mentor provides valuable advice on everything from ring gear to in-ring psychology. They can introduce you to other wrestlers and promoters, which can be invaluable for making connections in the industry. Mentors can be found almost anywhere, from your wrestling school to independent shows. Take advantage of the opportunities to learn from those who have already been where you want to go.

Develop Your Mental Toughness and Stay Positive

Pro wrestling is a tricky business. The physical demands of the job are merely the beginning. You must deal with rejection, disappointment, and injuries. Therefore, you must be mentally tough and able to handle adversity to succeed in this industry. The best way is to stay positive. Focus on the things you can control, and don't get discouraged by those you can't. Instead, believe in yourself and your abilities, and keep pushing forward.

Set Realistic Goals and Stick to Them

One of the aspiring wrestlers' most significant mistakes is setting unrealistic goals. While it's important to dream big, setting achievable goals is also essential. It means setting short-term and long-term goals. For example, short-term goals include getting booked for several matches in a month. Long-term goals could be getting signed to a major wrestling promotion. Once you have set your goals, it's essential to stick to them. Stay focused and committed, and keep going even if things don't happen as quickly as you would like.

Network with Other Wrestlers and Promoters

Finally, networking is crucial to success in the pro wrestling industry. Making connections with other wrestlers and promoters in the industry is highly beneficial. Attend wrestling shows and conventions and introduce yourself to people. Offer to help at shows and events and be willing to learn from those around you. The more people you know in the industry, the better your chances of getting booked for shows and advancing your career.

Tips for Women Wrestlers

Women interested in wrestling often shy away from the sport because of the perceived physicality and the dominant presence of men. However, the sport of wrestling is equally accessible to women as it is to men. All it takes is persistence, dedication, and an unwavering belief in oneself. So, let's dive into the top tips to help women wrestlers conquer this fantastic sport.

Don't Be Afraid to Speak Up for Yourself

Women wrestlers often feel intimidated being surrounded by men. However, everyone has to go through the process of learning the sport. Speaking up and asserting your boundaries and comfort zones is essential because nobody knows you better than yourself. Do not hesitate to ask for help or guidance from your coach and teammates. Being vocal about your needs will help you gain the respect and support of others.

Start Small and Build Your Way Up

Starting small means taking it step by step. Don't jump right into advanced training levels without mastering the basics. Start with the basics, focusing on your stance and footwork and getting the fundamentals right. Then, practice the techniques that suit you best, and build on them. You can create a strong foundation for future advanced learning by perfecting the basics.

Have Confidence in Your Skills and Abilities

Wrestling is intimidating, especially when seeing experienced wrestlers in action. But don't let that discourage you. Believing in yourself and your ability to learn and grow like every wrestler is a fundamental attitude. Go into the match with a positive mindset. Visualize yourself performing, give your best, and focus on the moves you excel in. Believe in your ability and skills, and you will surely ace the game.

Find Mentors Who Can Help You Grow as a Wrestler

Having a mentor makes a substantial difference in your journey as a wrestler. Look out for wrestlers who have been where you are and achieved the goals you set for yourself. Mentors provide you with guidance, motivation, and hands-on training while sharing their experiences. You can learn a lot from the people who have been through what you're going through.

Keep a Positive Attitude and Believe in Yourself

A positive attitude is crucial to success in any field; wrestling is no different. Keeping a positive attitude doesn't mean getting things right all the time. It means having a willingness to learn and improve from mistakes. No wrestler is perfect. However, every mistake can be an opportunity to learn and improve. Keep your spirits high and allow opportunities for yourself to grow and develop your skillsets.

Women can do it. Wrestling has no gender restrictions, and if you set your heart on the game and adopt the tips mentioned above, you can become an ace woman wrestler. Be bold and speak up for yourself, start small and build, have confidence in your skills and abilities, find mentors to guide you, and always keep a positive attitude. Believe in yourself, and you'll achieve your goals in no time. Remember, the more you practice, the better you become, and always be ready to learn more. Then, it's time to hit the mat.

General Pro Wrestling Tips

Whether you're training to become a pro wrestler or a novice, learning the basics and avoiding potential injuries is essential. This section shares some general pro wrestling tips to help you prepare mentally and physically for the challenges ahead.

- **Practice Safely to Avoid Injury:** Wrestling is a contact sport involving many physical contacts, which can result in injuries. Therefore, practicing safe techniques and using protective gear, such as helmets, elbow pads, knee pads, mouthguards, and groin guards, is essential. Always warm up before training or a match to help prevent injuries.
- **Learn the Rules of Professional Wrestling:** You must master the rules of professional wrestling to be a successful wrestler. Studying the different matches, understanding the ring's layout, and learning the specific moves and holds are imperative. Also, watch wrestling matches to learn from other experienced wrestlers.
- **Stay in Shape and Stay Hydrated:** In pro wrestling, endurance, and strength are crucial. Therefore, it's essential to stay in shape by following a balanced diet and an exercise routine that includes cardio and strength training. Also, staying hydrated is vital in any sport for optimal performance. Drink plenty of water before, during, and after training or matches.
- **Listen to Your Body and Respect its Limits:** Knowing your limits is vital in pro wrestling. Pushing yourself too hard can result in injuries, so listening to your body and taking breaks when necessary is crucial. Also, don't take unnecessary risks in matches; always prioritize your safety and that of other wrestlers.
- **Use Visualization to Reach Your Goals:** Visualization is an excellent technique to help you achieve your goals in pro wrestling. For example, imagining yourself executing a perfect move or watching your opponent's moves before the match can help you gain an advantage. Furthermore, visualize how winning feels, which can help increase your confidence and motivation.

A few key things genuinely matter for achieving success in wrestling. Firstly, you must be passionate about the sport. Wrestling is not something you can do half-heartedly and expect to excel. You must be willing to put in the time and effort to train physically and mentally. Moreover, you must have a strong work ethic and an unwavering commitment to your goals.

Whether competing to win a championship or improving your skills, you need an unyielding dedication to your craft. Finally, it would be best to surround yourself with people who will support and encourage you on your journey. Your coaches, teammates, and family members are crucial in helping you succeed on the wrestling mat. You can accomplish anything in wrestling and beyond with passion, hard work, and a robust support system.

Conclusion

Wrestling is one of the oldest and most challenging sports. However, it provides countless benefits and rewards for those willing to put in the time and effort to master its techniques. From posture and balance to advanced maneuvers and techniques, wrestling is a comprehensive sport requiring strength, agility, and a keen mind. So, whether you're a youth, high school, or college athlete or simply looking to get back in shape, wrestling offers an exciting and rewarding challenge to improve your life on and off the mat.

Wrestling involves grappling with an opponent to gain control and pin them to the ground. Several basic rules and techniques every wrestler must master include proper stance, hand placement, and grip. Wrestling aims to get your opponent to the ground and control them using combined moves, such as takedowns, joint locks, and pinning maneuvers. This guide covered the basics of wrestling, from the rules and techniques to advanced moves and strategies. It explored posture and balance fundamentals and how to perform penetrating and lifting maneuvers. It also discussed the art of attacking and countering and how to use reversal techniques effectively.

One of the most critical skills for wrestling success is proper posture and balance. This involves maintaining a low center of gravity, keeping your feet shoulder-width apart, and staying balanced and centered. This skill requires practice and discipline, developed through consistent training and coaching. Wrestling involves several advanced maneuvers and techniques demanding strength, agility, and precision. These maneuvers include penetrating moves, such as double-leg takedowns, single-leg attacks, and lifting and throwing maneuvers requiring quick reflexes and keen timing.

A key aspect of wrestling is to attack and counterattack effectively. This skill involves creating openings and opportunities to score points and anticipate and neutralize your opponent's moves. It necessitates strategic thinking, physical prowess, and mental toughness. This guide provides several exercises and drills to develop your offensive and defensive capabilities.

Wrestling requires a strong understanding of reversal and escape techniques, allowing you to get out of a vulnerable position and regain control of the match. These skills involve quick thinking, agility, and a willingness to take calculated risks to gain an advantage. Finally, wrestling consists of various pinning combinations using physical strength and strategic thinking. These moves allow you to gain control of your opponent and secure a win. But you must learn to adapt to changing circumstances and react quickly to your opponent's moves.

Wrestling is a unique sport that offers mental and physical challenges, making it an ideal choice for those looking to improve their health and fitness. Whether you're interested in competing at a high level or merely want to get back in shape and learn valuable life skills, wrestling is an exciting and rewarding challenge helping you build confidence, discipline, and resilience on and off the mat. So, why not try wrestling and discover how this ancient sport can improve your life?

Good luck on your journey to becoming a skilled wrestler!

Part 5: Karate

A Comprehensive Guide to Karate Techniques for Beginners Wanting to Go from Basics to Black Belt

Introduction

Have you ever wondered what it is like to be a student of karate? Have you always wanted to learn an ancient and powerful martial art but don't know where to begin? This book gives you all the information to get started and master this timeless art.

Karate focuses on enhancing the mind, body, and spirit. It's about striking and kicking and building character, discipline, and resilience. With each technique and form, you'll learn to focus your mind, harness your strength, and push your limits. You'll move through the ranks quickly when you practice karate diligently as your skills and understanding grow.

The dedication and commitment instilled in karate practitioners go far beyond the dojo walls and affect every aspect of their lives. Developing a karate mindset requires mental toughness, an unbreakable will, and a never-give-up attitude. With these traits, a karateka can overcome physical challenges and obstacles they face in life. Karate's fundamental principles and training methods are the foundation for any practitioner, regardless of belt rank. Properly understanding stances, blocks, punches, kicks, katas, and kumite is essential for a successful martial arts journey.

Karate belts are not just a piece of cloth tied around a martial artist's waist. They represent milestones and achievements in their karate journey. Each belt color has significance and symbolizes the hard work and dedication of the karateka. From the beginner's white belt to the experienced black belt, the journey is a never-ending process of learning and improving. The karate community is excited and proud when a karateka enters the dojo wearing a new belt. Each belt color is meaningful and vital to the karateka's journey. It brings a sense of accomplishment and proves that pushing yourself to the limit is worth it.

This comprehensive guide dives into the details of karate, from stances and blocks to katas and kumite. You'll discover the basics, advanced techniques, pressure points, and drills. You gain insight into karate culture and what it takes to master this martial art. From the importance of respect to the power of the karate mindset, this book teaches you everything about this ancient art.

Before you begin your journey, arm yourself with knowledge. Read this book and learn the information needed to succeed as a karateka. With the right mindset and dedication, you can defend yourself and impress your friends with impressive forms and techniques. So, get ready to experience the power of karate and take your martial arts journey to the next level.

Chapter 1: The Karate Mindset

Are you ready to master physical and mental prowess? Can you restructure your mindset and develop an unshakable spirit? Karate enhances your physical strength and agility and teaches you the value of self-confidence and discipline.

The karate mindset focuses on training your mind to be as strong as your body. [49]

The karate mindset is about training your mind to be as strong as your body. It's about pushing beyond your limits and tapping into a level of focus and discipline you never thought possible. Adopting the karate mindset, you become more patient, humble, and resilient. You learn to embrace failure as a steppingstone to success and develop a deep appreciation for the power of hard work and perseverance.

Whether a seasoned martial artist or a complete beginner, this chapter helps you understand karate's philosophical teachings and psychological aspects passed down for centuries. It briefly overviews the four main karate styles, their corresponding techniques, and the three main elements of karate in detail. Mastering these concepts will take your physical and mental skills to the next level.

Philosophical Teachings of Karate

To truly understand karate, you must delve deep and embrace its philosophical teachings. Karate has taught individuals to help them to become more self-aware, find inner peace, and develop discipline beyond the dojo. Understanding the philosophical teachings of karate is essential for unlocking the full potential and true essence of this ancient art. This section explores the connection between mind and body harmony in traditional karate teachings.

Awareness

One of the fundamental teachings of karate is awareness. karate practitioners are always taught to be present in the moment, aware of their surroundings, and alert to potential danger. This awareness is essential in self-defense and daily life. Knowing your surroundings, actions, and thoughts can help you navigate life with better clarity and avoid unnecessary distractions. The heightened awareness that comes with being a karate practitioner is a powerful tool for self-improvement and personal growth.

Mind and Body Unity

Karate teaches that the mind and body are not separate entities but interconnected. Practicing karate, you learn to master your mind and body, aligning them with each other. You know to use your mind to control your body and your body to support your mind. As a result, karate training enhances mental clarity and concentration, increases physical strength and flexibility, and improves overall health and well-being. By practicing karate, you develop a deeper connection between your mind and body – which is essential to achieving your goals and finding inner peace.

Discipline

Another critical teaching in karate is discipline. Karate requires discipline in everything you do, from training and practicing to daily life. Discipline is what separates a martial artist from a mere fighter. Martial artists are disciplined individuals dedicated to pursuing excellence in all aspects of life. You learn to respect yourself, others, and the world around you through discipline. Disciplined individuals can focus their attention and energy on achieving their goals without being distracted by negative thoughts or external influences.

Humility

Humility is a cornerstone of traditional karate teaching. Humility is recognizing your limitations, weaknesses, strengths, and abilities. Karate teaches that everyone should approach training with an open mind and a willingness to learn from others, regardless of skill or rank. Embracing humility, you see yourself and others as equal, developing tolerance and respect. Humility prevents arrogance and ego, which can significantly hinder personal growth.

Perseverance

Perseverance is the ability to persist in the face of adversity and to stay committed to your goals despite challenges and setbacks. Karate training can be physically and mentally demanding, requiring much perseverance to progress in skill and rank. Perseverance is essential in developing a strong spirit, crucial for overcoming obstacles and achieving success. By creating a resilient and determined mindset, you can overcome any challenge.

The philosophical teachings of karate are essential for unlocking the full potential of this ancient art. The teachings of awareness, mind and body unity, discipline, humility, and perseverance all contribute to a holistic approach to life. The ultimate goal of karate is not only to become physically strong or skilled in martial techniques but also to become a better human and live a more fulfilling life. A better insight into karate's more profound meaning and purpose can help you achieve mind and body harmony.

Importance of Right Kokoro

Karate is a physical sport and a mental discipline that requires a balanced blend of mind and body. Therefore, the Kokoro, the Japanese term for heart, mind, and spirit, is vital in the practice of karate. Your kokoro should be pure and focused, allowing you to concentrate on the task and perform it to your fullest potential. This section discusses why having the right kokoro is crucial in karate and how it impacts your overall performance.

A Strong Kokoro Helps You Overcome Challenges

A strong kokoro means having a clear focus and a positive mindset. When you practice karate, there will be times when you encounter challenges seemingly impossible to overcome. However, having the right kokoro enables you to push through these challenges with grit, determination, and a never-say-die attitude. It helps you keep your composure in adversity and makes you a better, more resilient karate practitioner.

A Clear Kokoro Helps You Develop Your Technique

The importance of the right kokoro in karate goes beyond mental fortitude. A clear mind helps you learn and master techniques effectively. When mentally distracted, your body will naturally follow, resulting in incorrect posture and movement. Conversely, when your kokoro is clear and focused, your actions become more precise, and your activities become more fluid. You will develop your technique faster and achieve better results on the mat.

A Pure Kokoro Helps You Connect with Your Training Partners

Having the right kokoro allows you to connect with your training partners deeper. When your heart is pure, your energy is positive, and your intentions are sincere. It creates an environment of mutual respect and trust, fostering an excellent training atmosphere where everyone can grow and learn together.

An Inclusive Kokoro Helps You Promote Unity and Camaraderie

Karate is an inclusive sport welcoming people from all walks of life. The right kokoro fosters a spirit of inclusion, promoting unity and camaraderie among practitioners. You become an ambassador for the sport and help spread its values beyond the dojo.

The Right Kokoro Helps You Find Inner Peace

Karate is not merely about winning medals and competitions. It is about finding inner peace and balance. The right kokoro helps you do just that. When you have a clear mind, a pure heart, and a focused spirit, you connect with your inner being and achieve serenity, positively impacting other areas of your life.

The importance of having the right kokoro in karate cannot be overstated. It goes beyond physical training and enables you to become a well-rounded practitioner in mind and body. A clear and focused kokoro helps you overcome challenges, develop your technique, connect with your training partners, promote unity, and find inner peace. To take your karate practice to the next level, focus on cultivating the right Kokoro and watch your performance soar.

Psychological Aspects of Karate

Karate is more than a series of punches, kicks, and blocks—it's a way of life. Beyond the physical benefits of karate, like improved fitness and self-defense skills, martial arts can have profound psychological effects. This section explores the psychological aspects of karate and how practicing this ancient art benefits you mentally and physically.

Mental Fortitude

Firstly, karate cultivates discipline and self-control. The mental fortitude required to become proficient in this martial art involves dedication, hard work, and perseverance. The practice of karate is a pathway to understanding the power of the mind and how it can be harnessed to overcome obstacles. A sense of purpose and achievement comes with mastering a new technique or belt level carrying over into all aspects of life and giving practitioners control over their destinies.

Support System

Secondly, karate fosters a sense of community and belonging. Practicing karate alongside others pursuing the same goal creates a support system beyond the dojo. This sense of camaraderie and belonging leads to improved self-esteem and greater well-being. Additionally, karate offers an opportunity to connect with traditions and cultures practiced for centuries so practitioners feel more grounded and connected to a larger community.

Coping Mechanism

Thirdly, karate builds resilience and mental toughness. Even the most experienced karateka (karate experts) have setbacks in the dojo and life. The practice of karate helps individuals develop the coping mechanisms necessary to weather these challenges and come out stronger on the other side. This approach to adversity applies to any area of life and leads to more excellent emotional stability and a positive outlook on the world.

Stress Reduction

Fourthly, karate promotes mindfulness and stress reduction. The practice of karate requires complete presence at the moment, helping practitioners experience greater focus and concentration in all areas of life. Additionally, karate provides a healthy outlet for stress and anxiety, which is especially beneficial for individuals in high-stress professions or those dealing with mental health challenges. The physical release of energy helps individuals feel more relaxed and at ease.

Spiritual Growth

Finally, karate offers a path to personal and spiritual growth. Whether through meditation, breathing exercises, or kata (prearranged movements), karate provides opportunities for self-reflection and personal development. This approach helps individuals explore their values, beliefs, and goals, leading to greater self-awareness and a more profound sense of purpose.

The psychological aspects of karate provide an avenue for personal growth and development beyond the physical benefits of martial art. It offers a way to cultivate discipline, mental toughness, resilience, and mindfulness while fostering a sense of community and belonging so that individuals thrive inside and outside the dojo. So, whether your goal is to improve your physical fitness, learn self-defense, or explore what karate offers, the psychological benefits of this ancient art are undeniable.

The Four Mindsets

One of the crucial elements of karate is a mindset, the four perspectives: Shoshin, Mushin, Fudoshin, and Zanshin. Understanding these mindsets can improve your karate practice and your daily life. So, let's explore each perspective, its significance, and how to develop it.

Shoshin

Shoshin is the beginner's mind. It means having an open mind, free of preconceptions, opinions, or biases. When you approach karate or any learning experience with Shoshin, you become receptive to new ideas, willing to learn from your mistakes, and humble enough to ask for help. Shoshin is the foundation of continuous growth and improvement. You must let go of your ego, breathe deeply, and focus on the present moment to develop Shoshin. Practice karate as if practicing for the first time, with curiosity and enthusiasm rather than automatic habits.

Mushin

Mushin is the mind of no mind. It means being in a state of flow where your actions are spontaneous, intuitive, and effortless. Mushin refers to an empty mind, free of distractions, doubts, or fears, where you act instinctively and confidently. Mushin is the goal of all martial arts practice, where body and mind become one, and you react instantly and appropriately to any situation. To develop Mushin, you must be fully immersed in your practice and free from external or internal distractions. You must create your intuitive sense and trust your body's natural reactions.

Fudoshin

Fudoshin is the immovable mind. It means having a calm, stable, and committed mindset, regardless of external circumstances. Fudoshin refers to a warrior's spirit, where you are prepared for challenges and unshaken by obstacles or setbacks. Fudoshin is essential in karate when facing opponents trying to intimidate or distract you. You must simultaneously train your mind to be unyielding and flexible to develop Fudoshin. You must cultivate mental toughness, focus on breathing, and visualize yourself as invincible.

Zanshin

Zanshin is the lingering mind. It means having an aware, observant, and reflective mind, even after an action. Zanshin refers to a state of heightened awareness where you remain vigilant, watchful, and prepared for follow-up action. In karate, Zanshin is crucial, as it allows you to anticipate a counterattack, escape, or defense. Zanshin is also applicable in daily life to remain vigilant and attentive to your surroundings, even after completing a task. You must train your mind to be mindful, observant, and reflective to develop Zanshin. You must stay connected to your surroundings, focus on breathing, and visualize yourself as alert and ready.

The four mindsets in karate are more than abstract concepts or philosophical jargon. They are practical skills enhancing your karate practice and life. By developing Shoshin, you become receptive to new ideas and continuously improve. By creating Mushin, you are in a state of flow and instantly react to a situation. By developing Fudoshin, you become resilient and unyielding in the face of challenges. Finally, by creating Zanshin, you are always aware and vigilant. So, cultivate these mindsets, and see how your karate and your life transform.

Karate Styles and Techniques

Karate is a martial art that has evolved from ancient Japanese traditions. It involves punching, kicking, and striking techniques for defensive purposes. Karate has various styles and designs depending on the region and instructor. As a result, you might be overwhelmed by multiple styles and designs if you're new to karate. To help you get started, here are some of the main karate styles and techniques you should know:

- **Shotokan Karate:** Shotokan is one of the most popular styles of karate. It emphasizes powerful and straight movements, with punches and kicks delivered linearly. In addition, Shotokan focuses strongly on stances and breathing techniques, which develop strength and stamina.
- **Wado-Ryu Karate:** Wado-Ryu is another popular style of karate. It emphasizes quick movements and evasion techniques. Wado-Ryu focuses on body shifting and positioning, allowing the practitioner to maximize strength and speed.
- **Goju-Ryu Karate:** Goju-Ryu is a karate style focusing on circular movements and body conditioning. It emphasizes close-range combat techniques, including grappling and joint locks. Goju-Ryu strongly focuses on breathing techniques, improving cardiovascular health, and enhancing the body's natural healing abilities.
- **Kyokushin Karate:** Kyokushin is a karate style emphasizing full-contact sparring and physical conditioning. It strongly emphasizes powerful strikes and hardening the body through repeated impact training. Kyokushin incorporates throws, joint locks, and powerful kicks to the body and legs.
- **Bunkai:** Bunkai is not a karate style but a set of techniques to practice karate moves in a realistic, self-defense context. Bunkai involves breaking down the movements of Kata (a prearranged set of actions) and practicing them with a partner. It emphasizes practical self-defense techniques that can be used in real-world situations.

Karate is a diverse and exciting martial art with a range of styles and techniques to explore. However, regardless of which type you practice, the benefits of karate are numerous. From improving physical fitness to developing self-discipline and self-defense skills, karate has something to offer everyone.

Three Basic Elements of Karate

Karate is an ancient Japanese martial art popular worldwide. The word "karate" means "empty hand," meaning the martial art does not rely on weapons. Instead, karate relies on three essential elements: kihon, kata, and kumite. These elements are crucial for every beginner to learn and master. They form the foundation of karate and every other martial art. This section explains these three essential elements of karate in detail so you can improve your skills and become a better karateka.

Kihon

The first and most important essential element of karate is kihon. It means "basic techniques" and includes different blocks, punches, strikes, kicks, and stances. Kihon is the foundation of karate and helps develop proper body alignment, balance, and coordination. Therefore, a karateka must master kihon before moving on to more advanced techniques. A karateka can perform the other two elements effectively with overwhelming kihon.

Kata

The second essential element of karate is Kata. Kata means "form" and is a series of prearranged movements simulating a fight against imaginary opponents. Each kata has a specific sequence of activities, and every move has a purpose. Kata helps develop muscle memory, timing, rhythm, and breathing. Practicing kata improves a karateka's balance, coordination, and focus. Remember, kata should not be performed mechanically but with spirit, emotion, and expression.

Kumite

The third fundamental element of karate is Kumite. Kumite means "sparring" and is karate's most dynamic and exciting element. Kumite is a simulated fight with a partner and the ultimate test of a karateka's skills. Kumite develops reflexes, timing, speed, and agility. It teaches a karateka how to react in a real fight situation. However, kumite should not be taken lightly, as it can be dangerous if not performed correctly. Therefore, a karateka must always practice kumite safely and under the supervision of a qualified instructor.

How to Master These Elements

You must continuously practice and refine your skills to become a skilled karateka. An excellent way to practice kihon is to repeat each technique until it becomes automatic. Practice kata by memorizing the sequence of movements and performing them with emotion and expression. You can practice kumite by sparring with a partner and gradually increasing the intensity of the fight. A karateka must practice breathing techniques, meditation, and visualization to improve their focus, relaxation, and mental clarity.

Karate is a martial art requiring dedication, perseverance, and patience to master. By mastering the three essential elements of karate, a beginner can develop a strong foundation for their karate journey. These elements are interconnected, and by learning one aspect, a karateka improves the others. Remember, always practice safely and under the guidance of a qualified instructor. Keep practicing, and never give up on your karate journey.

This chapter explored the karate mindset and how it is essential in martial art. From the four mindsets of Shoshin, Mushin, Fudoshin, and Zanshin to the four main karate styles of Shotokan, Wado-Ryu, Kyokushin, and Goju-Ryu, you must have the right attitude and approach to become a better karateka. Furthermore, the three essential elements of Kihon, Kata, and Kumite were discussed in detail so karateka could practice and refine their skills. A karateka can become a skilled martial artist with dedication, perseverance, and patience.

Chapter 2: Kihon I Stances and Blocks

Karate is a martial art that has gained popularity across the globe thanks to its unique techniques and intense training regimen. One of the fundamental aspects of karate is mastering the kihon. These stances and blocks are the building blocks for all other karate techniques, making them essential to any practitioner's training. From the robust and rooted Zenkutsu Dachi stance to the elegant twists and turns of Hidari Gedan Barai, each kihon requires discipline, focus, and an unwavering commitment to excellence. Students can perfect these moves through extensive practice, increasing agility, coordination, and overall strength.

This chapter introduces you to the basic karate stances and blocks. It guides how to practice them properly and highlights their importance in proper training. When you master the core kihon, you open yourself to more advanced techniques. The confidence gained through only a few months of practice can last a lifetime. By the end of this chapter, you will be well-versed in basic karate stances and blocks. The aspect of karate will seem much less intimidating and more achievable.

Stances

Karate is not just about throwing punches and kicks. It's about mastering the art of stances. Known as Tachikata, stances are the foundation of every move and technique in karate. Each stance requires precise alignment and balance, from the classic front stance to the more advanced horse stance. It is essential to hold the stances correctly and move between them with speed and ease. When executed perfectly, stances give karate practitioners the power, speed, and flexibility to perform any move effectively.

Tachikata and Requirements

With its origins traced back to Japan, karate has become a widely practiced sport with millions of devotees worldwide. Known for its strength and lethal strikes, karate emphasizes the importance of a good stance in executing powerful punches and kicks. This section explores the basics of Tachikata and the requirements for a good stance in karate.

Basic Stances

Tachikata, or karate stance, forms the foundation of all the movements in karate. A good stance is essential in karate since it provides balance and stability to the body, which is critical in generating power for strikes. There are three basic stances in karate: Zenkutsu-dachi, Kiba-dachi, and Kokutsu-dachi. The Zenkutsu-dachi stance, known as the front stance, is the most common in karate. It involves placing one foot forward and the other back, with your knees bent and weight distributed evenly between the legs.

The Kiba-dachi, or horse stance, is standing with your feet shoulder-width apart and knees bent as if you were sitting on an imaginary chair. The Kokutsu-dachi stance, known as the back stance, requires you to stand with one foot back and the other foot forward, with your body leaning backward.

Achieving a Good Stance

Practitioners must meet specific requirements to achieve a good stance in karate. First, you must maintain proper balance by keeping your center of gravity low and distributing your weight between your legs. Your hips should be tucked in and aligned with your spine, and your back should be straight. Finally, controlling your breathing, inhaling deeply through the nose, and exhaling slowly through the mouth is imperative.

Secondly, foot placement is crucial to developing a good stance in karate. The distance between your feet and the angle of your toes must be adjusted for each stance. The foot placed at the front should be pointed toward the intended target, while the rear foot should be angled slightly to the side, providing stability and balance.

Thirdly, the knee position is vital in achieving a good stance. Your knees must be bent, but not too much that they extend past your toes, as this can put too much strain on the knee joints. Be mindful of your knee alignment with your toes; they should always point in the same direction.

Furthermore, your hands should be positioned at the right height in a good karate stance. The hands should be held up to protect the face, with the elbows tucked in to save the ribs. Avoid dropping your hands as it weakens the defense. Finally, maintaining eye contact and focus is crucial for a good karate stance. Your gaze should be permanently fixed on your opponent, allowing you to anticipate incoming strikes and react quickly.

Types of Stances

Karate techniques are rooted in a solid stance, providing stability to the practitioner, and channeling the power generated from the ground up. Stances are much more than just standing or walking in karate. They're the foundation of every move you execute. Therefore, understanding the various karate stances is crucial for any student aspiring to master the art. This section dives deep into the four stances in karate, their benefits, and how to execute them correctly.

Natural Stance

The natural stance is karate's most important stance and the starting position for most moves. It's a simple yet effective stance characterized by your feet being shoulder-width apart, toes pointed straight ahead, and knees slightly bent. This is your default stance and the position you'll return to after each move. The natural stance sets the foundation for balance, strength, and mobility. Keep your core engaged and distribute your weight evenly on the balls of your feet. Remember to keep your head up, shoulders relaxed, and chin tucked in, facing straight ahead. This stance particularly benefits beginners, as it helps develop coordination and balance.

Heiko-Dachi, the natural stance.

Unstable Stance

Unstable stances, known as kiba-dachi, require placing your feet further apart, with your toes pointing outward. This stance focuses on developing your leg strength, stability, and balance. This stance can lower your center of gravity, allowing you to generate more power for techniques like punches. Place your heels together; toes pointed out about 45 degrees, shift your weight back on your heels, and bend your knees evenly. Keep your back straight, chin tucked in, and your core engaged. This stance is particularly beneficial when delivering strikes with the feet or engaging in close-range combat.

Kiba-dachi, the unstable stance

Outside Tension Stance

The outside tension stance, or soto-tension, is more advanced. This stance is about maximizing the power of your techniques by creating tension in your muscles. Turn your front foot out to a 45-degree angle and push the heel of your back foot away from your body while keeping your toes on the ground. The movement engages your hips and core, emphasizing your side muscles. It stresses the lower back, hip joints, and leg muscles. The outside tension stance improves kicking ability, including high and spinning kicks. Additionally, it creates a more comprehensive, longer, and stable base that strengthens the lower body.

Outside tension stance

Inside Tension Stance

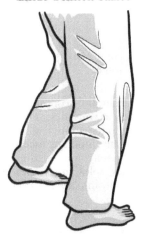 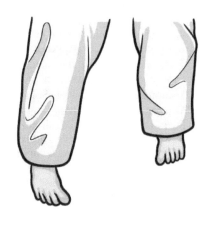

Uchi-tension stance

The inside tension stance, or uchi-tension, is like the outside tension stance but with the placement of the front foot reversed. It emphasizes the inner muscles, creating tension from your buttocks to the lower abs. It puts more pressure on your knees, making it a great stance for developing stability and power. The primary emphasis is mobility and to quickly move your hips and legs. Place your front foot at a 45-degree angle but position the back foot facing straight ahead. Lower yourself into the pose by bending your back foot knee. Ensure your back is straight and your head is up. This stance is ideal for offensive moves, like knee strikes and close-ranged techniques.

The natural and unstable stances are beginner-level stances that help develop coordination, flexibility, and balance. In addition, they allow the practitioner to generate power for strikes and kicks. On the other hand, the outside and inside tension stances are more advanced for offensive and defensive techniques. These stances emphasize the side and inner muscles, creating tension that channels energy to the hips, legs, and core. The correct execution of stances is crucial in karate, as it is the key to mastering powerful and decisive moves. With the proper technique and practice, perfecting the different stances in karate can take your game to the next level.

Stability in Karate

As a karate practitioner, mastering stability is a crucial aspect of the art, as it enables you to transfer your body weight effectively, control movements, and deliver precise blows. Unfortunately, karate practitioners often focus on techniques, forgetting that stability is the foundation of a successful attack or defense. This section explores practical tips and tricks to help you achieve stability in karate, from lowering your center of gravity to positioning your knees, ankles, soles, and hips.

Lowering the Center of Gravity

Lowering your center of gravity helps you stabilize your movements and maintain a balanced stance. This technique relies on bending your knees and dropping your hips slightly, allowing your body weight to spread evenly across both legs. To achieve this technique, do the following:

1. Start from a natural standing position and bend your knees, picturing yourself sitting on an imaginary chair.
2. Keep your feet hip-width apart, aligning them with your shoulder blades.

---

3. Engage your core muscles by pulling your belly button into your spine and exhaling slowly.

4. Distribute your weight evenly between both feet and avoid leaning too far forward or backward (keep your back straight).

5. Regularly practice this stance until it feels natural and comfortable. The lower your center of gravity, the more stable your movements will be.

Positioning Knees, Ankles, Soles, and Hips

Proper positioning of your knees, ankles, soles, and hips significantly contributes to stability in karate. Your knees should point in the same direction as your toes, and your ankles should remain flexible and relaxed. Your sole should grip the ground, allowing you to pivot and turn during techniques. Your hips should rotate smoothly, following the movements of your upper body. Stand sideways in front of a mirror and perform a basic punch to test your positioning. Watch your knees, ankles, soles, and hips, and correct any misalignment. Good habits in your stance will positively impact your overall stability and technique.

Do's and Don'ts

To further enhance your stability in karate, here are some do's and don'ts to consider:

- Keep your shoulders relaxed and your chin tucked in to avoid neck tension.
- Don't lock your joints or hyper-extend your limbs, which could cause instability and injury.
- Engage your core muscles and breathe deeply to increase stability and focus.
- Remember to warm up before training to prevent muscle strains and stiffness.
- Practice on different surfaces, such as soft ground or sand, to challenge your stability and balance.
- Take your time with your techniques and movements, ensuring stability and precision.

Mental Stability

Mental stability is as important as physical stability in karate. Mental strength is developing a clear, focused mind, free of distractions and negative thoughts. Practice meditation and mindfulness regularly, visualize your goals, and stay motivated to achieve mental stability. Use positive affirmations and celebrate small achievements along the way. Mental stability will improve your martial arts abilities and overall well-being.

Breathing Techniques for Karate

Karate is a martial art that involves a great deal of physical exertion, speed, and precision. You must master many techniques, including breathing, to become a skilled karate practitioner. Proper breathing techniques help generate power, focus the mind, and maintain balance. This section discusses breathing techniques for karate to improve your performance and take you one step closer to mastering this exciting martial art.

- **Abdominal Breathing:** Abdominal breathing, known as belly breathing, is an essential breathing technique in karate. It involves breathing through your nose, filling your belly with air, and exhaling through your mouth. This technique helps maintain a steady flow of oxygen to the muscles, increasing stamina and reducing fatigue. It calms the mind and regulates the heart rate.

- **Reverse Breathing:** Reverse breathing is a technique that involves inhaling while contracting the abdominal muscles and exhaling while expanding them. This technique helps generate extra power during strikes and blocks and strengthens the core muscles. However, this technique requires proper guidance as it can lead to dizziness and fainting if not performed correctly.
- **Breath Control:** Breath control is an essential aspect of karate. It involves synchronizing your breathing with your movements. For example, you could inhale while raising your arms and exhale while delivering a punch. This technique improves balance and coordination, making your movements more fluid and efficient.
- **Ki Breathing:** Ki breathing is meditation involving deep relaxation and controlled breathing. This technique increases your awareness of Ki, the life energy flowing through your body. Ki breathing involves inhaling slowly and deeply through the nose, holding the breath for a few seconds, and exhaling slowly through the mouth. This technique calms the mind, reduces stress, and improves overall health and well-being.
- **Dynamic Breathing:** Dynamic breathing uses short, sharp exhalations when striking or blocking. This technique increases power and speed and helps intimidate opponents. Dynamic breathing involves exhaling with force through the mouth while tightening the abdominal muscles. It is essential to practice this technique regularly to avoid hyperventilation.

Breathing techniques are an essential aspect of karate, and mastering them helps you improve your performance and achieve your goals. Whether a beginner or an experienced practitioner, incorporating these breathing techniques into your training routine helps you develop a deeper understanding of the art and takes your skills to the next level. Remember, practice these techniques slowly and steadily, and always seek guidance from a qualified instructor before attempting advanced techniques. With consistent practice and patience, you can become a karate master and take control of your mind, body, and spirit.

Blocks (Uke)

Karate is best known for its uke. [50]

Karate is an ancient martial art known for its powerful blocks (uke). The primary purpose of a block is to defend against an attacker's strikes and kicks. Karate blocks are not just simple movements but a combination of technique, speed, and power. This section delves deeper into the world of blocks, their types, and their importance in karate.

Basics

Blocks are among the fundamental techniques of karate, and every beginner must master them. A block, or "uke," is a defensive movement protecting the defender from attack. The most common blocks in karate are the rising block (age uke), inward block (uchi uke), outward block (soto uke), and downward block (gedan barai). Each block is crucial, and a karateka must master them all.

The rising block (age uke) is a rising motion deflecting an upward attack. The inward block (uchi uke) raises the forearm to block incoming punches or strikes. The outward block (or soto uke) deflects blows from the outside, and the downward block (gedan barai) aims to defend against low kicks and attacks.

Another essential block is the combination block, combining several individual blocks in rapid succession to defend against an attacker's continuous assaults. Combination blocking is crucial in modern-day karate, and a karateka must practice different combinations to react instinctively to an attacker's movements.

The importance of blocks in karate cannot be overstated. Besides protecting the defender from an attack, mastering blocks in karate provides the karateka with many benefits. Practicing blocks improves your muscle strength, speed, and flexibility, making it easier for you to execute more complex techniques. Blocks improve awareness and reaction time, essential qualities in martial arts.

A karateka must practice blocks regularly to perfect their techniques. Regular practice sessions should include warm-up exercises, drills, and sparring with an opponent to simulate a real-life attack. Practicing with a partner helps you to master defensive techniques while building confidence and learning to react instinctively.

Each block, ranging from inward and outward blocks to combination blocks, aims to protect the defender from an attacker's attack. Blocks provide countless benefits to the karateka, including improved muscle strength, speed, flexibility, awareness, and reaction time. Therefore, regular practice and training are essential for a karateka to master blocks and other karate techniques.

Timing the Blocks

Karate is a martial art focusing on self-defense techniques. Therefore, it requires much practice and discipline to master the various moves and techniques. This section discusses how to time your blocks and turn them into effective counterattacks in karate. This technique is crucial for martial artists because it can give you the upper hand in a fight and help you defend yourself effectively.

Timing Is Everything

Timing techniques will make or break your game. Timing blocks are essential to stopping the opponent from attacking you, but timing blocks and turning them into counterattacks is even better. When you time your blocks just right, you can land an effective counterpunch and subdue your opponent. You must stay focused and watch your opponent's movement and body language to time your blocks correctly. If you time your block too early or too late, your block could be ineffective, and your opponent will have an opportunity to attack you.

Striking Back

Once you timed your block correctly, it's time to strike back. When you counterattack, you take advantage of the momentum your opponent has generated and use it to your advantage. You should aim for vulnerable points like the ribs, throat, or groin to make your counterattack effective. These areas are sensitive and can cause immense pain to your opponent. When you land an effective counterattack, your opponent might be forced to back off, allowing you to escape or launch another attack.

Turning Blocks to Counterattacks

Timing blocks and turning them into counterattacks requires a lot of practice. The best way to practice is to pair up with a partner and practice different moves and techniques. During the practice session, your partner will play the role of the attacker, and you, the defender. When your partner attacks, you must focus on timing your block correctly and immediately launch a counterattack. You'll learn to time your blocks better with practice, and your counterattacks will become more effective.

Remember that timing blocks and turning them into counterattacks require patience and discipline. It would be best to wait for the right moment to strike and not rush into an attack. It takes a lot of practice to master the technique, so don't get discouraged if it doesn't work the first time. Keep practicing, and you'll eventually get better at it.

In addition to the basic blocks discussed in this chapter, a karateka can practice plenty of more advanced techniques. Blocks such as split blocks, cross blocks, and palm-heel blocks can further protect the defender from an attacker's attack. These techniques require more practice and skill but provide even more excellent protection once mastered. When practicing these advanced blocks, it is essential to keep the same principles of timing in mind. Correctly timing these blocks will ensure the defender's counterattack is more likely to succeed.

Maintaining a good stance is critical to effectively performing kicks, punches, and blocks. A proper stance requires Tanden or the center of gravity to be at the body's center. This ensures the weight is evenly distributed and the movements are precise. Good Tachikata differentiates a novice from a seasoned karateka, and regular practice can help improve their stance. Developing a balanced and stable posture is critical to advance in karate and is a journey worth undertaking. So, kick off your shoes, stand up tall, and let's get ready to strike the perfect stance.

Chapter 3: Kihon II Punches and Kicks

Punches and kicks are just a tiny part of what makes karate so forward-thinking. When you watch a skilled karate practitioner, you'll observe that their movements are almost effortless yet incredibly powerful. Likewise, the kicks and punches in karate are meant to be quick and deadly, making karate highly effective in self-defense. Mastering the karate techniques takes time, but understanding the basics is an essential starting point.

This chapter breaks down the basics of karate punches and kicks so that you can confidently begin your karate journey. First, it covers the essential grips and punches, from simple straight punches and jabs to advanced techniques like reverse punches and katas. Second, you learn the basics of kicking, from front kicks to crescent and reverse crescent kicks. Finally, it touches on advanced karate kicks, leg attacks, and non-traditional kicks.

Punches

From the classic front punch to the roundhouse and uppercut, karate is a martial art where the power of the punch reigns supreme. Each punch requires precision and technique to execute flawlessly, making it all the more satisfying when you finally master them. You won't forget the adrenaline rush from throwing a punch in sparring or in a real fight. Karate punches seem intimidating, but they can become one of your greatest weapons with practice and dedication. So, put on those gloves, channel your inner karate master, and get started.

Holding a Punch Grip

Karate is a martial art involving striking, kicking, and punching techniques. The grip you use when punching is essential to the effectiveness of your striking techniques. It's necessary to have a solid punch grip in karate, as it contributes to the accuracy and power of your punches. This section explores the importance of holding a punch grip in karate, why it matters, and how to improve your punch grip technique.

Holding a punch is necessary for practicing karate.

Importance of a Punch Grip

A firm punch grip is essential in karate as it helps you build more power in your punching technique. The more muscle you put into your punches, the more you intimidate your opponents and offer a quick victory. A punch grip can also be an indicator of your technique. A correct punch grip will demonstrate your mastery of the method.

Improving Your Punch Grip

One way to improve your punch grip in karate is by strengthening the muscles in your hand. Hand-gripping devices can help, or even simple exercises like squeezing a tennis ball or gripping resistance bands. You can improve your grip by focusing on the position of your fingers. For example, they should be positioned close together in a fist. It ensures you make contact with your knuckles on the punching bag and protect them from injury.

Tips for Holding a Punch Grip

During karate practice, it's crucial to maintain a loose punch grip to prevent injury. With a loose grip, your hand can quickly adapt to the movement of the punch and prevent your wrist from injury. In addition, you must ensure your wrist is straight during the punch, as bending your wrist can damage the tendons. Furthermore, the angle of your wrist and the flexibility in your hand should remain consistent throughout each punch. Lastly, tuck your thumb away firmly at all times. Keeping your thumb out of the way prevents it from getting injured as you punch.

Perfect Punch Grip

A perfect punch grip in karate is natural and comfortable. Your grip should provide enough power to break boards. However, avoid gripping tightly, which will result in damaged knuckles and injury. Instead, aim to strike at the correct angle, with your knuckles aimed at the target. With the proper technique, it will become second nature. Focus on strengthening the muscles in your hands, positioning your fingers correctly, and maintaining a loose grip to improve your punch grip. During karate practice, master the art of the punch with a firm punch grip and good technique; your punches will have greater power, accuracy, and a good chance of success.

Four Basic Punches

Karate emphasizes punches as one of its primary striking techniques. The art of karate is known for its powerful and precise punches that can bring an opponent to the ground in one strike. This section discusses the four basic punches in karate to unleash your full potential as a practitioner. Mastering these punches will improve your physical strength and cultivate mental discipline.

Straight Punch

The Seiken punch is fundamental in karate.

The straight punch, known as the "Seiken" punch, is the most fundamental in karate. It involves striking with a straightened arm and pushing forward with your body weight. This punch is aimed at your opponent's face, solar plexus, or ribs. When performing a straight punch, keep your elbows close to your torso and turn your wrist at the end of the punch to add more force. Mastering this technique requires a lot of practice, focusing on perfecting your posture, balance, and timing.

Lunge Punch

Oi-Zuki is more powerful than a straight punch.

The lunge punch, known as the "Oi-Zuki" punch, is more potent than the straight punch. It involves stepping forward with one foot while throwing a punch simultaneously. The force generated in this technique comes from your body's momentum as you lunge forward. Aim for your opponent's chest or stomach with this punch. Keep your back straight and rotate your back foot as you punch to achieve maximum power. This technique is more advanced than the straight punch and requires more training in speed and accuracy.

Reverse Punch

Gyaku-Zuki generates more power and speed than a straight punch.

The reverse punch, known as the "Gyaku-Zuki," is thrown from the hip. This punch can cause more damage than the straight punch since it generates more power and speed. To execute this technique, turn your back foot 90 degrees and twist your hip, creating torque in your body. The punch is delivered in a straight line, aimed at your opponent's ribcage or head. The reverse punch is a signature move in karate and can knock down your opponent in one blow with correct execution.

Jab Punch

The jab punch, known as the "Oi-Tsuki," is a quick, sharp punch to distract your opponent. It is often thrown as a setup to other punches or as a counterpunch to the opponent's jab. This technique is executed by extending your arm straight and quickly retracting it, aiming for the opponent's face. Keep your elbow close to your torso and snap your fist back to its starting position. This punch is a valuable tool for sparring since it can disorient the opponent and provide openings for other attacks.

Oi-Tsuki can be used as a setup for other punches.

Karate is an art requiring years of training and discipline, but mastering the four basic punches is the foundation of becoming a skilled karateka. The straight punch, lunge punch, reverse punch, and jab punch are techniques every student must learn to become proficient in karate. These techniques help build strength, speed, and precision and are used during sparring or self-defense. Remember, practice these techniques until they become intuitive, and you'll be well on your way to becoming a skilled karate practitioner.

Advanced Punches and Katas

Karate is more than just a discipline. It's developing your mindset, body, and spirit. As you progress in your training, you'll learn more powerful techniques and moves demanding precision, strength, and balance. This section explores advanced punches and katas in karate. Whether you're a veteran or a newbie, you'll find valuable insights to help unleash your power and elevate your skills.

Mechanics of Advanced Punches

Punching is one of the basic karate skills, but it takes years of practice and dedication to master. In advanced karate, punches become more complex and powerful. The key is to use your entire body, not just your fist, to generate maximum force and speed. You must coordinate your breath, stance, and hips to deliver a punch to knock down your opponent. Some of the advanced punches in karate include the reverse punch, double punch, and spinning back fist. You must train your muscles, reflexes, and timing to execute these punches. Work with your sensei or instructor to learn the proper technique and gradually increase intensity and accuracy.

Kata: The Art of Moving Meditation

Kata is a sequence of movements simulating a fight against multiple opponents. It's a fundamental aspect of karate training, developing your coordination, balance, focus, and martial art skills. Kata requires precision, grace, and intensity. It's not just about moving your arms and legs randomly. Each movement has a purpose and meaning. It's like a dance telling a story. In advanced karate, kata becomes more complex and demanding. You must memorize longer and more intricate sequences and perform them with incredible speed and power. Kata is a physical, mental, and emotional exercise. It teaches you discipline, patience, and resilience.

Double-Hand, Fore-Knuckle, and Spear-Hand Punches

Now that you know the basics of punching, let's explore more advanced punches. These punches are crucial in fighting and self-defense situations. Learning them teaches you to throw a punch and deliver maximum impact properly. Here's a brief overview of each punch:

Double-Hand Punch

The double-hand punch is a technique used by many martial artists worldwide. It uses both hands to strike an opponent. To deliver this punch, you must execute a step forward with your lead foot bringing both hands to your chest. Then, thrust both hands forward while holding your fists together and planting your body weight behind your punch. This technique can cause significant damage to your opponent's organs, ribs, and spine. When executed correctly, this punch can deliver a knockout blow.

Fore-Knuckle Punch

The fore-knuckle punch is one of the most effective punches in martial arts. It is a technique involving striking an opponent with the knuckles of the index and middle fingers. To execute this punch, form a fist with your thumb on the outside of your fingers. Extend the knuckles of the index and middle fingers so that the fingers protrude forward to form a punch. Deliver this punch by thrusting your arm forward and leading with your shoulder. This punch can cause significant damage to your opponent's face, nose, and jawline. Therefore, accuracy and proper alignment are critical to maximizing this punch's impact.

Spear-Hand Punch

The spear-hand punch is a technique in which the hand is fashioned into a spear. It involves driving the fingertips straight into vulnerable regions of the opponent's torso. When executed with force, this punch can cause damage to vital organs, such as the solar plexus, liver, and heart. To perform the spear-hand punch, form a fist and extend your fingers forward, keeping your fingers straight and the thumb tucked alongside your index finger. Next, thrust your arm forward, pushing your fingertips toward your target while maintaining a rigid wrist.

The advantages of the spear-hand punch are that it is lightning-fast and more directly powerful than an ordinary hand strike. The key is to deliver this punch with a solid and stable forward drive to drive your fingers into your opponent's body. In addition, proper training of the wrist and forearm muscles to deliver an effective spear-hand punch is vital.

These three punches are very effective and must be learned by those wanting to be proficient in martial arts. They are versatile and can be used in various fighting and self-defense applications. However, these techniques should only be used in self-defense and never violently or aggressively. Hone your skills through constant practice and learning to execute these punches' powerfully. Master these techniques and become a more powerful martial artist willing to defend yourself and others.

Combining Punches and Katas

Punches and katas are like two sides of the karate coin. They complement each other and enhance your martial art skills. Combining punches and katas creates a dynamic and versatile training routine challenging your body and mind. You can incorporate different advanced punches into your kata sequences to add variety, strength, and surprise. You can use katas as a warm-up or a cool-down before or after a punch session. The key is to balance punches and katas and avoid overusing or underusing each element.

Training Tips for Advanced Punches and Katas

To improve your performance and avoid injuries, here are some tips for training to perform advanced punches and katas:

- Warm up properly before starting your training. Do some stretching, cardio, and joint mobility exercises.
- Focus on quality, not quantity. Don't rush your punches or katas. Instead, focus on the details and form.
- Progress gradually. Don't try to master all the advanced punches and katas at once. Instead, start with the basics and work your way up.
- Take breaks and rest between sessions. Your body needs time to recover and adapt to the stress of training.
- Listen to your body and your sensei. Don't push too hard or ignore your pain or discomfort. Instead, talk to your sensei about concerns or questions.

Kicks

Watching a skilled karate practitioner execute the perfect kick with graceful movements, precision, and lightning-fast speed is genuinely mesmerizing. It's like watching a work of art in motion. Moreover, karate kicks are incredibly effective self-defense tools. So, whether a beginner or a black belt, perfecting your kicks is essential to mastering the art of karate, but don't forget the fun factor. There's something incredibly satisfying about feeling the impact of your foot connecting with a target. It's a rush that keeps karate enthusiasts coming back for more. So, get your leg muscles fired up and your focus sharpened because this section dives deeper into karate kicks.

Key Tips for Kicking

- **Choose The Right Karate School:** The first and most crucial step in becoming a successful karateka is choosing the right karate school. There are many karate styles, so it is vital to find a school that teaches a style you are interested in. Additionally, finding a school with experienced and qualified instructors is essential.
- **Set Realistic Goals:** One of the biggest mistakes people make when starting karate is setting unrealistic goals. Remember, karate is a lifelong journey rather than something to master overnight. So, instead of setting goals like "I want to be a black belt in six months," set goals like "I want to attend class three times per week" or "I want to learn one new technique per week."
- **Be Patient:** karate takes time and patience to master. There will be days when you feel you are making significant progress and days when you feel you are not making any progress. It is essential to stick with it and be patient with yourself. Remember, every great skill needs nurturing at first.
- **Practice, Practice, Practice:** The only way to improve at karate is to practice regularly. In addition to attending class, it is essential to practice at home. You can do this by shadowboxing, practicing techniques on a heavy bag, or even doing push-ups and sit-ups. The more you practice, the better you will become.
- **Stay Healthy And Injury-Free:** It is crucial to stay healthy and injury-free to be a master in karate. It means eating a balanced diet, sleeping well, and stretching before and after each training session. It is essential to listen to your body and rest when sore or tired.

- **Have Fun:** Remember, karate is supposed to be fun. If you are not enjoying yourself, then there is no point in doing it. Instead, find an activity you will enjoy, and have fun with it.

Essential Kicks to Master

Karate is a martial art known for its fast-paced movements, powerful strikes, and dynamic kicks. While there are many techniques in karate, mastering the different kicks is essential for any practitioner. However, with so many kicks to learn, it can take time to know where to start. This section reviews the essential kicks to master karate. Whether a beginner or seasoned martial artist looking to revisit the fundamentals, this guide will help you develop your skills and improve your performance.

- **Front Kick:** The front kick is one of the most basic kicks in karate, and often the first beginners learn. To perform a front kick, stand in a fighting stance with your dominant foot behind you. Lift your knee toward your chest and extend your leg, striking your opponent with the ball of your foot. Again, keeping your toes pointed up and your heel down is crucial to avoid injury.
- **Side Kick:** The side kick is powerful and can knock down your opponent if executed correctly. To perform a sidekick, lift your knee toward your chest and turn your body to face your target. Extend your leg out while keeping your toes pointed up and your heel down. Aim to kick with the blade of your foot, the area on the outer side of your foot.
- **Roundhouse Kick:** The roundhouse kick is a versatile kick targeting your opponent's head, torso, or legs. To perform a roundhouse kick, start in a fighting stance and lift your knee toward your chest. Then, pivot on your standing foot and kick out with your leg, aiming to hit your target with your shin. Retracting your leg quickly after striking is vital to avoid leaving yourself open to counterattacks.
- **Crescent and Reverse Crescent Kicks:** Crescent and reverse crescent kicks are advanced techniques requiring a lot of practice to master. To perform a crescent kick, lift your knee toward your chest and extend your leg out while making a circular motion with your foot. The aim is to hit your opponent with the blade of your foot while swinging your leg around their head. Reverse crescent kicks are done in the opposite direction, with the leg hanging toward the back of your opponent's head.

Mastering different karate kicks takes time, practice, and dedication. So, whether you're learning basic front kicks or advanced crescent kicks, focus on the details, such as posture, foot position, and timing. By incorporating these essential kicks into your training routine, you'll become a well-rounded karate student and improve your technique and performance in the dojo. As always, remember to train safely and under the guidance of a qualified instructor.

Advanced Kicks and Leg Attacks

You must work hard on your kick's speed, power, and accuracy to be an excellent karate fighter. Training in advanced kicks and leg attacks in karate is a challenging but rewarding experience teaching you various techniques to keep your opponent guessing. This section explores the world of non-traditional kicks and leg attacks.

- **Spinning Back Heel Kick:** The standard kicks in karate, such as the front, roundhouse, and side kick, are well-known and commonly used, but there are plenty more kicks to add to your arsenal. The first non-traditional kick is the spinning back heel kick. Start by spinning and raising your back leg, then snap it around to kick your opponent with the heel of the foot. This kick is excellent as a surprise attack and for changing direction quickly.

- **Hook Kick:** Another effective kick is the hook kick or "Ura Mae Geri." Swing it in a circle using your back leg to generate momentum and extend your leg mid-swing into a kick. This kick is hard to see coming and for your opponent to block due to its unique motion. Please take advantage of this kick's unpredictability by using it at the right moment to confuse your opponent.

- **Low-Spinning Back Kick:** A low-spinning back kick is highly effective and underused. This kick sweeps low and can take down opponents by aiming at their ankles. To perform this kick, start in a low stance, spin to turn your back toward your opponent, and sweep their legs away from them with your heel.

- **Knee Kick:** Despite its name, the knee kick, or "Hiza Geri," is an incredibly effective attack when done correctly. The motion of the knee kick is excellent for delivering a devastating blow to your opponent's stomach or chest. To start the kick, bring your knee up toward your opponent's chest and extend your leg. It is essential to practice this non-traditional kick carefully; otherwise, you could injure your knee.

- **Stomp Kick:** Another overlooked kick that catches many fighters off guard is the "Fumikomi" or stomp kick. This kick is done by stepping with the lead leg and driving it down onto your opponent. A well-executed stomp kick can disrupt an opponent's movements or break their bones.

It would help if you had a wide-ranging collection of kicks and leg techniques to become an excellent karate fighter. The classic kicks are essential, but the non-traditional kicks discussed can catch your opponent off guard, confuse them, or lead them into a trap for your next move. Train thoroughly to make your moves as fast and accurately as possible and become a skilled karate fighter. You can master these advanced kicks and leg attacks and become a deadly karate fighter with lots of practice and dedication.

Readers can find a comprehensive glossary at the end of this guide covering all the topics discussed here. This glossary provides detailed information about each punch, kick, and attack discussed in this chapter. Now that you understand the basics of punches and kicks, the next chapter discusses white and yellow belt katas kumite.

Chapter 4: White and Yellow Belt Katas and Kumite

Karate belts are a fascinating component of the martial arts tradition that has captivated people for generations. The first two belts of the belt system, white and yellow, signify new beginnings, but they mark an important milestone in karate practice. Not only do they represent the first steps in a student's journey toward mastery, but they also come with unique challenges and rewards. Whether you're a beginner looking to take your first steps in karate or simply curious about the intricacies of a martial arts practice, the white and yellow belts are vivid reminders of the dedication and determination that go into mastering this fascinating craft.

This chapter focuses on the kata and kumite required for white and yellow belt karate practitioners. It explores the Heian Shodan, Heian Nidan, and Heian Sandan katas. It provides embusen/floor diagrams to help illustrate the flow of movements. The second part of this chapter looks at the Gohon Kumite and Sanbon Kumite. This chapter aims to give budding martial arts practitioners a clear understanding of the basics to build solid foundations and progress in their training.

Katas

As a beginner in the karate world, white and yellow belt katas seem daunting at first but don't worry. These katas teach the fundamental moves and techniques of karate while also honing your focus and concentration. Whether practicing the basic punches and kicks or moving into more complex sequences, correctly executing the katas improves your physical abilities and provides an incredible mental workout. As you progress through your training, you'll look back on your early belt katas with pride and appreciation for the solid foundation they provided. Here are the three katas you'll be focusing on:

Heian Shodan

Performing the Heian Shodan.

Karate is not just a physical art form; it is also an expression of mental and spiritual prowess practiced and refined over centuries. Kata, a legendary practice of karate, is a unique collection of martial art movements honing a karateka's strength, endurance, and flexibility. Heian Shodan Kata is the first Kata of the Heian Kata series and among the most popular katas in karate, particularly among beginners. This section explores the intricacies of Heian Shodan Kata, how to execute it flawlessly, and its significance in karate.

Heian Shodan Kata comprises 21 movements that must be executed in a specific sequence. Each movement must be completed with precision and focus. The kata begins with the "Ready" posture, followed by the "Kamae" posture and "Oi Tsuki" movements. The "Oi Tsuki" movement is a forward punch aimed at an imaginary opponent.

The "Gedan Barai" movement comes next, a sweeping downward motion, followed by the "Age Uke" movement. The "Age Uke" motion is an upward block aimed toward the face of the imaginary opponent. Next, the "Gedan Barai" movement is repeated in the opposite direction, followed by the "Shuto Uke" movement and "Oi Tsuki" again. The "Shuto Uke" movement is a Knife-hand block aimed toward the neck area of the opponent.

In the Heian Shodan kata, are several leg movements, such as the "Kekomi" and "Mawashi Geri" kicks, requiring perfect execution, as a fault could lead to a disastrous outcome. Moreover, every movement must be completed precisely and with perfect timing, including the "Tate Zuki" movement involving a vertical punch aimed at the opponent's solar plexus.

Regularly practicing Heian Shodan Kata improves physical technique and provides a deeper understanding of the practical application of karate. The kata comprises different techniques like blocks, kicks, and punches, and every move must be executed with precision and focus. Perfecting the sequence of movements of this kata and correctly performing them leads to mastery. Explore the intricacies of this kata and embrace the beauty and discipline of karate.

Heian Nidan

Heian Nidan movement pattern. [51]

Karate is self-defense and a way of life. Kata, like Heian Nidan, is an essential part of karate and helps students develop their self-defense skills, flexibility, and concentration. Although Heian Nidan is considered a fundamental kata in karate, it still requires practice, patience, and discipline to master. Anyone wanting to learn karate should start with Heian Nidan and focus on the basic movements before moving to other advanced katas. This section explores Heian Nidan Kata and explains how to perform it.

Heian Nidan Kata is the second kata in the Heian series, consisting of 26 movements. Heian means "peaceful mind," and Nidan represents "second level." The kata is relatively simple and is an excellent starting point for anyone learning karate. Here are the steps to perform Heian Nidan:

- **Step 1:** Starting Position. Stand still, bow to the front, and take a left footstep into Heisoku Dachi or a closed stance.
- **Step 2.** Chamber your right fist at your right hip and punch with your left hand on the left side. Move two steps forward while punching.
- **Step 3:** Chamber your left hand by your left hip and punch with your right hand on the right side.
- **Step 4:** Bring your left foot into the Kiba Dachi stance and perform two consecutive lower-grade blocks, left then right, with the opposite-hand leg forward.
- **Step 5:** Rotate your left foot 90 degrees and step forward with your right into a forward stance with a simultaneous downward block with your right hand.
- **Step 6:** Without pausing, rotate your right foot 180 degrees to face backward, executing a right downward block.
- **Step 7:** Bring your left foot back, pivot your left foot to face backward, and move your right foot backward, transitioning to a new forward stance. Perform an overhead block with your left hand. Simultaneously, your right open hand will be pulled back behind to the right side of the hip.
- **Step 8:** Bring your feet together and move into the starting position, facing front.

The above steps are the first half of the kata. As mentioned earlier, Heian Nidan consists of 26 movements; every action is essential. It takes practice, focus, and discipline to understand and master the kata completely. Here are some additional steps you will perform when completing the kata:

- **Turn and Blocks:** From your starting stance, perform a series of turns and blocks to defend yourself against the imaginary assailants.
- **Kicks:** Perform various kicks, like Mae Geri, Kekomi, and Mawashi Geri. Proper balance and leg strength are essential for performing kicks.
- **Punches:** Like other katas in karate, Heian Nidan includes various punches, such as Age Uke, Yoko Uchi, and Uchi Uke.
- **Combination of Techniques:** You must display various techniques, including blocks, kicks, and punches. It requires focus and precision to perform all the movements correctly.

Heian Sandan

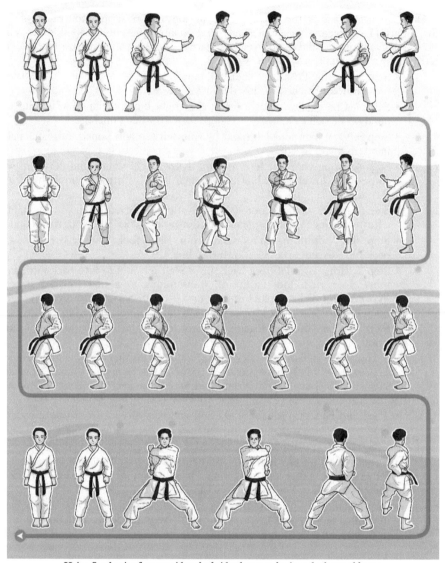

Heian Sandan is often considered a bridge between basic and advanced katas.

For karate practitioners, the Heian Sandan kata is an essential part of their training. This section explores the Heian Sandan kata, one of the five Heian Katas in karate. This kata is often called the "bridge" between the basic and more advanced katas. You will learn to perform this kata, its meaning, how to practice it, and its benefits in martial arts and everyday life.

The Heian Sandan kata consists of 20 movements to teach you powerful techniques, such as age uke (upper block), shuto uchi (knife-hand strike), and gedan barai (lower block). The kata starts with a step forward and a downward block, followed by a double punch. The arms are then raised, and you perform a knife-hand block and a reverse punch. Next, you perform a low block and a rising elbow strike.

As you continue through the kata, you perform various techniques, such as front kicks, strikes, and blocks. The Heian Sandan kata shows how to transition fluidly from one method to another and how to use the power generated from the hips to deliver effective strikes. This kata emphasizes timing, speed, and agility, essential elements in karate.

The Heian Sandan kata has a more profound significance beyond learning self-defense techniques. The kata reflects the spiritual and philosophical aspects of karate. It teaches humility, respect, and self-discipline. Every move should be executed with intention and focus as you strive to become a better karate practitioner and person overall.

It is vital to maintain good posture and balance to practice this, Kata. Focus on the transition between each move and perform each movement with precision and intent. Practice the kata slowly, gradually increasing your speed and power. It is helpful to practice the kata in front of a mirror to ensure your techniques are correct and monitor your progress.

The benefits of practicing the Heian Sandan kata go beyond becoming more robust and agile. Practicing this kata builds character, fosters self-discipline and respect, and enhances mental clarity and focus. The kata increases stamina and flexibility and improves overall physical fitness.

Kumites

Karate's appeal lies in its physical and mental challenges. Therefore, *kumite* (or sparring) is crucial to karate training. As a karate student, you have the opportunity to engage in kumites at various levels, beginning with the white belt learning and practicing basic techniques. Once you master the basic skills and graduate to the yellow belt, you will participate in more competitive kumites. This section discusses the white and yellow belt kumites, their rules, and how to train for them.

The white belt kumite is the starting level for the karateka. In the white belt kumite, you spar with a partner following predetermined techniques you learned in class. The kumite allows you to apply your learned techniques in a controlled and safe environment. The kumite helps you develop a strong fighting spirit and learn to fight respectfully and with good sportsmanship. The yellow belt kumite is the second level in the kumite progression. At this level, you engage in more competitive kumites. In the yellow belt, you fight against someone in the same belt level or higher. Yellow belt kumite focuses on developing good timing, rhythm, and distance. You learn to assess your opponent's movement and intents. The yellow belt kumite is an opportunity to take on a more challenging fight and learn to adapt to different fighting styles.

To practice for the kumites, you must improve stances, balance, and posture. Additionally, you must master basic techniques such as blocks, punches, and kicks. Practicing sparring with a partner, using protective gear like a karate gi and helmet, will help you simulate the kumite and test your skills. It would be best to practice hitting a makiwara, a punching bag, to develop strength in your punches and kicks.

The karate kumite provides a practical way to develop martial arts skills. The white and yellow belt kumites are great starting points for young karate enthusiasts. Along with learning basic techniques, students will understand the importance of sportsmanship. As you continue your journey in karate, you learn to adapt to different fighting styles and improve your fighting spirit. By practicing regularly and giving your best effort, you will progress to higher belt levels while enjoying the thrill of kumites.

Gohon Kumite

Gohon Kumite technique.

Karate is known for its rigorous training and demanding techniques, such as the Gohon Kumite. Gohon Kumite is a five-step sparring exercise for advancing karate students. It involves defending against five different attacks while responding with predetermined techniques.

You will need a partner to perform Gohon Kumite. The exercise should be performed at a steady pace, and it's essential to maintain control throughout. Here are the steps to achieving Gohon Kumite:

- **Step 1:** The first attack is a straight front punch. Your partner punches with their lead hand, and you block with your front arm, simultaneously stepping in with the opposite foot. Then counterattack with your lead punch.
- **Step 2:** The second attack is a lead roundhouse kick. Your partner throws a roundhouse kick at your ribs, and you block with your forearm, then step in and counterattack with a punch.
- **Step 3:** The third attack is a straight punch followed by a reverse punch combination. Your partner throws a straight punch with one hand, immediately following with a reverse punch with the opposite hand. You block the first punch with the opposite hand, the second with the same hand, step in, and counterattack with a punch.
- **Step 4:** The fourth attack is a lead front kick. Your partner throws a front kick at your chest. You block with your front arm while simultaneously stepping in with the opposite foot. Then counterattack with a punch.
- **Step 5:** The fifth and final attack is a simple grab and punch. Your partner grabs your front wrist and punches you with the opposite hand. You escape

the wrist grab, block the punch with your opposite hand, and counterattack with a punch.

Gohon Kumite is an excellent technique for advancing karate students. It helps them gain control, improve their timing, and enhance their response to different attacks. Remember, approach the exercise steadily, maintain control, and focus on technique. With practice, you'll master Gohon Kumite in no time.

Sanbon Kumite

Karate uses strikes, kicks, and punches as self-defense mechanisms. Sanbon Kumite is commonly practiced in most schools. It is a three-step sparring technique to improve students' reflexes, agility, and coordination in real-world situations. This kumite requires basic techniques such as jabs, front kicks, and reverse roundhouse kicks. This section discusses the steps to perform Sanbon Kumite.

- **Step 1:** Starting Position: The starting position requires standing 6 feet from your opponent. The attacker and defender stand in a Sanchin Dachi stance with their hands up to their face. The attacker initiates the sparring by throwing a jodan punch toward the defender's face. The defender blocks the punch with a rising block and moves in for a punch of their own.
- **Step 2:** The First Exchange: After the initial block, the defender throws a jodan punch toward the attacker's face. The attacker blocks the punch with a rising block and returns with a chudan punch toward the defender's chest. The defender blocks the punch with a lower block, completing the exchange.
- **Step 3:** The Second Exchange: Once the first exchange is completed, the attacker initiates the second exchange with a gyaku-tsuki or reverse punch to the defender's solar plexus. The defender blocks the attack with an inside or outside block and counter-attacks with a Mae Geri or front kick. As the defender throws the front kick, they must keep the attacker at a distance and return to the starting position.
- **Step 4:** The Third Exchange: In the third exchange, the attacker initiates the sparring with a mawashi geri or roundhouse kick. The defender blocks the kick with a rising block and counterattacks with a gyaku-tsuki or reverse punch toward the attacker's face. The attacker blocks the punch with an inside or outside block and returns to the starting position.
- **Step 5:** Repeat the Process: Once the third exchange is over, the roles of the attacker and defender switch, and the steps are repeated. The defender becomes the attacker, and so on. This process is repeated thrice to help students master the Sanbon Kumite technique.

Sanbon Kumite is an essential technique in karate, improving a student's defensive and offensive sparring capabilities. By understanding and mastering the steps in this kumite, students establish fluidity in fighting and ultimately become better karatekas. It takes time and practice to perfect the Sanbon Kumite technique, but by following these steps, anyone can learn and execute it expertly. So, the next time you're in karate class, try out Sanbon Kumite and become a better martial artist.

As you begin your journey into the martial arts world, the white and yellow belt katas and kumite (sparring) are the foundation for your practice. These initial levels enable you to develop precise movements and defend yourself in real-life situations. Kata is a prearranged exercise allowing you to hone in on your technique and fluidity. As you move on to kumite, you'll face an opponent and focus on timing, distance, and strategy. Don't let the color of your belt discourage you. These basic skills are essential to advancing in martial arts and giving you the confidence to conquer any challenge. So, get ready to kick, punch, and chop your way to success.

Chapter 5: Orange and Green Belt Katas and Kumite

As karateka progresses through the ranks, they are introduced to a series of katas and kumite, which help them improve their technique and master the art of self-defense. Orange and green belt students are required to learn a specific set of katas and kumite to test their physical and mental abilities. These katas and kumite help the students become more disciplined, focused, and confident in their approach to karate. With rigorous training and consistent practice, students can progress to become black belts, the highest rank in karate.

If you're an aspiring karateka, ready to put in the effort and dedication to unleash your true potential, this chapter is for you. From the Heian Yondan to Kihon-Ippon Kumite, this chapter provides an in-depth look at the techniques orange and green belts learn to progress. In addition, it aims to give you a better understanding of the katas and kumite to master when training for the middle-order belt ranks.

Heian Yondan Kata

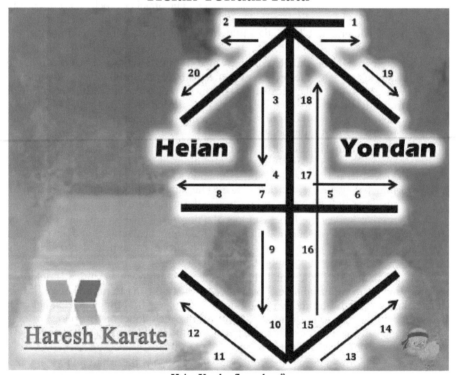

Heian Yondan floor plan. [52]

One of the critical components of karate is kata, a series of movements practiced in a sequence to simulate a fight against multiple opponents. Heian Yondan Kata is an intermediate-level kata typically learned after practicing the first three Heian katas. This section breaks down the Heian Yondan Kata and provides tips on how to master it.

Understand the Concepts

Before attempting to learn the Heian Yondan Kata, it is crucial to understand its concepts. This kata involves a series of movements simulating fighting against multiple opponents. It includes techniques like blocking, striking, kicking, and shifting positions. Understanding the rhythm of the movements and how they flow together to create a fluid sequence is also essential.

Practice Techniques

First, practicing individual techniques making up the Heian Yondan Kata is essential. Focus on perfecting them before moving on to the next one to ensure you have a strong foundation before attempting to perform the kata. Some techniques to focus on include:

- **Front Kick:** This primary kick involves kicking with your front foot. Practice maintaining proper form, keeping your balance, and chambering the kicking leg.
- **Downward Block:** This block involves bringing your arm down from the outside to the inside of your body to defend against an overhead strike. Focus on keeping your arm and wrist aligned and your elbow down.
- **Double Punch:** This technique involves punching with both hands simultaneously. Practice maintaining proper form, including aligning your elbows and fists with your shoulders.

Learn the Sequence

Once you have a strong foundation of techniques, it is time to learn the Heian Yondan Kata sequence. Break it into smaller sections and practice each until you can perform it seamlessly. Slowly build up and practice the entire sequence until you can achieve it confidently and fluently. Record yourself practicing so you can identify areas for improvement.

Focus on Breathing

Proper breathing is an essential aspect of karate. When practicing the Heian Yondan Kata, maintain a regular breathing pattern. Inhale deeply before performing a technique, and exhale with each strike or block to maintain rhythm and control your movements. The more stable your breathing, the more fluid and powerful your kata will be.

Practice with Partners

Practicing with partners is essential to mastering techniques and kata in karate. Find a training partner and practice the Heian Yondan Kata together. It will refine your movements and timing and build confidence and endurance. Communicate with your partner to help each other improve.

Mastering the Heian Yondan Kata in karate requires patience, discipline, and dedication. Remember, focus on the concepts, practice individual techniques, learn the sequence, focus on breathing, and practice with partners. With consistent practice and an unwavering commitment, you can master the Heian Yondan Kata in karate.

Heian Godan Kata

Heian Godan

Heian Godan floor plan

The Heian Godan Kata is your next challenge if you are a green belt. This traditional kata requires focus, precision, timing, balance, and coordination. This section provides an overview of the moves and explains their translations to help you master this kata.

Preparation

The first step is to stand at the center of the mat, facing the front of the dojo. Keep your feet shoulder-width apart, arms on your sides. Bow to show respect to the dojo and your sensei. Bring your hands up to your chest and take one step forward with your left foot. This is the starting position for Heian Godan Kata.

Movements

Heian Godan Kata consists of 23 movements, divided into four parts. The first part includes three moves to the left, followed by a right-handed block. The second part moves to the right and consists of a series of strikes and kicks. The third part comprises stepping back and blocking, followed by a spin and a strike. The fourth part includes a series of blocks and punches, ending with a right-handed hammer fist.

Timing

Timing is crucial in karate, and Heian Godan Kata is no exception. Every move must be executed with precision and timeously. Ensure to count the steps and focus on each technique. Don't rush, but don't hesitate, either. Remember to take a deep breath before each move to stay focused, centered, and relaxed.

Visualization

Visualization is a powerful technique to help you improve your karate practice. Before you start the kata, do the following:

1. Visualize yourself performing each move flawlessly.

2. Picture yourself moving fluidly, with perfect timing and technique.

3. Imagine yourself feeling confident, strong, and focused.

4. Visualize yourself succeeding, and it will become a reality.

Practice

Heian Godan Kata requires dedication and effort to master. Repeat the kata several times slowly and gradually increase the speed. Practice with a partner or in front of a mirror to get feedback and improve your technique. Don't be afraid to make mistakes. Instead, learn from them and keep going. If you put in the hard work, you will soon master Heian Godan Kata. Remember to prepare yourself mentally, execute each move precisely, focus on timing, visualize success, and practice consistently. With dedication and effort, you can master Heian Godan Kata and progress in your karate journey.

Tekki Shodan

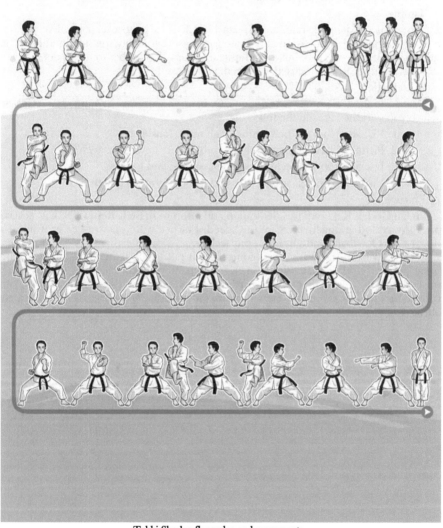

Tekki Shodan floor plan and movements.

A green belt in karate symbolizes you have learned the fundamental concepts in your martial arts journey and are on your way to mastering your techniques. One of the requirements for this rank is mastering the Tekki Shodan Kata. This kata focuses on developing soft, fluid movements to engage with your opponent effectively. The Tekki Shodan Kata is a primary series of sequential actions of stepping in different directions while executing various kicks, punches, and blocks. This section walks you through the Tekki Shodan Kata, highlighting the critical steps necessary to achieve mastery.

Learn the Basic Stance

You must learn the basic stance to execute the Tekki Shodan Kata correctly. Start by standing with your feet together, then move your right foot forward while pivoting on your left foot. Your feet should be shoulder-width apart, with your back foot at a 45-degree angle to maintain balance. The knees should be slightly bent, and the hips should be tucked in, allowing you to transfer your weight between your feet.

Master the First Three Steps

The first three steps in the Tekki Shodan Kata involve a sequence of punches, kicks, and blocks:

1. Punch forward with your right arm, then place your left arm parallel to your stomach while turning your hips.
2. Raise your left leg and pivot on your right foot, executing a front kick.
3. Step forward with your left foot and execute a downward block with your right arm.
4. Perform the same sequence, but this time using your left arm to punch, your right leg to kick, and your left arm to block.

Polish Your Movements

As you continue to practice, focus on your movements. They should be fluid, fast, and powerful. Your punches should land squarely on your imaginary opponent, and your kicks should be quick and secure. Practice moving swiftly and gracefully while maintaining a solid stance.

Internalize the Correct Breathing and Timing

Correct breathing and timing are vital in executing the Tekki Shodan Kata correctly. Inhale sharply as you pull your arm back for a punch, then sharply exhale when you perform a strike. The sound created by your exhalation should be audible and sharp. Appropriately timing the breath will synchronize your movements with your breathing and make more effective strikes.

Practice with Sparring Partners

Take your practice to the next level by testing your skills with a sparring partner. As you practice with a person, you will appreciate the importance of timing, distancing, and precision in your movements. Observe how your partner moves and adjust yourself accordingly. Sparring allows you to develop the right mindset of calmness, focus, and awareness and enhances reflexes.

Mastering the Tekki Shodan Kata is no small feat. It requires dedication, patience, and commitment to detail. However, as you become more fluent with the sequence, your techniques evolve, and your movements become naturally more fluid. Therefore, take your time, practice regularly, and always remember that true mastery is a journey, not a destination. By following the steps outlined above, your journey to becoming a karate Purple Belt will be more enjoyable, rewarding, and, most of all, successful.

Kihon-Ippon Kumite

Kihon-Ippon Kumite is an essential element of karate training with one-step sparring techniques. This section looks closer at Kihon-Ippon Kumite and how to master it. From the basics to the advanced, it explores various approaches and drills to help you become a better martial artist.

Basics

Kihon-Ippon Kumite is a sparring technique performing a pre-determined sequence of moves with a partner. This technique is fundamental in karate because it helps students learn how to react quickly and effectively in various situations. The method is also excellent for improving focus and coordination.

Sequence

Kihon-Ippon Kumite consists of a series of moves divided into two parts. The first part involves the attacker executing an attack, which the defender blocks. The second part consists of the defender counterattacking with a pre-determined sequence of moves. The attacker and defender trade roles after each sequence, allowing both partners to practice their skills.

Sparring With Partner

Starting Kihon-Ippon Kumite with a partner at the same skill level or slightly higher is essential. This ensures that the technique is performed correctly and safely. The partners must wear the appropriate protective gear to protect themselves from injury. Protective equipment includes gloves, mouthguards, and groin protectors.

Form Practice

When practicing Kihon-Ippon Kumite, maintaining a proper stance is vital. The right karate stance is keeping your knees slightly bent, your feet shoulder-width apart, and your weight evenly distributed. Keep your hands up to protect your face, with your elbows close to your sides. Always keep your eyes on your partner. Practice the technique slowly at first and gradually increase the speed and intensity. Pay close attention to your partner and ensure you communicate effectively. Break the process down into small steps and practice each step until it becomes second nature.

Kihon-Ippon Kumite is a crucial element of karate training, helping students learn to react quickly and effectively. It is an excellent technique for improving focus, coordination, and physical strength. Practicing the technique safely and with a partner of the same or slightly higher skill level is essential. Remember to maintain a proper stance, communicate effectively with your partner, and practice the technique in small steps. With time and dedication, you will master this technique and become a skilled karate student.

Tips for Mastering Orange and Green Belt Katas and Kumite

Karate is a martial art emphasizing physical fitness, mental toughness, and discipline. Orange and green belts are significant milestones in this journey, representing intermediate ranks. Mastering katas and kumite at this level can be challenging, but you can achieve your goal with the proper training and guidance. This section shares tips and techniques to improve your orange and green belt katas and kumite.

Practice Daily

Consistency is vital for mastering katas and kumite. Set aside some time each day to practice and stick to it. Focus on at least one or two katas during each session and break down each movement into manageable steps. The same applies to kumite, to practice different moves repetitively until you perfect them. Take your time and don't rush, which can lead to bad habits. Instead, focus on mastering each step before moving on to the next.

Focus on Proper Technique

Ensure you're doing each technique correctly from the start. Focusing on the proper form will help you avoid developing bad habits that are hard to break later on.

If you need help executing a particular technique, ask your sensei or watch training videos to learn the correct way. The competition judges look for precision and accuracy, so ensure your techniques are on point. An excellent way to check your technique is by recording yourself and watching it.

Improve Your Fitness Level

Orange and green belts require significant physical fitness. You should have an excellent cardiovascular endurance level, strength, and flexibility. The better your physical fitness, the better you'll be at kata and kumite. Stability, fluidity, and control are essential for success, so ensure you incorporate fitness exercises into your training regimen. Incorporate a mix of strength, endurance, and stretching exercises into your training routine.

Diet and Rest

Proper nutrition and hydration are essential for mastering katas and kumite. Eat healthy meals with the right protein, carbohydrates, and fats. Pay attention to your hydration level, which is significant in performance. Lastly, get enough rest. Having adequate rest between training sessions is vital for your body and mind to recover. A good night's sleep can go a long way in improving your performance.

Weekly Assessments

Take time each week to assess your progress. Track the katas and kumite you learned and any difficulties you encountered. Keep a journal of your progress and use it to set yourself goals for the upcoming week. It will help you stay on track and ensure consistent progress. If you are struggling, ask your sensei for guidance and assistance. With their help, you can keep progressing in the right direction.

Believe In Yourself

One of the essential aspects of mastering katas and kumite is your mental state. Believe in yourself. Don't let fear or self-doubt hold you back. Visualize yourself performing katas and kumite without any mistakes. Set goals and work hard to achieve them. Remember, the mind is as crucial as the body in karate. If you think you can do it, you will.

Mastering orange and green belt katas and kumite in karate can be challenging but achievable with exemplary dedication and guidance. You can reach your goals through consistent practice, focusing on proper technique, improving your fitness, training with a partner, and believing in yourself. Remember, karate is a journey requiring patience, persistence, and hard work. Stay committed to your training, and you'll move up the ranks in no time.

Chapter 6: Purple and Brown Belt Katas

Karate enthusiasts know the journey toward the black belt involves mastering a series of katas, each more intricate than the last. The purple and brown belt katas are no exception. With their complex combinations of punches, kicks, and blocks, these forms challenge even the most seasoned practitioners. However, the key to success lies in discipline and practice. By dedicating themselves to the art and committing fully to each movement, karatekas can unlock a whole new level of skill and precision.

Whether you're striving for a purple or brown belt, the journey toward mastery is exciting and filled with challenges and rewards. This chapter covers four essential katas practiced by purple and brown belts. From the flowing movements of Bassai-Dai to the dynamic Enpi Kata, these katas are crucial for any serious practitioner. This chapter explains, translates, and illustrates the techniques to perform each form. By the end of this chapter, you'll be well on your way to mastering these complex katas and achieving your next belt.

Bassai Dai

Bassai-Dai floor plan and movements

Bassai-Dai is a Kyokushin kata emphasizing power and speed. It includes several techniques, like strikes, kicks, and blocks. These striking techniques must be performed with passion and precision. The kicks are fast and hard and highlight the importance of balance and agility. The basic movement in Bassai-Dai is the horse stance, which builds lower body strength. The featured techniques in Bassai-Dai enable the students to fight with confidence and power.

The Bassai-Dai Kata is performed in an intimidating stance with arms held high. This form focuses on powerful, swift movements requiring strength and agility. The key to mastering this kata is to move precisely with purpose, directing each punch and kick. This section explains the Bassai-Dai Kata, its translation, and essential techniques to perform this form. By the end of this chapter, you'll better understand what it takes to master the Bassai-Dai Kata and impress your friends and training partners.

Translation

Firstly, let's break down what the Bassai-Dai Kata translates to in English. Bassai-Dai means "to penetrate a fortress," which represents mastering your inner fortress and channeling that strength into practice. This form often symbolizes the strength and discipline to break through any obstacle.

Techniques

The beginning of the kata involves a series of movements aiming to destabilize your opponent by blocking and striking. You need a solid foundation and stable gravity center to perform this effectively. Focus on keeping your feet shoulder-width apart and your knees slightly bent, even as you move through the kata's steps. Use your core muscles to generate power and balance throughout your movements. Keeping a steady and grounded stance is critical.

Next comes the "hinge" technique. This technique involves using your arms to deflect your opponent's attack while simultaneously striking with a counterblow. First, use your hips to pivot sideways away from the attack. Next, keep your feet planted, bend your knees, and use your arms to block. As you block, use your hips to turn back towards your opponent, throwing a punch or strike. This motion should be fluid and snappy.

After the hinge technique, move into several combination movements focusing on taking down your opponent, controlling their limbs, and destabilizing their balance. You must learn moves like the "sweep" and the "hook." The sweep uses your foot to trip your opponent while simultaneously pulling their arm, throwing them off balance. The hooking technique uses your elbow or forearm to strike your opponent's arm or leg, to cause a stumble or fall. These moves require good timing and accuracy.

The Bassai-Dai Kata ends with a series of movements focusing on incapacitating your opponent completely. This involves delivering a final, powerful strike to disable them. To perform this effectively, you must focus on generating power from your legs, through your hips and core, and into your arms. By keeping a solid foundation and using your entire body, you'll deliver an impactful blow leaving your opponent stunned.

Mastering the Bassai-Dai Kata requires power, technique, and precision. You'll take huge strides toward mastering this powerful kata by focusing on your foundation, pivoting technique, destabilization moves, and final strikes. Remember, consistent practice and attention to detail are the keys to success in karate. So, keep at it; soon enough, you'll be a master of the Bassai-Dai Kata.

Kanku Dai

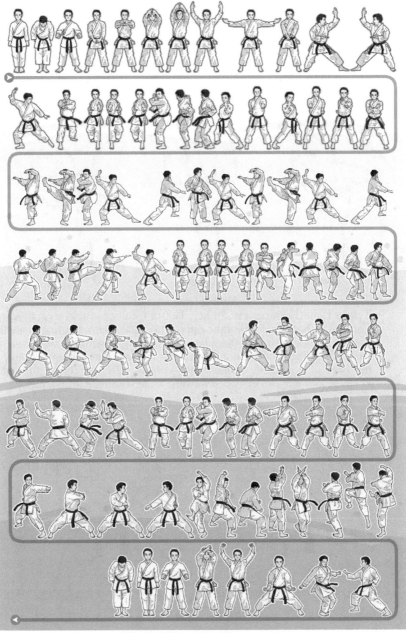

Kanku-dai floor plan and movements

Kanku-Dai Kata is one of the most complex and fascinating karate forms. It develops strong stances, fluid movements, and body alignment precision. With five stances, multiple strikes, and a series of intricate turns, it's no wonder beginners often need help executing it flawlessly. However, with practice and a deep understanding of the techniques, mastering the Kanku-Dai Kata is possible. This section discusses each technique in the kata, providing clear explanations and illustrations to help you perfect your form.

- **Mawashi Geri (Roundhouse Kick):** The Mawashi Geri is a unique kick that involves swinging the leg in a circular motion and striking the target with the ball of the foot. To perform this technique correctly, stand in a left-front stance and lift your right leg. Next, pivot your left foot and kick your right leg at a 45-degree angle. Bring your leg back to the starting position and return to a right front stance. Keep your arms close to the body as you kick, maintaining proper balance throughout.

Mawashi Geri. [53]

- **Tettsui Uchi (Hammer Fist Strike):** Tettsui Uchi is a crucial technique in the Kanku-Dai Kata as it strikes the opponent's vital points. Starting in a left hip stance, lift both arms to shoulder height. Make a tight fist with your right hand and bring it down in a hammering motion, hitting the opponent with the base of the hand. Maintain eye contact with your target throughout, keeping your left arm extended forward while your right arm strikes.

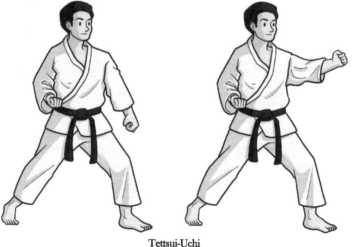

Tettsui-Uchi

- **Yoko-Geri (Sidekick):** Yoko-Geri is a versatile and powerful technique to attack the opponent's legs or the side of their body. Starting in a left front stance, bring your left leg up, pivoting on your right foot. Next, kick your left leg out to the side, striking your target with the blade of your foot. Return to your starting position and repeat the technique with your other leg. Keep your guard up and your arms close to protect yourself from counterattacks.

Yoko-Geri

- **Morote-Uke (Double-handed Block):** Morote-Uke is a defensive technique that blocks and controls your opponent's arms. To perform this technique, stand in a left front stance, lift your right knee, and bring both hands together in front of your chest. When the opponent attacks, use both arms to block their arms and push them away. Maintain a firm stance and proper balance throughout.

Morote-Uke

- **Gyaku-Zuki (Reverse Punch):** Gyaku-Zuki is a fundamental technique of striking the opponent with a powerful reverse punch. To perform this technique, stand in a left front stance, bend your left elbow, and pull it back toward your body, creating a powerful chain reaction to channel the strength of your entire body to your punching arm. Then, without shifting your stance, bring your right arm forward while twisting your hips, and throw a punch with your right arm. Keep your elbow down and your wrist straight as you punch.

Kanku-Dai is a kata that entails many complex movements, emphasizing speed, focus, and strength. It is a powerful and dynamic karate form demanding excellent balance and control. The kata has an elaborate sequence of moves, including several turning and jumping techniques. It enhances the student's reflexes and hand-eye coordination. This kata provides an excellent opportunity for students to showcase their skills in front of their peers and instructors.

Jion Kata

Jion

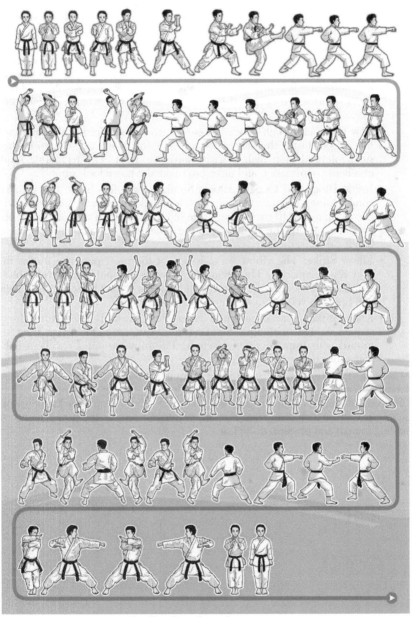

Jion Kata floor plan and movements.

Jion Kata is a traditional Okinawan kata emphasizing focus, balance, and footwork. It includes several blocking and striking techniques, requiring students to have excellent control. This kata develops the student's timing, helps improve their concentration, and teaches them to adapt to various situations. It is challenging and requires consistency and patience to master.

For karate enthusiasts, mastering the Jion Kata is a significant milestone in their journey to becoming black belts. This kata dates back to the 12th century and is revered for its strong, fast movements simulating a real-life fight. The Jion Kata is a sequence of movements requiring strength, speed, and execution. This section dives deep into the techniques to perform this kata correctly.

- **Front Snap Kick:** The front snap kick is performed at the beginning of the kata and requires executing rapid movements. The technique involves kicking forward with one leg, landing on the same foot, and immediately executing another kick with the other foot. Focusing on the technique's fluidity and speed is crucial while maintaining your balance to pull off this move.

- **Low Block and High Block:** These two moves are frequently combined in one action during the kata sequence. The low block is executed to the left side, followed by a high block towards the right. The technique requires excellent coordination and timing to make the move look smooth.

- **Inside Block and Outside Block:** Similar to the low block and high block combination, the inside and outside block techniques demand precise execution to be effective. The inside block is executed with one hand on the opposite side of the body, while the outer block is performed with both hands on the same side.

- **Elbow Strike:** The elbow strike is one of the most powerful moves in the Jion Kata sequence. The technique requires a rapid and forceful motion, emphasizing the elbow's use to strike and block. You must focus on balance and body movement to execute this move correctly.

- **Knee Strike:** The knee strike is executed toward the end of the kata sequence. The technique requires the swift execution of a knee strike toward your opponent's midsection. The move requires excellent balance and coordination to be effective.

Mastering the Jion Kata techniques requires much practice and patience. Understanding and focusing on the technique's fluidity, strength, and speed is essential. The abovementioned techniques form the foundation to level up your karate game. In all karate disciplines, including Shito Ryu and Shotokan Karate, the Jion Kata is crucial in building mental and physical discipline.

Enpi Kata

Enpi

Enpi kata floor plan and movements

Enpi Kata, known as the "Flying Swallow Kata," emphasizes mobility, speed, and agility. The kata includes several high kicks and strikes, and the movement is fluid and graceful. This kata improves the student's flexibility, speed, and precision. In addition, it teaches the students how to react quickly and swiftly change direction during a fight.

If you plan to learn the Enpi Kata, you're in for a thrilling ride. This kata is one of the most visually impressive in Shotokan Karate, known for its quick and sharp movements, kicks, punches, and blocks. Enpi Kata is a traditional Japanese martial art that is challenging to master. However, you can perfect this kata with the proper techniques and practice. This section takes you through some essential techniques to perform Enpi Kata successfully.

- **Stepping Technique (Fumikomi):** Enpi Kata's stepping technique is critical for creating momentum and producing power. To perform the Fumikomi technique, take three steps forward with your left foot, extend it firmly, and pull back with your right foot. This movement should create a sound known as Kiai that puts your whole body into the attack.

Fumikomi

- **Elbow Thrust Technique (Empi Uchi):** The elbow thrust technique in Enpi Kata is essential to its arsenal. After taking three steps forward with the Fumikomi technique, twist your body to the left, raising your right arm and elbow. Then thrust your elbow forward, hitting your imaginary opponent's head or throat, and pull back immediately.

Empi Uchi

- **High Block and Kick (Jodan Uke and Mae Geri):** Enpi Kata features many kicking and blocking techniques, including the High Block and Kick combination. To perform this technique, raise your left arm for a Jodan Uke (high block), lift your right knee, and perform a Mae Geri (Front Kick), striking your opponent's face.

Jodan uke

Mae Geri. [54]

- **Reverse Punch (Gyaku Zuki):** The Reverse Punch (Gyaku Zuki) is a fundamental technique in Shotokan karate and a crucial component in Enpi Kata. To execute the Reverse Punch, chamber your right hand by your hip, step forward with your left foot, pivot your left foot, and push your right fist toward your opponent's face.
- **Jumping and Spinning (Tobi and Kaiten):** Enpi Kata ends with a series of dynamic moves, including jumping and spinning. To perform the Tobi (jump), crouch down, propel yourself off the ground by extending your legs, and land back into your Kiba-dachi stance. As for Kaiten (spinning), rotate your body and strike your imaginary opponent in mid-air.

Enpi Kata is not easy to master, but practicing these essential techniques means you're on your way to becoming a pro. Remember, consistent and persistent training is the key to success. We hope these techniques provide insight to help hone your skills. Whether a beginner or an advanced karateka, these techniques suit anyone looking to improve their Enpi Kata.

The purple and brown belt katas, including Bassai-Dai, Kanku-Dai, Jion Kata, and Enpi Kata, are vital to developing a student's skills and proficiency. These katas help students improve their agility, speed, power, and concentration. In addition, they emphasize the importance of self-discipline, patience, and mental focus, crucial attributes a karate student should possess. So, if you are a purple or brown belt karate student, perfect these katas.

Chapter 7: Brown and Black Belt Kumites

The practice of kumite, or sparring, is a crucial component of martial arts training. For karatekas aiming for black belt, brown and black belt kumites are essential to the process. Once they have perfected the kumite basics, practitioners can move on to semi-free sparring (Jiyu Ippon Kumite) and free sparring (Jiyu Kumite). While the two have similarities, there are critical differences between them.

This chapter outlines the main features, techniques, and steps of Jiyu Ippon Kumite and Jiyu Kumite. Understanding these drills is essential as they are significant to brown and black belt practice. The knowledge acquired here will help karatekas perform these drills to the best of their ability. Mastering these kumites is essential before progressing to the next level. Read on to learn more about brown and black belt kumite.

Brown and black belts use sparring. [55]

Brown and Black Belt Kumites

Brown and black belt kumites test endurance, strategy, and skill. It involves full-contact sparring with an opponent of the same skill level or higher. The karateka must demonstrate their mastery of techniques, such as blocks, strikes, and kicks. The objective is not to knock out the opponent but to score points through proper execution of techniques.

Timing

One key component of brown and black belt kumites is timing. A split second can make all the difference in winning or losing. Karatekas must demonstrate effective distancing to control the distance between them and their opponent. Footwork is crucial to move quickly and evade an opponent's attack.

Control

Control is another crucial aspect that should be considered during brown and black belt kumites. Karatekas must strike their opponent with enough force to score a point but not enough to injure them. They must use control in their defense, being aware of their opponent's movements and anticipating their attacks. It requires physical mastery and mental focus, and sharpness.

Character

Brown and black belt kumites test a karateka's character - respect for their opponent, following rules and regulations, and demonstrating humility in victory and defeat. Karatekas must show perseverance in improving their skills and techniques. These are essential qualities a true martial artist must possess. The ability to control emotions and stay focused are vital traits to develop.

Courage

Lastly, brown and black belt kumites allow karateka to test their limits and face their fears. It takes a lot of courage to go against a skilled opponent and risk being hit. Failing in a brown or black belt kumite seems discouraging, but it's an opportunity to reflect on what went wrong and to improve. In the end, karatekas emerge more potent and confident in their abilities.

Brown and black belt kumites are more than sparring with an opponent. They test a karateka's physical and mental abilities, courage, and character. It's about something other than winning or losing but about each karateka honing what they've learned in training to demonstrate their skill, intelligence, and control. Brown and black belt kumites push karatekas to their limits, but they become more robust, disciplined, and resilient.

Jiyu Ippon Kumite (Semi-Free Sparring)

Jiyu Ippon Kumite, known as semi-free sparring, is a popular method in traditional karate training. It is one of the most challenging yet satisfying exercise forms helping practitioners improve their technique and sparring skills. In addition, Jiyu Ippon Kumite allows karatekas to showcase their agility, timing, and precision skills. This section explores the main features, techniques, and steps to master Jiyu Ippon Kumite.

Main Features

Jiyu Ippon Kumite is a combination of technique and sparring. Practitioners are allowed to use any methods provided they are controlled and do not cause harm to their opponents. During Jiyu Ippon Kumite, there is no pre-planned attack sequence, and the opponent moves spontaneously to attack or counterattack. This training incorporates speed and distance management, allowing practitioners to perfect footwork and body coordination.

Techniques Used

Jiyu Ippon Kumite allows practitioners to apply techniques in a controlled but more realistic environment. A masterful Jiyu Ippon Kumite requires knowing and executing basic techniques on the spot. Here are the most effective techniques in Jiyu Ippon Kumite and pointers on improving your technique.

- **Use Your Footwork to Your Advantage:** Footwork is crucial in Jiyu Ippon Kumite. Moving your feet quickly and efficiently to outmaneuver your opponent is essential. One tip is to practice moving in all directions and dodging to avoid being hit. You can quickly step in or out of striking range, making it difficult for your opponent to land a clean hit.

- **Focus on Blocking:** Effective blocking is essential in Jiyu Ippon Kumite. Practicing blocking with precision and using your hands and arms to protect your vital areas is necessary. One technique is to block to the outside of your opponent's strike, known as Uke. You can use kicks to block strikes. Blocking immediately once your opponent initiates a move is crucial.

- **Apply Counterattacks:** Counterattacks are significant in Jiyu Ippon Kumite. Once you block your opponent's strike, you can strike back. Some techniques include Jodan, a punch to the head, and Chudan, a punch to the torso. You can also use kicks and sweeps to take your opponent off balance. It is essential to ensure your counterattacks are precise and controlled.

- **Take Advantage of Distractions:** Distractions are effective for catching your opponent off guard and creating an opportunity to attack. Some techniques include Feints – faking a move to deceive your opponent, and Moving Targets - moving your head or body to make it harder to hit. By using these techniques, you create openings to strike your opponent.
- **Stay Focused and Calm:** Lastly, staying focused and calm is critical to mastering Jiyu Ippon Kumite. Maintaining a clear and focused mindset is essential, even when under pressure. Avoid becoming agitated and losing your cool, which leads to mistakes. By staying focused, you anticipate your opponent's moves and react accordingly.

Steps of Jiyu Ippon Kumite

The steps to practice Jiyu Ippon Kumite vary from dojo to dojo, but the basics remain the same.

1. Firstly, start with a thorough warm-up session to avoid injuries.
2. Face your opponent and bow to begin the sparring session.
3. Decide who will be the attacker and who will be the defender.
4. The attacker decides which technique to use while the defender performs a block, then quickly follows up with a counter-technique.
5. Stay relaxed, manage your distance, and maintain good footwork during sparring.
6. Lastly, bow to your opponent to indicate the end of the session.

Jiyu Ippon Kumite is an excellent training mechanism for improving your karate skills. It tests your technique and sparring abilities and helps build confidence. You can master this karate form and develop essential skills such as agility, timing, and precision with regular practice. The techniques are vast and allow for endless creativity. The key is to stay relaxed and focused and maintain good footwork during sparring. Regularly practice Jiyu Ippon Kumite and see how it enhances your karate skills.

Jiyu Kumite (Free Sparring)

Martial arts are more than just learning forms and techniques. It's about testing yourself physically and mentally against others. For karate practitioners, Jiyu Kumite allows them to show off their skills and learn from their mistakes. Jiyu Kumite, known as free sparring, is crucial in traditional karate training. This section dives into Jiyu Kumite's main features, techniques, and steps of this dynamic and exciting practice.

Main Features

Jiyu Kumite is a sparring practice teaching students how to react quickly and effectively to different fighting styles. Unlike predetermined kumite, Jiyu Kumite doesn't rely on choreographed moves. Instead, students must create their attacks and defenses on the spot. This approach helps practitioners develop thinking on their feet and adapt to changing situations. Additionally, Jiyu Kumite emphasizes the importance of control and respect toward your opponent, keeping both martial artists safe during the sparring session.

Techniques Used

Jiyu Kumite is one of the most exciting and challenging aspects of karate training. Like a real fight, it requires quick reflexes, strategic thinking, and adapting to any situation. In Jiyu Kumite, you must be prepared to work with a wide range of attack techniques, from punches to kicks to elbow strikes.

Firstly, punches (tsuki) are a fundamental technique in Jiyu Kumite. Keeping your guard up is one of the most important things to remember when throwing a punch when sparring. Your opponent will look for weaknesses in your defense, so keep your hands up to protect your face and body. Aim for the chin, solar plexus, or ribs when throwing a punch. Use your whole body, not just your arm, to generate power.

Elbow strikes (empi) are another crucial technique in Jiyu Kumite. Elbow strikes can be used in close-range combat and are incredibly effective when thrown correctly. To throw an elbow strike, bring your elbow up and to the side of your body, then drive it forward using your whole body. The target for an elbow strike will typically be the temple, jaw, or collarbone. Elbow strikes are powerful and can stun or incapacitate an opponent quickly.

Knife-hand strikes (shuto) are commonly used in Jiyu Kumite. Shuto strikes involve striking with the side of your hand and are used in various ways. For example, you can use a shuto strike to the neck or temple to stun your opponent or hit the ribs to knock the wind out of them. To execute a shuto strike, keep your fingers together and your thumb tucked in, then strike with the fleshy part of your hand.

Kicks are essential in Jiyu Kumite and include three main techniques: front kicks (mae geri), side kicks (yoko geri), and roundhouse kicks (mawashi geri). Front kicks are powerful and can keep your opponent at bay. When throwing a front kick, aim for the solar plexus or chin. Side kicks are helpful when your opponent moves laterally and can be delivered to the ribs or knee. Roundhouse kicks are powerful but slower than other kicks. They target the side of the head or the ribs.

Steps of Jiyu Kumite

Before the sparring session, students must warm up and stretch properly. Then, typically perform predetermined exercises to refine their skills and techniques. Once the sparring session starts, there are a few key steps to know.

1. Start with a bow and assume a fighting stance.
2. Test each other with light jabs or footwork before exchanging more advanced techniques.
3. Be aware of your distance and positioning when engaging with your opponent.
4. Use different techniques to attack, defend, and counterattack.
5. Be aware of your opponent's position, movements, and their reactions to your attacks.
6. Use light contact and remain in control at all times.
7. Be respectful of your opponent and their skills.
8. When the bout is finished, bow and shake hands.

Jiyu Ippon Kumite is the second sparring drill practiced by brown and black belts. This sparring is more structured than Jiyu Kumite and follows a predetermined sequence of attacks and blocks. In this drill, students practice prearranged techniques from an offensive and defensive perspective to score points. The methods in this drill include punches, kicks, elbow strikes, and knife-hand strikes.

Jiyu-Ippon and Jiyu Kumite are essential for mastering karate and developing critical martial arts skills, such as focus, balance, precision, and respect. In addition, these kumites help build self-confidence and decision-making abilities, making them valuable practice in the physical and mental aspects of karate. Whether a beginner or an experienced martial artist, these kumites provide an interesting and exciting challenge to take your karate skills to the next level.

Chapter 8: Black Belt Katas I

Take your martial art skills to the next level with advanced black belt katas. These intricate forms are not for the faint-hearted but for those willing to put in the time and effort. The Jitte brings sharp, precise movements to keep your opponent guessing. Tekki Nidan and Tekki Sandan provide a challenge with their focus on strength and balance. The Bassai-sho emphasizes power and speed, always keeping you on your toes.

As a black belt, these katas are the ultimate test of your abilities and showcase your dedication to the craft. This chapter helps you take on the challenge and add these impressive forms to your martial arts arsenal. It covers each kata's meaning, techniques, steps, timing, and tips. You'll be ready to confidently take on the advanced black belt katas by the end.

Jitte Kata

Jitte

Jitte floor plan and movements

Karate is about throwing kicks and punches and encompasses artistic movements called katas. Kata is a sequence of actions mimicking a fight against an imaginary opponent. One of the katas every black belt karateka should learn is the Jitte Kata. Unfortunately, this kata is a hidden gem only a few can perform correctly. This section guides you through learning to perform the Jitte Kata correctly.

Meaning

Jitte means ten hands in Japanese. The purpose of the kata is to show that with proper technique and timing, the karateka can defend against ten opponents. The Jitte Kata helps improve your balance, focus, and coordination. It teaches awareness of your surroundings and uses combat strategies.

Techniques and Steps

The Jitte Kata consists of 24 movements divided into two parts. The first part contains ten moves involving blocking techniques, while the second includes fourteen actions involving striking techniques.

1. Start in a left stance, with fists and open hands on the hips.
2. Step to the right in a horse stance and simultaneously execute a down block (Gedan Barai).
3. Step forward with the front foot and execute a middle inner block (uchi uke) while pivoting on the back foot, ready for a front kick (mae geri).
4. Step forward with the back foot and execute the front kick (mae geri).
5. Land and pull back the front foot and perform a downward middle block (Chudan Gedan Barai).
6. Feint with the front hand and employ a lower-level modified spear-hand strike to the groin (Nage-Azuki).
7. Without retracting the modified spear hand, pivot 270 degrees clockwise.
8. Shift to a front stance and execute a rising block (age uke).
9. Step forward with the back foot and execute a front kick (mae geri).
10. Land and pull back the front foot and perform a middle inner block (uchi uke).
11. Slide the left foot in and raise the right foot to perform a left front kick.

The second part involves striking techniques and has fourteen movements. Like the first part, all the movements require excellent footwork, balance, and coordination.

Timing

The Jitte Kata requires precision and timing. Each move is a response to an attack from an imaginary opponent. Therefore, it's essential to clearly understand the sequence of movements before practicing the kata. Practice each step methodically and ensure each movement flows smoothly to the next. When practicing, please observe your breathing and ensure it syncs with your actions.

Tips

- Practicing with a partner helps you understand the timing and flow of the movements.
- Understanding the meaning behind this kata helps you perform it with the proper perspective.
- Focus on your stance. Ensure it is solid and your hips and shoulders are aligned.
- Consistency is vital to mastery. Practice regularly and aim to improve in every session.

The Jitte Kata is a vital kata every karateka should learn. Learning and mastering the kata requires dedication, practice, and patience. However, when performed correctly, the kata shows your coordination, balance, and focus. If you follow the guidelines in this section, you can complete the Jitte Kata quickly and confidently.

Tekki Nidan (Ne2)

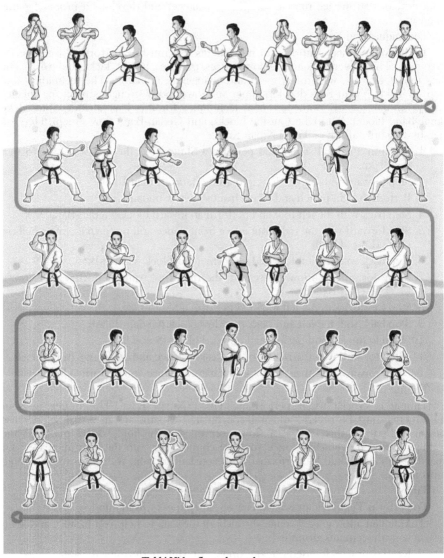

Tekki Nidan floor plan and movements

Kata is the cornerstone of traditional karate practice, and Tekki Nidan is one of the most important and popular forms. A kata is a series of pre-arranged movements and techniques simulating a self-defense situation, and Tekki Nidan Kata is considered one of the most advanced forms. This ancient kata is a foundation kata, excellent for students to learn and perfect. This section explores the meaning, techniques, timing, and tips for performing Tekki Nidan Kata.

Meaning

Tekki Nidan, known as Naihanchi Nidan, is a powerful and dynamic kata to simulate close-quarter fighting. Its name comes from the Japanese word "Tekki," meaning "iron horse," and "Nidan," meaning "2nd level" or "second step." In this kata, you move linearly, firmly planted on the ground like an "iron horse." Tekki Nidan Kata develops strong leg muscles, improves balance, and develops a proper fighting mindset.

Techniques and Steps

Tekki Nidan Kata comprises 24 movements that must be performed with precise execution. The movements include low stances, punches, blocks, kicks, and twists. The kata moves linearly, with many turns and changes in direction. The techniques and steps in Tekki Nidan Kata develop upper and lower body strength, enhancing balance and promoting agility. Some essential techniques for this kata include Shuto Uke (knife-hand block), Soto-Uke (outside block), and Gedan-Barai (low sweep). Here's a step-by-step breakdown of Tekki Nidan Kata:

1. Begin in a natural stance and perform a Shuto Uke, then pivot and perform a Soto-Uke.
2. Step forward with the left foot into a side stance (Jodan Uke).
3. Perform a right punch and take a front stance (Chudan Uke).
4. Step back with the left foot and perform an inward block (Gedan-Barai).
5. Step forward with the right foot into a front stance and perform an inward elbow strike (Empi-Uchi).
6. Step back with the left foot and perform a low block (Gedan-Barai).
7. Move forward in a low stance with the right foot while performing an inward block (Gedan-Barai).
8. Step forward with the left foot and perform a Shuto-Uke.
9. Step back with the left and perform a low block (Gedan-Barai).
10. Step to the left and perform an outward block (Soto-Uke).
11. Step forward with the right foot into a side stance and perform a front punch.
12. Step forward with the left foot into a natural stance and perform a Shuto-Uke.

Timing

Timing is crucial when performing Tekki Nidan Kata. The timing of your movements must be precise and well-coordinated to simulate an actual self-defense situation. Perform this kata at a slow, controlled pace until you've mastered the techniques and movements. Once you feel comfortable with the kata, increase your speed. The kata should be performed with constant motion, with no pauses between movements.

Tips

To perform Tekki Nidan Kata effectively, keep these tips in mind:

1. Maintain a low gravity center throughout the kata to help you balance and keep your movements grounded.
2. Keep your eyes focused on your opponent while performing the kata.
3. Breathe properly and continuously throughout the kata to maintain physical and mental stamina.

4. Practice the kata repetitively until your movements become fluid and aggressive.

5. Learn to control your body and actions to execute each technique with precision and strength.

Tekki Nidan Kata is an explosive and challenging kata that takes time and dedication to master. You must develop flexibility, strength, and endurance to perfect this kata. While Tekki Nidan Kata appears simple at first glance, it is a complex form requiring advanced techniques and precise timing. However, you can learn to perform this dynamic kata like a true martial artist with consistent practice and dedication. So, take your time, stay focused, and enjoy the journey as you unlock the techniques and timing of this ancient kata.

Tekki Sandan

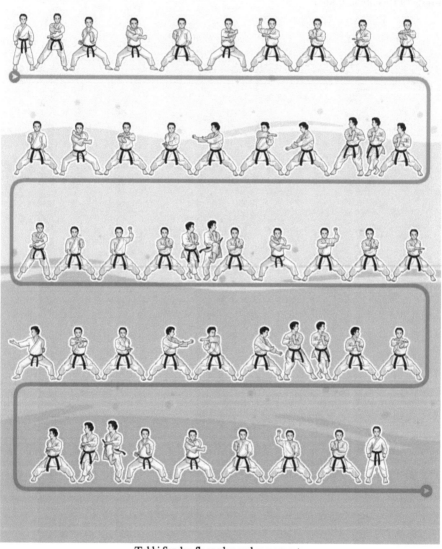

Tekki Sandan floor plan and movements

The Tekki Sandan Kata is a basic form taught after you've attained a blue belt. This section covers the meaning of Tekki Sandan Kata, the techniques, steps, timing, and tips to help you master this kata.

Meaning

Tekki Sandan Kata translates to "Iron Horse Three." It's an excellent representation of the movements and stances while executing the kata. The symbolic importance derives from the firmness of the horse and balance. The balance between the front and back of the feet must be precise, where both feet point in perpendicular directions and provide a stable foundation.

Techniques and Steps

The Tekki Sandan Kata involves fundamental techniques crucial to mastering martial arts. One of the more central techniques includes the "Shuto Uke" technique or the knife hand block. Other moves in this kata are the palm heel strike, punch, and front kick. The kata is quite complex in its stepping techniques and requires moving your legs laterally continually. Remember, practice makes perfect. Start with getting the footwork correct and then work on mastering the various techniques involved.

Timing

Timing is everything in martial arts. For Tekki Sandan Kata, the movements are fast-paced and quite intricate. However, to the untrained eye, they can appear slow. The kata comprises 26 movements and requires roughly 50 seconds to complete. The trick is to move at a consistent speed and ensure every action is in sync.

Tips

1. Focus on your breathing. Remember to inhale and exhale during the movements.
2. Pay attention to your posture and ensure it's correct. An improper posture could cause imbalance.
3. Ensure each movement is precise. It will take time to get it right, but you'll get there with practice.

Your stances must be rooted and stable. The technique becomes effortless when your stances are correct.

Learning the Tekki Sandan Kata will lay a solid foundation for mastering martial arts. First, it's essential to understand the meaning behind the kata, the techniques and steps involved, the timing, and to read the tips to help you master it. Then, you'll execute the kata effortlessly with regular practice, determination, and patience.

Bassai-Sho Kata

Bassai-Sho

Bassai-Sho floor plan and movements.

Bassai-Sho Kata is a martial arts form that originated in Okinawa, Japan. This traditional karate form is widely practiced by martial artists worldwide – and for a good reason. Bassai-Sho Kata embodies agility, power, control, and challenges body and mind. This section explains everything about this dynamic karate form, including its meaning, techniques, timing, and tips on improving your skill.

Meaning

"Bassai-Sho" means "to penetrate a fortress" in Japanese. The art of Bassai-Sho Kata is based upon the two concepts of infiltration and evasion. The movements of Bassai-Sho Kata enable a martial artist to overcome an opponent by making direct, consequential, and effective strikes. The basic principles of Bassai-Sho Kata include mastering footwork, proper alignment, and focus on breathing.

Techniques and Steps

Several techniques and steps are involved in performing Bassai-Sho Kata. However, the most essential include movements, such as:

1. **Hachiji-Dachi:** This stance forms a base for many movements in Bassai-Sho Kata.

2. **Chudan-Uke:** This is a middle block using your forearm to block an attack aimed at your torso.

3. **Age-Uke:** This rising block uses your arm to deflect attacks on your face.

4. **Kiba-Dachi:** This stance is for counterattacks, striking your opponent's legs.

5. **Empi-Uchi:** This is a powerful elbow strike to hit an opponent at close range.

Timing

Timing is an essential component of Bassai-Sho Kata. The art involves grasping the right moment to attack or defend against an opponent. Timing involves recognizing the suitable openings to execute a move, translating to heightened accuracy and precision. The key to timing is controlling your body's movements to avoid telegraphing your next move. Proper alignment, footwork, and breathing are crucial to timing in Bassai-Sho Kata.

Tips

- **Practice Regularly:** Like any martial art form, continued training of Bassai-Sho Kata ensures mastery. In addition, regular practice helps you become more comfortable with the moves and techniques to enhance your skills.

- **Strengthen Your Core:** Core strength is critical in executing Bassai-Sho Kata movements. Strengthen your core through exercises like sit-ups and planks.

- **Seek Feedback:** Your movements are as good as your ability to execute them in karate. Seek feedback from your sensei or peers to understand areas needing improvement.

- **Focus on Breathing:** Karate masters emphasize the importance of controlled breathing during practice. Focus on steady and deep breathing as you execute moves.

Learning Bassai-Sho Kata takes time, effort, and dedication. It requires constant practice, discipline, and focus on mastering the movements and techniques. However, you can achieve great rewards in physical fitness and mental strength with patience and persistence. Whether learning for sport or self-defense, Bassai-Sho Kata is an excellent addition to your martial arts repertoire. Always remember the critical components of Bassai-Sho Kata, including the meaning, techniques, timing, and tips, as they form the foundation of your growth in this beautiful martial arts form.

The black belt katas are an advanced traditional karate form. This chapter covered the meaning, techniques, steps, and timing of the most popular katas among advanced practitioners. With practice, discipline, and focus, you can acquire the skills necessary to clear the fortress of these katas and grow in strength, agility, and mental clarity. Remember, seek feedback when necessary, focus on controlled breathing as you practice, and strengthen your core to increase stability.

Chapter 9: Black Belt Katas II

The Black Belt Katas are a vital aspect of any martial artist's training regimen in karate. From Kanku-Sho to Gankaku, each form has unique challenges testing a practitioner's strength, agility, and mental focus. For example, Hangetsu emphasizes the importance of balance and breath control. Sochin challenges even the most skilled fighters with intricate hand movements and precise footwork. Whether a beginner or a seasoned pro, mastering these katas requires dedication and commitment. But nothing beats the feeling of executing each movement with precision and grace.

This chapter is dedicated to the four black belt katas, providing detailed descriptions. It covers the translation and meaning of each kata, outlines the movements, and offers valuable tips for mastering them. By this chapter's end, you'll understand the four katas and be well on your way to becoming a black belt. The journey is long, but the rewards are great.

Kanku-Sho

Kanku-Sho

Kanku-Sho floor plan and movements

Karate is a dynamic martial art requiring discipline, focus, and continuous practice. Like any martial art, it has its own katas or choreographed patterns of movements. One of these katas is the Kanku-Sho Kata, a second-level kata known for its intricate movements and symbolisms. This section explores the translation, meaning, and significance of Kanku-Sho Kata. Additionally, are tips to help you master this unique kata.

Meaning

Kanku-Sho Kata means "to look at the sky and beckon." This name is derived from one of the movements in the kata where the practitioner performs an upward block with one hand while the other is extended upward as if beckoning or calling forth something from the heavens. This action is believed to represent a moment of meditation where the practitioner takes a moment to reflect and connect with the universe. Most practitioners believe this Kata symbolizes the journey to enlightenment. It's a powerful reminder that with dedication and focus, anything is possible.

Movements

The Kanku-Sho Kata consists of 27 movements divided into three parts: the opening, the middle, and the closing. Each element has its actions and meanings. Initially, the practitioner performs a series of defensive and offensive movements symbolizing the need to protect from external threats. The middle part focuses on slow, deliberate movements emphasizing balance, control, and concentration. The closing part includes finishing moves to end the kata with power and grace. While executing each movement, the practitioner must remain focused and aware of their surroundings.

Tips

To master the Kanku-Sho Kata, start by memorizing the movements and their meanings. Practice each movement slowly and deliberately, focusing on form, stance, and breathing. Once you have memorized the movements, practice performing them with fluidity and grace, keeping your actions precise and controlled, and always maintaining eye contact with your imaginary opponent. Regularly practice the kata to increase your stamina and endurance. The more you practice, the better your execution will become.

Kanku-Sho Kata is a fascinating and profound kata requiring discipline, focus, and practice. Its movements and symbolisms represent the essence of karate, which is the pursuit of physical and spiritual perfection. Mastering this kata teaches you to defend yourself and develop a deeper connection with the universe. So, keep practicing, stay focused, and always remember to look at the sky and beckon.

Hangetsu

Hangetsu floor plan and movements

For karate enthusiasts, the Hangetsu Kata is a form that must be noticed. This particular kata is one of the most unique and challenging. Hangetsu translates to half-moon, symbolizing the balance between Japanese and Chinese martial arts. This kata is an excellent tool for honing mental focus, physical balance, and precision. This section explores the meaning and movements of Hangetsu Kata and provides tips on how to master it.

Meaning

Hangetsu Kata combines two forms, Gojushiho and Sanchin Kata. The half-moon symbolizes the balance between the physical body and the mind, external martial arts, and internal energy art. The core idea behind this kata is to develop inner strength, speed, and sharp movements. It emphasizes deep, stable stances increasing balance and stability while performing motions redirecting or neutralizing an opponent's attack. The end of this kata is marked by a stance symbolizing the moon at its fullest with both hands held up and palms open.

Movements

This kata is performed slowly and precisely, making it one of the toughest to master. It requires a lot of control and balanced weight to execute each movement correctly. Hangetsu Kata has many circular motions, blocks, strikes, and kicks. It opens with a slow Neko ashi dachi, known as a cat stance, preparing you for the following steady movements. The sequence includes a breathing exercise focusing on relaxing your body while maintaining a constant flow of energy.

Tips

You must have a fundamental understanding and body control of basic stances to master the Hangetsu Kata. It is essential to take things slowly, even slower than usual, and focus on executing each movement with perfect balance. Please pay attention to each movement and understand how it connects to the next one. Also, control your breathing, as this kata requires precision and attention to detail. Another critical aspect to consider is your footwork. Ensure you're grounded and your feet are correctly positioned to avoid losing balance.

The Hangetsu Kata is one of the primary karate forms helping martial artists to unlock their inner strength and achieve balance in their physical and mental state. Its complex movements and emphasis on the balance of mind and body offer a unique opportunity to develop your power, precision, and overall martial art skills. So, try it out and experience the joy of mastering this challenging but rewarding kata. Remember to take things slow, maintain proper breathing techniques, focus on your movements, and keep your feet grounded.

Gankaku

Gangaku

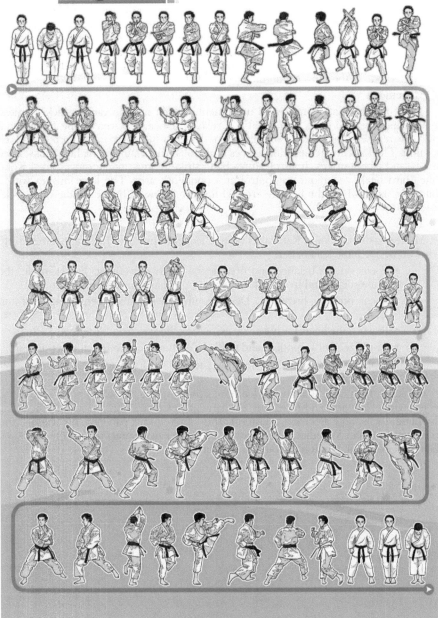

Gankaku floor plan and movements

Karate, a martial art that originated in Okinawa, Japan, has a wide range of kata (forms) with different techniques and movements. One is the Gankaku Kata, known as the "crane on a rock" Kata. This kata uniquely combines stances, kicks, strikes, and blocks and is known for its fluid movements and grace. This section delves deeper into the Gankaku Kata and explores its meaning, movements, and tips.

Meaning

Gankaku Kata, known as Chinto Kata, translates to "crane on a rock" or "fighting on a rock." It is believed to have originated from Chinese martial arts and was brought to Okinawa by a Chinese martial artist named Chintō. The kata is named after a small island near China with rocky terrain, resembling the crane on a rock position. The kata incorporates a crane's movements, symbolizing longevity, grace, and balance, and is considered one of the most beautiful katas in karate.

Movements

The Gankaku Kata contains 42 movements, which include various kicks, strikes, and blocks. The kata starts with a soft and relaxed stance, followed by the "crane on a rock" move, including a crane stance on one leg with the other raised in a front kick position. The kata progresses with stances of various heights, including high kicks, knee strikes, and elbow strikes. It also features hand strikes and a unique move called Koko - the "bird beak" technique to control an opponent's arm. The kata finishes with a "butterfly" kick, where the feet are crossed mid-air, followed by the "crane on a rock" pose.

Tips

Mastering the Gankaku Kata takes time, effort, and practice. Here are some tips to help you perform the kata better:

- Focus on the balance and precision of each movement. For example, the crane stance and front kick require good balance and coordination.
- Focus on your breathing. Deep, controlled breathing helps you relax and focus.
- Practice the kata slowly before increasing the speed and intensity.
- Visualize your opponent and perform each move with intent and purpose.
- Train with a partner or instructor to receive feedback and improve your technique.

Gankaku Kata is a challenging kata incorporating the movements of a crane to achieve grace, balance, and flow. It is a testament to karate's core principles, including discipline, focus, and precision. Mastering this kata requires patience, dedication, and consistent practice. Whether a beginner or an experienced practitioner, the Gankaku Kata is an excellent addition to your karate training.

Sochin

Sochin floor plan and movements

Sochin Kata, known as "the strength in tranquility," is one of the most prominent katas in karate. Originating from Okinawa, Japan, this kata is practiced by beginner and experienced martial artists due to its benefits for the body and mind. Sochin Kata is a powerful routine requiring focus, flexibility, and discipline. This section dives into the meaning of this kata, its movements, and some tips on how to master it.

Meaning

Sochin Kata is translated as the "tranquil force" or "strength in tranquility." This kata was developed by Chojun Miyagi, the founder of Goju-Ryu Karate, in the early 20th century. The kata combines hard and soft techniques, represented by the smooth and sudden transitions between different stances. The movements in Sochin Kata train the practitioner to become more stable, grounded, and powerful.

Movements

The Sochin Kata consists of 41 movements and is performed at a slow, controlled pace. The kata starts with a slow walking motion, followed by a series of strikes and kicks. The movements within Sochin Kata are done in a fighting stance while breathing in specific patterns. These movements are not only for physical training but also for the mind to focus on the techniques. Sochin Kata emphasizes strong, stable standing postures with wide-stance blocks and low kicks. The kata is performed slowly and deliberately to build concentration and discipline.

Tips

To perform Sochin Kata well, you must master breathing techniques and physical movements. As you exhale during the kata, let out a robust and forceful breath to enhance your power in each movement. Focusing on your technique and form is essential to ensure each movement is precise and accurate. Take time with each motion and practice until it feels comfortable. Then move on to the next movement. Practice the kata in front of a mirror to observe your technique and identify areas to improve.

Sochin Kata is a powerful karate kata to help you develop mindfulness, discipline, and stability. The slow and deliberate movements of the kata allow you to focus on your technique and breathing and strengthen your mind, body, and spirit. Sochin Kata is an impressive routine and a discipline to help you become a better martial artist. With consistent practice, focus, and discipline, you can accomplish greatness and fully embody the strength within tranquility.

Conquering the First Rank of Black Belt

Embarking on the journey to become a black belt in martial arts is no easy feat. It requires dedication, discipline, and perseverance. However, the sense of achievement and pride in earning that first rank is immeasurable. You must master 26 katas, each with unique techniques and movements, to reach this milestone. The glossary of terms at the end of this guide contains all the names and information about these katas, so you can research them further.

You can achieve your black belt through consistent practice and dedication and further your martial arts journey. This chapter discussed the three black belt katas: Kanku-sho, Hangetsu, and Sochin. By studying the fundamentals of these forms, analyzing the techniques, and mastering the proper movements, you will reach your goal of becoming a black belt. The journey is challenging, but the rewards are worth it. Now that you better understand these katas, you can practice and master them.

The following chapters of this book will guide you through the defense techniques, training drills, and dojo etiquette to become a karate master. It might seem daunting, but with the right mindset and guidance, you can conquer each and prove that you can achieve greatness. Imagine the satisfaction when you finally earn that coveted black belt and the sense of accomplishment that comes with it. So, keep practicing, and soon enough, you'll wear a black belt with immense pride.

Chapter 10: Understanding Belts and the Dojo

Understanding the intricacies of the old traditions and customs is essential to mastering the art of karate. The system of ranks in karate is based on colored belts; each color represents your skill level. As you progress in your training, you earn the right to wear a higher belt. But it's not only about the belt. It's about the journey. The dojo, or training hall, is a place where you can physically and mentally push yourself to new limits. It's where you learn discipline, respect, and humility and form bonds with other practitioners sharing your passion.

By understanding the nuances of karate belts and the dojo, you fully immerse yourself in the art and unlock its true power. This chapter closely examines the ten kyus and dan ranking system, titles in karate, and etiquette involved, and teaches you how to tie a belt. The journey of karate starts when you enter the dojo. So, let's begin.

Entering the Dojo

Are you considering joining a martial arts class to improve your physical and mental well-being? Look no further. Karate could be precisely what you need. This ancient Japanese martial art form fosters discipline, focus, and respect for self and others. Whether you want to improve your self-defense skills or experience the physical and mental benefits of training, karate might be the perfect activity. Read on to discover more about this great art form and why you should consider joining a karate dojo today.

The Physical Benefits of Karate

Karate improves balance, coordination, and flexibility. In addition, the nature of the movements and strikes practiced in karate helps develop a lean and agile body over time. As a result, regular karate training leads to a more robust and healthier body. Moreover, practicing karate reduces stress, as the focus required to perform the movements and techniques helps individuals clear their minds of negative thoughts and emotions.

Another reason to consider joining a karate dojo is the community aspect. A karate dojo is a welcoming space for individuals of all ages. It is a place to make friends, cross paths with people from various walks of life, socialize, and have fun. Moreover, practicing karate with people striving toward the same goals can be incredibly motivating and uplifting.

Tips

You must consider a few things when joining a dojo. First, it is crucial to choose the right dojo. Ensure the instructors are certified, experienced, and from a reputable dojo. Take time to observe a class or two before committing to a long-term membership. It is worth checking out reviews from previous or current members, the facilities, and the safety measures in place. As for the training, remember, karate calls for a certain level of respect and discipline. Arriving on time, performing the movements correctly, and being mindful of the other practitioners in the dojo is essential.

Dojo and Sparring Etiquette

Etiquette is taken very seriously in most dojos and is the foundation for a student's training. Part of the training includes sparring, which can be an intimidating experience for those new to the sport. This section discusses the dojo and sparring etiquette expected of beginners and advanced karate practitioners. By following these guidelines, you show respect to your fellow karatekas and become a better martial artist.

Bowing

The first thing you will notice when entering the dojo is everyone bows when they enter and leave the room. Bowing is a sign of respect and should be taken very seriously. Bowing to your training partner before and after each sparring session is an expected and accepted practice. Remember, while sparring, your partner is not your opponent but your training partner. Bowing shows you respect them and their abilities.

Dress Code

Wearing the appropriate attire is expected in the dojo. It includes the karate gi, or uniform, which should be cleaned and ironed before each training session. Long hair should be tied back, and jewelry should not be worn. Showing up dressed inappropriately shows a lack of respect for the art and your fellow karatekas.

Sparring Rules

Before sparring, ask your partner if they are ready to begin. You should also never strike someone who is not mentally or physically prepared. Strikes should be kept light enough to avoid injuring your partner, and any contact in the face or groin is strictly prohibited. Lastly, once a sparring session ends, thank your partner and bow to them as a sign of respect.

Respect for the Teacher

In the dojo, your teacher must be respected and looked up to. You should bow to them as a sign of respect and listen attentively to their instructions. When sparring, obey their commands and never argue. Remember, your teacher is there to help you learn and grow.

Respect for the Dojo

The dojo is a sacred place where students come to train and better themselves. Therefore, it must be treated with respect. Do not eat, drink, or chew gum in the dojo, and keep noise levels to a minimum. Clean up after yourself, and always keep equipment from lying around. By respecting the dojo, you are respecting the art of karate. A karateka must always strive to be humble and respectful, even when competing in tournaments. It gives a better impression of the art.

Understanding Japanese Words in Karate Training

Japanese words are infused into the art form. Knowing them is essential since they are used throughout karate training. This section unlocks the secrets of karate by deciphering Japanese words used in karate training so that you can confidently approach your practice.

- **Sensei:** Sensei means "teacher" in Japanese. This term shows respect to the teacher, who is seen as a mentor and guide. Therefore, correctly addressing your sensei is a sign of respect and an essential aspect of martial arts training.
- **Obi:** An obi is a wide belt worn around the waist with a karate gi. It represents rank and progression in the art, with different color belts representing different levels of achievement in the practice.
- **Shihan:** A Shihan is a master of a martial art. This is the highest title anyone can achieve in karate and requires many years of dedication and commitment to the art.
- **Reigi:** Reigi is the Japanese term for etiquette. Respectful behavior and manners are essential in karate and should always be observed when training and in the dojo.
- **Sempai:** A sempai is a senior to the Kohai or junior students. The sempai must show respect to their teacher and senior students. They often help Kohai understand the techniques taught.

- **Rei:** Rei translates to "respect.". It is the act of bowing in karate, which is a sign of respect and gratitude. It should be done before and after training and when greeting someone at the dojo.

Earning Belts in Karate

TAK Belt Ranking System

	Color Belt	Black Belt	
Yellow Belt			1ST DAN Black
Orange Belt			2ND DAN Black
Purple Belt			3RD DAN Black
Blue Belt			4TH DAN Black
ADV.Blue Belt			5TH DAN Black
Green Belt			6TH DAN Black
ADV.Green Belt			7TH DAN Black
Brown Belt			8TH DAN Black
INT.Brown Belt			9TH DAN Black
ADV.Brown Belt			10TH DAN Black
Master Brown			

Karate belt ranking system.

One of the most iconic aspects of karate is how students earn belts signifying their proficiency and dedication. In addition, the colorful progression from white to black belts symbolizes hard work, perseverance, and respect toward self and others. This section explores the journey to earning belts in karate and what it entails for students and instructors.

The Basics

Before students can earn belts in karate, they must master the basics of the art, including learning proper stances, footwork, strikes, blocks, and kicks. Basics are the foundation upon which all advanced techniques are built. With a strong foundation, students can progress. Therefore, instructors pay close attention to how students perform the basics, reflecting their discipline and commitment to the art. Students who take shortcuts or neglect basics will need help earning belts in karate.

The Journey of a Beginner

As a beginner in karate, the journey to earning belts often seems daunting. However, acknowledging the progress made at each step is essential. Beginners start with a white belt and must earn their way up the ranks through consistent practice, dedication, and hard work. The first belt is often the hardest to earn, as it sets the tone for the rest of the journey. Instructors work closely with beginners, offering guidance and encouragement to help them overcome challenges and improve their skills.

The Significance of Belt Colors

Each belt color in karate has a specific meaning and significance. For example, the yellow belt represents the sun rising and the beginning of a new day in the journey toward mastery. The green belt represents a growing plant, signifying growth and progress. As students advance through the belt ranks, they better understand the art and its principles. Belt tests involve proficiency in techniques and katas, etiquette, and respect toward instructors and fellow students.

The Role of Competition

While earning belts in karate isn't about winning competitions, competition is significant in the journey toward mastery. Competitions allow students to test their skills against others and gain experience in a controlled environment. Winning competitions isn't the goal; it's learning from the experience and improving skills. Instructors often encourage students to participate in competitions to help them grow in their understanding of karate and themselves.

The Rewards of Earning a Black Belt

The ultimate goal for many karate students is to earn a black belt, which signifies mastery of the art. Earning a black belt is a significant achievement representing years of dedication and hard work. More than just a physical symbol, a black belt means a mindset of humility, respect, and continuous learning. Students who earn a black belt often find the journey more rewarding than the destination, as they have grown in all aspects of their lives.

The 10 Kyu and Dan Ranking System

One essential aspect of karate is the ranking system outlining a student's progress and skills. The ranking system is known as the 10 Kyu and Dan systems, used worldwide by karate schools and organizations. This section details the 10 Kyu and Dan ranking system, the different ranks' meanings, and how to progress through the levels.

The 10 Kyu and Dan ranking systems are used to grade students' skills and knowledge of karate. The system comprises ten Kyu ranks, from the lowest to the highest. Colored belts represent the Kyu ranks, and each rank has its own set of skills and techniques. For example, the lowest rank is the white belt, followed by the yellow, orange, green, blue, purple, and belts. The different ranks represent the various stages of learning, with each color representing a proficiency level.

After the Kyu ranks, the Dan ranks. These are the black belt ranks and are divided into ten degrees. The first-degree black belt is Shodan. The highest rank is the tenth degree, awarded to masters. The Dan ranks signify a level of mastery and are a symbol of excellence in karate. Dan ranks are usually awarded after several years of practice and dedication. Achieving a black belt is no easy feat, requiring hard work, discipline, and perseverance.

One way to progress in the ranking system is by regularly attending karate classes. Consistent practice and training are essential to advance through the ranks. Many schools have a minimum waiting period for progression between ranks, usually three to six months. It ensures students have enough time to master the skills and knowledge required for the next level.

Karate students must take an exam to move up the ranks. Students are tested on their techniques, knowledge of karate, and physical ability. The exam is usually conducted by a panel of black belt instructors who grade the students' performance. The exam can include kata tests, a prearranged sequence of movements, sparring, and breaking boards.

Karate Titles

Karate is one of the oldest martial arts in the world and is practiced by millions of people globally. But did you know that karate comes with a unique system of titles? These titles signify the level of expertise and proficiency practitioners have achieved. This section looks at the different karate titles and their meanings. So, buckle up, and delve into the fascinating world of karate titles.

The Beginner Titles

In karate, the beginner rank is known as the Kyu rank. Usually, practitioners start at the 10th rank and progress from there. The Kyu ranks are numbered, beginning with ten and descending toward one. Any student below the Kyu rank is considered a novice. The Kyu rank titles are usually colored belts denoting the student's expertise level. For example, a yellow belt signifies a fifth Kyu rank, while a blue belt is the third Kyu rank.

The Dan Titles

After advancing through the Kyu ranks, a student progresses to a Dan rank. The Dan ranks begin from the first Dan, signifying the first-degree black belt. Dan ranks go up to the tenth Dan, the highest level in karate. The Dan titles are usually awarded based on the student's mastery of various karate techniques, performance during tournaments, and contribution to the karate community.

The Master Titles

The master titles are usually awarded to the highest-ranking karate practitioners. These titles include Renshi, Shihan, Kyoshi, and Hanshi. These titles are earned through decades of mastering different karate forms and techniques. A Renshi usually refers to a teacher who has completed their fifth Dan. A Shihan denotes a teacher who has met their eighth Dan and shown excellent teaching skills.

The Reference Titles

Besides the Kyu, Dan, and Master titles, karate has many reference titles denoting a person's contribution to karate. Some of these titles include Soke, Kokusai Budoin, and Kaiso. A Soke is a person who founded a particular karate style and is regarded as its father. The Kokusai Budoin is an organization recognizing outstanding karate practitioners worldwide.

The Ceremony of Awarding Titles

Awarding titles is considered the highest mark of honor in the karate community. During the ceremony, the practitioner is awarded their new title, and their achievements are recognized. The ceremony is usually attended by other karate students who have attained similar titles.

Step-By-Step Tutorial on How to Tie a Belt

If you're new to karate, one of the first things you must learn is how to tie your belt. Not only is it an essential part of your uniform, but also a symbol of your progress and dedication to the martial art. It might seem tricky the first time you attempt to tie your belt, but it becomes second nature with practice. This step-by-step tutorial walks you through the process so you can tie your belt like a pro.

- **Step 1:** Place the center of the belt on your navel and wrap it around your waist. Make sure you have equal length on both sides.

- **Step 2:** Cross the ends over each other at the back and bring them to the front again.
- **Step 3:** Take the right end of the belt and tuck it under both layers. Pull it up and over the left end of the belt. Next, take the left end of the belt and tuck it under the right end and through the loop you've just created. Pull both ends of the belt tight to secure the knot.
- **Step 4:** Adjust the belt by pulling the ends to make it comfortable. Ensure the belt is even around your waist and the knot is centered on your body.
- **Step 5:** Tuck any loose ends of the belt into the folds at your waist. Stand tall, proud, and ready to start your karate training.

Learning to tie your karate belt might be confusing at first, but if you follow the steps above, you'll have it down in no time. Remember, your belt is not just a piece of clothing but an important symbol of your karate journey. Therefore, always treat it with respect and care. Practice tying your belt before class so you don't feel rushed or pressured before practice.

Belts and ranks are not just symbolic in karate. They represent your skills, progress, and accomplishments. From the beginner's level, the ten kyus, to the advanced level, the dan ranking system, every level is challenging and rewarding. Remember the karate titles that inspire practitioners to become better martial artists, such as Sensei, Shihan, and Hanshi. Respect for the dojo, your instructor, and fellow students is crucial. Also, proper sparring etiquette and simple Japanese words like "oss" and "rei" will enhance your training experience.

Chapter 11: How to Defend Yourself with Karate

Learning karate is not only about mastering a new skill. It's about gaining confidence to defend yourself in any situation. Whether walking home late at night or confronting a bully, knowing how to protect yourself with karate can make all the difference. With its focus on discipline, fitness, and self-defense, karate gives you the tools to protect yourself while improving your overall health and well-being.

Karate can teach you discipline and help you defend yourself. [56]

This chapter explains why karate is an excellent tool for personal defense. It discusses how Shotokan karate was created as an art of self-defense and offers tips on how to use karate in different situations. Finally, it examines the vital points you should target to defend yourself effectively. Nobody should feel helpless or scared to go out in public. With the proper techniques, karate can give you the confidence and skills to stay safe.

Why Karate Should Be Your Go-To for Self-Defense

Self-defense has become a necessity in today's world. With the increasing number of crimes, protecting self has become a priority. As a result, many martial arts have developed, and choosing the right one for self-defense can be overwhelming. However, karate has stood the test of time and proven an effective tool for defense. This section explores why karate should be your go-to martial art for self-defense.

Karate is an excellent martial art to help you become physically and mentally demanding. It is a physical exercise and focuses on mental discipline. The practice of karate requires dedication and discipline, helping you develop perseverance, strength, and focus. In addition, by practicing karate, you become physically more potent and confident, helping you defend against a potential attacker.

Karate focuses on strikes, kicks, and blocks, making it the perfect martial art for self-defense. These strikes can incapacitate an attacker without causing severe harm. Moreover, karate does not rely on weapons, meaning you can defend yourself in any situation. The blocks and strikes taught in karate can be delivered with speed, power, and precision, neutralizing an attacker effectively.

Karate teaches you to avoid and evade attacks. The best way to prevent an attack is to recognize the danger signs early. Karate teaches you to be aware of your surroundings, identify potential threats, and act quickly. Techniques like body shifting and distancing can create space between you and the attacker, allowing you to defend yourself successfully.

Another benefit of karate is it can be practiced by anyone regardless of age and gender. It is a great way to get fit, stay active, and relieve stress. Learning karate gives you the confidence to protect yourself, your loved ones, and your property. By practicing karate, you learn self-discipline, self-control, and self-awareness, essential skills in any self-defense situation.

Shotokan Karate: An Art of Self-Defense

Learning self-defense has become necessary as violence continues to plague society. Regarding martial arts for self-defense, Shotokan karate should be considered. With its roots in Japan, this martial art provides a comprehensive system of strikes, kicks, blocks, and throws to defend against an attacker. This section delves deeper into the art of Shotokan Karate, explores its history, philosophy, and techniques, and why it's worth pursuing your fitness and self-defense needs.

History and Philosophy

Shotokan karate traces its roots back to Gichin Funakoshi, who developed this art in the early 20th century based on the principles of Okinawa Karate. Funakoshi's goal was to promote physical and mental discipline, character development, and mutual respect through martial arts training. He named his art "Shotokan," meaning "House of Shoto," his pen name. Today, Shotokan karate has become one of the most popular martial arts styles, with millions of practitioners globally. Its primary focus is basic techniques such as punching, kicking, striking, and blocking, designed to build strength, speed, and coordination.

The Techniques of Shotokan Karate

Shotokan karate is known for its powerful and explosive techniques, requiring much focus and precision. The art emphasizes solid stances, proper posture, and effective breathing techniques to generate power and speed. Here are common Shotokan karate techniques you'll learn in a beginner's class:

- **Punches:** There are four basic punches in Shotokan Karate, including the front punch (Jodan Zuki), reverse punch (Gyaku Zuki), uppercut (Chudan Tsuki), and hook punch (Kagi Tsuki).
- **Kicks:** Shotokan karate includes various kicks, including a front kick (Mae Geri), side kick (Yoko Geri), hook kick (Uchi Mikazuki Geri), and spinning kick (Chudan Mawashi Geri).
- **Blocks:** Effective blocking is essential to defend against incoming attacks. The art of Shotokan karate features several blocking techniques, including the high block (Jodan Uke), the low block (Gedan Barai), the middle block (Chudan Uke), and the inward block (Uchiake).

Benefits of Shotokan Karate

Shotokan karate training offers many benefits beyond self-defense. Here are some benefits you can gain from practicing Shotokan Karate:

- **Improved Physical Fitness:** Shotokan karate provides a comprehensive workout improving cardiovascular health, increasing strength and flexibility, and enhancing balance and coordination.
- **Boosted Confidence:** As you progress in your Shotokan karate training, you gain confidence in your abilities, translating into other areas of your life.
- **Self-Discipline:** Shotokan karate requires dedication, commitment, and focus, developing self-discipline and determination.
- **Stress Relief:** The physical and mental exertion involved in Shotokan karate training provides a cathartic release of stress and tension.

Shotokan karate is a holistic practice with numerous benefits to enhance physical and mental well-being. So, whether you want to improve your self-defense skills, build confidence, or boost your fitness level, Shotokan karate is an excellent choice. It's a discipline requiring patience, commitment, and practice, but the payoff is well worth it.

Performing karate Maneuvers against Unarmed Offenders

Do you get worried when walking home alone at night? Or do you have to walk through a bad neighborhood to get where you're going? If so, it's essential to know some self-defense techniques. Karate is one of the most common and effective forms of self-defense. This section covers a few karate maneuvers you can use against unarmed offenders.

- **Palm Heel Strike:** This technique is perfect for striking the nose or chin of an assailant who has grabbed your collar or shoulder. To execute this maneuver, make a fist with your hand and turn it so it's facing inward. Next, forcefully use your palm to strike your opponent's chin or nose. It should cause them to stumble backward, giving you time to escape.

- **Knee Strike:** The knee strike is ideal for an attacker standing before you. To execute this maneuver, bring your knee upward, and thrust your knee toward your opponent's groin with the toes pointing down. It will provide more than enough time to escape or fight them off.

- **Elbow Strike:** The elbow strike is a great technique when fighting in cramped quarters, like a bar or at home. Throw your elbow directly toward your opponent's jaw to perform this movement. This move can knock an attacker out, giving you enough time to flee.

- **Back Kick:** The back kick is perfect when someone sneaks up on you. To use this technique, bring your foot up behind you, then turn around to kick directly backward. This kick can catch an attacker off balance and send them reeling, giving you enough time to get away.

- **Hammer Fist Strike:** This technique is perfect for striking the back of your opponent's head. To perform a hammer fist strike, form your hand into a fist and strike your opponent's head with the flat part of your hand. This action can cause your opponent to lose consciousness long enough for you to escape.

Knowing basic karate moves can help you feel more confident when walking alone or in an unfamiliar area. You never know when you might need to use a self-defense technique to protect yourself. However, learning these five methods can provide the necessary tools to defend yourself effectively should the need arise. Remember, using self-defense techniques should always be a last resort, and calling for help from the authorities should always be your first action.

Defending Yourself from Armed Assailants

One of the most terrifying situations anyone could find themselves in is a confrontation with an armed assailant. Being a victim of armed assault is something nobody wants to experience. But what if it happens to you? How can you defend yourself and stay safe in such a situation?

- **Be Prepared:** Preparation is vital to any defensive situation. In case of an armed attack, your preparation should include knowing your surroundings and having an exit plan. Remember, every second counts when facing an armed assailant, so it pays to be prepared.

- **Stay Calm:** It is challenging to stay calm in a stressful situation, but it is crucial when facing an armed assailant. The attacker is already in an agitated state of mind, so getting worked up only escalates the situation. Being calm allows you to think and act rationally, helping you gain control of the problem.

- **Fight Back:** If you are being attacked, and running away is not an option, fighting back might be your only recourse. Knowing basic self-defense techniques like kicks, punches, and blocks can help you fend off the attacker and buy enough time to call for help or wait for the authorities to arrive.

- **Use Available Tools:** In case of an armed attack, any tool can be helpful. For example, items like keys, pepper spray, or a tactical pen can be used to defend yourself. These tools might seem small, but they can cause severe damage to an assailant, allowing you to escape or control the situation.

- **Seek Training:** It is essential to get training to defend yourself in an armed attack. You don't have to be a martial arts expert to defend yourself. However, basic self-defense training like Krav Maga or kickboxing can make a huge difference in a life-or-death situation.

Mastering Karate Moves to Defend against Different Weapon Attacks

Karate is a self-defense martial art useful in various situations, especially when dealing with weapon attacks. Knowing how to defend yourself against knives, bats, or sticks gives you a sense of security and empowerment. Here are some karate moves you can master to protect yourself from weapon attacks.

- **Against Knife Attacks:** To defend against a knife attack, position your hands in front of your face, with one foot back and the other forward. Wait for the attacker to move toward you and use your forearm to block the hand holding the knife. Then, quickly strike their face, neck, or groin with a punch or kick to distract and create an opportunity to disarm them.

- **Against Bat Attacks:** If someone is attacking you with a bat, move to the side to avoid direct impact and use your forearm to block the bat. Then, use your other arm to strike the attacker's neck or face with a punch or elbow strike. You can also kick their knees to destabilize them and create an opening for counterattacks.

- **Against Stick Attacks:** When faced with a stick attack, use your forearm to block the impact and strike the attacker's head, throat, or chest with a punch or knife-hand strike. If the attacker holds the stick with both hands, you can use a double-forearm block to deflect the attack and then counter with a punch or kick.

- **Against Multiple Weapons:** If the attacker has more than one weapon, you must be aware of all the threats and prioritize your defense. One strategy is to move swiftly and evade the attacks while looking for opportunities to disarm the attacker. Another approach is to defend against one weapon at a time and neutralize the attacker's balance and stance.

- **Against Surprise Attacks:** In case of a surprise attack, your reaction time and awareness are crucial. Maintain a relaxed but alert posture and use your peripheral vision to detect signs of danger. If you sense an attack, quickly move to the side, and use a combination of blocks and strikes to create space and time to react.

Karate moves can be a valuable tool in personal defense against various weapon attacks. However, mastering these moves requires practice, dedication, and the guidance of an experienced instructor. Remember, the best defense is to avoid dangerous situations and seek help from law enforcement or other authorities when facing threats. So, stay safe, and keep practicing.

Chapter 12: Daily Training Drills

Engaging in a karate training regimen can be one of the most significant decisions you'll ever make. It promotes physical fitness and cultivates mental and emotional wellness. Regular exercise can reduce stress and anxiety, improve focus and cognitive function, and alleviate symptoms of depression. But what sets karate apart from other exercises is its required discipline and dedication. As a result, you'll improve your physical prowess and acquire valuable life skills, such as patience, self-control, and perseverance.

This chapter outlines a daily karate training regimen you can follow at the gym or in the comfort of your home. It breaks down several drills and routines to enhance physical fitness, agility, speed, and power. The exercises cater to beginners and can be adapted for advanced practitioners.

Exercise can help you progress in karate. [57]

Warm-Up Exercises

Karate involves many high-impact movements, so a proper warm-up routine is crucial to avoid injury. A good warm-up should include cardio to raise your heart rate and stretching exercises to prepare your muscles and joints. Recommended warm-up exercises include jumping jacks, skipping rope, leg swings, and hip rotations.

Kicking and Punching Drills

Karate is all about mastering the various kicks and punches. Practicing them repeatedly, alone and with partners, is essential to perfect these moves. Training equipment like punching bags and kick pads can add resistance and intensity to your drills. Continuous practice builds muscle memory, leading to automatic movements and better overall technique.

Muscle Conditioning Exercises

Karate requires solid and powerful muscles to execute moves with speed and precision. Incorporating exercises like squats, lunges, and push-ups into your training regimen builds strength and endurance. These exercises strengthen the core muscles, which are essential for balance and stability. Using weighted bars or kettlebells can help you take your muscle conditioning routine to the next level.

Plyometric Training

Plyometric training is a specific workout to improve explosive power. In karate, this translates to higher jumps, faster kicks, and more decisive and quick strikes. Plyometric exercises include jump squats, burpees, and box jumps, focusing on rapidly contracting and extending the muscles. When done correctly, plyometrics can significantly improve physical performance. However, executing the exercises flawlessly and taking time with them is critical.

Resistance Band Exercises

Resistant band exercises are excellent for training the weaker muscle groups and preparing the body for high-impact moves. Focusing on specific muscle groups most used in karate training wraps up a comprehensive workout regimen. The resistance of the bands helps build strength, endurance, and flexibility.

Cardiovascular Training

Karate emphasizes overall fitness and health, including a solid cardiovascular system. Combining aerobic exercises, such as running or cycling, with anaerobic exercises, like jumping or sprinting, provides an effective training regimen that strengthens the heart and improves stamina. A good mix of high- and low-intensity exercises is ideal for a well-rounded workout. For example, complete a 30-minute cardio session at least twice weekly to boost endurance and cardiovascular health.

Stability and Core Training

Exercises focusing on promoting balance, stability, and coordination help execute various karate positions efficiently. These exercises include planks, mountain climbers, and single-leg balance exercises strengthening the muscles around the hips, lower body, and spine. While not directly related to martial arts, squats and deadlifts also strengthen core muscles. The core is essential for balance and stability in all martial arts, so incorporate these exercises into your routine.

Cool-Down Exercises

After completing a strenuous karate workout, it is essential to cool down properly to prevent muscle soreness and injury. Stretching exercises and slow cardio activities like jogging or walking reduce the heart rate gradually and aids in better blood circulation to the muscles, helping with muscle recovery. Take time to stretch after each workout to improve flexibility and prevent muscle tightness. If you feel incredibly sore after a session, taking an ice bath or using a cold compress can do wonders for keeping muscle inflammation at bay.

Meditation

Taking time off your busy schedule to relax and focus on breathing can improve concentration, reduce stress, and boost overall well-being. Use meditation to visualize certain moves or techniques to help you understand them better. There are many ways to meditate, so feel free to experiment and find the one that suits you best. Even a few minutes of dedicated meditation can help you stay focused and motivated while training.

Weekly Routine

Now that you know the basics, it's time to create a routine. Aim for 3-4 days of karate training a week, depending on your skill level and fitness goals. Supplement your training with other exercises, like running or swimming, for a complete workout. Ensure each session involves warm-up, plyometric exercises, resistance band exercises, cardio training, stability or core training, and cool-down exercises. It's important to incorporate rest and meditation days into your routine. Your body needs time to recover after a strenuous workout, so take at least one day off a week to allow your muscles to heal and prevent injury.

- **Monday:** Cardio Training – 30 minutes
- **Tuesday:** Plyometric Exercises – 20 minutes
- **Wednesday:** Rest and Meditation
- **Thursday:** Resistance Band Exercises – 25 minutes
- **Friday:** Core and Stability Training – 20 minutes
- **Saturday:** karate Drills – 40 minutes
- **Sunday:** Stretching and Cool-Down Exercises – 20 minutes

This routine will help you stay in shape, improve your technique, and increase your karate skills. However, everyone is different, so feel free to experiment with other exercises and routines until you find the one that works best.

A comprehensive karate training regimen helps you achieve your goals by focusing on your physical and mental well-being. A thorough karate workout that includes warm-up exercises, kicking and punching drills, muscle conditioning exercises, plyometric training, resistance band exercises, cardiovascular training, stability, core exercises, and cool-down exercises will pave your path to karate success. In addition, regular training, dedication, discipline in following your karate goals, and consistent practice with commitment result in achieving your karate goals and a well-balanced diet with proper nutrition. So, go ahead, build your regimen, and achieve excellence in karate.

Extra: Pressure Points Overview and Karate Terms

Whether a seasoned practitioner or just starting, understanding pressure points is crucial for mastering the art of karate. By targeting these specific areas of the body, you can quickly disable an opponent and gain the upper hand in a fight. Since karate has a unique vocabulary, this final chapter explores popular terms you should be familiar with. So, get ready to kick, punch, and chop your way to success.

Striking Points and Their Locations

In self-defense, knowing which vital striking points can take someone down is essential, especially if you're physically more petite than your attacker. Striking points are pressure points throughout the body that can cause pain, imbalance, and even unconsciousness. Here are some points to consider:

- **Temple Point:** One of the most common striking points is the temple. By striking the temple point on both sides of the head, near the hairline, you can cause a sudden shock to the brain, resulting in disorientation and confusion. It gives you time to react and defend yourself against the attacker.
- **Jawline Point:** Another crucial striking point is the jawline point below the ear. When struck correctly, it causes intense pain, disorientation, and damage to the attacker's inner ear, resulting in imbalance. On the other hand, a strong punch or elbow strike to this point can immobilize the attacker temporarily, giving you time to flee.
- **Collarbone Point:** The collarbone point is at the lower edge of the front of the collarbone. Striking this point can cause extreme pain and discomfort, leading to temporary paralysis and difficulty breathing. However, striking this point can buy you a few seconds to escape if you're being attacked from the front.
- **Solar Plexus Point:** The solar plexus point is in the center of the torso, just below the ribcage. Striking this point can cause a sudden loss of breath, resulting in temporary paralysis and even unconsciousness. However, punches, kicks, or even a quick jab to this point can be highly effective in stopping an attacker.
- **Groin Point:** The groin point is between the legs, below the beltline. Striking this point will cause intense pain, especially in males, resulting in temporary paralysis and disorientation. While not guaranteed to stop an attacker, it can give you time to escape or bring them to the ground.

Karate Terminology

Now that you know the essential striking points, it's time to learn the basics of karate terminology. Here are terms and phrases you should be familiar with:

26 Katas
1. Heian Shodan
2. Heian Nidan
3. Heian Sandan
4. Heian Yondan
5. Heian Godan

6. Tekki Shodan

7. Tekki Nidan

8. Tekki Sandan

9. Bassai Dai

10. Bassai Sho

11. Kanku Dai

12. Kanku Sho

13. Empi

14. Hangetsu

15. Jion

16. Jiin

17. Wankan

18. Meikyo

19. Unsu

20. Sochin

21. Nijushiho

22. Gojushiho-Te

23. Chinte

24. Jitte

25. Gankaku

26. Gojushho-Dai

Japanese Numbers

1. Ichi

2. Ni

3. San

4. Shi/Yon

5. Go

6. Roku

7. Shichi/Nana

8. Hachi

9. Ku/Kyuu

10. Juu

Karate Stances

- Zenkutsu-Dachi (Forward Stance)
- Kiba-Dachi (Horse Stance)
- Heiko-Dachi (Parallel Stance)
- Shiko-Dachi (Sumo Stance)
- Tsuru-Ashi-Dachi (Crane Stance)
- Neko-Ashi-Dachi (Cat Stance)
- Kokutsu-Dachi (Back Stance)
- Hangetsu-Dachi (Half Moon Stance)

Karate Techniques

- Uke (block)
- Tsuki (punching)
- Uchi (striking)

- Geri (kicking)
- Kihon (foundational training)
- Kata (form or pattern)
- Kumite (sparring)
- Tanden (center of gravity)
- Goshin-Jitsu (self-defense)
- Shime-Waza (grappling techniques)
- Atemi-Waza (vital point striking)
- Kime (focus)
- Jiyu-Kumite (free sparring)
- Ukemi (break-falling)
- Ikken Hisatsu (one-strike kill)
- Kyusho-Jitsu (vital point striking)

Now that you know the essential striking points, stances, and techniques of karate, it's time to start practicing. Find karate classes near you and start training with an experienced teacher. With practice and dedication, you'll master the art of karate and become a proficient fighter.

Conclusion

Karate is an ancient martial art practiced for centuries, originating in Okinawa, Japan. It is a highly disciplined form of self-defense focusing on physical and mental training to develop the mind and body. This martial art is about punches and kicks and developing a strong mindset, discipline, respect, and humility. This ultimate guide covered everything from the basics to the advanced techniques of karate.

The karate mindset is one of the most critical aspects of this martial art. karate teaches you how to be disciplined, focused, and mentally strong. It's a way of life requiring respect for yourself and others. You must be committed to your practice and persevere through challenging situations to develop this mindset. Also, aim to be humble with a positive attitude. Meditation and visualization exercises are essential to developing the karate mindset.

Kihon is the foundational training of karate and includes basic stances and blocks. These techniques are the building blocks for more advanced techniques. This guide taught you basic postures, like the front, back, and horse stances. You learned the basic blocks, such as the inward, outward, and rising blocks. These techniques are crucial for defense and are used in conjunction with strikes. This book covered proper punching techniques, such as the straight punch, hook punch, and uppercut, and explored various kicks, including the front, roundhouse, and sidekicks. Proper form and technique are essential for effective strikes.

Katas are prearranged sequences of movements simulating a real fight. Kumite, or sparring, is another essential component of karate training. This comprehensive guide covered the katas and kumite techniques for each belt level. You learned to perform the katas correctly, the importance of proper technique, and how to apply your techniques in kumite to defend yourself against opponents. In addition, this book provided a guide to understanding belts and the Dojo culture. It discussed the different belt levels, what they represent, and the etiquette expected within the Dojo environment.

This guide provided an overview of pressure points and a glossary of terms. Knowing the body's pressure points can immobilize your opponent and control the situation. Understanding karate terminology is essential for proper communication within the Dojo. At the end of this book, you should have a solid understanding of the basics, skills, and knowledge to take your karate training to the next level. With consistent practice and dedication, you can master the art of karate and develop a powerful mindset to serve you well in defending yourself.

From the foundational stances and blocks to the advanced black belt katas and self-defense techniques, karate provides physical and mental training for individuals of all ages and backgrounds. With consistent practice and training, you can improve your skills, develop a strong mindset, and achieve your karate goals. Additionally, check the glossary of terms at the end of this guide to refresh your knowledge and enhance your karate journey. Good luck, and happy training.

Part 6: Taekwondo

A Comprehensive Guide to Tae Kwon Do Techniques, Basics, and Tenets for Beginners Wanting to Master This Martial Art

CLINT SHARP

Taekwondo

A COMPREHENSIVE GUIDE TO TAE KWON DO
TECHNIQUES, BASICS, AND TENETS FOR BEGINNERS
WANTING TO MASTER THIS MARTIAL ART

Introduction

Like any other sport, getting started with Taekwondo can be daunting for beginners. While it bears some similarities to other martial arts forms, it is remarkably different in various ways, which is why you need to learn the basics to be able to lay a solid foundation for your journey.

Taekwondo, as a combat sport, has a history that spans several centuries. The early precursors of the sport date back over 2000 years. Translated as "the ways of hands and feet," the sport bears semblance to many ancient martial arts that were eventually unified during the 1940s and 1950s.

Taekwondo is a combative contact sport, but it's not an unruly free-for-all. There are rules, as well as specific techniques that the person has to adhere to. More than its physicality, there are unique principles and tenets that must be learned. Taekwondo also teaches discipline with an emphasis on developing the mind just as much as the body.

Taekwondo is for everyone and is a great way to work out, build your strength, develop excellent leadership skills, and improve yourself overall. Do you want to get started with Taekwondo and enjoy all of its benefits? Come along as we go through the basics, tenets, and techniques of this ancient martial art.

Chapter 1: A Brief History of Taekwondo

Taekwondo is a Korean Martial Art characterized by quick and powerful leg kicks. The name of the art translates to "the way of the foot and fist." Today, Taekwondo is one of the most well-known forms of martial arts and the easiest styles to learn for anyone of any age worldwide.

Although the original forms of martial arts from which Taekwondo takes its roots go way back, it has a very short history in its current form. It is young compared to other forms of Asian martial arts, like Karate.

The development of Taekwondo as we know it today began in the 1940s. The art came about through the work of various martial artists. It was born from a combination of older art forms like Chinese martial arts and Korean martial arts, such as Taekkyeon, which is focused on dynamic footwork and striking; Subak, the martial art predecessor of Taekkyeon; and Gwonbeop, which is the Korean version of the Chinese martial arts.

Ancient History

As mentioned earlier, even though Taekwondo is relatively young, it draws its root from ancient Korean martial art forms. Therefore, it is impossible to talk about the history of Taekwondo without making a brief reference to how these older martial art forms came about.

According to ancient Korean mythology, the Korean Nation was founded in 2333 B.C. by the Tangun or Dangun (god-kings). However, there are no records of any martial arts during this period. The first mention of martial arts is linked to the Three Kingdoms era. Our Taekwondo history begins with the establishment of these three kingdoms: Silla, Goguryeo, and Baekje, in 57 B.C., 37 B.C., and 18 B.C., respectively.

During the three kingdoms era, the Silla Kingdom, which was the smallest of these three, requested help from the Baekje to defend itself from the Goguryeo and pirates that terrorized it. The Baekje kingdom had a basic style of martial arts, which they taught the Silla soldiers to help them defend their kingdom.

Chin Heung, Silla's 24th king, elevated this martial art's popularity by incorporating it into fundamental military training programs. He formed a group of young fighters skilled in martial arts. Hwa Rang Do was their chosen name; it translates into "Flowering Youth."

The Subak, the martial art practiced by this group of soldiers, was one of the early predecessors of Taekwondo. They also learned to command weaponry such as swords, bows, and spears in addition to physical combat. Subak practice also included lectures in ethical rules that paralleled Buddhist monks' teachings. These included selflessness and dedication to serving the kingdom and its people and leading an exemplary lifestyle. These principles are similar to many of the tenets of Taekwondo that are still taught today.

The Hwa Rang Do troops were highly successful in military conquests, and through their help, the Kingdom of Silla defeated its enemies. This victory also led to the unification of the three separate kingdoms into a single kingdom in the Korean Peninsula.

In 936 A.D., Wang Kon formed the Koryo Kingdom, and the Subak (hand combat) was the adopted style of martial arts. In addition to being used for military combat, it was also practiced for self-defense and as a form of exercise.

As the art quickly became a favorite pastime of the people, men who practiced the art of Subak were widely respected. It was popular among citizens of the Koryo Dynasty, very much the same way American Football is well-known in the United States today.

During this time, Subak became more than just military combat training and was taught to commoners, boosting its popularity.

During the 1300s, the Subak martial arts style evolved into the Taekkyeon, a form of art that emphasized kicking. The history of the name "Tae-kwon-do" has also been linked to Taekkyeon.

During the Joseon Dynasty (Yi Dynasty), which lasted from 1392 to 1910, the country's military changed its philosophical ideals from Buddhism to Confucianism. An implication of this was that the once-popular martial arts of Subak and Teakkyeon became unpopular among the elites and the ruling class; they were only practiced by commoners.

Japanese Occupation

The Japanese invaded Korea in 1909 and occupied the country until World War II ended in 1945. During this period, all elements of Korean culture were suppressed, and the Japanese government banned all things connected to Korean heritage and art forms, including Teakkyeon and Subak.

Japanese and Chinese martial arts were taught instead of the traditional Korean martial arts. As a result of this suppression, many Taekkyeon and Subak masters had to go into hiding or escape to other countries to continue teaching and practicing their art.

Modern Taekwondo

Source[58]

The era of the modern Taekwondo began after World War II, which signaled the freedom of the Korean Peninsula. Once again, the Koreans were now free to practice their traditional martial arts.

From 1945, several new martial arts schools were opened in Seoul, South Korea, to teach the arts of Subak and Taekkyeon. These schools all claimed to teach "genuine" or "traditional" Korean martial arts methods. Not only were these arts diverse, but they also included elements of what they learned during the Japanese occupation, including Kung Fu and Karate techniques.

By the 1960s, nine notable martial arts schools (also known as Kwans), each practicing a slightly different style, existed. But they all bore some similarities to the ancient arts of Subak and Taekkyeon.

Despite being distinct in their techniques and incorporating characteristics of foreign martial arts, the many kinds of martial arts practiced in the Kwans are sometimes lumped together as "Traditional Taekwondo." Around this period, the South Korean military chose to elect traditional Taekkyeon as the official unarmed combat martial art, greatly increasing its popularity. In 1952 during a Taekkyeon demonstration by the military, South Korea's President, Syngman Rhee, was so impressed that he made it mandatory for all of the country's soldiers to be trained in the art. General Choi Hung-hi, a captain at the time, was saddled with the responsibility of formulating standardized training that would return the ancient arts of Subak and Taekkyeon to their roots. This involved uniting the nine different Kwans and stripping their various techniques of all Kung Fu and Karate influence.

By 1955, the masters of all the different Kwans had collaborated to form a single Korean martial arts technique. Tae Soo Do was the original name of the newly established style - from the Korean word *Tae*; to "stomp or trample;" *Soo*; as in "hand"; and *Do*; for "way" or "discipline."

General Choi Hong Hi later suggested that the word "Soo" be replaced with Kwon, meaning "fist." Hence, the name Tae Kwon Do was born." This unified name and newly established techniques were adopted by the various Kwans that taught the art.

The Taekwondo Associations

A few years later, in September of 1961, the Korean Taekwondo Association was officially formed as part of the efforts to further standardize the activities of the various Kwans. The KTA became the Taekwondo governing body for the entire country and was headed by none other than General Choi.

Under the General's administration, the art of Taekwondo received some major boosts. Masters of the art were sent to a number of locations worldwide in order to spread proper teachings of Taekwondo, in addition to establishing an esteemed representation of the country. He also laid the groundwork for the creation of an international body called the International Taekwondo Federation, which would have its headquarters in South Korea.

As head of the KTA, General Choi played an important role in the development and popularity of the art. However, his ambitious efforts to grow Taekwondo eventually brought him into disfavor with the people and government of Korea. He sent a delegation of Taekwondo instructors to North Korea for a diplomatic mission in 1966. This did not bode well with the South Korean government since the countries were at war with each other; General Choi was then relieved of his position.

Enraged, General Choi left the country and moved to Toronto, Canada. From there, he created the International Taekwondo Federation and dissociated himself from the KTA in 1972. The International Taekwondo Federation is focused more on the Traditional Taekwondo style that was created and refined by General Choi.

The South Korean government established a new national academy to teach Taekwondo a year after the ITF was formed. This academy was called the Kukkiwon. The World Taekwondo Federation was also created at this time. The purpose of the WTF was to promote Taekwondo at international levels.

The style and rules of Taekwondo adopted by the WTF are known as the Kukkiwon style or WTF style. It is also the same as the Olympic style or sports style. WTF's efforts ensured the recognition of Taekwondo as an international sport. Currently, Taekwondo is one of only two Asian martial arts (including Judo) that compete at the Olympics. In 2010, it was also recognized as a sport at the Commonwealth Games.

Taekwondo in America

In 1962, Jhoon Goo Rhee established the first Taekwondo school in America, in Washington DC. Rhee is often reputed as the Father of American Taekwondo, but prior to his arrival, there were other masters of the sport in the country. Taekwondo masters first arrived in the United States from Korea to teach the art in the 1960s. They came as representatives of the KTA at the time. In 1963, a Taekwondo demonstration was conducted in the United States and was favorably welcomed, leading to the formation of the United States Taekwondo Federation under the supervision of the Amateur Athletic Union and the United States Taekwondo Union. The WTF acknowledged the United States Taekwondo Union as the regulatory organization for tournaments in the United States in 1984. The United States Olympic Committee took over the Union in 2004 due to an internal problem, and the sport was renamed USA Taekwondo the following year. Haeng Un Lee founded the American Taekwondo Association in 1969 after going to meet General Choi in 1968 to learn traditional Taekwondo. The organization's headquarters are in Little Rock, Arkansas, and it boasts over 350,000 members who participate in the sport. The Songaham style of Taekwondo is the one used by the ATA (Pine Tree and Rock style). In this approach, students are referred to as a pine tree that grows from a weak little sapling to a big, magnificent tree with rock-solid roots. The ATA has highly rigorous requirements, and schools that are members are obligated to implement the association's business model. The ATA is run like a business, with a CEO (who is required to have a 9th-degree black belt) and a board of decision-makers.WTF and Olympic History

The World Taekwondo Federation has been linked with different Taekwondo schools in over 160 countries since 1973. The organization's headquarters are located in Kukkiwon, Seoul, South Korea. Since 1980, the International Olympic Committee (IOC) has recognized the organization as the sport's official governing body. According to the organization's official website, there are currently more than 5 million WTF certified black belt holders. Taekwondo made its Olympic debut as a demonstration sport in 1988 and then again in 1992. At the 2000 Olympics in Sydney, Australia, it was formally acknowledged as an Olympic sport.

WTF practices and training tend to lean more towards the sports-like form of Taekwondo than ITF styles, which are more centered on traditional Taekwondo. Many master teachers, however, maintain that certain traditional Taekwondo aspects are still present in WTF training programs. The World Taekwondo Federation sanctioned and promoted international, national, regional, and local Taekwondo tournaments. The WTF also promotes the sport in local communities through academic institutions (also known as Dojangs) that teach martial arts to adults and children to better their fitness and physical health. Its method is comparable to that of the ancient Hwa Rang Do technique, which taught the Subak art to commoners.

Chapter 2: The Original Masters of Taekwondo

The pioneer masters of taekwondo are a group of 12 South Korean martial arts instructors who created the Korea Taekwondo Association (KTA) in the 1960s to promote the latest forms of martial art. Many of the men on the list had prominent roles in the International Taekwondo Federation (ITF), but as time went on, the majority of them moved to North America, Australia, and Europe. The title "Original Masters" does not imply that these individuals were the first KTA masters, though. The KTA was founded by nine men who headed their own kwans, a distinct set of individuals than those on the list we'll discuss. But many of them practiced martial arts under different names, such as kong soo do and tae soo do, refusing to use the name taekwondo. Below is a list of the first men to ever adopt that name and actively promote it.

- Choi Chang Keun

C K Choi was born in Korea in 1940 and began his martial arts training in the Korean army in 1956. He began teaching taekwondo in Malaysia in 1964 and relocated to Vancouver in 1970. He was promoted to 8th dan in 1981 and 9th dan in 2002 after starting as a 7th dan in 1973. To this day, he is still living in Vancouver.

- Choi Kwang Jo

K J Choi was born in Daegu, Korea, in March 1942, and he began training in the martial arts as a child. Choi met Hong Hi Choi while serving in the South Korean army. He instructed students in taekwondo all over Singapore, Malaysia, Indonesia, and Hong Kong in 1966/67. Injuries experienced during training, however, led him to seek medical care in the United States in 1970. In 1987, he formed the Choi Kwang-Do organization and now resides in Atlanta. He is ranked 9th dan in Choi Kwang-do.

- Han Cha Kyo

Born in Seoul, Korea in 1934, C K Han trained under no less than three masters – Woon Kyu Um, Duk Sung Son, and Tae Hi Nam. In March 1959, he was the first original master to perform taekwondo outside of Korea while traveling to Vietnam and Taiwan. After quitting the South Korean army in 1971, he immigrated to the United States and resided in Chicago. In 1980, he founded the Universal Taekwondo Foundation and continued to teach until he died in 1996.

- Kim Jong Chan

Born in 1937, J C Kim taught taekwondo in the 1960s in Malaysia. In 1979, while ranked 7th dan, he traveled to Argentina to show and teach taekwondo. Chan was listed as the President of the World Tukido Council in a letter he wrote, which was later published in the Black Belt magazine in July 1985. Today, he lives in Vancouver, Canada.

- Kim Kwang Il

K I Kim made a significant contribution to introducing taekwondo in West Germany and, until 1971, he was the ITF head instructor in West Germany. In 1975, he was elevated to 6th dan, and in 1976, he promoted Rolf Becking, the leader of the ITF Germany Technical Committee, to 2nd dan. He operated his own restaurant in Stuttgart from 1974 to 1977 and finished his Brewmeister training before opening.

- Kong Young Il

Y I Kong was born in Korea in 1943 and began training in Shotgun Karate in 1952. He served in the South Korean army from 1963 to 1967, rising to the rank of Sergeant.

Throughout his time and after leaving the army, he took part in demonstrations worldwide and emigrated to the USA around 1968. In 1968, he and his brother, Young Bo Kong, formed the Young Brothers Taekwondo Associates, and in 1997, H H Choi advanced him to 9th dan in Poland. He is currently residing in Las Vegas.

- ### Park Jong Soo

Born in Chung-Nam, South Korea, in 1947, J S Park trained under H H Choi. He traveled to West Germany in 1965 to take over as coach of the German Taekwondo Association. He relocated to the Netherlands in 1966, where he established the association's Dutch division. He moved to Canada in 1968 and still resides there now, holding the level of 9th dan.

- ### Park Jung Tae

H T Park was born in Korea in 1943/44 (it's unclear which year) and learned boxing as a kid before moving on to judo and taekwondo. He was head of military taekwondo training from 1965 to 1967 in Vietnam before moving to Canada in 1970. In 1984, he was ranked 8th dan in the ITF but, due to political issues, he departed the ITF in 1989. He formed the Global Taekwondo Federation in 1990 and resided in Mississauga until 2002, where he died.

- ### Park Sun Jae

S JPark, one of the founders of taekwondo, visited Croatia in 1964 to deliver lectures on the martial art. He presented it in Italy in 1968 and was graded 5th dan at the time, rising to 7th dan in 1975. In 1976, during the foundation's inaugural meeting, he was chosen Vice-President of the European Taekwondo Union. He joined the WTF World Cup championship arbitration board in 2002 and was named Acting President of the WTF in 2004, following the resignation of Un Yong Kim. He is still the Vice-President of the World Taekwondo Federation for Italy, and he was elected President of the Italian Taekwondo Federation in 1998.

- ### Rhee Chong Chul

CC Rhee was born in Korea in 1935 and grew up practicing martial arts, gymnastics, boxing, weightlifting, and basketball. For three years, he served in the Korean Marines as an unarmed combat teacher, instructing the Marine Commandos, Marine Brigade Headquarters, and the Marine 2nd Infantry Division. Rhee was one of the pioneers in spreading taekwondo to Southeast Asia, primarily Singapore and Malaysia, as well as Brunei, Indonesia, and Hong Kong. In about 1965, he founded the Rhee Taekwondo Organization in Australia and still lives in Sydney.

- ### Rhee Chong Hyup

Born in Korea in 1940, C H Rhee helped introduce Taekwondo to Singapore and Malaysia in the mid-1960s. He moved to Melbourne, Australia, in 1970 and heads up the Melbourne operations of the Rhee Taekwondo Organization.

- ### Rhee Ki Ha

Born in Seoul, Korea, in 1938, K H Rhee began training at 7 or 8 years of age. He served in the South Korean army, where he met H H Choi and learned taekwondo. In 1964, he began teaching taekwondo to Royal Air Force personnel stationed in Singapore, and in 1967, he relocated to London, England. In 981, he was ranked 8th dan and attained 9th dan in St Petersburg in 1997. He is now renowned as the Father of both Irish and British taekwondo and is currently located in Glasgow.

Chapter 3: Grading and the Taekwondo Belt System

In Taekwondo, the colored belts are referred to as Kup Grades, and they symbolize the rank an individual has attained in the sport. Interestingly, the current grading system was not an original part of the sport; the complex grading system was introduced when Taekwondo made it to the western world.

Originally students merely went from white belt to black belt after years of dedicated practice and training. However, it was discovered that this format would not suit Western practitioners who preferred to have an incentive to continue participating in training. Therefore, the belt grading system was introduced.

In addition to achieving the main solid colors, tags were further introduced to create 9 different belts (stages or gups). Students must work their way up from white to yellow, green, blue, red, and finally, the black belt.

The frequency of grading or promotion depends on how often a student trains. The more lessons you attend and the harder you practice, the more likely you will get your next belt. The grading system includes a test for physical techniques, and students are also required to have the right attitude based on the tenets of martial arts.

Grading is scheduled on a 3-months basis, but students may not grade every time unless they have been practicing consistently and are extremely dedicated. There is a minimum number of lessons that a student must complete before grading for the next stage. There are also specific techniques that must be mastered and a list of translations on which you will be tested. All of these are typically spelled out in a syllabus.

Students typically need 3 to 4 years of rigorous practice to get from white to black belt. However, this duration could be longer or shorter depending on specific circumstances and how hard a student practices.

While instructors assist and guide you with your training, every student's responsibility is to practice and master their grading requirements. Once a student has covered the required number of lessons for grading, the instructor will include them in the pre-grading assessment to determine if they are ready to be graded for the next stage.

What to Expect on Grading Day

Your instructor will inform you of the day and venue of your grading. Students are expected to turn up in a clean and well-ironed uniform with the completed grading form on grading day. At the venue, students line up as if in a regular class. The examiners introduce themselves and give them a breakdown of the order for the day.

Typically, students sit at the back of the hall in their respective grade groups and will be invited forward when it's time for their exam. The exam gauges students based on the standard techniques for each grade, including the basics, routines, sparring, and breaking techniques. Additionally, students will also be tested on Taekwondo theory and translation.

When you are called to do your exam, your name will be announced, and you will be pointed to the starting position for your grading, usually marked with an X on the floor. When your name is called, reply with, "Yes Sir," and run to the spot. Take an attention stance, raise your hands, and mention your name and grade level, e.g., John Doe, 10th Kup, Sir, bow, and take a ready position as you wait for the examiner's instructions to begin.

Who Are the Examiners?

Taekwondo grading examiners usually consist of top instructors. They will observe going through the grading requirements of your grade's syllabus and grade you based on your performance. If you have practiced well, you should be confident you'll perform well and please the examiners.

Grading Results

Grading results are typically announced about a week after a grading exam by your instructor during a normal lesson. New belts or tags and a graded certificate will be assigned to students who have passed. You would also receive a graded certificate. The standard Taekwondo grade results are either pass or fail. If you did not pass, your instructor must explain the reasons and work with you to prepare for your next grading test. If you only narrowly pass, your instructor may require you to take more lessons for an extended period before taking your next grading test.

An A pass may also be assigned for students who pass excellently. But this is rare as it requires the student to have a high mark in every area of grading. In this case, they may be able to take their next grading test as soon as a month of training for it.

Time Requirements and Grades

It takes time to go through all the grades of Taekwondo, and the standard time requirement between each grade gets progressively longer as you go from white to black belt. The blue and the black belts are the two major milestone grades that indicate a substantial step up.

Your Taekwondo syllabus contains details of the requirements for each grade, including the number of hours of lessons you participate in to qualify for a grading test. Note that these times are only considered a minimum. Your instructor may choose to delay your grading based on his assessment of your performance.

- White Belt (10th Kup) – Minimum of 3 months training and 20 lessons
- White Belt, Yellow Tag (9th Kup) - Minimum of 3 months training and 20 lessons
- Yellow Belt (8th Kup) - Minimum of 3 months training and 20 lessons
- Yellow Belt, Green Tag (7th Kup) - Minimum of 3 months training and 30 lessons
- Green Belt (6th Kup) - Minimum of 3 months training and 30 lessons
- Green Belt, Blue Tag (5th Kup) - Minimum of 3 months training and 40 lessons
- Blue Belt (4th Kup) - Minimum of 6 months training and 60 lessons
- Blue Belt, Red Tag (3rd Kup) - Minimum of 6 months training and 70 lessons
- Red Belt (2nd Kup) - Minimum of 6 months training and 70 lessons
- Red Belt, Black Tag (1st Kup) - Minimum of 6 months training and 80 lessons
- Black Belt (1st Dan)

While the black belt is often considered the ultimate, it is, in fact, only the beginning. There are additional Dan grades and other Taekwondo qualifications to attain even as a black belt holder.

What a Grading Test Entails

During your grading, you will be tested on various things. In addition to demonstrating the moves for your grade level, you will also be tested on translations, breaking, and your sparring performance.

Translations

The translations you will be required to learn according to your grade level are included in the syllabus, but the list is only a guide. You may be tested on any translation that the examiner feels you should know for your grade level and lower grades. The translations include the Korean terms used for moves and stances in Taekwondo; hence you should be familiar with them.

Breaking

Demolition grading is not for everyone, and only students over the age of 16 will be required to participate in this as part of their grading. Each grade has a specific set of techniques you must use to break bricks or boards made of wood and tile. Your assessment will be based on your technique, accuracy, power, and ability to break the board.

Before attempting to break, you will demonstrate the technique by slowly touching the target. This way, the examiner can assess your technique and judge if you are doing it correctly and striking the board safely. After this, you have a few attempts to break the board.

Be sure to have practiced the various breaking techniques for your grade before the grading test. Aim at the center of the board and strike through it (not just at it). Confidence is one of the things examiners look for, so take a deep breath and hit the board without hesitation.

Partner Work

While demonstrating some techniques, such as sparring and self-defense, a partner will be required. Usually, the examiners will select a partner who is another student attempting the same grade.

The examiner's assessment of your performance is based on your technique, respect, and control as you work with your partner. You may also be required to work with different partners during a performance, as examiners do this to assess how you respond to different people based on their skill level compared to yours.

At the start of any of these activities, your examiner will give you clear instructions before calling you to attention.

Chapter 4: Fundamental Movements in Taekwondo

There are over 3000 movements, which are the basic elements of Taekwondo, often likened to musical notes. When linked correctly, they produce a harmonious result adding grace and beauty to the sport.

The fundamental movements in Taekwondo involve all parts of the body, performed harmoniously based on the theory of power. Students at all grade levels are expected to practice these movements and gain mastery over each. This way, they can make use of them as needed.

Mastering the fundamental movements is the core of Taekwondo training. These movements are typically a combination of designated positions with specific hand and foot techniques, but other body parts like the head and knees are also involved. In addition to mastering the basic movement, Taekwondo students are expected to know about hand attacking weapons and the vital spots of the opponent's body. A combination of all these movements constitutes a formidable attack or effective defense.

In Taekwondo, each of the basic moves signifies an assault, counterattack, or defense against a specific target region or an action against a real or imagined opponent (or opponents). It's critical to understand how these fundamental motions tie into your overall competency as a learner while studying them. It determines how they will be applied in actual combat.

With constant practice, the Taekwondo movements will become second nature to you. Students must strive to improve the power and balance of their moves and shift stances to block or attack an opponent without losing form.

You will learn to physically use these fundamental motions against actual moving opponents during sparring once you have mastered them in individual training.

The Stances

The stance refers to how you stand and is arguably the most important aspect of learning Taekwondo and any other form of martial arts. The stance is an essential elemental factor on which all your future lessons rest and the reason it must be mastered from the onset.

In Taekwondo, there are numerous stances that students should learn and master. Each stance has an important role in developing the attack and defense and is also essential for developing a student's physical strength.

Taekwondo stances are the foundation on which all the offensive and defensive moves are built. Maintaining the proper stance is vital for performing any kick, punch, or block correctly. Not appreciating the importance of maintaining a good stance will result in loss of balance and power. The appropriate posture also allows you to throw punches and kicks with more accuracy.

The Principles Proper Taekwondo Stance

Each stance in Taekwondo has a specific purpose. For instance, the walking stance gives you a strong base for forward and backward techniques. The sitting stance gives you a solid base to perform lateral strikes improving your forward technique. The L-stance is primarily a fighting stance.

It is extremely important that you master the principles of maintaining the proper posture for each stance from the onset of your Taekwondo training. This will aid you in developing some muscle memory, gradually making each movement smoother and more effortless. As you progress in your training or applied sparring challenges, your movements will become more complicated, and your body will naturally utilize any needed stance that was previously learned.

You only need to understand the principles and familiarize how a correct stance feels, and with time, you will perform them correctly without a need to check. Some principles of a correct stance include:

- **Balance:** Like every other form of martial art, balance is important in Taekwondo. Instructors often stress the importance of balance; without it, there will always be flaws in your stance and consequently in your attack and defense.

- **Relax:** A tense body cannot produce the correct moves, so you must relax your body while in every stance. It gives more fluidity to your moves and helps you quickly react when it's necessary. Later in this book, you will learn about meditation and how it helps calm your mind in Taekwondo.

- **Keep Your Back Straight:** For every stance, your back must be straight and aligned. If your spine isn't aligned as it should be, your base will most likely be off.

- **Tighten Your Core:** Your core (your abdomen) needs to be tight while you're in a stance, as this helps you control your movements better. Research and practice different methods to tighten your abdomen without tensing your body.

- **Foot Placement:** Your foot is the base of every stance and must be placed correctly. With every stance, you need to stand on the balls of your feet to ensure even weight distribution and boost your reaction time.

- **Breath:** One of the ways to ensure that your body is relaxed is to breathe evenly; it makes it easier for you to maintain a proper stance.

There are several different stances in Taekwondo. Each Taekwondo association has its list of stances that must be mastered, and the following are basic ones that every student should know.

The Walking Stance

As the name implies, the walking stance looks like you are taking a step forward. The left foot is positioned forward and at an angle of about 30 degrees while the right foot faces straight forward. In this stance, the entire body is turned to about 45 degrees to the natural angle. This positioning aids balance. In most cases, your weight is evenly divided across both feet. The placement of feet in this stance makes it suitable as an offense.

The Horse-Riding Stance (Juchum Seogi, or Annun Seogi)

The horse-riding stance is similar to the positioning of one's leg when riding a horse. The specific placement of the feet varies depending on the style of Taekwondo practiced. In the Kukkiwon or WTF style, the feet are positioned at about two shoulder widths apart. The ITF style is less wide, at about one-and-a-half shoulder widths apart.

Both of your feet should point in a forward direction. The knees are deeply bent in an outward direction from your body. The extent of the bend required varies from one school to the other. In the horse-riding stance, there is an even distribution of weight between both feet. The hip is pushed forward, and the torso is kept straight and vertical. Your fists should be connected to the sides of your belt with the abdomen tight.

The Horse-Riding Stance

The horse-riding stance is used to help students build their leg strength and is usually used for exercising. However, the horse-riding stance may also be an offensive stance from where you can throw punches and kicks.

Back Stance (Dwi Kubi Seogi)

Back Stance (Dwi Kubi Seogi)

This style is also known as the L-stance in the ITF style. The back stance is also called the fighting stance in some traditional Taekwondo styles.

One foot is positioned in front of the other to do this stance. The foot at the back is placed in a perpendicular direction from the front foot. The positioning of the two feet should form the letter L.

The leading foot should be about one stride, around 3-foot, ahead of the rear foot. In the back stance, most of your weight should rest on your rear legs. The knees should be slightly bent, and both feet should be flat on the ground.

The naming of the back stance does not follow the normal convention in Taekwondo. Typically, the correct version of every stance implies that your right foot is the leading foot, and the left foot is behind. But for the back stance, this rule does not apply. In the right-back stance, the right foot is placed behind the other and is called the *trailing foot,* while the left plays the forward role.

Tiger Stance or Cat Stance (Beom Seogi)

For this stance, the front foot is placed forward with the heel slightly elevated, about 4-5 inches. This means that only the ball of your front foot should be placed on the ground. The rear foot should point outwards about 30 degrees.

Positioning your feet like this will shift most of your weight to the rear foot, and both legs should be bent at the knees. In the ITF version of this stance, your front foot should be forward by about a shoulder width.

Tiger Stance or Cat Stance (Beom Seogi)

Front Stance or Long-Forward Stance (Ap Kubi)

Front Stance or Long-Forward Stance (Ap Kubi)

This position is similar to the walking stance. In the front stance position, the forward foot is placed well ahead, up to two-and-a-half feet, of the rear foot. The front foot points straight ahead while the rear foot is positioned outward at an angle of about 25-30 degrees.

Your front knee is bent, and your shin is parallel to the floor. Typically, if you can still see the leading toes of your feet, then your knee is not bent enough. The rear leg is not bent, and the foot is positioned flat on the floor with no heel lift. The front leg bears most of the weight (around two-thirds) of your entire weight.

In this posture, there is a propensity to lean inward or turn the hips, but to accomplish it correctly, your hips must be held front to keep your body straight. These are the basic stances in Taekwondo. Learning and performing all the other moves will be much simpler if you have properly learned how to hold these stances correctly.

Blocks

Blocks are the most basic moves in Taekwondo. The goal of these maneuvers is to avoid being struck by an opponent. Almost any portion of the body can be used to deflect an approaching attack and strike an opponent.

Although a block is a defensive move, it also has to be strong and fast if you want to stop an attack. It is the purpose of learning this move from the early stages of mastering Taekwondo.

Each of the different block moves has a twist at its end to block the incoming blow effectively, and it takes a lot of practice to master the techniques for blocking. The middle block, high block, low block, knife block, and outside forearm block are all examples of block movements in Taekwondo.

- **The Low Block:** This is one of the most basic blocks to learn if you're starting Taekwondo. Position your fist on your opposite shoulder and sweep it downward in front of your pelvis; stop on the same side, near the base of your leg, as your blocking arm.

Low Block

Inside Block

• **Inside Block:** This is an inside sweeping motion used to protect the body by hitting attacks off to the side of the body. To do the inside block, bring the forearm of your blocking arm inside across your face or body to block an opponent's attack while stepping to the side.

• **Face Block:** To do the face block, shoot your arm up at an angle, stopping just over your brow. The move should be like you're forming a roof or church steeple. With this block, you can make a strike glance off you protecting your head. This type of block is excellent for weapon defense.

Face Block

• **Hand-Blade/Double Forearm Block:** This is a more complex block as it doubles as an attack move. To do this, one of your hands blocks the attack while the other is ready to deliver a follow-up strike to the opponent. There is a lot to this technique, and many beginners often misunderstand it.

Hand-Blade

Attacks

Initially, Taekwondo attacks only involved using the legs. The sport expanded throughout time to incorporate strikes and hits delivered with the arms. Attack maneuvers, on the other hand, are typically taught at higher levels of the sport since you can't learn to attack without first learning to defend. Punches have become an important weapon in Taekwondo, and thus, mastering them is crucial. Here are a few of the basic punch and kick attack moves you should be familiar with as a beginner:

• **Straight Punch:** To do the straight punch, the fist begins from the chamber of your hip and is thrust straight forward. The two big knuckles are used to make an impact. This punch should be delivered from the front stance or horse stance.

Straight Punch

Front Kick

• **Front Kick:** This is the foundation of almost all kicks in Taekwondo. Almost every other kick begins with a front kick chamber.

• **Knife Hand Strike:** This is often referred to as the karate chop. The attack is delivered down towards the outside with your palm facing downwards. It can also be done towards the inside with your palm facing up. The impact is made with the knife or meat of the hand. As an attacking move, the knife hand strike typically targets the side of the neck, trachea, or the opponent's temple.

Knife Hand Strike

Side Kick

- **Side Kick:** This is another very popular attack move in Taekwondo, and it is common for an individual's overall Taekwondo ability to be judged based on their sidekick. The sidekick is performed as a simple forward kick off the back leg. It requires you to bring your leg all the way to the side and thrust it forward at an opponent. This move can be a bit of a challenge to master.

- **Round Kick:** The round kick is also popular in many other martial arts, but the Taekwondo execution method is unique. On a back stance, turn your hips with your front foot as you bring your back leg knee upward. Kick your leg through to the target. It can be quite useful for sparring purposes.

Round Kick

Other Common Attack Moves

- Punching hand twists
- Double knife-hand strike
- Front kick
- Back kick
- Ax kick

Apart from these basic moves, many variations also exist to open the door to more advanced taekwondo techniques. The key to learning and mastering these moves is practice. The more you practice and improve your skills, you will execute these moves with greater confidence and scale up to more complex ones.

Chapter 5: Meditation and Taekwondo

Believe it or not, Taekwondo goes hand in hand with meditation. Meditation has been a very useful tool in the world of martial arts for years and always will be. Scientific research has proven that meditation possesses excellent health benefits, including but are not limited to:

- Decrease in insomnia
- Intelligence increase
- Reduced risk for illnesses
- Easy focus and concentration
- Increased personal development
- Lower blood pressure
- Reduced risk of cardiovascular diseases
- Lower stress and anxiety levels

Terrific right? It seems that meditation gives a much stronger and healthier body to whoever partakes in it. Meditation has all-around importance for everyone. Children use it to calm themselves before taking on that important math or calculus test. Adults with shyness or public speaking fears have been advised to practice meditation to calm themselves down before that job interview or presentation. Anyone in a stressful situation can calm themselves sufficiently through breathing and focus - two preeminent factors taught in meditation.

Breath and Focus

Meditation does a lot to improve Taekwondo performance, like giving you a much-needed energy boost that is beneficial for your training. For those new to meditation, the best way to begin is to focus solely on breathing. A few minutes of focused breathing goes a long way, and it is best to start with small steps and develop a good breathing pattern when accessing the inner self. Ensure to close your eyes while you're at it.

Source[59]

When immersed in Taekwondo, controlling your breathing pattern is of utmost importance because your movements require proper breath management. Taekwondo requires you to move with skill and precision. Of course, these movements are complex, but they must be done fluidly. Meditation training increases your lung capacity, which translates to better breathing patterns, and advanced meditation will fine-tune this further.

While performing Taekwondo movements, an unparalleled focus is needed. Focus is everything in Taekwondo, a miscalculation or slip-up can result in a loss for you, and one way to polish your focus is through meditation because it also utilizes one's focus. Consistent meditation gives your mind a rhythm that makes unparalleled focus effortless.

Many people erroneously believe that martial arts are all about physical strength. Even though the role of physical strength in martial arts cannot be underestimated, as it is very instrumental, there are several cases where a much smaller opponent overpowers a physically strong man or woman. Intelligence and focus take precedence over brute force in any situation. Most times, these biggies fall to smaller opponents due to the lack of a focused mind. Staying calm and focused during a fight allows you to execute the right movements with effective react time to your opponent's advances.

Mastering Meditation - Tips to Begin

We have outlined the excellent benefits embedded in meditation. It is a fact that Taekwondo athletes who incorporate meditation in their training outperform those who don't. So, how do you infuse it in yours?

Like anything else, there are several ways to meditate. As a beginner, twenty minutes of meditation practice per day should be good enough to get you started.

Find a quiet place. It's impossible to meditate amid a racket or a place steeped in noise and unhealthy sounds. Remember, your mind needs to concentrate. This quiet place can be anywhere - like your bedroom or office, for example; the important thing is that you must be uninterrupted. It shouldn't be a place where anyone can easily reach and disturb you. Most Taekwondo training clubs use the dojang. It's pretty powerful, and it's something you can take advantage of, too.

What's your intention with meditation? What are you looking to focus on at that moment? Or for the day? Meditation is about focus, and focus is about intentionality. You've got to be intentional about what you want to focus on. Do you want to perfect your techniques? Imagine playing both sides. Strategize. Meditation needs intention, or else the goal won't be achieved.

Start by breathing in and exhaling. Breathe slowly from the lowest part of your abdomen. Hold it in for as long as you can, then exhale slowly through the mouth. When you do this three times, your body enters a state of calm and relaxation, and so does your mind. Then, merely focus. Focus on your breathing and enjoy each breath so that random thoughts are lessened.

Your thoughts will undoubtedly be running around in your mind; this is inevitable; acknowledge them and let them saunter away. If you find yourself bogged down by too many thoughts, go back to focusing solely on your breathing until your timer goes off. You'll feel a lot calmer and more relaxed.

It's best to meditate with a timer. It helps keep you on track in case you lose track of time; this often happens when you get into the flow state. When this happens, twenty minutes feels like five minutes. Practice makes perfect, and as you meditate more often, you'll find it easier to meditate for more extended periods.

As a beginner, you have to learn to be patient with yourself and not engage in unnecessary pressure. Meditation differs for each one of us, and everyone responds to it differently. The one thing you must understand is that the flow comes with consistency. Meditation works best if and when it is done at the same time every day or regularly before Taekwondo tournaments or practices. Don't panic if you notice that you cannot meditate for long periods or your mind is always overwhelmed with thought processes. It doesn't always start out great for everyone. It takes time. As you harness the habit through consistency, you will become more proficient.

Understanding the Connection between Martial Arts and Meditation

Meditation embedded within fighting didn't begin today. It has been around from the beginning of time. Before participating in deadly fights, ancient warriors employed different breathing methods to soothe their minds and bodies. Meditation, on the other hand, did not become a part of martial arts until several decades later.

Traditional martial arts possess several philosophical concepts to improve the mental and physical capabilities of students. One of them is a calm mind and control over mental physique and emotions. These are crucial to carrying out and executing complex martial arts moves. There are distinctive breathing techniques that are recognized as meditation.

Source[60]

Martial arts training and competitions are not for the fainthearted. They are very stressful, and their intricacies are quite complicated, especially for beginners. If you are a newbie in the Taekwondo world, you can probably relate to consistent failure or struggle to suppress your anger on the mat when your opponent gets the better of you. This is why you need to meditate. It calms your mind and increases your concentration.

Meditation can take a person into a mental state known as The Flow State or Zone. Entering this state of intensive focus increases your fighting performance, changing how you perceive and understand pain; this will help you maintain a consistently high level of energy during fights. Listed below are three popular methods and exercises you can use to meditate before you jump into a Taekwondo session or training:

Breath and Body Control

Because of its ability to link the mind and body, a martial art such as Taekwondo does not discount the importance of breathing. When battling, you must inhale as you prepare to perform your move and exhale as soon as the motion is completed. You can pull off both defense and attack techniques by focusing on your breathing.

Deeper Meaning

Often certain things prevent a true martial artist from attaining his full potential. It could be a great and deep personal loss, the fear of death, or colossal injuries. To unleash the true fighting potential that invariably leads to excellence, the artist needs a comprehensive understanding of the world around him and his true self.

Self Defense Practice

This is all about awakening your subconscious and focusing on mentally integrating techniques you've previously learned. The goal is for your subconscious to have an automatic response. Although it sounds basic and oversimplified in context, it can take time to perfect.

Mindfulness and Taekwondo

"Mindfulness means paying attention in a particular way, on purpose, in the present moment, and non-judgmentally" - Jon Kabat Zinn

Mindfulness is one of many meditation techniques available, but it is especially important in Taekwondo. It requires you to deliberately pay full attention to the present without judgment or criticism. Practicing it formally requires you to set aside some time for it every day, informally requiring you to pay attention to what you are doing at any time of the day.

Source[61]

The good thing about mindfulness is that you can begin with the mundane - showering, dressing, eating, and so on. I'd recommend starting and mastering the informal practice before going on to the formal. Why? You get to start small and easy and then work your way up. The key is your attention and lack of judgment.

Now, do it formally. Find a comfortable position in a quiet place, close your eyes, and inhale. Let your attention be solely on your in-out breathing rhythm and nothing else. Your mind will wander around, and your senses will be heightened. Take note of your experiences but always return your attention to your breathing. In time, you will find yourself relaxing. Relaxation is important in Taekwondo, as sports psychologists and analysts have determined that anxiety is a huge cause of failure. So, the less anxious you are, the better. Your energy levels will also be regulated, but the focus is perhaps the most significant benefit of mindfulness.

Now with mindfulness, your mind is allowed to wander. But your task is to return your mind to your chosen focus of attention without judgment. When doing it, you will find that this exercise is perpetual. Distraction pops up, but you re-focus again and again. Eventually, you will gain the power to focus on what you want rather than what your brain wants. This focus is vital in Taekwondo because you must focus on your opponent's actions rather than emotions, like fear or doubt.

Conclusively, the greatest advantage of meditation in Taekwondo is its ability to aid you in breaking free from any fear, doubt, or shame as you step onto the mat with a clear mind and a single goal. It helps you learn and grow significantly and harness the pertinent factors to succeed. Since the beginning of time, it has been a part of the combat rituals of skilled warriors, and new trends, studies, and analyses keep emerging.

Not all coaches incorporate meditation into their teachings, but you will do well to engage in it consistently as a beginner. It will help you go a long way in your martial art success.

Remember, everything you want is on the other side of consistency.

Chapter 6: The 24 Essential Patterns in Taekwondo

Patterns in Taekwondo refer to the basic movements of both defense and attack in sequential order, against single or multiple imaginary opponents. Also known as Forms (toul), these patterns form an intricate part of Taekwondo training and are used to measure how far you've come as a student and the skills you have developed.

Patterns are taught and practiced for students to improve their knowledge of Taekwondo techniques, many of which are unique to Taekwondo. By practicing these patterns, you build flexibility and movement, improve your sparring ability, control of your breath, tone, and build of your muscles; you will also notice an increase in balance and coordination. These patterns are typically carried out in accordance with the books written by General Choi Hong Hi, the founder of Taekwondo.

Why Are There 24 Essential Patterns?

The 24 patterns of Taekwondo are based on the philosophy of Grandmaster General Choi Hong Hi. He thought that in order to obtain immortality and live a meaningful life, we should endeavor to leave a spiritual legacy to the future generation. The General opined that man's existence on Earth occupies a very short time in space, and he used the 24 patterns to represent this. In his legacy, he said,

"Here, I leave Taekwondo for mankind as a trace of man in the 20th century. The 24 patterns represent 24 hours, one day or all my life."

He created these core patterns to depict the life of man in just one day. The designs symbolize many significant events and well-known persons who affected the Korean people's history. Taekwondo has 24 patterns stretching across 19 to 72 movements.

Each of the 24 patterns carries a message that inspires you in your everyday life and when performing the movements. These synchronized movements range from simple to complex. The first ones are a combination of symmetrical movements executed with both sides of your body. Each pattern starts and finishes in the same location, allowing you to gain mastery over basic kicks and block techniques and develop a proper solid stance.

These patterns are also aimed at honoring Korean history and impacting each student with Korean historical knowledge and a full grasp of the Taekwondo techniques. Each pattern has a diagram and a specific number of movements that tell of an event or a heroic person in history. The stories chosen are realistic, and the struggles of each of the characters are relatable to people from other nations and cultures that are not Korean. The patterns in Taekwondo teach universal morals and inspire its students to strive for a life of legacy and devotion to a greater good.

The 24 Essential Patterns in Taekwondo

Chon Ji

The first of the essential patterns contains 19 movements that begin from a ready posture of parallel ready stance and end with left foot returns. It is translated as "Heaven the Earth." It refers to the history and creation of mankind and is usually the initial pattern a beginner learns in Taekwondo. The movements in this pattern are divided into 2 similar parts; one part symbolizes Heaven and the other, Earth.

Dan Gun

This is the next essential pattern. It is named after the man who founded the nation of Korea in 2,333 B.C. It involves 21 movements, requires a ready posture of parallel ready stance, and ends with a left foot return.

Do San

This pattern is named after the national Patriot Ahn Chang-Ho, who went by the alias Do San. He dedicated his entire life to Korea, fighting for its independence and educational rights. The pattern requires you to perform 24 moves, beginning with a ready posture of parallel ready stance and ending with right foot return.

Won Hyo

In 686 A.D., during the Silla dynasty, a monk named Won Hyo was credited with introducing Buddhism to the country, and this pattern was named after him. When performing Won Hyo, you make 28 moves, starting with a closed, ready stance, ready posture, and ending with right foot return.

Yul Gok

Famously dubbed the "Confucious of Korea," Yul Gok was a pseudonym of the 16th-century Scholar and Philosopher Yil. This Taekwondo pattern requires you to perform 38 movements that represent the 38th-degree latitude of the philosopher's birthplace. It starts with a ready posture of parallel ready stance and ends with left foot returns. The word "scholar" is represented by the graphic exhibiting this pattern.

Joong Gun

The sixth Taekwondo pattern is named after Ahn Joong Gun, a Korean nationalist who killed the first Japanese Governor-General following the unification of Korea and Japan. At the age of 32, he was imprisoned and hanged at Lui-Shung Prison in 1910. The 32 movements required of this pattern represent Joong Gun's age when he was killed. The pattern starts with a closed, ready stance and ends with left foot returns.

Toi Gye

This pattern was named after the pseudonym of the 16th-century renowned scholar and guru on Neo-Confucianism, Yi Hwang. For this pattern, you must perform 37 moves, starting with closed, ready stance B ready posture, and ending with right foot returns. The 37 movements indicate the guru's birthplace's 37th-degree latitude, and "scholar" is portrayed on the diagram for this pattern. ## Hwa Rang

During the Silla Dynasty in the early 7th century, a company of soldiers known as Hwa Rang Do was formed. This pattern was named after them, and to perform it, you are required to make 29 moves, beginning with a closed, ready stance C ready posture and ending with right foot returns. The 29 movements of this pattern represent the place where Taekwondo was fully developed as a martial art; the 29th Infantry division.

Choong Moo

This pattern was named after the reputed admiral of the Yi Dynasty, Yi Soon-Sin. In 1592, he was credited with the invention of the Kobukson, the pioneer armored battleship. His inventions are said to have paved the way for what is today's submarines. The pattern requires you to perform 30 moves, starting with a ready posture of parallel ready stance and ending with left foot returns. The last move of this pattern is a left-hand attack that represents how the great admiral died.

Kwang Gae

The Kwang Gae pattern is named after the famous 19th ruler of the Goguryeo Dynasty, Gwang-Gae-Toh-Wang. He is known for recapturing most of Manchuria and all other territories that were once lost. To perform this pattern, you need to form 39 movements, starting with a parallel stance with a Heaven hand-ready posture and ending with left foot returns. The 39 movements of this pattern represent the first two numbers of the year Kwang Gae started ruling, 391 A.D. The diagram for this pattern shows the territories recovered and consequent expansion.

Po Eun

Po Eun pattern is named after the pen name of a famous 15th Century poet and subject of the Koryo dynasty. He was one of the most important physicists of his time; he authored a poem, "I would not serve a second master though I may be crucified a hundred times," that is still widely known in Korea. For this pattern, you are expected to perform 36 moves beginning with a ready posture parallel stance with Heaven's hand and ending with left foot returns. The diagram for this pattern shows Po Eun's unending loyalty to his country and the ruler of that time.

Ge Baek

This pattern requires you to perform 44 movements, beginning with a ready posture of parallel ready stance and ending with right foot returns. It was named after Ge Baek, one of the most famous generals of the Baek Je Dynasty in 660 A.D. The general's military discipline is depicted in the diagram of this pattern.

Eui Am

Eui Am refers to the alias used by the leader of the March 1st, 1919, Korean independence movement, Son Byong Hi. The pattern requires you to perform 45 moves beginning with a ready posture of closed, ready stance D and ending with right foot returns. This pattern's 45 movements correspond to Byong Hi's age when he transformed Dong Hak to Chong Kyo (Oriental Culture to Heavenly Religion) in 1905. The diagram of this pattern showed his insurmountable character when he led his country.

Choong Jang

General Kim Duk Ryang, a Yi Dynasty general in the 14th century, was given the pseudonym General Kim Duk Ryang. It requires you to perform 52 movements starting with a ready posture of closed, ready stance A and ending with left foot returns. The final movement of this pattern is a left-hand attack that represents the untimely death of the General in prison. He was 27 years old.

Ko Dang

Ko Dang pattern requires you to perform 45 movements beginning with parallel stance with a twin side elbow and ending with right foot returns. It was named after the alias of one of Korea's national patriots, Cho Man Sik. He devoted his life to the independence movement of his country and fought for the education of Koreans. The 45 movements of this pattern represent the last two digits of the year Korea gained freedom from the Japanese: 1945.

Juche

Juche is the philosophical view that man is the ruler of the world and consequently his destiny. That is, man has authority over everything in this world and determines his path. This concept came from the Baekdu Mountain, which is supposed to reflect the Korean people's spirit. Performing this pattern requires 45 movements ending with right foot returns. The diagram of the Juche pattern symbolizes the Baekdu Mountain.

Sam-IL

This pattern represents the historical period of the Korean Independence movement that began on March 1st, 1919. To carry out this pattern, you need to perform 33 movements, starting with a closed, ready stance C ready posture and ending with right foot returns. The 33 movements of this pattern symbolize the 33 pioneer patriots who organized the independence movement.

Yoo-Sin

This pattern requires you to perform 68 moves, starting with a ready posture of warrior ready stance B and ending with right foot returns. General Kim Yoo-Sin, one of the Silla Dynasty's leading Generals, is the inspiration behind this design. The warrior stance B ready posture represents a sword drawn at the right side instead of the left side. This portrayed the General's error in obeying the King's instructions to fight alongside foreign forces against his own nation. The last two digits of the year Korea was united, 668 A.D., are used as symbolism throughout the 68 movements.

Choi Yong

General Choi Yong, the 14th century Koryo Dynasty Commander-in-Chief and Premier of the Armed Forces, has an influence on this pattern. He was well-liked and respected for his sincerity and devotion. He was assassinated by a number of his subordinate officers, commanded by General Yi Sung Gae, who went on to become the first emperor of the Lee Dynasty. This pattern requires 45 moves to complete correctly, beginning with a closed, ready posture C and concluding with right foot returns.

Yon Gae

Yon Gae Somoon was a well-known General during the Goguryeo period; this pattern was named after him. To perform this pattern, you need to perform 49 movements beginning from a ready posture of warrior ready stance A and ending with left foot returns. The 49 movements correspond to the year Yon Gae forced the Yang Dynasty to flee Korea after destroying over 300,000 of their warriors at Ansi Sung. It was the year 649 A.D.

UL-JI

This pattern requires you to perform 42 moves starting with a parallel stance with an X-back hand-ready posture and ending with left foot returns. It was named after General Ul-Ji Moon Dok, who is credited with defending Korea against a nearly one-million-strong Tang invasion in 612 A.D. Using hit-and-run guerilla tactics, the General was able to annihilate a substantial portion of their forces. This pattern's schematic is in the shape of an "L," which represents the General's surname. The 42 movements of the pattern represent the age of the author who designed the diagram.

Moon-Moo

The Silla Dynasty's 30th King, who was buried at Dae Wang Am (which translates to Great King's Rock), inspired the Moon-moo Taekwondo pattern. The King requested that his body, after his death, be placed in the sea so that he could protect his country from Japan. The Sok Gul Am (Cave Stone), a noteworthy artifact of Silla Dynasty culture, was created to protect his grave after he was buried. This pattern necessitates 61 movements, which correspond to the last two numbers of the year Moon Moo attained the throne, 661 A.D.

So-San

This pattern calls for 72 movements, beginning with a closed, ready stance, ready posture, and ending with left foot returns. Choi Hyong Ung, a 16th century Lee Dynasty monk, was given this pattern's name. The pattern's 72 movements indicate the monk's age when, in 1592, he and his student Sa Myung Dang assembled a battalion of monk soldiers to resist Japanese pirates on the Korean Peninsula.

Se Jong

This pattern is named after Se-Jong, the great Korean King and a renowned meteorologist credited with inventing the alphabets of the Korean language in 1443. To execute this pattern, you need to perform 24 moves, starting with a ready posture of closed, ready stance B and ending with left foot returns. The 24 movements depict the 24 letters of the Korean alphabet, while the "Z" diagram for this pattern symbolizes the

King.

Tong-IL

This pattern requires you to perform 42 moves starting with a ready posture of parallel stance with an overlapped backhand and ending with left foot returns. It symbolizes the union of the Korean nation that has been separated since 1945. The diagram of the pattern is shaped as "I," signifying a uniform and single race.

Important Tips to Note When Performing Taekwondo Patterns

You are expected to start and end each pattern at the same location. It shows how accurate you are in performing the pattern.

- You must maintain the correct posture and face correctly at all times.
- You need to ensure your muscles are either tensed or relaxed at the crucial and precise moment when performing the pattern.
- You must perform each pattern with a rhythmic movement that is void of stiffness.
- You need to ensure acceleration and deceleration of patterns per the instructions given.
- You must perfect each pattern before moving to the next one.
- As a student, you are expected to know the purpose of every movement.
- As a student, you are required to perform every pattern with realism.

Chapter 7: The Five Tenets of Taekwondo

If you have attended any standard Taekwondo class in the past, then you must have heard this phrase at some point. The tenets of Taekwondo are often recited as part of the Taekwondo student oath in most schools. At the beginning of class, the pupils recite the oath, either in unison or by repeating after their instructor.

The Taekwondo student pledge serves to remind students of their responsibility to themselves, the art, their instructor, their fellow students, and society. So, the tenets form an integral part of the oath that students are expected to be familiar with.

Luckily as a beginner reading this book, you can become acquainted with them earlier than most. More than just learning how to fight, you get to understand some of the fundamental ideas of the sport and appreciate them.

To begin, we need to understand what a tenet is. A dictionary or an encyclopedia defines a tenet as an opinion, dogma, principle, or doctrine that a person or an organization believes, practices, and maintains as true.

An encapsulating definition, perhaps, but it does not do justice to the rich history and heritage from where Taekwondo tenets were derived. The point is to understand the role of these tenets. They were created to give the ancient warriors powerful motivations, and the same remains true as the driving force behind all the learning processes, even today.

- Courtesy
- Integrity
- Perseverance
- Self-Control
- Indomitable Spirit

These are the five tenets of modern Taekwondo, but they haven't always been like this. The old tenets of the ancient art were known as the Hwarang code of conduct and comprised of five rules. They have the same meaning as these modern ones but are written in a more flowery and superfluous language. The Hwarang code is:

- Rigid loyalty to the King and country
- Respect and obedience to one's parents
- Unswerving loyalty and trust to friends
- Display of courage and never retreat in battle
- Prudence in the use of violence and taking a life

While connecting how one came to become the other would be tricky, it's easy to see their similarities. Respect and obedience are synonymous with courtesy. Loyalty and trust are a significant part of integrity. Prudence in the use of violence and killing is self-control. "Display of courage and never retreating" shows perseverance and an indomitable spirit.

As always, Taekwondo stays true to its roots.

The five tenets are a source of guidance to serious students of the art. They are a moral code and must be adhered to, not merely every time you're in the dojang, but every time you use the skills. Taekwondo is spiritual philosophy, and it is just as much of a mental discipline as it is a physical one. Your success in understanding the mental part of Taekwondo will also determine your physical success.

Respect for the rich history and tradition of Taekwondo must always be freshly embedded within the mind. It is why most coaches and instructors will recite all the tenets once the students have bowed on the mats to remind students that Taekwondo revolves around self-improvement and humility. The greatest thing about the tenets of

Taekwondo is that they can serve you in your everyday life, too.

Analyzing the Tenets

Source[62]

Courtesy (Yah Yie)

Courtesy is another word for politeness and humility and enduring respect for oneself and others. It is immense consideration for others and is usually seen and displayed in the dojang. Shoes are removed in the dojang as a sign of respect for the training facility, and students bow to the Grandmasters and Black Belts to demonstrate respect for their accomplishments. Whenever the Grandmaster or instructor is giving a lesson, students must remain silent and listen actively; side discussions symbolize disrespect. If you are a beginner who has never been inside a dojang before, you must remember these things.

Often as students progress through the ranks and become friendly with their tutors and seniors, complacency about courtesy creeps in, which is when vigilance is required. Being friendly is great, but being a perfect embodiment of one who adheres to the tenets at all times is even greater. Courtesy also requires respect without seeking gratification. Sometimes, students are courteous only to their seniors for what they can get, but never courteous to newcomers; this is unacceptable.

The truth is that your dedication to the tenets will not be tested at your inception stage. It is easy for a beginner to adhere to them, but as you gain more expertise, you will need more self-awareness and understand the necessity of constantly renewing your dedication. It isn't surprising to see young artists courteous when they are at the lower rung of the ladder only to attain the black belt status and turn into what no one recognizes.

Integrity (Yum Chee)

Integrity is steadfast adherence to a strict moral and ethical code. Taekwondo has its ethics, and instructors, grandmasters, black belts, students, and beginners must all adhere to them. For instance, instructors must teach or demonstrate techniques that are deliberately harmful to the student's opponent. Even when students are taught the bone-breaking moves of self-defense, emphasis is placed upon the principle that they are only executed when the use or threat of force is life-threatening.

As a budding martial artist, you must recognize that integrity is one of the virtues you must hold dear. You must learn to be true to yourself, your dojang, your Grandmaster, and your training institute. Understand that moral codes and ethics are as important as learning Taekwondo techniques. In Taekwondo, integrity also means staying true to your word. You are a beginner today, but one day you'll evolve to the point of teaching others. How will you handle it? You must be able to teach and willingly help those who need help. Integrity means respect and loyalty. It means staying true to your word and yourself. It means defining right and wrong and listening to your conscience.

Perseverance (Inn Nae)

An old Asian Proverb says: Patience leads to value or merit. Perseverance is a trait needed for the growth process, and, as a beginner, it cannot be more strongly emphasized how important this is for you. Taekwondo is a complex sport, and you cannot be weak at heart and hope to excel in this sport. Learning to perfect your techniques - polishing them until they gleam - is only attainable by perseverance. *Those with black belts didn't get there by chance!*

Perseverance at a task is in itself a skill. As you progress within Taekwondo, you will discover your unique set of strengths and weaknesses. There will be certain moves you'll find easy to perfect and others not so easy. But no matter how tough or arduous the process is, you must learn to be persistent and dedicated to never giving up on perfecting your flaws. Perseverance is the one tenet that will lead you to excellence and give you a sense of fulfillment when you achieve what you have worked assiduously for.

At all levels, you have to renew your dedication to perseverance. There will be times when you feel safe and assured about certain moves you think you have perfected, only to receive a rude awakening at a training practice or, even worse, during a tournament. It is perseverance that will drag you back to the mat and ensure you refine and fine-tune what you thought you knew.

As a beginner, the best way to handle the steep learning journey is to take it one day at a time. For every day you show up, strive to be better than what you were yesterday. When you constantly have that principle at the back of your mind, you'll be more proficient at Taekwondo until you become top-notch.

Self-Control (Kook Kee)

Taekwondo is a combat martial art that features foot strikes, kicks, and punches. It requires you to learn how to control yourself because it's very easy to cross the line. Imagine, for one instance, that you become a black belt, and you're sparring with someone you intensely dislike. It could be tempting to beat them to a pulp by executing flawless moves, and yeah, that could make you feel good about yourself, but that's not what Taekwondo is about. A lack of self-control can prove to be disastrous for the opponent and student.

Self-control is also about paying attention to your instructor and not moving an inch until you are instructed to. It means maintaining your calm while your opponent trashes you hard. It means you respond well to criticisms no matter how angry they make you. Besides Taekwondo, all martial arts require years of understanding and patient practice. If you have no self-control, you wouldn't be able to last.

Indomitable Spirit (Back Jok Bool Kool)

Taekwondo is all about self-improvement. Whenever you find the terrain difficult, remind yourself why you began training in the first place.

Have you seen the epic movie, Troy? It starred Hollywood Powerhouse actor Brad Pitt as the legendary Greek warrior Achilles. In the first battle where the Greek army advances, Achilles and his Myrmidons singlehandedly take on the fearsome warriors of Troy at the beach. They were resilient enough to take down a city that had never previously been conquered.

Source[68]

Let's use a more martial arts example. Remember the movie "Karate Kid"? (Fun fact, the movie should be called "Kung Fu Kid" because Dre Parker actually learns Kung Fu and not Karate). During the tournament, Dre was badly wounded and was told his injury was so bad that it was advisable to quit fighting, yet he persisted because he was determined to conquer his fears that night.

One final movie reference to drive home the point; do you remember the battle movie 300? Leonidas and his army of 300 Spartan warriors faced the powerfully superior army of Xerxes and displayed one of the most profound acts of courage the world has ever seen. Their epitaph reads: Here lies 300, who did their duty.

These movies are used as examples because they are warrior movies. Even if you are a beginner, you must understand the day you decided to step onto the mat in a training center; you became a warrior. And as a warrior, you must show courage, even in the face of overwhelming odds.

Perseverance is the physical effort required to face challenges, but an indomitable spirit is the will of the soul that is necessary to conquer the opposition. You display an indomitable spirit when you consistently choose to rise above the fears gnawing at your heart. You display an indomitable spirit when you choose not to be weak-willed and face your opponent without fear. You display an indomitable spirit when you choose to keep competing at tournaments, even though you have lost so much. You display an indomitable spirit when you have trouble mastering your moves, but you don't stop showing up for practice. You need a fighting spirit to succeed in life, and Taekwondo is not an exception.

Contemporary martial artists largely ignore the five tenets of Taekwondo, even though they're chanted like a mantra in school. It might be tempting to do the same, and you might even meet those who tell you that these tenets are old-fashioned. Yet, be assured with all confidence that adhering to these tenets is a sure guarantee of success.

Additionally, these tenets can serve you well in life. Self-control teaches you how to keep cool under fire. There is a saying that you can regret the harshness of your words after your anger dies, but you can never regret the silence you kept. Integrity will help you keep your word and stay loyal in your relationships. Courtesy ensures that you respect everyone, including strangers. Perseverance and an indomitable spirit will give you immense willpower and courage to attain whatever dreams you have outside Taekwondo.

Taekwondo isn't just a combat skill. It's a life skill, too. Living by the five tenets helps you become not only a better fighter but a better human being. It gives you the physical and mental discipline to improve all areas of your life. The tenets can fit in effortlessly with any religious or philosophical beliefs you might have. So, study the five tenets and let them be a source of guidance throughout your martial arts journey. It will be one of the best life-changing decisions you'll ever make.

Chapter 8: Taekwondo Hand Techniques

Most people believe Taekwondo is a martial art that is all about the kicks, and they aren't entirely wrong. But, while kicks were a predominant staple of the sport at its onset and still remain an integral part of it today, there are a variety of hand techniques also still commonly used. This chapter focuses on some of the hand punches you will learn in Taekwondo and tricks and strategies to improve them.

Throwing the perfect punch in Taekwondo, like in any other martial art, takes time and practice. You must learn how to execute each technique correctly in order to obtain the necessary skills; it will give you an edge, especially in competitive matches.

There are several hand technique combinations in Taekwondo. Some are more popular than others, and the complexity also widely varies from one technique to another. Here are a few things to know about Taekwondo hand techniques.

Punches Are a Secret Weapon

Punches are mostly underutilized in Taekwondo, especially in competitive games. Most people focus on kicks without paying enough attention to their hand skills. This could be an advantage for an opponent who invests their time and effort in developing hand techniques.

Not only do people forget to throw punches, but they also hardly defend against them. It is quite interesting considering you can earn between 1 to 2 points for landing a punch, depending on the rules of the competition.

The Mexican national Taekwondo team takes advantage of this. They are currently one of the top teams globally and have dominated for more than two decades. You'll notice that their performances incorporate more punches than most, which contributes to their dominance in the sport - further proving that you can stack up valuable points with punches if you know how to apply your hand techniques correctly.

How to Throw a Good Punch in Taekwondo

Contrary to popular belief, you need more than just your hands to throw good punches. Many hand techniques in Taekwondo require you to use your entire body. In addition to your hands, your arm, abdomen, and feet can contribute to the effectiveness of your punch.

Source[64]

- **Your Feet:** In Taekwondo, your feet are your solid base and foundation. You must be as stable and balanced on the floor as possible to generate enough power for your hand technique. Most moves require you to stand on the balls of your feet to stop, turn, and pivot your punches properly.
- **Abdomen:** This is the center of your body. In all physical sports, including Taekwondo, the abs serve the purpose of connecting your hands to your feet. Power generated from your feet is transmitted to your hands, so you need to learn to tighten your core to ensure you're not losing the power behind your punch.
- **Arms:** While most hand techniques in Taekwondo involve the hand, the arms are equally important since they do the movement. Your fist and wrist must be at the correct level of firmness during a punch to avoid injury.

Taekwondo Hand Techniques

There is an assortment of punches and hand techniques in Taekwondo; below are some of the most popular ones.

The Jab

This method is employed in Taekwondo for both defense and distance measurement. The jab can also be used to bait an opponent, leaving them vulnerable to a counterattack. The jab is designed to provoke your opponent into attacking while you counter with a kick. The jab is delivered as a direct blow from a distance, with your arm over your leading foot. This technique should be executed with speed and timed explosiveness if you want to catch your opponent off guard. It is typically accompanied by a slight rotation of the hips and torso. The fist is rotated at a 90 degrees angle through the punch, becoming horizontal on impact.

Bring the lead shoulder up to guard your chin while the hand is completely extended; the other hand remains next to your face to guard your jaw. Retract your lead hand into a guard position in front of your face as soon as you make contact with the target. Instead of only striking with your hand while throwing jabs, transfer some of your body weight into your punch to sustain the blow. For maximum effect, aim for a 10 to 15cm hit behind the target surface. When in combat, try to strike through your opponent rather than merely making contact on the surface.

As a note of precaution, you should ensure that your wrist is in proper alignment when you deliver a jab. You risk an injury if it bends on impact, especially against a solid surface.

Straight or Cross Punch

A straight or cross punch is similar to a jab, but instead, you strike the surface or opponent with the rear of your hand and not the forward fist. Because you have to twist your body into the strike when delivering it, a straight punch normally has more power than a jab. You strike your opponent with the first two knuckles of your fist when doing a cross or straight punch. Depending on the rules of the competition, it might be hurled towards the head or the body. When your opponent is approaching you, straight punches are the best option.

Uppercut

The uppercut is a strike that involves moving your first in an upward motion while striking an opponent. Turning your torso upward to load the arm and shooting your hands upward to hit an opponent is how this punch is accomplished. In a close fighting situation, an uppercut is best employed to land a body shot on your opponent. For maximum effect, your shoulder must be lowered along with your knees. Then, propelling your body upward and forward, you extend your fist towards the opponent's chin and face.

Uppercut

Hook Punch

It's a more compact or shorter variant of the standard straight or cross punch. It is usually thrown with the front hand and targeted to an opponent's sides. When delivering the hook punch, your body makes a slight tight turning movement.

Hook Punch

In Taekwondo, the hook punch is considered a more controlled and effective alternative to the more traditional haymaker punch. Use this punch to land a body shot in close combat or to get beyond an opponent's guard; it's also more difficult to parry a hook punch.

You can use the hook to lead a cross punch or as part of a combined sequence of punches, with the last being the hook. The hook is also effective as a counter strike against an opponent. Push into your hook punch with your leading leg and perpendicularly turn your foot while throwing the punch to give it more strength.

Back Fist

In Taekwondo, there are different types of back fists. The most common type is performed with your front hand, similar to the jab. But in this case, the padded part of your backhand is used. At the end of this punch, flick your hand as it hits the side of the opponent's head (depending on the organization, hitting with the padded end of your hand may be prohibited).

There are two versions of a back fist in Taekwondo; the Turn Back Fist and the Spinning Back Fist. The difference is very subtle.

The turn back fist; Before striking an opponent with the back of your hand, the hand should be rotated around 180 degrees.

The spinning back fist; there is a 360-degree spin of the hand. This type of punch typically follows another strike that initiates the spin. Both types of back fists are typically set up with a punch or kick.

Back Fist

Hammer Fist

To perform the hammer fist technique, make a motion similar to if you were swinging a hammer. With the fleshy part of your hand, you should execute a downward motion. The hammer fist can be used to attack above an opponent's guard and can also be thrown off a spin or turn for extra impact.

Hammer Fist

Swing your fist downward towards the target to execute this technique. One major advantage of the hammer fist, especially for beginners, is that it is quite safe, and there's no risk of injury to your hand or knuckles since you hit the target using the bottom padded part of your fist.

Extended Knuckle Punch

An extended knuckle punch is a variation of the traditional fist configuration used to deliver a normal punch. To throw an extended knuckle fist, one finger protrudes forward (usually the knuckle of the middle finger). The knuckle is used to generate the impact, concentrating more force on a smaller area for a greater impact.

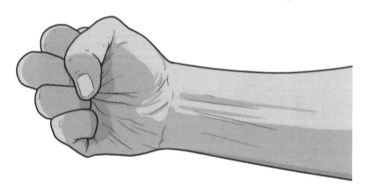

Extended Knuckle Punch

The extended knuckle is often used to attack the pressure points. The technique takes its roots from traditional Kung Fu. However, it is considered a high-level Taekwondo move only used by advanced students because it requires a level of accuracy and conditioning most beginners don't have.

To deliver this punch right, you are expected to relax your body as much as possible during the strike and tense it right at the point of impact, relaxing it again when recoiling your hand. The sequence of relaxation and tensing the body helps to attain the highest possible velocity while also achieving a maximum transfer of force.

Spear Hand Strike

The spear hand strike is an open hand strike. Aptly named because the hand is fully extended, giving it the appearance of a spear. The strike is delivered with the tips of the fingers and is usually targeted at the eye, throat, or other more sensitive targets. One significant advantage of this technique is that it extends the range of the hand by a few inches.

Spear Hand Strike

Note that the spear hand strike must be used with caution. If you miss and hit a hard target, you risk injuring your fingers. Also, while this technique is commonly taught in Taekwondo, it is considered illegal in tournaments.

Ridge Hand Strike

The Ridge Hand Strike is another common open hand technique. When executing this punch, your hands and fingers are extended while you strike the target with the thumb side of your open hands.

This strike is quite effective; it is delivered in the same manner as a hook or overhand punch. However, to prevent injury, you are expected to tuck your thumb into your palms to avoid injury when you hit the target.

Differences in Hand Technique Rules between Taekwondo Organizations

There are different rules regarding the various hand techniques in Taekwondo. The WTF, ITF, and ATA each have specific rules about which punches are allowed and what body part is off-limits.

World Taekwondo Federation (WTF): Martial arts fighters are only allowed to strike in straight blows using the knuckle area of their hands, according to WTF guidelines. In addition, punches can only land on the abdomen, truck, or uppercuts; hooks are not permitted.

International Taekwondo Federation (ITF): The ITF's rules for hand punches are similar to the WTF's, with the exception that the ITF allows hits to the head. In addition, the ITF permits contestants to throw a variety of blows rather than just straight punches.

American Taekwondo Association (ATA): The rules for ATA sparring are comparable to those of the WTF. Only straight abdominal blows are legal.

Tips for Improving Your Hand Techniques in Taekwondo

Consistent practice and training are needed to sharpen your Taekwondo hand techniques. Like everything in Taekwondo, the more you practice, the better you get. It is also important that you understand your hand techniques' philosophy of push and pull and hard and soft execution.

The principle of push and pull has a major impact on the delivery of your punches. When you push your punching hand forward, you must pull the non-punching hand backward with as much power you are pushing the punching hand. The same principle applies to blocking. When you block, pull the non-blocking hand with equal power as the other hand to maximize its full potential.

Additionally, it's imperative to master how to be soft and hard in various aspects of your technique. Being completely hard is not good, and conversely, all soft is also not great. Finding the sweet spot between both ends of the extreme is essential. A martial artist must learn to relax before executing a technique and tense up just at the right moment to focus all of his power behind a punch for maximum effect.

As mentioned earlier, hand techniques involve your entire body and not only your hands. Everything from your feet (your lower energy center) to the tip of your finger has to be involved in delivering a blow. Your hip is used to crack that whip to generate enough power and speed for your blows.

Also, you must have safety considerations in mind for each hand technique and pay proper attention to them. You can risk a sprain, dislocation, or even breaking your hand if your hand strikes are executed ignorantly.

Exercises to Improve Your Hand Techniques

There are different methods of training you can use to improve your hand techniques. Three of the most common ways to boost your punches include:

- **Train with a Punching Bag:** Taekwondo schools usually have a punching bag you can use to train. To strengthen your hand techniques, your coach should lead you through sessions of bag practice.

- **Mitt Training:** Another method that instructors use to assist with this practice is to use a punching bag. It requires teaching pupils how to synchronize punches while holding mitts for them to hit. Conditioning training is also conducted with this technique.

- **Technical Sparring:** Students are sometimes paired with a sparring partner, encouraging them to practice various hand techniques on one another. Note that Taekwondo punches and strikes are best practiced under the supervision of your instructor.

Chapter 9: Taekwondo Foot Techniques

It is no secret that Taekwondo boasts some impressive kicks. They are called Chagi in Korean, the most recognizable aspect of the sport. Taekwondo kicks can be performed through a variety of methods, including jump kicks at various heights, spin kicks, or a combination of these. The type of kick to be used depends on the specific situation. While some kicks are great for self-defense, others are more suitable for attacks in competitions. This chapter looks at some common Taekwondo kicks, what they're used for and how they're executed.

The Front Kick ("Ap Chagi")

The front kick, also known as the flash kick or snap kick because of how fast it is executed, is among the first sets of kicks you will learn as a beginner. It is a powerful kick useful at both beginner and advanced levels of the sport.

When executing a front kick, you raise the knee of your kicking leg high to your waist level. Then, move your foot forward towards the target; this exerts a forward force that pushes the target backward. The front kick can be used to inflict significant damage.

With any Taekwondo kick, the resting or off leg is just as important as the kick itself during execution. For this kick, you bend your off-leg slightly to execute the kick. Your weight should be rested on the ball of your foot and not flat on the floor. You may also lift your foot slightly off the floor but be careful not to overdo it. During the kick, the off foot rotates slightly away from the target.

The position of your arm and torso are important, too. Bring your fist up towards your chest as in a blocking position. As the kicking leg is brought forward, the arm on that side should be brought downward and pulled back.

In WTF and ITF styles of the sport, the toes are bent upward when executing this kick to ensure that you strike the target with the balls of your feet. In some other styles, the toes are pointed straight in the same direction as the rest of the foot. This way, the topside of your foot is used to hit the target. In this style, the reach of your leg is also extended.

The Side Kick ("Yeop Chagi")

This is another move that you'll probably be expected to learn early on in your Taekwondo career. The sidekick is also a powerful kick that can have different implications depending on the Taekwondo rules you are following.

To perform this kick, you need to raise your knee while also rotating your body about 90 degrees. You then exert force by straightening your leg. When executing this kick, you should pivot your non-kicking foot on the ball so that it is fully turned away from the target at the moment of impact.

Your torso must be bent to one side during a sidekick; this is particularly important if you are doing a high sidekick. If you're kicking with your right leg, your right arm lowers down behind your kicking leg as you kick it forward. The left arm is pulled to the chest area with the fist closed in a blocking stance.

As with the front kick, the part of the foot used to hit the target depends on the Taekwondo rules you are following. But the options are either between the outside edge of your foot and the heel.

The Roundhouse Kick ("Dollyeo Chagi")

The Roundhouse kick is arguably the most referenced Taekwondo kick in pop culture. This kick is very powerful when mastered. To perform the roundhouse kick, the knee of your kicking leg is raised and aimed towards the target. Next, you pivot the balls of your resting foot and turn your hip slightly; this will turn your body sideways towards the target. Then, straighten your leg, moving the shin parallel to the ground as you kick.

In some versions, the top of your foot is the striking surface for this kick. In this situation, you hold your ankle straight to align with the rest of your leg and point your toes along the same line. In other versions, the kick is executed with the balls of your foot. If this is the intention, your ankle and toes should be bent upward.

Your non-kicking leg is a vital part of the roundhouse kick. It propels your body as it rotates to turn your side towards the target. It is important that you pivot on the balls of your resting foot. Typically, the non-kicking foot must be turned away from the target at the moment of impact.

When you turn to do the roundhouse kick with your right leg, you have to bring your right arm down to the right; it provides counter-rotation to your kicking leg. Some people prefer to bring the right hand behind the right leg at the moment of impact.

The Back Kick ("Dwit Chagi")

One of the more complex Taekwondo techniques is the back kick. As the name implies, you have to perform this kick by setting yourself up away from the target. Do this the wrong way, and you will end up losing your balance or falling over.

To execute the back kick, you have to pivot away from your opponent and execute a kick linearly backward once you are facing away from the target. It is important to note that although many people refer to this kick as the Spinning Back Kick, the kicking leg does not make a spinning motion, and the spin only refers to how the martial artist turns their body during the kick.

Your torso should lean slightly forwards as you execute the kick to increase the height of this kick. Also, turn your head to the side as you execute the kick so that you can see where you are kicking.

The Outer/Inner Crescent Kick ("An Chagi / Bakkat Chagi")

There are two variations of the Crescent kick; inner and outer. They are also commonly referred to as the inside and outside crescent kicks. Both variations involve forming an arc; in one, the arc goes from the inside to the outside, and from the outside to the inside in the other variation.

Both types start the same way, with you raising your leg and bending it like you're about to do a front kick. The knee is then pointed to the target's left or right side. When the snap's energy is deflected, your leg whips across the target in an arc, striking from the side.

This move is great for aiming for an opponent's defenses – striking the head or knocking down their hands before launching a close attack.

In the case of an outward crescent kick, the arc forms at the center of your body and moves outward. You kick the target with the blade (outside edge) of your foot in this manner.

For the inward crescent kick, the arcing motion begins from the side of your body and gradually moves inwards to the center. This way, the kick is executed with the inside edge of your foot.

The Hook Kick ("Huryeo Chagi")

The hook kick is a newer Taekwondo technique. In execution, it is just like the roundhouse kick but with a twist. At the end of the kick, when the foot is extended, there is a backward sweeping motion as your leg impacts the target creating hooking motion.

When doing the hook kick, strike the opponent with the heel of your foot (or the flat of your foot when sparring). The start of the hook kick is similar to the sidekick. You raise your kicking leg's knee forward towards the target, whereupon you pivot your off foot to the side, moving your kicking leg's hips over.

When kicking past the target with a hook kick, you consciously angle your leg towards your kicking foot toes. By the time your leg hits the target, it is extended a little to the side. Your heel strikes the target at full extension, then you bend the knee while in position and snap it to the side.

Typically, the back of your heel is used to deliver a hook kick, but at a closer range, the back of the calf or back of a bent knee may also serve to strike.

The Ax Kick ("Naeryeo Chagi")

This is another very recent addition to competitive Taekwondo. As the name implies, executing this kick is similar to the motion you make when bringing down an ax to cut a log of wood. You begin by raising the ax above your head and swinging it down towards the log (at a slight angle for better impact).

The ax kick works the same way. You pull your leg down by exerting a downward pressure while keeping your heel directed down to the ground after raising it high up towards an opponent. Any area of the body above the torso can be a target area for this kick, including the torso, head, collarbone, or shoulder.

The ax kick is different from the other kick in its execution. While most other kicks involve bending your knee first, this is not the case with the ax kick. Instead, your kicking leg is held straight as it is raised (slightly to the side of your target) and brought down forcefully.

Like the crescent kicks, there are two variations for the ax kick. It is called the inside-outside ax kick if your leg is raised towards the center of your body and brought down slightly outside as you do your downward strike. In contrast, if the kicking leg is raised towards the outside of your body and brought down slightly in the center, it is an outside-to-inside ax kick.

The Ax Kick

The Knee Strike ("Mureup Chigi")

If we're strict with the definition of the word, then the knee strike isn't exactly a "kick." However, the knee is an essential part of any good kick and executes a powerful blow on its own when used correctly.

The Knee Strike

The knee strike can be done in a variety of ways. Even yet, the main premise is that they all require getting the opponent into the knee or driving the knee towards them. Knee strikes are more prevalent in mixed martial arts (MMA) and other kinds of martial arts. In Taekwondo, a knee strike is directed at the head or body of your opponent. To execute this move, you must control your opponent's body or head and bring the knee forward. Simultaneously, the knee is raised to strike at the opponent. When making this move, keep your striking leg's ankle straight (pointing downward).

The Scissor Kick ("Kawi Chagi")

This is a more advanced kick performed by jumping up into the air. The scissors kick is not commonly used in competitions or even for self-defense because of its complex execution. Instead, it is reserved for demonstrations.

The Scissor Kick

Executing the scissors kick involves jumping up to execute a kick that hits two opponents simultaneously, and each leg is used to target an opponent. Of course, this is a very impressive move if executed correctly, but hardly practical in a combat situation.

Flying Side and Back Kicks ("Twi Myo Yeop Chagi / Twi Myo Dwi Chagi")

These two kicks are perhaps the most legendary in Taekwondo. They are an advanced version of the sidekick and the back kick, with the key distinction being that they're performed while "flying."

To understand how this kick works, it is important that you understand the distinction between a jumping kick and a flying kick. The term "flying" is often used to indicate that the martial artists' body has significant momentum when performing the action. To perform a flying kick, the martial artist needs a running start to generate enough momentum for the kick.

For instance, for the flying back kick, you run forwards towards the opponent, rotate your body 180 degrees so that you are facing away from the target then deliver the kick. The flying back kick is delivered linearly, meaning the leg does not arc as it makes its way towards the target, and instead, it is thrust directly at the target while still in midair.

The flying side kick and flying back kicks are mainly used in demonstrations than in actual combat situations, but they may sometimes be used in sparring.

Tips for Improving Your Kicks in Taekwondo

To add more power and speed to your kick in Taekwondo, you must work on increasing your muscle strength. A combination of exercises, a stretch routine, and consistently practicing and perfecting the technique of your skill will help boost your form and ensure the proper execution of your kick techniques.

Exercising Your Vital Muscle Groups

However, first, you must become familiar with the main muscle groups that determine the strength and speed of your kicking techniques. Your quads, calves, abs, lower back muscles, and lateral obliques play an important role in your execution of the various Taekwondo kick techniques.

Targeting these muscles during your workout routines will improve your performance since they make up an interconnected network that contributes to the overall results of your kick in Taekwondo. If any of the links in this connection is missing due to an error, weakness, or injury, it will be impossible to reproduce a Taekwondo skill with the right speed and power. Therefore, your training routine should include specific exercises that target each of these muscles to prevent this. The goal is to improve the strength and flexibility of each muscle to boost overall performance.

Exercises for the Quads

The quadriceps are made up of four muscles that coordinate movement. Squats, leg extensions, and lunges are ideal exercises for targeting these muscles in particular. The good thing is that you can do these workouts in your home with no need for specialized workout equipment. You can also boost the intensity of these workouts in your home or public gym with barbells, dumbbells, kettlebells, and other weights.

Hamstrings

You need your hamstrings for foot rotation during a kick. The strength of your hamstrings is also crucial for achieving the hip extension and knee flexion required for good kick execution. Excellent exercises that target this muscular group are lunges, glute and ham raises, and deadlifts. Squats and kettlebell swings are also beneficial for increasing explosive power.

Calves

Most people believe that the calf muscles have a minor role in kick production. However, they are missing out on a lot. They are an important part of the interconnected chain, and without them, your kick will be weak. Some workouts you can do to boost their strength include step-ups, calf raises, and lunges.

Abs

Your core muscle is the center point of the body, and you need a strengthened core not only for kicks but also for punches and blocks. In almost every martial art, including Taekwondo, emphasis is placed on core strength, and routines like pushups, deadlifts, pull-ups, and crunches are often recommended for stronger abs and core muscles.

Lower Back

Your lower back carries a lot of weight when performing kicks. Strengthening your lower back boosts the power and speed of your kicks and prevents strain and other injuries. To develop your lower back muscles, try exercises like pull-ups, chin-ups, face pulls, pullovers, and dumbbell rows.

Lateral Obliques

This muscle group is particularly important for executing turn and spin kicks. Because they demand a lot of lateral flexion and trunk rotation to produce optimal outcomes, techniques like these rely on the lateral oblique. Exercises such as lateral pull-downs and side planks are excellent for strengthening your lateral obliques.

Stretching Exercises and Taekwondo

Most kicks in Taekwondo require you to be as flexible as possible for proper execution. Therefore, to master the art, you must include a stretch routine in your training regimen because it boosts your muscle flexibility. Stretching exercise also helps to condition your muscles and prevent injury.

Source[66]

However, it's imperative not to go straight to stretching workouts. Before you begin stretching, you should complete a short warm-up session to get your blood flowing properly. Warm-up for 3-5 minutes; you can include shadowboxing or jump-roping before beginning stretch activities.

Pull Down Stretch

One of the most typical stretch exercises for increasing flexibility is the pull-down stretch, which is also relatively basic. Reach down to the floor while maintaining your legs at shoulder width. Try holding this position for about 10 seconds before moving your hands from one side of your body to the other.

Crouching Stance

Lean over to one side of your body with one of your knees bent to one side, and the other knee is kept straight. Try holding this position for about 10 seconds before shifting to the other side and repeating the same procedure. Do this for both sides of your body about 2 or 3 times.

Horse Stance or Ready Stance

This stance has been explained extensively earlier in this book. The horse stance is halfway between a squat and a lunge. To maximize the stretch's tension, keep your back vertical, draw your chest out, and push your legs outwards while pushing your hands outwards. Hold this position for 30 seconds to one minute.

Splits

Splits are common in martial arts, and Taekwondo is not an exception. It is included as part of the practice in almost every Taekwondo school. Do a split for about 30 seconds (or more if you can hold it longer). You may not be able to do splits properly at first, but if you follow a stretch regimen, you will eventually be able to execute it.

Stretch Kicks

Source[67]

Stretch kicks are more difficult to master since they require you to emulate the actions of a kick. Begin at your hip, then gradually raise your leg higher until you are good enough to kick up to your head level.

Other Exercises to Increase the Speed and Power of Your Kicks

Run a Few Miles

Good old running can help build your muscle strength and improve your performance. You should run for roughly 4-5 miles at least three times a week if you're an athlete who is serious about your performance. However, you don't have to travel that far straight away; you can start with 2 miles and work your way up.

Swimming Works Too

Swimming is a terrific way for martial artists to get a proper body workout. It builds your muscles and is also a great way to boost your endurance. It can be used as an alternative to running or done in addition to your routine.

Box Jumps

This exercise requires you to move in swift and explosive motion. Workouts like this are great because you need that explosive energy behind your kick. Try doing 5-10 reps of box jumps up to 3 to 5 times. You can do this at a comfortable height so that you don't over-exert yourself.

Practice Your Kicks

If there is anything you should often do often, as a martial artist, you should practice. The more you practice, the more refined your kicks will be. Practice throwing your kicks to master them. Daily practice is recommended.

Tips for Effective Kick Practice in Taekwondo

It should be noted at this point that repeated practice does not do much good if your technique is bad. Your brain will only end up memorizing the wrong moves. Since muscle memory serves a lot in executing kicks in Taekwondo, correctly practicing them will give better results than when you merely practice without paying attention to form or the accuracy of your techniques. Here are some helpful tips to improve the effectiveness of your Taekwondo practice.

Learn the Proper Technique

Every Taekwondo move has a specific sequence of movements that must be followed for maximum effect. It's also a good idea to use the correct techniques to avoid injuring yourself.

Set Up Your Kicks Right

As mentioned earlier, a big part of this is the setup; it's about getting your technique right. If you continue to throw uncontrolled kicks, you may wind up losing your balance; not setting up your kick right can lead to serious injuries.

Maintain a Stable Base

To achieve the desired power and speed with a kick, you have to maintain a solid base throughout the entire move. For instance, always stand on the balls of your feet instead of flat-footed, and it will allow you to drive enough force into the ground to throw your kick with maximum speed and power.

Angles Matter

Kicks appear faster than they really are if you angle them right. If you master how to angle your kicks, you will add more speed to them.

Don't Try to Match Your Opponent's Speed

Take this advice for when you are sparring with an opponent that is a faster kicker than you. The worst thing you can do is try to match their speed. You will always trail behind because you are slower, and that's an almost certain defeat.

So, what can you do? It is recommended to go for the one thing you have control over, which is strategy. In the absence of speed, wisdom is your only shot at beating a faster opponent. If you can strategize properly, you will be able to observe your opponent's movement and time your move to counter or block them more effectively.

It is important to note that the list of kicks in this chapter is not an exhaustive one. There are several other types of kicks in Taekwondo that you should become familiar with. They are included in your syllabus, and you will learn them gradually as you move from one level to the other. Of course, learning the kicks is only half of the battle. You have to master them and learn how to boost your speed and power. For this, you will need the tips covered in this chapter to improve your kick training and strategy in a sparring situation. The more you're willing to put in the effort, the stronger and faster your kicks will get.

Chapter 10: Self-Defense in Taekwondo

Self-defense is one of the major reasons people become interested in learning martial arts in the first place. At some point in everyone's life, we are faced with a life-threatening situation, and some are unlucky enough to encounter these situations more frequently than others. Learning a few basic self-defense techniques will prepare you mentally and physically to deal with intimidating situations so that you are not entirely helpless in dangerous situations.

Of course, Taekwondo is one of the most popular forms of martial arts worldwide that is learned for this very purpose. Although it was once a brutal form of martial arts, it is no longer practiced that way in modern times. Today, people learn Taekwondo for tournaments and to defend themselves in difficult situations.

Taekwondo has various attacking techniques and blocking moves that are very handy for self-defense purposes. Its efficiency is proved by the fact that it was used in Korean and Vietnam battles for self-defense. It is a fighting style that is fun and easy to learn; still quite relevant today.

Even though Taekwondo is now being taught as a combat sport, it can be applied for self-defense; one only needs fine-tuned active thinking in self-defense combat scenarios. The type of Taekwondo training you get depends on the martial art school you attend. Some schools specifically include Taekwondo training against an armed attacker, multiple attackers, or when at a disadvantage in their lessons. For example, you are with a child or an elderly person. When your attacker has a weapon, the whole scenario changes entirely. Any careless move could leave you with serious injuries or may even cost you your life. At times, self-defense involves the need to identify and make use of improvised weapons. You are taught how to react and defend yourself in bad situations against an attacker, regardless of whether a mugger, thief, or stranger harassing you.

When you train consistently and correctly, you reach a point where Taekwondo becomes natural, and your body reacts to attacks instinctively.

Importance of Taekwondo Self-Defense

When you have adequately trained in martial arts, your self-respect and confidence are boosted. Walking down that unavoidable lonely street alone or defending yourself from a mugger does not sound all that scary to you anymore - well, at least, not as much as it used to.

The more you train, the more confident you feel about your capabilities, your self-esteem is enhanced. Even more pivotal to how you react, you feel less terrified in times of danger. Your newly attained confidence can also be applied to other specific areas of your life, like work. It is one of the best things about self-defense in Taekwondo. Your increased self-confidence makes you feel empowered and in control of certain situations in your life, and your mental strength plays an active role in successful defense fights.

Taekwondo can also help to improve concentration, self-discipline and develop a solid, strong will. As your training sessions intensify, you will notice that your ability to focus and observe even the tiniest details increases.

Taekwondo lessons are repetitive. Consistently repeating the same move over and over again until perfection is attained requires a lot of self-discipline. Like your self-confidence, you can intentionally apply your improved self-discipline and concentration skills to other areas of your life for more productivity. Mainly, you apply these skills to relevant situations instinctively, especially when you have trained hard, and Taekwondo has become part of you.

Self-Defense Techniques

"Hosinul" is a term used to describe Taekwondo self-defense mechanisms. With hosinul, you can quickly disarm your opponent and restrict his movements. The theory of self-defense techniques in Taekwondo is that you should be able to take out your attacker with a single move. However, a significant period is needed to require the skills to achieve this feat.

Short-range, long-range, and ground rage attacks are also important techniques to master for defense because you're never sure which style your attacker will use against you when. A deficiency in any of these techniques could put you at a great disadvantage.

The size, stamina, and aggressiveness of your attacker are also important factors to consider during the confrontation. Furthermore, the type of training you've had, your dedication to practice, the ability to read your opponent, and attack timing are also essential. Consistent training and body conditioning practices are key success determinants in fights; they determine how effective Taekwondo is in actual combat.

You Only Need the Basics

You need to devote yourself to mastering the basic techniques consciously. Advanced techniques, though they appear elaborate, are not suitable for self-defense fighting in a real-life situation. They leave you more prone and open to attacks and are not practical in actual fights. Your primary goal in a defense fight is not to show off your fancy fighting skills but to defend yourself and get away from threats as soon as possible.

You have to learn how to use the right move combinations to your advantage. While practicing or going through drills, focus on carrying out the moves correctly. Some of the key techniques you need to learn are: Joint dislocation, break boards, throwing powerful kicks and punches, hand strikes, and elbow and knee strikes. It is also necessary to know how to locate pressure points and use them to your advantage.

You must have invested enough time in Taekwondo to know that it focuses on kick techniques even though arm strikes are biologically faster. The idea behind this is that, since your legs are stronger and longer than your arms, they are more effective during fights. This notion is quite valid when you have trained so hard that you can move your legs as fast as your arms.

Another very important thing to note is that it is not advisable to use blocks against kicks in self-defense. If you are going to use it at all, it must be your very last resort because blocking against powerful kicks could easily cause injury to your hands. The best way to avoid attacks is to be well versed in evasive techniques, as they allow you to easily avoid incoming attacks from your opponent and conserve strength to counter-attack from their blind spots.

Basic Taekwondo Moves That Are Useful for Self-Defense

Kicks

Like punches, there are also different types of kicks used for specific purposes. Powerful kicks can keep your attackers at a safe distance from you. For example, for swift recovery during battle and to properly deliver attacks to your opponent's lower body, use the forty-five kick or the roundhouse kick. Round kicks are very versatile moves. The advantage is that this move can be used near an opponent and at a distance. They can cause your enemy to lose strength in their ribs, legs, or any other place you decide to attack. Attacks are even more efficient when you combine roundhouse kicks and punches to an enemy at close range.

Front and push kicks are useful in pushing your opponent away, and they are effective when you want to move an attacker away from your escape route. Defensive sidekicks are powerful kicks that serve the dual purpose of countering incoming attack kicks and causing pain to your opponent. A hard fast kick to the groin is a good way to incapacitate your opponent.

Straight Punches

There are different styles to throwing an efficient punch. Punches differ based on the technique used and the amount of power being applied. It is therefore essential to learn and know the appropriate time to throw a particular punch. An efficient punch in a specific scenario may be useless and irrelevant in another. A straight punch is particularly effective in Taekwondo because it is hard and quick, and it is quite difficult to detect and evade straight punches. Usually, your attacker is not prepared for it, so you get more chances of knocking him out fast. The combination of straight punches, front kicks, and low blocks are good building blocks in self-defense combat.

Your Fighting Stance

The stance is one of the most important things to get right in a fight situation. They differ according to various styles and techniques, and a proper fighting stance ensures that you are protected from dangerous openings and avoidable attacks. With the fighting stance, you stand with your feet firmly placed on the ground at shoulder width and ensure you are well balanced. Keep your chin down and your hands up, ready for an attack. Your stance should be flexible enough to allow for a quick attack, counterattack, and defensive movements.

Source[68]

Elbow and Knee Strike

You might need to use every part of your body in self-defense situations, especially if you don't have a weapon. Even your elbows can come in handy here. Most people are unaware of how much damage can be caused by an elbow during a fight. Striking someone's head with your elbow, or being struck in your head by an elbow, can be quite painful. You can cause excruciating pain to your attacker when you grab his head and hit him with one clean elbow strike. Knees strikes are just as effective, too. It must be noted that you need to stand firm and well balanced to land a proper knee strike. Never launch a knee attack into an open space. It could leave you vulnerable to attacks or counterattacks; it is advisable to pull your opponent in before you use your knee strike.

Hand-Blade Block

This move is also commonly known as the double forearm block. With this move, one of your hands blocks an attack while the other hand is ready to block the next incoming attack.

Palm and Face Blocks

Instinctively, you usually raise your hands to protect your eyes, face, and head during a provocation from strikes. Palm block lessons are good at reducing injury without sparing you any composure or balance. They also help you get ready for a successful counterattack.

Knife Hand and Back Fist Strikes

The knife hand strike is mainly targeted against your attacker's trachea, neck sides, and temples, used with the palm facing outwards or inwards. The back strike is quick and used to attack the head or the gap between the nose and the upper lip.

Palm Heel Strikes

These strikes are great for hard attacks without causing serious injury or damage to your hand. A palm heel strike is a perfect option if you are not too eager to break your hand or bruise your knuckles in a fight. So, you don't need to worry about severe damage or pain to your hand as you deliver hard attacks to your opponent in a self-defense situation using this strike.

Footwork

Sidestepping is a defensive footwork move and is great for performing counterattacks and dodging blows. It's a skill that takes time and effort to master. Skip movements come in handy when your opponent makes use of the whole leg length, such as in a situation where your opponent is armed with a knife, and you can move in and out of his kick range, kick your opponent, and disarm him.

Self-Defense Techniques in Different Situations

In situations where you need to defend yourself, lower your expectations; maybe your attacker will not be fair. So, to save yourself, there is absolutely no need to stick to the rules you adhere to in class and tournaments. For instance, punches to the body and a full-force kick to the head are not allowed in some competitions. But, when it comes to life-threatening situations, no one cares if you stick to the rules or not. In fact, you put yourself at a disadvantage when you adhere to some rules. Here are a few common attack examples used in a confrontation and how to defend yourself as a beginner.

Frontal Choke

In this type of attack, your attacker is trying to squeeze your neck from the front. Use the knife strike to hit your opponent in the chest around the ribs to distract them. Open block with both hands and strike your assailant on his neck.

Collar Grab

When your opponent does this, you can discontinue the grab by forcefully moving one of your opponent's hands down and raising the other. Then you can deliver an elbow strike to his chin.

Shoulder Grab

Grab the opponent's attacking hand and hold his elbow with your other hand. Widen your stance for balance and press the hand down to incapacitate your attacker.

Rear Shoulder Grab

In a case where your shoulder is grabbed from behind, the first thing you should do is keep your shoulders relaxed. Look behind and raise your arm to circle your opponent's elbows, locking them tightly in place. You can then deliver a strike to the rib cage area with your other free hand.

Hair Grab

When the opponent grabs your hair from the front, move to the side and palm block the attacking hand. Then, deliver a hard punch to the stomach of your attacker. Your fast response determines how efficient this counterattack will be.

Linear and Circular Taekwondo Self-Defense Techniques

In Taekwondo, the techniques can be grouped into Linear and Circular categories of movement.

Linear Techniques

Also referred to as Hard Techniques, this group consists of direct strikes, punches, kicks, and head butts. These moves need great strength for proper execution. Your technique choice largely depends on the distance between you and your attacker. If your opponent is very close, the use of your knees or elbows would be your best bet. If he is a little bit more distant, make use of punches, and use kicks when your attacker is out of arm's reach. Your attacker should be taken out with a single attack with the proper technique, especially when you are faced with more than one opponent.

Circular Techniques

This group is also labeled as the soft techniques. The moves in this category are mostly circular, as indicated in the name. Circular moves largely depend on delivering counterattacks to your opponent. This category of techniques is a more defensive approach, and a lesser amount of strength is needed than direct linear attacks.

The circular technique aims to redirect the attacks of your opponent and put you at an advantage. In other words, when your opponent attacks, you carry out a circular motion to throw him off balance and manipulate the attack, so your attacker is forced to be destabilized or remain in a lock position, giving you an edge over him. Then you have the chance to apply the finishing move.

Chapter 11: The Art of Blocking in Taekwondo

Blocking is the act of deflecting or halting an opponent's assault from making contact with one's body in Taekwondo and other martial arts. A block usually entails putting a limb across the attack line. However, even though blocks are the most direct sort of defensive technique in martial arts, they are not the only ones. Other evasive strategies include evasion, trapping, and slipping, all of which are referred to as "soft" or evasive techniques. When blocking, you are expected to relax your body as much as possible prior to the block but tense your muscles just enough on impact. It is then followed by recoil and relaxation after the block is completed. This cycle of relaxation and recoil ensures that the block achieves the greatest possible effect. The relaxation gives the blocking limb good velocity, while rigidity at the point of impact ensures an optimal transfer of force.

Basic Principles of Blocking

When doing a block, several basic principles must be observed to ensure your safety and to maximize the effects. Here are a few:

Source[69]

1. Keep your arm bent at an angle of about 15 to 45 degrees. This way, you intercept the attack at an oblique angle rather than head-on.
2. Do not extend your blocking arm beyond the point of focus of the attack
3. At the moment of impact of the attack, lower your blocking arm slightly
4. Besides a few exceptions, always withdraw your blocking arm immediately after making contact with the attack
5. At the contact point of the attack, the blocking arm forms a triangle with the attacking arm.

How Blocks Are Classified in Taekwondo

There are different types of blocks classified based on the relative position of the blocking hand, the facing posture, type of blocking tool, and the method of the block, as well as the purpose of the block, of course.

Classification of Blocks Based on the Blocking Level

Blocks can be classified as high, middle, low, inward, or outward based on the orientation of the blocking motion you make during the block.

High Block (Nopunde Makki)

A block is considered a high block if your fist reaches the same level as your eyes at the moment of impact. A high block is used to intercept an attack directed at an area close to or above your neck. You can execute a high block from nearly all stances. This block can be performed as a forearm block, knife hand, reverse knife-hand, palm, side fist, or double arm block.

Middle Block (Kaunde Makki)

If your fist or fingertips reach the same level as your shoulder during a block, it is considered a middle block. This type of block is used to fend off an attack directed at your solar plexus and any area above it. Like the high block, the middle block can be executed from any stance. The middle block involves the hand and the foot. The side sole, foot sword, side instep, ball of your foot, and back sole can play a vital role in executing this block.

Low Block (Najunde Makki)

A low block is used to intercept an attacking hand or foot directed at your lower abdomen or an area below it. Your blocking hand or foot must take the impact from the attack at the same level as the target area. You can perform a low block with your outer forearm, reverse knife-hand, palm, or side sole.

Inward Block (Anuro Makki)

If your blocking tool meets the attack with an outward to the inward trajectory to your chest lines, this is called an inward block. You can execute this type of block from any stance. An inward block is used to block an attack directed towards your chest line. This block can be performed with any blocking style except the backhand and inner forearm.

Outward Block (Bakuro Makki)

When your blocking tool hits the target from an inward to an outward trajectory, it is considered an outward block. This block can be performed from any stance, but you cannot execute an outward block with your palm.

Front Block (Ap Makki)

A block is considered a front block if your body is facing the target fully and your blocking tool is at the center of your body. The front block is performed from any stance regardless of the initial position of the opponent. You can execute a front block with your outer forearm, twin palm, knife hand, or your palm.

Side Block (Yop Makki)

A side block is when your body faces your opponent at the point of executing a block. It is executed from any stance regardless of the position of your opponent. A side block can be executed with any blocking tool and is often focused on the center of the defender's shoulders.

Other Ways Blocks Are Classified

A block can be classified based on the height of the block, the position of your hand, orientation, and so on.

Classification of Blocks Based on Hand Position

Several modifiers are used to name blocks based on how your hand is positioned during the execution, often mentioned in the section above. Some common hand positions used to execute a block include knife hand, ridge hand, palm heel, and so on.

Classification of Blocks Based on the Orientation

It is possible to refer to the hand's direction when the block is executed to describe it. Whether your palm is up or down when executing a block determines the side of the forearm that serves as the blocking surface. In a conventional outside block, for example, the blocking surface is your outer forearm, which means your fist is palm-down as you execute the block. Conversely, if the inner forearm is used, the fist is palm-up when executing the block.

Classification of Blocks Based on the Position of Your Off-Hand

For most types of blocks, the default position of your off-hand should be in a direction opposite the motion of the block. This opposing motion contributes to the action-reaction effect, which is one of Taekwondo's key principles. However, in some situations, your off-hand may be included in your block. Here are several examples:

- **Support Block:** Your blocking arm should be resting on your off-arm in this situation.
- **Assist Block:** The block is deemed an assisting block if your off-hand offers an additional push to the blocking arm.
- **Augmented Block:** If the off-hand is near the blocking arm and not drawn back, your block is strengthened.

It is important to note that these different descriptions of the blocks are not always consistent and may vary based on the organization standard that is applied.

Common Blocks in Taekwondo

In this section, we will briefly go over some common blocks in Taekwondo. While most of the blocks listed here are basic, some advanced ones that require high-level technique are also included.

The Outer Forearm Block (Bakat Palmok Makgi)

The outer forearm block can be done in three different ways: high, middle, or low. To complete this block, your forearm should snap forward in a horizontal frame. Impact with the attacking force is made with the outside of your forearm. In a walking stance, this type of block is frequently used. Typically, you begin your block in a ready stance and transition to the walking stance as you execute the block.

Inner Forearm Block (An Makgi)

This is the opposite of the outer forearm block in that it is performed with the inner forearm. You take a step forward and move your arm in a chopping motion. The arm is held vertically with the palm facing inward, and the blow is delivered to the interior of the arm.

Rising Block (Chookya Makgi)

A rising block is a high block that is used to defend against blows to the head and shoulders. Raise your arm over your head horizontally and let the inside of your forearm take the blow. In circumstances where your opponent has a weapon, this block is also useful for self-defense.

Guarding Block (Daebi Makgi)

In the ITF style of Taekwondo, a protecting block is more often used. The guard block is commonly executed in an L-Stance or as a rear foot stance. Your forehand is pushed forward to meet the opponent's hit at the point of impact with the offensive force, while the resting hand is placed on the side of your chest. In this position, the guard hand should provide sufficient cover for most of your body.

Twisting Block

A twisting block occurs when your torso turns in the direction of the strike. One of the biggest advantages of this block is that you can subsequently grab your opponent. The knife hand twist block is created when this block is combined with the knife hand.

Scissors Block (Kawi Makgi or Gawi Makgi)

The scissors block is a combination of a downward block and an outer forearm block. Both actions should be done simultaneously, with both arms producing a scissoring motion across your chest. The scissors block allows you to protect different parts of your body simultaneously with a single move.

Cross Block or X Block (Otgoreo Makgi)

In the ITF Taekwondo style, the cross block is also referred to as the X-fist block. Cross your wrists in front of your body on the same side as your leading leg, palms facing outwards. Using your fist or knife hand, you can defend against high, middle, and low assaults.

Palm Block (Sonbadak Naeryo Makgi)

This block entails putting your open palm in front of your face to shield it. For a proper palm block, all of your fingers should be linked rather than stretched out. When you meet an attacking punch or kick with a thrusting motion, the recoil will keep you from hitting yourself in the face.

Single Forearm Block (Wae Sun Palmok)

The single forearm block can be used to block kicks directed at your torso area. Your lead hand is aimed at your opposite shoulder, while your other arm is swiftly lowered downward to meet the opponent's kick. The forearm is used to perform this type of block.

Twin Forearm Block

This is a version of the single forearm block that is used to defend against both high and intermediate attacks at the same time. You usually start with your arm crossed across your chest. Then you execute a high block with your outside arm and a middle block with your inner arm.

Double Knife Hand Block (Yangsonnal Momtang Magki)

The double knife hand block is identical to the outside block, with the exception that it is executed with a knife hand while standing in a back stance. This move can be used to block a high or low attack.

Double Forearm Block (Doo Palmok Makgi)

This block is comparable to the forearm block that most people are familiar with. But, for this move, you place your supporting hand behind your blocking hand, giving the blocking arm extra support. It also makes it easier to block a secondary attack if necessary.

Nine Block (Gutja Makgi)

The nine block is a more complex blocking technique for defending your midsection against a variety of attacks. The name of this blocking technique is derived from the hand's position when you're executing this block. The nine-block is usually executed in a walking stance.

Push Kick (Mireo Chagi)

Although the push kick is not strictly speaking a block, it can still be used to deflect an opponent's strike; hence it being included in our list. Bring your knee to your chest and thrust your leg outwards at your opponent. It will not only deflect your opponent's strike but will also provide you with ample room to counterattack.

Cut Kick

The cut kick, like the push kick, can be used to deflect an opponent's attack. It has the appearance of a sidekick and is frequently employed to counter spinning blows during a sparring bout. If your opponent executes a spin kick, throw a cut kick at their hip or lower back to knock them off their feet. The cut kick also gives you enough room for a counterattack.

Mountain Block (Santul Makgi)

This is a more popular move in the WTF style. It is used to block multiple attacks directed at your face simultaneously. The inside edge of one wrist moves clockwise while the outside edge of the other wrist moves in the opposite direction when performing this block.

Tips for Practicing Your Taekwondo Blocks

The various Taekwondo blocking techniques described in this chapter are easy to execute, and there are many other variations of each of these types. As with every other aspect of the sport, the key to improving your blocks in Taekwondo is practice.

To practice your blocks, you can either do so on your own by practicing different Poomseas (patterns) or by practicing with a sparring partner. When training on blocks with a teammate, you should alternate taking turns practicing specific blocks. If your partner takes an attacking position, you take the defense and vice versa. During practice, attacking kicks and punches should be thrown at less than half their regular speed to allow space and time to perfect your block.

When practicing the Poomseas of your blocks alone, do so in front of a mirror. This way, you can observe if you're performing the blocks correctly and placing your hands in the proper position.

There is an extensive library of blocking techniques in Taekwondo. As you go through the various levels, you will be taught some of these blocks.

Chapter 12: Stretches and Drills

Taekwondo is a portmanteau of many things - martial arts, defense mechanisms, a pathway to a more energetic and enriching life experience, and a rich combination explosion of Chinese and Korean traditions. However, at its core, it is a weaponless traditional fighting skill that emphasizes jumping kicks, head-high kicks, sidekicks, and striking. The average Taekwondo lesson includes kicking drills, striking drills, and speed targets. These drills are engineered to improve motor skills and flexibility.

Taekwondo has bountiful physical fitness benefits. Research shows that it dramatically improves cardiovascular health, boosts athletic ability, and improves balance and coordination. In 2014, researchers found that Taekwondo athletes exhibited good endurance, upper-and-lower body strength, increased flexibility, and anaerobic power. These benefits are also products of good drills and stretches.

Since it is a physically defensive art, drills are usually combined with other calisthenics exercises and more strength and conditioning drills to provide a complete workout. They are advantageous because they boost your ability as you continually advance further. There are distinctive ways to stretch. Stretching often follows a warm-up to activate cold muscles. A warm-up is necessary because cold muscles do not stretch well. Some Taekwondo sessions are also concluded with stretching. The idea is to take advantage of the fact that all the muscles are warmed up fully at that point. Let's take a look at the importance of stretching before analyzing the various types.

Importance of Stretching

Source[70]

- It increases flexibility. The body needs a good deal of flexibility, but it is more pertinent for martial artists, especially in the hips, lower back, and legs.
- The range of motion is also increased. Good stretching helps you attain higher kicks or become better at challenging moves or positions.
- Fewer injuries usually occur during training and competitive matches when your muscles are conditioned through stretching.
- Often, stretching plays a role in injury recovery. Physical trainers make use of gentle stretching after injuries to restore flexibility and strength to the body.
- It increases blood flow and enhances muscular development. Stretching also enhances mental focus because of how much concentration it requires. Many artists use it as a meditation of some sort.

- It reduces muscle soreness after workout sessions and gives better motion flexibility, which helps you punch or kick well and move as fast as lightning.
- Stretching helps prevent injuries because it allows a full range of motion when performing Taekwondo techniques without pulling or tearing up the muscles. Taekwondo requires excessive use of the legs. When you stretch properly, it allows you to put your legs in proper positions without straining too much. It is impossible to achieve this with tight muscles, and incorrect moves can lead to nasty injuries.
- Since stretching gives more flexibility, your muscles become less and less resistant to fighting movements or positions. The result is a burgeoning speed that improves your performance. Enhanced speed paves the way for greater power, and better flexibility and range of motion improve your overall performance as a Taekwondo warrior in speed and power.

Stretching must be done properly and consistently. It is a key component of any sport, but it's more important for Taekwondo due to the explosively defensive nature of the sport. As a beginner, understand that stretching only on training days is dangerous. Stretch on non-training days at home to increase your flexibility as fast as possible.

Work with the pace your body demands; otherwise, you could be dealing with complicated injuries. But if you only stretch on your training days, your flexibility will be slow to improve, and you will be frequently outperformed by those who prioritize stretching. While stretching at home, consider doing it in the morning rather than at night.

Different Kinds of Stretches

Note: As a beginner, it's best to do these stretches with your instructor or trainer first. Most martial artist instructors are professionals with finely tuned experience. Some of the stretches below are risky, so only attempt them at home when you have a good grip and understanding of what you are doing.

Standing and Sitting
- **Neck Rotation:** Simply rotate your neck in a clockwise, circular motion. Another technique is to stand or sit with a straight back and stare directly ahead. Bring your arms in front of your body and straighten them, then clasp them tightly together. Turn your head so that your chin is above your shoulder. This stretch goes all the way from your jaw to your collarbone.
- **Neck Stretch:** Stretch your neck to the front and back and then to the side. Push or pull your neck to extend the stretching if you want to go further.
- **Shoulders:** Bend your arms so that your fists are near your shoulders and rotate your arms in clockwise and counterclockwise motions. To stretch your shoulders, hold an arm out straight and pull it to your upper chest using your other arm. Place your other arm just below the elbow of the stretched arm and squeeze it into your chest to further increase your stretch. The aim is to feel a stretch across your shoulder.
- To stretch the front of your shoulder, stand with your feet a shoulder's width apart and look straight ahead. Bring your hands behind your back and intertwine them while keeping your arms straight. Now gently ease your hands back, as far back as they will comfortably go, and squeeze your elbows toward each other.
- Stretching the back of the shoulder starts by standing with your feet a few widths apart and looking straight forward. Bring your arm straight up so that

it's parallel to the floor. Bring your arm over your chest while keeping your shoulders down. Use your other arm to squeeze the arm into the chest by placing the forearm just below the elbow of the stretched arm.

Back Stretches

- **Lower Back:** Lie on your back on the floor with your knees bent. Pull your knees towards your chest. When doing this stretch, do your best not to arch your back.
- **Back:** Kneel on the floor and keep your knees firmly together. Put your arms upward, and then bend from the waist, fold your chest onto your knees and place your hands flat on the floor. Leave them out straight. Sit back on your heels after a while to feel the stretch seep into your lower back. For a backward stretch, bend as far backward as possible, looking backward over your head. Let your legs stand a shoulder-width apart and place your hands on your hips.
- **Kneeling Back Stretch:** Kneel on all fours. Look at the floor with your back straight. Arch your back upwards and let your head drop to the floor. Return to the starting position and drop your stomach (not your chest) towards the floor. Stay facing forward, and keep your knees and hands shoulder-width apart when doing this stretch.

For a partner backstretch, interlock elbows and stand back-to-back. Take turns lifting each other off the floor by bending forward.

Waist Rotations

Rotate your waist in a circular motion with your hands on your hips and legs at a shoulder-width apart. Careful to twist slowly. For a side stretch, bend your waist over to one side and then bend to the other. Try raising your arm over your head as you do this.

Besides waist rotations, a ball stretch is also required. Lie flat on the floor and grab both feet with the aim of pulling them over your head. The goal is for your feet to touch your forehead and hold it there for at least a minute.

Leg Stretches

Lie flat on your back, bend one knee and bring it up to your chest; finally, ease it towards your opposite shoulder. This gives you a stretch across your bottom from the top of your leg to your lower back. For your outer hip, lie flat on your back with your arms slightly outstretched. Bend one knee upwards, then grab it with your opposite hand and bring it across your chest onto the floor. Still, keep your other leg straight and your shoulders on the floor. The aim is to stretch the outer leg up to your hip.

An excellent stretch for your groin is to sit on the floor with a straight back with your legs stretched out. Spread your feet as far out as you can, keeping your legs straight. Maintain a straight back while lowering your chest to the ground and stretching your arms out in front of you. Go as forward as you can, then let your elbows hold the stretch.

When stretching the front of your thighs, stand on one leg and bring the opposite heel up to your bottom. Grab your foot and gently pull upwards.

For the back of your thighs, stand with your legs straight, and bring your feet together. Raise your hands above your head and fold yourself down, and try touching your toes.

Understanding Taekwondo Drills

Taekwondo is a weaponless defense mechanism, meaning that you rely solely upon your sparring skills to carry it out safely and effectively. Sparring is at the core of

Taekwondo, and the most important thing is to always infuse control and not let it get out of hand. If you are scared of getting hit or injured or doing even hurting another person, this doesn't mean Taekwondo isn't for you.

Your fears are understandable because the human body possesses a strong in-built sense of self-preservation. However, drills were designed to aid you in your sparring. So, to succeed in tournament combat or mat training sessions, you must learn to work more effectively on your sparring skills. Sparring is a fight without actually fighting; it helps you develop a wider understanding and spurs the development of skills such as speed, distance control, and power.

Before starting any drills, the first thing to do is to have an open space of about 100 square feet (10 feet wide and 10 feet in length). It will be more than enough space to accommodate you if you are training alone and at home. But as a beginner, it's better to start drill practice at a training center to have a partner for the drills.

Shadow Sparring

Shadow sparring is usually performed in front of a mirror. You will need to throw kicks, punches, and elbows; you will also need to use proper footwork as you maintain a good range in your flow motion. The good part about shadow sparring is that you can see yourself, so you can easily identify your flaws. But, if you are shadow sparring with a partner, you need to focus on your opponent and not yourself, or you will get hit.

Heavy Bag Sparring

This is a great starting point for beginners wanting to practice their drills. Striking a heavy bag gives you an idea of what to expect when you come face to face with a real opponent. You get to understand how much force and speed you need to incorporate. It's a bag, so feel free to be brutal with your throw kicks, punches, elbows, and hand strikes. When the bag swings forward, use this to practice evasive tactics before striking again.

Dummy Sparring

This is also great for beginners who want to improve their defensive skills. Dummies are used a lot in martial arts and even in gun control because they are much safer. A dummy will be instrumental in learning offensive and defensive strikes and the use of both hands simultaneously. As with the bag, feel free to throw your strikes, but there is no need for evasion since the dummy cannot react. So, focus a lot on your power levels.

Circle Sparring

This is quite advanced, but even if you are a beginner, you will still have to face this at some point. The main focus of this drill is to learn awareness of your environment. In circle sparring, you are surrounded by six or more people who attack you one by one. Circle Sparring tests your speed, power, skills, and ability to react intuitively under pressure. There is no time to think. You either act fast or lose. Ordinarily, your fellow combatants are at the same skill level as you. But when your skills grow, circle sparring can become more intense because you will have more than one person attacking you at once. As a beginner, you might need to save this for last and understand other drills sufficiently first before taking on attacks from six people.

Additional Things to Note

Speed is of monumental importance in Taekwondo. Currently, how fast are you? How fast do you think you can be going forward? Sparring matches are very short, and they usually don't last for more than two minutes. Improving your kicks is an excellent way to improve your speed, plan your next move even before executing a strike, and plan for more than one kick in your attacks. When you have adequate preparation, you do not need to be outlining your next move while on the mat mentally. It should be done before you even step up on the mat.

- Faster kicks come from relaxed muscles, and this is why meditation and stretching are important. Tight, tense muscles will always react slower, never faster. Before practicing your kicks, relax your muscles so that your kicks come in a fluid, easy motion.

- Power is also of colossal importance in Taekwondo sparring. You must consistently hone your strength. Keeping this in mind maximizes the impact of your kicks or punches, and you can time your kicks or punches so that it collides with your opponent rushing at you. It multiplies the power of your attack and the counters speed of your opponent. To increase your power, you should also learn to incorporate squats and jumps in your warm-up exercises as they; build up thigh muscles. Remember to be cautious and careful with exercises and to perform them in the presence of a professional. Too much of these exercises might cause too much pressure that inevitably leads to injuries.

- One final thing to always have in mind is to be accurate with your kicks, strikes, or punches. One way of improving accuracy is to practice kicking small objects until you consistently hit your targets accurately. You will mostly find this challenging as they are smaller than what you are used to in usual target areas. Small targets don't only help you improve accuracy; they also help you to train your reaction towards a moving object. This training is vital because your opponent is a moving object in the ring, and you'll be skilled enough to direct your response with speed. Training with friends is also a good way to improve accuracy. Just ensure you're both outfitted in protective clothing.

Conclusively, Taekwondo is not the easiest sport or martial art. It will test your physical and mental capacity in numerous ways. Some will fly sky high, and others who crash and burn. As a beginner, you need to figure out what side you want to be on. Study the habits of the high performers in this art, and you'll find that they don't joke with their stretches, nor do they slack on their drills. They are also powerful combinations of accuracy, speed, and power. Strive to be the perfect embodiment of these things, and you are set for astronomical success.

Chapter 13: The Taekwondo Habit: Training, Discipline, and Mindset

Learning Taekwondo has several benefits. It is one of the most beneficial martial art forms to learn, as it improves your ability to defend yourself, and this sport also impacts various aspects of your life. Taekwondo improves your health, fitness, and mindset, and you will experience an overall boost in your quality of life by participating in this sport.

The many benefits of this sport stem from the diversity of technique and the discipline and mindset required to reach mastery. More than just a physical exercise or competitive sport, Taekwondo is a lifestyle that can empower an individual in various ways. People who engage in this sport can expect to gain a certain level of confidence and excitement in their life.

What Can One Learn from Taekwondo?

A good number of people take up Taekwondo classes for self-defense or to gain physical strength and agility. However, as time passes and you continue to train, you will realize that the benefits of Taekwondo transcend its physicality. You might not know this yet, but mastering the way of feet and hands can help you change your view of life and improve yourself in various ways. Some of the additional benefits of Taekwondo include:

Courtesy and Respect

If there's anything you'll learn from your very first Taekwondo lesson, it is that you have to bow to everyone and anyone. This act is not only done by beginner students, but even teachers and seniors take a bow in Taekwondo before proceeding with any action. One simple explanation for this is that it teaches respect.

Source[71]

By bowing before anyone regardless of their age, rank, or skill level, you learn courtesy, scaling down on your ego as well. You cannot bring your real-life status with you everywhere. Taekwondo also involves you bowing before an opponent. While this may seem ridiculous, this act packs in an important lesson; in real life, you must learn to show respect to people even if you have differing opinions or simply disagree.

Perseverance

There's a reason why perseverance and indomitable spirit are among the tenets of Taekwondo. It takes years to attain mastery of the art. You will practice continuously for weeks and months to move from one level to the other, building an attitude of perseverance towards your work. Even when you get to the highest point and earn your black belt, learning in Taekwondo can still be a sustained and sustainable aspect of your lifestyle.

This teaches you to invest in your tears and sweat to become a better version of yourself. That's how it is in the real world. Adversity will come your way, but you must stay strong and persevere if you are to harvest the fruits of your labor.

You Will Learn Something New Every Day

In Taekwondo, you will realize that learning never ends. No matter how much you have learned or the belt colors you've achieved, you have to learn new skills and develop yourself continually. The best martial artist is one who never closes the door on an opportunity to learn something new.

Discipline above All Else

As you begin your Taekwondo training, always keep in mind that discipline is vital to your success in Taekwondo and your daily life. Many things will try to push you off your chosen path. At some stage during your training, it might seem like you're not progressing as much as you should. In moments like these, it is up to you to decide how you want to respond going forward.

Taekwondo Training

By now, you probably know that Taekwondo is highly physically demanding. You will need a lot of physical power, stamina, and flexibility if you want to perform at higher levels. It is why Taekwondo training is best suited for the young and agile, but age is just a number, and anything is possible for anyone with enough willpower regardless of age.

Being young and strong is not enough to excel in Taekwondo, and many young people still have trouble keeping up with the pace of training. You will have to push yourself to the limits to build the right attitude and habit required to become a successful Taekwondo warrior.

Compared to many other forms of martial arts, Taekwondo is quite aggressive, but it has a very low injury rate or chance of permanent or serious injury. However, it is still important that you're aware of the dangers and rigor of what you're getting into. Taking up martial arts is more dangerous than painting or any other soft hobby. Therefore, you must take into consideration important safety tips and follow training instructions to reduce the chances of injury. The misconception that Taekwondo is a safe sport isn't the only one out there.

Getting Started? We Have News for You

There are two, actually. There's good news, and there's bad news. Let's just dump both on you right away and leave you with it. We'll start with the bad.

Taekwondo is hard; never begin with the illusion that you're going into a soft sport that is easy to master. As you will discover when you start your journey, going from white belt to black belt requires a high level of dedication and consistency from you.

The good news is that it is possible to fast-track your mastery and achieve impressive results. First, congratulations. The fact that you have read this book up to this point and have not stepped on the training mat is great. To celebrate this feat, you get a white belt, which is more than if you didn't step onto the mat at all. So, go ahead and give yourself a pat on the back.

Know that the decision to take up Taekwondo lessons means you have committed to do something challenging but amazing. But, as you will soon figure out, the journey from here to the top is an uphill climb. It is possible to feel lost at the onset, and you might even feel silly as you mess around trying to imitate moves of others who seem to move around gracefully with their fancy footwork and elaborate spin kicks.

So, how can you make Taekwondo easier for you to learn and fast-track your training? (Note - easier, and not easy. Taekwondo isn't easy, but you can make it easier by following a few simple tips). Keep the following things in mind as you begin your training and develop the proper habits.

Relax

If there's anything you need to know, it's that tense muscles don't work well in martial arts. Your moves will be slower, and your kicks and punches will be weaker if you're tensed up. You will also lose steam quickly during your training.

So, loosen up and relax. You will need to if you want to develop the right techniques. Practice how to relax not only your limbs but also your mind. Meditation and mindfulness practices are essential for this aspect. Practice regularly with a clear and relaxed mind, and you will see significant improvement in your technique. The more you do this, the more automatic and fluid your moves will become. You may have to actively will yourself to relax at the onset, but with time, you will find you don't have to think so much about it anymore.

Practice Regularly

You must attend classes and pay attention to your lessons. However, you will achieve remarkable results with more practice, meaning you need more time than the regular classes you spend with your instructors. You have to practice at home on your own. People who practice Taekwondo on their own at home are likely to do better than those who don't.

Your training should include solitary sessions to develop your form and build your technique at your own pace. Still, sparring is an important part of Taekwondo training as well. Research has shown that practicing under conditions you're likely to use as a motor skill will improve your mastery significantly. It is particularly essential if you're learning Taekwondo for self-defense or competitive purposes. It is important to note that as a beginner, you will be allowed to spar right away, but as you get a few levels higher, it will be an integral part of your training routine.

Exercise

Regular exercises are important for strengthening your muscles and improving flexibility. You need to focus on stretches and other routines that help improve the strength of targeted muscle groups.

It is recommended that you do stretch routines after your daily training (not before). Stretching out at the end of your workout helps keep your muscles from becoming tight and boosts flexibility. Your muscles are already warm and elastic after a workout, and you will achieve better results with your stretches.

You should also do routines that strengthen your core and hammies (hamstrings, hips, and glutes). You will be doing a lot of kicking in Taekwondo, and the effectiveness of your kicks depends on the strength of your core and posterior chain. Workouts like crunches, squats, and jackknives are quite beneficial for this muscle group. Also, include pushups, pullups, and other routines that strengthen your upper body for better punches.

Meditate and Visualize

Sometimes the most beneficial workouts are those you do without moving a muscle. With meditation and visualization routines, you can improve your skills and sharpen your mind while you're at work, cooking, or even in bed.

A lot has been said about meditation techniques in chapter four of this book. Go over it again if you need a refresher. Visualization involves you picturing yourself going through the motions of techniques to perfect them. It's like practice but in your mind. Research has shown that the same area of your brain that is involved in physically performing those moves is stimulated when you visualize yourself doing them. It helps build strong neural pathways to improve your skills.

These non-physical skills will also come in handy when you're too busy, injured, or too sick to practice physically and you have to be out of action for a while.

471

Conclusion

Taekwondo is one of the easiest forms of martial arts to learn, but that does not mean it is simple and rosy through and through. It takes determination and perseverance to go through the various levels of the sport and excel.

There is a wide variety of techniques and styles to master. You may notice that there are many variations in what you have read in this book to what you will find elsewhere. Many of Taekwondo's techniques have been developed by different masters. The sport is also globally governed by various organizations that adopt different rules and conventions. While you will find the lessons you have learned in this book instructive and beneficial, we implore you to listen to your instructors. Not only do they have the final say on the techniques you must master, but your instructor will also determine the pace at which you should learn them. You need to do what your instructor tells you if you want to get the best results.

Don't get ahead of yourself. Focus on mastering the basics and gradually work your way up. The spin hook might look fancy and sexy, but you must resist it until you are mentally and physically ready. The advanced moves and techniques will come later, and many are simply variations of the basics you are already learning. If you don't get the basics right, you are likely to struggle in the advanced stages.

Lastly, we hope this book was of benefit and that it will effectively supplement your training journey.

Part 7: Kung-Fu

The Ultimate Guide to Shaolin Kung Fu Along with Its Movements and Techniques

CLINT SHARP

Kung-Fu

THE ULTIMATE
GUIDE
TO SHAOLIN
KUNG FU
ALONG WITH ITS
MOVEMENTS AND
TECHNIQUES

Introduction

Most people's first introduction to martial arts was either through movies or TV shows. Strong, steadfast, disciplined heroes fight seemingly impossible odds with nothing more than their arms, hands, legs, and feet. These heroes are ambassadors. They introduced the art form to audiences outside of China and Hong Kong. You don't have to live in either of those places to learn Kung-Fu properly.

This book is your portal to the dojos and kwoons. From the comfort of your own home and working at your own pace, you too can perform the dazzling kicks and purposeful movements of Kung-Fu. Whether you're a novice or already have some training under your belt, this book is designed to not only further your knowledge of martial art but to enhance the positive ripples that learning it can spread into every facet of your life.

Kung-Fu is more than just learning how to throw punches and kicks. It is all about discipline. This martial art is a fantastic way to get in and stay in great physical shape. In today's hectic and often demanding world, it can be a fantastic outlet to relieve stress and anxiety. Sharpening your body sharpens your mind and improves concentration.

On your journey with this book, you can discover the self-confidence you may lack or bolster the one you already have. By learning Kung-Fu with this guide, you will be connected, if not physically, in spirit with all the practitioners who came before you. You will join an ancient community, all sharing the goals of learning self-defense and improving themselves.

Kung-Fu is an art that promotes self-expression. You can take the foundations and expand on them to form something uniquely your own. Like a painter, this book will provide you with the paint, the brushes, and the canvas. And it'll teach you how to paint while leaving the final product up to you.

Chapter 1: What Is Kung-Fu?

Before learning Kung-Fu, it is paramount to understand where it came from. To get the most out of this book's lessons and the martial art itself, obtaining a firm grasp on its history and origins is essential. These are the building blocks that the discipline is built on. Like those of a house, these foundations help keep the whole structure together and prevent it from falling apart.

There are several accepted definitions or translations of "Kung-Fu." Some interpret it as "work and effort." Others feel that the translation to "hard work of a man" is more accurate. Whatever your interpretation, there are always two elements: hard work and dedication. Mastering martial art requires both.

The origins of Kung-Fu are disputed. With a country as old and as rich in history as China, narrowing it down to a single source is seemingly impossible. That said, there are mythological and historical breadcrumbs that you can follow to establish a rough timeline of the martial arts' origin.

Many believe the beginnings of what would eventually become Kung-Fu started with the introduction and spread of martial arts through China. Later known as "The Yellow Emperor," Huangdi was thought to have written some of the first guides on military tactics and self-defense techniques that would evolve into a fighting discipline.

According to legends, the stars foretold the Yellow Emperor's birth and great destiny. Born into a time of great strife and warring tribes, Huangdi would unite the different tribes that lived along the Yellow River. Unified, these groups became the first version of the Chinese State.

The Yellow Emperor not only influenced the political and military landscape of China, but he also was the forefather of Chinese medicine. His philosophies and medical discoveries would later evolve into some of the central tenets of Kung-Fu. Those writings are some of the oldest ever discovered in the history of mankind.

After the legendary Yellow Emperor passed away, his martial arts teachings continued and were built upon. Centuries of small-scale warfare between feudal lords over everything from land rights to personal affronts enveloped a still young China. In this phase, Huangdi's philosophies on martial arts, warfare, and self-improvement were adopted and adapted by different regions of the vast country.

The Yellow Emperor's philosophies evolved into Ancient China's "Six Arts." Extremely similar to the western concept of a "renaissance man," Chinese men, especially those in the upper class, we're encouraged to learn. These Six Arts were: archery, calligraphy, chariot riding, music, mathematics, music, and rites.

During the Han Dynasty, another influential figure in the development of Chinese martial arts came to the forefront of the movement. He was an infamous physician and surgeon named "Hua Tuo." Besides being credited with discovering anesthesia, the well-known doctor filled in the gaps regarding medicine in The Yellow Emperor's teachings.

Another gigantic contribution from Hua Tuo to Kung-Fu was the development of exercise techniques that had numerous health benefits for his patients. These techniques were based on animals he'd observed. He developed a system that would later be used in Shaolin-born Kung-Fu techniques using those movements he observed.

More centuries passed with various fighting styles, techniques, and life philosophies cultivated in mainland China. It wasn't until a foreign Buddhist monk from Southern India, Bodhidharma, visited the country that Kung-Fu was formed.

Bodhidharma came to mainland China sometime between 450-500 A.D. The details of how he got there and his travels across the country are unclear. There aren't a lot of records of his travels. What is known is that he originally came to teach and spread the word of what would become known as Xiao Sheng Buddhism.

The arrival of Bodhidharma was heralded by Indian royalty, requesting that the Kingdoms of China take good care of their monk who came to spread the teachings of Buddha. Wherever he went, the Chinese were eager to see him, hear him speak, and learn from him. But they were surprised when instead of speaking, he simply meditated. Some were intrigued, others confused, and there were even those who were angered. Whatever their reaction, most of the Chinese populace he came across didn't fully understand what he was preaching. With that said, word of him and his radical teachings spread.

Eventually, tales of Da Mo (Bodhidharma), the Indian meditating monk, reached the ears of the ruler of China's Southern Kingdom, Emperor Wu. A devout Buddhist, the emperor, made a point to erect monuments, statues, and temples dedicated to the religion. So, when he heard of this Indian monk with a new take on what he loved, he had to meet him.

There's a famous story of the first interaction between Emperor Wu and Bodhidharma. The Emperor inquired whether or not the monk thought that the leader's dedication to Buddhism and generous donations to the religious institutions were good and moral. To his surprise, the monk said "no." When he asked if a Buddha was living in their world, again, the monk said "no."

It probably goes without saying, but Bodhidharma's answers upset Emperor Wu. Their reasoning was simple and demonstrated how the monk saw the world and what he promoted through his teachings. Emperor Wu's grand donations to temples and Buddhist institutions weren't something to brag about or be proud of. As the monk saw it, this was a leader's duty. Even asking if a Buddha was living among them displayed a clear lack of faith in the religion. Bodhidharma was ordered to leave the kingdom and never return.

After his exile from Emperor Wu's kingdom, Bodhidharma's trip up to the Northern Part of China brought him to a gathering in the village of Nanjing. There, he came across a former prolific general named "Sheng Guang." Guilt over all the people he'd killed, directly or indirectly, and the effects that had on his victims' friends and families led him to become a Buddhist Monk.

On this day in Nanjing, Sheng Guang addressed a crowd of villagers, teaching them traditional Buddhist lessons. Bodhidharma listened to him and reacted accordingly, whether he agreed with what was being said or didn't. The fact that this foreigner would have the nerve to shake his head and not agree with his lessons angered Sheng Guang. That anger boiled over to the point that the former general snatched the Buddhist beads from around the monk's neck and threw some of them at him, hitting him in the face, bloodying him, and knocking out a few teeth.

Naturally, Sheng Guang thought his angry outburst would produce a confrontation with the South Indian monk. Surprisingly, Bodhidharma simply smiled and walked away. This act of self-control and the ability to turn the other cheek profoundly impacted the former general. It also demonstrated a core tenant of Kung-Fu, discipline, control, and the ability to manage one's anger. This so profoundly impacted Sheng Guang that he followed Bodhidharma all the way to the Shaolin Temple.

Legend has it that when Bodhidharma reached the Shaolin Temple, he was greeted by enthusiastic monks who'd heard about him and his teachings. They were excited. But he just walked past all of them without saying a word or even acknowledging their presence. Instead, he made his way towards the back of the temple. Once there, he found a cave, sat down, and started meditating.

It is said that Bodhidharma sat in that cave, staring at a wall, not even the entrance, for nine whole years. Can you imagine that? Sitting in place for almost a decade without even muttering a single word? They said that his meditating and praying was so intense that his silhouette left a print on that wall.

The Shaolin monks were blown away by Bodhidharma's dedication and faith. They made and offered him a room there at the temple. Though he never said a word, the Indian monk got up after nine years and walked into a room that was offered to him. He sat down and meditated for another four years.

A mystic grew around Bodhidharma. His unorthodox teachings started to catch on with the Shaolin monks. They began to appreciate his approach to the religious teachings they'd dedicated their lives to. Though they weren't physically or spiritually strong enough to follow in his footsteps, the foreign monk thought they could be strengthened.

Back in Southern India, Bodhidharma was part of the warrior caste, a Kshatriya. Using techniques he'd learned as a warrior, he started training the Shaolin monks. Using his learned breathing techniques and movements, he unknowingly started laying the foundations for what would later be called "Kung-Fu."

This primitive form of Kung-Fu was very much stylized after Bodhidharma's Buddhist philosophies. Primarily it focused on mastering your inner self. He believed that by improving your health, focus, and the control of your mind, you could get closer to Buddha.

Bodhidharma's teachings at the Shaolin Temple led to the further development of martial art. From this infamous site, Kung-Fu spread throughout the country and eventually the world.

7 Kung-Fu Disciplines

There are hundreds of sub-disciplines under the Kung-Fu umbrella. While going through all of them in this book would not only be *near impossible*, it wouldn't help give you the foundations you need on your martial arts journey. Instead, you will see seven of the most popular and basic disciplines that will be the perfect base to start with.

1. Baguazhang

Originating in nineteenth-century China, Baguazhang, or "eight trigram palm," is a soft style of Kung-Fu. This refers to its technique which emphasizes using an opponent's power and weight against them. This involves re-directing strikes to knock opponents off-balance. A primarily defensive style, it requires a great deal of inner peace and a clear mind to effectively employ.

What makes Baguazhang unique is its integration of a wide variety of fighting techniques into one system. It is designed to allow a practitioner to engage up to eight opponents at once.

Part of what makes Baguazhang so effective is its constant movement and intricate footwork. With a practitioner constantly moving, twisting, and contorting their body, hitting them is extremely difficult. Using these techniques eliminates the need for excessive blocking and instead allows you to use deception and evasion instead.

With opponents thrown off balance, strikes can be delivered using virtually any part of the practitioner's body. Utilizing an enemy's body weight and momentum, Baguazhang also uses throws, submissions, and grabbing techniques to neutralize an attacker.

Baguazhang training starts with strengthening the mind before learning the movements. It is an inner style of Kung-Fu. It demands the ability to center yourself spiritually and mentally. Being all about flow, like a raging river around the rocks that jut out of the water, the practitioner of this discipline needs to be able to adapt.

After reaching an adequate mental level, a martial artist must first learn the circular movements central to Baguazhang. Circle walking is believed to create a sort of vortex of natural Earth energies that can be exploited to defend oneself. There is a second, straight-line method, which adds to the diversity of this well-rounded Kung-Fu discipline.

2. Northern Praying Mantis

Suppose you've ever seen Kung-Fu displayed or represented in popular media. In that case, there is no doubt you've been exposed to the Northern China-born Praying Mantis discipline. Those representations, however, are often inaccurate and do little to portray the complexities of this three-and-a-half-century-old collection of techniques. What started with a monk observing a praying mantis kill a cicada turned into one of the core variations of martial art.

Akin to Baguazhang, Northern Praying Mantis style relies on technique and movement over raw power. Using short, somewhat jerky, recoil-like movements, the Seven Star Style variation is the most dominant and generally regarded as better than the original developed at the Shaolin Temple. Because it generates strength from the waist and core, practitioners with less physical strength can help even the odds when facing stronger opponents.

Northern Praying Mantis style focuses more on a practitioner's legs than their upper body. This makes perfect sense if you think about it. Your legs are likely the strongest part of your body. This style can deliver devastating strikes with minimal effort or strain using quick-fire core power-propelled kicks. This fits perfectly with this technique's philosophy of the efficient use of energy.

3. Tai Chi

It is one of the more popular forms of Kung-Fu. It is a discipline that you probably have been more exposed to than you realize. Think about it. Have you ever seen a group of people, very often elderly, practicing what looks like slow martial arts forms in parks? They're practicing Tai Chi.

Tai Chi is all about harmony. The controlled movements and breathing techniques are designed to generate chi, also known as life energy. That promotes benefits both inward and outward.

It is exceedingly difficult to define a discipline as complex as Tai Chi. To truly understand it, you have to practice it. Using water as inspiration, similar to Baguazhang, its curved, rounded movements are meant to re-direct energy. Unlike Baguazhang, this discipline is intended to fortify and compliment a practitioner's skills and health, not for offense or self-defense.

In many ways, the harmony that Tai-Chi provides compliments a martial artist. Practicing it can improve your flexibility, expanding your array of physical capabilities. It can strengthen your muscles, bones, and tendons. Repeating and mastering the controlled movements can improve your agility and fortify your balance. There are so many potential health benefits from the discipline that medical professionals have borrowed some of its forms and principles to treat their patients.

The endless list of potential benefits of practicing Tai Chi doesn't begin and end with the *physical*. It has been shown to improve mental health as well. The balance and harmony it is based on requires a sound mind. Luckily, that's not a prerequisite to start learning the discipline as it works to improve it in practice.

There's a mystery to Tai Chi. No one really knows where its limits lie. Its wide array of physical and mental benefits makes that limitless potential all the more intriguing to martial artists and ordinary people alike.

4. Xing Yi Quan

Try to imagine a spear and how it is wielded – picture in your head the thrusting of the sharp spearhead. Take a moment and think about how that weapon is used, how it uses subtle movements to reroute enemy attacks. The spear uses the same basic ideas behind the Xing Yi Quan Kung-Fu discipline.

While some Kung-Fu disciplines are pretty, even fancy using elegant, extravagant movements, Xing Yi Quan is much more utilitarian. Its forms are built for effectiveness in battle rather than showing off and displaying the art behind it. This seemingly simple approach hides a deep complexity. That makes learning it an earnest endeavor and should be avoided by those who can't dedicate a lot of time to it.

The complexity of Xing Yi Quan starts with the fact that it requires a relatively even mix of internal, soft power techniques with more traditional martial art forms. In other words, it requires mastering the mind and soul and physical prowess. But that's not where the complexity stops.

Consisting of a large variety of connected complex forms, learning Xing Yi Quan requires a very methodical approach. Mastering it requires repeating each in a drill-like fashion, with each step building upon the one that came before. This less-than-personal approach makes it ideal for instructing large groups at once. That led to many theories that its origin was from the military – for its training regime and the technique itself.

Practitioners of Xing Yi Quan rely heavily on direct attacks and counterattacks. They use potent punches to break through the opponent's defenses. Some sub-disciplines use quick kicks like the northern Praying Mantis Style, while others focus on joint manipulation. It is a diverse style with strong utilitarian properties making it one of the more practical Kung-Fu disciplines.

5. Shaolin Style

When you think of Kung-Fu, what comes to mind? What are the first images that flash through your mind? You probably think of old-school martial arts movies or sinewy iron muscled monks in orange robes. These are all influenced by the famous spiritual mecca of the martial art, the Shaolin Temple.

Perhaps the most famous style of Kung-Fu is Shaolin Style. Not only did it originate from the same place the martial art itself originated from after the arrival of Bodhidharma, but it is also one of the most colorful and extravagant disciplines. This has led to it bleeding into almost every facet of popular culture, from movies and television to video games and music.

The practical use of Shaolin Style Kung-Fu focuses on defeating, disabling, and disarming your opponent with various strikes and blocks. Mostly shunning the use of throws and joint manipulation, this discipline emphasizes wide stances, powerful kicks, and open and close hand punches.

Where Shaolin Style differs from many other Kung- Fu disciplines is in its many sub-disciplines. Often theatrical, these branch styles often use highly agile acrobatic moves that can dazzle onlookers. Sometimes they focus on hardening parts of the body resulting in thrilling displays of strength and pain tolerance. Other sub-disciplines are based on animals or features of the natural world.

When most of us think of Shaolin Style, the aspect that stands out the most is its sheer beauty. Truly the most artistic of all the world's martial arts. This discipline is still practiced today. Initially, this variation of Kung-Fu was known for its power and how formidable its practitioners were. Today, it transitioned into more of a form of entertainment and is mainly used to build inner strength.

6. Bajiquan

Suppose you're more interested in explosiveness, sudden powerful strikes that can shatter an opponent's defense. In that case, Bajiquan might be up your alley. It gains its formidability from the idea that the human body has inherent power and protections that can be taken advantage of in self-defense.

Bajiquan is all about getting in close to your opponent, closing the distance, and using not just your fists or feet. Knees, elbows, shoulders, and even your head are natural and powerful weapons often overlooked in other Kung-Fu disciplines. In fact, they are so strong that, if used correctly, they can offset any lack of strength or physical prowess a practitioner might have. That means that it is an ideal system for beginners or those who might be at a physical disadvantage.

The power of Bajiquan doesn't just come from which extremity you use to hit your opponent. It also focuses on learning how to generate the strongest blows possible through technique. Though it has some soft power aspects, the overwhelmingly strong power needed requires an aggressive mindset. You have to continuously advance and be as efficient as possible with your movements and strikes to save energy for impactful explosive strikes.

In order to learn Bajiquan, you first need to condition and strengthen your bones to endure the arduous training required. Plus, your bones need to be able to support the powerful strikes you will deliver in your training and in practice. Though friendly to those without expansive Kung-Fu knowledge, it is one of the most demanding disciplines to learn due to what you have to endure.

Bajiquan is used today in Chinese and Taiwanese special forces. This is due to how effective a discipline it is. It can also be deadly, making it indispensable in the arsenal of those who regularly are tasked with putting their lives on the line. Even though its origins are Chinese, its principles can also be found in martial arts in countries like Israel, Brazil, Russia, and the United States.

7. Wing Chun

One day at the Shaolin Temple, a monk, Ng Mui, watched a rat and a stork fight. Though the rat was vicious, scratching, clawing, and even biting, the bird managed to hold the vermin off. By using the combination of its wings and legs, the stork prevailed, driving off the rat.

Ng Mui was one of the most formidable warriors in all of China. She took the lessons she learned from watching the stork and rat fight to develop a new Kung-Fu discipline. Once developed, she named her new art "Wing Chun."

Young by Kung-Fu standards, Wing Chun was born from Ng Mui's desire to simplify martial art. She packed all the strengths she had learned from other disciplines and tried to eliminate their inherent weaknesses. Speed, precision, and adaptability were key in making it an effective fighting technique.

Developed to work in the densely populated and often urban environments it was born in, Wing Chun can be used in more cramped spaces. It was designed to be used in tight spaces like alleyways or stairwells. It requires the use of fast strikes and superior reflexes to hold off any assailants, even armed ones.

Though inspired by a battle to the death between a bird and rat, Wing Chun's principles are based on human anatomy. A strong understanding of how the body works and how to get the most out of it has led to a style that takes less time to learn and master than other Kung-Fu disciplines. Unlike other styles, it can be adapted to different body types. There's a long history of women actually being more skilled Wing-Chun fighters.

Wing Chun, like traditional Shaolin Styles, is often heavily featured in pop culture. One of the most famous products, actually an off-shoot of the discipline, was

Hollywood action movie star Bruce Lee. Using its philosophies and principles, he created a looser, more freestyle version called Jeet Kun Do. His version was more like jazz. There's more improvisation, and it has a natural flow to the way moves are made.

The most famous traditional Wing Chun fighter, and the one who saved it from almost being lost in the annals of history in the midst of the Chinese Cultural Revolution, is Ip Man. He became a rare modern Kung-Fu legend. Ip Man's fights and life have been immortalized in an extremely successful film franchise and countless books.

Chapter 2: Shaolin Kung Fu vs. Other Styles

Kung Fu is a term that can be used to encompass many different styles of martial arts. There are, however, six primary styles in the world. In this chapter, we'll look at how Shaolin Kung Fu compares to other Kung Fu styles. We will compare Shaolin with Wing Chun, Tai Chi, Northern Praying Mantis, Baguazhang, and Xing Yi Quan to see what makes it unique.

What Makes the Different Styles of Kung Fu Unique?

Many people have a hard time differentiating between Shaolin Kung Fu and other forms of Kung Fu. Each style is distinguished based on its origins, geography, characteristics, techniques, and philosophies. Apart from the above-mentioned Kung Fu styles, there are several other ancient styles. However, those are not commonly practiced.

Each unique style was developed depending on how the core art form was taught. While Shaolin Kung Fu is the oldest and most significant one, the other types like Wing Chun and Tai Chi have been prevalent for hundreds of years. While Shaolin Kung Fu is known for its wide stances, kicks, and hand strikes, Tai Chi is more of an internal martial art that focuses on mind and energy with slow physical movements. Similarly, other forms like Wing Chun and Northern Praying Mantis, while less popular outside of China, are a few of the most powerful self-defense techniques, thanks to their agile, close-range explosive movements and animal postures.

This chapter will compare Shaolin Kung Fu with other styles to see what makes them unique.

Understanding Shaolin Kung Fu

Shaolin Kung Fu is one of the oldest martial arts styles in China. It was developed at a Shaolin temple by Buddhist monks over 1500 years ago. The most popular form, which has been studied for centuries across Asia, is Wushu (Kung Fu Sport). However, few know that there are several other types of Kung Fu based on different schools and styles.

Shaolin Kung Fu emphasizes several techniques, including wide stances, kicks, and open-closed hand strikes. Shaolin Kung Fu is perhaps one of the most well-known and sophisticated among all Kung Fu styles.

Shaolin Kung Fu emphasizes animal styles, including tiger, leopard, snake, crane, and dragon.

Philosophy of Shaolin Kung Fu

In Shaolin Kung Fu, the practitioner aims to improve their physical and mental condition through rigorous training. In this style, the movements are very fluid in battle, which is why it is often called "The Dance of a Thousand Hands."

Shaolin Kung Fu emphasizes several characteristics, including power generation from stillness, sensitivity, stability, and speed. One of the most important things to remember about Shaolin Kung Fu is that it is a fighting style, an art form, and a life philosophy.

It is the only martial art form encompassing all combat styles, from grappling and ground fighting to long-range strikes, including kicks and punches.

Here are some of the main objectives behind Shaolin Kung Fu:
- To build strength and endurance
- To increase mental and spiritual awareness
- To learn how to use internal force known as chi/qi

Fighting Techniques and Methods of Shaolin Kung Fu

In Shaolin Kung Fu, the practitioner tries to make their opponent lose balance and stability by using low stances. This ancient style is considered one of China's best martial art forms because it makes full use of every part of the body for self-defense purposes.

Shaolin Kung Fu also emphasizes several attacking and blocking techniques, including long-distance kicks, open-closed hand strikes, and punching combinations.

Shaolin Kung Fu is renowned for using weapons such as staff, swords, knives, etc.

Wing Chun

Wing Chun is a type of Kung Fu developed by Buddhist nun Ng Mui and her student Yim Wing Chun. It is a martial art that focuses on close-quarter combat and involves several types of blocks, punches, kicks, and strikes used to take down an opponent quickly. The system has been taught in secret for generations until one of its students, Ng Chung-sok, published the first manual with his master's consent during the 1930s.

Wing Chun focuses on close-range combat, punches, defensive tactics like ducking and sidestepping, and agility. Wing Chun is particularly famous for its arm strikes that target pressure points on the body, which can help practitioners quickly knock their opponents out in a fight. It includes several types of blocks with crossed arms to nullify an attack before launching a counterattack.

Wing Chun is often referred to as one of the most powerful styles of Kung Fu because it emphasizes powerful strikes and blocks and focuses on speed.

Wing Chun is a practical form of self-defense used in real-life situations to defend oneself against attackers or muggers without causing any lasting injuries. However, one needs to practice the techniques regularly and under the supervision of an experienced teacher to properly master their skills.

Wing Chun is the only variation of Kung Fu to be named after women.

Wing Chun vs. Shaolin Kung Fu

Wing Chun is one of the most practical styles of Kung Fu to learn because it focuses on fighting from a short distance. It emphasizes speed and agility rather than powerful strikes that easily knock out an opponent or cause lasting injuries. Wing Chun practitioners use "soft" techniques during training sessions to avoid getting injured while practicing.

Today, Shaolin Kung Fu is practiced more for show rather than for self-defense purposes. However, it can be a very effective style of Kung Fu if practiced the right way.

Tai Chi

Tai chi is a form of Kung Fu that involves slow and gentle movements instead of quick strikes or blocks. It is more of a meditative art where the practitioner focuses on the spirit rather than technique. It is considered one of the best martial arts for health because it promotes muscle flexibility, body coordination, and improving breathing capacity.

Tai Chi is practiced chiefly in China and has been around for centuries. It was developed from older styles of Kung Fu, such as the Tiger-Crane style. It is a soft martial art that emphasizes defense rather than attack because practitioners use slow movements to evade an incoming strike before launching a counterattack against their opponent.

Tai Chi is an excellent style of Kung Fu to learn if you want to improve your health and physical well-being. Its gentle movements can help relieve stress, calm the mind, and increase muscle flexibility in elderly people.

Shaolin Kung Fu vs Tai Chi

Tai Chi is a soft form of martial art that can be used to defend oneself against an attacker without causing lasting injuries. Its movements are slow and gentle, making it perfect for people who want to learn Kung Fu but don't have the physical strength or stamina to practice other styles.

On the other hand, Shaolin Kung Fu is an aggressive martial art form with several powerful blocks and strikes. It is considered one of the best styles to learn because it can help improve physical strength, stamina, and mental capabilities in people who practice it regularly.

Northern Praying Mantis

Northern Praying Mantis Kung Fu is one of the most popular styles practiced in China. It was developed during the Song dynasty by Wang Lang, who wanted to create his own version after observing several praying mantis insects fighting each other for food and territory. Northern Praying Mantis focuses on speed, agility as well as quick counterattacks against opponents.

Northern Praying Mantis Kung Fu is a practical martial art that can be learned in just a few months. Still, it takes years to master appropriately and use effectively against opponents during training sessions or real-life situations without causing lasting injury.

Shaolin Kung Fu vs. Northern Praying Mantis Kung Fu

Northern Praying Mantis is an excellent form of Kung Fu to learn if you develop speed and agility in your movements. Its fast counterattacks make it one of the most practical styles. Still, its lack of powerful strikes means that one needs years of training before effectively using them during self-defense situations against an attacker without causing lasting injury.

Baguazhang

Baguazhang is a soft Kung Fu style developed in China by Dong Haichuan during the 19th century. It is considered one of the most effective styles because it utilizes all parts of your body, including arms, legs, and even the head, to counter an opponent's attack or block their strikes. Baguazhang practitioners don't use brute force to attack their opponents. Instead, they try to stay calm and focus on evading an incoming strike before launching a counterattack.

Baguazhang is considered one of the most graceful styles because it uses circular movements combined with quick steps to defend against an attacker's strikes without causing lasting injury during situations that require self-defense.

It is an internal form of martial art suitable for people who want to learn Kung Fu but don't have the physical strength required to practice other styles.

Baguazhang means "eight trigram palm," referring to the trigrams of the I-Ching, a Chinese classic text written thousands of years ago. The style's movements are based on the theory behind them. Its practitioners spend many years learning how to use their hands to deflect an incoming strike before launching their counterattack against opponents during training sessions or self-defense situations without causing lasting injury.

It is one of the most popular styles practiced in China today. Dong Haichuan first demonstrated Baguazhang at the Beijing opera house, where he defeated several attackers without using any weapons or physical force.

Shaolin Kung Fu vs. Baguazhang

Baguazhang is an internal form of Kung Fu that focuses on defense rather than attack. Its circular movements combined with quick steps make it one of the most graceful styles. Still, its lack of powerful strikes means that practitioners need years of training before they can effectively use them during self-defense situations without causing lasting injury or damage to their opponent.

Xing Yi Quan

Zhang Sanfeng developed it during the 14th century, and it is based on Taoist theory that says all things share common life energy, which can be controlled using breathing patterns and mental capabilities. The style focuses on quick movements combined with powerful strikes to defeat opponents without causing lasting injury during self-defense situations.

Xing Yi Quan means "Form and Intention," referring to the need to use both body movements combined with mental capabilities to understand your opponent's actions during training sessions or real-life situations.

Xing Yi Quan is an external Kung Fu style that has many practical applications during self-defense situations. Practitioners spend years perfecting their muscle movements, breathing patterns, and mental capabilities to understand the theory behind each form of attack before they attempt them against an opponent to avoid lasting injuries.

Shaolin Kung Fu vs. Xing Yi Quan

Xing Yi Quan is an external form of martial art that focuses on attacking opponents rather than defending yourself against them. Its quick movements combined with powerful strikes make it one of the most aggressive styles. Still, its lack of defensive moves means that practitioners need to spend years perfecting their muscle movements before they can effectively use them during self-defense.

Bajiquan

Bajiquan is a popular Chinese martial art that was developed during the Tang Dynasty. This style of Kung Fu focuses on explosive short-range strikes or punches with elbows or shoulders.

The term "Baji" can be translated into "eight poles" or, more literally, "eight dividing sections." This refers to the eight divisions of the body which are used during training sessions.

Bajiquan is an external style that focuses on using punches to attack opponents rather than kicks or other moves. Its quick movements combined with powerful strikes make it one of the most aggressive styles. Still, its lack of defensive moves means that practitioners need to spend years perfecting their muscle movements before they can effectively use them during self-defense.

Jin, a power delivery method, is at the very core of Bajiquan. Jin and the eight hitting methods are the essences of Bajiquan.

Shaolin Kung Fu vs Bajiquan

Bajiquan is an external style that focuses on attacking opponents rather than defending yourself against them. Its quick movements combined with powerful strikes make it one of the most aggressive styles.

Benefits of Kung Fu Practice

Kung Fu has many benefits such as:

- Building strength and stamina
- Improving flexibility
- Increasing bone density to prevent fractures in old age. Kung Fu training can reduce the risk of falls among older people by up to 20 percent. This is because it trains your mind and body coordination, balance, and equilibrium which helps you maintain good posture and ultimately avoid falls.
- Teaching self-control, discipline, patience, and respect for others. Kung Fu training can help improve your awareness of the world around you and give you a sense of purpose in life. It also encourages people to interact with each other during sessions, creating a sense of belonging within different communities worldwide.

Which Kung Fu Style Should You Learn

There are many different styles of Kung Fu, including Shaolin, Wing Chun, Tai Chi, Northern Praying Mantis, and Baguazhang. The best martial art style you should learn depends on your reason for wanting to do it in the first place. Some people want to do it purely for looks. They love how Kung Fu moves look when practiced, whereas others want to do it because they enjoy the challenge of learning a new sport.

You should also consider how much time and effort you are willing to put into training. For instance, some styles of Kung Fu require less physical strength than others but still provide plenty of benefits for your mind and body if practiced correctly.

What is the Deadliest Kung Fu Style?

Wing Chun may be the deadliest style of Kung Fu because it is an external form that focuses on defensive moves designed to counter opponents' attacks. Wing Chun uses many kicking techniques and hand movements and blocks, making it one of the most effective styles when fighting against opponents who use different physical combat methods.

Most Practical Kung Fu Style for Self Defense

Wing Chun is the most practical style of Kung Fu for self-defense because it focuses on using defensive moves designed to counter attacks. Wing Chun uses many kicking techniques and hand movements and blocks, making it one of the most effective styles when fighting against opponents who use different physical combat methods.

Deciding which Kung Fu style to learn depends on your reason for wanting to do it in the first place and how much time and effort you are willing to put into training. The availability of master trainers can also play a big part in what style of Kung Fu you decide to learn.

Kung Fu and the Modern World

Kung Fu is a traditional Chinese martial art style that dates back hundreds of years. Its history can be traced way back to 500 BC when Bodhidharma, also known as Ta Mo in China, created what some people believe to be the first Kung Fu school.

The sport has evolved into an extremely popular practice around the world with an estimated 200 million practitioners. It has made its way into modern-day martial arts, appearing in films such as Kill Bill and Enter the Dragon.

Kung Fu became more popular when it was introduced into the modern martial arts world. It has since been incorporated into other styles of fighting that have become very well known throughout media around the world, including Krav Maga, which is a mix between Kung fu, and Karate moves.

This style started to get used in movies during the 1970s and has since been used in countless films and TV shows such as Crouching Tiger, Hidden Dragon (2000), The Matrix trilogy (1999-2003), and the Ip Man series.

Some modern martial arts, such as Taekwondo and Karate, were developed from traditional styles of Kung Fu. However, some people believe that some forms of Kung Fu are not practical for self-defense because some moves cannot be used in a real situation.

The Popularity of Kung Fu Styles in Western Countries

Kung Fu has become very popular among western countries over the last few years due to its incorporation into many different modern martial arts forms used in movies and TV shows. These days, you can even take Kung Fu classes in some gyms.

However, people might not realize that there are hundreds, if not thousands, of Kung Fu styles, and not all of them are suitable for self-defense. Some styles focus on using defensive moves that counterattacks, whereas others focus on attacking the enemy or protecting themselves from harm.

Some styles of Kung Fu are more popular in Western countries compared to other forms, which can be linked to the availability of master trainers, available training time, and how well-known the style is across media.

Shaolin Kung Fu and Tai Chi are two of the most popular styles in Western countries, whereas Wing Chun and Northern Praying Mantis are less well-known.

Kung Fu styles evolved, and numerous styles came to be practiced for their varying benefits. Today, seven styles are still practiced. Some focus more on attacking the enemy or protecting from harm, whereas others focus on using defensive moves to counter attacks.

All the Kung Fu styles focus on posture and footwork, internal and external training of the body. These styles aim to provide health benefits like improved muscle tone and increased flexibility, among many others.

Kung Fu has evolved from a martial art into an exercise regime for good health, which is why so many people in Western countries are taking classes to improve their fitness.

Shaolin Kung Fu and Tai Chi are two of the most popular styles in Western countries, whereas Wing Chun and Northern Praying Mantis are less well-known. Deciding which style to learn depends on why you want to get into Kung Fu, as well as how much time you're willing to put into training.

Chapter 3: The 5 Animal Patterns of Kung Fu

Inspiration for the different Kung Fu disciplines often came from a multitude of sources. Some were developed out of a simple need for self-defense. The China that many of these disciplines originated in was a violent place. Feudal Lords were often at war, leaving the citizens to bear the brunt of the effects and deal with roving gangs of bandits or wayward soldiers determined to take, rape, maim, and sometimes even kill.

One of the main drivers of developing Kung Fu styles was self-improvement. Spurred on by the teachings of The Yellow King, segments of the Chinese population were motivated to become better. This included a focus on mental health as well as physical health. Aligning the two became crucial for people to find the balance necessary to become the best versions of themselves.

As shown by Bodhidharma, religious piety can be bolstered by practicing martial arts. One of the most popular paths to understanding Buddha's Nature came in the form of Kung Fu. The meditative and humble nature of its many disciplines is inspired by providing a wide selection of possible choices that fit a practitioner's needs and attributes.

Lastly, one of the most well-known inspirations for the different Kung Fu styles comes from nature itself. That wasn't limited by elemental forces like the wind, fire, water, and earth. Animals were observed, copied, and learned from to develop five main animal-inspired techniques that eventually became synonymous with martial arts.

Let's take a look at the five animal patterns and techniques significant to Kung Fu.

Tiger

Tiger

The largest cat and one of the most formidable predators in all of nature is the Tiger. Today, the tiger population is slowly declining, and it is being added to the list of endangered species. However, in Ancient China, they were far from endangered. These dangerous creatures were a real threat to farmers and travelers alike. With that danger came profound respect. Kung Fu practitioners steadily developed an admiration for the fearlessness of tigers. Their courage and fierceness represent inner strength, which helps lead one towards straightforward forms with clear intent. This makes one courageous and a force to be reckoned with.

Style and Technique

Kung Fu practitioners find inspiration in one of the most vicious weapons at a tiger's disposal, which is their claws. The tiger style utilizes very strong hand movements and techniques, the "tiger fist." A practitioner's hands are actually formed into a claw-like shape to mimic the big cat. In order to turn their hands into something just as tough as the talons at the ends of the massive creature's paws, a tough, painful training process had to be employed.

Several popular training techniques are used to strengthen one's hand when practicing the Tiger style. One such technique is often referred to as the "Clawing Jar." With your hand folded in a tiger fist, grab a large empty glass or a ceramic jar. Fill the vessel with water up to its brim. You can also fill it to just half to practice in the beginning. Try to move it around in your hand as much as you can for about five to ten minutes. Every day, add another cup and keep adding until the jar is filled to the top. Next, repeat the same process with sand. This training will help strengthen and fortify every part of your hand and parts of your arms. It is simple, and you can easily find everything you need at home to practice and build your skill.

Exercises

Another exercise to build up a powerful tiger fist is called "Taming the Tiger," in which you build up the muscles and tendons in your fingers. Start by getting into a push-up position. Extend out your fingers until they're supporting your entire body's weight. With your fingers still extended, bend your arms, and lower your body to bring it close to the floor (but do not let it touch the surface). After holding your body in this position for a few seconds, pull it back up to return to your original position.

You can practice Taming the Tiger at your own pace and perform as many reps at once as you want. However, increase the number of counts and time period every time you practice. Take at least one hour every day to practice and try to do at least thirty to fifty of these finger-supported push-ups before getting to the actual training. One popular Tiger-style training technique is called the "Piercing Beans." The first thing you need to do is get your tiger fists (hands) in a tub or a basket as wide as your shoulders and filled with dry beans.

Get into the horse stance position and keep your spine straight. Both thighs need to be parallel to the ground, the mat, or the floor. Lift your hands, stick your fingers out straight (keep them rigid), and thrust them alternately into the container of beans. Try to hold back the power you're putting into this motion. Besides being designed to strengthen your hands, this exercise will also help you naturally generate more strength and build muscle memory. Repeat it a few times.

Dragon

The dragon represents the mystical and spiritual energy in Kung Fu. The three empowering or fundamental entities of this martial art are jing (internal force), chi (intrinsic energy), and shen (mind power), which collectively make one unit and thrive in harmony. They are known as the "three treasures." Despite being a mythical creature, the dragon is taken seriously in Chinese culture and philosophy. The animal represents one's fighting spirit and converts its energy into a physical force. It also stresses the importance of flexibility and grace, thereby representing the "chi" energy.

Dragon

Characteristics and Symbolization

The dragon represents prosperity, success, and luck. Hailing from water, the creature holds an important position in Chinese mythology. Its flowing movements and undulating force are well-respected in Shaolin Kung Fu. In fact, some of the toughest moves in this martial art are inspired by the swift movement of the Dragon. Its water-borne identity helps one develop inner strength and bring flexibility in their moves. Shen refers to "spirit" or "mind," and the Dragon motivates practitioners to build internal strength. At the same time, it also inspires them to stay mentally healthy, fresh, and peaceful to practice Kung Fu with grace.

The Dragon is extremely powerful and works at its own will. It can appear or disappear at any time and transcend into a supernatural state whenever it pleases. Dragons are strong, unpredictable, and deceptive. The four Shaolin animals collectively represent internal and external strength and combine several kicks and fists combinations. It is necessary to stay relaxed and focused on your movements when taking inspiration from the dragon to improve your skill. By contrast, the dragon can be extremely dangerous or act as a pacifist when unhappy or surrounded by negative energy. This opposing characteristic is also reflected in their exercises and technique.

Exercises and Techniques

The two famous moves in Kung Fu inspired by the dragon are "Dragon Claw" and "Dragon-tail Kick." Both training drills use quick movements, snapping kicks, and full fists as their main strategy. The techniques also combine several movements and exercises from other animals. Basically, masters train practitioners to become more agile, flexible, and strong. "Swimming Dragon Plays with Water" and "Green Dragon Shoots Pearls" are two other techniques related to the dragon. As mentioned, the moves inspired by the dragon can be confusing. You are moving gently with grace at one instance, and at the other, you are completely in action and ready to strike the opponent.

Basically, you can adapt to every move, technique, and fight based on your surroundings and the opponent you are fighting with. You are the complete opposite of the other person, which gives you enough flexibility and freedom to win the fight. Typical dragon-style Kung Fu warriors react to their opponent's moves after scrutinizing their moves and counterattacking by deciphering their weak points. They are also known as counterpunchers. Northern Dragon Style and Southern Dragon Style are two types of Dragon-inspired Kung Fu.

The former skill motivates the fighter to keep their ground, while the latter keeps the fighting fluid and flexible. Some spinning evasion moves are paired with rapid kicks and blocks in Northern Dragon Style Kung Fu. On the other hand, fighters confuse and evade their opponents in Southern Style Kung Fu to win the game. The "Dragon Claw" technique is one of the most common yet unique moves in Kung Fu. It strengthens your claw power and helps you win against your opponent using the power of your hand.

To practice this move, curl your middle finger, index finger, and thumb like a pincer to grab the ligaments or tendons of your opponent to win the fight. If you are trained for it, you can also use an open palm or your palm's heel to bring your opponent down.

Crane

Crane

The crane represents poise, grace, and steadiness in Kung Fu. The techniques inspired by this animal relatively need less strength and are based on evasive movements. When calm, the bird stands elegantly on one leg. However, when it sees rising tides and winds, it takes action and pecks with precision to combat the situation. The bird inspires several Kung Fu techniques for this reason. The crane can also inspire you in your daily life. It teaches elegance and grace. If you are clumsy or seeking to develop elegance, learn from the crane and boost your self-improvement process.

Characteristics

The crane represents the "jing" energy. It portrays essence and elegance as its main features. Ideally, the crane stays silent, poised, and calm at all times. However, when needed, it can strike with action. Even when in action, the movements are kept bare minimum and extremely straightforward. The famous Shaolin quote, "The spirit of the crane, resides within the stillness," is the main motivation behind the Kung Fu moves. The bird takes less offense and focuses on the weak points of the opponent. Despite being less popular than other animals in Kung Fu, the crane's energy and defense mechanisms are probably the strongest and basically unbeatable.

Some vital and soft areas targeted by the bird include the throat, eyes, ribs, sides of the head, and heart. Just like the crane, the practitioner needs to be tall and possess strong concentration levels. They should also have a good balance and have the ability to use as little energy as possible. More importantly, they should be able to remain still and calm for a longer period, which means that they should be extremely patient. When in crisis, the crane uses its weightlessness to keep things in control and drive results with accuracy.

Exercises and Techniques

As mentioned, practitioners need minimal strength when practicing Kung Fu techniques related to the crane. They focus on the upper body parts of the opponents during a strike. Critical areas like the throat and the eyes are the primary attack points. The techniques are also based on self-defense mechanisms that give the practitioners optimum strength and help them keep their opponents off balance. A famous soft style exercise inspired by this animal is the "Crane Beak." Practitioners finding trouble in gaining strength or the ones who are physically weak can rely on the Crane Beak technique to win their game.

When practicing this technique, you need to bunch your index finger, middle finger, and thumb together to make a hook-like shape resembling a crane's beak. You then need to focus on just one point and sway your hand into a pecking motion with a thrusting force. Kicks are also an integral part of the crane-related Kung Fu movements. Combined with the "Phoenix-Eye Fist," Crane Beak moves become stronger as they collectively attack the vital points. "Satisfied Reincarnated Crane" and "Crane Stands Amongst Cockerels" are two other forms or techniques developed from the crane's pose and movements.

Snake

Snake

As the Shaolin saying goes, "Hard like steel and soft like a rope of silk," the snake can be strong and deceptive. It is fast, agile, precise, and accurate in its moves. It can easily intimidate people by hissing at them but not necessarily attacking them. The reptile stays aware at all times and can scare its enemies by repeating coiling motions and utilizing its thin yet quick muscles. It can also easily hide from them, thereby giving it a chance to attack with precision. Every move and bite from the snake is poisonous, which is why the one on the receiving end must be more aware when tackling the creature.

Symbolization

The snake represents "chi" energy, which relates to profound sensitivity and awakening. The creature is aware at all times and therefore ready to attack its opponents at any given point in time. It is known as the "earth dragon" and glides smoothly to achieve its goals. The spirit and energy are intricately connected, just like the serpent's characteristics. It thrives in harmony with the chi energy, which collectively represents endurance and fluidity. It drives one's internal force and keeps the practitioners' movements smooth. When the snake is completely aware, it can use all of its muscle power and memory to make targeted strikes.

The serpent also acts as a revelation to promote good values in your everyday life. For example, it instills the importance of being grounded, precise in your moves, and more self-aware. It also symbolizes luck and health. It inspires you to keep training and working hard. Your weaknesses can be turned into your strength if you are dedicated and consistent. In Chinese astrology, the serpent is an important symbol used by the emperor. The snake also portrays certain signs possessed by the other four animals in Shaolin Kung Fu, thereby creating harmony among all creatures.

Techniques

One of the most popular techniques inspired by the serpent is the "Snake Hand form," which is a powerful defense technique. It uses one or two fingers to exert a thrusting force on the opponents. This movement can also take every opponent by surprise as it is extremely agile and explosive. The practitioner must work on building their muscles as the technique demands major muscle power. They should also be quick on their feet and build a thin silhouette for swift movements. The main body parts attacked through this technique include the throat, face, and eyes, considered the opponents' weak points.

The "Snake Hand" and "Spear Hand" are two other popular techniques in Kung Fu inspired by the serpent. Some other lesser-known techniques are "Snake Basking in Mist," "White Snake Crosses Valley," and "Poisonous Snake Shoots Venom." An important part of training for the serpent techniques in Kung Fu includes the development of self-awareness. Some trainers ask their students to build self-awareness and improve focus. This can help them become more aware of their subconscious thoughts and surroundings, which is necessary to improve self-defense and beat opponents with precision. This, in turn, also saves a lot of energy.

Leopard

Leopard

The leopard in Shaolin Kung Fu represents the saying, "Bend fingers hard, like iron." The leopard represents speed, calculation, efficiency, stealth, and strength. Leopards are also known for their hunting skills and high speed, especially when covering a short distance. When they spot prey, leopards hide or lurk stealthily, ready to pounce. Without alerting their prey, they look for the perfect moment to attack the smaller animal.

Characteristics

The leopard symbolizes instantaneous speed. Its moves are explosive in nature, and it focuses on counterattacks to win the game. It signifies the "Li" energy, which stresses the importance of muscular strength. When you train as a leopard, you can easily combat everyday struggles and move swiftly through your daily tasks. You can also notice an increase in your speed as you tackle important tasks and take necessary actions. Some compare the characteristics and techniques of the leopard with the tiger as both belong to the same family. However, there is a major difference between both animals in terms of movements and efficiency.

The tiger focuses on power and strength, whereas the leopard pays attention to precision and quickness. Just like a leopard, practitioners need to build supple strength to pounce easily and retract their limbs to throw an efficient strike. The leopard is brave, courageous, and fierce. Instead of being scared, the animal intimidates its opponents by simply showing up. The practitioner also needs to build torso strength and develop agility around their waist as that area helps them make swift movements. At the same time, high speed and power are the two other qualities the practitioner must improve on and maintain.

Techniques

The main strategy deployed by Kung Fu moves related to the leopard is *stealth and quickness.* Just like the leopard attacks with speed, Kung Fu practitioners attack to inflict pain to distract their opponents and thrust a major blow to go for the kill. In a way, they use distraction to win. The main attacking areas are the armpits, groin, neck, ears, and temples, which are basically all the regions with soft tissues. The practitioner must build strength and develop muscles to pounce on their opponent to inflict pain and cause distraction. Another requirement is supple strength. "Golden Leopard Watches Fire" and "Golden Leopard Speeds through Forest" are some of the other typical techniques.

The main technique used in this form of Kung Fu is the "Leopard Paw," in which the practitioner makes a half fist and attacks the opponent with two knuckles. This blow is intense and can make painful contact with the surface. Sharpening the Leopard Paw technique is extremely crucial as it is the first instinct of any attack. The stronger the blow is, the weaker the opponent becomes to fight right from the beginning. It should be lightning-fast, efficient, and sharp. Masters suggest that their students work hard on improving their precision as the strike should be placed at accurate spots and points.

Chapter 4: Stances in Kung Fu

There are several stances in Kung Fu, and most of them are derived from the five primary stances. This chapter focuses on five stances: the Horse Stance, Cat Stance, Forward Stance, Twist Stance, and Crane Stance. It begins by outlining the importance of stances in Kung Fu and also highlights other positions that may be of interest to you.

Significance of Stances in Kung Fu

Stances play a fundamental role when you are practicing Shaolin Kung Fu. They form the basis of learning this type of martial art, but most students usually take a long time to realize their importance. On the first day of learning Shaolin Kung Fu, every student is introduced to basic stances, including Forward Stance, Horse Stance, and Cat stance. During the introductory lesson, most students will develop a keen interest in knowing more about these stances. At this stage, the student becomes eager to learn high kicks, some fancy movements, and other fighting techniques.

After training for a long time, this is when you can fully appreciate the significance of stances in Shaolin Kung Fu. While the stances are basic and are usually taught in the first lesson, constant training determines whether you have mastered the skill of properly applying them or not. Novices are usually interested in watching the hand movements, but experienced practitioners observe the stances and bodywork when they view performance. The stances drive the hand motions, which give them power.

Furthermore, the stances are crucial because they allow you to use your body effectively. With a proper stance, you can control the motion of your body. All body movements pass through various stances, which help provide hand techniques and a solid foundation for coordinating different parts of the body. The stances also help you harness ground power when you execute various moves. The following section discusses the basic stances of Shaolin Kung Fu.

Horse Stance

Horse Stance

The Horse Stance is the first stance you will learn when you start your journey in learning Kung Fu. The Horse Stance basically means horse-riding stance, and it represents a wide squat. You can easily get into this stance where you stand with your feet and make sure they are positioned wide apart. The width of your shoulder should be parallel to your feet. When you are in this stance, bend your knees and try to rest your body down.

This stance constitutes basic training for different styles used in Kung Fu. First and foremost, the Horse stance plays a crucial role in strengthening the legs. To be an effective fighter, your legs should have sufficient power to maintain your balance. In other words, the major purpose of this stance is endurance training, which helps strengthen the tendons and leg muscles. It also teaches students how to relax in their stance in such a way that their center of gravity is low. There is no need to push the chest outward in this position. This is essential since the power in Kung Fu is obtained from the ground. Students can also sit in a particular stance when practicing different hand moves. For instance, you can use it to practice punches while at the same time learning how to evade attacks.

When you practice this stance, make sure you keep your feet out, and they should be wider than your shoulders. While maintaining your feet facing forward, slowly squat into a position that resembles a person riding a horse. Make sure that your posture is flat and the spine is in a straight position. How low you get in this stance significantly varies depending on the Kung Fu style you want to practice.

If you want to train using the Horse stance, you should first get a stick and assume the position. While in this position, put the stick on top of your knees and hold your arms outward. The palms should be parallel to your body. You should not allow the stick to fall. Repeat the exercise until you familiarize yourself with this stance.

Forward Stance

This is a crucial step in Shaolin Kung Fu. It is useful for moving your body forward, and it helps form a stable base to allow you to generate power and perform advanced movements. When you are attacking an opponent, you must utilize this stance to ensure that you are in a proper position. Your weight will be on the front leg, and it determines the action you will take.

Forward Stance

In this stance, bend your front knee while your back leg is straight. When you view the stance from the side, it will look like a drawn bow. As such, its other name is the bow stance. Others prefer to call it the forward-leaning stance, and it is used in different styles of martial arts. The shoulders and hips should remain facing forward. Essentially, the main purpose of this stance is to teach the practitioner musculoskeletal alignment, which plays a crucial role in adding the earth's mass to the strike. With this stance, you have a great chance of generating forward power. However, very little power can be generated in the reverse direction.

In Kung Fu, the Front Stance is practiced using different variations depending on the particular style you wish to undertake. The other function of the stance is to give you stability while you project the weight of your body forward. This often happens when punching to deliver a powerful blow to your opponent. When you strike, you should make sure that the punch is strong enough to have a competitive advantage over the opponent.

Your straight rear leg will push the center of gravity forward to ensure that the body's full weight is behind your strike. In this case, the bent front leg will help support body weight. Additionally, you can also use the front stance to move forward or backward as long as you are sure that the center of gravity or bodyweight is projected forward. The center of gravity is critical since it determines the power of the strike and its impact on the victim. In contrast, the back stance is used when you place the weight of your body on the rear leg. For instance, you assume this position when you lean backward to evade an attack.

Cat Stance

The Cat Stance is primarily meant for mobility and other transitional movements from one position to the other. All your body weight will be on your back leg while the front leg will rest on the ball of the foot of the toe. Your front leg should resemble the way a cat puts its paw out when it takes a step. There will be no weight on the paw, and this is where the name came from. You can use the front leg to shift to another stance or to kick your opponent.

It is still fine if you start your stance from a higher level then move down slowly with your training. This stance is versatile, and it allows you to move quickly and to remain light on your feet. When using this stance, you must visualize the cat as it readies to swiftly spring forward swiftly to catch its prey. You should aim to do the same when you use this particular style.

Cat Stance

If you want to practice the left cat stance, step the right foot back from the starting position. Turn the right foot you moved back clockwise at an angle of about 45 degrees so that you can get a better balance. The next move is to bend your right knee in such a way that you place about 90% of your weight on that leg. Your left foot should reach out in front, and you use the ball of the foot to place it on the ground. Do not use the base of the foot when grounding your left foot. You will only place very little downward pressure using your left leg. The benefit of this move is that little harm will be caused if the opponent tries the trick of sweeping your lead leg. Furthermore, you can also use your lead leg to avoid the sweep.

The Cat Stance offers excellent balance when you use it as a front kick snap in such a way that you keep the opponent at bay. Since there is little weight exerted on your front leg, you can quickly deploy it and use the ball of your foot as a weapon. The stance is an effective way of attacking your opponent if you use it as self-defense.

Twist Stance

The Twist Stance is a transitional stance, and your legs will appear twisted to help you execute your next move. Your front foot should be turned outward, while your back foot should be resting on the front foot's ball. You can use this stance to advance toward the opponent or to retreat when you realize that you are under pressure. You can also use it to change the position of the body. If you want to change direction, you untwist the legs and resume the stance once positioned correctly.

Twist Stance

You can also use the twist stance to execute a concealed sidekick. It is good in that it helps you get good balance which helps you perform various moves when facing the opponent. When the opponent attempts to sweep your front leg, you can keep your balance because of the little weight on that side. Furthermore, you can counter the attack by attempting another sweep on the opponent. The stance is also used to dodge low attacks.

The Twist Stance is useful in several ways, depending on how you want to use it. The way you get into this stance or come out of it determines how you can effectively use it. You can pivot into many throws or utilize your twisting momentum to bring the opponent down. You can also perform a sweeping technique when your hands move in the opposite direction.

Crane Stance

The Crane Stance resembles the way a crane stands on one leg. With this stance, you stand on one leg while the other one is raised. The stance is commonly used in Kung Fu and other forms of martial arts since it helps develop body coordination and balance. Essentially, the stance is focused on training the student to maintain balance while standing on one leg.

Crane Stance

You can use the stance to kick the opponent or evade and attack. When you kick the opponent using this stance, you can reach higher. You can also use it to perform sidekicks while maintaining the balance of your body on one leg. You build this stance by raising your knee to its maximum height while facing the opponent.

Remember that, with the crane stance, your supporting leg should be bent at knee level. This helps you maintain balance and enhance the execution of your kicks. If you lock your knee, it becomes very easy to lose balance, creating room for the opponent to attack. You may also have trouble performing follow-up techniques if your knee is locked. Eventually, this will render your stance useless.

The sidekick that you execute from a Crane Stance can be combined with a back strike. When you use your sidekick on the opponent, they will fall toward you, and this is when you can strike their head with a back fist. If you follow this stance and execute your kicks well, you will gain a competitive advantage over your opponent.

These are the five basic stances in Shaolin Kung Fu you should know if you want to become a master in this martial art. As you progress through your training, you will realize that there are also several other stances you must know. The following are some of the stances that you may need to know as you advance in your journey of mastering Kung Fu.

Bow Stance

Bow Stance

The bow stance is a variation of the forward stance, and it plays a critical role in Kung Fu. This basic stance involves moving your body forward, which gives you the stability to generate more power and advance your movement. When you are in this stance, you can pivot the center of your weight on the front leg to ensure maximum force when you hit your target. Your back leg should be straight, while your front knee should be bent. If you view this stance from the side, it looks like a drawn bow, which is why it is also known as the bow stance. You should make sure that both heels line up. Do not forget the back heel when you move forward.

Lower Stance

Most Kung Fu students don't like this stance because it requires you to assume a very wide horse stance. You will place the entire weight of your body on one leg, and you should squat as low as you can. This stance is primarily meant to help you avoid high attacks, knee, ankle, and groin attacks. Since you will be squatting very low in this stance, it tends to exert some pressure on your lower muscles which can cause pain.

If you are looking forward to learning Kung Fu, your first lesson will cover different stances. You must pay attention to these stances since they affect almost every move you make, and coordinate elements like body movement and footwork. Therefore, you should not neglect different stances as they affect almost everything you do in Kung Fu.

Chapter 5: The Lohan Pattern

The Lohan Pattern is one of the most important aspects of Kung Fu. It is a series of 18 hand movements used for many purposes, including self-defense and their health benefits. The Lohan pattern comes from Buddhist scripture but has been modified over the years to fit different styles of Kung Fu. In this article, we will discuss each movement in detail to become more familiar with them.

Origin of the Lohan Pattern

The Lohan Pattern was first introduced to the Shaolin monks in the 18th century when Daai Yuk came across Buddhist scripture that detailed hand movements described as "18 Hands of Luohan". This became known as The Lohan pattern and has been used in many styles of Kung Fu ever since then.

According to an ancient legend, a Buddhist monk, Bodhidharma, credited as the founder of Shaolin Kung Fu, meditated for many years to reach enlightenment. During this time, he had lost all his energy and strength because of his lack of movement. He decided that if he were to regain these powers, it would be through rigorous exercises. These exercises were designed to teach others how they too can improve their health and spiritual well-being.

The Lohan Pattern is meant to be one of the foundations in Wushu training because it helps develop a person's awareness and coordination through movement. It also teaches how to defend oneself when necessary, which can become useful for many different reasons (i.e., self-defense or if you're attacked). The patterns are meant to be forms of meditation where your mind can focus on the movements. You can relieve stress, improve coordination, and have a more focused mindset by practicing these hand patterns.

Importance of Lohan Hand Patterns for Kung Fu

Understanding Lohan hand patterns can help you improve your Kung Fu. It is a series of 18 exercises originally meant to develop strength, flexibility, and coordination within the body. However, many schools have modified them over time to work on self-defense skills as well. For example, some movements are used to trap or grapple opponents, while others help relax the body after fighting.

The number 18 is significant in Buddhism, so The Lohan Pattern has become an integral part of Kung Fu. Though everyone may have their own interpretation of it, each style emphasizes knowing these patterns inside and out. By gaining a complete understanding of this pattern, you will improve your Kung Fu skills.

These hand patterns are also called Qigong exercises and were kept secret for many years in the famous Shaolin Temple. Though they were shared with monks and other Kung Fu masters, the movements were kept secret so no one could copy their fighting style.

The Importance of Chi Kung for Kung Fu

Chi kung (also known as Qi gong) is an aspect of Kung Fu that focuses on cultivating and controlling energy throughout the body. This includes harnessing it to make your body stronger, more flexible, or even heal certain ailments.

Chi has been around for many years but was first mentioned in ancient China by the Yellow Emperor. He stated that there were two energies within all living things: Yin and Yang. Yin is considered to be female energy, while Yang is male energy. They work together in harmony to create Chi (energy). This can then lead to good health and even enlightenment if harnessed correctly.

The Lohan Pattern is one of many exercises that can help you with your Chi Kung. Performing these movements helps improve flexibility, strength, and coordination, eventually leading to better Kung Fu skills.

For Wushu enthusiasts, this means that they must learn how to perform these hand patterns to become better martial artists.

Practicing the Lohan Pattern

The Lohan Pattern is often mistaken for merely physical exercise. However, it is much more than that. It is a Chi Kung exercise, which engages both the mind and the body to achieve miraculous results.

It is therefore vital to learn how to perform this pattern correctly. The most common mistake is the lack of focus and concentration when performing these movements. You must put your heart into it to better understand the purpose of learning Kung Fu in general.

To gain maximum benefits out of the Lohan exercises, they should be performed along with Chi Kung breathing. This will help build the energy within your body and allow you to feel a stronger connection with each movement.

Importance of Practicing with a Master

The exercises described in this chapter are merely physical forms of the exercise. To get the full benefit of practice, learning more about the mind and energy is crucial. The masters of Shaolin teach these techniques of the internal dimension. Hence, whenever possible, you should practice with a master of Shaolin Kung Fu.

The Basics of the Lohan Patterns

Here is a brief explanation of the 18 movements with some images to help you better understand them.

Lifting the Sky

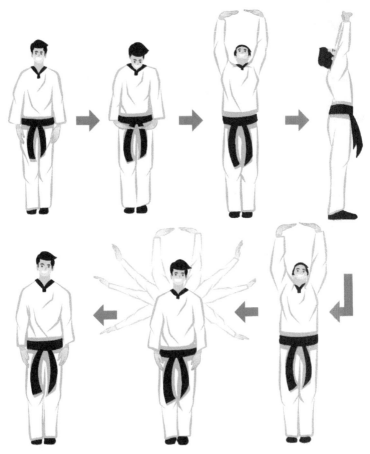

The first pattern begins with both hands reaching up to the sky. They are then brought down on either side of your body.

This means that you must stretch out forward and raise your arms above your head as if picking something heavy like a sack of rice. When doing this exercise, your palms should be facing upward, which is the opposite of what you might expect.

After reaching up, the hands are brought down on either side of your torso to form a level line with both arms fully extended.

Shooting Arrows

Shooting Arrows

The next movement is where things get a little more complicated. Here, one hand shoots out while the other pulls back in an arrow-like fashion.

A common mistake here is to move both hands together so they are parallel or even pointing slightly downwards. Instead, make sure to move one arm at a time. This ensures that you are properly engaging your core muscles while performing this exercise.

Plucking Stars

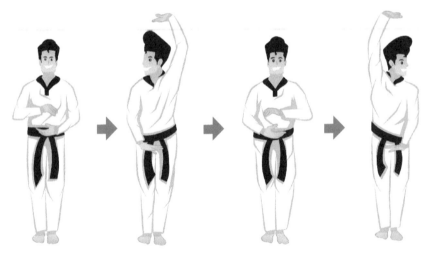

Extend one hand skyward, palm facing up, and extend the other hand downward, palm facing down. Keep your arms close to your body and stretch out skyward.

You should then bring that arm back to your side while extending the opposite arm in an upward motion.

As your hand reaches the top of its movement, it should be palm facing up while your other arm is still at your side. When you bring that arm back to rest, extend the other one in a downward motion again.

Turning Head

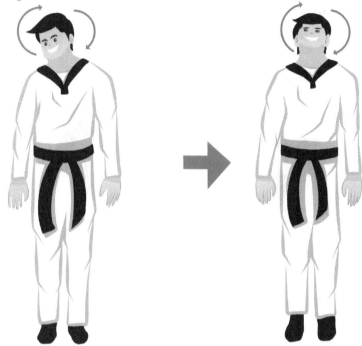

Turning Head

Rotate your head in a circular fashion as if you are turning your head around to look at the sky.

The head is a very important part of this exercise as it connects our mind with our body. Therefore, make sure that you keep your neck straight and do not awkwardly push or pull forward when performing these movements.

This pattern is known to have numerous benefits for the nervous system.

Merry-Go-Round

Merry-Go Round

Bring your hands together, join them and intertwine your fingers. Now imagine you are holding a stick in your hand. Circulate your arms, outstretched, around your body. Move from your waist.

This exercise works well to wake you up and stimulate your blood flow.

Thrust Punch

Thrust Punch

Assume a wide stance, toes pointing in 180-degree angles. Now, just like practicing a punch, thrust your arms forward with one arm on top of the other.

As you move them out, extend both fists together to form an L shape in front of your body. Then bring it back down to rest by crossing both hands over each other at chest level while still keeping a wide stance.

The Thrust Punch pattern is a great exercise for your heart, lungs, kidneys, and digestive system.

Carrying the Moon

Carrying the Moon

This pattern starts with you bending forward at the waist without bending your knees. Try to bend as far as possible towards your toes. Now, in the next step, lift your arms skyward to perform the core position. In the final step, separate your hands by bringing them down sideways.

This exercise boosts youth and vitality and is excellent for your back ailments.

Nourishing Kidneys

Nourishing Kidneys

Start with your arms on your waist. Bend backward. In the second step, bend at the waist and touch your toes with your fingers without bending your knees.

Kidney function is closely related to reproductive wellness. This position is crucial for fertility, vitality, and sciatica-related issues.

Three Levels to Ground

This is a basic squat where your arms are stretched out sideways. This exercise is well-known as the "frog position" and is very effective for your legs.

Doing multiple repetitions will raise your heart rate and improve cardiovascular fitness.

Dancing Crane

Bend your knees and shift your weight to one leg. Now move the other foot forward while keeping the knee bent to a 90-degree angle, forming an L shape with both legs.

This exercise is great for increasing joint flexibility and building strong bones by stimulating calcium production in the body.

Carrying Mountains

Stand in an upright position. Raise your arms sideways to a shoulder level. Now twist through your waist so that your lower body is facing the front, and your upper body (waist up) is facing sideways. Repeat this on both sides. This position is ideal for chronic back pain.

Drawing Knife

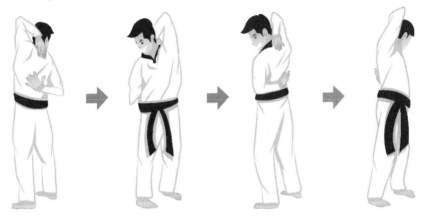

Start by standing in an upright position, feet together. Hold stance. Now imagine holding something behind your back with one arm. Raise the other arm and now put it behind your head to touch the other arm. Imagine pulling out an arrow from your quiver.

Presenting Claws

Presenting Claws

In a wide stance, raise your hands to your chest, palms facing outward. Now bend your fingers like claws. This is your starting position. In the second step, move one hand to your side and raise the other skyward. Now to reach the final position, bend sideways at the waist so that the raised hand bends in the opposite direction over your head. Repeat for the other side.

Pushing Mountains

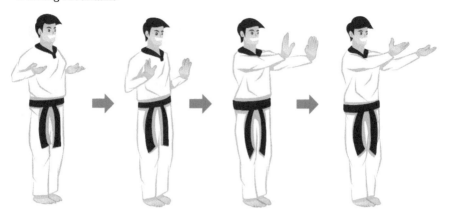

Pushing Mountains

Keep your knees slightly bent. As if you were pushing against a wall, push the palms of both hands together, like they were stuck to each other.

This pattern is great for relieving mental stress and builds strength throughout the body. It will also tone your legs and arms over time because it assists with circulation.

Separating Water

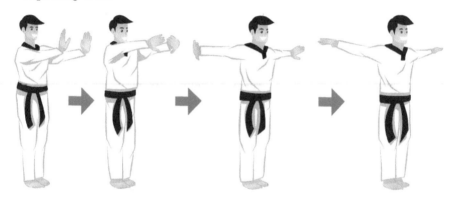

Start with your feet together, arms by the side. Now lift both arms sideways to your shoulders. Next, bring them to the front and sweep them sideways as if swimming. This pattern is very useful for developing arm strength.

Big Windmill

This is an easy one. Simply rotate your arms in 360 degrees while standing upright. Repeat for both arms.

Deep Knee Bending

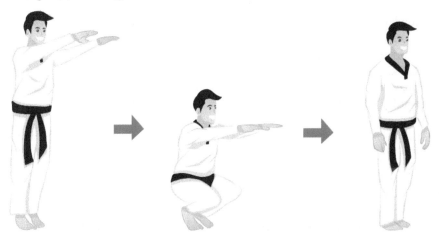

A deep knee bend is nothing but a squat on your toes and arms stretched out in front of you. Arms should be parallel to the ground. This is also an excellent cardiovascular exercise.

Begin in an upright stance. Now bend forward and hold both your knees with your hands. Slowly move both knees in a circular motion, clockwise followed by anti-clockwise direction.

This exercise is useful for relieving knee pain and also helps in toning your legs. It should be repeated multiple times for the best results. However, be mindful of your posture and do not go too fast and sprain your knee.

Practicing the Lohan Pattern Exercises

As mentioned earlier, these patterns effectively enhance your physical strength and calm your mind. Try to practice them at least once a day for the best results.

Here is a sample workout plan:

Monday - Rotating Knees (20 times clockwise & anti-clockwise)

Tuesday – Deep knee bending (50 times)

Wednesday – Carrying Mountains (20 times each)

Thursday – Drawing Knife (15 times on both sides)

Friday - Dancing Crane (50 repetitions) & Pushing Mountains (25 times each arm).

Saturday – Big Windmill (25 times clockwise & anti-clockwise)

Sunday - Separating Water (100 repetitions)

If you follow this plan for a month, your physical and mental health will improve significantly. Make sure to avoid foods with preservatives and processed sugar during the course of Lohan Pattern exercises.

Once you get familiar with all of the exercises, aim to do at least a couple of repetitions of each one on a daily basis.

Finding a Kung Fu Master Trainer

Performing the exercises by yourself could be overwhelming. So, we suggest hiring a Kung Fu master trainer to guide you through the process. However, finding one could be tough and your best bet is to ask around or look for one online.

Alternatively, you can also check out a few videos on YouTube that teach these exercises in detail.

Lohan Pattern Exercises for Beginners

If you are a beginner, starting with an easy exercise like rotating your knees or arms is best. Start off slowly and gradually increase your speed over time until the movement becomes fluid.

Once you build up enough stamina for this pattern, move on to other patterns. Some of the more advanced exercises, such as drawing a knife and dancing with a crane, can take months before you get used to them. So be patient and don't rush through your workout plan.

Also, it is important to focus on getting the stance right rather than focusing on repetitions. A good stance is what provides support to your body and aids in strengthening the muscles evenly throughout.

Lohan Pattern Exercises for Weight Loss

If you are looking at these patterns from the perspective of losing weight, then you're better off starting with the deep knee bend. This is because of its high intensity and will help you lose weight faster than other exercises.

However, it is suggested that beginners start small if they are not used to such strenuous activities. Rotating knees or arms is perfect for losing those extra pounds.

The Lohan Pattern is a series of exercises that are designed to have both physical and mental benefits. These exercises can do wonders from helping with weight loss, improving posture, alleviating joint pain, or just providing you with the opportunity for some deep breathing. However, they're not exactly easy. Start off slowly and take your time mastering each pattern before moving on to more difficult ones like drawing knives or dancing cranes. Also, remember to focus on getting the stance right instead of focusing solely on repetitions when performing these patterns. A good stance will provide support for your body and help strengthen all your muscles if done correctly.

Though all of these exercises look simple to perform, they are not easy. It takes a lot of focus and patience to perfect each movement pattern. So, we suggest that you don't rush through your routine and spend at least 15 minutes every day on Lohan Pattern exercises if you want the best results.

Chapter 6: Chi and Zen in Kung Fu

When practicing Shaolin Kung Fu, it is essential to keep in mind that there's more to it than just the physical aspect of the martial art. It also encourages practitioners to grow spiritually alongside their improvement in combat, and it does so by focusing on two concepts, Chi and Zen.

Understanding Chi

Chi, sometimes known as Qi, is a Chinese word that can literally be translated to "vapor," "air," or "breath." More metaphorically, it is often translated as "vital energy," "material energy," "vital force," or simply "energy."

This concept is critical to a number of traditional Chinese beliefs and practices, including Taoism, traditional Chinese medicine, and Chinese martial arts, including Kung Fu.

A simple way to understand it is to look at how the word is written in Chinese. The symbol for "Chi" is a combination of two other Chinese symbols, those for "steam" and "rice."

When understood according to the way the word is written, Chi literally represents the steam rising from rice or, more accurately, the energy the rice is giving out.

In the more basic sense, that's precisely what Chi is. The energy or the life force that animates the world. It encompasses a variety of phenomena known to the Western world and represents the flow and vibrations happening continuously at the molecular, atomic, and sub-atomic levels of nature.

Though Chi is little understood – and even less accepted – in the modern Western world, a variety of other cultures has theorized the idea of a life force that flows through all living things. This life force is known as:

- Ki in Japan
- Prana or shakti in India
- Ka by ancient Egyptians
- The Great Spirit by Native Americans
- Pneuma by ancient Greeks
- Ashe in Hawaii
- Ha or mana by Native Hawaiians

Indeed, some theorists even equate Chi to the Christian understanding of the Holy Spirit.

Types of Chi

There are numerous different types of Chi/Qi, as identified by practitioners of traditional Chinese medicine. These include:

- **Yuan Qi:** The innate Chi that we're born with. It is also known as Ancestral Qi.
- **Heaven Qi or Tian Qi:** Made up of natural forces, including the rain and the sun.
- **Earth Qi, or Di Qi:** Affected by Heaven Qi. For example, too much sun leads to drought, while too little sun causes the plants to die.
- **Human Qi, or Ren Qi:** Affected by Earth Qi in the same way humans are affected by the earth.

- **Hou Tain Qi (also known as Postnatal Qi):** The Chi that you absorb from food, water, and air that you consume during your life.
- **Wei Qi (or Protective Qi):** The Chi that acts as a protective sheath around your body.

Additionally, each internal organ has its own Chi. Some of these include the spleen, the liver, the lungs, and the kidneys.

Taoist cosmology holds that there are two other important forms of Chi: Yin-Qi and Yang-Qi, primordial masculine and feminine energies flowing through the world.

On the other hand, the practice of Qigong often involves using both Heaven and Earth Qis, while Feng Shui is the balancing of all three – Heaven, Earth, and Human Qis.

Each type has its own effects and uses.

Feeling Chi

In Qigong and traditional Chinese medicine, balanced and free-flowing Chi results in good health. On the other hand, if you have stagnant or imbalanced Chi, you will suffer from the disease. This holds true at both the micro (human) and macro (ecosystem) levels. Imbalanced Chi can lead to issues in the natural world.

There are numerous ways to re-establish free-flowing Chi through your body, including through the practice of Qigong and Feng Shui. One of the abilities that helps with this is the ability to perceive the flow of Chi, both in you and in others (both animate and inanimate) around you.

It is essential to keep in mind that the ability to feel Chi is a skill, which means that some people are simply naturally more gifted at it than others. In fact, if you're skilled enough, you may even unknowingly perceive the Chi around you.

Consider this, have you ever spoken to someone and gotten a "bad vibe" from them? Or walked into a room and was able to tell things were tense? Both of these are essentially your ability to feel the Chi of the people and things around you manifesting themselves.

Aside from making you more perceptive, the smooth flow of Chi in your body also enhances creativity and stabilizes your mood. Furthermore, it helps you reach a higher state of consciousness.

Working with Chi

There are numerous ways to work with your Chi. Some common techniques include:

- **Acupuncture:** Acupuncture points can be used to redirect the flow of Chi through the meridians of your body. The meridians are the "strings" connecting acupuncture points and serving as the "passageways" through which energy flows through your body.
- **Qigong:** A system of body movements and poses that help with Kung Fu training and cultivates and balances your Chi. Tai Chi is closely associated with Qigong. It is an internal martial style that involves more complex movements that are choreographed with breathwork and can be used for self-defense. Many scholars consider Tai Chi to be a subset of Qigong rather than a different style altogether.
- **Yoga and Meditation:** This helps unify the body and the mind. Certain yoga poses can help in the accumulation and blockage of Chi, which is released when you exit the pose, allowing the gathered Chi to flow through your body. Meditation helps you focus so you can get rid of any other blockages

hindering the flow of your Chi.

Chi Exercises

Here are two exercises you can use when working with your Chi:

Breathing Exercise

For this exercise:

- Find a comfortable position. It can be sitting, standing, or even lying down.
- Inhale through your nose and exhale through your mouth, extending the exhalation for as long as you can.
- Let your body inhale automatically. When the air enters your lungs through your nose, open your mouth and let it all out.
- Repeat for as long as possible. Aside from helping you with your Chi, this exercise can also help you catch your breath when you're feeling breathless and can even help boost your energy levels.

Ball of Energy

To activate the ball of energy you will be working with, you should:

- Rub your hands together vigorously.
- Bring your hands in front of your face, holding them in a relaxed prayer position. However, do not let them touch each other.
- Focus your energy on the center of your palms. You should start to feel a sensation similar to a magnetic force between your palms.
- Try to imagine this force or energy coalescing into a small ball of light energy between your palms.

Now, you can start working with the ball of energy. To do so, you will need to:

- Separate your hands slowly, and then close them again (without letting them touch). You should feel a slight resistance between your palms, kind of like two magnets are repelling each other.
- Repeat the step above so that you can get familiar with the feel of the energy.
- Once you're ready, practice throwing the ball of energy from one hand to the other, throwing with one hand and catching it with the other.
- While maintaining equal distance between your palms, try to rotate the ball between your hands.

Blending Chi

In the exercise, you will start to become aware of the forms of Chi that surround you and start understanding how you can blend them together harmoniously. To perform the exercise, you should:

- Stand with your knees slightly bent and your feet shoulder's width apart.
- Shift your weight to the balls of your feet, staying aware of your body's front side. Concentrate on the energy passing through your legs, chest, torso, the tops of your arms and hands, and face.
- After holding this position, shift your weight to your heels. Now it is time to concentrate on how your energy passes through the back of your body, from the back of your head to your arms and spine, all the way down to your legs.

Note: While you will start out holding this position and the one above for only about a minute, after practice, you should be able to hold it for up to 5 minutes at once.

- Repeat the steps above, this time focusing on the left and right of the body rather than the back and front.
- Repeat the first three steps carefully. Repeat them in a way that the motion is as invisible to the naked eye as possible. Instead, use your mind to move your weight while you feel your Chi flowing through the front and back of your body.
- Try feeling the way your Chi flows through the front and back of your body simultaneously, rather than differently.

Chi, Qigong, and Shaolin Kung Fu

There are two aspects in traditional Kung Fu: Neigong (the external, physical exercises) and Neijing (internal exercises focusing on the Chi).

Practicing Qigong and working with your Chi helps you improve your skills at Neijing. This, in turn, is used to gain an advantage when using martial art in combat. For example, you can use Neijing to collect the energy you possess and direct this energy into an opponent through the contact point on their body. This contact point is the only gateway through which you can conduct Neijing energies.

Without conscious control of your Chi, Neijing is difficult (if not impossible) to learn. Starting small with a few exercises will help you build up to a point where you can control Chi well enough to employ it in Shaolin Kung Fu.

Understanding Zen

Zen is the Japanese term for the Chinese word "Chan," which, in itself, is the Chinese pronunciation of the Sanskrit word "Dhyana" ("meditation"). It is a name given to a particular school of Mahayana Buddhism that developed in China during the Tang Dynasty, before traveling across East Asia to Japan. Before it spread to Japan, it was known as Chan Buddhism.

Zen Buddhism emphasizes the practices of meditation, rigorous self-restraint, and an exploration into the nature of the mind and the nature of things. This insight is meant to be expressed in daily life, especially as a way to benefit others.

Essentially, Zen Buddhism focuses less on doctrine and sutras and more on actual spiritual practice to better understand the self, the world around you, and Buddhism itself.

While it is undeniable that Zen Buddhism has been influential in the way the outside world views Buddhism as a religion - think of how the word "zen" is used today - this doesn't explain how it is relevant to Shaolin Kung Fu.

Zen and Shaolin Kung Fu

Shaolin Kung Fu is known as such because it was developed in China's famous Shaolin Temple. While Chinese martial arts existed before the development of Shaolin Kung Fu, the rise of the temple represented the first time one was institutionalized.

The Shaolin Temple was also home to the monk Bodhidharma, who is traditionally credited with spreading Chan Buddhism in China.

Legend holds that Bodhidharma first reached and requested entry to the Shaolin Temple about 30 years after it was founded. When he was denied, he climbed into the mountains and meditated in a cave for nine years before he was finally allowed entry.

In those nine years, Bodhidharma is said to have exercised as a way to stay fit. These exercises were what would become the foundation for Shaolin Kung Fu. Thus, he is credited with being the creator of Shaolin Kung Fu.

While there are questions about the credibility of this story, it cannot be denied that the Shaolin Temple was both the center of Chan (or Zen) Buddhism and Kung Fu.

In 618, monks from the Shaolin Temple took part in battles to defend the Tang Dynasty, and in the 16th century, they defended the Japanese coastline from pirates and fought bandit armies.

Due to this link, Shaolin Kung Fu has long been generally considered a form of practicing Chan Buddhism and Zen. In fact, it was given the term "wuchan," or "martial chan," and was considered to be a form of inner cultivation in Chan Buddhism. Chinese Buddhism would later go on to adopt these cultivation exercises as a way to increase concentration. Indeed, in some ways, Shaolin Kung Fu can be considered the physical path to achieving Zen.

Zen is considered as a way to distinguish Shaolin Kung Fu and other East Asian martial arts like Judo from other sports.

It provides Shaolin Kung Fu practitioners with the ability to understand themselves better, going as deep as the core of their minds. Every Kung Fu movement involves energy control and mental awareness, which is heightened through the practice of Zen.

In combination with Shaolin Kung Fu, Zen helps people live a balanced and positive life.

While the Shaolin Temple went into decline during the Qing Dynasty, it remains a practicing Buddhist temple where Shaolin Kung Fu is still taught. While many people believe that the Shaolin Kung Fu taught at the temple today is the original form, others claim that the original Shaolin Kung Fu was too powerful, so the monks switched to teaching a less aggressive version.

Whatever the truth, the Shaolin Temple serves not only as the birthplace of Shaolin Kung Fu but also as a reminder of how Zen and Kung Fu are intrinsically connected.

Finding and Mastering Zen in Your Daily Life

You do not have to be an expert at Shaolin Kung Fu to work on mastering Zen. In fact, you don't even need to take too much time out of your day to focus on it. Here are some simple ways you can find and master Zen in your daily life:

Breathe

Zen emphasizes finding the stillness and peace in your life. However, the chaos of the day can often lead to worry, which is not conducive to finding peace.

One simple way to bring yourself back into balance is to take the time to breathe deeply. This doesn't have to take too much time. The next time you find yourself spiraling, take a time out and breathe deeply for a few moments. With each breath, breathe calmness in and breathe your worries out. You will be stunned at how effective this can be.

Close Your Eyes

Closing your eyes as a way to drown out the world may sound like a cliché, but it can actually work.

If you're feeling overwhelmed by life, take a moment to stop, lean back, and close your eyes. Focus on your inner self, not the chaos of the outside world, and appreciate the sense of stillness it brings.

If you've never done this before, you may have to build up your abilities slowly. You may notice that intrusive thoughts start to creep back into your mind after a few moments of stillness when you first start.

However, keep focusing inward when necessary, and you will soon find that you're able to revel in the stillness of your inner world for longer each time.

Take a Pause and Meditate

You don't need to have hours of free time in order to meditate. Five minutes between tasks will do just fine.

Here's how you can hold a mini-meditation session in the middle of your office:

- Sit in a comfortable position.
- Close your eyes
- Take deep, full breaths in and out. Breathe through your nose.
- Repeat the last step while observing your thoughts. Do not focus too much on what you are thinking, as that can distract you. Instead, just watch your thoughts go by, like cars on a highway.

Admit How You Feel

Many of us try to use the stress and chaos of everyday life as a way to escape challenging, difficult, and inconvenient feelings. However, denial only serves to exacerbate your inner restlessness and strife.

It is important to be honest and admit what you're feeling, even if it is only to yourself. If you're not ready to talk to a trusted friend, your partner, or a therapist, writing down your feelings in a journal or talking aloud to yourself can help.

Remember to be compassionate and non-judgmental when you acknowledge what you feel. Self-deprecation will only make things worse.

For example, if you're worried about an upcoming job interview, it is important to:

- Acknowledge that you're worried.
- Stay confident without denigrating yourself for being worried. Saying or thinking things like "I'm so stupid for worrying," or "I'm not qualified, of course, I will not get the job" will only make your inner strife worse. Instead, consciously try to shift your thought patterns to compassionate ones, like "Being worried is understandable, but I'm confident I'll do well," or "There's no reason for me to worry. I'm qualified and know my stuff inside and out."

Let Go

Holding on to thoughts, worries, and really anything negative whatsoever can not only lead to physical and mental clutter in your life, but it can also make it difficult for you to appreciate the here and now. While it isn't possible for us to simply let go of everything, practice it as much as we can.

Take a moment to clear out your workspace and discard items you no longer need or journal your thoughts so that you can move past them and leave them behind in the past. Declutter both materially and mentally as much as possible.

Now that you understand the importance of Chi and Zen in Kung Fu, it is also important to keep in mind that Kung Fu focuses on both the spiritual and the physical. Chi and Zen help you understand the value of the spiritual aspects of Kung Fu, but there's more to it than just the spiritual.

In the next chapter, you will move back to the physical aspects of martial art once more and look at the 18 weapons of Kung Fu.

Chapter 7: Weapons of Kung Fu

While many types of martial arts consider the body itself to be a weapon, in Kung Fu, actual weapons are simply extensions of your body. You need to be able to use them well to master Shaolin art effectively. It takes a particular set of physical and mental skills to imagine, believe, and accept a weapon as a part of your body. Methodically swinging a heavy broadsword should be as easy as gracefully deflecting a blow with Crane's Beak. Perfectly handling a staff needs to be second nature to you.

Years of training and practice go into mastering the numerous Kung Fu body forms, techniques, and katas, but it may take you several more years to become proficient in using weaponry. That is because there aren't just one or two swords or staffs to practice with but 18 different weapons that are believed to be sacred in the world of Shaolin, alternatively called the Eighteen Arms of Wushu. However, once you can combat and defend with each one expertly, you can protect yourself against any type of weapon.

Here, we will guide you through the nature, use, combative abilities, and defensive purposes of each of the 18 sacred weapons in Kung Fu. However, be very careful while handling those. Each weapon is insanely powerful yet extremely secure in the hands of a Shaolin master, but it can be equally dangerous for both the wielder and the opponent if used by an amateur. That said, you can't just magically master Kung Fu weaponry, so don't forget to practice with each weapon every day in a carefully controlled, safe environment.

1. Staff

Four weapons are revered more than the remaining 14. Those are the Straight Sword, Broadsword, Staff, and the Spear. The Staff is the most fundamental, highly reputable piece of them all. It is the "chief/father of weapons." There are several different types of Staff used in Kung Fu. To name a few, there is the khakkhara with an artistically designed top edge, the gun, which is a regular lean staff with a slightly broader hold, and the three-section staff that consists of three strong sticks connected with ropes or metal rings. Of these, the gun or the Bo is ideal for training purposes.

The Bo Staff is usually made out of wood, and it is best used for both offensive and defensive purposes. While it may look much like a snooker cue stick, it is not held in the same way. You need to grab it with both palms, face-up from the underside, and practice your moves from there. Being a long-range melee weapon, the gun has an exceptional reach in combat, and it can easily fend off most other Shaolin weapons. Balance is the key to mastering the art of Kung Fu, but you need a tad bit more of it to handle the Staff properly.

2. Straight Sword

Who doesn't love the look and feel of the Straight Sword? After all, it was the weapon of choice of many of our childhood heroes, mythical or real. It is not without good reason that the Shaolin Straight Sword is called "the gentleman," for it is indeed the weapon preferred by the admirably gentle yet extraordinarily valorous individuals. For the past 2500 years, Chinese Kung Fu specialists have used a double-edged Straight Sword (called jian), but you are free to practice with a single-edged one as well.

The jian may look like a ninjaken or a katana from afar, but the differences between the legendary Japanese ninja weapons and their Shaolin counterpart are starkly apparent up close. For one, the jian has a longer and wider hilt to protect your palms better from the opponent's sword. Secondly, double-edged Shaolin Straight Swords are more popular, unlike the single-edged ones preferred by the Japanese.

Many martial artists believe that the jian is the only weapon through which they can express their unique Kung Fu style. Its blade is generally forged from steel with a special technique called sanmei. It involves sandwiching a hard steel plate between two relatively softer ones. However, if you are a to-dai or a beginner in Kung Fu, then you will start off with a wooden Straight Sword with blunt edges.

3. Broadsword

A Broadsword is heavier than a Straight Sword but can be easily held in one hand. A Chinese Broadsword is nothing like those in Arthurian legends. Its blade grows wider from the hilt before curving at the top. Forged with a single-edge, it is referred to as dao in Shaolin culture. It comes in many different lengths, but Kung Fu masters believe that your chosen sword should reach your eyebrow when it is held vertically in your palm, pointing toward your face.

Of all the Eighteen Arms of Wushu, the dao is the "marshal" or the "general," implying that it assembles and leads all the other swords into battle. Regular Chinese Broadswords have a wider blade, but there are also daos with a small width, alternatively called sabers. The Broadsword is primarily an offensive weapon, most used for slashing and chopping actions. The hilt is curved in the opposite direction to the blade, maximizing the thrust of your cut.

The dao was once the most used weapon in the Chinese military, for it took only about a week to master its basics. Don't get your hopes up too high, though. Read that sentence again. *A week to master its basics.* Kung Fu is an advanced martial art, and it may take you several months, or even years, to effectively use the dao for offensive purposes.

4. Spear

The Kung Fu Spear may look and sound like an ordinary weapon, neither a full Staff nor a complete Sword, but its use in Shaolin is extraordinary. It is not without good reason that the qiang (Chinese name of the Spear) is called the "king" of all the Eighteen Arms. It has a leaf-shaped blade affixed on top of regular staff, giving it unparalleled reach in one-to-one combat.

Unlike the Chinese Sword, which features a tassel wrapped around its pommel, the qiang has one tied just below the blade. The color of that tassel denotes the rank of the infantry, and it is best used to distract the opponent in fast-moving, close-quarters combat. It is also ideal for absorbing and stopping the blood flowing down the handle, thus keeping it clean.

At Kung Fu training centers, the qiang is among the first weapons taught to the to-dai, for it is the perfect piece to learn the weaponized extensions of various Shaolin styles. The edges during training are blunt, and the handles are furnished out of wax wood to improve performance. Its length may vary, right from nine feet to over 21 feet, depending on the handler's height and capability.

5. Kwan Dao

As you may have guessed from the name, kwan dao, often stylized as guandao, is a lengthier version of the dao (Broadsword). The blade's width is more pronounced to maintain a healthy balance with the long handle, but its shape is almost the same as that of the dao.

The kwan dao is also akin to the Spear (dao blade fitted atop a long wooden pole), only the former's handle is usually carved out of metal, and its blade is more like a Broadsword than a knife. The sharp bend at the top of the blade coupled with its long reach makes the guandao exceptional for locking the opponent's weapon down, effectively parrying their attacks.

6. Pu Dao

The pu dao is almost exactly the same as the kwan dao, the only difference being that its handle is usually shorter than that of the latter. The remaining structure, down to the blade's curvature and its use in parrying and defending attacks, is the same as that of the guandao.

7. Shaolin Fork

Alternatively called a Tiger Fork or a Trident, the Shaolin Fork is used just like any long-range Wushu weapon. A three-pronged steel fork is attached to a metal staff, and a tassel is usually wrapped just below the trident to confuse the opponent. Quite a few of its Kung Fu styles are similar to the Spear and the kwan dao, but its techniques vary in many other forms and katas. The Shaolin Fork is perfect to set up a counter-attack in long-range melee fights.

8. Tri-Point Double-Edged Sword

From afar, the Tri-Point Double-Edged Sword can be easily mistaken for a Shaolin Fork, but upon taking a closer look, you can clearly notice the differences between the two. If you are an artist at heart, you will immediately realize that the blades in the Tri-Point are shaped like a lotus, with two side curvatures bending outward and the one in the middle shooting upward. The rest of its structure, right down to the material used, is similar to the Fork. It is typically used in parry-and-thrust styles of combat.

9. Ax

There is nothing different between a woodcutter's ax and a Wushu Axe. A wooden handle latched onto a solid, curved steel pane makes any kind of ax deadly in the hands of a Shaolin monk. Its Kung Fu variants usually include the varying length of the handle and the material used to forge it. Sometimes, you may also come across a double-edged Axe with a sharp peak, just like a Tri-Point. Hacking and slashing is the main purpose of the Axe in Kung Fu, but it is often done with artistic grace, conforming to the pre-existing styles of the combat form.

10. Monk's Spade

A Wushu defensive weapon similar to the Fork but greatly varies in its practice styles. The Monk's Spade is twice as heavy as the dao, which brings the strength factor of the martial artist into the equation. While any to-dai can train with a wooden Shaolin Spade in a dojo, very few can actually use a real one in combat. It consists of a crescent-shaped blade affixed to a long pole, with the other end metal-forged like a spade. Given the blade's sharpness and curvature, it is mostly used for defensive moves and for maiming the opponent without inflicting any fatal injuries.

11. Da Mo Cane

Also known as the Bodhidharma Cane after the founder of Kung Fu and Zen, the Da Mo Cane is one of the most ancient weapons in the art of Shaolin defense. Shaped like a typical cane with no sharp edges, it is ideal for learning the Tiger Claw Wushu technique. Simply pick a Da Mo Cane based on your height so that it is well-suited for treading mountain paths, and begin your defensive katas in sync with the basic blocking and parrying stances.

12. Nine Section Whip

Simply called a Chain Whip. Its name was modified to the Nine Section Whip to denote the number of chain sections it contains. There may be fewer or more sections in different Chain Whips, and they are named accordingly. The Nine Section variant has been in use in Chinese martial arts for generations. In fact, in the earliest Wushu period, only the Seven Section and Nine Section Whips were available, but today, you can find ones with up to 13 sections.

Each segment of the chain is made from stainless steel. There is a wooden handle at one end and a metal dart at the other. The Nine Section Whip is widely considered to be the hardest weapon to master. You should be able to twirl and lash it around in quick motions, so much so that the dart becomes an invisible blur.

13. Hand Dart

A Shaolin Hand Dart is longer and heavier than a regular Dartboard dart. A feather-light tassel is bound to the pointy end of the dart just so that it could better guide it through the wind. Traditionally made out of stone, it is currently forged from iron and steel. It is generally used as a long-range projectile to take down far-off targets.

14. Flying Dart

A Flying Dart is customarily lighter than a Hand Dart, and it is called so because it flies back into the attacker's hand. A long rope is tied to the blunt end of a metal dart, which allows the martial arts specialist to swing the weapon around as they please. An accomplished Flying Dart user can pierce the opponent from all sides, even from the back. This weapon and the Nine Section Whip are a part of the Rope Dart family of ancient Chinese weapons.

15. Iron Pen

Pick any item in your house that looks like a long, thin pen. That becomes your Iron Pen. It requires a delicate hold, and its complementary Kung Fu moves are also quite gentle and elegant. A typical Shaolin Iron Pen is usually much heavier and longer than a regular pen carved from brass. It is ideal for strengthening your fingertips with the Chin Na technique. If the tip is sharper and the grip in the middle is more pronounced, you can also use it for some offensive and defensive maneuvers.

16. Thorn

There really isn't much to say about the Thorn because the name speaks for itself. The Shaolin Thorn is like any other thorn, only longer and pricklier. Depending upon the user, it may or may not be laced with poison. It is generally a weapon of choice for female Kung Fu specialists, for they can easily hide the Thorn in their long hair or tie it up in a bun with it. The weapon is flung at the opponent with precision and the intent to draw blood and weaken the person. Don't mistake it for the African tribal thorn, which is pelted at the opponent through a thin, circular mouthpiece.

17. Iron Flute

The Iron Flute is just that, a flute made of iron. It can be played to whisper a sweet melody, helping you meditate and soothe your senses, calming your mind, and getting ready for the next session of Wushu katas. At the same time, the Iron Flute doubles up as a weapon that can be used the same way as the Iron Pen. That is primarily the reason why the Chinese don't prefer the wooden flute over the iron-made one. The latter may generate a better sound, but it cannot be used as an effective weapon.

18. Shaolin Sickles

Many of the ancient Chinese Kung Fu practitioners were farmers. Hence, they naturally transformed the sickle, one of the most commonly used farming tools, into a deadly Wushu weapon. Shaolin Sickles are normally wielded in pairs. They are made of solid iron with a curved top edge and another short curve sprouting from the bend. The latter is most important for defensive moves, locking the opponent's weapon away while aiming an offensive strike with the second Sickle.

As you may have guessed by now, most of the Eighteen Arms of Wushu are merely modified renditions of everyday working tools, except the four primary weapons, the Staff, the Straight Sword, the Broadsword, and the Spear. In essence, a vastly experienced martial arts master can use any available item as a weapon. So, if you do not have easy access to any of the 18 weapons, don't hesitate to pick any tool from your garage that resembles a weapon and practice your Kung Fu forms with it.

The ideal environment in which you can wield and practice each of those weapons is a dojo under the watchful eye of a Shifu. However, if there isn't a dojo in your neighborhood and you are forced to practice at home, be sure to clear out your room of any delicate, breakable items, especially the TV set, lamps, chandelier, and vases. The basement would be perfect for weapons training, and if you have a spare room with minimal furniture, that's even better.

Chapter 8: Striking and Lama Pai Kung Fu

Lama Pai Kung Fu is one of the most sought-after Chinese martial arts involving animal-style strikes and precision techniques. Striking in Kung Fu is placed under the umbrella term "Lama Pai," which means Lion's Roar. The practice evolves from a Tibetan tradition and can be traced back to the Qing Dynasty. In fact, Hop Gar and Tibetan White Crane are the older versions of this martial art and are collectively known as Tibetan Lama Pai today. All the relative techniques, movements, and sub-categories of Lama Pai fall under one figure called "Sing Lung." In Lama Pai, the striking movements are inspired by the crane, and the grabbing techniques can be attributed to the ape.

The system is believed to have been devised by a monk called Dai Dat Lama, or Ah Dat-Ta. The monk explored and traveled across Qinghai and Tibet with his nomadic tribe to find peace and meditate in seclusion. Ah Dat-Ta found a secluded spot and resided among the mountains to study Buddhist writings and find inner peace. The monk also diligently practiced his martial art skills. One day, as his meditation was disturbed by a fight between a crane and an ape, he saw the scenario as an inspiration to devise a new martial art involving movements based on the crane and the ape.

Striking Fundamentals of Lama Pai

Typically, Ah Dat-Ta's martial art is based on some effective grabbing moves inspired by the ape and the white crane's vital point striking techniques. He witnessed the bird fighting for its life using its giant wings and pecking at the ape's weak points, whereas the ape resisted and fought back with his powerful hand movements and swings. With this, the typical Lama Pai system consists of eight elbow strikes, eight palm strikes, eight fist strikes, eight kicking techniques, eight stepping patterns, eight stances, eight clawing or seizing techniques, and eight finger strikes. This makes the martial art system a set of 8 striking with eight moves in each set.

The fighting pattern and techniques also incorporate traces of Shuai Jiao (Manchurian wrestling), Mongolian wrestling, Indian hand techniques, and long arm techniques. Several foot movements also steadily became a part of Lama Pai. Ideally, this martial art is limited to these eight parts of divisions and was never open for exploration or to be broadened by practitioners and masters of Kung Fu.

Different Striking Techniques

Several techniques related to striking in Lama Pai Kung Fu are important for beginners and professionals as well. Practitioners learn a variety of strikes that involve a lot of hand and elbow movements.

Source[72]

Ideally, every fighter closes their hand to turn their fists into a weapon to attack or protect themselves. While the ancient Chinese developed their own form of using fists as self-defense, the ancient Greeks also devised another way to incorporate closed fists during the fighting. Among all martial art forms, Lama Pai particularly has a lot of fist strikes in a circular motion. The most basic forms of fist strikes are Uppercut - Paau Choih, Straight Punch - Chyuhn Choih, Horizontal Backfist (the thumb pointing towards the sky), Overhand Punch- Kahp Choih, Hook Punch- Gok Choih, Forearm Strike, Inward Sweeping Strike- So Choih, and 45 Degree Backfist Strike - Gwa Choih (the palm pointing towards the sky).

Some other forms of fist strikes include Chopping Fist - Pek Choih, Whip Strike - Bin Choih, and Small Trapping Strike - Siu Kau Dah. Even though fist strikes are powerful and act as strong, instant weapons, they need to be combined with other striking forms for effective results and to establish a strong attack and defense mechanism. Lama Pai also focuses on the principle of distributing the strikes among the upper and lower parts of the body, thereby improving the game. If the practitioner attacks the opponent's head multiple times, the rib cage is exposed, allowing them to attack their completely undefended legs.

When using the fist combinations in Lama Pai, the opponent takes continuous blows on their upper body, slowing them down and weakening their footwork. In turn, they are unable to use their hands and fists. Even if the opponent can intercept punches, a Lama Pai practitioner can dodge the moves by deploying the Right Side Stance or the Whip Strike. When combined with the Inward Swing Strike, the practitioner can attack and defend with maximum power.

Jaang Fat

The eight most basic forms of elbow strikes are:
- Hyuhn Jaang (round elbow)
- Tai Jaang (upward elbow)
- Chum Jaang (downward elbow)
- Deng Jaang (straight elbow)
- Kahp Jaang (overhand elbow)
- Bong Jaang (inverse rising elbow)
- Bui Jaang (elbow to the rear)
- Bouh Jaang (folding elbow)

Some can be used independently, whereas others need to be incorporated with other techniques to form effective combinations.

Jeung

The eight most basic forms of palm strikes are Twin Pushing Palms, Shoveling Palm, Chopping Palm, Single Thrust Palm, Groin Striking Palm, Propping Palm, Stamping Palm, and Slicing Palm.

The palms and claws are the strongest weapons in Lama Pai as they can be extremely versatile. When you keep an open hand, your fighting power gets stronger as it can be difficult to break an open hand. Unlike a closed fist, an open hand can make several movements and swing around multiple directions, thereby making palm and claw strikes more effective than fist strikes (not necessarily in every case but in most cases).

An open palm gives the fighter two ways to combat: the palm face and the edge (primary striking surfaces). When used in a circular or chopping motion, you can attack the opponent's upper body, specifically areas like the collar bone, the neck, the underarm, and the floating ribs. Edges of the palms can also be deployed in a thrusting motion. The face of the palm can cover larger parts of the upper body and face. Some fighters cup their ears using their palm's faces. In some cases, you can also use the palms to create space by pushing your opponent and causing them to lose balance.

8 Clawing or Seizing Techniques – Jau

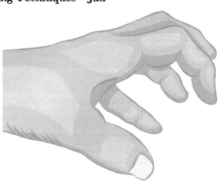

Jau

The eight most basic forms of clawing strikes are Single Tiger Climbs the Mountain, Upward Arm Seizing Claws, Crane Claw, Twin Downward Claws, Greater Trapping Claw, Lesser Trapping Claw, Bodhisattva Subdues a Tiger, and Inward Sweeping Grab.

Like the fists and the palms, a fighter can use their claws to grab or seize the opponent. Claws act as pulling weapons used to create imbalance and defend yourself from oncoming attacks and strikes. You can use your claws to pull, press, and twist the opponent's muscles and skin, thereby inflicting pain and distracting them.

8 Finger Strikes - Jih

The eight most basic forms of finger strikes are Finger Spear to Eyes, Crane's Beak, Dragon's Head, Phoenix Eye, Slicing Fingers, Arrow Fingers, Thrusting Finger, and Needle Finger.

Finger strikes are another important part of hand movements in Lama Pai Kung Fu practices. It is necessary to build strength and resistance in the fingers to consistently use them in your Kung Fu practice. For this, learners develop the skill of "Biu Gung," which develops finger muscles and strengthens bones to keep them from breaking during attacks and heavy blows in fights. Practitioners use their fingers to fight some of the most delicate and trivial parts of the body, like the eyes and inner, soft parts of the body. Duhk Ngaan Jih refers to the fingers used to poison (attack) the eyes, and Biu Jih refers to the main thrusting or attacking fingers. At times, the thumbs and second knuckles are also used during fights.

8 Kicking Techniques

The eight most basic forms of kicking techniques are Front Heel Thrust, Back Kick, Side Kick, Hooking Sweep, Floor Sweep, Inside Crescent Kick, Tornado Kick, and Cross Kick.

8 Stepping Patterns

The eight most basic forms of stepping patterns are 7 Star Footwork, Plum Blossom Footwork, Baat Gwa Footwork, Meridian Footwork, Bik Bouh, Shuffle, Stealing Step Footwork, and Leaping Retreat.

8 Stances

The eight most basic forms of stances are Drop Stance, Single-Leg Stance, Kneeling Stance, Cat Stance, Cross Stance, Horse Stance, Figure 8 Stance, and Bow Stance.

Lama Pai and the Importance of Self-Defense

Being a traditional martial art, Lama Pai is often questioned on its self-defense or counterattack capabilities. Since some skills focus just on attacking, the opponent can easily counterattack and win the game. Typically, many Kung Fu styles and techniques allow one arm to swing below the waist or behind the body, which leaves room for a counterattack. Unless the practitioner is experienced or extremely skilled, they must be aware of these stances and apply their techniques with precision to defend themselves. This is taken care of by Lama Pai Kung Fu techniques.

In this martial art, the practitioner automatically swings their lead hand, places it in front of their body, and swings it back to defend themselves. They strike with their rear hand. This form and technique can also be seen in Western boxing, part of which is instilled by Lama Pai. However, the practitioner may be perceived as an open target, and the lead hand movements may be mistaken for an opening. In reality, the lead hand movement deflects a blow or strike to the opponent and protects from an attack. With this, you can easily strike the opponent's control with your rear hand while defending yourself. In turn, you get complete control of the game.

Even though Lama Pai places great importance on self-defense and counterattacks, it also stresses the points where the participants must attack to control the situation and turn things in their favor. Like a Western boxer, a Lama Pai practitioner brings his fists close to his upper body and face to attack the opponent while saving themselves from a counterattack. Western boxing and many modern martial art practices can learn valuable lessons from Lama Pai Kung Fu, especially those involving self-defense techniques. Since a Western boxer leaves a lot of vital points open to the opponent's attacks, Lama Pai can teach them effective ways to counterattack or defend themselves.

Three Forms or Categories of Lama Pai

These eight divisions were simplified into distinct categories or forms to understand and learn martial art with ease. These forms are "Dou Lo hands," "Maitreya hands" (Neih Lahk Sau), and "Flying crane hands" (Fei Hok Sau).

Dou Lo Hands

This moniker comes from an Indian indigenous plant with an interior soft as cotton and an exterior hard as a coconut. The hard shell protects the soft inner seeds. The form "Dou Lo Hands" does not necessarily focus on the outer or main aspects of Lama Dai but on the internal factors and teachings. The "vein changing skill" is an integral part of the striking system.

Maitreya Hands - Neih Lahk Sau

This form is an advanced version of the basic Lama Pai martial art and incorporates several new hand techniques to hold, seize, or twist the opponent's vital parts or arms. This skill needs a lot of practice and is named the "vein seizing hand," inspired by its original name.

Flying Crane Hands- Fei Hok Sau

Fei Hok Sau

This form primarily involves open hands and fist movements to attack the opponent at their weak or vital points. It mainly uses the fundamental levels of Lamai Pai and the striking techniques, along with evasive footwork and kicking techniques. It also involves a lot of hand strikes and circular movements to keep the opponent alert.

To date, Lama Pai, or Lion Roar's Kung Fu, is taught across China and some Eastern parts and gaining traction across the Western world. Over time, martial art has evolved as several masters stepped in to explore the skill. Buddhist guardians known as the Gam Gong (diamonds) and saints known as the Lo Han inspired many hand moves and strikes. After Lion Roar's Kung Fu turned into Lama Pai, it was gradually overtaken by the new form, and the fundamentals were taught only to curious or advanced learners. However, the eight fundamentals were carefully recorded by teachers in the past, which is how we know about Ah Dat-Ta's developed Kung Fu martial art system.

Chapter 9: Kicking in Kung Fu

Kicks are an important part of many martial arts techniques, particularly in Kung Fu. Even though kicks are usually the second line of defense in Kung Fu, they are still regarded as a useful tool. Due to the prevalence of hand techniques in Kung Fu martial arts, many people assume there are very few or no kicking techniques in Kung Fu. On the contrary, Shaolin Kung Fu specifically has about 36 kicking techniques, with more than one type of kick in each technique. Although basic Kung Fu training only covers five kicking methods, if you learn the fundamental principles of each technique, advanced techniques will become easier to master.

Kicks, however, aren't as commonly used as strikes in martial arts because of their innate weaknesses. Although your legs are supposed to have 70% power while your hands give 30%, there's also a greater risk when you use your legs to attack. There is a greater chance of losing your balance when you use kicking techniques than striking practices. Because kicking is a more difficult technique to learn and has numerous safety risks, it is critical to learn as much as possible about the various techniques before you start to learn.

The Characteristics of a Good Kick

Because of the many safety risks, kicking techniques are more difficult to master and require certain characteristics to be effective. A good kick should have the following characteristics.

1. Instinctive Accuracy

A good kick should be thrown accurately to hit the opponent correctly. As a martial arts practitioner, you should also be able to select the correct kicking technique based on the situation. Many factors affect this, including the spatial distance, exposed pain points, and how much damage you want to inflict. Your instincts should be able to predict which point you want to hit while also keeping in mind your own safety. For example, if you hit your opponent's bone with your toes, it would cause a severe fracture and render you unable to kick for a while, not to mention the immense pain it would cause.

2. Power

Although legs are said to exert more power than your arms, they can be completely useless if you don't know how to throw your power correctly. If your kick doesn't exert a specific amount of power on your opponent, it will be of no use, and your opponent will not suffer any damage. This is why it is important that you understand each technique and how to power your kicks precisely in order to induce maximum damage.

3. Speed

The speed with which you kick plays an important role in how effective your kicks are. If you keep your speed high, there will be fewer chances of being intercepted or dodged, whereas slower kicks will only make you vulnerable to attacks on the lower part of your body. Your opponent will easily be able to trip you if your kicking techniques are too slow, not to mention, the power wouldn't be maintained either. However, kicking fast is an advanced skill that requires hard work and practice, but your techniques will become infinitely better once learned. Make sure that you work on other skills, too, like power, balance, and instincts, because without them, speed will not do you much good.

4. Timing

Every fighting situation is different and requires a different time set to throw your kick accurately. First, you've got to identify if there is enough time to throw a kick without alerting the opponent of your move. Second, you will need to consider which kicking technique you can use in said time. When you time your kick correctly, the chances of it hitting your opponent effectively are increased. Otherwise, you can miss your target and make yourself susceptible to tripping or falling.

5. Muscle Chain

When you use the maximum number of your body's muscles to throw a kick, it can be infinitely more powerful than a regular kick. This is because utilizing the muscle chain reduces the chances of interrupting energy flow in your movements and will require considerably less effort than a normal kick.

6. Unpredictability

One of the most important characteristics of a good kick is its unpredictability. If your opponent is a good fighter, they will be easily able to identify your movements and either block or deflect your kick or attack your lower side to make you trip. This is why you should first learn every technique and apply these characteristics to improve your kick throwing skills significantly.

Basic Kicks

There are six basic types of kicks you need to learn about first if you want to understand the advanced kicking techniques in Kung Fu. If you understand the basic principles and movements of these types, it will be significantly easier for you to learn the complex techniques we'll discuss later on.

1. Back Kick

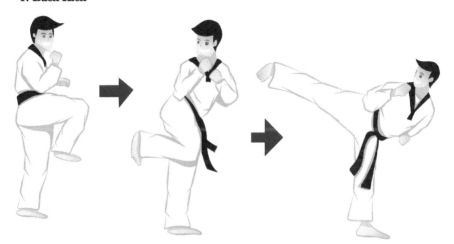

Back Kick

This is one of the most widely used kicking techniques across numerous martial arts. Back kicks are powerful and inflict maximum damage to your target. Follow these instructions to master your back kick.

- Use your rear leg for this technique, get into a kicking stance, and turn your body to the right until you are facing directly away from your target.
- Continue turning to your right while keeping an eye behind your right shoulder.

- Lift your right knee to your chest and drive back the heel of your foot straight to your opponent.
- After hitting your target, you quickly resume your kicking stance in a defensive position and get ready for the next kick.

2. Front Kick

Front kicks are simple, precise, and hit the target with maximum power to cause considerable damage. Front kicks usually involve hitting your target with the ball or heel of your foot. Follow these instructions to learn the front kicking technique.

- Raise your dominant leg's knee and thrust your foot forward
- Hit your opponent with the ball or heel of your foot - make sure to avoid hitting with your toes.
- Bend your toes upward prior to the kick to avoid any damage
- After hitting your target, withdraw your leg to avoid being grabbed or tripped.

Front Kick

3. Ax Kick

Ax kicks are used to target the opponent's head or clavicle. The following instructions will ensure that you correctly use this technique.

- Raise your rear leg (the dominant one) as high as you can in the vertical direction.
- Hit the target with the heel of your foot. The hard bone of your heel is more effective than striking with the ball of your foot.
- Target either the face or shoulder bone of your opponent to induce maximum damage.
- Be careful of your lower body, as this technique will leave it exposed to any attacks.

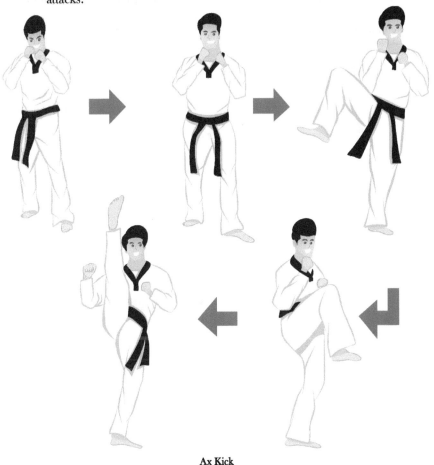

Ax Kick

4. Side Kick

Although sidekicks are considered to be powerful, they are much slower than the other techniques and leave your body wide open to counter attacks. This kick can be done using your rear leg or front leg and requires you to chamber in power before releasing your leg. Follow the instructions given below to ensure you can throw an effective sidekick.

- Rotate your body until it is at a 90-degree angle from your opponent
- Pivot 180 degrees on your front leg
- As you rotate, bring your rear leg forward until your knee is near your waist. Your foot should be facing the attacker.
- Your knee should be almost 270 degrees from the starting position if you want to launch your kick correctly.
- Thrust your foot forward and use the heel or blade (outer edge) of your foot to strike your target.

Side Kick

5. Roundhouse Kick

The roundhouse kicking technique is one of the most commonly used kicks and one of the easiest in martial arts. Also, unlike the other types, this technique doesn't focus on attacking a specific part of your opponent's body and can instead be used to target any part. Whether you want to attack your opponent's knee or chest, or head, you can power your kick accordingly and deliver an efficient and strong kick. The basic roundhouse kick can be mastered by practicing the following steps.

- Use your front or rear leg depending on your preference
- Get into your fighting stance by taking a big step forward with your left leg and letting your right leg naturally pivot towards the side
- Bring your leg up and bend it back upon itself so that it is touching the thigh.
- Bring your bent leg to the side so that your knee chambered
- Snap your leg forward and pivot on your lower foot - make sure you make contact with the target before your leg is fully extended for maximum effect.
- After hitting your target, retract your leg and get back into your fighting stance.

Roundhouse Kick

6. Crescent Kick

The crescent kick has many advanced techniques, but the most basic ones are the inside and outside crescent kick. Follow these steps to ensure you do it correctly.

- Bend your kicking leg similar to how it is done in a front kick.
- Point your knee deceptively towards the left or right point of the actual target.
- Whip your leg into an arc, and hit your target from the side
- According to the technique used, the arcing motion starts from the center of your body and moves outward or inward.

Crescent Kick

Advanced Kicks

Advanced kicking techniques are basically derived from the basic kicking techniques and should therefore be easier to master. Listed below are a few of the numerous advanced Kung Fu kicking techniques available. Follow the steps for each of the following, and practice on your own first before moving on to a real opponent.

1. Butterfly Kick
    - Make sure you're facing the direction you want your kick to hit.
    - Get into a forward bow stance by placing your legs apart and placing both your feet at 45 degrees.
    - Extend your arms out to build momentum for your kick
    - Lift your heels from the ground and pivot your feet 90 degrees
    - Swing your arms to gain momentum
    - Bend your body forward and pivot 180 degrees on one leg, then lift your leg and extend it behind you
    - Jump off your other leg and pivot it to hit your target, and land back on this leg

Butterfly Kick

2. Cartwheel Kick

- Place your right foot behind your shoulder and shift your weight to the right.
- Raise your left forearm to defend your exposed area.
- Transfer your weight to the left and bend sideways, push into the floor with your left leg and hand
- Lift your right leg up and hit the target

Cartwheel Kick

3. Uppercut Back Kick

- Get into a fighting stance similar to the one in back kicks. Make sure you keep an eye on your opponent over your shoulder
- Raise your leg in your back until it reaches your thighs
- Use the heel of your foot to hit the pain points of your opponent
- Ensure you keep your hands in a protective stance to deflect counterattacks

Uppercut Back Kick

4. Spinning Hook Kick

- Get into a fighting stance with bent knees and legs far apart
- Swing your arms around with the non-kicking leg to build momentum for the kick
- Spin 180 degrees and look over your shoulder to gauge kicking power and distance
- Lift up your kicking leg and throw a hook kick to your opponent's chest or shoulder

Spinning Hook Kick

Although practicing these kicks might seem like a harmless activity, you should make sure you get the guidance of a Kung Fu martial arts specialist. Plus, if you're trying these kicks on an opponent, make sure you don't exert damaging force onto your opponent's body as it can cause permanent damage. It is a good idea to first learn in detail the basic types of kicks before moving onto the advanced ones because the underlying principles remain the same throughout. You will find numerous advanced techniques, which will be almost impossible to master if you don't learn the basics of a good kick first. Practice makes perfect, and you should practice as much as you can if you want to master these kicking techniques to perfection.

Chapter 10: Self-Defense in Kung Fu

Kung Fu is much more than just a martial art. It is an art form that teaches us multiple life lessons. While many people assume that all martial arts are focused on attack, only a few are aware of the defensive aspect of these arts. Wing Chun is a truly unique style of Kung Fu that focuses primarily on defending oneself. It is a very intricate and beautiful style of Kung Fu that teaches a person the ability to defend themselves against almost every possible attack.

Wing Chun is so popular that it is a widely recognized sport in multiple parts of the world. There's a very logical reason behind this popularity, and it is the fact that Wing Chun is the most in line with today's needs. Martial arts aren't what they used to be because we live in a relatively safer society regulated by law. Since we don't need the lethal forms of martial arts in modern society, Wing Chun provides an excellent alternative to those who seek to learn self-defense.

The core elements of Wing Chun are simultaneous blocking and striking coupled with trapping the opponent, attacking from a close distance, pressurizing the opponent with movement, and a flurry of punches. Many more elements give Wing Chun its unique reputation, but these are the most well-known and visibly apparent characteristics. The unique quality of Wing Chun that separates it from other forms of martial arts or even Kung Fu is that it is especially effective when applied in a self-defense scenario. Perhaps, this is because Wing Chun can cripple an aggressor without lethally harming them. The ability to defend oneself while staying on the right side of the law is something that everyone wants, and that's where Wing Chun shines the most.

Wing Chun Today

Before we further explore how Wing Chun can help with self-defense, it is important to know a little bit about the current state of this martial art. Most of the training provided in Wing Chun by non-native masters are either focused solely on training or completely wrong. While it is perfectly fine to focus on training during the initial phases, Wing Chun is a practical art that must be regularly practiced.

Training can't provide the same level of experience and knowledge as practicing Wing Chun with a partner or in competitions. These unrealistic training methods have led to Wing Chun developing a much softer image than what it actually is. The extremely complex techniques each have their own merit, but not in the case of self-defense scenarios.

We'll be discussing many techniques that aren't as emphasized as some of the fancier ones because of aesthetic reasons only. These lesser-known techniques are in no way less effective than the ones being taught in almost every martial arts dojo. On the contrary, the techniques we'll discuss are some of the most important ones to learn from a self-defense standpoint.

Wing Chun has slowly been turned into an exercise in showmanship, and all the techniques and methods utilized are absolutely redundant in a real-world scenario. Problems like these usually arise because of the changing nature of Wing Chun. When we talk about Wing Chun as a self-defense martial art, we need to understand that it differs from the regular forms. However, the same can be said for every martial art that has both showmanship and self-defense applications.

Fundamentals of Self-Defense

1. Structure

Wing Chun is a martial art that's performed with a focus on offense as well as defense. The main goal of a Wing Chun practitioner is to trap, lock, or jam their opponent's limbs to create windows of attack. Not only does a Wing Chun practitioner need to develop their strength, but they also have to focus on developing their technique in a structured manner so that their strength is multiplied. All the different techniques fall under subgroups like punches, blocks, and kicks. If you can learn to use these techniques in conjunction with the forward motion aspect of Wing Chun, you will be able to overcome any opponent.

2. Offense vs. Defense

I have stressed this point many times in this chapter, but its significance requires that I repeat it again. Wing Chun is a Kung Fu style that demands symmetry between being offensive and defensive, which means that a strike will accompany every block you make. The same thing applies to strikes. You will learn to use different strikes to deflect attacks. This feature is only present in a few other martial arts like Muay Thai. The remainder of martial arts don't utilize this sophisticated style of fighting, and this is why Wing Chun is a lot more technical in nature. Practitioners will need to balance their offensive and defensive training at all stages of their development.

3. Trapping

Trapping is one of Wing Chun's aspects that declined in popularity due to poor teaching and practice methods. While the experts can utilize Wing Chun trapping to subdue an opponent effectively, the vast majority of practitioners have absolutely no clue how to do that. Due to a lack of regular practice and sparring, the fighters choose to rely on other more dominant aspects of Wing Chun. Because of this, most of the sports community believes Wing Chun sparring can't be applied in scenarios like an MMA fight or a self-defense scenario.

Trapping is something that every fighter should focus on. Knowledge of the various Wing Chun style traps will help amplify a practitioner's strength. However, it is important to understand that the fancier traps are nothing but a series of smaller traps layered on top of each other. They will never be as effective as the simpler, less flashy, and much more effective traps.

4. Sparring

Sparring is the eventuality that all practitioners of Wing Chun must face after they've been training for a while. No matter how much training you've done, you wouldn't be able to defend yourself against enemy attacks unless you practice all your moves in a real-life scenario. This is why sparring is such an important aspect of Wing Chun. It helps you push your boundaries with a partner without risking any fatal injuries.

The reason sparring is so effective is that the movements of your opponent are unpredictable. The proper way to spar is to do it lightly without any intentions of hurting your partner, more of a dance than a fight because you have to reciprocate with equal force. The major mistake made while sparring is that both the fighters practice their Wing Chun techniques. While this is perfectly fine from the competitive perspective, it will not be very useful in a street fight! One partner should ideally mimic the moves of an untrained fighter because it is highly unlikely that your opponent in real life will also be adept at Wing Chun.

Techniques of Wing Chun

Whenever a fighter, a warrior, or a soldier goes into battle, they have to bring the proper tools to fight. In the case of self-defense, your techniques are your tools. You should have perfect mastery over those to be able to defend yourself. Every fighter should have a variety of tools to counter the various situations they may find themselves in, and this is why you need to be an expert in multiple techniques.

In this section, we're going to explore the various techniques you should try to master for self-defense purposes. While the fancier moves are definitely a crowd-pleaser, our focus here is on efficiency and being able to defend yourself. This is why we'll only be looking at the essential techniques you should master first before moving on to more complex moves.

1. Hand Strikes

Hand strikes are some of the most important ones in any martial art because our hands are the most intuitive part of the body. Striking with hands isn't as emphasized in Wing Chun as blocking is, and that's primarily because of the defensive nature of martial art. However, these strikes play an important role nonetheless, and we'll be looking at some of the most important hand strikes you should learn.

Bin Sau: Also known as the Thrusting Fingers technique, Biu Sau simply involves darting your hand forward with tremendous force to damage the soft spots on your opponent's body. Remember that the fingers play a critical role here, and conditioning them properly should be your foremost priority.

Lin Wan Kuen: This isn't just a single strike like the previous attack. It is known as the Chain Punch due to the flurry of strikes that the practitioner must learn to throw. The main goal here is to overwhelm your opponent, and it is one of the most surprising attacks you can do to defend yourself.

Punches: This is a broader category than the previous two and involves multiple types of punches in Wing Chun. You should aim to practice the One-Inch Punch, the Double Punch, and a few other basic punches so that your arsenal isn't limited and, thus, predictable.

2. Kicks

Unlike kick-centric martial arts such as Tae Kwon Do, Wing Chun focuses more on upper body attacks and blocks. However, learning how to deliver a well-executed kick is still very important as kicks help increase your range and damage output. Every martial artist should know a few basic kicks like the Straight Kick, Side Kick, Hammer Kick, and Round Kick. You don't need to learn fancy kicks like the Roundhouse or the Tornado Kick for self-defense, as you will not have the time to use these in a real fight.

3. Elbow Strikes

Mostly associated with martial arts like Muay Thai, elbow strikes can be particularly devastating if executed properly. The biggest benefit of using elbow strikes is that you can surprise your opponent and deliver a lightning-fast blow that's almost guaranteed to cripple them for a brief moment. The most popular elbow strike in Wing Chun is the Pai Jarn, and it generally involves hitting the opponent's head to increase the amount of damage done.

4. Blocking

Blocking is one of the most significant aspects of Wing Chun, and an attack usually accompanies the blocks executed by a Wing Chun fighter. This means that you can deal massive damage while reducing the chances of you getting hurt in the process.

Biu Sau: We discussed Biu Sau in the hand strikes, and it is a highly versatile move that can be used to divert, attack, and counter-attack at the same time.

Chi Sau: Also known as the Sticking Hands technique, Chi Su involves rapid hand movements supported by the executor's reflexes and speed. You can easily and rapidly deflect a flurry of attacks from your enemy by utilizing this technique which will provide you with ample openings to strike the enemy.

Huen Sau: This technique is sometimes also referred to as the Circling Hands technique, and it is very useful if you want to change positions while still retaining control over an opponent's arm.

Kwan Sau: The Rotating Hand technique is most useful when you want to block simultaneous low-level and high-level attacks from your enemy. Your opponent will often try to overwhelm you with such attacks in a real fight, and when you execute this block, you will be able to nullify them entirely.

Pak Sau: This technique is also known as the Slapping Hand Block, and it is very useful if you need to deflect an incoming attack with ease. This involves utilizing your palm to deflect the attack, and it can even divert the direction of attack, which can cause your opponent to lose their balance.

Chapter 11: Daily Training Drills

Source[78]

Having covered all of the different techniques, styles, and exercises that go into creating a well-rounded Kung Fu routine, as with many other things in life, practice makes perfect. Even simple routines such as basic strikes and kicks need to be thoroughly practiced if you want to gain mastery of these moves and take your Kung Fu to the next level.

Without regular practice and proper focus on improving your skillset, it will be close to impossible to improve as a martial artist. Whether you are a complete beginner who has only learned the basics or someone more advanced learning the more technical moves, it always requires constant work. Martial arts relies on you knowing about the move and theoretically understanding the concept and shifting that knowledge and applying it to your body, and teaching it to move in a certain way. Just like boxing, mixed martial arts, and any other kind of physical activity, repetition will burn this information into your muscle memory and hardwire it into your nervous system. This is crucial when it comes to really perfecting a move. More importantly, when you need to use one of these moves in a match or even in everyday life, you will not have the time to think about it. You need to be able to react quickly and efficiently.

If you look at professional football players, you will see that they practice the same routine hundreds of times throughout the year, during training and competition seasons. This way, when they are actually in a match, they don't have to do any thinking since their bodies already know what needs to be done. This applies to nearly every sport and is an effective solution for both game strategy and specific moves that a player uses.

It is no different in Kung Fu. As you progress, you learn more complex skills, and your muscle memory becomes even more important. You don't want to learn new things at the expense of older and often more fundamental skills. Staying in touch with basic movements will also keep your body nimble and ready to absorb more advanced skills that build on those basic movements.

If you have the time to enroll in a martial arts academy, you should definitely do that. You will not only be training in the things you need, but you will also have the chance to immerse yourself in a great atmosphere and be surrounded by like-minded people. You will have access to lots of equipment and skilled teachers who will be vital in improving your practice sessions. However, don't let your lack of resources or time limit your Kung Fu training. Even if you are on your own and don't have any equipment to train with, you can get in a very good session that will help both your physical fitness and your Kung Fu.

However, if you really want to be self-sufficient, you should definitely consider getting some basic equipment. This doesn't have to be extremely expensive. In fact, most of the basic equipment you need can be quite cheap. For instance, a medium-sized wooden dummy, a few stretching bands, and some basic resistance equipment are not very expensive and portable. You can easily take these things with you if you need to be out and about frequently. These items are also very easy to manage and store at home. If you are serious about developing your Kung Fu, good equipment is a must-have.

To make daily training a bit more manageable, let's look at some specific things you can do to improve particular aspects along with some holistic training routines you can use.

Stretching

Source[74]

This is a critical part of any good training routine and important if you want to perform moves properly. Nearly every kind of move you come across, whether a flip, kick, or punch, will require you to have solid joints and the ability to fully and properly extend your limbs and torso. Even simple breathing techniques require you to fully expand and contract your entire torso so you can get the maximum amount of oxygen into your system and generate the maximum amount of force in strikes. Similarly, flexibility in the hips, lower back, and waist are extremely important for martial arts. Whether you are punching, kicking, dodging, or doing anything else, this central part of your body is what allows you to generate momentum.

Any stretching routine you do should incorporate a portion, especially for your core and the rest of your spinal column. It is also important that when you are stretching at the start of the workout, you take it nice and slow and don't force any fast or explosive movements. You can incorporate stretching as part of your warm-up routine, or you can do it separately, where you focus on certain areas of your body that feel tight. Ideally, you should have a bit of both where stretching is part of your warm-up and cool-down routine. You also have a separate time when you only focus on stretching and flexibility.

Warm-Up

Source[75]

If you ask any seasoned martial artist what the key to a healthy and sustainable routine is, they will tell you it is proper body management, and this starts with the warm-up. You can easily avoid many problems and significantly reduce your chances of injury if you just spend an extra ten minutes before the workout properly warming up and a few extra minutes after the training to cool down properly. Warm-up routines don't have to be related to your martial arts training, and you can do anything like going for a walk or swimming or jogging or even just doing some cardio to warm up. In fact, the Shaolin monks and many other eastern martial artists always start off their day and their training with a run.

This could be a short 10-minute run or even a thirty-minute run, but the point is that it serves as a gentle warm-up that gets the entire body ready for a workout. If you have a treadmill at home, that's fantastic. If you don't, just go for a little walk outside and get yourself properly warmed up before you start training. If you are about to do some explosive movements, getting warmed up is key. Similarly, warming up is about your cardiovascular system just as much as it is about getting good blood flow to your muscles. With both areas properly warmed up, you are ready to train.

Combat

Source[76]

Essentially, the purpose of all the intense Kung Fu training is to make you a better fighter and to give you all the skills and knowledge you need to construct a better fight routine. However, even with the different skills, there are a variety of ways to apply them. Using the various combat styles such as the Tiger style, Dragon style, Praying Mantis style, Leopard style, and others, you can better perform your skills and take down your opponent more efficiently. These different kinds of combat techniques involve their own unique moves and strategies. If you want to really master a certain style, you need to learn the minor variations of each one.

The small differences, such as the slight variation in the way the hand is held between the Dragon style and the Tiger style, can have a big impact on how the move is executed. More importantly, the different styles also influence your overall combat strategy. While some styles such as the Tiger style are more aggressive and require you to be more offensive other styles such as the Dragon style will allow you to be more elusive and strike more strategically.

Also, the kind of style you wish to pursue will also have a big impact on the kind of training you do and how you build up your body to support a certain fighting style. For instance, if you wish to pursue the Tiger combat style, there will be a higher focus on physical fitness. It requires more calisthenics, and there is a greater importance on sparring instead of just perfecting moves.

Striking

Source[77]

In any kind of martial art, the purpose is self-preservation. You are trying to protect yourself from an attacker. To do this effectively, you need to be able to strike with power, accuracy, and speed. Without a good combination of these three factors, you may still fight, but your attempt to stop the attacker will not be effective, and they will continue to attack while you continue to run out of energy and eventually get defeated.

When you practice striking, you want to make sure that you are unleashing a good strike. This means that your strike is quick, powerful, and targets the right areas. If you are about to launch a very complex attack, but you don't have sufficient power behind it, or your strategy is not good enough to break through the opponent's defense, the complexity is of no use.

When striking, the first thing to consider is your stance, the base from which you launch the attack. You need to be in a good position, and you need to learn how to efficiently position yourself in the ring or wherever you are to formulate a good attack. The most important things in a good stance are the position of your feet and the equal distribution of weight.

Next, you need to be aware of your distance from the opponent. Whether you are using your hands and legs for punches and kicks or using a weapon, having the right range of motion will help you get the most out of the strike. If your opponent is too far or too close, it will undermine the amount of power you can generate, and you might not even be able to land the shot where you want to. So be aware of your distance from the opponent at all times.

A good strike has to take the quickest route and be a rapid movement. There is no need for a big flowing movement when you want to land a reverse heel kick - more movement reduces efficiency. To make the strike hit hard, it must be fast, and it must have excellent momentum from the launch to the final point of impact. Also, you want to make sure you are using your Chi to drive additional energy into the strike. Keep things simple and be quick in your movements to generate as much force as possible.

Whether you use a weapon or your hand, you want to be able to put as much mass into the move as possible. This means incorporating your entire body into the movement. Mass combined with speed creates power, and when you put your entire body into the movement, you increase mass exponentially. Be very careful which direction your body is moving in when launching an attack, and try to streamline your entire body to create a solid strike.

Another great way to add momentum and force to your strike is with rotation. Spinning on your heels, spinning from the waist, or simply shifting the weight from one foot to another is a great way to make use of torque. What you want to eliminate is counter-rotation, as this reduces momentum and slows down the movement.

When launching a strike, you also need to pay extra attention to the angle from which you are launching it and the angle at which the strike will land on the opponent. This can often be the difference between a strike that has a very small impact and one that ends the match. Understand where you are hitting the opponent and what kind of angle is most effective for that area, then change your attack angle accordingly.

Kicking

Source[78]

You can use countless kicks in Kung Fu to defend yourself, but generally speaking, these can be categorized as forward-thrusting kicks, lifting kicks, and spinning kicks. Moreover, other kicks can be used for close-range or long-range fights, but they too will be based on either a thrust, a lift, or a spin. Ideally, you want to be proficient in a wide variety of kicks. Kicks help keep a distance from the opponent and create a lot more force than what you would be able to with a punch.

Self-Defense

Source[79]

If your aim is self-defense, then Kung Fu is something that can come in handy. It originated on the battlefield as a form of fighting that will incapacitate an opponent with many kinds of strikes that can be fatal when done right. To make your Kung Fu lethal, you don't need to know very advanced skills, but you do need to be extremely proficient in the execution of basic skills. However, as important as attacking is, it is also important to be very proficient in defensive techniques and dodging techniques to protect yourself properly. With the right combination of defense and attack, you can outplay any opponent. Relying on just one of these two things will not help you in most situations.

General Kung Fu Workout Ideas

Source[80]

As you can tell, a good Kung Fu routine addresses a lot of things and one in which training is balanced. You need a good mix of everything to have a solid foundation in Kung Fu that you can use to learn more advanced skills. To this end, there are a lot of masters and even grandmasters who still practice very basic training every single day.

The fact is that these basic things are taught to new fighters not because they are simple but because they are the foundation. The horse stance is a perfect example of something so important in so many ways. Simply holding the horse stance every day for thirty minutes is a fantastic exercise.

However, you can also use some general workout principles to help you train more effectively.

Warm-up – 15 minutes of running or jump rope or 30 minutes of walking.

Workout

- 4-second stretch (4 times per side)
- 2-second stretch (4 times per side)
- leg swings (10 times on each leg, both to the front and to the side)
- low kicks (5 times on each leg)
- 9-count pushups (a minimum of 10 or as many as you can do)
- knuckle pushups (however many your target does it in one set)
- sit-ups (again, do your daily target in one set)
- Horse stance (start by holding the position for 1 minute and increasing it by 30 seconds each week. Beginners should aim for a total time of 5 minutes, intermediate students 10 minutes, and advanced students 20 minutes)
- hamstring stretch, straddle stretch, butterfly stretch, dragon drop stretch, twist stretch (2 minutes each, total 10 minutes)

This is a sample workout that you can easily do every day, as it doesn't require a lot of equipment, it is quick, and it is effective. Of course, if you have a certain kind of training that you are focusing on, you can carve out a routine that better addresses that. However, as a daily training routine, you want something that will work on your overall strength, flexibility, and the basic requirements for Kung Fu movements.

Conclusion

In this ultimate guide to Kung Fu, we have provided a comprehensive and practical look into this type of martial art. The book covers critical elements of Kung Fu like stances, different patterns, weapons, self-dense, and daily training drills. You need to understand how to execute different moves against the opponent before you actually employ any of the moves for self-defense. Read this book to learn a step-by-step approach to this amazing martial art.

Many people have heard of Kung Fu, and some believe that it is an exceptional art for highly talented and skilled individuals. However, with the appropriate knowledge under your belt, you can also become proficient in this form of martial art. This book offers you the information on critical techniques and stances you need to understand how to overcome opponents. It also explains how Kung Fu differs from other types of martial arts.

If you are interested in developing your knowledge and skills in Kung Fu, it is vital to know where it is similar and where it differs from other forms of martial arts. The information you get from this book is there to help you familiarize yourself with the discipline of Kung Fu while also preparing you for real action. When you read this book, you will gain theoretical knowledge and easy-to-apply techniques.

The volume is full of images and well-explained instructions about the different moves and stances you should know. You can easily practice each move thanks to all details provided. You will also find plenty of images that will help you get a better idea of what some of the moves and stances look like.

The book is unique in that it is specifically designed for novices and those interested in Kung Fu. All the terms are explained in a simple and easy-to-understand way. It is also up to date, and it presents comparisons to other forms of martial arts. Kung Fu continues to evolve, and this text provides you with the latest information you may need to improve your skills.

If you are looking to gain expert tips to improve your Kung Fu skills, this book is for you. It provides a hands-on approach to help beginners master different techniques. While you require a coach to train you in different elements of this martial art, with this book, you will realize that some of the other things are self-taught. More importantly, all the information is easy to understand, and you can perform some of the drills without any assistance. If you're looking for the ultimate way to start your Kung Fu journey, this book is your best option.

Part 8: Judo

A Simple Guide for Beginners Wanting to Learn Techniques for Self-Defense or Competition

CLINT SHARP

Judo

A SIMPLE GUIDE FOR BEGINNERS
WANTING TO LEARN TECHNIQUES FOR
SELF-DEFENSE OR COMPETITION

Introduction

Judo is a Japanese martial art that focuses on grappling and throwing techniques. It's an Olympic sport and can also be used in self-defense. The philosophy behind Judo is to use your opponent's strength against them, which makes it perfect for smaller people who need to defend themselves against attackers. You don't need any experience or special equipment to start, either! This guide will teach you everything you need to know about the basics of Judo so you can start practicing today!

This book introduces self-defense and competition aspects of martial arts as a practical guide for people interested in Judo. It illustrates techniques, strategies, mindset/philosophy, and discipline. The focus is on using these elements in real-life situations, such as defense against armed opponents or more than one opponent and in competitive matches.

The book presents a well-written, beginner-friendly, error-free guide to everybody interested in Judo. The author imparts a good amount of his Judo knowledge and experience to the reader, each chapter building on the previous one.

The author's passion and love for Judo are evident on each page. Together with high-quality illustrations, it is ideal for beginners. Readers will feel like they are learning from a friend who wants them to succeed rather than just an instructor or coach.

The high-quality imagery and photos illustrate the techniques given in the book, making it easier for the reader to understand the basic concepts of grips or throws.

This book covers all the basic throws and takedowns that are essential for anyone wanting to learn how to throw their opponents around easily. We also go over some of the most common submissions and locks, so even if someone gets hold of you during a fight, there are ways out of almost every situation! Finally, we discuss what Judo is like at its highest level – competition rules and strategies to win matches against other skilled players. Whether you want something fun to do after work or dream of becoming an Olympic champion someday, this book has everything you need!

The art of Judo is a great way to get in shape and stay active. It's also an excellent form of self-defense that can help protect you from harm.

This book will teach you the basics of Judo so you can start immediately. No experience necessary! Once you understand the fundamentals, practicing at home or in your local dojo will be easy.

Chapter 1: Judo Rules and Philosophy

Origins

Judo is very different from any other kind of martial art. It is a very young martial art and has only been around for a little over a century. Unlike other martial arts, where the development of the sport is a culmination of input from many people over the course of time, Judo can be accredited to one person alone, Kano Jigoro.

Born in 1860 in Japan, Jigoro was a polymath, an educator by profession, and an avid martial artist. Even as a young adult of 17 years old, Jigoro was a very thin and slender man. As he was always getting bullied throughout his school years, he was very interested in learning martial arts to defend himself. During the mid to late 18th century, Ju-Jitsu was falling out of popularity, and Jigoro found it very difficult to find an instructor. Moreover, his small frame wasn't doing him any favors, and the few teachers he could find would not accept him due to his size.

Later on, he successfully became a mentee of Fukuda Hachinosuke. However, this relationship didn't last too long, and a little over a year after he commenced training, Hachinosuke became ill and died. Jigoro moved on to find another teacher, Iso Masatomo. Under Masatomo, he learned a great deal and made good progress. Very soon, he was able to earn the title of Master Instructor (Shihan) and become an assistant instructor.

Jigoro's last teacher was Likubo Tsunetoshi, from the Kito-Ryu school, a different school to the Tenjin Shin Ro-Ryu School of Martial Arts his initial two teachers had been from. However, throughout his training, Jigoro always learned from Masters, who all placed a great deal of emphasis on free practice and focused on perfect form rather than intense energy. This focus on form, free movement, and the core principles of Ju-Jitsu laid the foundations for the new techniques that Jigoro developed and essentially created Judo as we know it today.

Judo and Ju-Jitsu

As you can see, Judo was born out of Ju-Jitsu but was developed for a very different purpose. Where Ju-Jitsu was born on the battlefield, Judo was born in a time of peace when the focus was on strategy, discipline, control, and sportsmanship. In fact, the very name "Judo" refers to gentleness, softness, and suppleness and can help us understand that Judo is all about the "soft method."

Where traditional martial arts were all about force, power, and energy with the aim to severely injure or kill the opponent, Judo is all about understanding the opponent and using techniques to use their power against them. This is why rather than hard attacks and blocks, Judo uses many leveraging moves in which a Judoka attempts to catch the opponent off balance, redirect their momentum, and rely more on smart moves rather than brute force.

Similarly, rather than simply being a way of fighting, Judo is more about a way of thinking and living with an aim to improve a practitioner physically, mentally, emotionally, and even spiritually. Therefore, those who aim to learn Judo are not only learning a martial art but, more importantly, a way of life.

Etiquette

A Judo teacher is known as a Sensei. A student, on the other hand, is known as a Judoka, although, traditionally, the term "Judoka" was reserved for students who had attained 4th dan or higher. Fresh students up until the 3rd dan are referred to as Kenkyu-sei (trainees). The outfit that Judo practitioners wear is known as a Judogi. The same uniform is used by many other martial arts and was initially developed by Jogori in 1907.

In major competitions and in the Olympics, you may notice that one player wears white while the other wears blue. This simply makes it easier for judges, referees, and spectators to distinguish between the players. In Japan, however, this trend is looked down upon. In Japan, both competitors wear white with a red belt.

The Bow

Good etiquette is paramount in a Judo match, and bowing plays a big role. While bowing is important in Japanese culture in general, it is vital in the sport of Judo. Players are expected to bow to instructors when they enter or leave a match. During a match and both before and after a match, competitors are also expected to bow to each other. This is a sign of sportsmanship and courtesy that shows the players want a professional and fair match.

Modesty

Loud celebrations and emotional reactions are not expected of Judo players. Any kind of boasting, bullying or abusive language is completely unacceptable. Judo players are to respect their opponents before, during, and after a match. Winners are not expected to create a lot of commotion over their win, and losers are supposed to take the defeat with dignity. Overall, Judo players are supposed to be extremely considerate of the opponent and everyone else who may be watching the match.

Respect

As well as displaying modesty, Judo players are expected to treat one another with the utmost respect and be very wary of how they use their skills. Some of the skills that they have learned can cause serious injuries to opponents, and Judo players are expected to use this knowledge according to the situation and in line with the aim of the game rather than in an emotional frenzy with the aim of hurting the opponent. This is another one of those things that helps build strong character, integrity, and humbleness in players that resonates in other areas of their lives.

Perseverance

Judo can be an especially challenging sport, particularly when you are up against a more technically skilled opponent. It can be exhausting and mentally stressful to not be able to counter an opponent's moves, and players are always motivated to keep on going. Even if they lose a match, they are expected to continue training with the same focus and discipline and to continue to learn. There are many levels of Dan in Judo and many moves that can take quite a while to master, so it is a fundamental principle to be a lifelong student of the art.

Modern Day Judo

Kodokan, the word for a school of Judo, literally translates to a place to teach the path'.

At its core, Judo consists of various rolls, falls, takedowns, chokes, and locks. Seldom do Judo players rely on punches and kicks, but they are familiar with them and can use them when necessary.

The primary focus in Judo is on throwing (nage-waza) and grappling (katame-waza). Furthermore, throwing can be subdivided into standing techniques (tachi-waza) and sacrifice techniques (sutemi-waza). Similarly, the ground fighting techniques can also be divided into three main categories of attacks in which a player fights against joint locks (kansetsu-waza), strangleholds (shime-waza), or pinning techniques (osaekomi-waza).

As players progress and get more technical, they start to learn about more intricate and complex techniques used in each area of the fight. For instance, standing throwing techniques can be further divided into hand, hip, foot, and leg. Then there are multiple techniques under each subcategory of these moves. There are so many moves that most players don't practice all of them. Instead, they focus on the most useful techniques that are going to help them win a match. This has become more common ever since Judo became a mainstream sport, and it was less about the art of Judo and more about scoring points to win.

In Judo, there is a practice known as Randori, which is "free practice." This is a kind of practice session in which players are not bound by the rules of contest-level Judo and can bring such things as kicks and punches into their game. Similarly, they can also involve knife and sword techniques" However, this kind of practice is usually only allowed for more senior students. The main reason for not allowing this -even in practice -is for the safety of students. These kinds of weapons and styles of practice can be extremely dangerous, and only students of a certain age or rank are allowed to do this.

The structure of a randori is similar to many formal tournaments in which players fight each other until one taps out. The whole aim of the game is to get the opponent in a lock or a choke and have them tap into submission.

Judo as a Sport

Modern-day Judo games are broken into five-minute matches between opponents of the same weight class. Before you can understand how a match is won, other than tapping out submissions, it will help you to understand the points and scoring system that is used.

Scoring in Judo

Formal Judo consists of three main kinds of scores and two kinds of penalties.

Points

1. **Ippon** - This is awarded in response to a "full" throw. For a throw to qualify as a full throw, a fighter must be able to throw his opponent onto the mat with power and speed so that the opponent lands on his entire back. If a fighter can manage to pin down the opponent for 20 seconds or more, or if the opponent passes out or taps out during grappling, this also earns an Ippon. An Ippon instantly ends the match.

2. **Waza-ari** - This is awarded in response to a very good throw that isn't quite as precise as an Ippon throw. Also, if a player can immobilize the opponent with a grapple for 15 to 20 seconds, that earns a Waza-ari. If a player earns two waza-ari during a match, that is the equivalent of an Ippon, ending the match.

3. **Yuko** - This is awarded for a throw that largely displays the three main components of a good throw which could be lack of speed, lack of force, or when the opponent didn't land on his back. A Yuko is also awarded if the player can immobilize the opponent for 10 to 15 seconds. Yukos do not accumulate to create a waza-ari or an ippon and are a separate grade in themselves.

When you watch a match, you will usually see three columns that depict each score category that a player has earned so far during the match. A simpler version of this scoring is to look at it in terms of cumulative points where:

Ippon = 100 points

Waza-ari = 10 points

Yuko = 1 point

Penalties

1. **Hansoku-make** – This is a major error that disqualifies the fighter instantly. Intentionally trying to injure the opponent, unprofessional behavior, continuous infringement of rules, and other foul behavior will all earn a fighter a hansoku-make. This is the negative equivalent of an Ippon.

2. **Shido** – This is a slight infringement and can include things such as not being active enough in the match, being too defensive, palming the opponent's face, etc. Under standard regulations, there is a limit of three Shido warnings. If a fourth Shido is issued, those shidos become equivalent to a hansoku-make and result in disqualification from the match.

There are a few ways that a person can win a match; these include:

1. Score an Ippon.
2. Score two Waza-aris.
3. The opponent earns a hansoku-make.
4. The opponent earns four shido penalties.
5. The opponent can't fight due to injury.
6. Opponent submits.

If the match completes the full match time, the winner is evaluated based on the number of waza-aris each player has earned. If both players have the same number of waza-aris, it comes down to how many yukos they have. If even the number of yukos is the same, it comes down to how many points each player has scored and who has the fewer penalties. If everything, including the number of penalties, is the same, then the match is decided by a golden score. This is a sudden-death situation. The golden score round has no time limit, and the match ends as soon as the first point is won. Also, if a fighter is given a shido in the golden score match, the opponent wins.

Main Rules in Judo

The main rules of Judo are quite simple:

1. Intentionally injuring the opponent is not allowed.
2. Punching and kicking are not allowed.
3. Touching the face is not allowed.
4. Attacking joints other than the elbow is not allowed.
5. Head butts are not allowed.

Benefits of Judo

Judo is a very explosive sport that requires a lot of strength and sharp critical thinking. From a standing position, it requires strength to pick up and throw down an opponent, and on the ground, it requires both skill and strategy to pin the opponent down in various locks and chokes.

From a physical point of view, Judo is a very good sport for developing functional physical strength. Just going through the exercises and through sparring, a player is able to get quite an intense physical workout. Judo players can develop larger and stronger physiques with a lot of flexibility. Rather than just having large muscles, they can actually translate their strength into everyday life and use it in many other areas, even outside Judo.

At a mental level, it is a fantastic strategy game. As the aim of the game is not to harm the other person but rather to outsmart them, it can be extremely beneficial to learn the tactics of this game. This requires a player to be a quick thinker, to be able to analyze situations on the move, to forecast what the other person is about to do, and to be prepared to handle any attack the opponent might throw at them. Combined with the high moral standard that Judo players are expected to abide by and the overall social environment of a Judo school or class, it can be a great way for young adults to learn social norms and develop key traits such as perseverance, discipline, respect, and sportsmanship.

Moreover, as it is a rather complex sport that can take quite a while to master, it helps develop patience and a thorough work ethic. Anyone who wants to be good at Judo or compete in the sport will soon understand that this is not simply about being able to push other people around.

How Judo Has Contributed to Education

Jigoro was both an academic teacher and scholar, as well as a Judo sensei. At the core of his teaching, his purpose was to improve the way young people were taught and also to enhance the way young people learn. Overall he wanted Judo to be a sport that added to the development of humans and helped us create a stronger society.

It is a sport that is a training of both the mind and the body and can help a person develop in every aspect of their life.

More specifically, one of the core tenets of the sport is "Seiryoku Zenyo" (or maximum efficiency). This teaches students the simple concept that anything can be achieved – but only when both the body and the mind are applied to that purpose with maximum efficiency. This applies to both Judo and life. Using these concepts of maximum efficiency, mutual welfare, and benefit, we can work toward creating a society that is ideal for humans and free of the many flaws we see in societies worldwide. Even though we have many religious, political, and philosophical ideologies meant to improve society, we still see a disconnection in every culture worldwide. By incorporating the principles of Judo into the education system all over the world, we can work toward instilling a greater sense of compassion, discipline, empathy, and integrity in our younger generation.

Cherry Blossom

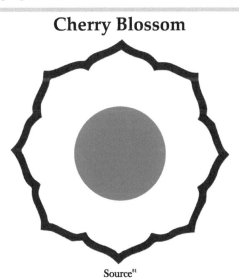

Source[81]

The cherry blossom tree and flower have a special place in Japanese Culture and Judo. The international sign for Judo is, in fact, the cherry blossom flower. However, this was made official long after the death of Jigoro. The cherry blossom flower has played an important role in martial arts and, more specifically, the life of a Samurai. The cherry blossom season is an important part of the Japanese year, and people visit Japan, especially for this season. Locals will spend their days in parks full of cherry blossom trees spending time with friends and relatives and soaking in nature.

For Samurais and Judogis, the cherry blossom plant symbolizes a thing of extreme beauty and fragility. The cherry blossom flower often falls off the tree at its peak -at the height of its bloom- which is important for a warrior to understand. When he is in top condition, he is most susceptible to death on the battlefield, and this is nothing to be embarrassed about. On the contrary, it is an incredibly beautiful thing to embrace death at the peak of your abilities and in a way that emphasizes your commitment to your role as a warrior. This is why in many martial arts schools, the focus of meditation is often the cherry blossom tree or flower.

Judo and Olympics

Judo first appeared on the main stage at the Olympics in 1932 in Los Angeles. Jigoro and nearly 200 disciples gave a live demonstration of the sport. However, it wasn't until nearly 30 years later that it became a formal sport in the Olympics. The first time that Judo was played competitively in the Olympics was in 1964 (when the Olympics were held in Tokyo). In the 1964 Olympics, it was still a sport only for men, and it was not until the 1992 Olympics that there was a female Judo competition as well. Currently, there are seven weight divisions in Olympic Judo for both men and women.

Chapter 2: Kata Judo vs. Randori Judo

In this chapter, we will compare these two methods of training and discuss the benefits of each. Everyone knows that practicing is the best way to learn a new skill. Practicing means doing something over and over again until it becomes automatic. It's the same with Judo, but there are two ways of practicing: Kata or Randori.

The Difference between Kata and Randori Judo

Kata is practiced following a formal system of pre-arranged exercise. In contrast, randori or sparring is freely practiced with opponents simulating live fighting as closely as possible. You can take the role of either an attack or defense and apply techniques that you have learned from kata to your advantage to gain control over your opponent.

Randori is about technique and form, gaining knowledge on what works best for different opponents so that you can adjust accordingly during live fights, while Kata training helps develop a deeper understanding of Judo. The more you practice randori, the better your kata training will be because it helps to develop a deeper understanding of Judo.

The Basics of Kata Judo

Kata Judo is based on pre-arranged exercises. Trainees practice techniques in a specific form so they can develop the principles of executing moves correctly and effectively. Pre-arranged forms are used to enforce discipline, attention to detail, accuracy, rhythm, timing, and distance control, among other things.

The Seven Official Kata

There are seven official forms of Kata.
1. Goshin-Jutsu Kata.
2. Itsutsu-No Kata.
3. Ju-No Kata.
4. Katame-No Kata.
5. Kime-No Kata.
6. Koshiki-No Kata.
7. Nage-No Kata.

Goshin-Jutsu Kata

Goshin-Jutsu Kata is the only Kata that deals with Self-Defense techniques. It has a very practical application, and its movements are similar to Ju-No Kata. They include techniques for defending against armed attacks (Dagger, stick, and pistol) and unarmed attacks.

Itsutsu-No Kata

Itsutsu-no kata is composed of five movements, each using a different technique. This Kata has more than one application, and its main purpose is to teach the students how to apply Judo moves and develop their speed and strength. The five techniques, known by number, are-direct push(ichi), deflection(Ni), Circular Energy(San), action and reaction(Shi), and void(Go).

Ju-No Kata

Ju-no Kata is a three-part routine that can be done by two people, one acting as a Uke and the other as a Tori. The three sets include techniques such as hand thrusts, shoulder pushes, holds, strikes, and turns.

Katame-No Kata

Katame No Kata has 15 techniques, categorized into three main techniques - holding, strangulation, and locks. This Kata is designed to teach the students how to defend themselves against attacks using hard and soft techniques. There are three groups of grappling methods, each with five distinct techniques. Your Katame No Kata training aims to master the skills needed to control your opponent in a fight.

Kime-No Kata

Kneeling (idori waza) and standing (tachi waza) are the two starting postures for each technique in this series. There are eight techniques. Both sets of techniques include defenses against both armed and unarmed assaults.

Koshiki-No Kata

This is a set of forms that comes from ancient techniques and was created for "Kumiuchi," the grappling of armored warriors in the feudal age, which was a popular practice. In this movement, both partners must imagine that they are wearing armor while performing the kata.

Nage-No Kata

Nage-No Kata consists of 15 techniques under five main categories. The techniques include -hand techniques, hip techniques, foot techniques, rear and side sacrifice techniques. Both right and left-handed techniques are completed twice, in the same sequence, on both sides.

Techniques Used in Contemporary Judo

There are a number of other techniques that have been added to the original forms. These include:

Okuri Eri Kata - This is practiced with one partner lying on their stomach while the other holds and then flips them over in various ways. This technique aims to develop timing and distance control for throwing techniques.

Koshi Guruma - This is a hip technique that sees the Tori lift and rotates the Uke over their hips.

Sumi Gaeshi - This is an extension of Koshi Guruma, where Tori drops to one knee as they throw Uke backward and over them.

Ippon Seio Nage - Literally meaning "One Arm Shoulder Throw," this technique is similar to Seio Nage, but it involves using one arm under the leg.

Yoko Guruma - This sees the Tori lift the Uke over their shoulders and ends up in a standing position with the opponent on their back.

Uki Goshi - A hip throw that involves lifting the Uke over the hip.

Uchi Mata - A throwing technique that involves lifting your opponent off their feet and dropping them sideways to take them down.

Nami Ashi Dori - Literally meaning "Waves Feet Handle," this is a foot-sweeping throw that uses one leg at a time.

O Uchi Gari - This requires the Tori to use their leg to hook the Uke's supporting foot from the inside.

O Soto Gari - A popular technique that is used to take your opponent down by sweeping their support leg on one side.

Ko Uchi Gari - This involves the Tori using their inside arm and shoulder as they bend forward at the hips while sweeping the outside leg of the uke.

Ko Soto Gari - A similar technique to Ko Uchi Gari, but this sees the Tori sweep outward with their arm and shoulder instead of using their hips.

O Guruma - This involves throwing your opponent over your shoulders by dropping down on one knee while grabbing hold of them around the waist.

O Goshi - A hip throw that combines a twisting motion as the Tori lifts the Uke and drops them to the ground on their back.

Banana Split (Yoko Sumi Gaeshi) - This is an advanced version of Uki Goshi, where you bend forward at your hips while holding onto the uke.

Juji Gatame - This is a reverse arm-bar and sees the Tori bend their opponent's arm into an "X" before pinning them to the ground.

Osoto Guruma - The outside leg sweep, which involves the Tori hooking the Uke's supporting foot from the outside while simultaneously sweeping it outward.

Sasae Tsurikomi Ashi - This is used to block the opponent's movements using your legs before sweeping their supporting leg outwards.

Soto Makikomi - A throwing technique where you wrap your legs around the Uke while lifting them off of the ground.

Kata Guruma - The shoulder wheel, a more advanced form of Uki Goshi that sees the Tori lift the Uke off of their feet while turning in a circle.

Okuri Ashi Barai - This is similar to Hiza Guruma, and it sees the Tori lift the Uke over their hips as they sweep one of their legs out from under them.

Harai Goshi - The sweeping hip throw is used to take your opponent down by sweeping the supporting leg on one side with your arm extended outward.

Hane Goshi - This involves grabbing the Uke's supporting foot on one side with your inside arm as you hook their ankle.

Hiza Guruma -The knee wheel, a more advanced form of Uki Goshi that sees the Tori lift the Uke off of the ground before dropping them to their back over their hips.

Ippon Seoi Nage - The shoulder throw, where the Tori drops down behind the Uke before sweeping one of their legs with their arm extended.

Kibisu Gaeshi - A standing ankle-reaping throw that sees the Tori sweep the Uke's supporting leg from the outside while simultaneously sweeping them inward and off of their feet.

Hikikomi Gaeshi - A backward foot-reaping throwing technique where you pull your opponent down by grabbing hold of one or both legs around their ankles while they attempt to move away.

Ko Soto Gake - A forward foot-reaping throw that involves the Tori hooking the Uke's supporting leg on one side with their inside arm while simultaneously sweeping outwards to take them down.

Kata Gatame - A shoulder hold, where you wrap your arm around their neck before dropping them down on the back of their head by pulling downward with your arms.

Ude Garami - A key lock, a shoulder hold that sees you bend their elbow inward while pushing the wrist upward to take your opponent down on their back.

Kesa Gatame - The scarf hold - where the Tori holds the Uke by wrapping one of their arms around the Uke's neck and grabbing hold of it with their opposite hand.

Ude Gatame - A shoulder lock, where you bend one of your opponent's arms at the elbow before pushing downwards on it to put them in pain. Using both hands, push down on their wrist until they submit or get knocked out from the pressure.

The Basics of Randori Judo

Randori Judo, which literally means "free practice," is free fighting. During randori training, opponents simulate live fighting as closely as possible. You can take the role of either an attacker or a defense and apply techniques you have learned from kata to your advantage to gain control over your opponent. Randori training allows you to develop your fighting spirit by teaching you how to adapt quickly in any given situation.

Randori is about technique and form. You must consider the distance, timing, and grip needed to apply your techniques properly without exposing yourself to counterattacks from your opponent. Randori training helps you develop self-confidence by learning how to be more creative in any given situation and gaining knowledge of what works best for different opponents so that you can adjust your stance accordingly during live fights. The more you practice randori, the better your kata training will be because it helps to develop a deeper understanding of Judo.

Randori Rules and Tricks

Randori Judo rules are similar to those of kata Judo. The only difference is that you can now use all your techniques with full contact during randori training, which means your opponent cannot counterattack like they would in a real-life situation.

When it comes to Randori Judo, there aren't any specific regulations since this type of training is done as a way to help you develop your Judo skills by applying what you have been taught about the kata system.

There's no winner or loser in Randori, so just go at it freely without thinking about getting thrown. Relax and allow your body and mind to move freely. Keep your arms loose. Keep a hold on things lightly, but don't let go.

Follow through with each strategy. Avoid developing the habit of leaving a strategy halfway and trying new techniques.

Maintain solid contact with the mat using your feet. For added power, let out a loud kiai. Keep track of your breathing to remain in control. Keep your elbows tucked in tight against your body, where they are more effective. Always face your opponent and never turn your back on them. Do not put your feet together.

Importance of Mastering Kata

It is important to master Kata before progressing to Randori sparring because Kata helps you develop the technical skills needed to win when applying any given technique in randori.

Kata training is how Judo was formed, and it's what will make up most of your training. It's where you learn everything about different types of techniques, grips, and counters with the help of a partner who practices with you on the mat.

Kata training is what will help you learn how to apply different techniques when you get into randori fights, where it's no holds barred, and anything goes. So make sure that your Kata skills are on point before even attempting Randori sparring so that you can effectively use the techniques needed to win against an opponent.

The Importance of Following Judo Safety Rules and Etiquette

The main aim of following Judo safety rules and etiquette during sparring is to keep you and your opponent safe while training.

Be sure to warm up and stretch all the muscles in your body before getting into a sparring session. This is essential to avoid muscle strains, sprains, and other types of injuries, which can be caused by sudden movements during randori training sessions. Always make sure you are wearing the proper protective gear, such as mouthguards or head protection.

During randori training, be respectful and take it easy -don't waste your energy, especially if you're new to Judo or only have a little experience. To become a better Judoka and gain a better understanding of everything Judo has to offer, you can always work on developing your techniques by sparring with more experienced players and other people who practice the art form at a higher level than you. Make sure you are aware of your surroundings and the people around you during randori training or sparring sessions so that no one gets hurt during the practice session. This is especially so if a lot of people are attending or involved in an event. It would be best to have a set of rules agreed upon by the people taking part in randori training, especially for those just starting out.

Always take your time and focus on what you are doing during sparring so that you can improve your technique without rushing to finish every round as soon as possible. Knowing how much force to apply when performing different techniques is important, so you don't hurt your opponent.

Stop when the referee blows the whistle.

Don't attack your opponent when they are down on the mat after being thrown or pinned.

Always bow before and after sparring matches regardless of whether it was a win or loss for either competitor.

Make sure your opponent is ready before starting randori. If they are not, politely wait until they are fully prepared to fight.

Always start off easily, and gradually increase the intensity of sparring as you get more comfortable with Judo training or practice sessions.

Don't make any sudden movements while your opponent is applying a technique on you because this could cause injury to them or yourself.

You should always bow to your opponent before and after the sparring match, showing respect for their training, providing courtesy, and avoiding misunderstandings that could lead to injury. You can also show good sportsmanship by bowing toward the referee if you feel they have made an unfair call.

The Benefits of Judo Sparring

Judo sparring provides you with a good cardio workout and helps to boost your stamina. It's also an intense way of training that can help improve your speed, endurance, and strength by using the right techniques at the right time during randori or free practice sessions. Sparring is great for building confidence in yourself when fighting with fellow Judo players.

Randori is a great way to put the techniques you've learned into practice and apply them to different scenarios, especially if you want to push yourself beyond your limits or challenge yourself to be better. Daily training with new people of varying levels of experience will challenge you mentally and physically. It's also a good opportunity for you to learn from your mistakes and correct them in future training sessions and a time to improve your technique through experience.

Mastering Nage No Kata and Katame No Kata

Mastering nage no kata (throwing techniques) and katame no kata (grappling techniques) through repetition is the only way to learn new Judo techniques and improve on them. Since nage no kata are pre-arranged forms, you can easily follow the sequence of steps without having to think about it as they become integrated into your practicing or randori training sessions.

Kata practice teaches you how to apply Judo techniques in a safe and controlled environment, so practicing these forms with 100% focus is important. This will help you learn how to apply Judo throws correctly. This is where your Sensei can coach you and correct your mistakes while simultaneously building up stamina, ready for randori training. Randori training allows you to fight against opponents who can attack from any direction at any time. Randori also requires Judo players to be mentally focused and prepared for anything, which is why both forms of practice are important when it comes to learning the art and sport of Judo.

Nage no kata and Katame no kata are Judo's key technical training exercises. This is because they allow you to practice your throwing and grappling techniques without the pressure of randori or fighting against an opponent during free practice sessions. Nage no kata also provides a great opportunity for players to improve their timing and distance awareness –as well as learning new throwing techniques that they may not be familiar with through katame no kata practice.

These techniques will be explained in detail in the upcoming chapters.

The two forms of Judo (Kata and Randori) have their own benefits. The key to bettering your skills is practicing the right form at the right time to master these techniques. Practice Judo sparring with caution so you don't injure yourself or others while maximizing your training by focusing on different aspects such as speed, endurance, strength, and confidence through randori practice sessions.

Chapter 3: Judo Basics and Ukemi, or Falling Safely

In this chapter, we will discuss Judo basics and ukemi. Ukemi is the Japanese term for the art of falling safely. We'll start with a brief overview of what Judo is, why it's so popular in Japan, and how to perform basic poses and movements correctly. Then we'll talk about shisei, or posture – the ideal form you want to strive for when practicing Judo. Finally, we'll be discussing various ways to fall safely from either being thrown by an opponent or executing a throw on him/herself.

Shisei (Posture)

Shisei

Shisei is the Japanese term for posture. During Judo practice, you will strive to maintain perfect shisei at all times -that means standing straight with your head up and back arched slightly backward. Your feet should be shoulder-width apart so that they are pointing forward perpendicular to your upper body, which should be facing forward. Your knees should be slightly bent, and your stomach pulled in, and your shoulders back.

The concept of shisei is that your body should be in a natural standing position for maximum balance. There are three main postures: shinzei-tai (natural standing), shinzen-hontai, migi-shizen-tai, and hidari-shizen-tai.

Shinzei-Tai (Natural Standing)

Shinzei-Tai

This posture is the most common for beginners, and you should aim to progress from this stance. Your weight is evenly distributed on both legs, with your feet pointing straight forward. This means taking a natural standing posture. Pull your chin in, straighten the back of your neck, and tighten the butt cheeks. It may seem difficult to maintain at first – but with time and continued practice, you will get used to it. The upper body should be upright and not leaning forward. Hips should be slightly pushed back with a 45-degree angle between the upper part of your body and hips.

The natural standing position is composed of shinzen-hontai, migi-shizen-tai, and hidari-shizen-tai

Shizen-Hontai

Shizen-Hontai

The shizen-hontai is the most natural of all postures because it is the position in which you are standing when at rest. Your body weight is distributed evenly with your heels and hips in line so that both legs form a right angle with each other. Your feet should be shoulder-width apart and pointing straight forward. Knees should be slightly bent, but not more than at 15 degrees angle from your upper body. Your head is up, your chin pulled tight against the neck, and your back arched ever so slightly backward.

Migi-Shizen-Tai

This posture is another natural standing position where the body weight is evenly distributed on both legs with your right foot pointing forward. Your hips and shoulders should be in line with your legs. Your chest is up, chin pulled back into the neck, and knees slightly bent just as they were for shizen-hontai.

Migi-Shizen-Tai

Hidari-Shizen-Tai

The last natural standing position is hidari-shizen-tai, where you stand with your left foot pointing forward. Your body weight is distributed evenly on both legs with hips and shoulders in line, just as they were for the migi-shizen-tai posture. The only difference between this position and migi-shizen-tai is that you will face to the right side instead of straight ahead.

Hidari-Shizen-Tai

Defense in Judo

In Judo, the whole idea of defense is not to defend yourself from an attack but rather negate the momentum and redirect it into a throw. It's about using the opponent's power against him/her. The best way to do this is by using their forward momentum against them.

To stop an opponent from throwing you, remain calm and relaxed. Most often, you will see your opponent tense up when they're trying to throw someone because it takes a lot of exertion on the part of the person doing the throwing -it's like pushing or pulling something with all your might.

If an opponent is trying to throw you, try not to resist and tense up because that just makes it easier for them -that's why staying relaxed and calm works best against a bigger, stronger opponent. If they're throwing you backward, make sure you don't step back with the same foot they are using (if their right foot is forward, you should step back with your left leg). If they're trying to throw you sideways, use the same principle - step in the opposite direction of which way he/she is throwing.

Importance of Posture in Defense

When you are practicing throwing someone, keep in mind that your posture is important. If you're weak and not able to pick up the person as easily as usual, it's probably because your balance isn't right; you may be off-balance or leaning too much forward/backward, etc., so make sure when practicing you don't unbalance yourself.

Defensive Postures in Judo (Jigo Tai)

Jigo tai, or defensive postures, are a series of stances that you will learn while training in Judo. They allow you to absorb the force from being attacked and then redirect it back to your opponent. These stances are used as a way to protect yourself from harm or injury.

There are three basic postures which are jigo-hontai, migi-jigo-tai, and hidari-jigo-tai.

In Judo, the posture that lowers your hips and opens both legs is called Jigo-hontai.

Jigo-hon tai

Open your feet widely if you are in the Right Leg Forward Posture for migi-jigo-tai.

Migui-jigo-tai

Similarly, the posture of lowering the body and opening both feet widely from the left foot forward position is referred to as Hidari-jigo-tai (Left Defensive Posture).

Hidari-jigo-tai

Suri Ashi (Footwork)

When you're learning the art of Judo, one thing that will be crucial to your success is footwork. Being able to move around without tripping over yourself and being able to get into a good position for throwing someone down either by taking their balance or getting them off-balance so they can't defend themselves as easily is key.

When you're fighting in the dojo, make sure to use the correct footwork. If you don't know what it is or how to use your feet properly when Judo-ing someone down, ask a more experienced classmate for help. They will be able to show you and teach you everything from proper posture and stance to different throwing strategies.

Suri-ashi is the term used to describe Judo footwork. When you are training, don't just walk around during practice. Use suri ashi (moving your feet quickly by sliding them along the floor) instead of taking big steps. Make sure to keep your back straight and move forward without taking unnecessary steps!

The term "Suri ashi" refers to the footwork used during a contest or Randori, which is meant to keep one's balance while moving.

The contestant avoids lifting his leg too far off the ground by stepping with this Suri ashi (Footwork) methodology, which allows him to shift quickly while keeping his body weight balanced.

Ayumi-ashi and the Tsugi-ashi

The term "Ayumi ashi" refers to the footwork used during tai sabaki (body shifting body techniques). It allows for quick, large steps without losing balance or posture. The contestant should step forward quickly by sliding his feet along the ground to keep himself from being knocked off balance while still keeping his body weight evenly distributed.

The term "Tsugi-ashi" is a footwork technique used to move forward quickly without losing balance or posture and is done by sliding the feet along the floor instead of lifting them up and taking large steps. This technique is also known as shuffling.

Slide your feet along the ground when you fight in Judo, and make sure you keep a strong posture. Using proper footwork and stance will give you an advantage over your opponents who don't know how to use their fighting strategies properly during practice, so try different stances out until you find one that works for you!

In order to ensure safety during Judo practice/sparring, make sure you keep your balance and posture so you don't get injured. It is important to know the footwork involved in Judo as well, whether it be Ayumi-ashi or Tsugi-ashi – make sure to practice them both!

Tai Sabaki (Body Shifting Body Techniques)

One of the most important things that you will learn in Judo is tai sabaki, or how to move your body efficiently and effectively. The type of tai sabaki required depends on whether there are throws or groundwork involved in your practice or free fighting. Regardless, knowing how to properly move your body is one of the most important parts of Judo.

When you are trying to throw someone down, it's best to use tai sabaki to get into position for throwing them. Make sure when using tai sabaki during practice or a match that you keep good balance and posture. If not, you could easily get thrown – and you don't want to let your opponent take advantage of that!

Tai sabaki is an important part of Judo, so make sure you practice different tai sabaki techniques until you find the one that works best for you.

"Tai-sabaki" (Japanese) refers to the way a contestant's body position and orientation change when performing or receiving a Waza.

The four fundamental tai-sabaki (Body shifting / Body control) techniques are as follows:

1. Mae-sabaki is when you step forward to put your foot in front of the other person's foot. One foot needs to be in front of the opponent.

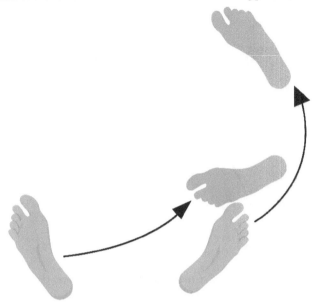

2. Ushiro-sabaki is when you step back with one of your feet, putting it next to the other person's foot at a right angle. You need to do this while staying in position.

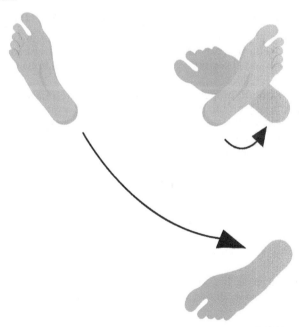

3. Mae-mawari-sabaki is a move in which you step forward with one foot and spin around in front of the person.

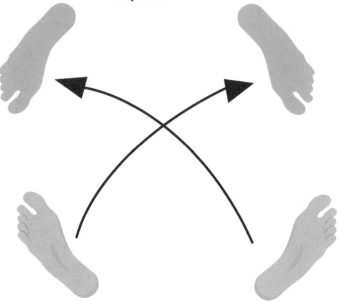

4. Ushiro-mawari-sabaki is a move in which you move one foot back before spinning around to face the other way.

Learning these different tai-sabaki techniques is one of the most important parts of learning Judo, so make sure you practice these different tai sabaki repeatedly until they become second nature!

Avoiding Injury Using Ukemi Techniques

It is vital to avoid injury while doing ukemi (falling techniques) in Judo. People who know how to do ukemi properly and safely will be able to avoid injury, while people who don't know how to fall correctly could very well end up injuring themselves during practice or a match!

You need to learn the proper way to land when you are practicing/doing ukemiis, which is on the side of your hip or your arm. You should avoid landing on your lower back at all costs – especially if you are a beginner!

The main reason that it's important to know how to do ukemi correctly is that when you don't practice this way in training, it can be very easy to get injured.

Ukemi Tips

Understanding Form and Balance

One of the most important parts of doing Ukemi is having good form and balance.

Depending on your sex, height, weight, and build, you can alter the angles and round off the corners of your body as it enters and exits ukemi until you are satisfied and at ease.

Imagine that you are feeling the mat with all of your body; *listen to what your body has to say.* While you take advice, remember to pay attention to what works for you and what does not.

Relax and Breathe

Being nervous or tense while doing ukemi will only make things worse and increase your chances of getting hurt.

If you feel yourself tensing up, try to relax by taking a deep breath and letting it out slowly while thinking about something calming.

Do Not Resist Your Tori's Technique

Do not resist the Tori's (player executing the technique) attempt to do a throw or other Waza. If you tense up, your chances of being countered are much higher and will increase the chances that both players get injured!

Energy and Confidence

When doing ukemi, you should be confident and full of energy in your actions. This will make it easier to get in position for the throw and much harder for the Tori (Player executing the technique) to counter.

Practice, Practice, Practice!

The more you practice doing Ukemi, the better your balance and form will get. You'll also be able to tell what works for you in terms of angles, speed, etc., so that way, it is easy to do ukemi anytime during a match or training session.

Ukemi Methods

To improve in ukemi techniques, you must have fluid motions and dedication, which comes with practice. The best way to learn is to get thrown and practice your ukemi. Begin with a sitting fall, then a squatting posture, and eventually work your way up to standing.

The three types of falls are firstly to fall straight to the ground, dissipating the energy through your arms and legs. Secondly, it is to roll with the ground, and thirdly, it is a combination of the two.

The ability to fall correctly is essential for Judo practice and competition. A common mistake that many people make when first learning how to do Ukemi during a match or training is over-rotating the body and twisting their head too far around, which can be dangerous since it causes whiplash.

While you may think falling is easy, it takes a lot of practice and patience to do so without getting injured.

Mae Ukemi (Forward Breakfall) and Ushiro Ukemi (Back Breakfall)

The forward or front breakfall is essential to learn since it will keep a student's head from striking the ground if attacked from behind.

One person should fall straight forward from the upright position. Ensure that your upper body remains rigid. It should not bow forward.

The head is turned to the left or right and raised slightly just before making contact with the ground to avoid hitting your face (or nose) on the floor. Raise your arms with your thumbs at ear level; avoid shoring up with arms to avoid elbow injury.

The back breakfall is an essential Judo technique to learn since it can harm your back and head if you fall incorrectly when thrown. It involves kneeling and falling on a rolled back, protecting your head at all times with arms drawn in the front. This fall is difficult as one cannot see and judge behind himself.

Yoko Ukemi (Side Breakfall)

This hardfall is practiced when one leg is blocked or swept away. Push one leg to the side on which you want to fall. Move this in front of the other foot in a sweeping motion. As you do this, keep bending in your knees until you fall to your side.

You must roll on the tatami with a straight flat arm, hip first. It is important to keep the angle of the arm with the body axis between 20 to 40 degrees to avoid injury. Be careful to avoid head injury as well.

Tips for Falling Safely

- Make sure you are relaxed, but be confident that you can take whatever your opponent throws at you!

- Practice Ukemi techniques to improve balance and form. You'll also be able to tell what works for you in terms of angles, speed, etc. - so that it is easy to do ukemi anytime during a match or training session.

- To learn to do Ukemi, you must have fluid motions and dedication, which comes with practice. The best way to learn is by getting thrown and then practicing your ukemi. Begin with a sitting fall, then a squatting posture, and eventually work your way up to standing.

- While you may think falling is easy, it takes a lot of practice and patience to do so without getting injured. One common mistake many people make when first learning how to do Ukemi during a match or training is over-rotating the body and twisting their head around too far, which can be dangerous since it causes whiplash.

- While the forward or front breakfall is essential to learn, another important technique to know is the back breakfall, as it will keep a student's head from striking the ground if attacked from behind. To do this, fall correctly, kneel, and fall on a rolled back, protecting your head at all times with arms drawn in at the front. You must also remember to keep your upper body rigid and not bow forward, as well as maintaining a head-neck relationship by turning it slightly to one side so that your nose does not hit the floor.

Another common mistake many people make when first learning how to do Ukemi during a match or training is not tucking their head into the chest. This causes excessive neck injuries! To avoid this issue, you must roll on your side with a straight, flat arm (and hip first). Keep in mind that it is important to keep the angle of the arm with the body axis between 20 to 40 degrees, which will allow you to avoid injury.

Judo is a sport that requires both agility and endurance. Proper posture, or shisei, will not only make you more agile but can also help protect your back from injury if thrown to the ground. These techniques are essential for any competitor in Judo as they'll keep them on their feet no matter how many throws an opponent makes during a match! Make sure to practice these basic Judo poses and movements while feeling out what works best for you when practicing Ukemi. Once mastered, you'll be able to tell what angles and speeds work best for you when doing Ukemi. Be sure that while they may not seem easy at first, practicing these techniques will come with time, dedication, and, most importantly, practice!

Chapter 4: Te Wazsa: Hand Techniques

Nage Waza is a class of throwing techniques in Judo. This includes sweep, lift, trip, hold-downs, and many more submission holds. Te Waza is the name for throwing techniques that involve the use of your hands or arms. After throwing an opponent with your arms, you immediately have control of your opponent while they are still on the ground or trying to get up.

As always, in Judo, there are no rules regarding how to throw an opponent. There is only one goal which is to get them on the floor. However, for larger opponents, sometimes standard throws will not work. If this is the case, then you can turn to Te Waza techniques. These are considered safer than Nage Waza because they do not require full-body contact. In this chapter, you will venture deeper into the details of Te Waza techniques, which can be used to easily control or even take down larger, stronger opponents. It'll also cover the 15 Te Waza techniques.

Te Waza and Nage Waza

Te Waza is the first of the three major categories in Kodokan Judo that were created by Jigoro Kano. They consist of thirty-six techniques or waza, which are executed from a standing position with the opponent's balance broken. The main difference between Te Waza and the other two Judo techniques is that this category does not include any groundwork or mat work.

The idea behind Te Waza is to use your arms or hands in a way that makes them safe for you and dangerous for your opponent. If you can take control of your opponent's balance without using your legs, then there will be nothing they can do to counter the throw. After you gain control over them, getting them on the floor will be extremely easy.

This is completely different from Nage Waza, which requires full-body contact. If your opponent does not fall, they are free to counter you. However, after throwing an opponent with Te Waza, there will be nothing they can do once you take control of their balance. It will allow you to pin them down, immobilize them, or do anything else you want to do.

Te Waza's goal is simple. Take control of your opponent before they take control of you. Always having perfect balance will allow you to fight against any sized opponent, whether they're bigger than yourself or not. The techniques found in Te Waza will greatly increase your chances of getting on top in a grappling situation.

Te Waza Techniques

A total of 15 Te Waza techniques can be used to throw an opponent. The first three will allow you to take down even the strongest opponents safely and easily. The last twelve work better against normal-statured people who have already been taken to the floor.

1. Kata Guruma (Shoulder Wheel)

This basic Te Waza technique is performed from the Kumi kata. To break it down a little more, you can do a standard harai goshi with your right leg and then throw the opponent on their back after turning to your left side. The rotation motion will allow you to easily scoop them up by lifting them under their shoulder so they cannot resist.

2. Morote Seoi Nage (Two-Hand Shoulder Throw)

The second technique is done similarly to Ippon seoi nage. You can use both hands to grab the opponent by their neck and then throw them over your body with the help of momentum. This will be easiest if you've already got them off balance or knocked them down by trapping one of their arms behind their back.

3. Tai Otoshi (Body Drop)

The third technique is a little more dangerous. It's done by trapping one of your opponent's arms against their back, scooping them up with both hands, and then throwing them over the top of your body. This will be extremely easy if they're leaning forward, which makes it perfect for Judo competition.

4. Morote Gari (Double Leg Reaping)

This Te Waza technique is a little more difficult to get down because it's done from the feet. However, it's extremely easy if you already have them on their knees or stomach since it'll be easier to trap one of their arms under your leg. After that, it will only take a little bit of a push from you and a pull from them to make them land on their back.

5. Ippon Seoi Nage (One Arm Shoulder Throw)

Just like the other Seoi Nage techniques, this is a pretty basic throw to get to grips with. It can be done from a standard harai goshi which allows you to lift the opponent's arm under their shoulder. After that, all you have to do is grab their other hand and throw them on their back. This technique works best against weaker opponents who don't expect to get thrown.

6. Sukui Nage (Scoop Throw)

This technique is extremely useful because it can be done from almost any position. If you have your opponent trapped under their arms, then all you have to do is scoop them up and then throw their center of gravity over your shoulder. Alternatively, you can set it up by tripping their leg to get them down on their knees. The possibilities are endless, which makes this a favorite for Judoka.

7. Obi Otoshi (Belt Drop)

The next Te Waza technique is best done when you have your opponent up against the wall. Anytime their feet are off the floor will be useful, but you can also do it when they're standing on one leg. To break it down further, grab them by the belt with both hands and then push them backward and away from you. This will make it easy to knock them off balance, take them down, and land on top of them.

8. Kibisu Gaeshi (Heel Reversal)

This one is done by throwing the opponent by their heel after getting them flat on their back. It will only work well if you have a large enough gap between them to grip their heel with one hand. Once this is done, it's a simple matter of sitting straight up, lifting them by the heel, and throwing their center of gravity over your stomach.

9. Kuchiki Taoshi (Dead Tree Drop)

The next technique is done by trapping one or both of your opponent's arms with your legs before pulling them over you. This will make it extremely easy to knock them down and land on top of them. If done correctly, you will end up sitting straight up with the opponent flat on their back as you pull them over you.

10. Morote Gari (Two-Hand Reap)

This throw technique is done by throwing the opponent over your shoulder after trapping one of their arms. It's generally easy to do because you only need one of your arms to block their arm and then scoop them up when they are off-balance. Sit straight up, pull them over your shoulder, and then land on top of them.

11. Sumi Otoshi (Corner Drop)

The next is done by throwing the opponent sideways after trapping their arm. Then all you have to do is trip them to get them off-balance and pull them over your body. This will make it easy to land on top of them while they're flat on their back. After that, you only need to sit straight up to get them flipped over.

12. Uki Otoshi (Floating Drop)

This is executed by pulling your opponent over your shoulder after trapping their arm. You will need to be quick to knock them off balance and pull their arm before they can grab the mat. Once you've done this, sit straight up and pull them over your shoulder to throw them on their back. You can increase the power by pulling them up and over with both arms.

13. Uchimata Sukashi (Inner Thigh Throw Slip)

The next Te Waza technique is done by pulling your opponent over your hip after tripping their leg. This will make it easy to knock them off balance and pull them over your hip while you sit straight up. Then you can land directly on top of them with either one leg between theirs or both legs outside of theirs. With either technique, you will end up sitting straight up with them flat on their back.

14. Yama Arashi (Mountain Storm)

This Te Waza technique is done by trapping one or both of their arms before pulling them over your hip. This will allow you to easily knock them off balance and then throw them on their back. It also works if they have both arms over your shoulders because then you can simply pull them over one side of your body.

15. Seoi Otoshi (Shoulder Drop)

The final Te Waza technique is done by throwing your opponent on their side after trapping one of their arms. Just hold onto their arm and pull them over your body to flip them onto their side. All you have to do from there is sit straight up for an easy throw. You must get your hips under them before they hit the ground.

With Te Waza being the first major category in Judo, you should master this category before moving on to others. Practicing these techniques will boost your overall Judo abilities and get you ready to begin studying more complex throwing techniques like Osaekomi Waza. The main thing to remember with Te Waza is that you should always try to trap both of the opponent's arms before throwing them so they can't grab onto the mat. If you can manage to trap both of their arms before they are thrown, then the throw will certainly be easier to do.

The fifteen techniques, or waza, in this Judo text are performed by trapping one or both of the opponent's arms before the throw. They are meant to be done from a standing position with the opponent off balance, which will make it easy to take them down and land directly on top of them. The fifteen techniques are often combined to make even more effective combinations that flow smoothly from one technique to the next. It should be easy to find a Te Waza technique that works well with your particular body type and level of Judo knowledge.

Chapter 5: Koshi Waza: Hip Throws

The main idea of Koshi Waza is to break the opponent's balance by pulling them towards you and throwing them down with the help of your hip after breaking their balance. Koshi Waza is usually performed from a static position or during Tai-Otoshi, but they can also be used as counter techniques after being improperly thrown. This chapter explains the main idea and proper movements of all 11 Koshi Waza techniques.

The Basics of Koshi Waza: Hip Throws

This group of techniques is used to throw the opponent by using your hip as a driving force. When a Judo practitioner first starts Judo, they learn Koshi Guruma as a first technique. It is important to learn Koshi Waza from the beginning because it will be easier to learn them as a foundation for later Waza. By using Koshi Waza, you can perform powerful techniques that appear as if you are "pushing" the opponent. The strength to execute these techniques comes from your entire body rather than just your arms. Instead of using the force of the arms, you use the whole body to execute these hip techniques. You can use Koshi Waza as throwing techniques or counter techniques after being thrown.

For all Koshi Waza, the first thing to do is to get a hold of the opponent's body with two hands. It starts by grabbing the opponent's clothing. However, this is not the traditional grip called "Sumi-Kakae" (Corner Sumi Grip). You must grab your opponent's lapel with your blocking hand and your opponent's sleeve with the other. Be careful not to change the traditional grip called Sumi-Kakae while performing Koshi Waza, or it will become a different technique.

For some of the Waza, you must break your opponent's balance by taking a step and blocking your opponent with the same foot. The first thing to do is step diagonally forward with your right foot. If you want to throw your opponent using your hip, you must quickly place your left foot on the ground so that you can use your hip as a driving force. If it is necessary, you must block your opponent's right foot with your left foot.

Now you must try to grab the opponent's belt or pants with your right hand and keep your left arm straight. Then, while using your right hand and your left foot as a guide to block the opponent's foot, you must pull the opponent toward you. You must then use your right hand and hip to throw the opponent.

When throwing the opponent, you can either try to lift them high and throw them down (Kata-Guruma) or throw them straight to the ground (Uki-Goshi). When performing Kata-Guruma, you must try to lift your opponent high and throw them straight down. When performing Uki-Goshi, you must first lift your opponent high, but instead of throwing them down straight, you must jump up and throw them down to the side.

Koshi Waza Techniques

There are 11 Koshi Waza techniques. They are explained below, together with the rules for using them. However, it is important to remember that with a few minor changes, you can use these techniques in an infinite number of ways. This is the beauty of Judo.

1. Daki Age – High Lift

This technique can be applied by lifting your opponent high and then throwing them straight down. However, the Daki-Age Waza starts by grabbing the opponent's shoulders or sleeves and can be applied in many different ways. Once you have grabbed your opponent, you must use the strength of your arms to lift them. Then, while maintaining your grip with both hands, you must lift your opponent straight up to the level of your shoulders. The next step is to quickly raise your left leg while still holding your opponent. Now you must land on your left foot while throwing the opponent down with the help of your hip.

2. Hane Goshi – Spring Hip Throw

This technique must be applied when you are in a standing position, with your left foot forward and your right foot back. You must grab the opponent's shoulders or sleeves with your hands. The next step is to quickly use your outside hand to pull the opponent toward you by using your right hand. The right hand must move in a small circular motion, with your elbow being the center so that you can break the opponent's balance with your pull. Then you must use your hip to throw the opponent.

3. Harai Goshi – Sweeping Hip Throw

This technique is applied in a very similar way to Hane Goshi. This time you must grab the opponent's left lapel with your right hand, the outside hand. You must then grab your opponent's sleeve with your blocking hand. The right arm will act as the driving force for this technique, so you must pull your opponent toward you by turning the right hand in a circular motion. When you have pulled the opponent, you have to apply Harai Goshi by using your hip to throw the opponent.

4. Koshi Guruma – Hip Wheel Throw

To successfully perform Koshi Guruma, you must be in a standing position with your left foot forward and right foot back. You must grab your opponent's belt or pants with both hands. The next step is to quickly block the opponent's left foot with your left foot. You must then throw the opponent by using your hip and right hand. You must not use your arms to lift your opponent, but try to keep them as close to the ground as possible. The rotation will happen around an axis that passes through your opponent's leg and your own body. Koshi Guruma is a hard technique to pull off, but it is possible for someone with good physical strength and flexibility.

5. Goshi – Major Hip Throw

This technique is very similar to Koshi Guruma. The only difference is that O Goshi does not block the opponent's foot to throw them. O Goshi is a gentle technique, which may be hard to get used to if you are accustomed to throwing people around with force. However, it is very effective for throwing children or smaller opponents. All you need to do is pull the opponent toward you by using your arms. You must pull them up high and then quickly move one foot forward while throwing the opponent down to the ground on your knee.

6. Sode Tsurikomi Goshi – Sleeve Lifting and Pulling Hip Throw

This technique can be applied by grabbing the opponent's left sleeve with your left hand and the back of the opponent's collar or belt with your right hand. The right hand is the driving force for this technique, so you must pull the opponent toward you by using your elbow as a center and rotating your right hand in a circular motion. You must then pull your opponent while using your hip to throw them down.

7. Tsuri Goshi – Lifting Hip Throw

This throw is almost identical to Sode Tsurikomi Goshi. However, in this case, you must grab the opponent's belt with your left hand and the back of their collar with your right hand. Once again, the right hand is the driving force for this technique, and you must pull your opponent toward you by using your elbow as a center and rotating your right hand in a circular motion. Then you must throw your opponent down to the ground, using your hip as a pivot point

8. Tsurikomi Goshi - Lifting and Pulling Hip Throw

Tsurikomi Goshi is a variation of the technique Sode Tsurikomi Goshi. In this case, you grab your opponent's sleeve with your left hand and the back of their belt or collar with your right hand. You then pull the opponent toward you by using your elbow as a center and rotating your right arm in a circular motion. You must then lift your opponent and pull them down to throw them.

9. Uki Goshi - Floating Hip Throw

This is a very traditional technique, and it is normally only taught to black belts. It is a more difficult hip throw to pull off, so you should not attempt this one until you are very familiar with the basics. Uki Goshi is performed by grabbing your opponent's belt with your right hand. You must then pull the opponent toward you, lifting their left leg high into the air. After that, you quickly move your right foot to the outside of your opponent's left foot and throw them down to the ground.

10. Ushiro Goshi - Rear Throw

This one is normally taught to white belts. You must stand behind your opponent, with your arms around the body and your back arched a bit backward. After that, you must lift them into the air by using your hip and then throw them down to the ground over your shoulder. You must not bend your knees when throwing Ushiro Goshi, and you must keep your feet in the same position throughout the technique.

11. Utsuri Goshi - Hip Shift Throw

This is another hip throw that will not be taught until you are a black belt. It is a hard technique to learn and to pull off because it relies on very subtle movements. You must first pull your opponent into you by using their shoulder or wrist, forcing them to shift their weight onto one leg so that they lean toward you. After that, you must lift them and shift your hips to the outside of their leg to throw them down to the ground.

Judo Koshi Waza (hip throws) uses the hip as a pivot point and requires that you break your opponent's balance. The main technique in all the hip throws listed above is to pull and then throw your opponent down by using your hip. It can be very difficult to learn and execute hip throws, which is why you will only be taught them when you have advanced past the beginner stage. You should focus on perfecting the basics before attempting any of these advanced techniques. All of these techniques, with the exception of Ushiro Goshi and Utsuri Goshi, can be performed by both men and women. You can perform any of these Judo techniques at any competitive level, and they can be very useful in a fight. As always, it is essential to practice these techniques with a trained Judo coach to ensure that you are doing them correctly. Once you master these hip throws, they can provide a very effective means of self-defense.

Chapter 6: Ashi Waza: Foot Techniques

Ashi Waza is a category of techniques in Judo that includes sweeping, hooking, and reaping throws, as well as sacrifice throws. The term Ashi Waza can be broken down into two words "ashi," which means foot, and "waza," which means technique. Thus, Ashi Waza can be translated as foot techniques. This chapter focuses on the 21-foot techniques that are recognized by the International Judo Federation (IJF).

Ashi Waza's Main Principle

The main principle behind any Ashi Waza technique is to unbalance your opponent by using foot sweeps, hooking motions, or reaping motions. Once the opponent has been unbalanced, they must then be thrown or pinned to the ground. As the name implies, Ashi Waza involves the use of the feet rather than the hands to throw an opponent. There are 21 recognized Ashi Waza techniques. These include all of the sacrifice throws, sweeps, hooking motions, and reaping motions. Although many of these 21 techniques are similar to the hand techniques of Katame Waza, they are still unique and important to learn.

Judo Ashi Waza: Foot Techniques List

The following are the 21 Judo Ashi Waza techniques that are recognized by the IJF. Each of these techniques should be practiced in two distinct phases: the attack and the execution. The attack is when you sweep or hook your opponent's foot attempting to unbalance them. The execution is when you press down on the opponent's foot, apply a throwing technique, and throw your opponent to the ground.

1. Hiza Guruma (Knee Wheel)

This technique involves sweeping or hooking your opponent's lead foot with your lead leg. Sweep the foot outward in a circular motion while placing pressure on their lead foot with the arch of your same side leg's calf. Sweep your opponent's lead foot into your chest while flinging your other leg over the opponent's lead leg.

2. Kosoto Gake (Small Outside Hook)

This move involves hooking the outside of your opponent's lead foot with your lead leg. Hook your opponent's foot just above or below the ankle with the instep of your foot. It is important to keep your hands on your opponent's chest or shoulders as you hook their foot. Then, throw your opponent backward

3. Kosoto Gari (Small Outside Hook)

This sequence is similar to Kosoto Gake, but your opponent does not have their hands on the mat. Using your lead leg, sweep your opponent's outside foot at the ankle or further up the shin. Sweep your opponent's foot in a downward motion while keeping contact between your chest and your opponent's back. Then, sweep your opponent backward and to the ground.

4. Kouchi Gari (Minor Inner Reaping)

Similar to Kosoto Gari - except your opponent's lead foot will be on the inside of their body. Sweep low at your opponent's outside foot with your lead leg. Sweep the foot inward and out as if throwing a Sumi Gaeshi (corner reversal throw). With this throw, the opponent's back will be to you, and you will be facing their opposite side. Before throwing, lean your upper body in front of the opponent so that you are parallel to the ground.

5. Guruma (Large Wheel)

This is performed when you swing your opponent's lead leg with your rear leg. Keep the hands on the opponent's shoulders or chest as you sweep your opponent's foot in a large circular motion. Push or pull the sweep and then throw them down. Remember to keep your hips away from the opponent's hips when performing this technique.

6. Okuriashi Harai (Following Foot Sweep)

This technique is performed when you sweep your opponent's forward foot with the back of your same side leg's calf. Swing low at your opponent's forward foot with your lead leg. Sweep the opponent's front foot quickly to unbalance them while keeping your hands on their chest or shoulders.

7. Ouchi Gari (Major Inner Reaping)

Similar to Kouchi Gari, except your opponent will be facing in the opposite direction. Sweep low at your opponent's inside foot with your rear leg. Sweep the foot inward and back, throwing your opponent back to the mat. Before throwing, lean your upper body in front of your opponent so that you are parallel to the ground. Your opposite side arm should be pressed against your body for support and balance.

8. Ouchi Gaeshi (Major Inner Reversal)

Similar to Ouchi Gari, except you will be throwing your sparring partner over your opposite side shoulder. Sweep low at your opponent's inside foot with your rear leg. Sweep your opponent's foot inward and back, turning your body as you sweep them off their feet. This will result in your opponent landing on their upper back and shoulders.

9. Osoto Gari (Major Outer Reaping)

This technique is similar to Kosoto Gari, except for this move, you will be sweeping your opponent's lead foot with your rear leg and facing in the opposite direction. It is important to keep your hands on the opponent's chest or shoulders as you sweep their foot. Sweep your opponent's lead foot outward in a circular motion while keeping your outside foot glued to the mat. You must keep contact between your chest and the opponent's back as you swing their foot out to unbalance them. As you sweep your opponent, lean forward with your upper body so that you are parallel to the ground.

10. Osoto Gaeshi (Osotogari Counter)

This technique is performed when you sweep your opponent's lead foot with your rear leg and they are facing in the opposite direction. Keep contact between your chest and the opponent's back as you sweep their lead foot. Swing your opponent's foot out, throwing them to the mat. As you sweep your opponent, lean forward with your upper body so that you are parallel to the ground.

11. Osoto Guruma (Larger Outer Wheel)

When sweeping the opponent's forward leg, sweep with your same side rear leg and turn 180 degrees as you sweep. It's similar to Osoto Gaeshi, except you will be turning your back to the opponent. Press your opposite arm against your body for balance and support. This technique is useful if you are facing an opponent with a strong defense since the opponent will be unable to stop your sweep or counter it.

12. Osoto Otoshi (Larger Outer Drop)

In this move, you will swing your opponent's forward leg with the same side rear leg. Just as in Osoto Gari, sweep low at your opponent's forward foot with your lead leg. Without putting energy into the sweep, quickly bring both legs together and turn slightly to sweep your opponent's front foot. Keep your weight shifted forward as you move, swinging the foot and dropping to one knee for support. As you sweep, lean slightly forward with your upper body to make your opponent fall over the top of you.

13. Sasae Tsurikomi Ashi (Lifting Pulling Ankle Prop)

This technique is used when your opponent is either standing still or moving toward you. Just as in Kouchi Gari, sweep the inner part of your opponent's forward foot with your rear leg, pulling it up and back to unbalance them. Sweep the foot inward and back. Lean your upper body in front of your opponent. Keep your hands on your opponent, using them to push them off balance or for support if needed.

14. Tsubame Gaeshi (Flight Reversal)

This Ashi Waza is used when sweeping the opponent's lead leg to the opposite side. Hook your opponent's forward foot with your rear leg, sweeping it out and to the side. Lower your body by leaning in the same direction as you sweep. Lower yourself even lower after you sweep, sending your opponent out and over you. Pull the opponent's body past you with your same side arm while maintaining contact with their back for balance.

15. Uchimata (Inner Thigh Throw)

For this one, your opponent will have their weight centered over the front leg. Sweep the opponent's lead foot with your rear leg, sweeping it inward and back. This will unbalance your opponent and dump them onto their back. Lean forward with your upper body to add difficulty to the throw. Keep contact between your chest and the opponent's back, and use your opposite arm for support. Keep the opponent close to you as they fall to unbalance them further and lessen the chances of a counter-attack by your opponent.

16. Ashi Guruma (Leg Wheel)

Your opponent will be in a forward-facing stance. Swing the opponent's lead foot with your rear leg, pulling it out and around in front of you. Keep the opponent close to you as they fall onto their back by keeping contact between your chest and their back.

17. Deashi Harai (Forward Foot Sweep)

When your opponent is standing with their weight centered over their feet, sweep their lead foot to the inside with your rear leg and pull it forward and up, dropping you and your opponent to the ground. Lean your upper body slightly towards their back for control as you sweep. Sweep high enough to make sure your opponent cannot grab your leg on the way down.

18. Hane Goshi Gaeshi (Hip Spring Counter)

This technique is used when your opponent sweeps at you with their lead foot. Sweep the outside of their lead leg inward, towards the center of your body. Lower your upper body and hips to make it harder for your opponent to follow up with a throw. Use the momentum from the sweep of their lead leg to throw your opponent past you and off-balance.

19. Harai Goshi Gaeshi (Hip Sweep Counter)

This technique is used when your opponent sweeps at you with their rear leg. Hook the inside of their forward leg inward, towards the center of your body. Keep your hands on their hips to unbalance them and complete the throw. This technique requires no backward movement on your part.

20. Harai Tsurikomi Ashi (Lifting Pulling Foot Sweep)

This technique is used when your opponent is off-balance or sweeping from the other side. You will sweep the inside of their lead leg just below the knee with your rear leg. Sweep straight in and up, keeping most of your weight on your rear leg. Keep your hands on the opponent's hips to help unbalance them and complete the throw.

21. Hiza Guruma (Knee Wheel)

Your opponent will be off-balance or standing straight. Sweep the outside of their rear leg with your leading leg, pulling it behind them and up. Keep your leading hand on their shoulder for control as you sweep, making sure to keep some of your weight on the rear leg during the sweep. Once the sweeping leg is behind them, use your opposite arm to pull your opponent's body past you and down onto their back.

Ashi Waza could be useful to learn if you want to make your throws more effective and help unbalance your opponent. Training with a partner and slowly adding more speed to your throws will help you develop the body control and timing needed for this effective style of throwing. This chapter explained 21 of the most common Ashi Waza, or foot techniques. It explored the main principle behind these techniques and explained how to apply them in practice. This includes the sweeping, reaping, hooking, and countering principles. These techniques can be useful to learn if you plan on participating in Judo or want to learn effective throws.

Chapter 7: Sutemi Waza: Sacrifice Techniques

In Judo, Sutemi Waza, which is the Japanese term for sacrifice techniques, falls under the throwing techniques, or Nage Waza, category. A sacrifice technique consists of two components, which are the Tori and Uke.

The Tori is the practitioner who is executing the technique, and the Uke is the opponent receiving their attack. To execute a sacrifice technique, the Tori wraps the Uke's body around his own and continues to fall with the Uke.

The term "Sutemi" can be translated as "throw away the seed." However, the term is most commonly translated into the word "sacrifice." The word "Waza" refers to a technique, particularly a throwing one. The name illustrates the fact that a Judoka must throw themselves on their back, sacrificing their balance, to perform the throw.

The sacrificial throws are useful when both opponents fall to the ground, but as a strategy in free fighting. Using sacrificial throws can be a quick way to turn the situation around.

Some Sutemi Waza moves are not as powerful as the Uke Waza, which is also known as the floating technique. However, other moves, such as Tomoe Nage, or the circle throw, can be very strong ones to execute.

Sutemi Waza is further divided into two groups: Ma-Sutemi Waza and Yoko-Sutemi Waza. Ma-Sutemi Waza refers to rear sacrifice throws, while Yoko-Sutemi Waza refers to side sacrifice throws.

This chapter will explore the Judo sacrifice techniques in further depth. We'll also discuss the importance of Ukemi and explain how the sacrifice techniques can be detrimental if not performed correctly. You'll find a list of the different Ma-Sutemi Waza and Yoko-Sutemi Waza, as well as an explanation of how they are performed.

Ukemi in Sutemi Waza

The technique of Sutemi Waza requires the practitioner to intentionally throw themselves on the ground along with their opponent. If not done correctly and carefully, the damage the attacker suffers can be similar to that which the opponent suffers.

In any fighting discipline, practitioners always have a plan or strategy. In addition to these factors, the practitioner must account for the fall when planning to perform a Sutemi Waza.

Ukemi, which has been discussed previously, is the correct way to fall and is very important in preventing injuries. Practicing Ukemi is an important part of learning and executing Sutemi Waza. The application of this technique should become an instinctive movement, which is possible due to muscle memory.

Ukemi can generally be practiced in four directions, as was discussed in a previous chapter. These are Ushiro Ukemi for backward falls, Mae Ukemi for forward falls, and Yoko Ukemi for right-side and left-side falls. This means that there is always a way to break your fall, regardless of whether you decide to do the Ma-Sutemi Waza or Yoko-Sutemi Waza.

The development of great Ukemi skills requires a lot of practice and repetition, and doing this repetition will make you a good Judoka because Ukemi techniques are key to good Judo skills. Not only can they help you correctly and safely execute Sutemi Waza, but they can also help you easily and quickly recover from your opponent's attacks.

Potential Risks

Sutemi Waza moves work because of the momentum of your opponent. When executing the move, the practitioner does not try to stop the opponent. What they do is accept their momentum and use it to their own advantage. They redirect the adversary's efforts, using their movement and balance.

These throws, when done incorrectly or hesitantly, can be very risky. This is because the attacker has to put themself in a disadvantageous position; this is the sacrifice part of the technique. If a faulty break fall technique is applied, the results can be devastating. Similarly, hesitation gives the opponent power. Since the attacker's position in Sutemi Waza is already not ideal, being slow or hesitant gives the adversary leverage.

While it can be risky, Sutemi Waza is comparatively easy to do. The momentum that comes from the falling body adds a lot of power to the throw. This means that very little strength is required, as surprising as it may sound. Though, the effect of the throw can be incredible.

This is why performing Sutemi Waza must be a very smooth process from start to finish. One should move with their opponent's body, accept their momentum, apply Ukemi to fall safely onto the ground, and continue to execute their throw quickly and cleanly.

Ma-Sutemi Waza

There are five rear sacrifice throws or Ma-Sutemi Waza techniques that can be applied.

1. Hikikomi gaeshi

Hikikomi gaeshi means pulling in reverse. This technique requires the practitioner to pull their opponent forward and then proceed to throw them over and then behind their head.

To perform the Hikikomi gaeshi, you need to move forward and place your foot halfway between your opponent's feet. You should then use your Hiki-te, or pulling hand, to pull the opponent forward. This will cause them to lose their balance. When they start falling forward, use your Tsurite or lifting a hand to reach over their shoulder. Then get hold of their belt. At the same time, use your Hiki-te again to scoop up your opponent's side or grab their pants. Following that move, shift your center of gravity backward. While grasping your opponent, you continue to roll them back and throw them over and behind your head. While throwing, you need to kick upward and against their thighs to project their body.

2. Sumi Gaeshi

Sumi gaeshi means corner throw. This technique requires the practitioner to pull the opponent forward, destabilizing and unbalancing them before falling back and throwing them over your head.

To get in position, stand in the Kenka yotsu position, and use your Tsurite to grab hold of your opponent from the back of their uniform. Then, use both your Tsurite and Hiki-te to pull the opponent forward. When they lose their balance, you'll start to secure your opponent at the back with your leg hooked to the opponent's crotch. You need to kick upward quickly to throw them over your head.

3. Tawara Gaeshi

Tawara gaeshi means a bag of rice throw. This technique requires the practitioner to throw their opponent over their head and behind it as if the opponent was a bag of rice.

This technique is typically used as a counter-attack to the Morote-gari or two-hands reap. So, when the opponent's hips are lowered, and they are prepared to move forward to grab your torso, you need to reach behind their shoulders. You should then hold them in what looks like a reach-over hug. Their head, at this point, faces downward. You need to tightly hold your opponent's upper body and destabilize them to the front. Then, roll onto your back, throwing them over your head and behind it in the process.

As explained above, you don't really use your strength or arms in the process. However, it is your opponent's destabilized body's momentum, along with your own rolling motion, which causes a shift in their center of gravity that helps you execute the technique.

4. Tomoe Nage

Tomoe nage means circular throw, which is also known as a submarine technique. This is because the technique requires the Tori to submarine under the Uke and use a leg throw to launch them.

While standing in a natural posture, the opponent performs a lateral move that you anticipate. As they execute it, you need to bend your knees and kick off. Then use your body to project a forward roll, which causes your body to curl tightly into a ball. From that position, you end up submarining underneath the opponent. You need to place your foot on your opponent's upper thigh, near their torso, and use all your force to extend your knee. The extending knee's spring force kicks the opponent upward. Then, use your Tsurite alongside your Hiki-te in harmony with your kicking force.

5. Ura Nage

Ura nage means rear throw. If you're familiar with professional wrestling, you'll find that the technique is similar to the backdrop. This technique requires the practitioner to hug their opponent from behind and throw them upwards and behind their head.

When your opponent attempts an attack and they step forward to hold the back of your collar, you should hug or grasp them with both arms. You can even bend your knees for resistance if they try to hook one of your legs. Then, you need to pull your adversary backward, shifting your own center of gravity. At this point, they'll be up onto your stomach. Extend your legs to use your knee's spring force, throwing your opponent over and back.

Yoko-Sutemi Waza

There are 15 side sacrifice throws or Yoko-Sutemi Waza techniques that you can apply.

1. Daki Wakare

Daki wakare means rear trunk turnover. The Tori is required to hug and throw the Uke from behind.

When your opponent attempts a Seoi-nage or a similar attack, you counter-attack by seizing their side with one hand. This causes them to widen their stance and fall off balance. At that moment, you need to wrap your other arm around their neck, grasping the back of their collar or shoulder on the counter side. Then, push their back toward one side, bending their knee and placing one foot in front of them. Stop your opponent from turning to the side by holding their knee. Then, throw them to the side, hugging them midway while twisting your own body powerfully. This brings your opponent near your abdomen. Thrust your abdomen out, resembling a bridge posture, and then plant your elbows on the floor. Execute a side sacrifice while throwing them in a twisting motion.

2. Hane Makikomi

Hane makikomi means springing wraparound throw.

After attempting a failed Hane-goshi or hip spring, you can go for a Hane makikomi. What you should do is release your right hand, extending it outwards and twisting to the left. This will cause you to wrap your opponent's body around you. Finally, throw them over by rolling and falling forward onto the mat.

3. Harai Makikomi

Harai makikomi means hip sweep wrap-around throw.

To execute the throw, take your opponent to their right front corner or front corner to throw them off their balance. After being in Harai-Goshi, you need to let go of your right grip and twist to your left. You will then wrap your adversary's body around your own by taking their right arm underneath your armpit. Finally, they will fall forward, and you'll take them down with your throw.

4. Kani Basami

Kani basami means crab or scissors throw. This sacrificial throw, however, has been banned in all Judo and the majority of BJJ competitions around the world.

5. Kawazu Gake

Kawazu gake means one-leg entanglement and is also forbidden in competition.

6. Osoto Makikomi

Osoto makikomi means large outside wrap-around throw.

An Osoto makikomi needs to be picked up from an o-soto-gari. If you're in that position, your right hand should be on your adversary's lapel. You need to let go with that hand and spin to the left. At that moment, bring your arm over the adversary's right one. This will cause their body to wrap around yours. Resume your movement to execute the throw.

7. Soto Makikomi

Soto makikomi means outer wraparound.

Start by throwing your opponent off-balance, directing them to your right front corner. Then, release your right hand and turn to the left. Make sure to wrap your right arm around your opponent's right arm and use your armpit to squeeze on it. This will make their body wrap around yours. Then, continue moving in that position to throw your opponent forward.

8. Tani Otoshi

Tani otoshi means valley drop.

To execute the Tani otoshi, you need to throw your adversary off balance into the right back corner. Afterward, you have to move your left foot to the outside of their foot behind both of their feet. To finish it off, you have to sacrifice yourself to the left, throwing your adversary to the right back corner in the process.

9. Uchi Mata Makikomi

Uchi mata makikomi means inner thigh wraparound.

To get into this position, you need to take it from Uchi mata or the inner thigh reap. Then, you have to let go with your right hand and twist to your left. Bring your right arm to the outside so that your opponent's body wraps around your own. Continue turning and then bring yourself to a fall, bringing your opponent down with you.

10. Uki Waza

Uki waza means floating technique.

You need to throw your opponent off-balance to the right front corner. Then, widen your stance and extend your left foot, blocking the outside of your opponent's right foot. Finally, quickly fall onto your left side to throw your adversary over.

11. Uchi Makikomi

Uchi makikomi means inner wraparound.

To get into uchi makikomi, you need to take it from an ippon-seoi-nage or one-armed shoulder throw position. Then, thrust your hips in a great motion outside the throw's direction. You need to wrap your opponent's right arm in your elbow's crook. Then sacrifice yourself and throw your opponent over.

12. Yoko Gake

Yoko gake means side body drop.

You need to throw your opponent off-balance to the right front corner, in the direction of their left fingers. Then, start taking it to the opponent's right side and use your left foot to sweep their right foot from beneath them. You should then fall with your opponent to the left.

13. Yoko Guruma

Yoko guruma means side wheel.

You need to counter your opponent's Waza by moving around to the front. Then use your leg to throw them around in a wheel-like motion.

14. Yoko Otoshi

Yoko otoshi means side drop.

This technique throws your opponent off-balance to their right. Then, move your leg to the outside of their right foot. Finally, you need to drop to your left and throw your adversary over.

15. Yoko Wakare

Yoko wakare means side separation:

You need to throw your opponent off-balance to either the right front corner or forward. Then drop to either your left side or back, extending your legs in front of your opponent. Finally, throw them over your body.

Judokas, wrestlers, and those who practice other fighting styles are all likely to go off balance when caught off-guard or by surprise. If they don't act quickly, these situations can be very threatening to their positions in the match. Fortunately, the Sutemi Waza can turn a Judoka's undesirable stance into an advantageous one.

The key to any sport, not just the fighting techniques, is to be in control of your body, mind, and movement. Therefore, losing your balance is never a good sign and is rarely intentional. However, executing Sutemi Waza allows Judokas to willingly sacrifice their balance to throw the attacker. This way, they regain control of their own body, their decisions, and the match – as well as gaining leverage over their opponent.

Chapter 8: Osae Waza: Pinning Techniques

There are many things people do to defend themselves, both physically and mentally. One form of self-defense is through grappling techniques called Osaekomi Waza or pinning techniques. Osaekomi Waza is the act of using bodyweight to hold an opponent down on their back. Pinning movements are an integral part of self-defense because you can hold someone down until they submit, or help arrives. These movements will help the fighter hold their opponent on their back, which is an essential part of the fighting.

Judo players must know how to use Osaekomi Waza because grappling is a big part of Judo. Many Judokas train hard to perfect their ability to pin an opponent, even for an entire match. This technique developed into its own distinct set of movements called Katame Waza. Because Osaekomi Waza is such an important part of the sport, it needs its own category, and students need to learn all there is to know about this type of movement. This chapter will help you learn the proper Osaekomi Waza techniques with step-by-step instructions and pictures.

The Main Principle of Osae Waza

The main principle of Osae Waza is that one player must pin their opponent down by lying on top of them using their entire weight. The goal is to immobilize your opponent, which can lead to a submission or a transition from one technique to another. A good way for beginners to remember the proper positioning is by imagining themselves as a heavy blanket that must cover their opponent.

The attacker first grabs the uniform of the defender with both hands and places their chest on top of themselves. The weight should be minimized by keeping your forearms, elbows, palms, and knees in contact with the mat at all times. These body parts are used as the pivot point to shift the weight from one side to another.

The defender must keep their elbows in contact with the mat and try not to move too much while the attacker is on top of them. The technique can easily be finished by moving your hips slightly off-center, which will allow you to grab the opponent's collar while using one of your legs to pin down their leg next to their body.

Both the attacker and defender must aim to keep their hips low by keeping both their knees on the mat. If one player raises their hips too high, then the other person will be able to roll them over and go for a counter-attack. By maintaining proper body positioning, both players can conserve energy while attempting to pin down their opponent.

1. Yoko Shiho Gatame - Side Control Pin

This is the first and most basic of all Osaekomi Waza techniques, but it's also one of the most significant since there are variations that can be used to defeat your opponent. You will need good hip movement to perform this technique. Otherwise, it won't work. This technique can be used to get your opponent to submit by chokes or arm locks, so it's an important part of students' training.

If you are performing this move on someone who is standing, they may try to throw their weight into you, so you need to have good posture when you move in for the pin. When practicing Shiho Gatame, make sure your opponent feeds you their shoulder so that you can create pressure on the side of their neck.

2. Kuzure Yoko Shiho Gatame - Side Control (Variation)

Different from the normal Yoko Shiho Gatame, this technique is performed when your opponent is lying down. When you are practicing, make sure you keep your hips low and use a good amount of pressure to pin your opponent.

When you perform this variation on a standing person, they can grab one of your legs and try to pull you towards them. If this happens, use your arms to pull yourself forward so that you keep the pressure on your opponent's neck and shoulders.

3. Tate Shiho Gatame - Mount Control

Once you are in the Tate Shiho Gatame position, your opponent will try to use their hips to make space between you and them. To stop this from happening, put one of your arms under their neck, which makes it hard for them to move out of the way. Once they realize they can't escape, they'll try to move their hips back, but you can use your weight to pin them down.

When practicing this technique, make sure that your arm underneath your neck is locked. Otherwise, they'll be able to get out of it. If they are trying to bring their hands up by their face, then grab hold of one of the arms and lock the elbow using your shoulder.

4. Tate Shiho Gatame - Mount Control (Variation)

This is another variation of the Tate Shiho Gatame that can be used on a standing opponent. When striking using this method, keep your hips low and apply pressure to their arm. When an opponent is trying to bring their elbow up to their face, grab hold of one of their arms with both hands and lock the elbows using your shoulder. If they are trying to lift their hips, then push your hips down so that they are unable to get out of the technique.

With this technique, it's important to keep your hips low and maintain your center of gravity. One common mistake beginners make with this movement is that they stand too high, which makes it easy for their opponent to escape from the hold. In addition, if your opponent keeps their hips low, then you can use this move to submit them.

5. Kesa Gatame - Scarf Hold

The Kesa Gatame is a very famous, straightforward pinning action that doesn't require much strength to pull off. This move requires the use of your entire body along with good hip movement. Practice this on both sides of your opponent's body so you're ready for any situation.

Once an opponent has their arm under your armpit, they can throw their weight on you so that you don't have a chance to get them in the Kesa Gatame. To get out of this position, pick one of your legs and hook it around their hips and pull forward. This should force them onto their back and allow you to set up the Kesa Gatame.

6. Kuzure Kesa Gatame - Scarf Hold (Variation)

The Kuzure Kesa Gatame is another variation of this popular pinning technique. To get into position, your opponent needs to move their hips out and try to escape. Instead, grab hold of their lapel with one hand and put the other arm under their armpit. Then slide it up across their neck and lock your forearm with your opposite hand.

With this variation, keep your chest up and use your knees to help you get the pressure required to pin them down. If they try to bring their elbow up by their face, grab hold of one of their arms with both hands and lock the elbow using your shoulder. You must use good posture when you're pinning your opponent.

7. Kami-Shiho-Gatame - Top Four Upper Corner Hold

The Kami-Shiho-Gatame is another variation of the Kesa Gatame, where you need to get your opponent to open their legs. To get into position, put your arm under their armpit and slide it upward across their neck while grabbing hold of their collar on the other side. Then grab the sleeve with your opposite hand and sit down on their stomach.

With this variation, remember to keep your chest up and put pressure on them using your body weight. As soon as they try to bring their arms up, then grab hold of one of their arms with both hands and lock the elbow using your shoulder.

8. Kuzure Kami Shiho Gatame - Top Four Upper Corner Hold (Variation)

The Kuzure Kami Shiho Gatame is another variation of this popular pinning method. To get into position, an opponent needs to bring their hips out and try to escape. Instead, put one arm under the armpit and grab the collar on the other side with your free hand. Then bring that arm across their neck so that the arm is now in front of their other arm.

To get into position, you'll need to use good hip movement. When an opponent tries to bring their arms up by their face, then grab hold of one of their arms with both hands and lock the elbow using your shoulder. You must keep your chest up and use your knees to pin them down.

9. Morote Shiho Gatame - Two-handed Four Upper Corner Hold

This is an effective pinning technique using both arms. This move requires the use of your core strength and hip movement, so it's not an easy move to master. To get into position, you need to bring your arm up under your opponent's armpit and then slide it upward across their neck. You also need to move fast so that they don't try to push your arm away. Then grab hold of the sleeve with your opposite hand. Your legs should already be in between theirs, so you just need to move your hips over them and apply pressure.

It takes a lot of energy to pin someone down, so you must maintain good posture throughout the hold. If they try to bring their elbows up towards your face, then grab hold of one of their arms with both hands and lock the elbow using your shoulder.

10. Makura Kesa Gatame - Pillow Scarf Hold

This pinning technique is more difficult to get into position than it looks. Instead of grabbing the sleeve with your free hand, you need to get your arm under your opponent's opposite armpit and grab hold of their collar on the same side. Then bring that arm across their neck so that it's in front of their other arm.

This position begins by bringing your legs up to lock around their waist. Then lean forward and bring the arm across their neck under the armpit of your free arm. As soon as they try to push themselves up, then sit down on them and use your weight to keep them pinned down. Use good posture so you don't tire yourself out.

It is important to remember that these pinning techniques put a large amount of pressure on the opponent's back and chest. This means it is difficult for them to use their arms, and they cannot move as freely as usual. Once pinned down like this, your opponent can't counter you as easily. This gives you a great opportunity to go for a submission.

These ten pinning techniques will help you keep an opponent on their back as long as possible so you can go for a submission. Although it is important to know how these pins work, mastering the skill through practice and training is what will give you an advantage in competition. But always remember to keep safety in mind.

Chapter 9: Shime Waza: Choking Techniques

There are three main types of chokes depending on where the compression takes place. They are the neck, the trachea, or the chest. These are considered "subtle art" because of the dangers posed to the opponent and should only be practiced under the supervision of a trained Judo instructor. Choking techniques can positively incapacitate an opponent with less force than striking, making them particularly useful in Judo for self-defense applications. This chapter will explore the three types of chokes and describe and illustrate a total of twelve Judo choking techniques.

Choking techniques are executed from various grappling positions, with the goal being to cut off the blood flow to the brain while limiting an opponent's movement. Choking techniques have been used in Judo for decades, if not centuries. Several of these techniques were practiced and taught in traditional Japanese jujutsu schools as early as the mid-19th century.

Choking techniques work by blocking the carotid arteries on both sides of the neck, which is normally how we breathe, with our bodies getting oxygenated blood from each side of the neck. In Judo, chokes don't block those arteries completely but instead limit the blood flow just enough to gradually affect the brain.

The Main Principle of Shime Waza

In Judo, the main principle of Shime Waza is to take a person's balance and standing position from them by using their weight against them. Although this sounds complicated, it can be achieved through a variety of movements which include lifting, tripping, and throwing. When an opponent is thrown and lands on their back or neck, they will not be able to continue with the proper defensive maneuver. While they can land squarely on the ground and maintain a standing position, as long as Shime Waza is controlled properly by the practitioner applying the pressure, there should be no injury involved.

In Shime Waza, one of the most important things to consider is that the opponent must be rendered unconscious. Since the opponent is standing and their movement is restricted, they will not be able to tap out. That's why it's very important for the person executing Shime Waza to be careful about how long they apply the pressure. They can lose consciousness by applying the proper amount of pressure, but using too much force will cause serious damage, so it's imperative you don't use too much force. In general, it's a good idea to practice only under the supervision of a trained instructor while you are in class.

Shime Waza Techniques

There are a total of twelve different types of choking techniques. They are called Shime Waza, or "strangling" techniques. All the Judo choking techniques are similar to those used in other martial arts, such as aikido, jujutsu, and karate. Some of the Judo choking techniques are similar to those used in the street. For example, gi chokes can be applied to a person who is not wearing a Judo uniform. This makes the techniques important for law enforcement and related professions to be proficient in their execution.

1. Do Jime - Trunk Lock

Do Jime

This choke is also known as the "trunk lock." To apply this technique, your opponent will have to be lying flat on their back. Grab your opponent's arm, and twist it so that the palm is facing upward. Now slide your right arm underneath their head and neck. Using your forearm, press down on the trachea so that it is below your opponent's arm. If you are successful, your opponent will tap out.

2. Gyaku Juji Jime - Reverse Cross Choke

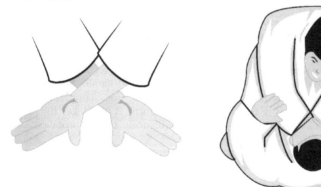

Gyaku Juji Jime

This choke is applied in the same way as the Do Jime. However, when you are applying pressure on your opponent's trachea with your forearm, use the opposite side of your arm. This means that the trachea is pressed from underneath your opponent's arm instead of above it, which makes the choke tighter, which will increase your chances of getting a tap-out in a matter of seconds.

3. Hadaka Jime - Rear Naked Choke

Hadaka Jime

This choke is applied by grabbing your opponent's collar, then wrapping your arm around your opponent's neck. Once you have done this, grab the back of your hand with the other hand. Keep both hands close to your opponent's neck. Now pull toward you and upward so that your opponent's chin is pushed down, and his neck is lengthened. This is the same way that you would apply this choke against a standing opponent. This is extremely effective because it takes your opponent by surprise.

4. Kata Ha Jime – Single Wing Choke

To apply this technique, your opponent will have to be lying on their back with you standing next to them or kneeling beside them. Place your right arm over your opponent's chest and grab the collar of their uniform. Turn your hand so that it is facing downward, and pull upward so that your opponent's chin is brought up. This keeps your opponent's trachea exposed and makes it easier for you to apply the choke.

Kata Ha Jime

5. Kata Juji Jime – Half Cross Choke

Kata Juji Jime

This choke is also known as the "diagonal." It is applied in the same way as the Kata Ha Jime. The only difference is that you will have to apply your wrist lock from the opposite side. It is applied from your opponent's left side, meaning that you will have to use your right arm. Remember to move your right arm underneath your opponent's neck and place it on the right-hand side of their trachea. Pull up so that your opponent's neck is lengthened, and the trachea is exposed.

6. Kata Te Jime – Single Hand Choke

Kata Te Jime

To apply this method, your opponent will have to be lying on their back with you standing next to them or kneeling beside them. Your right arm will be around your opponent's neck and arm. The only difference is that you will be grabbing your left hand, which means you can use one of your hands. The most notable part of this technique is to make sure that both of your arms are close to your opponent's neck. You need to do this because it will give you more leverage and also makes the choke tighter.

7. Nami Juji Jime – Normal Cross Choke

Nami Juji Jime

This choke is applied in the same way as the Kata Te Jime. However, you will need to use both of your hands. This means that you will have to bring your left hand from around your opponent's neck and grab your right arm. This applies pressure on your opponent's trachea, and if you are successful, they will tap out straight away. Just like the Kata Te Jime, make sure both of your arms are close to your opponent's neck. If you are using the correct technique, this will make the choke tighter and increase your chances of getting a tap-out.

8. Okuri Eri Jime – Sliding Lapel Choke

Okuri Eri Jime

Apply this choke in the same way as the Kata Ha Jime. To do this, grab your opponent's collar with your left hand and then wrap your arm around their neck. As you are doing this, grab the back of your right hand. Keep both hands close to your opponent's neck. Now pull towards yourself and upward so that your opponent's chin is pushed down, and their neck is lengthened. This choke can be done from a standing position or a lying one. If it is done from a standing position, remember to pull your opponent towards you and get them off-balance.

9. Ryo Te Jime – Two-Handed Choke

Ryo Te Jime

This choke is applied in the same way as all the above techniques. The difference with this method is that you will need to use both hands. This is usually applied when you are in a lying position and you have managed to get past all of your opponent's defenses. To apply this choke, you will have to grab your opponent's right hand with your left and then place your right arm around their neck. Once in this position, make sure that both of your hands are close to the opponent's neck. This will give you more leverage and make it harder for your opponent to escape.

10. Sankaku Jime - Triangle Choke

Sankaku Jime

To apply this choke, your opponent will need to be lying on their back. You will be kneeling with your left knee by the side of their head and your right leg over their chest. You will need to grab hold of your opponent's collar with your left hand and place your right arm around the opponent's neck. Once this is done, hold onto the back of your left arm with your right arm and place it close to the opponent's neck. To make this choke tighter, you will need to push down on your opponent's shoulder with your left knee.

11. Sode Guruma Jime - Sleeve Wheel Choke

Sode Guruma Jime

This choke is applied in the same way as the Kata Te Jime. The only difference with this routine is that you will be using both hands to grab your opponent's right sleeve. To apply this choke, grab both of your opponent's shoulders with your right arm and then place it around their neck. Finish the move by grabbing your left sleeve. This, in turn, creates the choke and forces your opponent to tap out.

12. Tsukkomi Jime - Thrust Choke

Tsukkomi Jime

To apply this choke, you will need to be in a standing position facing your opponent. You will then grab the collar of your opponent's Judogi with your left hand and place your right arm under their armpit. You will now need to grab the back of your left hand with your right. You will then pull your arms toward you and upward so that your opponent's shoulder blades are pushed together tightly. This creates a strong pressure around the neck and gives you a good grip. Your opponent will tap out, surrender or pass out before long.

The Shime Waza are valuable moves to learn when practicing Judo. They are extremely effective in real-life situations when you may find yourself needing to defend yourself against a street attacker or in class during sparring. If you learn these techniques properly and then practice them, they will soon become second nature to you, and you will be able to apply them confidently and competently. This chapter listed twelve of the most common chokes from the Shime Waza and showed you how to perform them. It also gave you advice on how to practice the techniques so that they become instinctive for you.

Chapter 10: Kansetsu Waza: Joint Lock Techniques

There are different joint locking techniques in Judo that you can apply to subdue your opponent. This chapter explains tips and techniques for the 10 common Judo joint locking techniques that you should know. It provides details about how you can use any of the techniques to render your opponent helpless by grappling their joint and locking it by bending it in the opposite direction.

What You Should Know About Joint Locks

A joint lock involves the manipulation of the opponent's joints in a way that they reach their maximum degree of movement. As the name suggests, a joint-locking technique causes severe pain and immobilizes the opponent. Joint locks can cause different forms of injuries like ligament, tendon, and muscle damage. They can also cause severe injuries like bone fracture or dislocation, depending on their impact. In martial arts, joint locks are often practiced in safe and controlled ways. There are different types of joint locks in Judo, and the following 10 are the official techniques that are allowed.

Ude-Garami Figure/Four Keylock

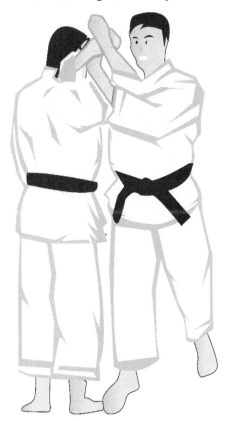

The four keylock is also known as the top shoulder lock, bent arm lock, or V1 arm lock. This is a grappling method that causes the opponent's elbow, shoulder, and – to a lesser extent – their wrist to flex. To target your opponent's right hand, you use your left hand. This will allow you to pin the arm to the floor in such a way that the elbow will fall at a right angle and the palm facing the upward direction.

The practitioner will subsequently thread their left arm under the opponent's upper arm. This will lead to the creation of figure four, where the name of the technique comes from. If you are the practitioner, you will gain an advantage over your opponent. You will need to slide the wrist of the opponent toward their lower body to complete the move. While doing this, you need to lift the forearm and elbow simultaneously in a sweeping motion. This caused your opponent's joints to flex and be painful. If the opponent does not submit on time, they could be injured.

Ude-Garami Figure

Ude-Hishigi-Juji-Gatame/Cross Arm Lock

Ude-Hishigi-Juji-Gatame

The cross armlock is a Judo technique that is also known as cross armbar, armbar, or straight bar. The technique also applies to other types of grappling martial arts. The opponent's extended arm is held by the practitioner at the wrist. This is done by squeezing the knees at the opponent's arm. To subdue the opponent, one of your legs must lie across their chest, and the other should be placed across the opponent's face (or just below their chin). Your hips will be tight into the armpit while the thighs hold the arm. If you hold the opponent's wrist to your chest, you can easily extend their arm, hyperextending the elbow. You can increase the pressure on the elbow joint further by pressing your hips against the elbow. The technique is commonly used in different forms of martial arts, including Judo.

Ude-Hishigi-Ude-Gatame/ Armbar

Ude-Hishigi-Ude-Gatame

You can perform this arm lock technique when the opponent is on their stomach and their arm is trapped with the elbow beneath your armpit. The other party's hand is lifted, and their elbow joint is overextended. If you are executing the technique, you first grab the extended arm with both hands, then hug it to your chest. You then pull the wrist to one side of their face and press the knee against your opponent's side. Their arm will not move easily, and this will cause some pain.

This will lock the side while you extend the bend on the arm to increase some pressure. When you pull the trapped arm toward your stomach, you will be applying the elbow joint lock. The opponent can give up at this stage when they fail to extricate themselves from the tight grip of the elbow lock.

Ude-Hishigi-Hiza-Gatame/ Knee Arm Bar

Ude-Hishigi-Hiza-Gatame

Like the arm lock explained above, the knee armbar technique is used to pin the opponent's knee joint. You can apply the armbar on the opponent's elbow using your knee when their face is down. You can also apply upward pressure on the wrist while you use the knee to apply downward pressure on the elbow. You can also use the inside area of the knee to stretch the shoulder or elbow from a bottom position.

After pulling the opponent's arm toward you, trapping it between your legs, and using your knees to lock the elbow joint, when the elbow joint is locked under the pressure of your knees, the opponent finds it difficult to move, and they will feel the pain that can lead to surrender.

Ude-Hishigi-Waki-Gatame/Armpit Lock

Ude-Hishigi-Waki-Gatame

This joint lock technique is dangerous, and it can draw a penalty. In the armpit lock, you twist the opponent's arm behind him and lock the elbow joint. When the opponent is down on the floor, you grab their arm firmly by the wrist and pull it strongly beneath your armpit. While executing this action, spread your legs widely for balance to prevent the opponent from escaping. This is a press-down technique that uses excessive force that can cause damage to the elbow ligaments or even break a bone.

Ude-Hishigi-Hara-Gatame/ Stomach Lock

Ude-Hishigi-Hara-Gatame

This maneuver is mainly used by fighters with large stomachs to lock one of the opponent's arms. While you kneel beside the opponent on all fours, you grasp the back of their collar and belt, then pull forward in a diagonal motion. This will make your opponent extend their arm, creating a gap between their side and arm. You then seize the opportunity to slide your leg into the gap and use it to press the opponent's arm against your stomach. The arm is trapped, and you can apply your body weight to the arm; this will help you lock the elbow joint.

Ude-hishigi-Ashi-Gatame/Leg Arm Bar

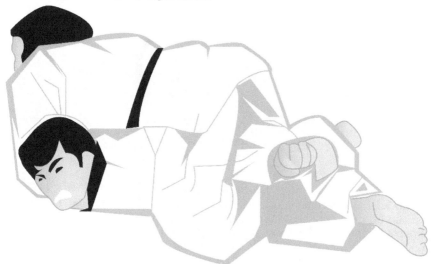

Ude-hishigi-Ashi-Gatame

When you use this technique, you use both legs to attack your opponent's elbow joint. You clasp their arm between your legs to lock the elbow joint. The leg lock term comes with several variations, and you can apply it to the opponent when they are down on the ground. When your opponent is facing downward on the ground, grab one of their arms and wrap a leg around it. At the same time, lower your upper body across the opponent's back. Clasp the leg that is around the opponent to create the shape of "4" and scissors their elbow. If you are executing the technique from this posture, you bend your body back so that you are able to bend the opponent's elbow in a reverse direction.

If the opponent is in the supine posture, wrap your arm around their neck from above and pull their body against you while clasping one of the arms between your legs. You then use your lower leg to lift the upper body of the opponent to apply pressure on their elbow using your thigh.

Ude-Hishigi-Te-Gatame/Hand Armbar

Ude-Hishigi-Te-Gatame

You will use both hands when you want to attack your opponent's elbow joint. There are several variations that you can consider to pin down your opponent's elbow joint. You can grasp their arm and lay it across the thigh of your leg, then press the arm's lower part downward so that you can bend the elbow backward. When you move it to a side four-corner hold, you hold the arm in the same way and execute the action.

You then squeeze the elbow to apply pressure with the back of the opponent's hand. Then clasp the opposite side arm firmly to exert pressure, at the same time preventing any movement. When you lock the hand in an armbar, the opponent cannot turn, and this will make them submit if there is no other way of escaping from the tight grip.

Ude-Hishigi-Sankaku-Gatame-Triangle Arm lock

Ude-Hishigi-Sankaku-Gatame

When executing this triangle arm lock, you clasp your opponent's arm between your legs and lock the elbow joint. The Triangle arm lock name derives from the scissored legs, which form a triangle shape while holding your opponent's arm. To complete this move, you grab your opponent's arm while they are down on fours and quickly twist with both your legs. You must firmly hold the other party's arm, together with the neck.

This posture might appear as if you are pulling the opponent down and forward, but your legs will hold them back. This will only allow the arm to be pulled forward. This posture allows you to thrust your stomach out to bend the opponent's arm backward, locking their elbow joint. This will exert pressure on the other player's arm such that they cannot freely move it.

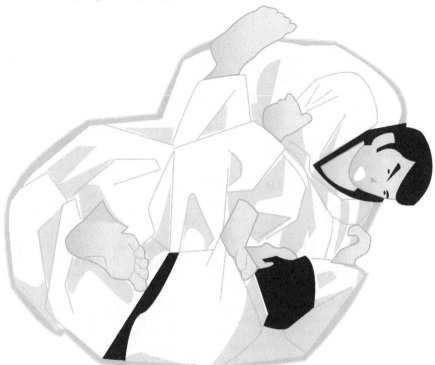

Ashi-Garami

When you are doing this technique, you clasp both legs around your opponent's legs. Twist their leg so that you lock their knee joint. The opponent is usually lying face down on the mat for this technique. Make sure your legs are firmly clasped around the opponent's legs as you rotate your body to the opponent's scissoring legs. The opponent is also likely to apply a twisting motion as well.

To make the lock strong and effective, grab the opponent's sleeve and pull them together with the leg action for a strong knee lock joint. This type of entangled leg can pose a high risk of injury to the other party's leg joints. The locking style is prohibited though you may need to learn it. You can use it for self-defense if you are facing a threat of harm or any unwanted action.

Joint lock techniques in Judo are specifically used to grapple the opponents' joints to subdue them. When pressure is applied to the joint such that it reaches its maximum motion level, the opponent becomes helpless. There are different techniques you can practice, but you should know when to apply them.

Chapter 11: Goshin Jutsu Kata, the Judo Self-Defense

Judo involves throws, grappling techniques, joint locks, and chokes, with the ultimate goal of being able to use any technique to attack an opponent and immobilize them. It was originally designed for self-defense purposes and called *Judo Goshin Jutsu Kata*, which means "self-defense form," and uses techniques from the standard Judo syllabus. There are four katas that include unarmed, knife, stick, and gun. These correspond to 12 techniques of unarmed attack, three of knife attack, three of a stick attack, and three of handgun attack. Some people combine the unarmed and knife katas into one, but the original is four separate ones.

Judo as Self-Defense

There are many reasons why Judo Goshin Jutsu Kata can be a good self-defense tool for everyone. One reason is that it focuses on taking down someone bigger, stronger, or faster before they get to strike you. Many martial arts teach the opposite of this, which is to strike first before they do. The Judo throws allow you to escape if there is a speed or power mismatch while at the same time giving you the ability to control an attacker if there is no speed or power difference. This allows for more options when dealing with violent encounters at almost any size advantage.

Another reason why Judo Goshin Jutsu Kata can be a good self-defense tool is its ability to use any attack against an opponent. Some people are thrown off by this idea because they don't understand that it means *any attack* rather than just punches or kicks. This includes weapons such as knives, sticks, and even guns. If you are not able to easily avoid these, you can use them against your attacker. For example, if someone tries to stab you with a knife, you can counter by using the "knife kata" technique to disarm them. Then you could proceed to incapacitate them with joint locks or chokes. Thus, training in Judo Goshin Jutsu Kata can provide a complete self-defense toolkit.

Lastly, Judo Goshin Jutsu Kata can be a good self-defense tool because it allows you to practice realistic techniques. Judo is designed upon the principles of motion and body mechanics, and momentum, so your technique will work regardless of strength or speed differences between you and an opponent. This means that if you were to use Judo Goshin Jutsu Kata techniques in a self-defense situation, they would most likely work against an untrained person or someone who has less practice than you do. In addition, the principles of motion and body mechanics allow for counter-techniques when doing drills. You can use the techniques to their full extent when training because you can practice technical execution at high speeds. This will allow you to perfect your technique for use in an actual fight.

Self-Defense against Unarmed Attacks

The "unarmed attack" kata consists of 12 techniques, such as punches, kicks, and palm strikes. These are arranged into three groups which are high attacks, mid-level attacks, and low attacks. The order of these groups goes from more difficult to less difficult. Even though some of the techniques require you to be low near the ground, all of them can be used against someone who is standing up. The principal idea behind this kata is that it starts with simple techniques and becomes more complex as you progress. This will allow you to expand your range of techniques while keeping it organized in a way that beginners can understand. It also makes sense because you should use simpler techniques when dealing with less dangerous situations.

Counter-Technique 1: High Attacks -Palms to the Face, Backfist to the Temple

This technique is a simple palm strike to your opponent's forehead. It teaches you how to move in closer to make effective strikes – and at the same time, protect yourself from counterattacks. This is a self-defense technique for when someone attacks with an overhead strike, such as a baseball bat or howling palm to the face. To execute the defense, you would step in and redirect their attacking arm while striking them with your own palm at their temple.

Counter-Technique 2: High Attacks -Jaws of Hand to the Chin, Knee Strike

This movement starts with an opponent's strike to your jaw with a back fist. You see this attack coming by watching their hips and shoulders drop as they start to wind up for the strike. Immediately after blocking the strike, you move in closer to jam both of your fingers into their eyes. Your other hand is also free to grab their hair and pull them down toward the ground. Then you can stomp on their knee or shin with your heel, then throw them over your shoulder with a hip throw.

Counter-Technique 3: High Attacks -Forearm Block with Knife Hand to the Solar Plexus

This move starts by blocking a punch from an opponent with your raised forearm, then grabbing their punching arm by the wrist with your free hand. Now you can strike them in their solar plexus with a knife-hand strike to disrupt their breathing, which will make it much harder for them to fight back. You can also yank your opponent's arm up and step through so that you are behind them. From there, you can apply a wrist lock to take them down.

Counter-Technique 4: Mid-level Attacks -Forearm Block with Punch to the Groin

This technique starts by blocking your opponent's punch with your forearm, then punching them hard in the groin. It is important to make sure you are close enough to strike an opponent at this height. If you are too far away, your punch wouldn't have enough reach, so it is important to get an idea of the distance required for punches by studying kata.

Self-Defense against Dagger Attacks

In this kata, you will learn how to defend yourself from a person who has a knife. The three techniques in this segment are meant for when the opponent is slashing at you with their blade.

Counter-Technique 1: Low Blocks with Parries and Kicks to the Groin

This maneuver begins with you blocking your opponent's stab with your forearm, then using that energy to strike one of their legs with your free hand. Your next move is to kick hard into the side of their knee exactly where it bends, which will disable their leg and make them useless for the rest of the fight. Then you can knee them in the face while they are bent over from the pain.

Counter-Technique 2: Low Blocks with Knife Hand to the Neck

This opens off with you blocking your opponent's stab with your other arm while simultaneously pulling them closer to you. When you are close enough, pull their head down and strike them with your knife hand to the side of their neck, disrupting their central nervous system. If they are still standing, you can kick them hard in the knee to buckle them and then throw them over your hip.

Counter-Technique 3: Low Blocks with Forearm Block and Punch to the Side of the Head

This technique commences with blocking your opponent's stab with your forearm, then blocking their punch with your other arm. Without letting go of their wrist, strike them in the side of the head to knock them unconscious. Then you can pull your feet back and wait for them to fall before stamping on their face or neck.

Self-Defense against the Stick Attack

In this kata, you will learn how to defend yourself from a person who is attacking you with a stick. The first one is designed to defend you against a strike from the opponent's arm in which he is holding a stick or club, and the second two moves are meant to be used when your opponent swings a club at your head.

Counter-Technique 1: Stepping Through and Guillotine Choke

This move is initiated by stepping in front of your opponent when they try to strike you with their stick. As soon as they miss, turn quickly and grab their wrist with the hand that is holding the stick. Grab their other arm from behind with your free hand and pull it down while dropping your weight onto your opponent. As you do this, slide your free hand around to the back of their neck and lock it in place with a guillotine choke.

Counter-Technique 2: Forearm Block with Punch to the Side of the Head

This technique starts by blocking your opponent's stick strike with your forearm. After they miss, quickly punch them hard in the side of the head to disorient them. Then you can use their own momentum against them by pulling on their shoulder and back-flipping them over your hip.

Counter-Technique 3: Low Blocks with Knife Hand to the Neck

This is done by firstly blocking your opponent's strike with both arms, then moving your hands together so that your opponent's hands are locked. Now you have a hold of their weapon, use it to pull them forward while stepping back and letting yourself fall to the ground. When you hit the floor, push off with your feet and flip your opponent over your head.

Self-Defense against a Pistol Attack

In this kata, you will learn how to defend yourself from a person who is attacking you with a firearm. The three techniques in this segment are meant for when the opponent pulls out and fires their pistol at you.

Counter-Technique 1: Intercept and Punch to the Face

Firstly, you start by stepping forward and raising your arm in front of your head when you see your opponent pull their firearm. As soon as they fire, block the bullet with your arm and immediately punch them in the face with your free hand to disorient them. While their head is turned, grab their wrist and twist it around so that they drop the pistol, and you can knee them in the groin.

Counter-Technique 2: Forearm Block and Punch to the Side of the Head

This technique is done by blocking your opponent's shot with your forearm. When the bullet misses, immediately punch them hard in the side of their head to disorient them. When they are dazed, kick them as hard as you can in the kneecap so that you can throw them over your hip.

Counter-Technique 3: Low Blocks with Knife Hand to the Neck

This technique starts by blocking your opponent's shot with both arms, then moving your hands together so that your opponent's hands are locked. Now you have a hold of their weapon, use it to pull them forward while stepping back and letting yourself fall to the ground. When you hit the floor, push off with your feet and flip your opponent over your head.

Recommended Goshin Jutsu Kata for Self-Defense

As an alternative to the three techniques in each section, you can learn to incorporate any of the following katas into your routine:

- **Kime No Kata** -A great offensive kata. Practice combinations until you know what attack flows out of which setup.
- **Ikkyo** -The standard beginner's kata. Use it to get your basics down before moving on to something more complex.
- **Nikyo** -Another beginner's kata, allowing you to get out of difficult situations using joint locks.
- **Sankyo** -This kata has various ways of breaking free from grabs and can be used against an opponent who is trying to strike you.
- **Yonkyo** -Practice this kata so you gain a good understanding of how to control your opponent.
- **Gokyo** -This is a beginner's kata but can easily be made into an advanced technique if you have the strength and energy to maintain constant pressure.
- **Kansetsu-Waza** -If someone grabs you from behind or attacks you with a knife, use this kata to break yourself free.
- **Koryu Dai San** -If you are ever attacked from behind by an opponent with a stick or stick-like object, use this kata to turn the tables on them and beat them senseless.
- **Kodokan Goshin Jutsu** -This is a compilation of various techniques from many different katas. Use it to get an overall idea of self-defense in Judo, and you can use any of the techniques depending on your situation.
- **Aikido No Kata** -If your opponent attacks you with punches and kicks, this kata will show you how to get out of such a situation using throws and joint locks.
- **Aiki Nage No Kata** -Similar to the Aikido No Kata, it teaches how to end up on top in ground fighting situations; it also covers striking your opponent while they are down and choking them until they pass out.
- **Ju No Kata** -If you use this kata while your opponent is trying to punch you, it will teach you how to redirect incoming force and momentum and use that against them.
- **Kime Katame No Kata** -A great kata for learning how to defend yourself from a grappler. Use it if someone ever tries to tackle you or take you down in a fight.
- **Suigetsu No Kata** -If someone ever tries to take you down and pin you, use the techniques in this kata to get out of their grasp.
- **Kodokan Academy 1st-3rd Kyu Katas** -Practice these simply for the sake of practice and repetition! They will help your Judo no matter what.
- **Kodokan Goshin Jutsu Kata** -Use this kata to get an overall idea of how to defend yourself in a fight.

Judo makes for an excellent self-defense tool due to its focus on taking down your opponent, regardless of their size or strength, to gain control of them so you can take them into custody. This makes it useful for everyone, not just those who are physically fit or want to become professional fighters. Goshin Jutsu Kata is a compilation kata that you can use as an alternative to the techniques listed above to learn how to defend yourself against any kind of weapon. If you are ever in a bad situation, these techniques will either help you to escape or protect you sufficiently until help arrives.

Judo is a great self-defense tool that anyone can use! If you want to learn how to defend yourself against unarmed attackers, weapons, or grappling attacks, practice Goshin Jutsu Kata. There are many different katas included in this book for beginners and advanced students alike. Whatever level you are at, focus on improving your Judo, and this kata will be a useful tool in your arsenal.

If endangered on the street, use Judo techniques from other katas and those in Goshin Jutsu Kata. Practice this kata for any level student who wants to have more experience practicing with different types of attacks. If you are ever attacked from behind by an opponent with a knife, use Koryu Dai San kata to turn the tables on them. If your opponent attacks you with punches and kicks, use Kodokan Goshin Jutsu Kata to escape or defend yourself. Practice these techniques for a way to better protect yourself from all types of dangerous situations!

Chapter 12: The Competitive Side of Judo

In the previous chapters, we mentioned all the different types and techniques of Judo. Now it's time to talk about *shiai* in Judo. Shiai refers to a competition or a Judo contest between two Judo fighters. It's important to note that Judo is not only a fighting style but also a form of martial arts and sport. In this chapter, we'll discuss rules, rankings, and promotional tests and give you some insider tips on how you should prepare for them.

Judo as an Art Form and Sport

Let's talk about Judo as an art of self-defense. If you are interested in learning Judo, you have to immerse yourself in its culture and what it entails physically and mentally. Japanese Samurai practiced Judo as well as other types of martial arts. It was an important exercise because it taught them the art of combat without the use of weapons.

The physical movements of Judo involved combinations of hits, kicks, throwdowns, and techniques in holding their opponents down to the ground while inflicting enough pain to gain - and keep - the advantage. Mastering the art of Judo provides fighters with the techniques to get out of these entanglements and regain their stance. This is one of the main tactics of Judo, where the fighters stop resisting when they're in a compromised position and wait until their opponent loses their balance to overthrow them. This is how Judo gained its name, meaning "gentle" or "soft."

Let's explore the techniques with an example. Assume your opponent is stronger than you and pushes you with all their strength. You will be thrown to the ground no matter how much you fight back. This is the result of direct resistance to a forceful attack. However, if you choose to stop resisting, you will be able to keep your balance by moving backward with equal strength. This will cause your opponent to lose their balance because they normally will be moving forward. Their position at that moment is more vulnerable due to the odd posture, making them weaker than you. Since you keep your balance, you will be able to retain your strength and fight back. Even if we assume you are stronger, it's better not to resist from the beginning, as you should hold your ground, waiting for your opponent to slip up.

In another position, your opponent may try to lift you and throw you on the ground. If you resist, you will still fall because of your vulnerable position. A good defense is to grab onto your opponent and deliberately throw yourself to the ground while pulling your opponent with you and easily bringing them down. With these examples, you have an idea of how Judo emphasizes the use of your opponent's strength and movement momentum against them by not resisting them. Of course, this doesn't always work. For example, if your opponent grabs your wrist and you don't resist, you won't be able to wiggle away from this position. Instead, you should lift your whole arm so that you can use your body's strength to resist his grip. (This technique is opposite to the previous one as you used your strength against theirs.)

A Judoka (practitioner) develops physical strength with regular practice, but they also benefit mentally as they have to be smart when competing. There are numerous ways to learn the techniques, which gives each Judoka a unique style and allows them to develop on their own. The beauty of Judo is that it welcomes people of all ages and strength levels. The ultimate goal is to teach players how to have excellent body and mind control and make them ready for any sudden attacks.

Judo students are trained to be aware of their opponent's strengths and weaknesses so that they can use this information to win a fight. This mental training is just as important as physical training, and if done properly, the student becomes confident and precise in their movements. A good Judoka is decisive and knows how and when to react to a sudden move. This state of mental awareness makes the participant alert at all times to remain focused so they are not beaten by their opponent. It's a good idea to research and watch Judo regularly fight to learn from people's mistakes and successes. In Judo training, you will learn how to use your imagination, logic, and judgment to win a fight.

The regular practice of Judo is demanding and vigorous. You will learn how to develop your physical fitness by improving your strength, speed, accuracy, endurance, balance, and flexibility. Offensive and defensive maneuvers will help improve your reflexes and body coordination and boost your confidence. Your physique will drastically improve after a few months because Judo training works on all your muscles. It only takes mastering a few techniques to be a successful contender in competitions.

Apart from the physical and mental benefits, Judo teaches you how to manage your emotions and impulses. Judo students are taught to control their anger and emotional outbursts, or you risk wasting your energy, giving your opponent the chance to beat you. This emotional stability will benefit you in all aspects of your life. We often experience a lack of motivation and can be easily discouraged from performing our jobs or projects. Judo teaches you how to use your body and mind in principle called Seiryoku-Zenyo or maximum efficient use of energy. You can use this principle to motivate you to overcome your rough patches.

You will learn a lot about work ethics and etiquette. Young Judo students exhibit bravery and the ability to work under pressure by not letting fear paralyze them. The high standards of Judo emphasize the principles of justice and fair game. It is more than a sport, as the morals and lessons learned during the training instill humility and decency among students of the art that they carry with them into the world. It teaches learners about the importance of helping their communities and contributing to them. The world of Judo revolves around its unique traditions and culture of gentleness. It's one of the most popular martial arts and is taught in many schools and centers around the world.

You will learn how to build friendships and partnerships while practicing Judo because players who train together spend a lot of time pushing their limits and being in their most vulnerable and strong states. When participating in Judo, you will learn that each movement has a meaning. It's not just about learning certain movements and repeating them. There are limitless combinations you can use to fight an opponent. That's how Judo transcends from being a regular fighting style to a form of art.

The International Judo Federation

As a sport, Judo contests started to take form officially at the beginning of the 1900s. In 1932, The European Judo Union was created in Germany. Two years later, the first European championship took place in Dresden. The European countries of Germany, Austria, France, The Netherlands, Italy, and Switzerland were joined by Argentina. The name of the union was switched to the International Judo Federation (IJF), founded in 1951. It took a while for Judo to be part of the Olympic games due to World War II. After the end of the war, the sport became more and more popular in many countries. Judo finally became a part of the official Olympics in 1964.

The role of the International Judo Federation is to organize Judo events around the world and protect its integrity. The IJF participates in organizing Judo games in the Olympics, and it aims to spread the practice of Judo as a martial art to people of all ages and categories. The IJF today is affiliated with 200 federations in many countries, with around 20 million people practicing this martial art globally, as per IJF surveys.

The IJF also holds World Championships and World Judo Tour every year since 2009.

If you want to put your Judo skill into practice, we urge you to watch the events organized by the IJF each year. There are also many YouTube videos you can watch while you practice Judo.

Judo Contest's Rules, Format, and Scoring

Weight Categories

There are seven weight categories for each of the male and female teams in Judo:

Judo Weight Classes For Men:

- Extra Lightweight-60 kg (132 lb.)
- Half Lightweight -66kg (145 lb.)
- Lightweight -73 kg (160 lb.)
- Half Middleweight -81kg (178 lb.)
- Half Heavyweight -90 kg (198 lb.)
- Heavyweight-100 kg (220 lb.)
- Open Weight +100 kg (+220 lb.)

Female Judo Weight Classes:

- Extra Lightweight-48 (105 lb.)
- Half Lightweight-52 (114 lb.)
- Lightweight-57 (125 lb.)
- Half Middleweight-63 (138 lb.)
- Half Heavyweight-70 (154 lb.)
- Heavyweight-78 (171 lb.)
- Open Weight+78 (+171 lb.)

Cadet and IJF Junior Judo Weight Classes

Cadet Men Under 18

- Featherweight-50 kg (110 lb.)
- Extra Lightweight-55 kg (121 lb.)
- Half Lightweight -60 kg (132 lb.)
- Lightweight -66 kg (145 lb.)
- Half Middleweight -73 kg (170 lb.)
- Middleweight -81 kg (178 lb.)
- Half Heavyweight-90 kg (198 lb.)
- Heavyweight +90 kg

Note That the Kg does not convert perfectly into LBS

Junior Men's Under 21

- Featherweight-55 kg (121 lb.)
- Extra Lightweight-60 kg (132 lb.)
- Half Lightweight -66 kg (145 lb.)
- Lightweight -73 kg (170 lb.)
- Half Middleweight -81 kg (178 lb.)
- Middleweight -90 kg (198 lb.)
- Half Heavyweight-100 kg (220 lb.)

- Heavyweight +100 kg

Cadet Women's
- Featherweight-40 kg (88 lb.)
- Extra Lightweight-44 kg (97 lb.)
- Half Lightweight -48 kg (105 lb.)
- Lightweight -52 kg (114 lb.)
- Half Middleweight-57 kg (125 lb.)
- Middleweight -63 kg (138.9 lb.)
- Half Heavyweight-70 kg (154 lb.)
- Heavyweight +70 kg

IJF Women's Junior
- Featherweight-44 kg (97 lb.)
- Extra Lightweight-48 kg (105 lb.)
- Half Lightweight -52 kg (114 lb.)
- Lightweight -57 kg(125 lb.)
- Half Middleweight 63 kg (138.9 lb.)
- Middleweight -70 kg (154 lb.)
- Half Heavyweight-78 kg (172 lb.)
- Heavyweight +78 kg

All players must undergo a weigh-in a day before the competition. Each country is permitted to include two players in each weight category, with a maximum of seven male and female players in the team. The final eight players in the game compete in repechage contests. Players who lost in the quarter-finals will compete in two additional repechage contests for the bronze medal.

Format

In a Judo contest, two players compete on a mat or tatami. One player is dressed in a white Judo suit or Judogi, and the other is dressed in a blue suit. The referee signals to the players to approach the mat, face each other, and take a bow. The referee proceeds to start the game by giving the verbal command, "hajime." Each game lasts for five minutes for both men's and women's categories. The referee may stop the game with the verbal command "matte" and then proceed again by calling "hajime." The clock is stopped during this break. In case both players score equal points by the end of the game, it does not stop. They are given an unlimited extension or golden score period. The game is ended if a player scores a point and wins or receives a penalty and loses.

Rules

The contest area should be covered completely by Judo mats or another material that is accepted in the sport – in the color preferred by the International Judo Federation. The area is split into two parts. The size of the innermost area or the contest area ranges between 8x8 and 10x10 meters. The size of the outermost area or the safety area is at least three meters wide, and both areas should be in different colors.

Scoring

The referee performs hand signals when a player scores a point or receives a penalty. It's how they communicate instructions and scores to the players. The biggest score in Judo is called an *ippon*. If a player scores an ippon, they win the contest, and the game is ended. There are four ways to score an ippon. The first way is using speed and strength to throw your opponent on their back.

The second way is pinning your opponent to the ground using the holding technique "osaekomi waza" and preventing them from disengaging for 20 seconds. If your opponent taps out twice or more with their hands or feet or calls out "maitta," this means they submit due to strangulation (or shime waza) or arm locking (or kansetsu waza).

While ippon is a full point, waza-ari is a half-point. Waza ari is scored if an element is missing in the throwing technique or if you pin your opponent between 10 and 20 seconds. If you score two waza-ari, you win the game. There were two other lower scores called koka and yuko, but they were canceled in 2008 and 2017, respectively.

The final score is the penalty score or shido. There are many ways to gather points from an opponent's faults in a Judo contest. Shido can be rewarded if a player spends too much time not engaging or being unaggressive in a contest. If both players score an equal number of shidos, they cancel each other out and are not counted in the winning score. Shido refers to minor penalties, while hansoku make refers to major penalties. It can also be awarded if a player scores three shidos. A hansoku-make is a serious penalty because the player is eliminated from the whole tournament.

Safety Procedures and Etiquette

The players should not harm each other on purpose, and they are not allowed to use kicks, punches, or similar attacks during the game. They are also not allowed to touch each other's faces at any time. They are not allowed to wear any hard objects in their suits like rings, watches, or any protective gear, as all these call for a hansoku-make. The players are also not permitted to perform head dives or attack joints other than the elbow joints. Two additional techniques are not permitted: kawazu gake (a leg entanglement technique) and kani basami (a foot sweep move).

In terms of etiquette, the players must bow first before stepping on the map. They then proceed to face each other and bow again before and after the contest or training session. Players must maintain decent behavior, so no bad language or gestures are permitted. During the game, the players are not allowed to stall, use a defensive stance, or ignore the referee's instructions.

The Judo suit or Judogi has specific criteria for safety and to allow grip techniques. The sleeves should not be too short; they must be 2" above the wrist when the arm is extended in front of the player's body. The pants must be long enough to reach 2" above the ankle. Sponsorship logos must be kept to a minimum on the suit. The uniform must be appropriate, or the player will be subjected to penalties.

Judo Ranks and Promotional Tests

Judo is graded by a ranking system where each belt color represents the student's level. The black belt signifies the master of the sport. There are two main grades in Judo, which are kyu and dan grades. Kyu or mu-dan-sha is for students who are just starting to learn Judo. This grade is further divided into six levels. In ascending order, the brown belt is called Ikkyu, the blue belt is Nikyu, the green belt is Sankyu, the orange belt is Yonkyu, the yellow belt is Gokyu, and the white belt is Rokyu. After the white belt, the student takes a promotional test to upgrade their level to enter the dan grades.

The dan grades or black belt group is named yū-dan-sha, meaning a black belt holder. This ranking is divided into 10 levels or degrees of the black belt. The players can all wear a black belt or other colored belts on special occasions. Players who achieved the sixth, seventh, and eighth black belt levels can wear a red and white belt. Those who reach the ninth and tenth levels can wear a red belt.

Before your promotional test, you need to master the falling technique. It's important to learn how to fall to prevent yourself from getting seriously injured. You must educate yourself on all the rules and etiquette of the game. You need to learn about the terminologies in Japanese and be courteous and respectful at all times with your teachers and fellow players. You need to remember to keep your Judogi clean before your test and to trim your nails before every game. If you have long hair, you must tie it well with a rubber band and ensure that you don't have any metal objects in your hair. Women are allowed to wear a white t-shirt under the jacket. Your behavior and attendance are important in Judo, so you need to be fully committed to the sport to achieve high rankings.

By now, you have learned how Judo is more than just a fighting style. It is a form of art and an esteemed sport. There are tremendous benefits you can gain by learning Judo, from physical fitness to anger management, all of which can be carried with you in your everyday life.

Chapter 13: Daily Training Drills

Judo is one of the most demanding martial arts. Though it is not as physically taxing as other styles like Karate or Taekwondo, it requires a great deal of mental discipline and focus. Not only that, but there are many different areas you can take your Judo skills - everything from submissions to throws to groundwork to self-defense. And each area, if you train hard enough, will take up a significant amount of time to master.

This chapter is about helping you find the time to do daily training and succeed in this martial art.

Below you'll find some drills and routines that will help you spend more time training on a daily basis. These can be used in addition to your gym sessions or at home with a training partner. Included is a list of things you can practice for Judo-specific training, which includes muscle conditioning and warm-up routines.

Also, you will see this chapter includes information on strength training. Not only is conditioning important, but it is also important to train your muscles so you don't get injured. Even if you do not participate in any other martial arts, it is important to train your muscles to support the movements of Judo. You will find that many of these routines include a set amount of repetitions and sets for each activity. You can choose to do as many as you would like for each set, but do not go over the recommended amount, or you might get injured.

At the end of this chapter, some helpful stretching exercises are important to do after you are done with your training routine. It doesn't matter what style of martial arts you participate in; you must stretch to prevent injury and muscle pain. This is especially important for Judo, as you use your entire body when choking, throwing, or pinning your opponent.

Warm-Up Exercises

Judo is a sport that uses your entire body, so not only should you train your muscles, but you should also warm up to prevent injury. Here are a few warm-up exercises you can do before your Judo workout:

1. Half Get Up

Start on all fours. Bring your right knee toward your chest and then extend it back. Next, bring the knee up to about shoulder level, making sure to keep your abs tight. Finally, bring the knee up to chest level again, but this time return it to the starting position on all fours. Perform three sets of 12 reps, then repeat the same number of reps with your left side.

2. Child's Pose

Start on all fours, but instead of bringing your knees up to your chest, you are going to bring them out. Bring your hips back until your forehead is touching the ground. Keep your arms outstretched in front of you, with your palms flat against the ground. Hold this position for 30 to 60 seconds.

3. Quad Stretch

Start standing and bend one of your legs behind you at a 90-degree angle. Grab onto your foot, or bring your foot up to your butt and hold it with both hands. Your leg should be outstretched behind you. Slowly lean forward, making sure that your knee does not go past your toes. You will feel a stretch in the front of your thigh and throughout the back of your leg. Hold this position for 30 to 60 seconds, and then switch legs.

Warm-up Drills

After you have stretched and warmed up, here are some drills that will get your heart pumping and blood flowing:

1. Running Man

This is a drill you can do anywhere, though it is easiest to do outside. It is a great cardio exercise as well. Start by standing with your arms outstretched above your head. Then jump up and touch the tips of your fingers together. Jump again, but this time bring your hands over to touch the opposite side of your head. Keep switching back and forth. To increase your skill, jump and touch your fingers on one side, then switch arms and jump with the opposite arm. 2. High Knees

Run-on, the spot, bringing your knees up to about waist level. Keep your arms outstretched in front of you, almost at a 90-degree angle. Try to bring your knees up as high as you can. If you feel like you are slowing down, try pumping your arms harder.

2. Butt Kicks

Another drill that is good to do outside. Run in place, bringing your knees up towards your chest. Try to kick yourself in the butt with your heels. Keep pumping your arms for more intensity.

3. Skips

This is similar to the Butt Kicks drill, but you are going to bring your knees up to about chest level. You will be jumping straight up and down, but try to get a little height on your jumps. Pump your arms while you are jumping to increase your intensity.

Strength Training for Judo

Judo is a full-body workout. It not only uses your arms and legs but also uses your core muscles. After you have warmed up and stretched, it is time to do some strength training. Here is a list of some exercises you can do at the gym to supplement your Judo training:

1. Pullups/Chinups

A pull-up is when your palms are facing toward you. A chin-up is when your palms are facing away from you. Pull-ups and chin-ups are great exercises to strengthen your back muscles. They also help you lift your opponent off the ground. The best way to perform these is to use an overhand grip, meaning your palms are facing away from you. Grip the bar with both hands shoulder-width apart and hang from the bar. Pull yourself up as high as you can, then lower yourself back down. Perform three sets of 12 reps.

2. Bench Press

This is a great exercise for developing your chest and triceps muscles. Lie down on a bench with a barbell resting on your chest. Grip the bar with both hands shoulder-width apart, and press it up until your arms are fully extended above you. Slowly lower the barbell back down to your chest and repeat. Perform three sets of 12 reps.

3. Deadlift

The deadlift is a great exercise to increase your leg strength, as well as strengthen your back. This needs to be done with caution, so make sure you know what you are doing before performing it. The best way to perform this exercise is to use an overhand grip with your arms shoulder-width apart. Stand with your feet shoulder-width apart and bend your knees slightly. Then slowly lower the barbell to around knee height. Keep your back straight and lift the barbell back up, then repeat. Perform three sets of 12 reps.

4. Squat

The squat is a great overall workout. It focuses on your lower body and core muscles, as well as strengthening your back. Stand with your feet shoulder-width apart and lower yourself down as if you were about to sit. Keep your back straight by sticking your butt out behind you. Ensure that your knees do not go over your toes, as this can cause you to injure yourself. Slowly raise yourself back up and repeat. Use a weight that is challenging for you but is still doable. Perform three sets of 12 reps.

5. Tricep Dips

This is an exercise that works your triceps muscles. It can be performed at home or in the gym, but it is easier to do at the gym if you have a bench or chair available. Grip the edge of a bench with your palms on the edge and your fingers pointing towards you. Push with your toes to lift yourself, then lower yourself back down. Keep your elbows tucked in by your sides throughout the movement. Perform three sets of 12 reps.

Muscle and Conditioning Drills

1. Pushups

Start with your hands slightly further than shoulder-width. Keep your back straight and lower yourself down until your chest is just above the ground, then push yourself back up. Keep your abs tight to prevent putting pressure on them and hurting them. The recommended reps for this are 40-50. Do as many as you can without stopping, but do not go over the recommended number, or you may hurt yourself. If you are not strong enough to do that many, start with your knees on the ground rather than your feet. Do as many as you can to start, then add reps as you get stronger.

2. Sit-Ups

Sit on the ground and place your feet under something sturdy. The sturdier the object you place your feet under, the more difficult it will be. Place your hands behind your head and crunch up, curling your torso towards your knees. Hold this for a moment, then bring yourself back to the ground slowly. Make sure you do not touch the ground with your back, as this will cause it to arch, and you may hurt yourself. Instead, bring your upper body down to the ground. The recommended number of reps for this is 40-50. Again, do as many as you can without pausing, but do not go over the recommended number.

3. Leg-Raises

Lay on your back and bring your knees up to a 90° angle. Keep them at that angle and lift your feet off the ground. If you need to, put a small weight on your feet to keep them from coming down. Bring your legs up until they are perpendicular to your torso, then slowly lower them down. Keep your head on the ground, and do not roll back to get yourself back up. The recommended number of reps for this is 20-30.

4. Bicycle Crunches

This is another full-body exercise that will work your ab muscles and legs. Get into the same position you used for leg raises. Instead, move your legs so that your right knee comes up next to your left elbow, then your left knee comes up next to your right elbow. Continue alternating in this pattern one after the other until you have gone all the way across your body. The recommended number of reps for this is 20-30.

5. Planks

Lay on the ground with your elbows directly under your shoulders and your legs out straight behind you. Keep yourself up on the balls of your feet and the backs of your hands, keeping yourself as flat as possible. You can keep your knees on the ground if this is too difficult for you. Hold this position as long as possible. The recommended time is 30 seconds.

6. Burpees

Start in a standing position. Drop down to the ground and put your hands on it. Kick your legs back so that you are in a push-up position with your arms extended. Do a push-up, then bring yourself back to the standing position and jump into the air. When you land, bend over and touch your fingers to the ground. The goal is to get your feet back up into the air while you are touching the ground, but it is not required. This exercise will work your legs, arms, chest, and core. Do as many reps of this exercise as you can.

7. Lunges

Stand with your feet shoulder-width apart. Step forward so that one leg is out in front of the other. Keep your back straight and lower yourself down until your back knee is almost touching the ground. Push yourself back up and step forward with your other leg, repeating this motion on that side. Make sure you are moving forward throughout all of this rather than just stepping out to the side. The recommended number of reps for this is 20-30. You can hold dumbbells in both hands if you want to add some extra resistance.

Stretch after Training

After you have finished your training, it is important to stretch out. Doing so will help your muscles to relax and prevent injury. Standing stretches include:

- Touching your toes.
- Reaching up high in tree pose.
- Bending over, trying to touch the ground with your fingers, if possible.
- Lying on your back and bringing both legs up to a 90° angle.
- Lying on your back and bringing both legs behind you at a 45° angle.
- Standing up tall and reaching your hands up high, then reaching to the right and left.
- Standing on one leg and bringing the other in front of you, bending down to touch your knee.
- Standing on one leg and bringing the other out to the side, again bending down to touch your knee.

Seated Stretches

- Pointing your toes away from you and then bringing them back toward you.
- Lying on your back and bring both legs up to a 90° angle. Then bring them down and touch the ground in front of you.
- Lying on your back and bringing both legs behind you, again at a 45° angle, then touching the ground in front of you.
- Sitting down with one leg crossed over the other, then reaching out to grab your toes and pull them toward you.
- Sitting down, holding onto one leg, and bringing it to your chest. If possible, grab the bottom of the foot with the opposite hand and pull it closer to you.

Judo is a martial art that requires discipline, training, and hard work to reach the black belt level. However, it can be beneficial for everyone to add some Judo training into their workout regimen. Training in Judo can help you to improve your overall coordination and balance, build muscle, and you will also burn calories during this process. This chapter has offered some great workout ideas that you can do to help get yourself started on your Judo training or just to add a little variety to your current workout plan. These movements can all be done at either the gym or at home and do not require any special equipment other than a workout mat to help cushion your falls.

Training for Judo can be done with other forms of exercise, but it is best if you do it on its own. It is recommended that you train for at least three days per week, but you can train more often if you want. Just remember to take it easy and listen to your body's limits. As always, you are returning to the standing position after practicing any of the throws/takedowns is important for preventing injuries in Judo classes. You should also remember to stretch out when you are done and drink plenty of water after a workout.

Conclusion

This book is aimed at giving you a wide overview of Judo in terms of its principles, techniques, and rankings. We began by mentioning the history of Judo, explaining how it originated from Jiu-Jitsu and how it was practiced by the Samurai. We discussed how etiquette is an important aspect of Judo - as players must bow before stepping into the mat and before and after each game. The whole idea of Judo is to achieve maximum efficiency while retaining your energy, so it's not about exerting your strength against your opponent. It's all about maintaining your balance and waiting for the right moment to overthrow your opponent. There are plenty of techniques and variations you can use during a Judo contest, as mentioned throughout the book.

In chapter 2, we mentioned the two major methods of learning Judo, which are Kata Judo and Randori Judo. You learned how to anticipate your opponent's offensive moves and how to respond to any sudden attacks. We mentioned the seven kata techniques and which ones are still used to this day. Randori Judo refers to the more freestyle form of Judo, where you are taught to be more creative with your techniques. Judo is a fluid sport, and it takes more than simply memorizing a few techniques or fighting combos to win a contest. In Judo, you'll need to know how to turn the odds in your favor when you're in a vulnerable position. Randori techniques teach you how to spar either standing or on the ground. You need to be fully conversant with the Kata techniques first before proceeding to the Randori style.

In Chapters 3 to 10, we mentioned all the essential techniques of Judo, starting with the most basic one, which is learning how to fall and land safely to avoid injuring yourself. This is vital because Judo entails a lot of throws and falls. The most important aspect of any sport is to maintain safety procedures and to practice self-control, so you will not be tempted to hurt your opponent on purpose (or you'll be disqualified from the game). We discussed the hand techniques and how to use your upper body to throw an opponent by learning the 15 te-waza techniques. Learning about hip throws is also very important because it's all about making your opponent lose their balance. We then proceeded to the 21 ashi-waza or foot techniques and sacrifice techniques, where you trick your opponents by falling on your back to overthrow them.

In Chapters 9 and 10, we talked about the pinning, choking, and joint lock techniques that are very necessary to score a full point or an ippon, which is how you win the game. You need to be careful with all these techniques and must only practice them under supervision. After that, we talked about Judo as an art of self-defense and explained how you can take a bigger and much stronger opponent down, as well as how to survive armed attacks. We mentioned the competitive side of Judo, how it transcends to an art form, all competition rules, format, and scoring, and how to train before promotional tests. In the final chapter, we explained how to set out a daily routine for Judo training that you can apply at home or in the gym. We hope this book is useful in teaching you all about this magnificent martial art.

Part 9: Sambo

An Essential Guide to a Martial Art Similar to Judo, Jiu-Jitsu, and Wrestling along with Its Throws, Grappling Styles, Holds, and Submission Techniques

CLINT SHARP

Sambo

AN ESSENTIAL GUIDE TO A MARTIAL
ART SIMILAR TO JUDO, JIU-JITSU, AND
WRESTLING ALONG WITH ITS THROWS, GRAPPLING
STYLES, HOLDS, AND SUBMISSION TECHNIQUES

Introduction

Sambo is a martial art resembling the discipline of Judo but with some variations. In this book, you'll learn basic terminology and techniques on throws, grip techniques, self-defense moves in Sambo, offensive rolls, and strikes - even ways to improve your skills at this exciting sport.

Sambo is a Russian martial art; its name is an acronym meaning "self-defense without weapons." It was initially developed in the 1900s to provide unarmed combat training for the Soviet military. It is very similar to Judo, jiu-jitsu, and wrestling but has many unique aspects.

Sambo, although derived from Judo, has unique technical differences. Since the art form was initially developed for the military, Sambo inherently has a lot of combat elements. For example, Combat Sambo allows more aggressive maneuvers of strikes, elbow, knee kicks, etc. Sambo Masters do very well in Mixed Martial Arts (MMA) competitions – thanks to the martial art's versatility.

Mastering Sambo reaps many benefits for those who train in it. Firstly, Sambo is great for self-defense since the techniques are practical and efficient. Furthermore, this martial art is excellent for fitness and self-improvement. Sambo requires a lot of strength to perform throws against stronger opponents, ultimately building endurance.

Sambo has a variety of throwing techniques. There are throws to take your opponent down if they are standing, sitting, or lying down. The grips used in Sambo allow for many combinations and attacks on your opponent – so practicing them is very beneficial.

Sambo also has many grip fighting techniques which can be used to gain an advantage during a match. Depending on the situation, you can also use your hands or legs, and these moves allow you to control your opponent effectively.

Mastering Sambo requires diligent practice and training over many years. Becoming an expert Sambo practitioner is not easy, but the benefits are worth it.

This encyclopedia-style manual is a must-have for Sambo fighters of all levels. It contains everything from the history to grip techniques, submissions, and self-defense in a clear, concise format perfect for beginners looking to become experts or executives who want to take up the sport.

Putting the self-defense techniques in context makes this book an easy-to-follow guide that equips readers with the essential information they need to gain mastery over this martial art. No details are left out from Chapter 1: What Is Sambo? to Chapter 10: Improving Your Sambo Skills.

This essential guide introduces different throws and rolls and self-defense. Tap into our expertise.

In this Sambo guide, you learn the fundamental elements of Sambo. There's much for readers to learn, with detailed sections on throws and holding techniques, headlocks and chokes, arm locks, and pins. Look closer at the different styles of wrestling applied in Sambo, including Judo, Brazilian Jiu-Jitsu, and Wrestling Systems, which make up a larger percentage of all competitions worldwide.

Most books on this topic are theoretical surveys covering basic information about techniques, strategies, and observations without providing anything specific for one person's needs. This guide gives you all the raw knowledge to learn the basics through hands-on training with an experienced instructor. The book also gives detailed guidance on solo drills for self-practice.

You'll be walked through each step, from carefully explained procedures for moves like pins or throws to descriptions of style changes, position shifts, and general positions –providing clear instructions on how these transitions should be made.

Chapter 1: What Is Sambo?

Over the years, more people have become interested in learning martial arts. It's everyone's top priority to ensure their safety and mental and physical health. Luckily, nothing combines self-defense, physical strength and health, and mental well-being and stimulation like the practice of martial arts.

You might be surprised to learn there are over 170 martial arts. China, Japan, and Korea are known for being the ancestral homelands of various combating and self-defense techniques such as Karate, Jiu-Jitsu, and Taekwondo. However, Sambo is a renowned Russian sport.

Sambo was created as a universal combat system. Aficionados worked tirelessly to collect, select, and seamlessly combine a wide array of elements as a foundation for the universal combat sport that is Sambo. The sport's teaching programs are highly distinctive, making its practitioners masterful in numerous techniques and skillful in tactical thinking, as needed on the mat.

The acronym SAMBO derives from the phrase "Samooborona Bez Oruzhia," which translates into "Self Defense Without Weapons." It is structured based on defense rather than attack, which comes in handy in several situations we face in today's world. Aside from teaching invaluable self-defense techniques, Sambo can help individuals build strong character. It teaches perseverance and endurance, qualities we need to make indispensable life experiences and withstand their complexities.

Not only does Sambo help us guard ourselves against potential predators, but it also helps us stay safe during other everyday incidents. For instance, slip and fall accidents are among the most common reasons for injuries. Whether you twist your ankle while walking or slip on a wet surface, you can stay safe by employing the Sambo fall technique. A safe fall technique is a must-learn for any wrestling system.

This sport teaches countless incredible qualities and traits. It is about physical strength and is also concerned with producing strong-willed individuals. Sambo helps individuals develop important character traits such as self-discipline, control, diligence, persistence, and will. These character aspects can heighten a sense of self-awareness outside the training facility.

For some, Sambo is their fuel, even if they view it as a professional sport. Others think of Sambo as a hobby and a way to work on self-growth and development. Regardless of what this sport means to you, it can be an awesome complementary addition to your career. It can serve as a stress outlet, a timeout, or the perfect opportunity to get your creative juices flowing.

This book is perfect if you're considering giving Sambo a go. We delve deep into what Sambo is and where it derived from throughout this chapter. There is no better way to start your journey than understanding the sport and its history you're getting into. Some Sambo subtypes are covered, and the differences between them are explained.

Getting to Know Sambo

So, what is Sambo? Sambo is a Soviet combat sport and martial art. As mentioned, it is an acronym of a Romanized Russian phrase meaning self-defense without weapons. It is among the newest or most modern martial art forms. According to United World Wrestling, it is acknowledged as the third most popular international wrestling style.

It was initially created for the military to aid in ending fights as efficiently and quickly as possible. Not long after, Sambo became an international competitive sport.

Judo, Jujitsu, and other martial arts forms inspired Sambo's make-up, movements, and techniques. This collection of wrestling or combat systems is widely known as a *self-defense art*.

In Sambo, like other wrestling systems, the fighters must comply with specific regulations and rules. The fight involves two individuals who employ different tricks and blows. The points earned are an evaluation of their tricks, and, of course, the wrestler with the highest number of points wins. The match can be ended before its allotted time limit if a player successfully attempts various submission tricks and locks on their opponent.

As you have realized, this sport is not easy to grasp. Therefore, Sambo wrestlers must undergo rigorous training to acquire the needed skills and techniques. Wrestlers should be able to grapple and strike in the clinch.

Although Sambo is a defense sport, it still requires aggressive play, especially during matches. Success during the match depends on acquiring and mastering a wide range of skills.

Flexibility and agility are required for joint locks, throws, suffocation techniques, kicks, and strikes. These are skills and moves that must be tactfully used throughout the match.

To learn Sambo, you must understand it takes years of practice and dedication to master the art. It is not a sport for those lacking motivation, determination, and patience. Sambo is not only about executing the moves but also about gaining complete control over each skill and every move your body makes.

The Goals and Characteristics of Russian Sambo

The goals of Russian Sambo depend on the style, which is discussed later. However, the ultimate goal behind this combating style is to end a fight quickly and efficiently. It is typically done by taking the adversary to the ground, and the wrestler proceeds to execute a submission hold quickly. The practitioner usually follows the takedown with fast strikes in combat-oriented Sambo styles.

Anyone who practices Sambo must know three specific characteristics; leg locks, a seamless combination of Judo and other wrestling maneuvers, and fundamental control abilities. The employed style of Sambo also adds a few things to the basic mix. For instance, in combat-oriented Sambo, the practitioner must acquire great striking skills. Even so, Sambo is essentially an art of masterful grappling. Submissions and takedowns are its primary areas of focus.

The History of Sambo

The Origins

Sambo was developed to serve as a combination of all or the majority of the different martial arts. The main goal was to develop a style and system that offered the most efficiency. Russia, the metaphorical bridge connecting Asian and European countries, was the hubbub of various fighting styles and techniques.

Martial arts developed in either continent were quickly introduced to the Russians as they were in near direct contact with the Vikings, Mongols, Japanese, Tartar, and several other battles and fight-savvy civilizations. The styles and techniques these people donated to the Russians served as raw material for the foundation of what we now know as Russian Sambo.

Russia's elite Red Army Karate and Judo instructor, Vasili Oshchepkov, was one of the pioneers of Sambo. Like every other trainer's goal or dream, he wanted his apprentices to be the best, most skilled, and most competent in all combat systems and martial arts techniques.

Oshchepkov was among the few non-Japanese holders of a 2nd Dan black belt in Judo from Jigoro Kano. This accomplishment convinced him that he could develop a better martial arts style. He combined the moves and skills he thought were most efficient from Judo with those from Karate and several Russian native wrestling techniques.

During that time, Victor Spiridonov, a highly experienced man in Greco-Roman wrestling and other styles, worked on sorting and picking all the techniques from hand-to-hand fighting methods and leaving out what didn't work. Spiridonov was formerly injured by a bayonet during the Russo-Japanese War. This injury left his left arm lame, which undoubtedly affected his work.

Due to his injury, the style that Spiridonov employed was naturally a lot softer in retrospect. His injury made him think from an alternate, rather unusual perspective. Typically, practitioners aim to use power and strength in combat. However, Spiridonov hoped to develop an effective style that allowed him to use the opponent's strength against them. This technique would work if the practitioner deflected the adversary's aggression or power in a way they would not anticipate easily. His technique was invaluable to injured or weaker practitioners, allowing them to fight equally well. His style was officially known as "Samoz."

General Military Training, or Vseobuch, was developed in 1918 by Vladimir Lenin. This program aimed to train the Red Army under K. Voroshilov's leadership. NKVD physical training center, Dinamo, was created by Voroshilov. Several experienced and professional instructors were brought together to ensure success in this center. Spiridonov was among the first instructors who taught self-defense and wrestling techniques at Dinamo.

1923 was the year when the magic happened. Spiridonov and Oschepkov worked alongside each other to expand on and enhance the Red Army's weaponless fighting and combat system. I.V. Vasiliev and Anatoly Kharlampiev, who were exceptionally well-versed in global martial arts, also participated in this significant collaboration.

One decade later, an outline or general draft for what the world now knows as Sambo was finally ready. This outline combined all the techniques and styles that each thought to be highly efficient and effective.

Although they all worked diligently on the project, Kharlampiev is famously known as the Father of Sambo, perhaps due to his strong political connections. It's also an homage to his ability and perseverance to stay true to the martial art's formulation throughout its early initiation and developmental stages.

Additionally, Kharlampiev was the person behind the campaign for Sambo to serve as the official Soviet Union's combat sport. His campaigning dreams and efforts came to life in 1938. However, it is worth mentioning that evidence points toward Spiridonov as the first one to use the name "Sambo" in reference to the newly developed combat system.

Sambo was finally taught and employed by the Soviet military and police, and other organizations as soon as its techniques were refined and properly cataloged. However, keep in mind that the techniques underwent minor enhancements depending on the targeted or assumed group.

Sambo in the USA

It wasn't until the 1960s that Sambo started spreading outside of Russia. It appeared in other parts of the world when several practitioners of the fighting style took part in international Judo competitions. In 1968, FILA ("Fédération Internationale des Luttes Associées"), or the International Federation of Associated Wrestling Styles, recognized

Judo, Sambo, and Greco-Roman wrestling as international wrestling styles.

Boris Timoshin – a Russian-born politician and a Czechoslovakian refugee – traveled to the United States in 1968. He was a Sambo practitioner and champion in college and aimed to keep training while seeking a career in Sambo instruction. Upon his arrival, he was turned down by every martial arts center he went to. Despite all the rejection, he found a place to train and teach Sambo on 23rd Street at the YMCA in New York City and formed wonderful friendships along the way.

While his Sambo teaching career only lasted until 1971, he left an incredible mark, making him one of the most legendary figures in the Sambo community. He earned the title "America's first Sambo coach" since he was the USA's first Sambo instructor.

It was during the mid-1980s that Sambo competitions gained popularity. The sport received its own organization, FIAS or International Sambo Federation, in 1985. However, the combating style's true recognition and popularity took off when Oleg Taktarov, a holder of a Russian black belt in Judo and a Sambo competitor, won the UFC 6 in 1995. Only then did an exceptional number of UFC fighters add Sambo techniques to their moves and skillsets.

Today, there are two large American Sambo organizations, the AASF or All-American SAMBO Federation and the USA Sambo.

Sambo: Is It An Olympic Sport?

In 1980, the Summer Olympics' opening ceremony in Moscow featured a youth Sambo demonstration. Despite the talk revolving around the International Olympic Committee recognizing Sambo as an official Olympic sport in 1981, the combat style is yet to become one. However, the pressure and hope persist, considering that President Vladimir Putin, an honorary FIAT president, shows ongoing support for the sport and the Sambo community's heartfelt efforts.

Modern-Day Sambo

According to the International Sambo Federation, the World Sambo Championships in Sofia, Bulgaria, in 2016 housed over 500 athletes. These participants came from 80 different countries. The exact number of people globally practicing Sambo cannot be estimated. However, in 2013 there were over 410,000 individuals practicing Sambo in Russia alone.

Sambo has a very admirable philosophy, like any martial art. This conviction promotes principles of respect, self-discipline, personal growth and development, and friendship. These values are taught to all Sambo practitioners regardless of age, race, beliefs, geographic location, or nationality, not to mention the sport's great influence on endurance, stamina, and strength. These make Sambo the perfect sport and self-defense technique for children and adults.

Subtypes of Sambo

Various Sambo styles exist. While the definitive principles of Sambo remain more or less the same, numerous variations of this sport have emerged since its first formulation. Despite the countless styles, the combat style can be broken down into Sport Sambo and Combat Sambo. In addition to these two main categories or subtypes, only four more are widely recognized by the public.

1. Sport Sambo

Sport Sambo is mainly a competitive form of Sambo and is generally similar to Judo and wrestling. For instance, a competitor must rely heavily on grappling, takedown defenses, and takedowns to win the match. Leg locks, in all their forms, are also allowed within the rules of the competition. Leg locks are very similar to armbars.

However, as you can deduce from the name, they are carried out by the legs.

The current World Championship weight categories for men are 52 kg, 57kg, 62kg, 68kg, 74kg, 82kg, 90kg, 100kg, and over 100kg. For women, the weight categories are 48kg, 52kg, 56kg, 60kg, 64kg, 68kg, 72kg, 80kg, and over 80kg.

2. Combat Sambo

Combat Sambo was created solely for military use. Although Sambo stands for self-defense without weapons, Combat Sambo includes disarming techniques and weaponry. In addition to the basic Sambo moves, Combat Sambo requires executing excess grappling and striking.

Despite being created exclusively for the Russian military, Combat Sambo is now among the common competitive Sambo styles. It differs from Sport Sambo because it includes head butting, elbow and knee usage, grappling, groin strikes, punches, and kicks. It is similar to modern-day MMA. Competitors must wear shin and head guards and hand protectors in addition to the regular Sambo gear.

Combat Sambo is practiced by men only. The current World Championship weight categories are 52kg, 57kg, 62kg, 68kg, 74kg, 82kg, 90kg, 100kg, and over 100kg.

3. Freestyle Sambo

In 2004, the American Sambo Association developed the Freestyle Sambo subtype. It was an attempt to have non-Sambo practitioners participate in Sambo events, especially those who took part in Judo and Jujitsu. These events allowed several submissions typically not allowed in Sport Sambo, the chokehold executions.

4. Self-Defense Sambo

Self-defense Sambo is all about - you guessed it - defense tactics and techniques. The great thing about this Sambo subtype is it teaches practitioners to defend themselves against weapons and other attacks. The main strategy is to use the opponent's or attacker's power and aggression against them. As you recall, this was Spiridonov's main aim. His influence, alongside the spirit of Aikido and Jujitsu, is eminent in self-defense Sambo.

5. Special Sambo

Special Sambo was created for rapid response law formations and Army Special Forces. It is merely a more specialized version or subtype of the average Sambo technique. It was refined and perfected to suit the specific unit that would use it. Special Sambo is quite similar to Combat Sambo. However, each group adds a few particular aims to the mix.

6. Beach Sambo

Beach Sambo is the unconventional version of the combatting style. As the name implies, the fight is carried out on the beach, eliminating the mat wrestling tradition. A rule that the combat's duration lasts three minutes is also employed. There are no penalties, and the time count begins as soon as the first move is assessed. The usual competition uniform is also modified. For the 2016 Asian Beach Games in Danang, Vietnam, the weight categories for men were 62kg, 74kg, 90kg, and over 90kg. For women, the weight categories were 56kg, 64kg, 72kg, and over 72kg.

Sambo quickly became an international sport due to its incorporation of numerous national martial arts. The self-defense technique has already gathered enthusiasts in over 80 countries, and the number is still growing. International tournaments and championships are held globally, meaning specialized Sambo schools or instructors are in different parts of the world.

Sambo practitioners take great pride in their sport. Instructors, trainees, and even opposing wrestlers are united by solidarity and friendship. All wrestlers must show respect to their opponents.

Chapter 2: Comparing Sambo to Judo, Jiu-Jitsu, and Wrestling

This chapter examines the similarities and differences between Sambo, Judo, Jiu-Jitsu, and Wrestling. It explains each martial art's unique style to help you decide which best suits your needs.

Core Aspect Comparison: Sambo vs. Judo vs. BJJ vs. Wrestling

The Core Aspects of Sambo

Source[82]

Sambo is a martial art originating in Russia but is recognized and practiced internationally. It is a hybrid of Judo and Wrestling, developed during the early 20th century. The primary goal of Sambo is to neutralize or disable an opponent as quickly as possible with effective joint locks, chokes, throws, kicks, punches, and other techniques. In addition to being very functional on its own merits, Sambo relies heavily on Judo throws and techniques to be effective. A Sambo practitioner must have a solid foundation in the art and excellent takedown skills to takedown opponents. In contrast, other martial arts styles focus more on stand-up techniques and less on takedowns.

The Core Aspects of Judo

Source[83]

Judo is a martial art originating in Japan but recognized internationally. It focuses more on throws, grappling, chokes, armlocks, kneebars, and kicks to the head and neck area (not groin shots) than Sambo does. Judo is one of the most effective martial arts for self-defense against bigger, stronger, or heavier opponents and has its place in MMA (Mixed Martial Arts). It is an excellent choice for those looking to compete professionally in grappling tournaments.

The Core Aspects of Jiu-Jitsu

Source[84]

Brazilian Jiu-Jitsu is a martial art with roots in Jiu-Jitsu. It is mainly about grappling and ground fighting. They do not focus on stand-up techniques like kicking and punching. It is very effective for self-defense against bigger, stronger, or heavier opponents because they will most likely take the fight to the ground where your smaller stature won't matter as much. However, BJJ can be more dangerous than other martial arts styles because of its focus on grappling and ground fighting. If you are not trained properly, your opponent will use their superior size and strength against you and endanger your safety.

The Core Aspects of Wrestling

Source[85]

Wrestling is the oldest grappling sport, with origins dating back as far as ancient Greece (even further if we consider its common roots with hunting). In self-defense, wrestling is one of the most effective martial arts because it protects you from larger and stronger opponents by taking them down quickly. Considering an opponent's size and strength while fighting on your feet also makes wrestling a very practical grappling form for MMA, which is now one of the most popular sports worldwide.

Differences in Origins

Sambo was developed in Russia during the early 20th century. It combines Judo and Wrestling, making it very effective for self-defense purposes (especially against larger, stronger opponents) and limiting its practicality to grappling situations like MMA.

Judo originated in Japan and was introduced in 1882 by Kano Jigoro Shihan. Judo is an educational method derived from martial arts, focusing on throws, grappling, chokes, armlocks, kneebars, kicks to the head and neck area (not groin shots), etc. It is very effective for self-defense against larger and stronger opponents, but it can be dangerous if trained improperly because of its focus on ground fighting. It became an Olympic sport in 1964.

Brazilian Jiu-Jitsu is derived from Jiu-Jitsu but focuses primarily on grappling and ground fighting rather than stand-up techniques like punching and kicking. The Japanese taught their art to Brazilians. An expert Judoka, Mitsuyo Maeda, went to Sao Paulo and taught the Brazilian people his art.

Wrestling is a very old sport that started in the Sumerian era – 5000 years ago. It is one of the most practical grappling martial arts because it protects you from larger and stronger opponents by allowing you to take them down quickly.

Differences in Goals/Aims

Although Sambo was derived from Judo and has many similarities with other martial arts, it differs greatly in philosophy. Judo teaches mental calmness and focuses on avoiding conflict, which aligns with the philosophy of all Japanese martial art forms.

On the other hand, Sambo allows you to fight for victory by all means necessary, even if that means striking your opponent. It is especially true for Combat Sambo, where techniques like kicks are allowed. Conversely, Sport Sambo has a calmer approach similar to Judo.

Brazilian Jiu Jitsu's philosophy is that any smaller or weaker person can successfully defend themselves against a larger opponent. It allows them to apply, most notably joint locks, to defeat the other person. One of the main objectives of Brazilian Jiu-Jitsu is to lock and immobilize by using your hands and legs.

Finally, Wrestling idealizes the idea of control over the opponent rather than attacking them. Wrestling is about gaining a superior body position to pin your opponent onto their back and getting out of that position by performing a technique or executing an escape maneuver before you are pinned.

Differences in Technique

Sambo focuses on techniques for leg locks, throwing, groundwork, and submissions. Sport Sambo does not allow chokeholds in competition and has a few restrictions on specific gripping and holding techniques.

On the other hand, Combat Sambo was developed for the military and closely resembles Mixed Martial Arts. This Sambo variant allows MMA forms of striking and grappling and more combative punching, elbow and knee kicks, soccer kicks, chokeholds, and headbutts.

The distinction between Sambo and Brazilian jiu-jitsu (BJJ) is that Combat Sambo rules and regulations do not allow ground fighting without throws or other combative tactics, as opposed to BJJ's allowance of these maneuvers.

The objective of Brazilian jiu-jitsu is to force an adversary to the ground to neutralize possible physical or size advantages through ground fighting methods, chokeholds, and joint locks.

Judo and Sambo have very similar fighting styles. Both arts use a wide range of throws and grappling to take an opponent down. However, as discussed, Combat Sambo allows additional strikes and knee and elbow kicks that are not allowed in Judo competitions or training.

Wrestling rules allow opponents to continue fighting on their feet after gaining control over one another - known as "top position" or "top control." The objective of wrestling is to pin your opponent on his back for long enough to win the match by reaching an agreed-upon number of points.

Differences in Rules

The governing ruleset of any martial art usually addresses three major criteria:
1. Techniques allowed – for example, some martial arts allow chokeholds and strikes while others don't.
2. Winning Criteria - when can a competitor be declared a winner? It can be scoring the maximum points, having a specific point lead, or executing the perfect maneuver.
3. Foul or illegal moves and the penalties imposed.
4. A detailed point system awarding a specific number of points for specific moves (or deducting points for illegal moves)

Rules of Sambo and Combat Sambo

There are four ways to win a match in Combat Sambo:

1. Throw an opponent to the ground while standing. How you throw your opponent must show control and intent, i.e., perform a perfect throw while remaining in a standing position.
2. Get an 8-point lead over your opponent.
3. In a submission, the referee stops the match when the opponent becomes unconscious or taps out of fear (achieved by locking the opponent).
4. A competitor has gained more points than the opponent at the end of the match. This is achieved by performing throws, takedowns, and holds, leading to your victory.

Throws and Pins are scored for Combat Sambo.

If the opponent is pinned for 10 to 19 seconds, 2 points are awarded. If the opponent is pinned for more than 20 seconds, 4 points are awarded.

Throws are scored depending on your position during and after the throw and how the opponent falls. More points are given when you are upright during and after the throw.

Illegal techniques and stalling are penalized in a competition.

Rules of Judo

Judo's rules are identical to Sambo's because the objective is to throw, takedown, or immobilize an opponent onto their back. An ideal score or Ippon is awarded when you have an opponent pinned onto their back for 20 seconds. An Ippon immediately ends the match.

In Judo, all submissions are allowed except those resulting in a broken bone or joint lock on the elbow and fingers. In addition, there is no "scoring" position during competition other than gaining control of your opponent's body through pins or holds. Any amount of time with your opponent on their back is considered a legal pin.

A Waza-ari (or half a point) is awarded for less ideal throws or when the opponent is pinned down for a shorter duration than required to score an Ippon. Scoring two waza-aris in a match is an Ippon and immediately ends the match.

Finally, a yuko is the smallest score for less effective techniques.

The aim is to score a perfect Ippon to overtake the opponent and win the match with maximum points.

Rules of Jiu-Jitsu

Jiu-Jitsu matches are usually 3 to 5 minutes, depending on the category. Competitors are awarded 2, 3, or 4 points for achieving dominant positions or executing techniques. A victory is gained by the opponent with the most points or on successful submission.

Rules of Wrestling

Wrestling matches are broken down into two rounds, each lasting three minutes. Competitors get points by:

- **Takedown** - A competitor gets their opponent onto the ground with at least one foot on the floor between them and the edge of the ring or on the ground.

- **Escape** - A competitor gets away from their opponent's control and back to a standing position with at least one foot not touching the floor within the ring (or lines) without being controlled by an opponent.
- **Reversal** - A competitor is on the ground, and their opponent has full control of them; they can get points if they reverse the hold so that they have full control.
- **Penalties** - Competitors can get negative points for illegal holds or technical violations.

Differences in Uniform

These martial arts demand quick footwork, and techniques revolve around complex body movements. The uniforms for each sport are designed to allow maximum flexibility and movement. Sambo, Judo, and BJJ have very similar attire, with minor differences. However, wrestling has a unique uniform, quite different from the others.

Sambo uniforms consist of four pieces; the jacket, pants, shoes, and belt. The uniform is red or blue, and the jacket is often reversible. The uniform is called a Kurtka.

Judo's uniform usually only includes a judogi (similar to a karate gi). Judogi is usually white and comprises three parts, jacket, pants, and belt. It should fit similarly to Sambo or Jiu-jitsu uniforms without being too loose or tight on the body.

Jiu-jitsu's uniform includes a Gi similar to Judo, a jacket, pants, and a belt. It can be any color, but white is most common for competitions. It comes with a belt ranking system from white to black depending on the time you have trained and your rank within the school or association.

Wrestling uniforms are specific to the competition held. In college, folk style is the most common, with a singlet or tight shorts and shirt worn without shoes during practices. Freestyle competitions wear tighter uniforms and wrestling boots for footwear. Women's folk style wear spandex-like short suits instead of singlets to minimize the risk of skin infections from mats.

Belt System Comparison

Sambo, Jiu-Jitsu, and Judo have their own belt systems. These indicate the rank of a competitor within their sport. More often than not, expertise is also measured based on performance at a regional and global level. Similar to other sports, martial arts rank their practitioners at a global level. However, to feature in this ranking system, a practitioner must participate and compete against the world's best.

In Sambo, there are seven ranks. Each rank is held for one year, starting with Rookie or level 1 (white belt) to 7th year, 2nd Master (yellow, orange, green, blue, brown, and finally black). Various organizations issue the title of "master of sport" or "international master of sport" to those who excel nationally and internationally.

Brazilian Jiu-Jitsu belts are divided by color, ranked from white to red, and consist of eight belts. A minimum number of hours of training is required for each belt level before being tested; usually, the higher the rank, the more hours are required to achieve that next belt or title.

Judo also has a belt system progression, with black belts being the highest.

Wrestling does not have a defined belt system for competitors. Still, it does have a progression level based on practice. The world ranking is based on performance in competitions.

Cross-Training Opportunities

Many athletes compete in more than one sport and experience success due to their similarities. Sambo, BJJ, and Judo are very similar, offering cross-training opportunities. Wrestling is a form of submission grappling, and Sambo is heavily influenced by Judo. Wrestling uses similar submissions to BJJ, making it easier for those who do both to transition seamlessly from one art to the other.

Each sport has different rules. Still, they all work on similar concepts, movements, and techniques involving takedowns, submissions, and using the legs. The similarities between these arts make it easy for those training in one art to cross-train with another similar art increasing their success rates within each sport and making them more knowledgeable practitioners overall.

For example, a Combat Sambo-trained athlete will do very well in MMA competitions, thanks to cross-training in Judo (throws and grappling) and strikes, elbow, and knee kicks from Combat Sambo training. Due to these skills, Sambo fighters are rightly called the most ferocious of the lot.

Competitions

Dedicated training in martial arts usually culminates in a competitive mindset. All four art forms have developed over the years and have seen a significant rise in professional world competitions and local or regional events.

Sambo competitions are governed by FIAS (International Sambo Federation), the international governing body. Many events are held yearly, with medals awarded to winners based on their rank and belt system levels. The most noteworthy events are the World Cup and other World Championships. The Sambo Federation has recently acquired recognition from the IOC (International Olympic Committee), and it could soon become an Olympic sport.

Judo competitions usually have many athletes competing at major tournaments, such as the Olympic Games, world championships, or regional meets. In addition, smaller invitationals around the country offer chances for athletes to compete in their respective divisions.

Brazilian Jiu-jitsu is governed by the IBJJF (International Brazilian Jiu-Jitsu Federation), which organizes tournaments and championships. Many competitions are held worldwide for all belt levels, for men and women.

Wrestling is one of the most popular sports and also an Olympics sport. It is governed by FILA (International Federation of Associated Wrestling Styles), which organizes various meets and competitions.

Benefits of Sambo Compared to the Other Martial Arts

Sambo is a great opportunity for those interested in martial arts but has no idea where to begin. So, Sambo has many benefits making it a great choice for beginners.

Sambo is an effective martial art that offers fitness training by employing cardiovascular exercise, strength conditioning, and self-defense skills.

Those interested in learning Sambo can take classes with other students at their skill level, making new friends sharing the same interests. This interaction builds camaraderie and is a great way to meet others with similar goals.

Sambo offers many opportunities for those wanting to compete, increasing self-confidence and providing a great outlet for stress relief, often missing in other sports or activities. It encourages discipline, high physical fitness standards, mental strength, and perseverance.

Sambo can be practiced by anyone, regardless of age or fitness level; it is an excellent option for children because it teaches discipline without being overly aggressive. It also helps build self-esteem while increasing coordination skills that could improve academic performance at school.

The belt system in Sambo acts as a guide for students on their progress. The seniority of belts reflects a person's knowledge level.

The Most Effective Martial Art

Although in principle, all martial arts have their pros and cons in technique, a Sambo-trained individual will win in a fight. Sambo training, especially Combat Sambo, is hardcore and involves striking, grappling, kicks, and weapon-disarming techniques. It is the best martial art for self-defense and a great form of fitness training with plenty of mental and physical benefits.

Sambo differs from other martial arts because it utilizes takedowns using all parts of the body, including legs and head, making Sambo stand out among others. Judo is the mother of Sambo and BJJ, albeit with certain restrictions and less brutality.

On the other hand, wrestling teaches a trainee to manipulate the opponent's strength and use it against them. It is a sport where practitioners can apply their skills in real-life situations, making wrestling a great choice for self-defense and recreational activity.

To summarize, Sambo is a fantastic martial art and self-defense system that can be practiced by almost anyone, regardless of age or fitness level. It offers many physical and mental benefits, so it is an excellent choice for those interested in learning effective fighting techniques and seeking general health improvements.

Availability of Training Facilities and Trainers

Sambo is available at various locations across the country, including military bases and colleges. Perhaps not as many as Judo. However, visit online resources or contact the federation to determine a training center near you. As far as trainers are concerned, many experienced martial artists offer lessons in different hand-to-hand combat styles, including Sambo.

Judo is a sport practiced by millions of people around the world. Many are drawn to this martial art because it focuses on grappling techniques, which can be used in real-life situations more often than striking moves. Judo is taught at most gyms and fitness centers across the country, making it an ideal choice for those wanting to train regularly and in an organized discipline.

Jiu-jitsu is considered one of the most effective martial arts in ground fighting – with elements similar to Sambo, Judo, and Wrestling. Jiu-Jitsu has become increasingly popular across the world and can be practiced by anyone. Many Jiu-Jitsu training centers are across the country where practitioners can take classes, usually alongside a fitness program.

Wrestling is a combat sport involving grappling techniques and offers physical and mental benefits. So, it is an excellent choice for self-defense and recreational activity. Wrestling training facilities are commonly available at gyms and fitness centers nationwide.

All the martial arts described in this chapter have their philosophies, origins, techniques, rules, competitive advantages, and benefits. However, in some form, nearly all the art forms have been derived from Judo.

Choose the discipline based on the availability of training facilities and trainers and your physical capability.

If you aim to only practice for self-defense, any martial art will be helpful. If you want to compete internationally, go for Judo or wrestling, as it is easy to find qualified masters near you. Brazilian Jiu-Jitsu is a great choice for those interested in ground fighting, while Sambo offers an effective blend of technique and combat.

Chapter 3: Before Starting: Sambo Essentials and Benefits

If you're reading this book, you've decided Sambo is the martial art for you. Or perhaps your child has already taken to it, and now you want to know more about their chosen sport. Either way, read on. Chapter 3 gives you all the information before starting Sambo, including gear and uniform requirements, benefits of learning this particular martial art, why it's worth learning, and much more.

Types of Sambo

Sambo can be categorized into three types based on the techniques - Sports Sambo, Combat Sambo, or Freestyle Sambo.

1. Sports Sambo

Sports Sambo combines Judo and Wrestling - allowing techniques like leg locks and takedowns with a focus on throws. Sport Sambo does not allow chokeholds.

2. Freestyle Sambo

Freestyle Sambo is a more independent version of the sport allowing all techniques, including submission, striking, and grappling. This form focuses on throws, takedowns, and locks.

Freestyle Sambo was introduced by The American Sambo Association. Freestyle Sambo allows any grappling technique, including those not allowed in Sport or Combat styles. Techniques like neck cranks and twisted leg holds are allowed to gain submissions. Striking is not allowed. Mastering throws is key to winning the match.

3. Combat Sambo

Combat Sambo is a more realistic version of the sport, including striking and grappling, making it closer to Mixed Martial Arts.

Combat Sambo combines Judo, Wrestling, and Jiu-Jitsu, allowing techniques like grappling, striking, chokeholds, and leg locks. It also allows techniques of elbow and knee kicks, groin strikes, and headbutts. It is the most aggressive form of Sambo.

11 Compelling Reasons to Learn Sambo

1. Sambo Is a Superior Martial Art

Sambo was derived from Judo in the Soviet Union as a combat form for the military. This positions Sambo as a unique martial art - having the age-old grappling techniques of Judo and superior Mixed Martial Arts combat skills. A Sambo Master is skilled in grappling, takedowns, dominating, and on-ground submissions. Therefore, a Sambo Master is almost unbeatable in any combat situation.

2. Sambo Is a Perfect Self-Defense System for Everyone, Young and Old

Anyone can learn Sambo. It doesn't matter if you're old or young, big and tall, or small and quick because Sambo works well with every body type. This martial art will teach you to defend yourself while also teaching respect and discipline. The locks, holds, and groundwork learned in Sambo prepare you for any threatening situation.

3. Sambo Is a Competitive Sport

Many think Sambo only works as a self-defense system, but it is also competitive. You don't have to compete if you don't want to. But there are many competitions for those who do. It's fun and exciting and helps your fitness level improve quickly. Recently, the IOC recognized the sport of Sambo, and it might soon become an

Olympic sport.

4. Physical Fitness and Endurance

Sambo is an excellent workout for the body. It trains every muscle, leading to increased strength and endurance. Since Sambo involves so many rapid movements, it's a great cardio workout, too. Whether you want to get in shape fast or give yourself a full-body workout that'll leave you feeling amazing when it's over, Sambo is the way to go.

5. Sambo's Success in MMA

Sambo is a Mixed Martial Art. Sambo practitioners are trained in grappling and striking styles, allowing them to excel at ground combat and stand-up fighting. Sambo fighters are known to be the best at all MMA techniques - grappling, throwing, and takedowns. Sambo Masters are also very good at submissions and reversals. They are known as the most ferocious fighters in the sport.

6. Sambo Teaches Discipline and Respect

Sambo is a discipline and respect-based art. It teaches students to be aware of their actions on the mat and in life. Sambo practitioners are expected to show self-discipline at all times, not only while training. Sambo teaches students to be humble and respectful towards themselves and others.

7. Physical Strength and Dexterity

Sambo demands much from the body - flexibility, coordination skills, stamina, and endurance; it's an all-around workout for your entire body. You'll get in shape fast and develop unbelievable strength with Sambo training. Whether you want to get stronger or more flexible, Sambo will help you achieve your goals.

8. Sambo Is a Valuable Skill for Law Enforcement and the Military

Law enforcement officers and military personnel are often called upon to subdue aggressive people who could be armed with weapons. More often than not, this requires grappling skills. Sambo is a very useful tool in these professions as it prepares people to take on dangerous situations.

9. Mental Strength and Wellness

Sambo offers a great workout for the body and an excellent way to soothe frazzled nerves. The concentration and energy you'll gain from training in this martial art will also help keep your mind sharp. Physical activity has been proven to lower stress levels, making Sambo perfect for those who are always on the go or constantly dealing with stressful situations.

10. Learn to Prevent Injury

Sambo training is great for preventing injuries. At its core, Sambo is Self Defense. Sambo will effectively help defend against aggression and teach you to prevent injury while taking a fall. Those training in Sambo learns to protect themselves against injury, which can be helpful for those with jobs or lifestyles in dangerous situations.

11. Sambo Provides an Excellent Base for Other Martial Arts

Anyone interested in joining other martial arts skills would benefit from starting with Sambo. The groundwork learned as part of this particular martial art is very beneficial when adding other martial arts to your collection. In the previous chapter, we learned that Sambo is very similar to Brazilian Jiu-Jitsu (BJJ), Wrestling, and Judo. Due to this, many people begin training in Sambo before moving on to BJJ or Judo, as these arts are more popular than Sambo among the general public. However, you can't beat a good solid foundation.

Sambo Gear and Equipment

You'll need certain equipment and gear to get the most from your Sambo training. Sambo gear is very similar to MMA gear, mainly consisting of the Sambovka, Helmet, Guards, Gloves, and Mouth Shields.

The Sambovka

The Sambovka is a traditional vest worn by Sambists when training. It is designed to be tightly form-fitting and provides ample protection without compromising agility or movement. This jacket is usually red or blue and worn with a belt and shorts to match. A competitor is usually required to have both blue and red-colored sets so they can be visually distinguished on the mat.

Sambovka does not portray the rank or expertise of the competitor in any way - there is no identification of rank on the uniform.

The Sambovka has strict specifications for material and design. It uses a specific fabric variant with robust seams and wings on the shoulders. A belt is worn around the Sambovka to secure it during a match. Additionally, the sleeve should be no more than 10 cm in width and reach the wrist exactly. The jacket's flaps should be only about 15 cm below the uniform's belt.

Helmet

The Sambo helmet is like the boxing helmet and is worn to protect the competitor's head. It should be very lightweight so as not to hinder movement or cause discomfort during training sessions.

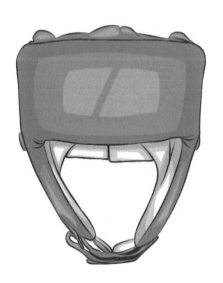

It is made from firm but soft plastic and has visors in front for proper visibility when sparring with competitors on all sides. Additionally, it provides protection from accidental knee or elbow strikes. The helmet has straps on the chin and back of the head to protect from accidental injuries.

Gloves

Sambo gloves are very similar to boxing and MMA gloves. They provide all-around protection for the hands, wrists, fingers, and knuckles during training sessions with competitors. The glove also helps secure a firm grip when grappling or fighting in matches while protecting you from accidental injury.

The Sambist should always have red and blue gloves.

Mouth Guards

The mouth guard is considered a vital piece of equipment in Sambo as it helps prevent chipping or broken teeth when taking falls. However, many people don't wear them because they can be uncomfortable and affect breathing during training sessions.

Groin Guard

Groin guards are not mandatory in Sambo but are highly recommended. They help prevent injuries to the groin during training sessions with competitors on all sides.

Shoes

Shoe specifications are not strict in Sambo. Ideally, you should wear wrestling shoes or boxing boots with a good grip for traction on the mat. These shoes should have a snug fit and adequately support the ankle and heels. Sambo shoes should not be fancy and have any parts sticking out, which could cause injuries.

Shorts

Sambo shorts must be the same color as the jacket. These should be about 2/3s the length of your thigh, reaching about 2.5 inches above your knee. Shorts with pockets are not allowed. The color of the shorts must match the jacket.

What to Wear to Training

You don't need any particular clothes or gear to train in, but you should wear something comfortable that allows your body a full range of motion.

Judogi is the most common uniform worn for Sambo training – it's required at higher levels (national and international competitions). A judogi consists of a jacket, belt, and pants. Some practitioners wear a Sambovka instead of the judogi when training with other Sambists.

You should wear socks but no shoes or slippers to training sessions as they can cause injuries during grappling and throwing.

Discuss the uniform with your trainer. Inform him about any financial constraints to purchasing appropriate gear, as many masters will donate or suggest alternate training attire.

What to Expect Before You Consider Training for Sambo

Consider the following before you decide to start Sambo training:

- Sparring and competition include a lot of throwing, takedowns, grappling, tackling, and lifting your opponent to slam them down or toss them across the mat. You might want to start with Judo if you're not prepared for such physical contact during training. Make sure you're in good health before you start.
- You need to have a calm mind or be able to control your emotions; otherwise, training can get very frustrating. New techniques are always being taught, so it's important to learn them quickly and don't let yourself become upset if someone beats you on the mat. Just keep trying until you get it right.
- You need to follow instructions and listen carefully. Otherwise, you won't learn what you should. Practice concentration during class - it'll come in handy later on.
- You need to be a self-starter. If you can't motivate yourself and work hard without being told, then Sambo isn't the martial art for you.
- You need to handle pain. Sambo is painful. Getting thrown, taken down, or held can hurt you, but your body will get used to it over time.
- You need to work well with others. Working in a team is important; you'll learn how quickly when training.
- You need to learn quickly. No matter your age, if you have trouble learning something, ask for help from the instructors. They are there to help you.
- You need to move fast when necessary. A lot of the throws and takedowns you learn will happen fast, so you need to be able to react quickly. Otherwise, you will end up on the ground.
- Sambo training could be expensive. You need to be prepared for the costs of uniforms, sparring gear, and training fees.
- Training can take a long time. Becoming good at the sport requires persistence and dedication.
- Sparring and competition can be dangerous, so training well before entering matches is important.
- You need to be ready for disappointment. If you don't win, keep practicing. Most athletes have lost more matches than they've won.
- Depending on where you live, you might need to travel for training. Sambo is practiced worldwide, but there are not many clubs in North America - you might need to travel.

You'll probably have lots of fun. Sambo involves a ton of physical activity and is a great way to get in shape while learning something new. There's nothing better than getting a takedown and pinning your opponent.

Sambo Practice and Training

Once you have all of your gear, it's time to get started with actual Sambo practice.

Sambo is a dynamic martial art involving many different throws and grappling techniques. To start this martial art, focus first on learning the proper technique for each throw or submission hold before applying them during sparring sessions against partners.

Although there is no formal curriculum for Sambo, it's best to start by learning the basic throws and grappling techniques before moving on to more advanced ones. You need to learn a few basic principles to practice correctly so as not to injure yourself or your opponent during training sessions:

- **Grip Fighting** - when you are both trying to gain a good grip on each other to execute a proper throw or submission move.
- **Takedowns** - where one person lifts their opponent and slams them down onto the mat, bringing them down with an arm across their chest while they land hard on the ground.
- **Throws** - where both practitioners are standing, one person throws their opponent down by tripping or pushing them.
- **Ground Fighting** - Once a competitor has been thrown to the ground, the attacker will set themselves in a position for better defense, preparing an attack on their opponent after gaining control of their body.
- **Submissions** - one competitor holds their opponent in a position that puts them at risk of injury, like limbs, joints, or the neck. The defender submits to end the fight.
- **Pinning Techniques** - After gaining control of your partner's body on the ground and immobilizing it with your weight to prevent escape, you can pin them down with these techniques.

How Much Does It Cost to Become a Sambo Master?

The cost of learning Sambo will depend on where you are located and what your instructor charges per lesson.

Sambo instructors are a rare find in regions outside of Russia. Hence, this could be an expensive art to learn. Typically, similar to an MMA gym, a Sambo gym membership could cost you between $100 and $150 per month.

With Sambo, like the other martial arts, some of your fees will go towards equipment and gear you need for training sessions.

Some other factors that will determine costs are:

- **Location:** If you are located in a big city, the prices of lessons can be higher due to demand.
- **Instructor:** Some instructors will charge more than others based on their experience and reputation as an instructor or competitor.
- **Group Class vs. Private Lessons:** Group classes usually cost less per lesson, but the number of sessions required to become proficient at Sambo is more than with private lessons.
- **Size of Training Arena:** If the training area is small, equipment will need to be shared, which can affect costs.

A Typical Sambo Training Session

Observing a training session with your instructor is best to learn more about Sambo.

Typically, there will be warm-up exercises led by the instructor. These exercises are designed to increase your strength and endurance and help you with breathing control before getting into sparring or grappling with a training partner.

After the warm-ups, you will learn the basic throws and takedowns. There are many different throws to learn, each with its benefits.

Once these techniques have been mastered, you can learn more advanced throws and grappling moves.

If possible, it would be best to get at least one sparring partner with experience in Sambo so they can give you feedback on your technique and help correct mistakes.

A training session will typically involve performing techniques repetitively until you develop muscle memory. Some sessions will also be set up to test your skill with a match. Matches are usually with opponents of the same skill levels.

Levels of Sambo Mastery

Sambo training is divided into seven years; each year gets you one step closer to becoming a master. You start as a rookie in the first year, and finally, in the seventh year, a student progresses to become a master.

This chapter outlined the basics of Sambo, a unique martial art. If you are looking for an intense workout that improves your coordination and reflexes while also learning some self-defense techniques in the process, Sambo could be just what you need. After reading this guide on how to get started, you will have a better idea about all the benefits available from learning this particular martial art.

Sambo is a unique art form with a rich philosophy that suits students of all mindsets. You have a Sambo form for those who want to focus on clean throws and also a variant for those wanting more aggressive kicks and strikes.

The chapter has discussed considerations to keep in mind before starting your Sambo journey, the costs involved, equipment and other essentials, and the benefits of becoming a Sambo Student.

Chapter 4: Throwing Techniques

For the most part, Sambo is practiced as a grappling art. Grappling is generally defined as two or more athletes competing against each other to achieve a position of dominance where they can apply submissions to their opponent, render them unconscious, or otherwise defeat them. This chapter focuses on the most basic throws in Sambo. The techniques chosen in this chapter are the most beginner-friendly and effective for grappling with a resisting opponent.

The Basics of Throws

When learning these techniques, understanding the importance of wrestling or grappling, in general, is essential. Grappling is about minimizing damage while maximizing control over the opponent. The most important part of any Sambo throw is the clinch, where the grappler secures a body lock on his opponent to limit his opponent's movement. Once the grappler has established his grip, he can use throwing techniques with proper execution and control over his opponent.

There are different variations when it comes to grappling. Each aims to limit the opponent's movements and attack.[86]

Effective grapplers in Sambo use the clinch whenever possible. It gives them a great advantage in controlling their opponents by limiting their movement and increasing grappling efficiency. For this reason, many throws involve gripping the shoulder or underarm area. However, other grips like waist-locks and hip-locks are also common.

Starting with a clinch gives you the advantage and opportunity to grapple.[87]

From this point, the grappler can execute his throw by placing his foot or leg behind one of his opponent's feet and pushing him off balance. This should be done immediately after gripping the opponent so he has no time to react before being thrown. The most important part of executing a technique is to push your opponent off balance, not lift them. Lifting your opponent can lead to many problems during the throw, such as floating or stalling in the air with no control over your opponent's body. Once you push them off balance and establish superior positioning on top of their body, it is easy to finish the technique by locking a submission hold or executing an elbow or strike on your opponent.

These Sambo throws are very effective in combat sports like MMA and self-defense because they attack the opponent's whole body and require little energy from the grappler, who has already established superior positioning over his opponent. Grappling is more efficient than striking, but it is harder to learn and execute effectively. These throws can be practiced as a warm-up or as a drill at the end of grappling training before transitioning to effective submission holds or strikes.

Understand the importance of proper positioning before attempting these techniques. Against a resisting opponent, it is imperative to use a superior position to gain control over their body so they cannot escape. Proper positioning is key to success when applying submissions or strikes to your opponent after a throw.

Remember, Sambo throws are based on pushing the opponent off balance rather than lifting them. Pushing them off balance gives you more control over his body and makes it harder for your opponent to resist as you transition into an effective strike or submission hold.

Do not try to lift your opponent during these techniques; it gives them a chance to stall and resist, putting you in a worse position than when you started. Attempting a throw with improper positioning is like punching someone while standing on one leg. You cannot generate the force necessary to do it effectively, and you will likely fall over while attempting to execute the technique.

Always look for the clinch when starting a grappling exchange with an opponent. Grappling is more efficient than striking in most cases, but it requires proper positioning before any technique can be applied successfully. Attempting a throw without controlling your opponent's body will lead to losing your positioning and neither of you gaining any advantage.

Training for these throws can be done after grappling exchanges or as a warm-up before transitioning into submission holds or strikes. The throws are meant to be executed quickly, so your muscles must be loose before attempting them.

Basic Sambo Throwing Techniques

1. Takedown

The single most important wrestling technique is the takedown. No grappling exchanges can be won in combat sports without the ability to execute a successful throw. Even when striking techniques are applied, throwing a grappler and establishing a top position on the ground is much easier and more effective.

Executing a Takedown: To execute a simple outside leg trip, you must first establish a good grip on your opponent. Once you have a stronghold over them, block the hips and push the outside leg back with your inside leg. You aim to send your opponent tumbling forward with his legs outstretched as he falls. Follow through by dropping down on top of them and securing a mounted position.

Takedown[88]

If your opponent turns or twists while you attempt this move, follow through and throw him to the ground anyway. It is not as efficient as the proper technique, but you will still be in a better position.

2. Judo Sweep

The basic Judo sweep involves establishing a double underhook grip on your opponent and thrusting your hips back as you pull forward with your shoulders. If executed correctly, this move should send your opponent tumbling over you and crashing to the ground.

Judo Sweep[89]

Attempting a Judo sweep without proper control over your opponent will result in you being thrown and placed on your back. So, establish the underhook grip before attempting this technique.

3. Back Toss

A basic Sambo back toss is executed by grabbing one of your opponent's arms, jumping up, and simultaneously pulling down on their shoulder with your arm. This move leads directly into a mounted position, making it efficient to take control of the fight from your opponent.

A back toss requires proper timing and positioning to be effective, so you need complete control over your opponent before attempting this technique. If you get thrown during the process, you will not be able to follow through and mount your opponent.

4. Knee Pick

The knee pick is the simplest of all Sambo throws. Hook your foot behind one of the opponent's knees and lift, forcing them over onto their back with you on top of them. This technique can only be used when both fighters face each other, so it is not as useful in MMA competitions as other throws.

Knee Pick

Grabbing both legs and pulling with your arms will give you more leverage than attempting to pick up only one leg. However, this move is still quite easy to execute without proper positioning or strength.

5. Back Drop

This technique is very similar to a Judo throw; the difference is that you must plant your feet against the ground before lifting your opponent. Take a wide stance, and bend down low while gripping both of their arms tightly with your head up. This move can be blocked or easily countered if you are not in the proper position, so it should be used as a surprise tactic instead of an ordinary throw.

Back Drop

Once you have pulled your opponent off balance, follow through by throwing them back onto the ground. If their legs are not completely outstretched, you might be forced backward instead of forward. The goal is to slam them down underneath you for a mounted position.

6. Arm Drag

A Sambo arm drag is like a professional wrestling move. You must grip both of your opponent's arms and pull them in one direction while pushing your legs against their legs. Like the knee pick, an arm drag only works when facing each other square-on instead of side-by-side.

An effective arm drag can be difficult to execute without proper control and positioning, but it is an incredibly powerful move. Since the Sambo practitioner is not on top of his opponent during this technique, he can easily transition into another throw or submission hold.

7. Leg Trip

This move requires minimal technical skill, making it an excellent move for beginners. Sweep your foot under one of your opponent's feet and pull it toward your body while pushing against their upper body with both hands. By utilizing this simple technique, you will swiftly bring them down to the ground.

An effective leg trip can be blocked or countered by an opponent who is ready for it, so this technique should be used at close range or as a surprise tactic. A leg trip is usually followed by additional grappling techniques like a clinch throw or half-guard throw that act as follow-ups to the initial throw.

8. Shoulder Roll

The shoulder roll is an advanced technique most effective when combined with other throws and takedowns. Grip your opponent's neck and shoulders, twist and pull in one direction while pushing forward with your hips. The goal is to quickly move from a standing position into a mount or side-mount position once the throw has been executed successfully.

Shoulder Roll

The initial grip must be incredibly tight to prevent the opponent from countering the move. The proper angle and rotation must occur to pull into a mount or side-mount position, so this technique is difficult for beginners.

9. Sprawl

The sprawl is a counter-throwing technique only used when escaping an opponent's takedown. Push your hips back, bend down low, and quickly kick your feet into your opponent's stomach, causing them to fly over you as you drop down to the ground below them.

This technique must be executed quickly for the best chance of success. So, it is best used when your opponent is holding you too close or attempting to knee your stomach. If they complete their takedown, you can fall back into a side-mount position on top of them.

The sprawl is also a defensive technique to prevent yourself from being taken down. It is an important technique used offensively or defensively during Sambo competitions and practice sessions.

10. Throat Push

When your opponent is holding you too close for other throws, the throat push is most effective, but it can also be a surprise move during grappling and wrestling matches. Jam your thumb into the side of the opponent's neck, pushing upwards towards their chin with all five fingers. Once you've pushed hard enough to create an opening between you and the opponent, use your other arm to push them back or off balance.

This move is difficult to execute without proper timing, but it is very useful against opponents unwilling to break the clinch or hold you too tight. It is also a great diversion tactic against opponents who think they have you cornered.

11. Hip Toss

The hip toss is a basic throwing technique effective against larger, stronger, or heavier opponents. Bend over and latch onto the opponent's shoulders with both arms to lift them from the ground. Once you've secured your grip, thrust your hips forward, forcing them upward and forward over your shoulder.

This technique can end in various ways, including landing in an immediate side-mount position or back-mount position, depending on where you throw your opponent. Since this move is so basic, it's an easy technique for beginners to get accustomed to Sambo quickly. Like the leg trip, it is very effective when used at close range. It can only be blocked or countered by an opponent who is aware of what you are attempting.

12. Suplex

The suplex is a basic move that can be executed in several ways depending on your preferences and the wrestling style you compete under. Pull your opponent up, lock your hands behind their head, and then fall backward, lifting them off the ground. It can also be executed by gripping lower on the torso and lifting them straight into the air.

Suplex

The suplex is regarded as a high-skill move requiring significant strength, balance, agility, and coordination to perform effectively. It is a great technique for beginners to practice against larger opponents, but it requires significant skill and training to execute properly.

13. Knee Pull

The knee pull is a beginner-friendly technique to stop opponents from completing their takedowns. Grip your opponent's torso or shoulder, and quickly drop down into a squatting position before sliding one of your knees between their legs. When in this position, stand and lock your hands behind their back.

This technique is used to sweep an opponent off their feet or trip them up extremely quickly. It's commonly used as a counter move to leg trips, but it can also be used if you are being held against the ropes by your opponent during wrestling matches.

14. Drop Toe Hold

The drop toe hold is another basic technique to take an opponent off their feet. Stand in front of your opponent and trap one or both of their legs between your thighs. Grab them around the back of the head with both arms. In this position, lean forward while keeping a tight grip on their head and shoulders.

This move can take your opponent down in several ways, depending on how you've caught them by the shoulders. If they are holding onto the back of your body or legs, trap one of their arms behind their back while turning around, facing away from them.

If they are holding onto your hips or lower thighs, trap their arms behind you while falling to the tatami. This move is great for beginners because it's easy to learn and simple to execute. It also provides incredible control over your opponent when executed against larger, stronger opponents.

15. Four-Point Takedown

The four-point takedown is a versatile technique to ground opponents quickly. Drop down into a squatting position next to one of your opponent's legs. Wrap your arm around the back of their knee. Simultaneously grip the inside of their opposite thigh with your other hand. Stand and toss or sweep them onto their back.

This technique is regarded as a high-skill maneuver requiring much strength and training to master, but it's an excellent technique for beginners to get used to the Sambo basics. It can be countered with some effort by experienced opponents, but they will have difficulty stopping it from being executed properly.

There are many different Sambo throwing techniques to take your opponent off their feet. These moves are most often used in real-life situations when grappling against an opponent to avoid being struck or taken hostage. Beginners must practice with a partner before attempting these techniques in competition, but they can provide a significant advantage over larger, stronger opponents. Once you get the hang of them, incorporate a few into your training routine while getting used to Sambo matches. The more experience you have with these moves, the easier they will be to execute in a real-life scenario.

Chapter 5: Grip Techniques

Sambo is a Russian martial art that focuses on grappling and striking. Sambo provides an excellent background for anyone interested in MMA or self-defense.

One of the best aspects of Sambo is its extensive use of different grip fighting techniques. This chapter provides an overview of what a practitioner must know before effectively using Sambo's gripping system. Included are some tips on how to get started learning about gripping.

Sambo Grip Techniques Overview

Sambo has several grip fighting methods. Students don't have to learn all these grips. Rather, they need to fully understand their capabilities and be aware of their limitations.

The first grip fighting type in Sambo is called Shime Waza; this is a grappling resource in Judo and related arts. It involves using any limbs and body parts, isolating an arm or leg, and applying pressure to deny that limb's use or cause damage. An example of Shime Waza would be the standard armbar from mount. However, instead of using the legs to elevate the opponent's hips and create space, the head is used as the third point of contact.

The second grip fighting type is called Kansetsu Waza, also used in Judo and related arts like catch wrestling and Brazilian Jiu-jitsu. It involves isolating the opponent's arms and legs, pinning them to the ground, and controlling them to create an attack with maximum efficiency. An example of Kansetsu Waza is heel hook submissions from side control or leg locking an opponent who is standing.

The third grip fighting type in Sambo is called submission wrestling. This grappling is a blend of Shime Waza and Kansetsu Waza. Submission wrestling involves arm locks, leg locks, chokes, and pins to subdue an opponent or force them to forfeit due to injury. It is called "submission wrestling" because it doesn't feature groundwork or pinning methods.

The fourth grip fighting type in Sambo is called Combat Grip Wrestling (CGW). This grappling involves life-and-death struggles with an opponent where there are no rules, and the only way to win is by applying a submission.

Now that you have a frame of reference for the four different grip fighting types in Sambo, let's look at some basic gripping methods from each type.

Sambo Basic Gripping Methods

In Sambo, there are several basic gripping methods from which a practitioner can move on to more complex ones.

667

Georgian Grip

The first gripping method is the "Georgian Grip." Place your forward arm over the opponent's back and grab the belt or gi with your hand. The opponent's head is tucked under your armpit, and you lean onto their body for extra weight. The other hand grabs the opponent's sleeve. Various throws can be executed from this position.

Georgian Grip

Figure-Four Grip

Figure-Four Grip

The second gripping method is called the "Figure-Four Grip." To achieve this gripping method, grab an opponent's wrist on one side with your hand, grabbing their opposite elbow with your other hand. You control the arm by bending it at the elbow and pulling it toward you.

Figure-Four Reverse Grip

Figure-Four Reverse Grip

The third gripping method is called "Figure-Four Reverse Grip," To achieve this gripping method, grab an opponent's wrist on one side with your hand while grabbing their opposite elbow with your other hand. You control the arm by bending it at the elbow and pushing it away from you.

Turtling

Turtling

The fourth gripping method is called "Turtling" because the arms are used to cover the head, neck, and face. Wrestlers commonly use this grip with the over-under grip and during standup grappling exchanges. Pull your opponent's arms towards you while pushing your head into their chest. This allows you to pivot around them and take their back.

Combat Sambo Grip Techniques

Combat Sambo combines the four basic grappling methods with striking techniques to create an explosive and effective style. Stylistically, Combat Sambo resembles Mixed Martial Arts (MMA) for a good reason. The rules of Sambo competitions allow striking on the ground, and an opponent can win by submission or technical knockout.

Head and Arm Throw

Head and Arm Throw

The first grappling technique is called the "Head and Arm Throw" because the arm controls your opponent's head while you use your opposite leg to trip them. Grab an opponent's head with your hand and pull it towards you, planting your foot on their hip. Drive the side of their face into the mat and push down on their shoulder until they submit or fall over unconscious.

Russian Twist

The second grappling technique is called the "Russian Twist" because it resembles a submission you might see in MMA. Grab an opponent's arms while they stand and pull them toward you while dropping down into a prone position. Transition into a seated guard position and loop your legs around their head. Roll them onto their back or side, forcing them to submit from the pain of a joint lock.

Reverse Head and Arm Choke

The third grappling technique is called the "Reverse Head and Arm Choke." You pull an opponent's arm towards their neck while pulling on their head with your

670

opposite hand. Grab an opponent's wrist using the inside of your arm and place it against the front of their shoulder. Loop your arm around their head and hold them in a headlock before pulling on both arms until they submit.

Turtle Guard Sweep

Turtle Guard Sweep

The "Turtle Guard Sweep" is the final grappling technique in Combat Sambo. This technique got its name because it resembles a turtle retreating into its shell. Grab an opponent's arms while they stand and pull them towards you as you drop down onto your back. Wrap your legs around their head and pull them to the side until they fall over or submit. This is not an easy technique but can be devastating if it lands successfully; end your opponent's winning streak with the Turtle Guard Sweep.

Leg Grips

When grappling in a Combat Sambo match, there is a good chance your opponent will attempt to apply these grips to your leg in an attempt to throw you. Here are some of the most common leg grips:

Triangle Grip

The triangle grip is one of the easiest ways for grapplers to pull a leg towards themself to execute a sweeping or throwing technique. Grab hold of the opponent's ankle and thigh before pulling the leg towards you. If you managed to pull them off-balance enough, you could execute a sweep while continuing with an attack to catch them off guard.

Single-Leg Slicing Grip

The single-leg slicing grip is exactly what it sounds like. Grab hold of an opponent's ankle and place the back of your neck against their knee before pulling them towards you. If they try to escape by stepping away from you, use this opportunity to execute a sweep or throw, allowing you to take control of the match.

Double Leg Grip

The double-leg grip is similar to the single-leg slicing grip; only you to control both of your opponent's legs. Grab hold of both ankles, placing the back of your neck against their knees before pulling them towards you. If they try to escape by stepping away from you, use this opportunity to execute a sweep or throw, allowing you to take control of the match.

Common BJJ and Wrestling Grips

When grappling in a Sambo match, there is a good chance you will encounter grips used by Brazilian Jiu-Jitsu or wrestling. Here are some of the most common grips your opponent will attempt:

Over-Under Grip

The over-under grip is one of the most common grips in Brazilian Jiu-Jitsu. Grab the opponent's wrist while simultaneously grabbing their opposite shoulder. Pull the opponent towards you until they are unable to move any closer.

Double Lapel Grip

The double lapel grip is another commonly used grip in Judo, Brazilian Jiu-Jitsu, and Wrestling. Grab the lapels of the opponent's gi and pull them toward you, shutting the distance between you. You will be in a position to break the opponent's posture and execute several throws.

Cross-Grip (or Under-Under Grip)

The cross grip is more difficult to apply than most grips but can be extremely effective if properly applied by an experienced grappler. Standing to the opponent's side, grab your opponent's wrist with one hand while reaching across their back onto their opposite shoulder. From there, pull them towards you until they are unable to move any closer.

Pendulum Grip (or Underhook)

The pendulum grip is similar to the over-under grip; the only difference is that your arms will be crossed over your opponent's shoulders. Grab one of your opponent's arms with both hands before pulling them towards you until they are unable to move any closer.

Lapel Grip with a Knee-In

The lapel with a knee-in is one of the most common grips used by Brazilian Jiu-Jitsu and Wrestling fighters. Grab your opponent's gi at the hips and simultaneously pull them toward you until they are unable to move any closer.

Other Gripping Techniques and Throws

Countless other grips and throwing techniques are used in Sambo competition, but they require a certain skill and dexterity level to pull off successfully. However, there are a few gripping techniques and throws that beginners can use to gain an advantage over their opponents:

Flying Armbar

Flying Armbar

The flying armbar is one of the best throws you can learn to use in a Sambo competition. Grab your opponent's right arm with both hands before pulling them towards you. Place a foot on their hip before jumping up in the air and simultaneously pulling down on their arm.

Leg Throw

This throw is extremely effective against opponents who like to grab onto your legs while fighting for control of the match. Pull your opponent towards you while sweeping one of their legs up and around. Then pull them towards you before moving your hips away from them to complete the throw.

Russian Hook-Sleeve Takedown

This takedown technique is used when your opponent manages to grab onto both of your sleeves at once, leaving you with no way to gain control over their waist or upper body. Pull your opponent towards you while pushing both of their sleeves in the opposite direction. From there, hook one of their legs with your leg before pulling them over and onto the ground establishing a pin.

Gripping for Back Control

This grip can be used when your opponent manages to get behind you, preventing you from taking control over any part of their body or even making contact with your arms or legs. Bring one arm over toward your opponent's back before grabbing underneath their waist. From there, slide their arm down across your chest, bringing it up to their neck and securing it against you for a choke or pin.

Sleeve Takedown from Standing

This move is used when your opponent reaches out and grabs your sleeves without having any control over your waist or upper body. It is a very common move in competition, but it can be avoided by turning away from it. Reach out to your opponent's grabbing arm and pull them towards you until they are unable to move any closer. Take their sleeve with the opposite arm and pull them down to the ground for a pin.

Scissor Takedown Method 1

The scissor takedown is one of the most commonly used throws in Sambo, but it can be avoided by keeping your distance from your opponent or positioning yourself behind them. Pull your opponent toward you by grabbing their sleeve and placing one of your legs in front of theirs. Scissor-kick your leg around them before bringing them down to the ground for a pin.

Scissor Takedown Method 2

This version of the scissor takedown can be used when your opponent stands in front of you with their calves against the back of your thighs, preventing you from gaining control over them using other methods. Pull your opponent toward you by grabbing their sleeves and placing both your feet on top of theirs. Scissor-kick your legs around them until they are unable to move anymore. Bring one of their legs over and push down on it with both of yours before bringing their torso down across your other leg for a pin.

Belt Grip Takedown Method 1

This first version of the belt grip takedown is used when your opponent reaches out and grabs the belt on the waist of your pants, preventing you from taking control of them from any other position. Place one hand onto their chest while grabbing onto their belt with the other arm and pull them down to the ground for a pin.

Belt Grip Takedown Method 2

This second version of the belt grip takedown can be used when your opponent manages to get hold of both your sleeves, preventing you from taking control over their upper body. Place one hand on their chest. With the other arm, grab the opposite side of their waist and pull them down to the ground for a pin.

Sambo wrestlers and submission grapplers can benefit from knowing how to effectively grip their opponents to make the most of every move they attempt. A competitor uses many techniques to grip and hold down an opponent. However, this chapter focuses on beginner-friendly takedown techniques to execute against opponents who have yet to develop an effective defense. These takedown techniques can also gain a significant advantage against opponents who are not expecting them, increasing their effectiveness. Sambo takedown techniques can be added to any BJJ or Wrestling game to improve your chances of successfully executing them against experienced opponents.

Chapter 6: Self-Defense in Sambo

If you want to take up any martial art, you must always know that mastering self-defense is an essential part of the process. It is especially true for Sambo, which we already know is a combat system providing weaponless self-defense tactics.

No one can depend solely on their ability to go on full-blown offense, throwing punches, kicks, joint locks, and whatever else they can think of. Practitioners can never succeed without mastering defense techniques, no matter how good or strong a wrestler or fighter is.

Learning self-defense proves beneficial even when you're not on the mat. Not only will you be able to skillfully and efficiently defend yourself against potential attackers, but learning self-defense also enhances your emotional, cognitive, and physical well-being in a plethora of ways.

Part of the self-defense learning process requires you to trust yourself and your abilities. The techniques you learn will grant you a great deal of awareness of your mind and body, which can push you to reach the limits you otherwise thought unreachable. You will also experience overall health improvements. These aspects will give you a confidence boost, automatically ameliorating other areas of your life in the process. Not only does great self-confidence boost your performance in the fighting ring, but it also helps you get that job promotion you know you deserve.

Every practitioner knows the key to mastering self-defense is discipline. It comes as no surprise that the level of discipline determines if we will succeed in any sport or area of life. When you're learning self-defense, you learn to avoid, withstand, and move on from attacks physically, mentally, and emotionally; this is generally a very useful skill in life. While life may not throw physical punches at us, it surely does have its fair share of obstacles.

Self-defense training also helps students to acquire the ability to set small and large goals and take the steps necessary to achieve them. Self-defense tactics are not easy to master. However, the process and how it's taught helps you learn to set goals for yourself and reach them even when they seem impossible. Everyone knows that success in life can't be achieved if you don't have solid goals.

When you're learning self-defense, it is never only about the current moment. Defense techniques encompass centuries of values, skills, and traditions. Think about everything an inclusive and comprehensive sport like Sambo has to offer. Knowing this, learning the skills doesn't only mean obtaining sufficient knowledge to execute them. However, the duty to constructively, properly, and responsibly use the skills is automatically passed on to you.

This chapter provides several tips on defending yourself against many of the throws discussed throughout the previous chapter. It also covers a few defense tactics for the submissions explained in the following chapters. You will also learn to defend yourself tactfully against someone with a weapon, including a step-by-step guide.

Sambo and Self-Defense

Sambo provides the most efficient and effective self-defense techniques among Karate, Judo, Boxing, and Jujitsu. Not only because it is a collection of their best moves but because it was designed to revolve around real-life problems, as well as struggles in combat.

Even if not on the battleground, law enforcement personnel require self-defense knowledge and skills to complete basic missions, like bringing criminals in for interrogation. Meanwhile, in combat and fights, individuals need an advantage over their opponents; for the Russian soldiers, Sambo offered that essential advantage.

Ultimately, Sambo is a combat system developed to purposefully gather only the best elements, moves, punches, submissions, kicks, sweeps, throws, trips, armbars, chokes, holds, and leg bars from various martial arts systems. Anything perceived as substandard was immediately discarded from this perfected system.

Real-Life Application

Sambo was developed for practitioners who needed to react to ever-changing situations immediately. It was for anyone having to incapacitate an opponent with nothing but the potential tools they already had, their hands, a chair, or a shovel. The system is developed to help its practitioners quickly disarm their opponents to minimize danger and make the mission as easy as possible. The purpose is to end a fight quickly, once and for all.

Although it was originally designed for Soviet soldiers, Sambo has become one of the best ways for the average individual to protect themselves and their families from the adversities of the modern-day world. Unfortunately, tragic incidents, such as robberies, assaults, and rape, have become quite common today. Even more terrifying is the majority of attackers have weapons. So, learning self-defense techniques encompassing disarming strategies is necessary to guarantee safety.

With regulated competition, you know what to expect. Participants know which moves and elements are allowed, the time allotted (if any), and are aware of everything off-limits. However, no one knows what the enemy has in store in real-life struggles. Sambo teaches its practitioners how to act strategically in numerous situations, what to use against one or more opponent(s), and how to act if they're armed.

Defense Advantage

You might not recognize this unless you see it for yourself. Although, it's still worth mentioning that a perfectly executed Sambo move can incapacitate the adversary; this particularly applies to opponents unskilled in properly breaking falls. At this point, you can expect a fight to end because the human brain is not very receptive to losing touch with solid ground or a reference point. If the opponent doesn't position themselves correctly for the fall, their entire body will absorb the shock or energy. When you factor in the increased acceleration produced by leverage, expect the results to be disastrous.

As someone well-versed in Sambo self-defense, this gives you an incredible advantage. First, learning the proper falling techniques helps prevent this from happening to you. Moreover, if your opponent is on the receiving end, you can use their self-defense deficiencies against them, as mentioned previously.

Many people think learning Sambo is about learning leg bars and seizing the opportunity to get in a few throws. However, this is not nearly enough. Sambo is an entire system; those who have never practiced it think it is all about grappling and throwing. An avid Sambo practitioner knows that the proper execution of Sambo techniques requires extensive physical preparation and an understanding of leverage and the fundamental laws of physics.

Unique Execution

Sambo teaches you execution techniques for the most stressful and difficult situations. It teaches you confidence and helps you incorporate it into your technique along with speed; this is where Sambo differs from other fighting techniques. People think Judo and Sambo are similar, and the practitioners of either discipline can do both. Yet, few realize that Sambo wrestlers can make incredible Judokos, whereas the opposite isn't necessarily true.

This is why choosing the right Sambo coach is crucial. One rule to always go by would be choosing an instructor who is dedicated and committed to Sambo instead of someone who is a 3-time Aikido championship and a black belt Judo holder. Their success in other fighting styles doesn't mean that they excel in Sambo.

You don't have to dedicate your life to Sambo or practice as a competitive sport to become successful. You know you are a great player when you find all you have learned useful and can easily implement it into your everyday life. Think of Sambo as one extra survival skill or a toolbox that can perhaps save your life.

Defense Essentials

The best thing about Sambo is its collection of most combat styles. This aspect makes its practitioners well-prepared for various fighting styles without having to take up different fighting techniques separately.

Grip-Breaking Techniques

1. Technique 1

To break free from an opponent's grip, grab their sleeve with a two-on-one grip. Push their hand at a 45-degree angle away from your gi. This movement should be done forcefully and quickly while maintaining a good posture. Make sure to move your body in the hand's opposite direction. At this point, their grip should be loosened. Don't loosen your grip and continue to push their hand away from your body.

2. Technique 2

If the sleeve on your power hand is the one under your opponent's grip, bend your arm at the elbow. The slack on your sleeve is released as soon as you bring your thumb up to your shoulder. Then, lift your elbow, and yank your arm free from them and toward your back. You will be free from your opponent's grip as you pull your arm away.

3. Technique 3

Another way to free your power hand is by bending your arm at the elbow. Bring your thumb to your shoulder to remove the slack from your sleeve. Then, move your thumb, in a circular movement, toward the adversary's wrist and bring your thumb up to your ear. Forcefully and quickly pull away from your opponent.

4. Technique 4

A third way to free your power hand is by arching your hand to the back and grabbing the adversary's wrist. Straighten and round your back as you push down on their wrist to release the grip. Push their wrist as far away as possible.

5. Technique 5

If the sleeve of your lead hand is under the opponent's grip, place your power hand on top of their wrist and straighten your arm as you push your power hand downward. Their power hand should catch on their sleeve arm to release the grip.

Takedown Defense

1. Footwork

Prevention is better than cure. If the adversary can't touch you, they can't take you down. Everyone knows that great footwork is the essence of self-defense. For someone to take their opponent down, they must be within a certain range. By circling, using lateral movement, and being evasive, you can prevent takedowns from happening.

- Do not remain flat-footed
- Don't stop moving your feet
- Stay mindful of your low kicks, as they can throw you off balance

- Try to kick and punch as you remain in motion

2. Pummeling

If the takedown begins from the clinch, you will probably have to resort to pummeling. It is a common wrestling technique that helps you keep the opponent from throwing underhooks. If they manage to do so, they'd have plenty of leverage. Your goal is to pummel for underhooks, get in double underhooks, and finally disengage. In this case, you can perform a takedown.

3. Sprawls

Sprawling is an effective way to defend yourself against single and double-leg takedowns. You can use sprawls to prevent the adversary from grabbing you. It also helps prepare you for back attacks.

When the attacker approaches for a low takedown, push down on their neck, head, or shoulder. As you do, drop your legs and hips behind you. At that moment, your body weight should be below them. Aim for a headlock or choke in this position, or circle them to take their back.

4. Chokes

Although they are not permitted in several Sambo subtypes, you can use chokes to protect yourself against a hostile attack. But this is a risky strategy. However, it can end a fight immediately. You can go for a ninja, Peruvian, or Guillotine choke.

5. Throw Your Knee

You can throw your knee to stop an opponent from taking you down. However, in this defense strategy, timing is key. Either leg can be used to catch the opponent off guard. You'll have a moment before they decide to attempt another takedown.

Striking Defense

1. The Low Roundhouse Kick

Low Roundhouse Kick

If you are not very well-trained, do not aim for above the knee. So, this is when a low roundhouse kick comes in handy. If your arms are struggling, move your dominant leg back a good distance to get the maximum power. Make sure you're in a stable, balanced position and rotate your non-dominant leg's foot outward while moving your shoulders in the same direction. Then, quickly use your dominant leg to kick the opponent. However, ensure to raise your knee as high as possible before extending your leg. Use the upper back of your foot, rather than the side, to kick the internal or external side of your opponent's knee. If you hit the right spot, they will suffer excruciating pain and will not be able to resume the attack.

2. The Open Palm Strike

Open Palm Strike

Avoid using your knuckles during a fight if you are unsure of your abilities. Instead, use the open palm strike. Pay attention to the moment when your opponent leaves their face unguarded. Bend your fingers' upper phalanges, exposing your palm, and direct all your strength to the base of your palm. The ideal spot to target the blow would be their nose or chin. If you target their chin, you must blow it from the bottom upward.

3. The Ram-Elbow Strike

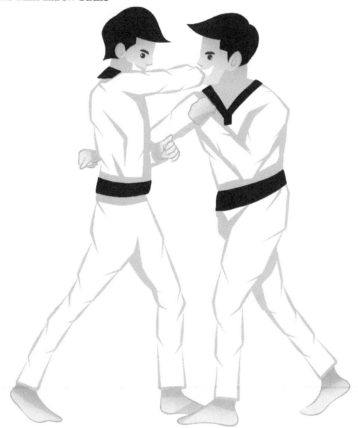

Ram Elbow Strike

Naturally, we are conditioned to protect our heads during an attack. If you're torn between covering your head and fighting for your life, go for the ram-elbow strike. If the opponent is going for your head, directing punches toward it, you must ensure your head is fully covered with your arms. Your elbows should be at the front, parted slightly to allow you to see. All your strength must be concentrated at your elbows, striking your opponent like a ram. Target the blows at the upper arm's inner side or the nose. If you hit the right areas with the right amount of force, the opponent will be in great pain, granting you time to plan your next move.

Submission Defense

Avoiding it altogether is the best way to deal with a submission move. Therefore, timing is crucial. It doesn't matter if you're new to Sambo or have mastered self-defense tactics for years. How you act right before the opponent locks in a submission determines if you will tap or not. Don't wait until a submission is locked to start defending yourself, as this should be your last line of defense.

When you start practicing the sport, you will discover several things to consider before going in for a submission move. You must ensure you have the right grips, get the right angle, and, most importantly, open their defenses. This gives you the time and opportunity to act.

1. Kill the Angle

Several submission attacks require the opponent to get into a specific angle. For instance, if they're aiming for a triangle, being square to you makes it harder for them to complete the attack because the pressure on the neck will be faulty. It is the case with leg locks, armbars, chokes, and almost all the other submissions. If you can throw them off the angle before they attack, you're on the safe side.

2. Center Line Control

You must remember that you're at a submission risk each time you cross the center of your or your opponent's body. For instance, for opponents to execute armbars, your arm must be in their body's center. Controlling your centerline will keep you safe.

3. Lines of Defense

There are various lines of defense you can utilize. The first ones happen before the submission is executed, like killing the angle and controlling the centerline. You can also defend yourself during the submission, which requires you to hide your arms in the case of an armbar attack. Your last line of defense is when you're in submission, right before you are forced to tap. This is when you can execute an armbar escape or a hitchhiker. You can pull the opponent's knee if you're in a kneebar submission.

Defense against Weapon Attacks

Make sure the opponent isn't looking, or don't make any sudden movements if they're looking or aiming at you.

1. Only attack if they're 5 to 10 feet away from you.
2. Duck out of the barrel's sight and move to the exterior side of the gun.
3. Whatever you do, don't move closer to the attacker's chest.
4. Use your dominant hand to chop down or strike the opponent's wrist to disarm them. You can also punch the outside of their wrist.
5. The chances are that the gun will fly out of their hand. In this case, quickly reach for it or push it as far away as possible.
6. If they still have the gun, quickly grab their wrist to stop them from shooting you. Grip their arm as strongly as possible.
7. Pull their armed wrist away and down to the ground. Move it in a circular motion to throw them off balance
8. Finally, twist their arm. They will probably drop the gun. If not, you can easily pull it away.

Similar to when you're in offense mode, you need intense movement to excel in self-defense. While it looks like you're learning just one fighting discipline or style, your approach differs widely depending on which end of the fight you're on. With self-defense comes an entirely different fitness routine your body will surely benefit from. You'll also be able to keep yourself safe during unfortunate situations.

Chapter 7: Offensive Rolls and Strikes

Rolls and strikes in the Sambo arsenal are crucial. Strikes are a very efficient way to put an opponent on the defensive and can be used as a setup for a high-scoring throw or takedown attempt. When thrown from standing, strikes also allow you to keep your body close to your opponent, making it difficult for them to defend against throws or trips you might attempt.

On the other hand, rolls are an offensive technique. Rolling is similar to tumbling. However, some additional rules in Sambo prevent flips and twists from being thrown at full strength. For example, if you want to perform a forward roll in Sambo, you must maintain contact with the mat with at least one of your shoulders. Also, as with takedowns, the direction of your roll is guided by the shoulder that makes first contact with the mat.

This chapter breaks down some fundamentals of Sambo rolling and shows you a few variations that can be used as an offensive technique. There are more complex rolls with plenty of potential for variation, which is discussed later in the book.

The Basics of Rolls

Before we can discuss the different variations of rolls, it's important to understand the basic mechanics of a roll. There are two ways for a competitor to perform a forward roll in Sambo:

- Lead with your head and shoulder
- Lead with your hips and keep your legs behind you

The first option is generally safer as it protects your head from an opponent kicking or kneeing you in the face. However, it has its disadvantages. If you do not turn your head while rolling, you will end up upside-down and completely vulnerable to attacks.

You must be familiar with the switch-stance transition concept to be able to lead with either shoulder when performing a forward roll in Sambo. A switch-stance transition is when you switch your dominant stance while moving in the opposite direction. It is commonly seen in most martial arts with strikes, like punching or kicking, as the strike is thrown from one stance but lands in another.

Leading with your hips and keeping your legs behind you is slightly more complex, but it's generally considered the best option for a forward roll in Sambo. It provides great momentum going into the roll and is good protection from strikes and takedowns from your opponent. Even if you lose contact with the opponent while performing this roll, you are still protected by your legs.

The most popular roll in Sambo is the forward roll. It is used to get behind your opponent quickly without running, which is crucial for any approach that requires attacking from a standing position. Here are a few points when performing a forward roll:

- Keep your back straight and extend your legs as far as possible.
- As soon as you start rolling, push off the mat with your hands and thrust your hips upward.
- Roll as far as possible, keeping your back straight the entire time.
- Keep rolling until you make contact with your opponent or reach a safe distance from him.

Other Offensive Rolls in Sambo

The Backward Roll

Backward Roll

The backward roll is not often used in Sambo, but it is still important to learn and master. For example, if you are near the edge of the mat during a match getting behind your opponent using a backward roll can be very useful if combined with an aggressive standup game. Here are some key points to know when performing this technique:

- Keep your legs and arms straight but not locked out.
- During the backward roll, keep your head tucked in and faced away from your opponent.
- If you need to change direction or stop the roll before it is finished, quickly plant both hands onto the mat and use them to redirect yourself.

As with forwarding rolls, backward rolls are started by pushing off the mat with your hands. However, you must push yourself away from your opponent instead of toward him. Once you complete the roll and want to return to a standing position, use both arms to push yourself up.

When throwing a strike during an offensive roll, remember it might take considerable time to complete your roll and return to a neutral position. Depending on the situation, this could be dangerous since it allows your opponent ample time to capitalize on your mistake.

The Head Snap Roll

When thrown from a standing position, this is one of the most popular rolls in Sambo. Its main purpose is to get behind your opponent while simultaneously moving him back, setting you up nicely for whatever follow-up technique you choose. Here are some key points to remember when throwing a head snap roll:

- Keep your legs bent and maintain tension on your legs and arms.
- As with other rolls, make sure the first contact you make with the mat is a shoulder strike.

- Upon making an impact on the mat, immediately thrust both legs forward and up as high as possible to knock your opponent back.

The Sideways Head Snap Roll

This variation of the head snap roll is very useful if you want to strike your opponent with your shoulder but also need to move him slightly away from you. Since it starts and finishes in a different position than the original head snap, it can also move your opponent sideways if necessary. Here are some key points when throwing this variation:

- Once again, keep your legs bent and maintain tension throughout the roll.
- Thrust both legs forward while simultaneously pulling your head back with all your might.
- Aim to put your shoulder squarely on the mat, so it becomes the first point of contact.
- Once the shoulder strike is made on the mat, thrust your legs forward and up to knock your opponent back.

The Knee Slider Roll

This Sambo roll is similar to a bicycle or kip-up because it uses the momentum from the legs while pushing off the mat to return to a standing position. The knee slider roll is useful because it does not waste time getting you back up again, allowing you to turn the momentum of the match in your favor quickly. Here are some key points when throwing this variation:

- Make sure your feet stay as close as possible to the mat during the roll.
- Kick your legs out and up as soon as possible, as if you are trying to sit on a chair directly behind you.
- Once your back touches the mat, immediately thrust both legs forward so that they help push you off it.

The Fireman Roll

This is another variation of the Sambo roll used to strike your opponent with your shoulder. It is very similar to the original head snap, but instead of thrusting both legs forward, kick them out and immediately bring them back in. This is useful if you need to move slightly away from your opponent after the roll. Here are some key points when throwing this variation:

- Once again, maintain tension in your legs throughout the roll.
- Keep your feet as close to the mat as possible until they kick out and return to it.
- Thrust both your legs forward once you hit the mat to knock your opponent back.

The Cross-Knee Head Snap Roll

There are so many variations of the head snap roll that it would be nearly impossible to list them all. However, this cross-knee head snap roll is unique because you tuck your knee up so you can grab onto it once you hit the mat. It is useful if you need to transition from one dominant position into another on the ground to regain dominance. Here are some key points when throwing this variation:

- Bring your leg up, so it's parallel to the floor once you hit the mat.
- When you make contact with the mat, use both hands to grab onto your knee right above the kneecap.
- Thrust both legs forward to help force your opponent down once you begin to stand up.

The Ankle Pick Head Snap Roll

Another great variation of the head snap roll is this ankle pick variation that allows you to maintain dominance while transitioning into a dominant position. This roll is very useful if your opponent tries to put his leg down as you attempt to stand up from the mat. Here are some key points when throwing this variation:

- Keep a wide base with both hands and feet to maintain balance throughout the roll.
- As soon as your head snaps back, grab onto your opponent's ankle with one hand.
- Use your other hand to prevent your opponent from using his hands to stand (which will probably be in a defensive position).
- Immediately after grabbing the ankle, use both hands and feet to stand.

The Single-Leg Body Hook Head Snap Roll

This is another variation of the head snap roll that uses only one leg to keep you balanced throughout the entire roll. It is particularly useful if your body feels far away from your opponent's leg, making it difficult to grab his ankle with both hands. Here are some key points when throwing this variation:

- Maintain as much balance as possible on one leg throughout the roll.
- Keep your other knee bent and ready to hit the mat hard.
- Use both hands to grab your opponent's ankle once you hit the mat.
- Roll back so your head snaps away from him, and immediately use both hands and one foot to stand up into a dominant position.

Sambo Strikes

Sambo is a full-contact martial art allowing you to use submissions, throws, takedowns, and strikes to knock out an opponent completely. The best part about Sambo strikes is that they are very simple yet effective. Here are some of the most popular Sambo strike techniques you should know:

The Jab

The Jab

In Sambo, a jab is a straight punch supported by your front leg. In BJJ, it's a front snap kick since your leg usually bends at the knee to get more power on your strike. A proper Sambo jab can be thrown at long or medium distances, meaning you can throw it while standing or on the ground. Here are some key points when throwing this variation:

- Bring your left shoulder back slightly to get more power on your punch.
- Lift your front leg just enough so that it's parallel to the floor for better balance.
- Your front foot should be turned outward slightly (referred to as Franklin Stance).

The Cross

The cross is simply a straight right punch, but it's thrown with your rear leg instead of your front leg, like in the jab. Since this one is thrown at a long distance, it can only be used on the ground. Here are some key points when throwing this variation:

- Follow through with your punch so your shoulder ends up in front of you.
- Your front foot should be turned inward slightly for better balance.
- Use your rear leg to lift your front leg just enough so it's parallel to the ground.

The Hooks

A hook is a roundhouse kick that can come from the inside or outside of your body. For example, if you throw an inside hook, your body should be turned so that your front leg is closer to the target. Alternatively, if you throw an outside hook, your body should be turned so that your front leg is further away from the target. Here are some key points when throwing this variation:

- Keep your leg as close to the ground as possible so that you can pull it back quickly if needed.
- Throw your hook with the ball of your foot to generate more power.
- Rotate your entire body with this kick for better balance.

The Knee Strike

Knee Strike

The knee strike is a straight punch with your knee instead of your hand. This strike can be extremely effective, especially on the ground. Here are some key points when throwing this variation:

- Keep your knee bent while turning your body slightly to make yourself a smaller target.
- Lean forward slightly so you can hit your opponent with the top of your knee instead of the bottom part.
- Use your rear leg to lift your front leg just enough so that it's parallel to the ground.

The Ax Kick

An ax kick is a roundhouse kick with your rear leg. This strike can be thrown at long or medium distances, so it can only be used on the ground or standing. Here are some key points when throwing this variation:

- Hold your front leg just enough to be off the ground at a 45-degree angle.
- Keep your rear leg bent and lift the front of your foot so you can strike with the ball of your foot.
- Lean back slightly so your weight is on your rear leg instead of the front leg to generate more power.

Ax Kick

The Uppercut

An uppercut is a straight punch thrown at close range that comes up from below. You can throw a punch at your opponent's ribs, chin, or abdomen (if you want to put him away fast). Here are some key points when throwing this variation:

- Keep your knees bent for better balance.
- Tuck your chin to reduce the chances of getting hit.
- Keep your hands up for protection.

The Front Kick

A front kick is a push kick with your front leg. The ball of your foot is used to generate more power. This strike can only be thrown when standing since it requires good balance and flexibility in the front leg. Here are some key points when throwing this variation:

- Keep your hands up to protect yourself while turning your body slightly to make yourself a smaller target.
- Keep your hands up while kicking with the ball of your foot for extra balance.
- Bend your front leg slightly for better balance.

Sambo is a Russian martial art and combat sport where a fighter uses a combination of grappling and striking attacks to defeat an opponent. Several tactics, including throws, locks, strikes, and joint-breaking maneuvers, are used to set up an arm or leg of a submission technique. You need good flexibility in the ipsilateral hip, knee, and ankle areas to perform forward rolls effectively. Additionally, forward rolls can be used from several positions on the ground, like when flat on your back or sitting up. If you want to add variation to one of the strikes explained above, you can use a combination of taekwondo roundhouse kicks. These attacks are extremely efficient and stylish. Good luck.

Chapter 8: Upper Body Submissions

Submissions play a critical role in Sambo since they subdue your opponent in the game. Different submission techniques can be applied to exert pressure and pain on the opponent to make them submit or surrender. This chapter focuses on neck cranks, chokes, and arm submissions. It also explains how to apply each submission and why it is effective.

List of BJJ Submissions

Submissions constitute a key component of Brazilian Jiu-Jitsu (BJJ) and provide an instant feeling of accomplishment and victory to those who subdue their opponents. The art of submission is still evolving and involves different forms from other arts like Judo and wrestling. The following are some of the popular upper body submissions, including chokes, joint locks, strangles, and cranks. These submissions are performed from different positions.

Chokes and Cranks

A neck crank (also called a neck lock) is applied to the opponent's cervical spine to cause hyperflexion, hyperextension, hyper rotation, or extension distraction. These submissions are applied through twisting, bending, pulling, or elongating the neck and head beyond their normal ranges of rotation. In the process, the submission will induce a choke, leading the opponent to submit.

Guillotine

Guillotine

The Guillotine submission is very versatile. The practitioner can use it to compress the opponent's neck from a close position. It is the first submission learned by white belt students and can be performed from various positions. Some positions you can consider undertaking this submission include open guard, mount, standing, gi, and No-Gi applications. You can choose the appropriate position depending on what you want to achieve.

Rear Naked Choke

Rear Naked Choke

This choke is Gi and No-Gi and involves a common grappling submission where you compress the opponent's neck from behind to immobilize them. You use both forearms to perform the rear-naked choke, usually from back control. You have more control when you are behind your opponent, and you can use your feet and hands for maximum balance and effectiveness. The rear-naked choke is also called, among others, the naked strangle.

Triangle Choke

Triangle Choke

The triangle choke involves grappling submission, using your legs and the opponent's arm to execute. The triangle choke originated from Judo but has since become a popular BJJ submission. You can perform the submission from various positions, including the gi and No-Gi settings. This move is versatile, performed from closed guard, mount, standing, half guards, back control, or open guards like spider and z-guard.

Bow and Arrow Choke

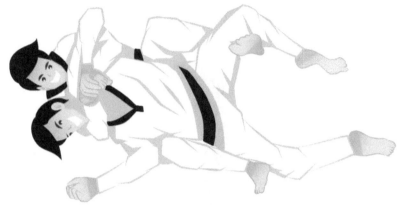

Bow and Arrow Choke

The bow and arrow choke involves the collar and is performed from back control. Use your opponent's lapel and a leg to finish the choke while controlling their movement with your legs. It is a Gi choke, and the name derives from the combination of two bodies during the choke. You can initiate this particular choke from closed guard, turtle, and side control.

Ezekiel Choke

Ezekiel Choke

This Gi choke is a sleeve choke. Wrap your forearms around the opponent's neck, and grip the inside of your sleeves for leverage. This submission choke is versatile and can be performed from your opponent's close guard, mount, back control, and side control. While choking the opponent, you have sufficient room to maneuver different moves out of harm's way.

D'Acre Choke

The D'Acre is another arm-triangle choke using your forearm together with the opponent's arm and shoulder. This Gi-based choke is similar to the Brabo choke that also uses the opponent's lapel. You can perform this choke from the turtle, side control, and half guard.

Cross-Collar Choke

Cross-Collar Choke

The cross-collar choke is performed when you grip your opponent's collar using both hands when they are crossed. Pull the opponent toward you and bend your wrist toward your opponent's neck crossing them. The cross-collar choke is very effective and is one of the submissions BJJ students learn because of how simple it is to execute. It has Judo roots like other BJJ submissions. The cross-collar choke submission is possible from different positions, including the mount, back control, and closed guard.

Baseball Bat Choke

Similarly, a Baseball Bat Choke is another example of a collar choke. Your hands grip the opponent's collar the same as gripping a baseball bat. Rotate your body while maintaining your grip, leading to a tight blood choke. Again, you can perform this choke from different positions like side control, bottom half guard, and knee on belly.

Clock Choke

Clock Choke

The clock choke is a collar choke against your opponent. Grab the opponent's collar and place your chest or hip on the back of their head. You can use this submission from side control or turtle, like other collar chokes.

North-South Choke

North-South Choke

As the name suggests, the North-South Choke is performed from the north to the south position. Use your bicep across the opponent's neck to add pressure on the head in this submission. Both players' feet are facing opposite directions. However, this choke can be challenging to finish because it requires finer details, so you must be very careful to avoid becoming the victim. The choke is often performed from side control.

Crucifix Choke

Crucifix Choke

This choke resembles the rear-naked choke, but the only difference is that it is performed using one arm from the crucifix position. This crucifix position looks like a Christian cross and is a back control. Wrap your legs around one of your opponent's arms and shoulders. (If the opponent is in the turtle position, this is when you can initiate the crucifix choke.) You can also use the crucifix choke to make the opponent submit using different armlocks. When you exert pressure on the arm, the opponent will feel the pain and quickly submit.

Thrust Choke

Thrust Choke

You can initiate the thrust choke as part of the guard pass or from the mount. Pull the opponent's lapel tight across your neck while moving your fist into the neck. Aim to exert more pressure on the subject's lapel so they feel the pain, making them relent quickly. You must be in the right position to execute this choke properly.

Anaconda Choke

Anaconda Choke

The Anaconda Choke resembles the arm triangle choke. Use your arms together with the opponent's shoulder to execute the choke. This move involves completing a rolling motion once you have established the grip. You can initiate this choke from an open guard or front headlock. You must choose the ideal position to execute this choke.

Peruvian Necktie

Peruvian Necktie

This is another variation of the arm triangle choke that you can do from the turtle position. Your legs must be on top of the subject's head and back to complete the choke.

The Japanese Necktie

Use your chest and arms at the back of your opponent's head. Also, use your opponent's shoulder and arm to complete the choke. This can also be a crank, depending on how you apply it. You can initiate a Japanese necktie from the turtle, side control, and half guard.

Loop Choke

Loop Choke

The Loop Choke involves a collar choke using your free arm to go behind the opponent's neck to finish the choke. You can use the loop choke as a counter to guard pass. Like other collar chokes, the loop choke is versatile and performed from various positions, including side control, open guard, turtle, and closed guard.

Step Over Choke

Step Over Choke

This choke is usually performed from the top side for control. Grip the opponent's collar and put pressure on the throat. Put your leg over the opponent's head to tighten the choke. You can initiate the step-over choke from the turtle or knee on the belly. However, you must be careful when performing this move.

Paper Cutter Choke

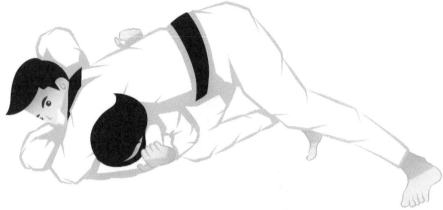

Paper Cutter Choke

This choke is a collar choke utilizing your forearm across your subject's neck. The choke is usually done using top-side control. This submission is sneaky, and many people do not anticipate or see it coming. To trick your opponent, consider using the paper cutter choke.

Gogoplata

Gogoplata

This is a rare submission using your hand and foot to create the choke around your opponent's neck. You must be flexible enough to wrap your leg around their neck and shoulder. Very few people can manage that feat with ease. You can perform the gogoplata in Gi and No-Gi, including different positions like mount, closed guard, and rubber guard.

Brabo Choke

Brabo Choke

This is a lapel choke often performed from the top half-guard. It requires you to loosen the opponent's lapel from the top and then grab its bottom. Wrap the lapel around your opponent's neck, changing the grips to complete. You can perform the Brabo choke from different positions, including the closed guard, half-guard, and side control.

Von Flue Choke

Von Flue Choke

To execute this choke, use your shoulder to push into the opponent's neck. This submission is usually performed when defending yourself from the guillotine using the top-side control. The way Von Flue Choke is applied often catches the opponent off guard.

Arm and Shoulder Lock Submissions

This section highlights different arm and shoulder lock positions you should know to make the opponent submit in combat. Likewise, these submissions vary, and you must take appropriate positions to execute them.

Monoplata

Monoplata

The monoplata is a shoulder lock you can initiate from a ¾ mount or mount. Use your legs to trap the subject's arm to complete the submission. This submission is versatile, and you can initiate it from spider guard, mount, failed triangle, and guard passing.

Americana

Americana

The Americana submission mainly targets the opponent's shoulder. To execute this submission, bend your opponent's arm and elbow in an upward direction while controlling your body and preventing the opponent from moving their arm. Americana submissions are versatile, and initiated from side control, mount, scarf hold, or closed guard.

Kimura

Kimura

Kimura is a BJJ submission originating from Japanese Jiu-Jitsu. Use both hands to push one of your opponent's arms behind their back. This action exceeds the normal range of motion, causing pain. Remember to control your body while simultaneously targeting the shoulder jointer. The submission was named after a Japanese judoka, Masahiko Kimura, who submitted Hélio Gracie leading to a broken arm. You can initiate kimura submission from side control, north control, closed guard, back control, and Z-guard.

Armbar BJJ Submission

Armbar BJJ Submission

The armbar is one of the oldest methods of submission that has existed for thousands of years. An armbar is a submission forced by exerting pressure on the arm at a specific angle to cause pain or injury. This submission continues to evolve and is used in different grappling practices. The armbar technique works the same way as you pull a lever. If you exert pressure on your opponent's elbow joint, they are likely to submit quickly.

You can perform armbar moves from different positions, like the guard and others. Performing this submission from the guard to subdue your opponent is the best option. You aim to grab the arm at the triceps and immobilize the opponent, preventing them from posturing. Your legs should also be in the right posture for easier control and to break their posture. Keep your knees firm as you perform the last steps of the armbar. The armbar submission is versatile, and you can initiate it from different positions, including mount, closed guard, side control, S mount, knee on belly, back control, turtle, and flying armbar.

Cutting Arm Bar

Cutting Arm Bar

This is another version of the regular armbar submission. Use your head and shoulder to trap your subject's arm and your knees to trap your opponent's shoulder. Complete this execution by exerting pressure on the backside of the opponent's upper arm. You can perform the cutting armbar from mount, closed guard, side control, and butterfly guard.

Bicep Slicer

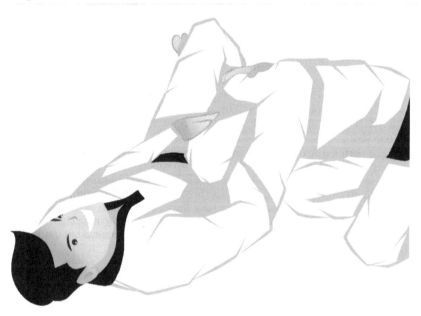

Bicep Slicer

The Bicep Slicer submission compresses your opponent's bicep against your forearm. This submission provides easy positioning and can be used to counter the armbar defense. Bicep Slicers are legal in certain belt levels, particularly brown and above. You can initiate this submission from closed guard, side control, and Armbar defense counter.

Omoplata

Omoplata

This submission is a shoulder joint lock using your legs to trap and control your opponent's arms. To complete the submission, you must sit in a position to be able to rotate your opponent's shoulder past its normal range of motion, like the kimura. You can perform this submission from several positions, including the mount, closed guard, half-guard, and spider guard. There are also other variations of Omoplata, listed below.

- **Marceloplata** - This omoplata version allows you to finish the move if the opponent blocks your bottom leg.
- **Baratoplata** - This omoplata version is used when your opponent hides your arm.
- **Tarikoplata** - This is a shoulder lock version against the opponent that attacks with a bent arm.

Wristlock

Wristlock

The wrist lock submission targets your opponent's wrist by forcing it to move past the normal range of movement. You can do this by rotation, hyperflexion, or hyperextension. To execute this submission successfully, immobilize your opponent's elbow and forearm first. Finish the action by forcing the palm forward or back, depending on your position. Wrist locks are versatile, and you can initiate them from different positions, including mount, side control, guard, and back control.

Calf Slicer

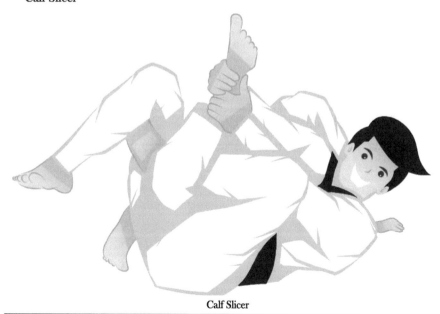

Calf Slicer

This is a compression submission. Place your forearm behind your opponent's knee, then pull the leg to compress the calf. This maneuver causes pain and leads the opponent to submit. You can initiate the calf slicer from different positions, including the turtle, half mount, truck, open guard, X guard, and knee on the belly. However, this submission is only legal for upper belts.

As you have observed in this chapter, several submission holds in martial arts are intended to subdue the opponent. The common upper body submissions include choke holds, compression locks, and joint locks, which can be applied from different positions. The next chapter focuses on lower body submissions and is required if you want to become a Sambo expert.

Chapter 9: Lower Body Submissions

This chapter focuses on the importance of groundwork and submissions in Sambo. As highlighted in the previous chapter, submissions help the participant to subdue the opponent. Here, we discuss the techniques of different leg locks, foot locks, ankle locks, and kneebars.

Leg Lock Submissions

Different leg lock submissions are available in Sambo, primarily based on exerting pressure on the muscles or joints of the legs. As a result, different leg locks come with different mechanical principles. Moreover, various leg locks have varying levels of success and are suitable for different situations. If the opponent's leg is trapped by two legs, it is extremely difficult for them to get out of the lock. Usually, submission is the only viable option to consider. The following is a list of lower body submissions you should know for games and self-defense.

Ankle Locks

Ankle locks are legal and used in competitions for each particular adult belt level. The ankle and the foot comprise a complex joint with about 26 bones, meaning several ligaments and bones can be damaged, resulting from the pressure applied under a lock. When you lock your opponent's ankle, they will feel pain and be immobilized.

Ankle Locks

An ankle lock is primarily concerned with causing torsion and hyperextension to the joint. Ensure you place your arms correctly around the foot. The bony part of your wrist must be positioned against the lowest part of the Achilles tendon, located above the heel. The palms should provide sufficient grip putting pressure on the tendons, leading to the opponent's submission if they cannot escape from the tight grip. When you apply this technique, you must ensure the opponent cannot easily escape your hold.

Toe Holds

A toe hold is a legal submission in Sambo, but you can only practice it at higher levels. For instance, brown belt levels or higher allow this devastating hold.

Toe Holds

The Toe Hold submission is primarily based on twisting mechanics. Use a figure four grip like the Kimura around the opponent's foot. Place your fingers around the pinky toe and twist in any direction, forcing it to exceed its regular movement. Pressure is formed when you squeeze the opponent's toe, causing great pain in the ligaments around the toe and making the opponent submit.

Kneebars

A Kneebar is a submission using your entire body power against one joint of the opponent, similar to an armbar. Tightly clamp down the opponent's leg to control its rotation. Apply pressure in the opposite direction of its natural bend on the knee you are holding. You will realize that your body position for a kneebar is similar to the posture you take for an armbar.

Your entire body must be positioned on the opponent's leg so your hips are above their kneecap. Also, consider other grips, like placing the foot in your armpit. However, these options are not as devastating. A kneebar submission is versatile and applicable from different positions, from the bottom, top, or standing. Additionally, kneebar submissions are legal for practitioners with lower ranks than the brown belt. It is one of the safest submissions to consider for different defense situations.

Heel Hooks

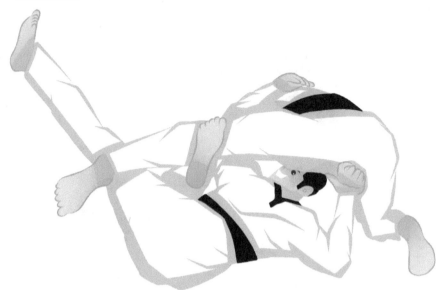

Heel Hooks

The Heel Hook submission is the leader in leg locks and is the most brutal. This technique affects the ankle and could easily destroy the knee's inner structure. Unless otherwise specified, this particular move is not allowed in all Gi competitions. However, it is a submission of choice for self-defense. You can perform the heel hook in two variations. The first one is the regular heel hook, and the second is the Reverse Heel Hook which is more dangerous.

However, both options share similar mechanics. Your opponent's toes are placed in the armpit, and the heel will be sticking out. Using one arm, cup the heel and place it under the thumb like the ankle lock. Pulling the heel using a twisting motion results in torsion of the knee and could completely tear most of the ligaments. When you undertake this submission, ensure you are in the correct position. Remember that this submission is illegal, so you can only use it for self-defense.

Straight Ankle Lock

The Straight Ankle Lock is known as the Straight Foot Lock or Achilles Lock. This lock is very common and uses your legs to control the opponent's leg. Apply pressure to their ankle and foot using your arms. Mainly two pressures will make the opponent submit when using the Straight Ankle Lock. The first involves the hyperextension of the ligaments and muscles above the foot. The second involves compression of the Achilles tendon at the back of the leg.

The Straight Ankle Lock technique forms the foundation for several other leg locks, like Toe Holds, Heel Hooks, and Steering Wheels. This submission also teaches you how to control the movement of the opponent's leg while using a safe mode of attack. Another important thing you should know is appropriate positioning.

Calf Crusher

The Calf Crusher submission, known as the Knee Slicer, resembles the Bicep Slicer lock, except you apply it on your opponent's leg, not their arms. However, the technique is illegal in many Gi tournaments up to the black belt level, like the Bicep Slicer. If – for some reason – you cannot complete the submission, it can transition nicely to the rear mount position. When you choose this particular technique, know your position to avoid mistakes that could backfire.

Figure 4 Toe Hold

The Figure 4 Toe Hold is a versatile leglock you can apply to your opponent's foot whenever you get close to them. You can use this submission as a primary attack. Alternatively, use this technique as a follow-up to other leglocks. The Figure 4 Toe Hold resembles the Heel Hook, but this one is a legal technique compared to other rotational leglocks. It means that you need to understand the situation to apply this technique and the action that follows.

Reverse Heel Hook

The Reverse Heel Hook submission is very effective, although it is illegal in most tournaments. Therefore, know when to apply this tactic. This submission is a rotational leglock that makes your opponent feel immediate pain and damage. With the flow of adrenaline, your opponent will quickly feel the impact of this technique, leading them to early submission.

Even if the technique is illegal, Sambo practitioners should still familiarize themselves with the Heel Hook for self-defense. If someone applies this to you and you cannot extricate yourself, early submission is vital to prevent severe harm to your heel. If you use the technique for training purposes, do it lightly so that you do not harm your training partner's ligaments.

Apart from the regular Heel Hook, the Reverse Heel Hook submission is worse and causes more harm. In Reverse Heel Hook, you rotate the opponent's leg outward instead of inward, causing a quicker submission. Likewise, you should not apply this technique during a training session. Also, know your limits when you use this particular technique.

Banana Split Hiplock

The Banana Split Hiplock is known as a groin stretcher, electric chair, and crotch ripper. This submission is an effective leglock that aims to attack the hips and groin areas. You can use this submission with other moves like foot locks and calf slicers. The electric chair variation uses the figure 4 leg lockdown position to control the action while the arms stretch out together with the other leg.

Leg Lock Positions

In different submission options, you should be in the best position for the best results. You cannot randomly use your legs without proper positioning since this could compromise your intended tactic. Using a leg lock to achieve quick submission might be ineffective due to a lack of control. Therefore, there are ideal leg positions you should know. Some submissions are attainable from several leg positions.

Ashi Garami

The Ashi Garami position is the best in the entire lower body submission system since it is controllable. This position stands for leg entanglement and is grounded in the Single Leg X Guard version. The only difference is the foot, which is kept on the butt in a single leg, now hooks on the opposite side.

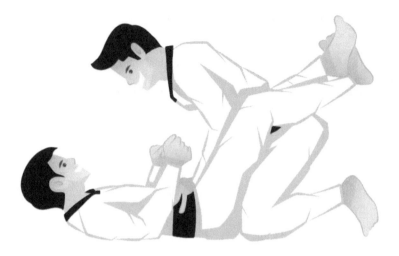

Ashi Garami

The position also gives you control over the knee, hip, ankle, and correct grips. When you are in this position, you can completely immobilize the opponent, giving you opportunities for different attacks. The heel hook is the best submission option for this position, followed by the ankle lock. When the opponent tries to escape, consider the toe-hold alternative. This position gives you sufficient control of the situation and increases the chances of submitting your opponent. This position is legal, and you can use it in Sambo competitions.

Outside Ashi Garami

The Outside Ashi Garami is the second-best position for leg lock options. It gives you better control than the standard Ashi. Depending on the situation, you also have better transitioning options with this position. Regarding different mechanics, the bottom leg will remain in the same position as in the standard Ashi Garami. The top leg you use to hook the opponent's side butt in Ashi will go over the hip on the same side of the leg that is being attacked.

Outside Ashi Garami

Essentially, both feet are placed to the outside of your opponent's hip, giving you more control over the hip. However, you might sacrifice some control of the knee. The good thing about this position is that it gives you control of different movements. The ankle lock and heel hook are the most appropriate submissions for this position. Toe holds are also attainable from a top position in the same way as Ashi Garami. Kneebar is another short transition from the Outside Ashi Garami.

411, Honey Hole, Saddle, Inside Sankaku

For the ultimate back control position, the 411 is the champion of the leg-locking system. It offers you full control of various submission options to subdue the opponent.

411, Honey Hole, Saddle, Inside Sankaku

You create a triangle using your legs around your opponent's leg with this position. This triangle structure gives you ultimate control over the limb you are attacking. In other words, the 411 position means your legs should form a triangle shape between the opponent's legs. Keeping your knee around the opponent's hip fold emphasizes the position's power and pressure.

The opponent's foot is also placed across your body, opening the inverted heel hook. Some submissions in this position include ankle locks, toe holds, and kneebars. It is difficult for the opponent to escape from this position, giving you more power and control. However, the 411 position is illegal. It can cause serious injury, like knee reaping. The inverted heel hook leads to instant disqualification if you apply it in a BJJ or Sambo event. Therefore, you must be careful when using this particular position in regulated games.

Sambo Knot

Another name for the Sambo Knot is "knee reap," implying it is a dangerous position that can cause severe harm. This position is placing one of your opponent's legs in a triangle and keeping the foot on the leg under attack on the same side. You can control the other leg by locking your feet around the opponent's ankle, keeping it on the ground and bent. The Sambo knot offers effective leg-locking positions. You can do heel hooks and toe holds using only one hand while transitioning to 411 positions. The 411 position is illegal in Gi competitions, but apply it in self-defense.

Sambo Knot

50/50 Guard

The 50/50 guard position is legal in Sambo and falls between the triangle and Ashi Garami in control. The position forms a triangle but is outside the opponent's hip. The submission of choice for this position is a heel hook, although you can also use it on toe holds and ankle locks. However, this position's major drawback is that the opponent will be in the exact position as you, meaning they can also attack at the same time using leg locks, putting you at a disadvantage if you are not careful.

50/50 Guard

The Truck

The truck position was developed by Eddie Bravo and is halfway between the back and side control. It provides different submission options to the host. You can easily apply this position to the Calf Slicer and the twister. Choosing this position, you must apply to the submission you want to initiate. When you are in the correct position, you can easily read the opponent's intentions and take appropriate measures to counter them.

Different leg locks are safe, and effective submissions help you control and subdue your opponent. While other submissions are illegal, you should learn them for self-defense and only use them in those scenarios. Remember, not every leg lock works every time and against everyone. So, it is vital to know when to switch to another attacking system before it is too late. More importantly, you must be wary of the Sambo game rules to avoid penalties. The next chapter focuses on tips and measures you can implement to improve your Sambo skills.

Chapter 10: Improving Your Sambo Skills

This final chapter focuses on sharpening the sword and applying more advanced training to your Sambo skills. Once you know the basics, it is important to train daily by performing body conditioning exercises, repeated drills, and legwork practices to build a strong foundation. The upcoming sections discuss advancing your skills with daily practice providing much insight into structuring your training program from beginner to advanced levels. Considering the availability of expert Samba trainers, the possibility, methods, and effectiveness of solo training and training at home are covered.

The Importance of Daily Training

Daily training is important not only to master Sambo techniques and tactics but also to maintain your physical fitness. Exercise is a part of a healthy lifestyle and should be considered an essential component of your training.

Daily Sambo conditioning exercises will better prepare you for competition when you have to perform under pressure at 100% capacity with precise technique. Moreover, they prevent injuries by strengthening the ligaments and tendons that support joints like knees and elbows.

Daily drills train you to react properly from various positions, whether pinned in the mounted position, side control, the guard, etc., so when an opportunity arises during sparring or competition, your body knows what to do exactly.

Solo Sambo drills are an excellent way to develop your technique and practice combinations and attacks or counters without interference from another person. You can also use them as conditioning exercises for specific positions like grappling, throwing, pinning, mounting, back control, etc. However, you cannot master Sambo by simply going through the motions of daily drills.

A proper understanding of the positions and transitions is important, which can only be achieved by working with an experienced instructor or partner who will watch your technique closely.

The Importance of Sparring Drills (Sparring with a Partner)

Solo drills are limited in practicing footwork and motion. When grappling with a partner, you can practice moving around the mat and transitioning from one position to another until you perfect your form.

You cannot execute certain throws without first establishing an effective grip on your opponent's uniform or person – so it makes sense to practice your grips and throws.

Sparring drills (or "randori" in Japanese martial arts like Judo and Aikido) are the best way to master Sambo techniques through repetition. It's impossible to predict what your opponent will do or how they will react, but it is possible to train repeatedly under conditions that closely mimic a real fight.

It's easy to simulate the fight, but you must be careful not to commit or get injured fully. Sparring drills allow full-contact resistance while minimizing the risk of injury due to their controlled nature. Both participants know what is expected during each drill. They start from the same position, and the drill ends when one participant submits or is pinned.

Practicing Sambo techniques progressing gradually from simple to more advanced is important if you are training for competition. If your moves fail during sparring or the match due to a lack of experience and preparation, you must work on your weakness and gradually improve. Practice makes perfect.

Most techniques in Sambo are performed with a partner, whether during sparring or competition. Sparring or competition is not a solo activity. You cannot think of yourself as an island and go through the motions without realizing how everything fits together with your opponent's actions and reactions.

Body Conditioning Exercises and Drills

Sparring and competition are physically demanding activities. Therefore, it's important to keep the body in good condition by doing daily exercises that strengthen muscles, ligaments, tendons, and anything that supports your joints, like knees and elbows. Regular conditioning exercises will prevent injuries from occurring during training or competitions to continue improving your Sambo skills.

What Is Body Conditioning?

Body conditioning is about keeping your body aligned, strong, and flexible.

Improving your conditioning is the only way to prevent injuries and maintain a high-performance level during sparring and competition. Conditioning exercises are used in all sports for this exact purpose, not only Sambo.

Conditioning is anything that improves your physical fitness through mental or physical exertion.

Common Body Conditioning Exercises

- **Squats/Lunges** - Improves strength throughout leg muscles.
- **Power Skipping Rope** - Builds endurance through the use of lower body muscles.
- **Double Lunges** - Strengthens legs by using triple extension at the ankles, knees, and hips.
- **Exercise Ball Donkey Kicks** - Enhances workout for abdominals and buttocks.
- **Dumbbell Press Downs** - Provides a balanced workout for chest muscles.
- **Push-Ups** - Uses primary muscle groups to strengthen the upper body, especially pectorals (chest), anterior deltoids (front of shoulders), biceps brachii (upper arm), triceps brachii (upper back), and serratus anterior muscles.
- **Fighter Dips** - It's a very intense exercise, so it's best to start with low reps before increasing the number.
- **Weighted Pull-Ups** - Targets upper body strength in the latissimus dorsi muscle of the back, biceps (arms), and deltoids (shoulders).
- **Plank** - Strengthens abdominals, lower back muscles, and gluteus maximus.
- **Leg Raises** - Workout for abdominals and hip flexors.

These are a few of the many-body conditioning exercises that can be done daily. These drills will improve your physical fitness and speed up muscle recovery after training sessions, sparring, and competition.

It's important to avoid doing the same conditioning exercises every day because this can lead to overtraining and injuries due to repetitive motions. It's best to mix these drills to condition different parts of your body weekly (i.e., squats/lunges one day, power skipping rope another day, and so on).

Mental Conditioning for Sambo

Mental conditioning is as important as physical conditioning for high-level performance.

It's about maintaining discipline, confidence, and focus to succeed during sparring and competition. Mental preparation starts with setting goals you want to achieve within a certain time frame, then breaking these down into weekly or monthly steps so you can track your progress and enjoy the journey of achieving these goals.

Maintaining focus is also an important part of mental conditioning because it's one thing to set a goal, but you need to stay focused on that goal for it to be achieved. It takes discipline and patience, as some days will be more productive than others (i.e., you're focused and determined one day, but the next day you might be tired and unmotivated).

Avoiding things that could distract you, like listening to music or watching TV before training or competition, is also important. This distraction will change your mindset (music) or take away from the mental energy needed to perform your best (TV).

Other ways to improve mental conditioning include visualization, inserting positive self-talk into daily conversations, and setting rewards when you achieve weekly or monthly goals.

Visualization is imagining yourself performing each step of a specific task, whether competing or training, before doing the drill. It's a way to prepare for the task and, if done regularly, helps develop confidence in your abilities.

Positive self-talk is another mental conditioning technique where you look at yourself as a winner regardless of the situation (i.e., whether you win or lose). It means disregarding any negative thoughts that could affect performance.

Rewarding yourself for achieving weekly or monthly goals is a way to keep your motivation high. It can be something as simple as eating out with friends or watching the latest movie, but whatever it is, reward yourself after each milestone because this will help maintain focus on future tasks.

These are a few ways to improve mental conditioning for higher-level performance in Sambo.

Solo Drills for Sambo Beginners

Solo Sambo drills are very important for beginners because it's the best way to familiarize yourself with the basic movements in Sambo.

Here are some solo drills which should be done regularly by beginners:

Rock and Kick

The Rock and Kick drill is a great way to learn to move your hips to defend against an opponent's takedown or submission attempts successfully. It also helps develop hip flexibility, which is important for maintaining the guard position and transitioning into other techniques.

Technique: Lie on your back. Roll upwards, raising both your legs with the knees bent slightly simultaneously, creating a rocking motion. Repeat this movement several times to strengthen your torso and get accustomed to creating momentum with your lower body.

Kicking Up

This movement helps master guard techniques for triangle chokes, armbars, and omoplatas.

Technique: Kicking up is an extension of the previous movement. Lie on your back. Lift your legs to the ceiling together, simulating a two-legged kick. Go as high as you can. Feel the tension in your lower abs.

180 Rock

The 180 Rock drill will familiarize your body with angle change while on the ground. It is vital to master this movement so that you can pivot around the mat easily when performing your guard.

Technique: Again, start on your back. Roll up with one leg bent and the other straight so you are now in a sideways position. Keep both of your hands near your face for protection. Roll over and do a 180-degree flip using your head and shoulders as a pivot. Repeat this multiple times.

Rocking S Sit

The Rocking S Sit drill lets you quickly get on your feet after being taken down.

Technique: Lie flat on the mat. Roll up into a sitting position and stay there for one second before rolling backward to get back into an upside-down L-sit position (legs still bent at 90 degrees). Roll back to the initial position. Repeat several times before doing other drills.

Alternating S Sit

This drill simulates the movement of getting up on your feet after being taken down.

Technique: Start in an L-sit position, then roll to one side into an S-Sit before rolling back again. Repeat this motion several times for each leg. This drill will help you develop the strength and speed necessary to get away from your opponent's side control.

Gyro Drills

The Gyro drill helps you learn how to create small pivots on your hips, a very important movement in Sambo.

Technique: Sit with your legs bent and feet flat on the ground about shoulder-width apart. Lean back as far as possible, lifting both arms towards the ceiling. Lean your body to one side and then the other, moving from a full-fledged sit position into an L-sit with straight legs. Repeat several times for each leg before doing another drill.

Rope Pulls

This drill will help you learn to use your legs to stand.

Technique: Lie on the mat with arms stretched forward at shoulder height. Swing both legs upward toward your head, keeping them together (it is easier if you bend them slightly). Bring one leg back and then the other. Pull yourself forward. Repeat this movement several times to master it before doing the next drill.

Shoulder Rolls

The Shoulder Roll Drill will help you develop strength in your hips, which is necessary for transitioning between different techniques during a match.

Technique: Lie flat with arms stretched forward at shoulder height and legs spread apart. Roll forward onto your shoulders and then backward. Repeat this movement multiple times.

Tuck Front Roll

The Tuck Front Roll Drill helps develop speed while getting up and improving your transitions between different techniques during a match.

Technique: Lie flat on your back with arms stretched forward at shoulder height. Roll up into a sit position and then quickly roll back to get back in the initial Tuck Front Roll starting position.

Bridging

This drill will help you learn to use your hips to get up quickly.

Technique: Lie on your back, legs bent at the knee and close to your buttocks. Slowly lift your buttocks and get into a tabletop position. Your torso should be extremely stable and straight so that a cup of coffee can balance on it. Come back to lying down on the mat. Repeat this movement several times.

Intermediate and Advanced Drills

These drills are meant for experienced players. Make sure you master the basic skills before moving on to these more difficult ones.

Shrimping

The Shrimp Drill will help you learn how to get back on your feet quickly.

Technique: Lie on your back. Bend your knees and bring your heels closer to your buttocks. Rotate to one side, pushing your arms and legs as if you are pushing something away. Repeat on the other side.

Leg Circles

This drill will help you improve your footwork and coordination skills.

Technique: Lie on the ground, raise your legs, and draw imaginary 360-degree circles. Repeat the movement several times. It is an excellent exercise to strengthen your core.

Bridges with Leg Switches

This drill will help you learn to use your hips to get up quickly and improve hand-eye coordination skills at the same time.

Technique: It is a bridge drill on alternate legs. Get into a bridge position and balance your body only on one leg instead of both. Keep alternating legs.

Crab Walk

The Crab Walk Drill will help you learn to quickly get back on your feet and improve your speed in transitioning between different techniques during a match.

Technique: Start in a sitting position with your legs extended forward. Keep both hands on the mat, palms facing downward. Lift your buttocks and move around the space in a tabletop-like position. However, you can keep your buttocks lower to the ground but not touching the ground.

Triangle Choke Variations

This drill will help you develop speed in getting up and improve your transitions between different techniques during a match.

Technique: A triangle choke is used when sparring. In this move, the attacker wraps his feet around the opponent's neck and wraps one of the opponent's arms in a leg wrap. This movement can be repeatedly practiced in a solo drill until it becomes muscle memory.

Quick Knee Cut

The Quick Knee Cut Drill will help you improve the speed of transitioning between different techniques during a match.

Technique: Start on your knees and hands perpendicular to your shoulders. Lift the left leg and the left hand and cut over to the opposite side by stretching your knee. Immediately go back to the starting position and repeat with the other leg.

Paper Mills

This drill will help you develop speed and improve your transitions between different techniques during a match.

Technique: Start in a high plank. Lift one hand and balance your entire weight on the other hand. Slowly move in circles, supporting your entire weight on one hand. Repeat with the other hand. Repeat a set on your elbow as a variation.

Bear Crawl

This is a great warmup and also increases core strength.

Technique: Performing a bear crawl is pretty simple. Get on your fours, hands perpendicular to your shoulders, and knees on the mat. Lift your knees and crawl around the area.

Exercises for Improving Balance

Balance is vital for improving your skills in Sambo. You will be thrown, grappled, and perform explosive and fast groundwork during sparring. This calls for a well-balanced posture and the ability to compose yourself in an imbalance quickly. So, you must train hard to achieve a balanced posture.

Here are a few exercises to help improve balance and posture:

1. One-Legged Standing, No Hands (2x 5 Min per Day)

This exercise is quite challenging for most people at first, but it improves balance and strength very quickly. You can challenge yourself by gradually increasing the difficulty, meaning you can gradually increase the time you can keep balanced on one leg without touching any surface for support.

2. Planks (3x 30 Sec per Day)

A plank is a simple and very effective exercise that strengthens your back muscles and is also great for posture since it trains your body to hold your back straight. The muscles responsible are often ignored but are very important in helping you maintain good posture at work or home.

3. Wall-Sits (2x 30 Sec per Day)

This exercise is simply sitting with your back against a wall and sliding down until the thighs are parallel to the floor. It trains your muscles to hold a sitting position that is "against gravity" for longer. If you're uncomfortable doing it against a wall, do it standing instead.

4. Neck Exercises (2x 10 Reps per Day)

This one's self-explanatory. Just move your neck in a clockwise and then counterclockwise motion.

5. Walking with Eyes Closed (5-10 Min per Day)

This is another exercise that trains you to focus better on balancing, so it's great for people who tend to get dizzy or feel off balance easily. Ensure to do it slowly and without distractions since it can be slightly dangerous if you don't pay enough attention to the environment.

This book has deep-dived into Sambo, compared with other martial arts. We have spoken at length about the various techniques, the essentials to get started, global competitions, and everything there is to know about this martial art.

In this concluding chapter, we spoke about improving your Sambo Skills using practice, group drills, and solo drills. The chapter also gives insight into a few drill exercises you can do to improve speed and transitions during a match.

Practice is crucial for achieving mastery in Sambo. Becoming an expert is not easy. However, it is easy to take the *first step*.

Conclusion

As you have observed, this book primarily focused on providing a practical and comprehensive understanding of Sambo and its critical elements like throws, holds, and movements. Sambo is a martial art that can be used for self-defense, and this book provided all the information about the basic moves. Before you consider using Sambo to defend yourself against an opponent, you must know how to execute different moves.

This informative book was carefully written to provide helpful details about submissions and throws. Many people have heard about the discipline of Sambo as a martial art, but the majority are scared of trying it. Indeed, performing different moves can be overwhelming to beginners. However, with the appropriate knowledge of the game, you will realize that everything is attainable. This book provided a step-by-step guide to understanding the crucial moves and throws to help you overcome the opponent.

Moreover, this book offered a basic understanding of Sambo and how it significantly differs from other martial arts. Martial art is a discipline that provides people with self-defense skills when facing threatening situations. There are different martial art styles, and each is designed for various purposes. However, Sambo significantly differs from other disciplines in several ways.

If you have a keen interest in Sambo, you should know its similarities and differences from other martial arts. The information provided in this book helps you familiarize yourself with the subject and prepares you for real action. You can significantly improve your skills when you have theoretical knowledge about Sambo. This essential book provided easy-to-apply techniques. Images are included to guide you as you learn to execute different moves.

You also got clear instructions from the book to help you understand the reason behind every move when practicing Sambo. Additionally, links for relevant videos are included to help you quickly grasp different moves you must familiarize yourself with. However, you need to follow the instructions laid out in the book carefully.

This book is unique since it is specifically crafted for beginners and those interested in Sambo. It is easy to understand, and all complex terms are explained in simple terms. In addition, the book is up to date and consists of information that might be new in the world of Sambo. It must be noted that this discipline has been evolving and is different today from how it was in its early days. Therefore, this book gives you the latest version of your favorite combat sport simplified.

It is great for beginners since it provides hands-on instructions to help them master different techniques quickly. While you need a teacher or coach to teach you Sambo, you can practice at home or with a sparring partner with the techniques detailed in the book. More importantly, the book is easy to understand, and you can execute various moves without seeking assistance from your coach.

We hope you enjoyed learning about Sambo!

Part 10: Capoeira

The Ultimate Guide to Capoeira Movements and Techniques for Beginners

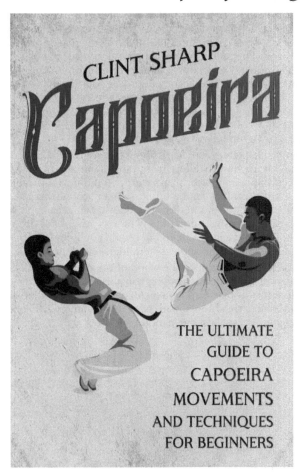

CLINT SHARP

Capoeira

THE ULTIMATE
GUIDE TO
CAPOEIRA
MOVEMENTS
AND TECHNIQUES
FOR BEGINNERS

Introduction

Capoeira is an expressive form of martial art that involves more than just fighting movements. Although it's considered a martial art, it is more of a dance than anything else. You will also learn about the music used in Capoeira performances and the history behind them. If you're interested in learning an elaborate and unique dance style, this book will help you get acquainted with the basic techniques and put you on the right track toward learning Capoeira.

Many martial artists learn Capoeira because it is a great way to work out. Most other forms of martial arts include stances or pauses to give fighters a chance to assess their opponents. Capoeira is nothing like that. You are constantly moving to the rhythm of the music. This enhances your physical and mental capabilities. Capoeira improves focus and teaches you how to anticipate your opponent's moves even while you're moving around. It also significantly improves your flexibility because you will be stretching all your muscles and bending in ways you never did before. Balance and good coordination with your upper and lower body are also things you will gain as you get used to using your core muscles, arms, hand, legs, and feet to perform Capoeira actions. It will give you a fun full-body workout.

In the upcoming chapters, you'll learn about the origins of Capoeira and its unique history. You'll also learn how it differs from other martial arts and what makes it so compelling! Street Capoeira performances are becoming more and more popular worldwide, and training centers can be found in many countries. The incredible skills and fluid movements of Capoeira performers are what attract people to learn it. If you are one of those people, but you don't know how or where to start, continue reading this book. This book was created with you in mind. You'll find the basics with detailed steps on how to do them at home and easy-to-understand illustrations.

With this book as a basic guide to the world of Capoeira, you will get an idea of this martial art's background and origin, making you a true capoeirista! We also encourage you to watch videos that display Capoeira techniques to get visual input as you read this book. We've combined the history and basic techniques you'll need to start your Capoeira training journey, so let's dive right in!

Chapter 1: What Is Capoeira?

Capoeira is a form of martial art that originated in Brazil by African slaves in the 16th century. It bears some resemblance to Brazilian Jiu-Jitsu. The key difference is that Capoeira fighters don't make contact with each other. The techniques involve many kicking movements incorporated with dancing and gymnastic performance. Unlike other martial arts, Capoeira is traditionally accompanied by music and singing. It's considered more artistic than other forms of martial arts as it's more expressive than combative. Martial artists who participate in competitions usually incorporate some Capoeira training to increase their range of movements, keep up their fitness, and improve their flexibility. Let's dive into the world of Capoeira and discuss its origin, history, and how it differs from other martial arts.

An Overview of Capoeira

Capoeira involves a lot of footwork and acrobatic movements. Capoeira fighters would move around each other inside a circle called a Roda. The performance is considered as a game as opposed to a fight. Fighters or players demonstrate their gymnastic abilities by doing back, front, and side flips with specific hand movements that resemble a dance. Music is an essential element in a Capoeira performance. The instruments played and the words chanted during the game guide the players through their performance. The music usually illustrates the history of Capoeira and how it came into existence. This unique martial art involves sharp movements that mirror the violence, racism, and eventual freedom that people went through when Capoeira was created. The whole routine is philosophical in nature, and it captures the essence of African culture when it was introduced to Brazil.

The music played during Capoeira consists of traditional songs that may differ a little with each group or region. Each community has created unique songs by adding a little bit of their own culture into them. The main instrument in Capoeira is the *berimbau*, and this wooden instrument is considered sacred as it's associated with slavery and the injustices slaves faced at the time. Traditional Capoeira songs include Samba de Roda, which is similar to samba tunes, and it incorporates a mixture of Brazilian and African music. Other songs are played to start a slow-paced performance with low movements closer to the ground. Some songs recall the game's history, while others are energetic and upbeat, which are usually celebrated by a fast and powerful dance.

When you watch videos about Capoeira, you might be intimidated by the skills and fitness of the performers. Bear in mind that it takes years to master this form of martial arts. It may take you a year of regular practice to get your first belt and even longer than that to reach the next level. Capoeira experts will be more than happy to help you advance in your classes because helping those less experienced than you is one of the main principles of this game. Remember to enjoy your journey and take it one step at a time. No instructor will rush you to learn backflips when you're just getting started. There's a lot of training you have to go through to gain the strength to do the movements without hurting yourself. You can get started using the instructions in this book and watching Capoeira-related videos using the information outlined throughout.

Capoeira training will help you stay focused and motivate you to improve your skills. Like with any other sport or martial art, Capoeira requires regular practice with maximum concentration and commitment. There might be a lot of information to ingest at first, but perseverance is key to reaching advanced levels. Make a habit of listening to Capoeira music and watching videos, whether performances or training sessions. It's always good to stretch regularly, even beyond your training hours. You'll be training your muscles by making them more flexible without feeling like it's a chore. Applying these practices in your life will help you understand, appreciate, and enjoy the world of Capoeira.

The Origin and History of Capoeira

Capoeira reportedly originated in the 16th century by enslaved Africans transported by the Portuguese to Brazil. The tradition of ritual dancing that involved kicks, slaps, hand walking, and elaborate movements was practiced by Africans originally from what we know today as Angola. This religious ritual was performed because people believed it linked them to their ancestors in the afterlife.

The Portuguese colonists enslaved Africans to work in the sugarcane fields. They were forced to work in inhumane conditions. They could not rebel against the colonists because they lacked weapons and knowledge of the new country. Capoeira was a way to escape the torture they faced every day. The movements were used to express how they could win a fight unarmed against the hostile colonists. Capoeira was also used as a dance to disguise the fact that they were actually training in a martial art.

In the next couple of centuries, the techniques of Capoeira remained intact, and the martial art thrived. Many enslaved people would take jobs beyond the work they had to do for their masters in return for a share of their wages. They would practice Capoeira during and after their working hours. This went on until the 19th century when the prohibition of Capoeira came into effect. The ruling regime saw it as a threat, so every person caught practicing Capoeira was arrested.

Rebellion Groups

Some of the enslaved Africans were able to escape their oppressors by forming external communities called quilombos. They moved to remote regions out of the colonists' reach and started to grow in size as they were slowly joined by other enslaved people, Brazilian locals, and even European outlaws. Some communities grew so much that they formed a state separate from Brazil and included various ethnicities. People were allowed to live freely and uphold their traditions as they pleased, far from the regulations of colonial law. Due to the mixing of cultures, Capoeira went from simply being a traditional dance to becoming a martial art with techniques that could be used during the war.

One of the largest and most famous communities was called Quilombo dos Palmares. It lasted for more than a hundred years and it included numerous villages. They were able to survive several attacks and invasions. The Portuguese colonial agents reported that it was difficult to bring the people down because they used oddly structured fighting movements when fighting.

Capoeira spread more in cities as those communities grew larger and larger, and more enslaved people were transported to major cities like Rio de Janeiro. At the time, the government passed laws to incriminate people who practiced Capoeira because it was associated with rebels against the current regime. Colonial agents used to track down Capoeira practitioners to execute them publicly. About a third of the people arrested at the time were charged for practicing Capoeira.

By the late 1800s, slavery started to come to an end. This was due to increasing attacks from rebellious groups that became more structured and heavily armed. The previously enslaved people were now left without jobs or homes and were discriminated against by local Brazilians. People then started to use capoeira in unique ways. They worked for gangs as bodyguards and even attacked cities. These criminal groups included Capoeira experts from different cultures and ethnicities. The new Brazilian government still criminalized capoeira, but people still practiced it in remote regions away from the reach of the police.

At the beginning of the 20th century, the discrimination laws against Capoeira practitioners began to loosen as martial arts instructors started to incorporate the movements into their training. They mixed the movements with other forms of martial arts to create self-defense techniques. Some trainers would exclude the musical part of Capoeira to disguise the practice from the police. Gradually, the Capoeira techniques made a comeback, but they lost the cultural aspect, which is why the original form of Capoeira started to fade as an art.

That was until a Capoeira master from Salvador called Mestre Bimba developed a training system called Luta Regional Baiana to teach the original form of Capoeira and established the first school in 1932. Eight years later, Capoeira finally became legal, and by 1941, Mestre Pastinha founded another Capoeira school called Centro Esportivo de Capoeira Angola, which was very popular among traditional Capoeira performers. The traditional style later became known as Capoeira Angola. Government officials still felt threatened by the practice of Capoeira, but in the 1980s, the current regime accepted the practice among students as a form of dance martial art, which is how it came to be known today.

Today, Capoeira is known as a unique part of Brazilian culture and is taught in many countries. This fantastic form of martial arts is popular among tourists who visit Brazil every year to watch street performances. Capoeira enthusiasts worldwide would strive to learn Portuguese so they could understand the songs played during the routines. Globally, Capoeira performances that involve acrobatic and rhythmic movements have become more common in recent years.

How Capoeira Differs from Other Martial Arts

Most martial arts originated from Asian countries like China and Japan. At first glance, a Capoeira performance will look more like a dance than a martial art. The movements are smoother and more fluid than the purposeful and powerful kicks and punches of other martial arts like Judo or Taekwondo. A Capoeira performer keeps himself in constant motion, and the Capoeira-related music guides their kicks and flips during their performance.

Capoeira movements are closer to the ground as the player relies more on their lower body to conduct intricate moves. The core movement of Capoeira is called *Ginga*. Unlike in other martial arts, Capoeira players don't stand still but rather rock back and forth and sideways in large steps. These techniques are used to make the player a hard target and to prevent the opponent from anticipating their next move. Compared to other Asian martial arts, Capoeira involves fluid dance-like movements, while other martial arts like Karate involve sharp movements and sudden stance changes.

Capoeira isn't exactly effective in this area when it comes to self-defense. Seeing how there is zero contact between people in a Roda, Capoeira is not a viable option for fighting an opponent. However, many martial arts instructors use Capoeira techniques to train students because it promotes flexibility, fitness, and strength.

Terminologies

Capoeira is celebrated as part of Brazilian culture by a performance or a game between two people. A Capoeira routine is performed as a presentation for the masses or for training purposes. It's not about hurting your opponent but more about displaying your own skills. As an expert Capoeira performer or a Capoeirista, you would stop your foot from actually hitting your opponent by a few inches since there's no need to hit them as you have already established that your skills are superior. This is usually how regular street performances happen, but private games with more advanced Capoeiristas can get more violent.

A Capoeira game can occur anywhere, but it's usually within a circle or Roda formed by the musicians and players. Musicians play traditional instruments and sing songs specific to the Capoeira culture. This music is used to dictate the pace of the game. Each game can end when a player leaves the Roda or when another enters it. It could also end if one of the berimbau players decides to stop. Street performances involve more acrobatic movements than serious fights, which involve more takedowns than public presentations.

Another term for a Roda is *Batizado* which is a ceremonial street performance. New Capoeira students are introduced in a Batizado as fresh graduates, and advanced students can get recognized for achieving a higher grade. Students usually enter a Batizado against their master or an experienced player. That usually ends with the student's takedown. A call or chamada can occur during a game to the tunes of Angola. The higher-ranking player initiates this part as they invite their opponent to participate in a dancing ritual. The newer player then responds by moving toward the caller, and they walk together side by side before continuing the game.

When two opponents conclude their current movements, they start to circle each other in opposite directions in a movement called *Volta ao mundo* or around the world. They use this movement to pause for a short while before resuming their game. Players need to possess the ability to anticipate their opponent's malicious intent, which is called *malandragem.* They can also use *mandinga* or magic – not in its literal sense but as a concept. This technique is used by smart players who can deceive their opponents.

Musical Instruments and Songs

We've already established that music is a big part of Capoeira culture. Musicians in a Roda are lined up in a row or a *bateria,* which means drum kit. This line is a popular concept in Brazilian samba. The traditional lineup includes berimbau, pandeiro, atabaque, agogô, and ganzá players, and their number varies according to each group's culture. Berimbau players set the tone for the entire musical piece by controlling the tempo of the music and the pace of the whole game. Low-pitch berimbau players play the bass tones, and the high-pitched player improvises a solo performance. The other instruments are played to complement the main performance of the berimbau player. All musicians must be in perfect harmony as they set the rhythm of the Capoeira game.

When it comes to singing and chanting, singers either call and respond to each other or narrate a story about the history of Capoeira. Some songs mention famous Capoeira artists, and others are chanted to motivate players to up their game. The Ladaínha is a song traditionally performed at the beginning of a game by the most renowned Capoeirista present in the Roda. This solo is followed by a louvação, which is performed to thank God in a call and response format. Each singer will call out a word, and then other singers reply with another word.

The second basic song is called the Chula, which is dominated by a solo singer with little response or backup singing performed by the choir. The soloist may sing up to eight verses, with the choir responding with one verse, but this format may vary according to each group. The third basic Capoeira song is called the Corrido, which involves singing an equal number of verses by the main singer and the chorus, usually two verses each. The last basic song is called the Quadra, and this involves singing one verse four times, where the main singer sings three verses and the choir replies with one verse.

Capoeira may seem impossible to learn because of its elaborate movements and techniques. However, like any other sport or martial art, it takes some time to get acquainted with the training, and it helps that music is involved. It makes the performances much more enjoyable than if you were practicing a combat-focused form of martial arts. People are usually attracted to capoeira because of how fascinating it looks. Although the footwork involves sharp and specific movements, these techniques are not used to hurt an opponent as there is no contact between players in a Roda. Capoeira players perform their routine for the love of dance, culture, and music of this marvelous martial art.

Chapter 2: Roda, Joga, and the Grading System

This chapter explains some of the key terminology used in Capoeira, like Roda and Jogo. It helps readers learn more about the ranking system and highlights some of the core concepts and ideas behind Capoeira.

What Is Capoeira Roda?

Source[90]

Capoeira is a Brazilian martial art that consists of acrobatics, dance, and music. Capoeira is usually performed inside a circle, and it has strong roots in Africa. Historically, Capoeira was practiced by Africans enslaved in Brazil during the 16th Century.

Capoeira includes complex maneuvers and acrobatics consisting of inverted kicks, and the hands are often on the ground. It mainly involves flowing movements instead of fixed actions. The term Capoeira originates from the Tupi word *ska'a* meaning forest, and paũ (round), which refers to areas low on vegetation. That's where runaway slaves used to hide in Brazil. A Capoeirista is the practitioner of this kind of art. Music and dance were added to disguise the fact that it was a martial art, and Capoeiristas who were caught training were arrested and even executed.

Capoeira is a combination of music, dance, philosophy, and ritual. All those elements form a special game known as the *jogo de Capoeira* (play of the Capoeira). The game has apparent Brazilian and African martial arts and cultural influences. It mainly involves elbow swings, kicks, headbutts, knee strikes, and sweeps in a way that emphasizes deception, fluidity, and flexibility. The aim is to block all the attacks thrown by the opponent while also trying to go along the flow of their movements until the perfect window of attack presents itself.

The game revolves around deceptive ground movement, dynamic acrobatics, and the strategic use of strikes. The excitement lies in the challenges players face when they try to outmaneuver each other. In addition to being immensely fun, Capoeira helps the players develop both their mental and physical skills. This game was initially created to preserve the African traditions that were facing extinction due to the harsh reality of slavery. This game was a way for slaves to rebel and helped them to preserve their heritage since it involved common African dances like *n'golo* from Angola and used traditional African instruments.

The person who controls *the Roda* is instrumental in the game, and not everyone qualifies for this opportunity. All the participants in the hodder are equally important, and the audience is usually big and includes up to about 100 people.

Understanding the Roda

The Capoeiristas play in a circle called *Roda*, and its radius is 8 to 10 feet. During the game, the two participants, or "Jogan," are inside the Roda, and the other Capoeiristas are outside the circle singing and clapping their hands. The spectating Capoeiristas are either sitting or standing. The Capoeira master has the highest authority and is responsible for the events that take place inside the Roda. Several rules shape the players' behavior in the game and help resolve any disputes that may arise.

When the two Capoeiristas are ready, they touch the ground with their hands. They may even touch the berimbau as a way to bless themselves. They may also raise their hands to the nape of their neck or forehead. That is a ritual specifically meant to ask for protection during the game, and it depends on the player's religious beliefs. The players shake hands before they start.

The Capoeiristas get into the Roda through a space called boca-da-roda. This space is usually in front of the instruments. Once inside, they will stop after a few steps and perform facing each other near the middle of the stem. If two Capoeira Mestres are playing, no one can challenge them. When you become a Mestre, you attain the highest authority to control the game. When one of the Capoeiristas wants to end the game, they extend their hand to the opponent. However, caution should be exercised since this can be used as a tactic to ambush unsuspecting players. Both players can then bless each other, and they leave the Roda through the same spot they used to enter it.

If you want to play the game, you must make your intentions known and choose the opponent before entering the Roda. Everyone has an opportunity to participate in the *hodder*, which is the highest level of Capoeira. However, the hodder often consists of many professors, making it difficult for the players from the lower court to participate.

Symbolism

Ancient Capoeiristas believed there was a perfect analogy between the Roda and the world. The good thing about Capoeira is that it emphasizes teamwork. Entering the Roda is like going around the entire world. The ground in Capoeira is equivalent to heaven in western cultures, and no one is allowed to enter without permission. Leaving the Roda also requires permission.

To become an effective Capoeirista, you should be able to both sing and play instruments. This will make you a complete player. While you can learn different techniques in school, you should always seek out further education. All the instruments play a crucial role in fulfilling the game's religious beliefs.

Summary of Joga

Jogo is a game played in a circle called Roda. The players are in the middle of this circle with the audience around them. Music is central to the practice of Capoeira. It consists of a bateria (orchestra), which has three-stringed instruments that resemble a bow (berimbau), pandeiros (tambourine), and an agogo (bell). At the start, players sing a ritual song called a *ladainha*. A corrido is sung next, and it is played for the rest of the game. The music helps control the action, inspires the players, and determines their rhythm. The true essence of Capoeira is felt when the music and the movements of the players flow together in perfect harmony.

The Capoeira Grading System

Before the advent of the belt system, Capoeira had only two ranks, the student and the master/*Mestre*. Colored scarves were once used for graduation purposes, but they have since been abandoned in favor of the chords system. This system represents the grading strategy in Capoeira which shows a clear linear progression, student, teacher, and Mestre. There are different progressions for each particular title. The following are the modern level progressions.

Aluno or Student (6-12 Months)

In Portuguese, *Aluno* means student, and there are several student belts among different groups. The student is expected to learn more things with every chord they earn. The chords symbolize your hard work and are presented to you during a ceremony to mark the chord change or *troca de cordeõs*, usually hosted once a year. Your school or the center in your area will host the occasion. You get your chord after six months to a year, and this event is known as *batizado*, and it introduces you to the world of Capoeira. It marks the beginning of your journey toward reaching Mestre level.

As an Aluno, your responsibility is to put the lessons you get from the teacher into practice. The students should always ask the teacher what different things mean in Capoeira and how to perform certain moves. Persistence and patience are key components that can help you master Capoeira. Constant training is critical since it helps improve your skills.

Graduado/Monitor

This is the advanced student chord, and it is attained after 5-7 years of experience. Different names are given to advanced students, and they are not the same across the board. Your responsibility as an advanced student varies depending on your relationship with the teacher. A monitor or advanced student can be requested to display warm-ups, or they can also be asked to instruct other students. This is when you begin to develop some sense of independence and confidence to teach others. Teachers have lots of responsibilities, and they are good at playing all the instruments. They must also be good at instructing others. New students will look up to you if you reach the monitor stage. You must ensure that you show complete commitment to your responsibilities so that students can learn from you and your work ethic.

Instructor/Professor

To become an instructor or professor, you must have at least 8-12 years of experience. The instructor is the commonly used title, and attaining this chord means that you are ready to teach others Capoeira. However, you must know that instructors and professors still need to continue developing their skills even after they get this chord. It is essential that you stay close to your Mestre so that you continue to learn from them. You can also use this opportunity to brush up on things you may have forgotten from when you were a student. Many people will test you one way or another when you reach this stage, so you must be ready for anything. When you play Capoeira at a higher level, you gain more authority, and you will face fewer challenges. At this stage, you may teach other players, or you could also be asked to play with another teacher or Mestre.

Conta Mestre

After 15 years in the low-end position, you become the right-hand man of the Mestre. This is the chord right before the Mestre. When you become the contra Mestre, you become one of the most advanced students, and you are one step closer to becoming a master. By being the right-hand man, the Mestre expects you to fill their shoes whenever needed. You will be expected to teach classes and help students to improve. You need to learn a lot of things before you attain this rank. Many people will often train for 20 or more years to achieve the rank of *contra mestre*.

Mestre/ Master

The Mestre is the highest rank in Capoeira, and it is attained after 25 years of experience or more. However, reaching this rank does not mean that you have reached the end. You will always have more things to learn in the world of Capoeira. It is impossible to learn everything there is in Capoeira, and this is the major reason people are always striving to learn new things.

Grao Mestre/ Grand Master

This chord is not an official one. You get it from the Capoeira community. It is a recognition for all the hard work you have done and all the things you contributed to Capoeira. This honor is usually reserved for people with 30 to 50 years of experience in teaching and training Capoeira. This title is not easily handed out. It symbolizes a person who has significantly influenced the world of Capoeira in many ways. While there is no belt for this title, it comes with great respect and admiration from the community members.

It can be noted that Capoeira's grading system is chord-based, and it differs significantly from other martial arts which use the belt system. In Capoeira, different color chords are used for each level to differentiate the players. The highest level you can reach in this martial art is *Mestre* or master. The next chapter focuses on defensive Capoeira movements.

Chapter 3: Why Capoeira as a Martial Art?

Capoeira is known for its acrobatic athletic style. This 500-year-old martial art infused with a form of dance originated in the northeastern region of Brazil. This high-energy Brazilian art form uniquely blends music, arts, dance, and acrobatics together and uses highly mobile techniques requiring strength and flexibility. Capoeira not only allows you to stay fit and healthy, but it also has plenty of other benefits. If you think that you will never be able to do Capoeira then, it is not true. You don't have to be an acrobat to do this. With enough practice, determination, and consistency, anyone can. No matter how old you are, you can become fitter and healthier with just a few months of training. There are no limitations when it comes to Capoeira. You can find the form of Capoeira that works for you depending on your age, size, or weight.

It is important not to hold yourself to impossible expectations. There is no need to rush. Enjoy this martial art as much as you can. You will need to start with Ginga, from which all other movements are formed. Ginga means to sway in English. You will learn that all Capoeiristas have their own individual styles that bring out your personality. You must try to make your own moves as you go rather than trying to be someone else who may be more proficient. The best part about Capoeira is that everyone will help you reach your highest potential. This will be a great chance for you to develop your skills.

Moreover, you can learn by mirroring your partner, and in this way, you will be able to learn quickly and then finally evolve your own style. There are numerous advantages of practicing Capoeira. Let's take a look at a few of them:

Relieves Stress

Exercising is a great way to release stress and relax your body and mind. As you immerse yourself into this art form, you will be able to find what works for you. Capoeira is a way to escape work, personal issues, and anything that causes you stress. Moreover, exercising amplifies endorphin levels in your brain, and that instantly improves your mood and makes you happy.

Makes You Stronger

Practicing Capoeira increases strength and makes you extremely strong. It requires you to use complex hand and arm movements, kicks, handstands, and many poses that allow you to work on your full-body strength. These movements strengthen your upper body by engaging your core and working your abs. Capoeira movements make you more flexible, improve breathing, enhance blood flow, improve hand and eye coordination, and build slow and quick-twitch muscle fibers.

Improves Your Coordination

Practicing Capoeira improves your coordination with yourself as well as with others. The types of movements may vary depending on the type of Capoeira you're practicing. However, fluidity is a staple of all the forms. Coordinating your movements with live music relaxes your mind, body, and soul and improves your sense of rhythm.

Makes You More Flexible

Source[91]

Capoeiristas are extremely flexible individuals thanks to the various movements that they have to practice. The flexibility and strength allow them to drastically reduce the risk of injury and enhance their mobility. So, if you're looking to do yoga to increase your flexibility, give Capoeira a chance instead, and it will make you stronger and more resilient.

Increases Your Stamina

A Capoeira workout is bound to leave breathless after just a few minutes. Even if you are an athlete or are used to doing high-intensity workouts, don't be surprised if a Capoeira session ends with you gasping for air. It exercises most of your muscle groups and makes a good cardio exercise. Capoeira increases your stamina and helps you withstand extended and rigorous workout sessions.

Gain More Confidence

Capoeira is a difficult art form that is both fun and challenging. When you finally start to get your bearings, you feel more confident, alive, and happy. Moreover, the thrill you experience knowing that your friends could never pull off the moves you can is unmatchable. This wonderful martial art provides you with a chance to express yourself through your body. It allows you to finally free yourself from the shackles of your own limitations and let your true, authentic self shine.

Become More Social

Capoeira is practiced in teams, and everything is executed in groups. It gives you a chance to meet wonderful new people who have the same interests as you. This martial art form gives you a chance to come out of your shell and to be less timid. It offers you unforgettable individual as well as communal experiences. A Capoeira group is more like a separate family that encourages you to be your true self. By practicing Capoeira with a group, you will gain more confidence and a great sense of pride, knowing that none of your friends will be able to pull off the same moves as you. Meeting new people and socializing with like-minded individuals is just one perk of Capoeira.

Not Just a Sport

Capoeira involves various art forms, including dance, music, and self-defense. Other than actually participating and being inside the Roda, you can instead become a composer or choreographer.

Inclusion

Practicing Capoeira with different groups of people that come from all sorts of backgrounds helps you understand other cultures and exposes you to their traditions. That makes you more inclusive and accepting of others. Moreover, respecting others is a core value of capoeira. This is because this martial art form requires you to express your authentic self to fully experience it. Having respect for your teacher is also a very important tenet of Capoeira as they are teaching you things from their own experience, but they also enable you to understand many values vital to your life.

Learn a New Language

While learning or practicing Capoeira with a group, you will interact with many people that speak Brazilian Portuguese. This will help you understand and maybe even speak the language without much difficulty.

Learn a New Culture

Unlike other forms of martial arts, Capoeira has still preserved its roots and maintains its traditional and cultural values. This way, you not only get to learn about a new culture, but you can also broaden your mindset and become more understanding and accepting of other people.

It's Fun!

Isn't a place with good music, dance and happy people called a party? Capoeira has all of that. Watching Capoeiristas practicing to the sounds of live music is a great experience. Their mesmerizing motions and movements will make you feel energized and happy.

Self-defense Techniques

Capoeira is a great and fun way to learn self-defense. Capoeira teaches you to detect the other person's movement and how to act quickly. Being able to swiftly spot the other person's intentions can help you protect yourself and even counterattack. It is important to note that Capoeira does not encourage hitting the opponent. However, it is still a great way to teach young children self-defense techniques while also emphasizing the idea that it is never wise to resort to violence.

Get Your Family Involved

This martial art can give you a chance to practice with your family. This not only teaches you a valuable skill, but it also allows you to spend quality time with your family to strengthen your bond with them. Anyone can practice this art form. Playing and learning with your children will open up more channels of communication between you. You will also learn to accept and understand each other as you are.

Overall Fitness

Capoeira is an excellent martial art form that is good for both your physical and mental health. It improves your flexibility, stamina, and strength while making you more relaxed and stress-free.

Challenges of Capoeira

With all that said, you must be thinking that since Capoeira has so many benefits, it must be impossible to learn and practice. That's not the case. Like everything else in life, Capoeira comes with its own set of challenges, but it's very doable. No matter how inflexible or weak you may think you are, you can still do it. As a beginner, you must recognize that you will encounter many obstacles in your journey. Knowing that, you must continue to learn and strive to achieve perfection.

Mobility

There are many exercises in Capoeira that will require you to stay mobile. Mobility is a blend of flexibility and strength. For example, high kicks, low squats, and wheel poses or bridges are all examples of mobility. Many people find it challenging since they start out by not being as flexible as they should be to perform some of the moves. Most beginners find low squats difficult because they lack flexibility in their ankles and hips.

Moreover, the lack of strength in the muscles around the hips and ankles may cause them to fall over or collapse. Due to this reason, they find that mobility is the most difficult part of Capoeira. However, once you work hard enough to overcome your challenges, you will be able to gain strength and mobility in no time.

Rhythm

While Capoeira might be the only martial art form with music, the characteristics of rhythm and timing are very common in boxing, kung fu, and MMA. If you do not have experience playing a musical instrument or you have trouble following a beat, then you may find the musical aspects of Capoeira difficult. The good thing here is that you can always learn. Rhythm, timing, and pitch can all be learned with proper and gradual exposure to music. You will need to remain patient and consistent to learn the musical aspect of Capoeira.

Proprioception

Proprioception is the concept of understanding where your body is in space. Individuals with poor coordination are likely to have bad proprioception. Doing a cartwheel requires you to have good proprioception. If you have poor coordination, doing cartwheels may be difficult for you. This is pretty common among beginners. You will gradually learn your way around it as Capoeira can significantly help you build the awareness you need.

Improvisation

Flow and improvisation in Capoeira are quite difficult to achieve because you need to coordinate with another member of the group. Improvising sequences on your own can seem quite impressive but doing it in sync with someone else feels even better. It is extremely difficult to achieve, but once you get the hang of it, you'll know just how great it feels.

Capoeira's Impact on Society

It is important to note that Capoeira has a great impact on society. Besides being a martial art that revolves around attack and defense, it also emphasizes community, positivity, spirit, and unity. Capoeira plays a vital role in bringing people together and raising awareness about important causes. It has its roots in slavery. The enslaved people were not allowed to train to fight, which led them to create Capoeira. They disguised this martial art as a dance so they could still learn self-defense techniques. As this is practiced in a group, it helps the community connect on a spiritual level and helps individuals feel supported and valued.

When young people don't find an outlet for their anger and frustration, they turn to violence. A Capoeira group offers young people a safe space to express their true, authentic selves without hesitation. Moreover, it promotes equality. This means that anyone will feel they belong in the group. Regardless of who you are or what you identify with, you will be accepted into the group. Your size, age, and abilities do not affect your chances of being accepted. You just have to be willing to try, and you will be welcomed without facing any judgment or bias. In Capoeira, everyone is different and has their own unique style. This is why you won't be rushed or even pressured into learning a specific style. One of the biggest reasons to join a Capoeira group near you is to insert yourself in an accepting space where you feel safe and understood. This will allow you to grow as a person and to learn how to care for other people. Capoeira groups are all about giving back to the community. So, why not start today?

Capoeira is a wonderful sport made up of various art forms, including dance, music, martial arts, and self-defense. It dates back to when slavery was widely spread in Brazil. Back then, slaves were not allowed to engage in any fights or even train. This is why they created Capoeira. It's a martial art disguised as a dance. Practicing self-defense techniques looked just like dancing to the unsuspecting. However, it is important to note that the purpose of Capoeira is not to hurt the opponent but to protect yourself from risk and dodge any attacks. You can only counterattack in self-defense. Otherwise, the practice itself is quite peaceful. This art form has various benefits and is known for its incredible effect on people and communities.

Capoeira as a martial art will make you stronger, more flexible, and more balanced, but it will also help you become more relaxed and stress-free. This sport will help you learn various art forms, including music and dance. It will encourage you to come out of your shell and to embrace your true self. However, like everything else in life, it has its own challenges. Some aspects of Capoeira may seem too complex and challenging for you to achieve. It is possible that you may not be as mobile or flexible as you want to be, or you may not be musically inclined. It is also possible that you suffer from coordination issues or the inability to improvise. None of that really matters. With practice and consistency, you will be able to reach your goals in no time and become better with each passing day. Another amazing aspect of Capoeira is the community. You will feel appreciated and understood. One of the core values of Capoeira is to respect everyone, especially the teachers. This is why it is a safe space where everyone can be themselves without fear of judgment. Seeing how anyone belonging to any age group can participate in this martial art, you can practice with your whole family to build stronger bonds and improve the unity among each family member. Capoeira is truly an inclusive, respectful, and fun sport that gives everyone the chance to reach their highest potential.

Chapter 4: Capoeira Angola vs. Regional Capoeira

Capoeira allows each individual to develop their style. It is divided into three styles: Angola, Regional, and Contemporanea. But, before we jump into the differences, let's learn a little bit about the history of these styles. Capoeira Regional and Capoeira Angola were introduced by Mestre Bimba and Mestre Pastinha respectively. Mestre Bimba introduced some movements from Batuque and some from Jiu-Jitsu into Capoeira to make it more effective and interesting for the youth. The reason behind this alteration was to reignite the interest of Brazilian people in this martial art form as they were getting more into other martial arts from different countries. Seeing the decline of Capoeira among his people pushed Mestre Bimba to make these changes to the art form.

This effort by Mestre Bimba led to creating a new style and legalized training in it, which was initially banned. Mestre Pastinha introduced capoeira Angola in an attempt to preserve the original form of Capoeira. The word Angola comes from the African country from which Capoeira originated. The efforts of these Mestres saved Capoeira from declining and brought it back to Brazilian society. It is important to note that Capoeira practiced back in the days of slavery was different from the form of Capoeira being practiced today. In those days, slaves from various countries and African tribes were gathered in one place. This led to Capoeira being more of a dance created by a diverse group of individuals. It is possible that each tribe had its style of Capoeira.

Another style of Capoeira is called Capoeira Contemporanea. This name is used for both Capoeira Angola and Regional Capoeira practice. Other than this, some people dropped these labels and adopted a Capoeira style where aesthetics and acrobatic movements are prioritized. As Capoeira allows everyone to develop and practice their styles, splitting Capoeira into just these categories can be difficult. Some people may refer to their groups by the name of their Mestres, and others may stick to the traditional categories of Capoeira Angola, Regional, or Contemporanea. However, one thing that is similar among all these Capoeira forms is the communal spirit.

Now that you have acquainted yourself with the history of the different styles of Capoeira, let's move to the original topic of discussion, which asked, "What is the difference between Capoeira Angola and Regional Capoeira?"

Capoeira Angola

Source[92]

Capoeira Angola is currently being practiced in many different ways, depending on the Mestres teaching it. Some Mestres are faster, and some are slower, some are calmer, while others are fiercer. Moreover, some Mestres like to play closer to the ground while others prefer higher stances. With that said, here are some elements that all the Mestres share:

Capoeira Angola utilizes the bateria, which consists of three berimbaus, at least one or two pandeiro, one agogo, one reco-reco, and one atabaque. This ensemble may be used with some variations, but for the most part, it remains the same.

Angola, Sao Bento Grande de Angola is the main rhythm that is played by the berimbau Gunga. However, Sao Bento Grande de Angola is rarely used even though it is taught in the academies that give lessons on Capoeira Angola.

- Capoeira Angola uses chamadas during the game
- It uses specific songs
- The Capoeiristas are required to stay seated in the circle or roda unless it is their turn to play.
- It is mandatory to recognize Mestre Pastinha as the main representation of Capoeira Angola.
- It is rare to use acrobatic movements.
- There is no color code used to identify the rank of the Capoeirista, and there is no graduation where a Capoeirista progresses from one level to another.
- The Mestres strictly adhere to the form of Capoeira Angola.
- The Capoeiristas are required to dress in short-sleeved t-shirts and tucked-in pants.
- They are often required to play and train with shoes on.
- They usually wear belts with their pants.

Other than these similarities, the differences may be visible in the color of the clothes, the rhythms played by the different berimbaus-medio and viola, and the different movements used to play in the game. The Ginga may vary as well in different groups and even among students who have been trained under Mestre Pastinha. Capoeira Angola includes many elements that are not found in the other styles as it is the most similar to the original form of Capoeira. Most of these elements revolve around rituals and religion. This is why many Mestres pay tribute to their religion through a song. That is believed to amplify the power of the practitioners. This has become a ritual ever since it started centuries ago.

It is important to note that Capoeira Angola is mainly defined by the energy it creates and cannot only be described by the elements involved. There is nothing that can describe this energy. It needs to be felt and experienced. As Capoeira Angola is usually played close to the ground, the energy it creates is quite intense, fluid, vibrant, and concentrated. This energy can also be referred to as primal and directly originates from the earth. Capoeira Angola does not maintain a chord system. It chooses to stick to tradition. A Capoeirista is awarded the title of a Mestre after a year of training based on many factors.

Regional Capoeira

Mestre Bimba incorporated structured and methodical training techniques into Capoeira because he believed that it should be seen as a self-defense martial art. Regional Capoeira mainly differs from other Capoeira styles because it is faster, the bateria involved is simple but compact, the blows are direct, and it gives a clear indication of how the game is played.

One of the elements that make Regional Capoeira unique is that it has an entrance exam, which is a physical exam with Capoeira movements to assess the student's abilities. This style of Capoeira also consists of sequences that are based on 17 core Capoeira attack moves that have corresponding defense moves. These are referred to as the "sequências." Moreover, it is important to learn the different rhythms of the game and the specific training movements: traumatic moves, projection moves, instability moves, and connected moves. Regional Capoeira has a diploma called "Formatura" and specific advanced exams called "Especializacdo" and "Emboscada." However, it is important to note that some of the groups practicing Regional Capoeira today have a very different style from that of Mestre Bimba. There are some commandments, principles, and traditions that Bimba curated that must be followed and the training method. These principles are still followed by some groups today. Here are some of Mestres Bimba's principles:

- The practitioners must not smoke or drink, which can seriously affect their performance.
- Surprise is a vital element when it comes to Capoeira. This is why a Capoeirista must avoid showing progress outside the academy.
- The practitioners must practice certain movements every day.
- The adversary must not be feared as it will help you improve defense and attacking movements while keeping the body relaxed.

Certain commandments were specific to Bimba's teaching method. Here are a few of them:

- "Gingar Sempre" means that you must always Ginga (the basic Capoeira movement) to be in constant flow during the fight.
- "Esquivar sempre" means that you must always dodge.
- All the movements must have an objective and must not be used purely for aesthetics. Both the attack and defense techniques must be coordinated.
- Stay on the ground. Being firm and avoiding jumps or acrobatic movements make you vulnerable.
- The Capoeiristas must play to the rhythm of the berimbau.
- Respect is a vital component in Capoeira. You must respect the integrity of the player if they can no longer protect themselves against an attack.
- The strongest player must protect the weakest member. The practitioners need to protect the moral and physical integrity of the adversary.

There are some traditions and rituals that have become a part of his training:

- Beginners must be trained using a chair.
- "Charanga" is the Capoeira orchestra that consists of one berimbau and two pandeiros.
- Bimba composed the songs to support the game (Quadras e corridos)
- The first time a student plays to the rhythm of berimbau is referred to as the "batizado" or baptism.

Capoeira Contemporanea

Capoeira contemporanea was started in the '60s by the Capoeiristas who felt the need to blend Capoeira Angola and Regional Capoeira. This style was formed by utilizing the acrobatic movements and other lost elements of Capoeira from the past. This was started after Mestre Bimba's influence. This style was formed to unify Capoeira. Capoeira Contemporanea is usually played to the rhythm of Sao Beno Grande de Angola in a clearer manner and at a higher pace. This style has a different method of training but utilizes technical bases that are similar to the training given by Mestre Bimba.

Capoeira Contemporanea is the most well-known of all styles. It is the style of Capoeira usually shown on TV, movies, shows, etc. The games are quicker, more technical, and consist of acrobatic movements. This is why players keep a distance from each other to ensure safety. The two core groups that have contributed to the development of this new style are Abada Capoeira created by Mestre Peixinho and Capoeira Senzala developed by Mestre Camisa Roxa and his brother Mestre Camisa. All Contemporanea groups have different ways of organizing and playing in a Roda. Here are a few elements that all Contemporanea groups practice:

- All Capoeiristas must stand in the Roda just like in Regional Capoeira, some Angola groups, and in the older types of Capoeira groups.
- Sao Bento Grande and Angola or Benguela are the two main rhythms used.
- There is a graduation system.
- Most of the groups play wearing white abadas and are barefoot.
- The games incorporate *floreios* (flowery movements).
- The games are quick, vibrant, compact, dynamic, and aerial.
- The bateria is quite similar to the one in Capoeira Angola as it consists of 3 berimbaus, 1 or 2 pandeiros, 1 agogo, 1 reco-reco, and 1 atabaque.
- It is important to note that each group is unique and that there will always be differences.

Graduation

Upon graduation, all the Capoeira styles have a common point of focus: the title of *Mestre* awarded after years of training. The Capoeira Angola group does not follow any chord system and abides by tradition. Moreover, in a Contemporanea group, the title of Mestre is recognized by a red chord. However, before getting the title of a Mestre, Capoeiristas are awarded different titles. The most common one is the title of Contra-Mestre. All groups and all styles recognize this title. The title of professor is also quite common. A professor is someone who is licensed to teach, whereas a Mestre is someone who his students and his peers recognize.

Mestre Bimba originated the graduation system, and it has evolved ever since. Originally, only the title of Mestre existed, and it was given to a Capoeirista who is recognized as someone who has mastered the art of Capoeira. When it comes to Regional Capoeira, the rules are specifically defined. It is played to rhythms created by Mestre Bimba. He specifically created the rhythm of Benguela to give the players of Regional Capoeira the ability to interact with the players of Capoeira Angola. This rhythm is based on the rhythm of Angola. However, the player would never make the same movements as a player from Angola. For example, there would be no *chamada* or any head movement. They would not be called back by the berimbau for a short suspension of the game for any reason, either. Nonetheless, the Madingua is still present even though it might be played in a different style.

Quiz

Still confused about the Capoeira style that might be the best for you? Here's a quiz:

1. Do you want to follow a strict set of rules for learning a martial art form?

    a. Yes

    b. No

    c. Maybe

2. Do you want to practice any acrobatic movements in your Capoeira style?

    a. No

    b. Yes

    c. Maybe

3. Do you want to have a graduation ceremony to pass to the next level?

    a. No, it is unnecessary.

    b. Yes, of course.

    c. I don't mind it.

4. Do you want to use specific songs in your practice?

    a. Yes.

    b. No.

    c. I would like to keep my options open.

5. Capoeira should be purely about defense and attack techniques.

    a. Yes

    b. Not really.

    c. It doesn't hurt to use some acrobatic techniques.

6. I don't want to be restricted by rules.

    a. No.

    b. Yes, rules are the worst!

    c. There should be some rules.

7. The emphasis of Capoeira should be on the technique.

    a. No, strategy and deception are also important.

    b. Yes.

    c. Absolutely.

8. How do you like your Ginga?

    a. Improvisational.

    b. Standard.

    c. Cadenced.

9. Do you want your attacks to be fast-paced?

    a. No, they should be slow and steady.

    b. Yes, they should be quick and compact.

    c. Absolutely!

10. Are you attracted to titles?

    a. No, not at all.

    b. Yes, they're great!

    c. Yeah, it doesn't hurt to have them.

Answer

If you selected option "a" the most, you should go for Angola.

If you selected option "b" the most, you should go for Contemporanea.

If you selected option "c" the most, you should go for Regional Capoeira.

Capoeira has a rich history and traditions that bring many benefits to its practitioners. The Capoeira Angola and Regional Capoeira may have some differences, but the inherent self-defense techniques and the elements of respect and using rhythms while playing are all common in every style of Capoeira. Capoeira Angola was introduced by Mestre Pastinha, who believed in sticking to the traditional principles of Capoeira which were used by the Capoeiristas of the past, whereas Mestre Bimba started regional Capoeira. He blended Capoeira with other forms of martial arts, including Kung Fu and Jiu-Jitsu. This was done to attract the youth back to the art of Capoeira as people had started losing interest in it and were getting distracted by other forms of martial arts. Mestre Bimba is recognized for his efforts in the sport of Capoeira and for bringing it back to the Brazilian community.

Another form of Capoeira is called Contemporanea. It is a blend of the two styles, Capoeira Angola and Regional Capoeira. It utilizes practices from both to make Capoeira more interesting, and it is the most well-known style out of them all. Contemporanea is almost always the style shown in TV shows, movies, etc. It is more appreciated due to its acrobatic movements and its focus on aesthetics. You must recognize which Capoeira style suits you best and which resonates with the kind of experience you are looking for. The best part about Capoeira is that everyone can find their own style. Take the quiz to get a clear idea of what you want, and then get started on your journey to becoming a Capoeirista.

Chapter 5: Core Capoeira Principles and Movements

Since the history of Capoeira is not that well documented, we don't know what the initial purpose of this art form was. Today, it is classified as a martial art. This chapter will provide more information about the moves used in this martial art that closely resemble *dance moves.*

It's important to understand that Capoeira was born under Portuguese colonialism in Brazil during a time when slavery was prevalent, and slaves were not allowed to practice their own traditions, religions, or cultures. Moreover, this region had slaves from all over the world, so it's hard to pin down a single culture it could have originated from.

It's hard to believe that it was envisioned purely as a form of fighting. It was cleverly disguised behind music and rhythm as a dance. The large flowing movements combined with explosive attacking power and elusive defensive strategies are difficult to decipher.

Keep in mind that Capoeira's main purpose is not to fight. It is considered a game, and both participants always aim to win instead of defeating the opponent. Winning does require taking down the opponent, and there is much more to it than just brute strength.

Let's look at some of the core principles in Capoeira and how they translate into the main movements.

Core Principles

1. Interaction

Capoeira can be played in many different ways ranging from an interaction that resembles a casual conversation to something that looks like the physical depiction of a heated argument. This interaction is a fundamental component of this martial art. You will notice that, during a game, opponents maintain intense eye contact and may even talk to each other. Their moves will reflect what they are saying and what is happening in that instant.

Capoeira is as much a mental game as it is a physical one. Each player is trying to study the other to develop a response that they hope their opponent won't be able to respond to, especially after breaking their defense or counterattacking.

In Capoeira, it is also common to see players distracting or taunting one another with slaps, pushes, pushback kicks, and various handstands. These are all things that can be done in a casual way to let the other person know that they need to pay more attention. The intensity behind some of these moves makes the difference between a gentle pushback kick and one that will leave you out of breath.

Players can be on the defensive or on the offensive. If a player is able to understand what the other is doing and has the skill to handle the attack, they can win regardless of their Capoeira style.

2. Movement

Source[98]

Movement and motion are fundamental pillars of this game. Even the basic stance a player holds is not a stationary one. Rather, players are constantly moving, changing places, and always ready to smoothly transition into another move.

This fluidity means that no attack is a hard movement, and no defense is a hard block. Instead, the focus is on dodging and using momentum from the constant movement to generate a powerful attack that the other player will not see coming. On the other hand, a player also must be fluid enough to dodge any similar attack.

For this reason, Capoeira can be extremely physically taxing, and it requires a lot of energy to stay in the fight and a lot of resilience to take on the brutal hits. Using all the momentum they gain from constantly moving around, Capoeira martial artists can generate very powerful punches, kicks, and even head butts.

3. Deception

All this movement gives rise to a lot of deception and false alarms. For instance, even in the initial stance, where a player is shuffling from one foot to another, you never know whether they are about to burst into an attack or whether they are preparing to defend themselves. The various stances are extremely open-ended, allowing the player to do anything they want to do and making it very challenging for the opponent to analyze and anticipate.

In fact, there is an entire set of moves known as "Floreios" that are designed specifically to trick your opponents. Anything and everything you can think of doing with the intention to distract or deceive the opponent is a part of this game. Whether you are pointing to something outside of the arena or pretending to be hurt, it all forms part of this martial art.

4. Resistance

Capoeira began with the slaves, and being oppressed, they knew that they couldn't get anywhere by using force. Rather, they relied on using clever techniques and altering the attacker's own momentum to work against him. This has translated into the various indirect resistance moves that cunningly work around an attack. In some cases, the player may just choose to dodge high-energy attacks until the opponent is drained, or they may weave through the attacks to find a weak spot that they can hit.

When it is happening in front of your eyes, you may think it is choreographed, but in fact, there is a lot of thinking and strategy behind every move, and it all relies on a strong body to execute those moves perfectly.

Main Movements

The entire dance of Capoeira consists of a few different kinds of clearly identifiable movements that are put together in a way that they seamlessly fit together. Some sequences are so seamless that the opponent cannot tell what is about to come next. This is only aided by the fact that any move can be created from any point if the player is skilled enough. Here is a brief breakdown of the main categories of movements and some of the most common maneuvers.

1. Basic Movements

Unlike other martial arts, in Capoeira, even the initial or idle stance of a player is, in fact, counted as a move. They are quite literally moving around, and while there are a few basic stances that all players use, with more experience, they are able to personalize them and have their own unique take on them.

The Ginga – Swinging Step from One Side to the Other

The Ginga[94]

The player is close to the ground, knees bent, arms out, and swinging in this move. The player shifts position from one foot to the other while maintaining a solid foundation at all times. This is a fantastic launching stance, and a player can use the momentum to explode into any kind of attack or defense.

The Ginga is the most common stance used in any kind of Capoeira. There are a few variations, but the core principle remains the same. As players get more advanced, they may modify their Ginga depending on their game plan and overall technique.

An Au – Cartwheel

An Au[95]

In essence, this is a cartwheel, but there are many variations that can be used for many purposes. In the most basic form, this is a slow circular movement in which players stay low and tight to keep a low center of gravity and a smaller profile. In some cases, the player might pause in a handstand to make a different move, or they may progress all the way through the cycle to land on their feet.

Like many things in Capoeira, the Au could be used as a transition to a move or an evasion of one. Moreover, it can be combined with several other moves to create a more elaborate maneuver.

One of the more advanced moves is the Bananeira, which is a handstand that resembles a banana tree. In this move, the opponent will have their hands about shoulder-width apart and may have their legs together or apart. The legs could be split sideways or front and back, and this is an effective block for many of the opponent's moves. This move stands out from other handstands because the player is still facing the opponent during the Bananeria and can modify the step move according to what he anticipates that the opponent will do.

2. Defensive Movements

The word "*Esquivas*" literally means "evading attacks."

When it comes to Capoeira, there are a lot of defensive moves, strategies, and techniques that players can choose from. The Equivas is one of the most commonly used defensive moves among all of these. More specifically, it is a technique in which a player tries to dodge an attack or counter an attack by using the momentum generated by the attack itself.

This is a sport in which each attack, especially if it is a kick, is launched with so much torque and momentum that trying to block it will still cause a lot of damage. The most efficient strategy is to dodge these power moves, find a weak spot, and counterattack, all in the flow of one smooth move.

3. Kicks

This is probably one of the highlights of Capoeira, kicks so powerful that you can seriously injure yourself just trying to block them. They can be used in various ways in this game and may take the form of an attack, a defense, or evasion.

One of the most powerful kicks in the sport is the Armada. This is a reverse roundhouse kick, also known as the spinning, inside to outside crescent kick.

This kick can either be done with the arms on the floor, or it can be done with a jump holding the upper body upright in midair. In either formation, the power is generated from the spinning of both the hips and the upper body, creating an incredibly powerful kick. Then there are many variations to the Armada depending on how it is done and whether it is meant to attack the upper body or the lower body of the opponent.

Armada

Another commonly used and very effective kick is known as the *Bencao,* which literally translates to "blessing." This is a straight frontal kick usually thrown from a standing position with the intent to hit the opponent with either the flat sole or the heel of the foot. It is a kick that has many uses and can be used as a defensive pushback or can be an attack on its own. It is usually aimed at the chest or the torso but can also be used to target the chin, face, or head.

Bencao

Another lethal kick is the *Martelo*. This is a kick in which the player takes a step forward and then targets the opponent's body with the lower part of their shin. This kick can hit any area of the opponent, but the most effective blow is aimed at the opponent's temple. This is usually a knockout move if the opponent fails to dodge or block it. The step forward creates momentum, and the overall movement of the entire leg adds more torque to the final blow.

Martelo

4. Hand and Arm Strikes

While footwork is the highlight of Capoeira, arms and hand strikes are also used extensively. They can be just as effective as a good kick with the right technique and move selection.

Similarly, hands and arms are also used as tools of deception. Players often wave their arms around or make over-exaggerated movements with their arms as if implying that a hand attack is coming while, in reality, they are about to launch a kick.

One of the most effective arm moves is known as the *Cotovelada*. This is an elbow move that can cause serious damage when performed right. If planted on the face, fractures of the skull, jaw, or damage to eye sockets are inevitable. This is a very powerful move used most in close-quarter combat.

Cotovelada

Another move is the Galopante, which is actually a slap to the face or the ear. This is used more as a distraction and as a message to the opponent, but it is also a very effective move when performed correctly.

5. Takedowns

Capoeira is a sport in which grappling and wrestling moves do not play a large role, but some types of takedown are used in particular situations. In most cases, takedowns are in the form of leg sweeps.

One of the reasons why takedowns are not used that much is because Capoeira does not really focus on the ground game. While many people do single-leg and double-leg takedowns, there is not much to do on the ground after that.

In most cases, takedowns are done with the legs as a defensive move and usually to counter other kick attacks. Timing is key to such a move, and this is something that you will witness when watching more advanced players.

6. Floreios

Traditionally, these are visually appealing moves and mostly acrobatic in nature. This doesn't mean they aren't effective as a defense or an attack, but the primary objective is to either create a distraction or just to display skill. Depending on the situation that they are used in, they could serve either purpose.

One of the most popular moves in this category is the helicopter kick, also known as the *Helicoptero*. In this maneuver, the player performs a cartwheel but lands with the foot that was the last to leave left the floor. In this way, they perform one and a half rotations with one leg and one big crescent with the other. This could be used as an attack or a defense, or it could be used as a fancy dodge to simply get out of the way on an oncoming attack.

Capoeira Today

Things have changed in the hundreds of years that this martial art has been around. In previous times, and even in some situations today, Capoeira can be a deadly sport. With the endless types of power move that a player has at his disposal, they can damage their opponent, and it can even be fatal.

However, modern Capoeira is more of an art, and the players aim to create a challenging strategic battle rather than to harm the other player.

Several moves were used in the past that are no longer used today in formal Capoeira. Things such as jabs to the eyes and kicks to the throat can easily be fatal and can impair a person for the rest of their life.

Rougher forms of street Capoeira that do not abide by formal regulation do not limit the kinds of moves players can choose from. In formal schools, these things are no longer taught, and there is more emphasis on strategic play.

To get more advanced in Capoeira and to be able to really increase the technicality of your game, you need to not only know the moves, but you also need to be in fantastic physical condition.

Many of the moves that players use double up as strength-building exercises and are used extensively in practice before a player can move on to more advanced techniques.

Chapter 6: Attacking Capoeira Movements

Attacks in Capoeira include moves that are directed toward the opponent, and they vary from palm strikes, kicks, and headbutts. Most attacks are circular kicks or straight kicks which come from Ginga. Since Capoeira is a non-contact sport, most of these attacks don't reach the opponent. This chapter specifically focuses on the basic Capoeira attacking moves you should know.

Capoeira Moves

Capoeira moves and techniques consist of unique movements that range from intense kicks to escapes. These moves are significant to the fluid nature of the game, and you should learn, remember, and use them. There are many types of effective moves, but they can be overwhelming for beginners. The following are basic Capoeira moves that you can use.

Common Types of Capoeira Move

The common types of Capoeira moves can be divided into five groups depending on their primary function. The following are the five groups.
1. Relocation movements (Movimentos)
2. Attacks (Attaka)
3. Defenses (Defensa)
4. Beautifiers/acrobats (Florelos)
5. Displacements/falls (Deslocamentos/Quedas)

Depending on how the moves are used, some of them can belong to more than one category. Your experience will determine your ability to connect different categories of moves.

Relocation Movements (Movimentos)

You can use relocation movements when you want to change your position or move continuously in Capoeira. A Capoeirista is constantly moving and changing directions. You can be moving up and down, forward, or backward. Basic movements offer you the foundation to play Capoeira since you can use them around the Roda. The basic moves for relocation you should know include Role and Ginga. These moves are commonly used as a defense, doing acrobatic taunts, and attacking. If you want to be good at Capoeira, it is essential to master the relocation moves.

Attacking Moves

This chapter mainly focuses on attacking movements that you use as a beginner. Capoeira does not include any physical contact but attacking is part of the game. Attacks can vary from kicks, headbutts, or palm strikes. However, in most cases, kicks are used the most. The attacks can be circular, round, or straight, and they all start from Ginga. As you will see in the following section, the Ginga helps hide attacks, which is why Capoeira is believed to be a dance. It provides some fun and also keeps the spectators entertained.

Ginga

This is a fundamental move in Capoeira that every player should be familiar with. It is a constant rhythmic movement that is employed by very few other martial arts. The Ginga comes in different forms, and its main purpose is to prepare your body for different types of movement like delivering attacks, evading, and throwing feints. In other words, it is the foundation for defenses, attacks, and florelos.

When you begin this move, your feet should be parallel to each other, and try to maintain the width of your shoulders. Take a step backward with your right leg and avoid going too far. While the leg is moving backward, move your right arm in front of your face and make sure the fingers are pointing to the left. This position is called the Ginga. You can start the process over and use your left leg and left arm pointing to the right. When you continue this motion by switching between the right and left, you are doing the Ginga. To familiarize yourself with it, start practicing it from one position, and then try to do it in a circle.

Since the Capoeirista is constantly in motion, this helps frustrate the advancing opponent. The move offers synchronization of the movement of the arms to avoid attacks; the legs and torso help to prevent high kicks while at the same time maintaining your balance. During the Ginga, you don't hold a static position and the rhythm coming from the bateria determines the speed.

Cadeira

Cadeira

The *paralelo* or the *cadeira* is a position found in the Ginga, and both legs will be squared off. This makes the move the appropriate base for the Ginga. The cadeira is usually a low position that resembles the one adopted by a shortstop. It also has many things in common with the horse stance often found in Eastern martial arts. You use one arm to protect the face while the other protects the opposite side in this move. You will use most of your body muscles to maintain your balance.

Several attacks, escapes, and movements can flow easily from this position. Those include balança, queda de rins, au, resistência, martelo, cabeçada, and others. The following section explains how you can perform basic Capoeira attacks.

Rolé (Ho-Lay)

This move is designed to help you remain low while you relocate to find a quick way to get up and return to Ginga. There are different methods you can use to get into Rolé. You can start with the Queda de Quatro position, where you will then decide the direction to go. If you want to roll to the right, your right foot should stick out, and your toes should point to the right. While lifting your left hand, try to reach your head and place it on the floor. Try to carry the left leg over the right leg simultaneously. You must end up with both legs parallel to each other on the floor with your hands flat as well. The next move is to get back to the Quatro, and you continue in the same direction. Your left leg should be under the right leg, and you should end up right where you started.

Role

When you want to utilize Rolé to get up, you need to make some adjustments to the steps above. You must do your Rolé to the right and keep your foot and toes sticking out to your right. Then try to reach your lifted hand and place it on the floor. At the same time, you must put your left leg over your right leg. Whatever move you choose, you will end up in a Ginga position.

Rolé is primarily used when you want to relocate in the Roda quickly. This helps you get up faster and create some attacking distance between you and the opponent. The direction of your feet is where you will go. You can use Rolé to defend against an attack or to hide an attack. You can also use it to initiate an attack if you want. This move is versatile, and you must know it to improve your Capoeira skills. You can also combine it with Aú to come up with "Aú Rolé."

Benção

Benção means blessing and refers to a straight push kick that starts from Ginga. You can use this move to attack the opponent, and it is one of the most important straight kicks you can learn in Capoeira. You will use the leg at the back to kick. Lift the back leg, put your knee to your chest, and then place your hands in front of you as if you are holding a board. Make sure you use the other leg to keep you balanced.

Do this as if you intend to break the board using the bottom of your feet. You will be using them to push upward while you pull your arm backward. Pull your extended leg back to the Ginga position to end the kick.

Benção is a kick that you mainly use to attack the torso or any spot between the hip and the neck. While the kick is easy to perform, it can be a great challenge to use effectively because of the distance and balance. You need to keep the following things in mind when using Benção.

- You should not be too close so that you are not vulnerable. The kick will have little impact if you are.
- Your kick will be ineffective if you are too far. You will be kicking the air, and there might be no reason for the opponents to react.

Therefore, it is essential to find an ideal distance to effectively perform this move. You must practice by slowly doing this kick and aiming at a marked position on the wall or at any other target you are comfortable with. You should aim to achieve a good distance when making contact with the wall, and you should not bend your knees too far upwards. You should aim to achieve a good distance before you contact the wall and make sure you do not bend the knees too far upward.

MeiaLua de Frente (Meya-Luwa Gee Frenchi)

This half-moon kick is one of the basic kicks you should master when you begin practicing. Seeing how this kick is in the form of a half-circle, it belongs to the round/circular category. When you perform this kick, your right leg will swing, and it starts from the back and moves across the body. Your right leg is at the back when you start from the Ginga position.

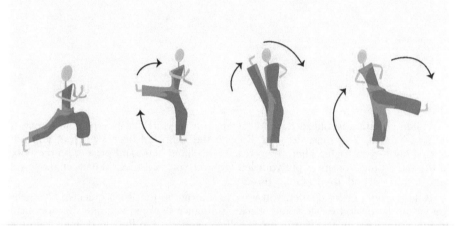

MeiaLua de Frente

This type of kick is considered one of the first that anyone should learn, and it is a perfect move when it is done with control and power. As this kick is in the form of a half-circle, it belongs to the round/circular category. When performing this kick, the leg swings from the back, making a semi-circle from the outside and moving across the body. You start from the Ginga position, and your right leg will be at the back.

Martello (Maar-Teh-Low)

Meaning "hammer" in English, this straight kick is used to attack. It is pretty much like a roundhouse kick used to attack the side of the body or head.

Martello

This straight kick is also known as the *hammer*. It is used when attacking your opponent. The roundhouse kick is specifically used when attacking the side of the body or head in Capoeira. When playing Capoeira, your intention is not to kick the partners' legs or their knees since this can cause serious injury. As a beginner, you should always aim to direct your kicks to areas above the torso.

Armada

This move is a circular kick where the entire body rotates, and you can use it for attacking. You start from the Ginga position if you want to do this kick and make sure your left leg is in the front while the right leg is in the back. Your posture should be like someone with their legs crossed when standing. The upper part of your body should be turned toward the direction of the right leg.

When you decide to begin the Ginga with the right leg at the back and your left leg in front, use your left leg to step to the right slightly. You should stand like someone standing with crossed legs. Turn the upper part of your body in the direction of your right leg.

Aú

Aú translates to *cartwheel* in English. It is performed differently from the cartwheel you already know. You walk using your hands with this move, but you look to the front, not toward the floor. You must place your chin on your chest to achieve this. The Aú move is specifically meant to improve the visual element of Capoeira, and you can use it for an attack or defense. Your intention will determine how you will use the Aú move.

Bananeira

Bananeira

The *bananeira* comes from a banana tree – and is a handstand. When doing Capoeira, you must be able to walk using your hands, and your legs will be on top. You must be looking straight ahead, not at the floor when you are walking with your hands. This will help you face the other player and improve the game's visual elements. You can use your legs to attack and defend. You can also use this move to take a short break or draw the opponent into a trap as they watch you perform your antics. This is another way of showing off your balance since the other purpose of Capoeira is to provide entertainment.

Tips to Learn Movements

It is not very easy to learn some of the attacking movements in Capoeira. The following tips can help you stay focused and learn quickly.

- Train with an experienced teacher. While it may appear simple to imitate different moves without an instructor, working with an experienced professional is essential. A good teacher has a lot of experience you can benefit from, and they also know what you need to master different techniques.

- Warm-up. You must warm up before you attempt any Capoeira move. Stretching will prepare your muscles for movements you are still new to so that you do not hurt yourself.
- Practice. Knowing something is different from doing it. Many people think that they can perform different things since they have theoretical knowledge, but this is not always the case. Practice helps you learn several movements, and you can only gain confidence after several attempts. You should never give up if your first attempt does not yield the desired results. Through constant practice, you will gain much-needed experience.
- Be attentive. You should always pay attention to every move to understand how to shift your weight or which position you should be in. You can hurt yourself if you fail to understand the basic sequence you should follow in each move.
- Be confident. You must be confident that you can perform whatever move you're practicing. Be confident in your abilities.

On top of these tips, you must closely work with your instructor to master different things. You must use every opportunity to ask about anything that you do not understand. You also need to repeat specific moves that are difficult to get right for beginners. Learning Capoeira is a long process. Practice helps you familiarize yourself with different movements that can go a long way in improving your skills.

When playing Capoeira, you should constantly be moving in the Roda. These moves are basic to the game of Capoeira, and they can also help you grasp more tactics. With these tips, you can significantly improve your skills. Keep in mind that learning Capoeira never ends. There is always something new to master.

Chapter 7: Defensive Capoeira Movements

In Capoeira, there should be no physical contact, but there are defensive moves you should know. When you are under attack, you should know how to protect yourself to avoid severe harm. This chapter discusses different defense moves and how to effectively perform each one.

Capoeira as Self-Defense

Wondering if Capoeira is the most effective martial art you can use for self-defense? Many people consider martial arts to protect themselves. However, Capoeira is viewed as a game and less effective for self-defense, but you can still use it to evade attacks. While it is widely believed that Capoeira is non-contact and predominantly for show, it can be the best option for self-defense. Capoeira is popular in street fighting since it prepares you to be agile and teaches you some versatile moves.

Defensive Capoeira Movements

There are different Capoeira moves that you can use for defense. The following are the most common defensive moves.

Ginga

Source[96]

In Capoeira, Ginga is the most basic movement you should know. To perform this move, you must move back, then forward, and then sideways while alternating between both legs. Your hands will also be moving along with your body to protect the parts prone to attacks. Ginga is a fundamental move of Capoeira, and very few martial arts utilize this strategy.

The main purpose of Ginga is to prepare your body for different movements that include feinting, evading, and delivering attacks. As a Capoeirista, you are constantly in motion, and this helps frustrate the opponent and keep them at bay. This is an effective defense technique that assists you in maintaining your torque. It also helps you avoid losing your balance in crucial moments.

Balanca

Balanca involves a combination of side-to-side feint moves that are specifically meant to deceive the opponent. It also makes it hard for the opponent to predict your next move. The Capoeirista's arms are always moving sideways in Balanca to protect the face. It is ideal to defend yourself against quick kicks, hand-strikes, and headbutts. In this move, you also shift the weight of your body from one leg to the other while maintaining balance. If you perfect it, you can execute unexpected strikes.

Negativa

Source[97]

Capoeiristas use this particular move to negate incoming attacks by lowering their bodies to the ground. You can lower your body to one side, and one hand will support it while the other protects the face. The legs are kept close to each other, and the body must be in a strategic position to avoid injuries. You can practice this move with your stomach lying parallel to the ground. It can also be utilized as a sweep. If the other player intends to deliver a standing kick, all of their weight is supported by just one leg. That is the perfect chance to use your extended leg to hook theirs from behind and sweep it. This move is a great way to protect your face.

Cocorinha

Cocorinha is a simple and effective defense move that protects you against round kicks directed at your torso or head. You must squat with your feet flat on the ground and your knees close to your chest to protect your body. Use one hand to protect the head while the other hand supports you flat on the ground. You can also squat with your arms crossed above your face. This way, your body can easily go lower, so you can evade all incoming kicks. If you are balancing using your left arm, the right arm's position will make it appear as if you are sniffing the right armpit. The right fist should be pointing to the left and vice versa if you are using the left arm for defense.

If you want to enter Cocorinha from the Ginga position, the right leg should be at the back while the right arm is up. Step forward with the right foot parallel to the left foot, and then squat as you move forward. Make sure both feet are flat on the ground, and the left hand is also on the floor. While you are stepping forward, make sure your right arm is above the head, and the fist is also pointing to the left side. You can resume the Ginga position once the kick has passed.

Esquiva

Source[98]

Esquiva is a low dodge or escape that you can use to avoid kicks by shifting down to the right or left depending on where the kick is coming from. Esquivas make Capoeira different from other types of martial arts in that it goes with the flow of the attack while at the same time releasing a potentially more devastating attack. Most Capoeira attacks are full kicks that can cause more injury if you try to block them instead of dodging them. There are mainly two types of Esquiva, namely Esquiva de Baixa and Esquiva Lateral.

Esquiva de Baixa

The move is similar to Ginga, but your body will be closer and lower to the ground. The hands and the legs move together while bringing the hips to the ground. You bend the torso forward, bringing your head lower, using your left hand to protect the face.

Esquiva Lateral

This move is translated as "side dodge" or "side escape," and you can move to the right or left side depending on the direction of the kick. You can use one hand to support the body while the other protects your face.

Esquiva Diagonal

Esquiva diagonal is another example of dodge that simultaneously goes with forwarding advancement. Instead of going off to the side to dodge an attack, you step diagonally to the right or left of the attack. This offers you a chance at counterattack where the right arm will protect the face, and the other arm maintains body balance.

Queda de Quatro

Source[99]

The Queda Quatro refers to "Fall on four" and consists of a defensive mechanism, a very simple move that you can do when you find yourself falling backward. This is more like you got pushed down and landed with your two hands behind you on the floor. However, your torso and butt must not touch the floor. You can use this particular move as a defense against a straight attack. The move is also effective against pushing or straight kicks as you intentionally fall backward to move away from the kick.

You can skillfully control your fall, and the move negates the impact of the kick. You can also fall into a crab-walk position and scurry away from the opponent. While you are down, you will be in a position to monitor the opponent and track their next course of action.

Resistência

Source[100]

A resistência move is similar to the negative, but the soles of your feet do not support your weight. The ball of your foot is the support point, while your arm on the opposing side helps. To protect your wrist, you must spread the fingers on the supporting hand on the floor. You should raise the other arm to protect the face and slightly extend the leg outward but with a bend. The bend is essential since it helps protect your leg against any pressure that could lead to injuries and support your gastro soleus and quadriceps muscles to prevent extended pressure on the knee.

While most beginners want to look at the floor when they are in this position, it is recommended that you look up. This will help you keep an eye on your opponent so that you can closely monitor their moves or attacks. You may not be able to defend yourself if you are not aware of the other player's intention.

Rolê

You can apply Rolê or the rolling motion together with the AU and Ginga to help you move around the Roda as a defense strategy. You can use this method to spin to one side and remain low on the ground while you watch the other player. When you perform this move, make sure you keep eye contact with the opponent and closely monitor all their movements. This move can end in Negativa, Ginga, or different types of esquivas. You can transition to different techniques to gain an advantage and watch all attacks from a safe distance.

Other Defensive Movements

You can also use different types of kicks for defense when playing Capoeira.

Armada

You can use this move as a Rabo-de-Arraia where your hands are not on the floor. The head will slightly fall below the waist, and you use the heel to execute your kick. Alternatively, you can also use Meia Lua de Costas or a half-moon from the back to execute a spinning kick with your body upright. You use the outside of the foot to strike the surface. The torque you place on your hips plays a pivotal role in determining the power of the armada. You will release your kicking leg to complete the arc and come back to become parallel to the other leg while your hands protect you against punches.

Armada Pulada

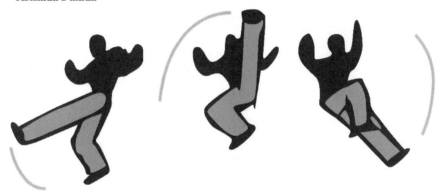

This is the kind of Armada that you release after a jump. Just like the regular armada, the Capoeirista can choose any side they want to release the spinning aerial kick. This should happen after the neck, head, and shoulders rotate toward the front.

Armada Dupla

This move is also called Envergado, and the major distinguishing feature is that your legs will remain together when you take off, execute, and land. The name also means double armada, and your torso will stay upright, but it will begin to gain power as you swing your legs upwards and around. Your body will assume the shape of a V when you reach the peak of this particular move. As your body readies for landing, your legs will continue to swing, and the move is known as a double leg. This is a trademark kick that is unique to Capoeira and also offers you defense against an opponent.

Armada com Martelo

This move is basically a spinning double kick, and it starts with an armada pulada and ends with a martelo. You will start with the same armada motion. When you raise your first leg, you jump off your back leg. When the first leg has completed the arc, the leg that you have jumped off will come around like a jumping martelo rotado.

Bênção

Source[101]

This is a straightforward frontal kick, and it is common when aiming at the chest or abdominal area. You will hit with the entire sole of your foot or the heel, and the impact varies depending on your intent and range. For instance, *chapa* is known as the sole of the foot, and it is used for straight kicks with the heel. You can use this type of kick to push the opponent away while you defend yourself. The following are the types of kicks that you can perform with the sole of your foot.

Chapa-de-Costas

This kind of kick resembles a horse kick, and you perform it by kicking the opponent while both your hands are on the ground. The kick can target the opponent's knee or groin.

Chapa-de-Frente

This is a straight kick that you perform facing the opponent, and it appears like a Bençao a Queda de Quatro.

Pisào

This is a sidekick, and the first player will start by lifting the knee of the leg they intend to kick with to hip level.

While Capoeira does not involve physical contact, there are specific moves that you should use for defense purposes. You can use each move for different situations. Try to find the appropriate defensive moves for each situation, and do not recklessly use a move that can harm you. More importantly, you should practice every single move you can find. You can never be *too ready.*

Chapter 8: Groundwork in Capoeira

When we look at the various movements used in Capoeira, it is easier to understand them in the middle of a game. For instance, Capoeira Contemporanea uses the same moves as Angola, but the purpose and the strategy are very different. Similarly, different kinds of games of Capoeira use different strategies, and depending on the situation, certain moves may be more appropriate than others.

Floreios in Capoeira can take many forms. Generally, Floreios is understood as being the "flowery," acrobatic, or aesthetic set of moves in Capoeira. Most players who perform these moves focus on handstands and flips, so Floreios has earned the reputation of being just flips. As we discussed previously, Floreios serve the core purpose of distraction and deception hidden under an acrobatic and visually appealing display of skill. Contrary to popular belief, Floreios are not only flips; they are much more than that.

Being very technical moves that require both skill and strength, they are not widely used. Most people who are interested in learning Capoeira or in the Floreios think of it as an acrobatic routine, an art, and forget that it is, in fact, a crucial component of the martial art that serves a very functional purpose.

More importantly, Floreios are a lot more than just flips. Similarly, there are many kinds of moves that fall under the category of Floreios that are not particularly beautiful to watch, but they do exceptionally well when it comes to fooling the opponent. More than just flips, Floreios can include a number of hand spins, kicks, head spins, ground moves, variations of the cartwheel, side flips, and many others. These are tools that a player can choose if the situation allows and requires.

One of the main reasons these are not used or practiced widely is that many games of Capoeira are so close-quartered that there simply isn't enough room. The players depend more on speed and agility than they do on deception.

In other kinds of plays, such as the Roda, there is a higher use of Floreios, but even in those, the players pay more attention to the aesthetic part of the move than to the deception aspect. In fact, many schools train their students in these moves specifically for their visual appeal. Some trainees are more interested in doing something that looks good instead of something effective that can be used in a match.

Floreios plays a big role in the groundwork in Capoeira. Below are some of the most effective groundwork moves.

Au

The cartwheel is a very dynamic movement that plays an important role in many Capoeira games. There are many variations to this movement to suit every need and every situation. Here are some of the most commonly used Floreios cartwheels that can be used to attack, defend, or distract. Also, cartwheels are a great way to cover space and change position very quickly. However, they can expose you, and it does take skill and timing to perform them correctly.

Au De Cabeca

This is a great starter move as it is easy and safe to do. This Au is more common in Angola games as it is a slow movement and not that effective in faster games.

1. Start off in the regular negative position with one hand on the floor toward the side of your body.
2. Lean on the hand on the floor, place the top of your head onto the floor, and then place your other hand on the floor.
3. As you start to move your body, shift the weight onto your head and begin the swing with your first leg.
4. Both legs are going to swing horizontally across the body away from your head, following the same line.

Au Fechado

This is a fantastic defensive cartwheel as it protects your chest during the spin. Unlike other cartwheels where your legs are stretched upward and outward, in this case, your knees will be closer to your chest. However, this is also what makes this cartwheel challenging.

1. Start the Au by placing your hand on the floor and getting into the motion to perform a side Au.
2. The key is to only lift your legs slightly while keeping your knees bent so that your thighs are protecting your chest.
3. This is a slow movement in which you are almost doing a handstand during the transition.
4. Keep your legs tucked in during the entire movement.

Au De Frente

The frontal cartwheel is a great move that will help you in many spinning kicks and other frontal moves. This is a faster move that requires rhythm to make sure you walk into this move and keep your hips up if you don't want to land flat on the ground.

1. Step into the move and place your hands onto the ground to begin the Au making sure you keep the momentum from the first step.
2. You want to land with the leg that left the ground first while bringing your body over your head.
3. During the transition, it's important to keep your hips up and keep the landing leg completely straight. If you have a downward slope on which you can perform the move, it will help you learn it much more easily.

Helicopter

This is a very popular Au that doesn't have a lot of use in combat but is very visually appealing. The key is to keep yourself straight during the Au so you can land it properly.

1. Start the Au with your legs slightly forward to avoid them going straight over your head.
2. The key is to bring your spinning leg back during the movement as if you were going to do another spin with it. That will allow your landing leg to be at the position it needs to be at.
3. In this Au, you are landing with the same leg you started the move with, so make sure to stay straight so you have enough time to bring that leg over.

Macaco

This is a move commonly used in Capoeira – which is probably why it is also a popular move that people always want to learn. This is more of a jumping squat than an Au with the difference that you don't jump backward.

1. Start from a squat position and place your hands behind you as far back as you can. The further back you are, the easier it will be.
2. With your hands planted on the floor, kick yourself off the ground with both feet.
3. Your hands need to quickly move into position to support your weight in mid-air.
4. Keep your core tight and keep your legs close to your chest during this and keep the momentum going in one smooth movement to finally land on both feet.

S-Dobrado

The main difference between this move and the Macaco is the lift-off; rather than launching with both legs, you launch with one leg, and that makes this move a lot more challenging. To overcome this, you can transition from an esquiva baixa, shifting legs and then launching into the S-dobrado. You could use a more direct approach if you have the strength.

1. From the esquiva baixa, shift your weight onto the other leg and stretch one arm behind you.
2. Move your weight to the planted arm and kick off from the leg that is on the floor.
3. Move your other arm into position and swing your body over.

Queda De Rins

The baby freeze is a core movement that will help you build the skill needed for many other moves. The key is to get your center of gravity right to build on this to do the other variations.

1. Start off by balancing yourself on your head, two hands, and two feet on the floor.
2. From this point, you can transition to taking your feet off the floor and supporting your weight with only your upper body
3. Once you can balance yourself in this position, you can move on to do a number of variations. Specifically, the baby freeze requires you to bring your knees close to your chest and hold them there in the fetal position.

Ponte

This is a somewhat difficult exercise for most people, so the best solution is to first try it on the wall to understand the movement. The aim is to move from a ponte into a quadruped position and then back into a ponte.

1. Place your hands behind you on the wall as you would when doing a bridge on the floor.
2. If you are moving to the right, then keep your right hand on the wall and flip your body over.
3. Try to avoid bending at the knees, as this will make it harder. The focus here is to rotate the upper body.
4. Once you can do this movement safely using the wall, you can move onto an inclined surface or go straight into practicing the move on the floor.

Corta Capim

This is another very popular Capoeira move you will have commonly seen other martial artists and even break-dancers performing. This is a very low-profile movement that can be used very effectively in many different situations in a match. It also helps generate the momentum needed for other moves.

1. Start off with your hands in front of you and hold up your weight as you squat down on one foot with the other leg extended out straight.
2. The aim is to rotate the leg in a circle underneath. Move your hands with your other leg over them to complete the movement.
3. You can also easily switch legs between the movement, and you can go as fast as you like once you are familiar with the movement.

Piao De Mao

In essence, this is a headstand with a spin, but it is often very challenging for people to perform and master. There is a bit of technicality that goes into this movement, and it requires you to perform this exercise in one smooth motion to maintain your balance.

1. Take a side step into a headstand so you have the momentum to proceed into the spin.
2. In the middle of the headstand, move into a one-arm headstand while keeping your head tucked closely into your armpit. Also, you must position your hand so that the weight is on your piriformis, which is the bone in line with your pinky and closest to your wrist.
3. You can start by doing just one spin. As you develop more stability, you can spin as much as you like and even perform a variety of leg movements during the spin as well.

Relogio

This is another very popular move that can be used in many areas outside of Capoeira. To build up for this movement, it helps to have mastered the Piao De Mao and the Queda de Rins as this is a combination of both those movements.

1. Start off with the Queda de Rins stand and move your weight onto the palm of one hand while making sure your elbow is tucked tightly into your body.
2. Keep your feet bent back as you initiate the spin. That will help you keep your weight centered and balanced.
3. With all the weight where it should be and your balance on the palm just right, you can move into a spin doing one spin or multiple.

Piao De Cabeca

While this move looks easy, it takes a lot of balance and strength. Also, make sure you have some good head protection before you do this. You can also do it on a well-padded surface as your entire weight is going to be resting on the top of your head. There is no flesh on the skull to provide any kind of cushioning, so it can be extremely painful. Also, it helps to build up your neck muscles for this move as you might not be able to support your weight if you have never trained for a similar movement.

1. Starting in a ponte position, you lift yourself up into a low handstand.
2. Place the top of your head on the ground and spread your weight equally using your palms and the top of your head.
3. At first, you can try to spin using your hands and your head. As you progress in this move, try lifting up your hands so that you are just using your head to spin.

A lot of these moves play an important role in other larger movements and other routines. Developing core strength and stability is key for any Capoeira move but more so for Floreios. If you want to master the movements in Capoeira, it is vital that you perfect the Floreios as this is the stepping stone that will help you build the strength and the skill you need for other movements. Be careful when performing these moves as they often require you to place your entire body weight on very small and delicate parts such as your neck, spine, wrists, and palms. The best solution is to start small and to do it slowly and gradually.

Chapter 9: Capoeira's Relationship with Dance and Music

As discussed in previous chapters, Capoeira has its roots in the enslaved people from West Africa who were taken to Brazil. The martial art is thought to have emerged as a way to bypass laws that prevented slaves from practicing martial arts and other cultural traditions.

In order to hide the purpose of the art, early practitioners created a unique style that could be disguised as a dance. Due to this, since its early days, Capoeira has had a special link with music and dance, one that lasts to the present day.

Capoeira and the Bateria

Music forms an integral part of the practice of Capoeira, especially when it is performed as a game rather than as pure martial art.

During the Roda, the circle into which Capoeira participants enter, the members determine the game's tempo by singing traditional songs and clapping their hands to go along with the music.

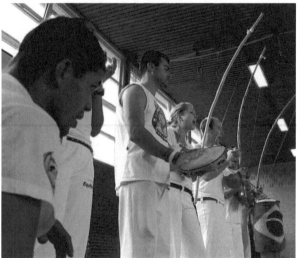

Source[102]

The music doesn't just determine the game's tempo; it also determines the style of the game being played. Different songs are associated with different types of Capoeira, and the two Capoeiristas within the circle alter their movements to reflect this.

The music can also determine when the game ends. One of the berimbau musicians in the circle can call an end to the game, though it can also end if one of the Capoeiristas decides to leave the circle or if the game is interrupted by another capoeirista.

Capoeira music is formed by both the singers and the instruments and features various rhythms known as toques that vary from very slow to very fast.

The instruments played during a Roda are arranged in a formation known as a bateria, which means "drum kit" in Portuguese and Spanish. The bateria is traditionally composed of three berimbaus, two pandeiros, three atabaques, and one agogô and one ganzá.

However, this arrangement may differ according to the Capoeira group and the style of the Roda. Other instruments are often added to the bateria, including the reco-reco. For example, Mestre Bimba, the founder of Regional Capoeira, preferred to use one berimbau and two padeiros in his Rodas. However, at least one berimbau will be present regardless of the group during the Roda.

The berimbau is always the lead instrument and determines both the style and the tempo of music that the rest of the bateria will play. The berimbau section of the bateria is composed of two low-pitched instruments (known as the medio and the gunga), which form the base, and one high-pitched instrument (also known as the viola).

The other instruments in the bateria follow the rhythm provided by the berimbau section, though they can improvise and vary the music a little depending on the traditions of the Capoeira group in question.

Because the music determines the style, speed, and aggressiveness, it is the driving factor of the game. Without it, the game would look significantly different.

Berimbau

The berimbau is a single-stringed instrument that resembles a bow. While its origin has not been thoroughly researched, it likely originates from Africa and is thought to be an adaptation of the African tradition of gourd musical bows.

Source[108]

There are three main sounds that a berimbau produces during a Capoeira game:

- The buzz sound
- The open string sound
- The high sound

While there are other sounds that the instrument can produce, these three sounds help determine the rhythm of the game.

There are three berimbaus played during a Capoeira game:

1. **The Gunga:** Played by the highest-grade Capoeirista around. Depending on the style of the Capoeira group, the gunga player can either improvise or stick to the main rhythm. The leader of the Roda usually plays it, and the other instruments follow its lead. Additionally, the gunga player is also often the lead singer of the Roda. The instrument is used to call players to the foot of berimbau, which is the place players enter the Roda from.

2. **The Medio:** The dialogue between the medio and the Gunga helps give the toque of the Capoeira its character.
3. **The Viola:** The viola makes variations and improvisations to the toque. It has often been described as the "lead guitar" of the bateria.

Atabaque

The *atabaque* is an Afro-Brazilian hand drum that is traditionally made of Jacaranda wood and calfskin, along with ropes and a metal ring on the body that serves as a tuning mechanism. It is sometimes also known as an atabaque de Corda.

Source[104]

The drums originally traveled with enslaved Africans when they were taken to Brazil by Portuguese colonizers. Aside from playing a role in Capoeira, they are also used in the Afro-Brazilian dance, maculelê, and are considered sacred instruments in Candomblé and Umbanda's religions.

The atabaque isn't as integral to a Capoeira game as the berimbau. Due to its size, it's often omitted during more spontaneous Rodas or replaced with another percussion instrument that creates a similar sound. Depending on the player and the Capoeira group, the atabaque can be played with either the hands, sticks, or a combination of the two.

Pandeiro

The pandeiro is a frame drum played (and held) in hand and is very similar to the better-known tambourine. It is one of the most popular instruments in Brazil and is often labeled the country's unofficial national instrument.

Source[105]

The most significant difference between tambourines and pandeiros is the sound each produces. The tones the pandeiro produces are drier, less sustained, and crisper than those produced by the tambourine. Like the tambourine, the pandeiro is also played with the fingertips, palm, and thumb, and the way the player alternated between them helps create the rhythm. This instrument is compact and easily portable, two factors that contribute to its popularity. They also mean that it is one of the most common instruments seen in Capoeira games - in fact, unlike the atabaque, it is part of nearly every Roda.

Agogô

The agogô is a double bell that originates from the Yoruba and Edo people of West Africa. It has the highest pitch of all the bateria instruments and is thought to be the oldest Capoeira instrument.

It is thought to be based on the single and double bells of the Yoruba people. The bell resembles a western cowbell and is played using a wooden stick. The name "agogô" is onomatopoeia for the sound it makes when played.

Ganzá

The ganzá is a rattle-like instrument used to provide percussion. It is a cylinder made from either metal or a hand-woven basket, and it is filled with metal balls, beads, pebbles, and similar items. It helps provide an underlying sense of rhythm to the music.

Reco-Reco

The reco-reco is a scraper that originates in Africa. It is traditionally made of bamboo or wood, though metal reco-recos are growing common as well. It is played with a wooden or metal stick, and the metal models produce a much louder sound than the wooden and bamboo varieties. The reco-reco provides rhythmic accompaniment to the rest of the bateria.

Other Elements of Capoeira Music

Some theorists claim that music is used during the Roda to create a sacred space. Both the formation of the circle and the music itself serve to create a connection to the spirit world. Even the instruments used are significant. The atabaque has religious significance in many Afro-Brazilian religions, while the berimbau was historically used in rituals in Africa and among the enslaved African diaspora as a way to communicate with the ancestors. Even the movements in some forms of Capoeira are thought to bring the capoeiristas spiritual power.'

Aside from the bateria, another important element of Capoeira music is the songs being sung along with the instruments. There is usually meaning and a theme to each song, including (but not limited to):

- Folk lessons
- An acknowledgment of history
- An acknowledgment of slavery and the roots of Capoeira
- An acknowledgment of the symbolic aspects of Capoeira
- An acknowledgment of the physical roots of Capoeira
- Biographies and autobiographies
- Mythology
- Metaphorical comments on the game being played
- Direct comments on the game being played
- Songs of greeting and farewell
- Songs that welcome women into the Roda

- Meta-Capoeira songs – those that directly refer to Capoeira by name

Of the themes mentioned above, one of the most interesting is that of directly commenting on the game being played. This form of singing often directly influences the game, though not in a way instantly apparent to a person who doesn't speak Portuguese.

During this type of song, the leader of the song starts a commentary on the game being played. This includes poking fun at mistakes and, crucially, telling a player what to do. If the leader feels the game is getting too violent, he can tell the Capoeiristas to slow down. Conversely, if he feels the game's pace is too slow, he can ask them to pick up speed.

There are three main styles of song that create the final piece: the ladainha, the corrido, and the quadra. There is also the louvação, which forms the start of the call and response section of the Roda.

Ladainha

This forms the beginning of the Roda and is a solo sung by the most senior member of the group present. The singer is also usually the person playing the lead berimbau.

While the songs can be improvised on the spot, there is also an existing canon of ladainhas that singers can choose from. They vary in length from as little as lines to as long as 20 lines.

Themes for the ladainha often include stories, mythology, history, and moral lessons. While they are almost always metaphorical, they can also be pure poetry or a topical theme depending on the occasion. The melody stays relatively consistent throughout the ladainha, though there may be some minor variations, and the first line is usually repeated.

Corrido

Corridos are overlapping call and response sections that are traditionally found in African music and are introduced with a louvação. This section is a short song that includes a response that is usually static.

The corrido provides a way for singers to communicate with the action taking place in the Roda and serves as a way to:

- Inspire the players
- Comment on the action
- Praise or warn the players
- Tell stories
- Teach moral values
- Invoke someone or something

There are different corridos that each serve different purposes. They can also be challenges. This happens when the lead sings one corrido and then, shortly after, sings another very similar one. The choir must pay close attention to the words in order to sing the correct response.

Corridos are rarer than ladainhas, requiring the singers to be more skilled. If the corrido is excluded, the challenge is made during the ladainha.

Each corrido has a different melody, though there can be corridos with the same melody as well. This allows singers to learn a vast repertoire of corridos without having to memorize too many things. The corrido response is sung in unison by the choir, and an occasional harmonization can be used as punctuation by one of the singers.

Quadra

In some Regional and Contemporânea Capoeira schools, the quadra takes the place of the ladainha. It is an innovation of Mestre Bimba and is a song that follows the louvação.

The main difference between the ladainha and the quadra is that the quadra does not have a standard melody (or melody model that the model draws from). There's a greater variety that the singers can draw from. Depending on the lyrics, quadras can also work as a variation on the corrido.

Louvação

The *louvação* is the start of the corrido, the call and response section of the Roda. While it is traditionally an invocation of God and Mestres and a way to give thanks, it can also have improvised content, which means that the choir must pay attention to the "call" section so that they can provide the correct "response."

Unlike the corrido and the quadra, there is no variation in melodies between louvaçãos. Like the corrido, the choir usually sings the louvação's response section in unison, and one of the singers can use an occasional harmonization as a form of punctuation.

Capoeira and Dance

While Capoeira is undoubtedly intrinsically connected to music, it also features a deep connection to dance. As you start to learn this art form, you'll soon realize that the movements appear similar to a fast, energetic dance.

While Capoeira can also be more violent than other martial arts, Capoeiristas often carried knives and bladed weapons with them in the art form's heyday. They were often hidden within the berimbaus act as dance-like rituals. In the early 20th century, Brazilian society and the government distrusted Capoeiristas. Capoeira survived this period by becoming a more sanitized dance form until it became more accepted by the general public again at the beginning of the 1940s.

In the 1970s, Capoeira Mestres started to emigrate from Brazil and brought Capoeira to the attention of the rest of the world. Many of them immigrated to the United States, including Mestre Jelon Vieira. Along with Loremil Machado, Mestre Vieira was the first Capoeira Mestre to live and teach in the United States.

At the same time as Vieira was teaching Capoeira in New York, breakdancing was becoming popular among the African-American community in the United States. While breakdancing can trace its roots to other dance forms such as the Lindy Pop and the Charleston and the dance moves of James Brown, it's very clear that breakdancing and Capoeira have eerily similar moves.

The parallels between breakdancing and Capoeira are so strong that some suggest that Capoeira significantly influenced the way breakdancing is performed today. Capoeira was prevalent in people's consciousness in the 1980s and 1970s, appearing in the pages and on the cover of the mass-market Black Belt Magazine. It was also examined in other publications aimed at primarily black audiences (the community which developed breakdancing).

Additionally, Vieira and Machado ran demonstrations and courses across New York. Vieira partnered with theatre director Ellen Stewart to run classes in the East Village, and Capoeira made its way to the South Bronx in the 1970s.

That said, this connection is far from a certainty. Journalist and dance historian Sally Banes, when describing reporting on breakdancing, noted that breakdancing's *"spatial level called to mind Capoeira, the spectacular Brazilian dance martial art form that incorporates cartwheels, kicks, and feints low to the ground, but the two were dissimilar enough in shape and timing that Capoeira seemed at most only a distant relative."*

Whether or not Capoeira directly influenced breakdancing, the similarity between the two styles definitely highlights the art form's deep relationship with dance, one that lasts to this day.

Capoeira may trace its history back, not to African martial art, but a ritual dance that incorporated several of the movements seen today, including headbutting, slap boxing, kicking, deception, and evasion. This dance was a religious dance that provided performers with a link to the afterlife and allowed them to channel their ancestors.

Capoeira's relationship with dance and music is undeniable. Without the influence of these forms of expression on the art form, Capoeira would look significantly different, both in terms of its movements and the culture surrounding it.

Capoeira is not only inspired by dance and music, but it also influences dance and music. It is a great form of cardio and is quickly becoming popular among fitness enthusiasts worldwide. Read on to the next chapter to learn more about Capoeira's relationship with fitness.

Chapter 10: Capoeira and Fitness

The rhythmic and fast-paced Capoeira is a great full-body workout. By incorporating a variety of kicks, handstands, and acrobatics into the dance-like moves, people of any fitness level can feel the burn almost immediately. But is it safe? Many people are intimidated by its intensity or worried about their body's ability to handle such athletic moves. Although exceptionally high-intensity workouts come with a degree of risk, if you enjoy Capoeira and practice it correctly, the risk of injury is minimal. The "correct way" means learning from a qualified instructor, taking it slow at the start, and following the right order of moves.

This chapter will shed light on the connection between Capoeira and fitness. It'll help you explore the various health benefits of this brilliant dance form imbued with exceptional aspects of martial arts. By the end of this chapter, you'll realize the effectiveness of Capoeira as an exercise and its amazing health benefits.

The Connection between Capoeira and Fitness

The beauty of Capoeira is that it provides a full-body workout. It requires you to use your entire body. Furthermore, it's an efficient way to stay active and improve your cardiovascular fitness. It boosts stamina, improves flexibility, and strengthens your core. Keep in mind that although Capoeira is a full-body workout, beginners are especially vulnerable to developing muscle imbalances. If you're new to Capoeira, it's important to schedule some time for stretching before and after class. It'll help your muscles relax and prevent injuries.

Source[106]

Capoeira builds a solid foundation for muscle endurance, coordination, and flexibility. It's a high-intensity workout that increases your heart rate quickly and keeps it elevated for a short period, especially if you include the berimbau into your moves. The speed and intensity of Capoeira movements cause a surplus of oxygen to circulate throughout your body. Remember that this is only true when the movements are done properly. If done improperly or if you rush through a sequence, your body won't receive the full benefits of Capoeira.

Capoeira is also an amazing calorie burner, especially when including the berimbau. The constant swinging of the berimbau generates heat in your body and causes you to sweat. The combination of swinging, jumping, kicking, and spinning can lead to a significant calorie burn after just thirty minutes of play.

Capoeira Honors a Variety of Fitness Goals

The main objective behind Capoeira is to keep your body moving. It's a dynamic workout that ensures all muscles get a workout. Depending on the intensity, tempo, and how you incorporate the berimbau into your moves, Capoeira can be adjusted to suit a variety of fitness goals. It can be low-intensity, making it more accessible to beginners and older people, or you can use the berimbau to increase the speed and intensity, turning it into a high-intensity workout.

Aerobic Capoeira vs. Anaerobic Capoeira

Aerobic Capoeira consists of slow, controlled moves to create a continuous flow of movements. It's mostly done at a moderate intensity and tempo. This type of Capoeira is better for toning and weight loss, as it's a low-intensity workout that doesn't push your body too hard. On the other hand, Anaerobic Capoeira consists of faster movements with higher intensity and power output. It uses the berimbau to increase speed and intensity, making it a great workout for people who want to strengthen their core and burn fat. The main difference between aerobic and anaerobic Capoeira is the speed of the moves.

Source[107]

Although Aerobic Capoeira is often considered less intense than Anaerobic Capoeira, keep in mind that this type of Capoeira is more accessible to people with a lower fitness level. Depending on each move's intensity, pace, and tempo, Anaerobic Capoeira can also be aimed at beginners or intermediate levels. The only difference between the two is that Anaerobic Capoeira uses the berimbau to increase speed and intensity.

What Are Some Benefits Associated with Capoeira?

There are many benefits associated with Capoeira. It's an effective way to stay healthy and improve your physical and mental fitness. It's a full-body workout that turns every movement into an opportunity to burn calories, strengthen your core, tone your muscles, and improve coordination and flexibility. Here are some of the main benefits associated with Capoeira.

Amazing Cardiovascular Workout

Capoeira is a great cardio workout that can be used to improve endurance, increase heart health, and strengthen one's respiratory system. Although it may seem like a less intense form of cardio, keep in mind that Capoeira is a fast-paced workout that can elevate your heart rate quickly. It's also an interval-based cardio workout, as it involves short bursts of intense activity followed by a recovery period.

Capoeira's constant swinging and kicking help strengthen your core and tone muscles in your upper body. The only equipment required for Capoeira is a good pair of shoes, which makes it an inexpensive way to stay healthy and fit. Incorporating the berimbau into your movements means that you can actively engage your core as you kick, jump, and spin. This means that you'll strengthen and tone your core no matter what move you're doing.

Tones and Trims the Arms and Legs

Although Capoeira tends to be neglected when people think of leg workouts, it's one of the best ways to tone your legs and lower body. The jumping and spinning involved in Capoeira help tone your quads, hamstrings, and glutes, while the kicks help strengthen your thighs. The pivoting and spinning actions also help strengthen your ankles, while the constant swinging of the hips helps sculpt your legs' muscles.

Source[108]

The constant swinging and kicking make Capoeira a great workout for your arms. It also improves upper body strength, as it involves several arm movements and activities involving your upper body and core.

Improves Bone Density and Reduces Osteoporosis Risk

Combining Capoeira with other forms of exercise is a great way to improve your bone density. Incorporating high-impact exercises into your routines, such as running or aerobic workouts, will help improve the strength of your bones and can reduce the risk of osteoporosis. Capoeira is an effective way to increase your bone density as it encourages you to perform several movements that require you to jump, including several moves that will help improve your balance, coordination, and strength.

Capoeira is a low-impact activity that doesn't put pressure on your joints and muscles. It can be used to improve your bone density and reduce your risk of osteoporosis, as it doesn't involve any high-impact stress on your bones. When you do Capoeira, the low-impact nature of the movements means that you won't be putting too much pressure on your joints. This makes it an ideal workout for people with weak bones or low bone density.

Mental Strength and Clarity

Capoeira may seem like a simple workout, but the fact that it involves several moves and positions means that it can be used to improve your focus, mental strength, and clarity. It strengthens your mind and your body as it involves a combination of aerobic and anaerobic activities that will work on your mind and your body. It can help to improve memory and problem-solving skills, as well as to reduce symptoms of depression. It also helps to improve your problem-solving skills and cognitive function.

The fast pace of the movements and the movements that require you to think quickly help improve your alertness and reaction time.

Source[109]

Reduces Stress and Anxiety

The fast-paced nature of the movements involved in Capoeira makes it an effective workout for relieving stress and anxiety. It doesn't require you to spend hours at the gym and can be performed in a short amount of time, making it an ideal workout to relieve stress and mental fatigue. The playful nature of Capoeira also gives you a chance to express any emotions you might be bottling up inside.

Helps You Become More Mobile

Although many people think that Capoeira is only a workout, in reality, it can also be used as a form of self-defense. It incorporates several moves that can help you improve your balance, agility, and coordination. It's also a great way to improve your flexibility and range of motion, as it incorporates several moves that require you to stretch. It's ideal for people who need to improve their mobility and is a great way for seniors to stay active.

Combats Obesity

Although it may not seem like it at first, Capoeira is an ideal workout for combating obesity. Incorporating various movements into your routine that require you to move around rapidly means that Capoeira is a great calorie-burner. It also involves several moves that require you to control your breathing, which helps you keep your heart rate up and improve your respiratory function. Increasing your heart rate and strengthening your respiratory function will help you immensely to improve your fitness.

Combats Arthritis

Capoeira is a great way to combat the symptoms of arthritis. It incorporates several movements that help improve mobility and flexibility. It can help relieve the pain associated with arthritis and prevent the deterioration of cartilage. It has also been found to reduce joint stiffness and improve hip mobility, enabling you to move around with greater ease. It is also beneficial for people suffering from rheumatism as it helps improve the range of motion in your joints, which can help reduce pain levels.

Improves Your Respiratory Function

Capoeira involves several moves that require you to control and coordinate your breathing. This is because, In Capoeira, you need to switch between fast, powerful movements and those that require you to use small muscles. This helps improve your respiratory function, as it makes you focus on breathing correctly and improves your lung capacity. It can help reduce respiratory problems such as asthma and chronic obstructive pulmonary disease (COPD). Also, since it encourages you to quickly switch between movements that require powerful breathing and those that require slow, controlled breathing, it can help improve your respiratory capacity.

Boost Metabolism

As it incorporates several muscle-toning moves and high-intensity movements, Capoeira is a great way to boost your metabolism. It can help burn calories and fat and help you maintain your muscle mass. The high-intensity movements involved in Capoeira are great for increasing your metabolic rate, even after you've finished working out. This means that it's an effective way to lose weight as it helps you burn calories and shed pounds. It's also a great way to improve your muscle definition and will help you achieve a toned body if combined with a healthy diet and an effective weight training program.

Helps Prevent Diseases

It's a great form of exercise for improving your circulation and respiratory function. It can also help improve your bone density and can help to prevent diseases such as osteoporosis, arthritis, and diabetes. Regular Capoeira training will help you maintain adequate circulation throughout your body and can help lower your risk of heart disease. It's also a beneficial form of exercise for people who suffer from diabetes as it helps control blood sugar levels and regulate insulin production.

Enhances Your Mood

Capoeira is a great form of exercise to enhance your mood. Incorporating high-intensity movements into your routine that requires you to focus on controlling your breathing is great for increasing your heart rate. As it helps to improve your respiratory function, it can also help you relax and reduce stress levels that are known to worsen any depressive symptoms you may suffer from. It can also help you achieve a deep state of relaxation as it encourages mindfulness, which will enable you to focus on the present and let go of stressful thoughts.

Source[110]

Improves Your Balance

Capoeira is a great way to improve your balance. It requires you to maintain stability when in motion, which can help you improve your coordination and overall balance. As it requires you to incorporate several movements that help you to switch between different stances rapidly, it is a great form of exercise for improving your sense of balance. This has several benefits, from enabling you to perform everyday tasks to preventing injuries, such as falls and broken bones.

Helps You Maintain an Ideal Weight

As Capoeira requires you to quickly change between high-intensity movements that use major muscle groups and low-intensity movements that mainly target your smaller muscles, it is a great form of exercise for burning calories. It requires you to maintain an elevated heart rate for the entire workout, which means that it's a great way to burn fat without spending hours on the treadmill. If you don't have access to a gym, practicing Capoeira regularly can help you maintain an ideal weight and tone your muscles.

Improves Your Performance at Other Sports

Capoeira is a great way to improve your performance in other sports, as it helps improve your agility, balance, and coordination. It is also a great form of exercise for improving your aerobic fitness as it requires you to incorporate high-intensity movements into your workout. This makes it a great way to improve your stamina, coordination, and mental focus, all of which are essential for excelling in any sport.

Prevents Injuries

Capoeira is a great form of exercise to prevent injuries as it incorporates several movements that can help improve flexibility and mobility. It's also a low-impact form of exercise that doesn't put too much strain on your body, which means almost anyone can safely practice it. It also helps improve your balance and coordination, which helps in preventing falls that can lead to injuries.

Increases Your Range of Motion

Capoeira requires you to switch between high-intensity movements that use major muscle groups and low-intensity movements that mainly target your smaller muscles. It is a great form of exercise to improve your range of motion. It's also beneficial for people with injuries, as it helps to strengthen the muscles in your arms and legs, which can help speed up your recovery. As a result, practicing Capoeira regularly can help improve your range of motion and prevent injuries that result from a limited range of motion.

Improves Your Posture

Capoeira is a great form of exercise for improving your posture as it requires you to incorporate several movements that improve your balance and coordination. This will enable you to perform everyday tasks with ease and prevent back pain and other problems that stem from bad posture. If practiced regularly, it will improve your breathing, which will enable you to maintain the correct posture without straining your body.

If you want to employ a form of exercise that will improve your overall well-being, then you should consider practicing Capoeira. It's a unique form of exercise that incorporates several movements that require you to rapidly switch between different stances. This makes it a great form of aerobic exercise that will help you maintain an elevated heart rate for the entire duration of your workout. It can also help improve your balance and coordination, which will enable you to perform everyday tasks with ease and prevent injuries that result from a lack of balance and coordination. Capoeira is also beneficial for people with injuries as it helps strengthen the muscles in your arms and legs, and that can speed up recovery.

Chapter 11: The Capoeira Workout

Capoeira has many different components. It is more than just non-violent movements as it requires great control and core strength too. Every form of Capoeira comprises several movements, each having a particular rhythm. The music is essential for the game, as it provides its rhythm and style. A common misconception about the acrobatics performed during Capoeira is that they are mere gymnastics or breakdancing moves, but this is not the case. The moves and fighting techniques in Capoeira are martial arts moves, but many moves require great strength and power to be effectively executed.

To help you on your Capoeira journey, this chapter has some basic Capoeira exercises and workouts that can be incorporated into your daily routine. This way, even if you don't go to a class every week, you can still practice and maintain your skill and be able to perform the different movements with ease.

The Preparations

To practice Capoeira, you don't need any special equipment. All you need is a flat space and enough room to move around freely. It doesn't matter if it's grass, concrete, or a wooden floor. As long as the surface isn't too smooth such as in a swimming pool, you should be fine. If you have a hard floor and want to reduce the impact of your falls, put something soft down like a mat or pillows.

You should wear comfortable clothing when you train in Capoeira. It's good to wear loose, light clothes that allow you to move freely without getting too hot. It is very important to have light clothes on because some movements can be quite acrobatic, and you need to avoid getting caught up in your clothes. Also, wearing tight clothing can be quite uncomfortable when you're upside down.

The first thing to do is make sure your shoes are right for Capoeira. They should be comfortable and allow you to move around easily. Sneakers or running shoes are the best for this as their soles provide good grip, which is useful for jumping and landing safely while still allowing you to slide around easily. You should avoid wearing high heels or flip-flops when training Capoeira.

Warming Up

Before you start practicing your moves, it is important to have a warm-up session. This will loosen your muscles and get your blood pumping. Stretch to move with greater ease and to avoid pulling a muscle. The warm-up session should usually take up to 10 or 15 minutes. The following exercises are good for your legs, hips, and shoulders:

Jumping Jacks

Jump up in the air with both feet while clapping your hands above your head. Then jump onto both feet and clap beside your waist. This is one repetition. Repeat it 20 times and then take a short break (15 seconds).

One-Legged Squats

Stand on your right leg and bend your left leg upward behind you with the knee pointing outwards. Keep your hips level and bend forward until your right thigh is parallel to the floor. Place your hands on the back of your right thigh and push upward until you're standing upright again. This is one repetition. Repeat it 10 times and then take a short break (15 seconds).

Repeat the exercise by standing on your left leg instead.

Lunges

Take three steps forward with your left foot. Your feet should be about 1 meter apart from each other. Keep your right knee pointing upward and bend it so that it is parallel to the floor. Your left knee should now be almost touching the ground. Push upward with your right leg until you are standing straight again. This is one repetition. Repeat it 10 times and then take a short break (15 seconds).

Repeat the exercise but this time, use your right leg.

Chair Pose

Stand straight with your feet hip-width apart. Bend one of your knees and lift the other leg out to the side, keeping it straight. Hold it for about three seconds, and then place your foot back onto the floor. This is one repetition. Repeat it 10 times and then take a short break (15 seconds).

Repeat the exercise but this time, use your other leg.

Now that you have finished the warm-up session, it's time to start practicing.

Capoeira Movement and Techniques

You will need to master several different kicks to be proficient in Capoeira. They are all different and serve particular purposes. There are also several rolls, cartwheels, pull-ups, and headstands that you will need to learn to advance. The first thing to learn is the set of basic movements. They are simple to perform and will give you a chance to get used to the flow of the game.

A Sweep

This move is used to capture your opponent's leg. You need to place your right foot in front of your opponent's left knee while they are trying to kick you. At the same time, grab them with your left hand by the back of their waist and lift them so they lose balance.

Making a "Wheel"

This move is harder to perform but very effective when you get the moves down. First of all, place your left foot behind your back and bend your right leg in front of you. Your left foot should be under your right knee and behind your right ankle. Now grab your left toes with your right hand and lift your leg. This will make you perform a backflip, landing on your hands. Now use the momentum to get up again, all while your right leg is in the air.

Cartwheels

You need to stand with your legs hip-width apart to perform this move. Bend your left leg and hold it with your hands a few centimeters from the floor but parallel to it. Now push yourself into a backflip until you stand straight with your arms parallel to the floor. Again, do this by using the momentum of your backflip.

Headstands

It is relatively easy to learn how to do a headstand. You need to place your hands on the floor in front of you and then push yourself up into a headstand. You need to make sure your legs are in the air when you do this, but your feet should be a few centimeters from the floor.

Pushups

All you have to do is get into position by leaning on your hands and toes to do a pushup. Now lower yourself until your chest is almost touching the floor, and then push yourself back up again by using your arms. Remember to breathe out when you push yourself up and to keep your back straight.

Airplane

The airplane is a relatively simple move to learn. Get into a pushup position but rest your weight on your bent arms to do this move. Now lift one leg at a time until they are parallel to the ground, then return them to the floor again. Your weight should be on your arms and your shoulders, not your feet.

Rolls

A roll is an essential move to learn if you want to avoid getting caught off-guard. To do one, you need to make sure your feet are shoulder-width apart, and your legs are slightly bent – but mostly straight. Now you need to bend your knees a little and lean forward. Now push yourself up until you are balanced on your hands so that your legs are above you and your back is facing the ground. From this position, push yourself up again to balance on your feet instead of your hands. Your head should be between your arms. Now all you need to do is lean back to balance on your hands again. Repeat this move until you reach the other side.

Kicks

There are four basic kicks in Capoeira: the Front Kick, Side Kick, Back Kick, and Axe Kick.

- **Front Kick** - This is one of the most basic kicks in Capoeira and is usually used to practice speed more than anything else. To do this move, stand in a fighting position and lift your knee in front of you so that it's bent at about 90 degrees. Now straighten it using your thigh muscles, not your back.

- **Side Kick** - This is one of the most useful kicks you will learn in Capoeira. To do this move, put your right foot behind you and bend your leg until your knee is almost 90 degrees. Now straighten your leg out so that it is perpendicular to the floor. Your weight should be on your right foot. You can adjust it by leaning forward.

- **Back Kick** - This kick is a little more complex than the other two because it involves a lot of hip movement so that you can gain enough momentum to kick your enemy. You must stand up straight and bend your torso forward a little bit to do this move. Now turn your body to the right and bend your left leg behind you. Lift your leg until it is parallel to the floor, then straighten it up using your thigh muscles. Your leg should be pointing at an angle of about 45 degrees from the floor; your weight should be on your right foot.

- **Ax Kick** is very similar to the back kick, but it does not require as much knee movement because your leg is bent at the beginning. The key to this move is the hip movement and its effectiveness. Stand up straight and turn your left leg to the right to do this move. Now bend it behind you and lift your leg until it is parallel to the ground. Again, straighten it by using your thigh muscles and pointing your toes slightly. Your weight should be on your right foot, but you can adjust it by leaning forward.

Advanced Capoeira Exercises

If you want to make your Capoeira workouts a little more challenging, consider trying some of these advanced exercises.

Side Kick with a Twist

This is a very effective move to try if you're looking to strengthen your hips and thighs, but it is very tiring. To do it, stand up straight and put your left foot behind you, bend your leg until the knee is about 90 degrees. Now lift your left leg so that it is parallel to the floor and twist it clockwise. Now bend your knee again and return your foot to its original position.

A-Frame

This move is an excellent way to develop your core strength and improve your balance. To do it, stand up straight and raise your arms so they are parallel to the floor. They should be roughly shoulder-width apart, but you can adjust it if needed. Now bend your left leg and put it behind you so that it's about 100 degrees from the floor. Keep this position for as long as possible.

Side-to-Side Punch

This is an excellent way to increase your speed and power, but you need to know how to do the basic punches and kicks before you attempt it. To do this move, simply run forwards and punch at your opponent like you would in a normal Capoeira fight. As soon as you punch, quickly turn to your right and do the same again. Keep repeating this until you reach the other side.

Back Hop

This move is very similar to the back kick, but it involves hopping so that you can get a little more momentum. This is the sort of move you would use if your enemy were charging toward you. Stand up straight and turn your left leg to the right. Now bend it behind you and lift your leg until it is parallel to the ground. Straighten it by using your thigh muscles and pointing your toes slightly. Now, using the strength in your leg, push yourself back until you are standing up straight again.

Sideways Hop

This is a great move if you want to try something a little more advanced. Stand up straight and turn your left leg to the right. Now bend it behind you and lift your leg until it is parallel to the ground. Straighten it by using your thigh muscles and pointing your toes slightly. From this position, lean to the left and push yourself back to stand straight again.

Switch Footed Hop

This move looks more complicated than it actually is. Stand up straight and turn your left leg to the right, but make sure it's slightly in front of your right leg. Now bend it behind you and lift your leg until it is parallel to the ground. Straighten it by using your thigh muscles and pointing your toes slightly. Now, using the strength in your left leg, push yourself back until you are standing straight again. To finish this move, switch your feet so that your right leg is forward and repeat the steps for a full minute.

Caterpillar Jump

This move is very similar to the switch-footed hop, but it is more of a cardio exercise and less of a Capoeira kick. You can use this to warm up or cool down. Stand up straight and turn your left leg to the right, but make sure it's slightly in front of your other leg. Now bend it behind you and lift your leg until it is parallel to the ground. Now, using the strength in your left leg, push yourself back until you are standing up straight again. To finish this move, switch your feet so that your left leg is forward and repeat the steps for a full minute.

Back Hop with Punch

To do this move, start in the same way as the back hop, but this time when you lean back to the right and push yourself up, punch at your opponent. This move is all about timing, so make sure you can complete the first two steps before attempting this. Remember to use the momentum from the back hop to help you with this move.

You should aim to achieve the following:

- Comfortable and controlled cartwheel.
- Handstand without support.
- 10 meters forward and backward walkovers.
- 15 meter headstand walkover.

- 10 to 15 consecutive push-ups.
- 30 seconds nonstop kick up from the floor, then a jump back onto your feet.
- 10 push-ups in a row with the feet only, then a jump back onto your feet.
- 15 to 20 consecutive side leg lifts, then a jump back onto your feet.
- 10 consecutive headstands, then a jump back onto your feet.

This is by no means all of the exercises that can be used to keep fit, but it's a good way to get your muscles used to what's involved in Capoeira. It is important to stretch and warm-up before attempting any of these exercises. If you're doing them with somebody else, then you should make sure you have enough space between you. This chapter has been designed to give you a head start and insight into what Capoeira involves. The movements and techniques may look complicated, but they aren't. If you do this workout every day and train hard, your skills will start to develop after just a few months, and you will see a big difference. Remember, Capoeira is all about working as a team, and practicing regularly is the only way to get better.

Chapter 12: Improving Your Skills

Slamming the ground with your hands is never fun, but it can be even worse when you realize that you were one inch away from catching the person trying to sweep your legs. You may also want to know when it's okay to unleash a barrage of punches on someone or how you can spin properly.

Capoeira is famous for its fluidity and expressiveness. There aren't any hard limits to what you can do, but here are some tips that will help improve your game:

1. Improve Your Flexibility

Right now, it may feel like your spine is one solid concrete pole. But if you do some stretches every day, you will notice some improvements in your flexibility. You'll be amazed at how much better you can move and how well you can execute moves.

Stretching is not enough though, you also need to strengthen your muscles to build up durability and endurance. If you practice too often without adequate muscle recovery, you will end up tearing your muscles, and you won't be able to practice for a long time. If your muscles get too strong, they won't be as flexible anymore. You should strike a balance between strength and flexibility.

2. Work On Improving Your Movements

Every move in Capoeira should be made quickly and smoothly. You'll want to become a lot more nimble in your fingers, hands, feet, and toes. If you're having trouble executing a certain move, try slowing it down and feeling how your body is moving at that moment. Then gradually speed it up to perfect that move.

If you're having trouble with a specific move, ask your teacher or somebody more experienced. They can point out which muscles you should focus on using and even help you to adjust your body.

3. Practice Fundamental Movements Everyday

At first, it will feel like learning to crawl all over again. You'll probably want to give up before you even start. Don't fall into that trap. Keep going and remember why you started in the first place.

You should probably start with the three fundamental moves Sacadas, Ginga, and Batuque. These will give you a strong base from which you can build later. Once you've mastered these basic moves, it will be much easier to learn more advanced techniques like the Berimbau Echo, Queixada, and Aú. If you're struggling with one move in particular, try slowing it down to half speed. This will allow you to feel each muscle and see where you go wrong

4. Watch Capoeiristas You Look Up to

This can be a great way to get inspired. You can see moves you want to incorporate into your own game and pick up some good cues from more experienced players. Try not to just mimic them. Instead, find out what makes their movement unique and add it to what you've already been practicing.

5. Practice Your New Moves with a Partner

The real key to timing and coordination is playing with a partner. If you're having trouble with this step as a beginner, try practicing next to somebody more experienced. Or even better, find somebody willing to spend some extra time helping you out.

Once you go beyond beginner moves, you'll notice that you need to go back and practice them from time to time. Try not to get discouraged. You may even find yourself looking forward to going back and practicing a basic movement because it feels so good when you finally master it for a second time.

6. Don't Be Afraid to Ask for Help

Remember that Capoeira is a community. We are all here to help each other out. If you're having trouble with something, just ask one of your friends for some pointers. They may not know the answer immediately, so don't be upset when they can't fix your problems in five minutes. The more you play with different people, the more exposure you will have to various movements and techniques. You may even come across new techniques you never even knew existed.

7. Keep Working on Your Endurance

Capoeira is an aerobic sport. It's really important to build up endurance with consistent physical activity over time. This doesn't mean running long distances or lifting weights. You can build up your endurance with lots of jumping, kicking, punching, and dance movements.

8. Keep Practicing and Don't Give Up

Even after you think you've mastered a move or technique, keep practicing it every day for another month just to be sure. Then wait another two weeks before you start testing yourself again just to make sure that the technique is truly ingrained in your muscle memory.

9. Get Excited about Capoeira

Remember, you chose this sport because there was something about it that made you want to learn more. If you're feeling disheartened or discouraged while learning, try taking a step back and remember why you started in the first place. Remember your original feelings of excitement and motivation every time you feel like giving up. This will keep you motivated to continue searching for new moves and techniques.

10. Try to Find a Role Model

Maybe there's a Capoeirista you admire. Maybe it's your Mestre, or maybe it's somebody from a group you regularly practice with. They might be able to offer advice or tips that will help improve your moves and make them smoother. Plus, if you show them what you've been practicing, they will probably be able to show you how it's supposed to be done.

11. Remember That There Are Always New Moves to Learn

Even after practicing for years and years, new moves are being discovered all the time. Don't get too comfortable with your current set. Keep an open mind and be on the lookout for new exercises to build your skill level.

12. Keep Practicing Your Baloes

Since Capoeira is a fluid, improvisational style of martial art, it's really important to be able to improvise and use what you already know during a real fight or confrontation. To do this, you must practice all of your moves and techniques until they become second nature.

13. Keep Practicing Your Rhythms

The more you practice these moves, the better they will flow together when you're in a game or *jogo* (fighting). You can practice by yourself or with another person. If possible, try to involve all four limbs in the rhythms you're practicing.

14. Keep Practicing Your Angolas

An Angola is a role that exists within the framework of Capoeira Angola, which is an older style of playing with more traditional roots than many modern styles of play. Some people might say these roles are outdated, but they are still very much alive today in some groups. Regardless of your group's style, the more Angolas you know, the better chance you have of being a true Capoeirista.

15. Keep Practicing Your Cuts (Golpes)

Cuts are movements that happen during game or jogo play that don't fit into the other categories like baloes, sambas, and angolas. These moves are very important because they can affect the gameplay of both you and your opponent. Plus, they often look really impressive when executed well.

16. Keep Practicing Your Sit-Ups (Agachadas)

Capoeira Angola is an art form that has its roots firmly planted in African tradition and many other cultures throughout the world. This is part of what makes it so interesting. One of these traditions includes a type of dance called "Agogô." You can practice your agogôs in many ways, but one way that is to incorporate them into your training is to do sit-ups while holding weights.

17. Keep Practicing Your Rolls

If you don't already know how to roll, start practicing as soon as possible, as it's a skill that will come in handy on many occasions. Whether you're rolling on the ground or trying to recover your feet when you are pushed down by an opponent, one of these well-practiced rolls can save your life or at least your pride.

18. Keep Practicing Your Cartwheels (Rolês)

Capoeiristas are artists at heart, and one of the most beautiful things to watch is a well-practiced cartwheel. It's also very impressive when you see someone who has mastered this movement while wearing their everyday clothes. Well-practiced cartwheels can make a huge difference during a fight.

19. Keep Practicing Your Backbends (Queixadas)

Although Capoeira moves are often thought of as very acrobatic, back bending is not something that is encouraged in many modern groups due to the risk of injury it poses. However, some Capoeira groups still incorporate this into their style, and it's worth learning if your group embraces them.

20. Keep Practicing Your Frontbends (Quebradas)

This is another acrobatic movement that falls into the "advanced level" category. Not all Capoeira Angola groups practice front bends, but some do. There are more risks involved with front bends than with backbends, which is why it's important to be careful and practice in a way that reduces the chances of injury.

Stretches for Capoeira

1. Calf Stretch

This stretch is very important because it's the foundation for many other stretches. Stand facing a wall with your hands outstretched at chest level to do this stretch. Keep one leg in front of the other and step back so that your heel is touching the wall. Make sure you are leaning forward and keep the knee of your front leg bent. Push against your hands and lean toward the wall until you feel a stretch in your calf muscles.

2. Quadricep Stretch

Stand with a chair to your left side. Place one foot onto the seat of the chair and keep it there for this whole stretch. Keep your other leg straight and push your hips forward and down towards the ground. You should feel a stretch in your right thigh muscles after you've done this for some time. Make sure you don't overdo it!

3. Hurdler's Stretch

Before doing this stretch, make sure that you have warmed up either through walking or running around. Sit on the floor and bring the sole of one foot in front of you towards your groin. Lean forward and place that foot onto the floor, keeping the other leg straight and stretched back behind you. You should feel a stretch in your groin area after doing this for some time.

4. Lower Back Stretch

Lie on your back with both legs facing upwards. Draw both knees up and hold them with your hands. Pull both legs upwards towards your chest while keeping your head on the floor. You should feel a stretch throughout your lower back at this point. Keep this position for some time to let the muscles relax before letting go of your knees and gently lowering your feet to the floor (use caution).

Making Your Spins Look Good

1. Work on Your Leg Work

This is all about finding your center of gravity and using the right muscles to create a beautiful cartwheel. Make sure you use your legs as much as possible during a cartwheel and that you look at where you're going so that you don't bump into anything once the cartwheel is finished. Remember, practice makes perfect.

2. Work on Your Hip Work

The hip movement helps create more momentum during your cartwheel, and you must focus on this aspect of the move. Make sure you aren't using your arms to push yourself off the ground as much as possible. Work more on using your hips so that you can gain more speed quickly.

3. Work on Your Torso Rotation

This is an important part of the cartwheel because you can't just jump into it. You need to do some torso rotation first to have momentum before getting up and flipping your legs over your head. Practice this movement with ankle weights on so that there is some resistance involved.

Capoeira Drills for Improving Skill Sets

1. Falling

This drill is all about increasing your coordination. Begin by standing with one foot in front of you for balance and fold your arms in front of you. Lean forward slightly and rotate your hips to the left so that you fall onto the floor into a controlled roll onto your back. Then repeat on the other side. Make sure that you don't turn your body or let go of your arms.

2. Rolling

Begin by doing the same thing as in drill number 1, but this time when you fall onto your back, roll to one side and stand up quickly. Repeat this on the other side.

3. Catching

This drill is similar to the previous one, except there is a ball involved which you must catch after your fall. Make sure you don't drop it! Repeat this for about 10 minutes, getting faster as you go along so that you can improve your coordination.

4. Catching with Leg Work

Throw the ball slightly upward after you've folded your arms for this drill. After catching it, do a leg sweep onto the floor and repeat on the other side. Remember to use your legs only.

5. Cartwheels with Weights (One Leg)

Start by standing on one leg with your arms folded in front of you. Lean slightly to the side and bend down, pushing off of your back leg, twisting your torso forward as you push yourself up again. Repeat this about 5 times on each side for best results.

Team Drills for Improving Capoeira Skills

1. Sit-Ups

Form two lines and make sure there is space between everyone. The first person in each line will start by lying down on the floor with their legs extended. Once they are comfortable, sit up quickly and pull one knee towards your chest with your arm. Pause and then repeat on the other side. This is a great drill that helps strengthen your core and helps your coordination as well.

2. Standing Up Drill

This drill is similar to the previous one, except you're standing up instead of lying down. Start by bending over slowly and pausing before extending your legs again. Focus on your core and make sure you don't lose balance, extending one leg carefully at a time.

3. Weights to the Front and Back

This drill is similar to drill number 2 but involves ankle weights. Pick up some light ankle weights and put them on before starting this drill. Bend forward with your legs straight and pause before standing back up. It may be difficult to get the timing right if you have heavier ankle weights on.

You can never stop learning new skills in Capoeira, and the more time you spend practicing, the more you will learn. Keep working on your moves until they're perfect. Don't get discouraged if you find yourself constantly tripping over at the beginning. Keep trying until you get better.

Once you feel like your basic movements are getting better, try to work on learning other Capoeira skills such as the road, how to swing a saber, and even play berimbau if you're interested. You can also look into starting your own Capoeira school or joining one if you want an even bigger challenge.

Conclusion

Capoeira is a Brazilian martial art practiced around the world. It combines dance, music, and acrobatics elements to create a unique blend of martial arts and dance, setting it apart from other martial art practices.

This art form originated from enslaved Africans in Brazil, who disguised their traditional martial arts to resemble a dance. This helped them avoid getting caught by government officials and being labeled as rebels.

This book provides you with a better understanding of the history of Capoeira and helps beginners start learning this martial art. It takes you through the many unfamiliar terminologies used by traditional Capoeira practitioners and explains the grading system used in Capoeira, as well as the significance and meaning of the Roda and the Jogo.

Additionally, it walks you through the two main schools of Capoeira– Capoeira Angola and Capoeira Regional–and also provides you with a quick glimpse into Capoeira Contemporânea. Some readers may be limited in the choice of which form they can practice because of the availability of teachers in their area. If you have the option to choose, this book will help you make an informed decision.

Next, the book took you through some of the core Capoeira principles and movements. This included the ginga, kicks, the au, and the esquivas. It guided you through the attacking techniques used in Capoeira, including round, circular, and straight attacks. While it is a non-contact martial art, you should better understand which techniques to use when playing the game in a Roda or just while practicing on your own.

It also walked you through defensive Capoeira movements and explained how you could defend yourself against an attacking Capoeirista during a game. While some techniques are similar to those used in attacking movements, others are unique to defensive Capoeira.

Another aspect of Capoeira is groundwork. This is also known as floreios ("flowery movements") and helps make Capoeira a visual treat. It involves taking basic movements and expanding upon them until they are beautiful enough to awe viewers. At the same time, they serve as a way to help Capoeiristas transfer their weight around and make the game smoother and more efficient. The book guided you through the basics of Capoeira groundwork, so you can integrate all the techniques you learned into a basic workout you can use to improve your skills.

The book expanded on Capoeira's deep relationship with music and dance and explained how these elements still play an important part in this martial art today. It also looked at the practice of Capoeira as a fitness method and gave you a basic Capoeira workout you can practice at any time. Finally, to evolve as a Capoeirista, it has provided you with ways to gradually level up your Capoeira skills over time.

Many people interested in Capoeira cannot learn directly from a teacher or are looking for supplemental material to help expand their practice of this martial art. This book served as a comprehensive guide to Capoeira for beginners, so you have a trustworthy source to turn to with any questions you may have.

References

(N.d.). Realbuzz.com. https://www.realbuzz.com/articles-interests/sports-activities/article/the-basic-skills-of-boxing/

Chen, L. (2021, June 15). The ultimate boxing workout for beginners. Byrdie. https://www.byrdie.com/boxing-workouts-5188633

Duquette, T. (2021, April 13). How to box at home - techniques for beginners. Joinfightcamp.com; FightCamp. https://blog.joinfightcamp.com/training/5-basic-boxing-techniques-to-learn-at-home-during-quarantine/

Evolve, M. M. A. (2022, October 2). 15 basic boxing combinations you should master first. Evolve Daily. https://evolve-mma.com/blog/15-basic-boxing-combinations-you-should-master-first/

Imre, B. (2020, August 14). 6 basic boxing punches & how to throw them correctly. PunchingBagsGuide. https://punchingbagsguide.com/basic-boxing-punches-guide/

Johnny, N. (2012, November 23). The BEGINNER'S guide to boxing. How to Box | ExpertBoxing. https://expertboxing.com/the-beginners-guide-to-boxing

Mahoney, K. (2020, May 2). 7 boxing fundamentals everyone should know. Muscle & Fitness. https://www.muscleandfitness.com/muscle-fitness-hers/hers-workouts/basics-boxing/

McNulty, R. (2020, May 29). The beginner's guide to boxing training. Muscle & Fitness. https://www.muscleandfitness.com/workouts/workout-tips/the-beginners-guide-to-boxing-training/

Ritterbeck, M. (2017, April 11). Boxing for beginners: Boxing basics for stance, breath, and punches. Greatist. https://greatist.com/fitness/boxing-workout-basic-moves-for-beginners

5 tips to improve your pressure jiu-jitsu style. (2020, February 24). Jiujitsu-News.Com. https://jiujitsu-news.com/5-tips-to-improve-your-pressure-Jiu-Jitsu-style/

40+ Brazilian Jiu Jitsu submissions you need to know. (2020, September 7). Bjjsuccess.Com. https://www.bjjsuccess.com/brazilian-Jiu-Jitsu-submissions/

Action reaction in Jiu-jitsu. (2020, January 29). Jiujitsu-News.Com. https://jiujitsu-news.com/action-reaction-in-Jiu-Jitsu/

Barra, G. (2014, July 31). 5 Tips on how to create pressure and be heavy on your opponent. - Gracie Barra. Graciebarra.Com. https://graciebarra.com/gb-news/tips-pressure-opponent/

Barra, G. (2021, January 25). Why Brazilian Jiu-Jitsu is the ultimate form of self-defense. Graciebarra.Com. https://graciebarra.com/chandler-az/why-brazilian-Jiu-Jitsu-is-good-for-self-defense/

Bjj, A. S. (n.d.). Learn BJJ Sequences - Combinations in Brazilian Jiu-Jitsu. Pureartbjj.Com. from https://www.pureartbjj.com/blog/bjj-sequences-combinations/

BJJ for self defence: A complete review by an ex cop. (2020). https://theselfdefenceexpert.com/bjj-for-self-defence/

BJJEE. (2020a, February 20). How to successfully use action-reaction principles when grappling. Bjjee.Com. https://www.bjjee.com/articles/successfully-use-action-reaction-principles-grappling/

BJJEE. (2020b, April 14). Marcelo Garcia on how to use combinations to finish opponents. Bjjee.Com. https://www.bjjee.com/articles/marcelo-garcia-on-how-to-use-combinations-to-finish-opponents/

bjjmindset. (2013, June 7). Action and Reaction. Wordpress.Com. https://bjjmindset.wordpress.com/2013/06/07/action-and-reaction/

BjjTribes. (2020, September 20). How many guards are there in BJJ? The Ultimate list of all of the guard positions in Brazilian Jiu Jitsu. Bjjtribes.Com. https://bjjtribes.com/list-of-all-of-the-guard-positions-in-brazilian-Jiu-Jitsu/

Brazilian Jiu Jitsu – everything about the gentle art. (2019, October 3). Bjj-World.Com. https://bjj-world.com/brazilian-Jiu-Jitsu/

Brazilian jiu jitsu what is it. (2020, April 29). Jiujitsu-News.Com. https://jiujitsu-news.com/brazilian-Jiu-Jitsu-what-is-it/

Brazilian Jiu-jitsu style. (2020, January 29). Jiujitsu-News.Com. https://jiujitsu-news.com/brazilian-Jiu-Jitsu-style/

Bryers, M. (2018, December 13). Top 3 Takedowns For Brazilian Jiu Jitsu. Jiujitsuct.Com. https://www.jiujitsuct.com/3-takedowns-bjj

de Los Reyes, J. (2016, June 15). The Strengths and Weaknesses of Each Martial Art for self-defense. Kombatarts.Com. https://kombatarts.com/strengths-weaknesses-martial-art-self-defense/

Evolve, M. M. A. (2018a, January 29). The first 3 submissions you should master in Brazilian Jiu-Jitsu. Evolve-Mma.Com. https://evolve-mma.com/blog/the-first-3-submissions-you-should-master-in-brazilian-Jiu-Jitsu/

Evolve, M. M. A. (2018b, March 31). 5 basic BJJ movements beginners need to perfect. Evolve-Mma.Com. https://evolve-mma.com/blog/5-basic-bjj-movements-beginners-need-to-perfect/

Evolve, M. M. A. (2019, January 6). The 3 best BJJ takedowns for beginners. Evolve-Mma.Com. https://evolve-mma.com/blog/the-3-best-bjj-takedowns-for-beginners/

Fanatics Authors. (n.d.). Five Essential BJJ Takedowns! Bjjfanatics.Com. from https://bjjfanatics.com/blogs/news/five-essential-bjj-takedowns

Four Esoteric Principles of Martial Arts Skill Development. (2019, December 3). Sonnybrown.Net. https://www.sonnybrown.net/principles-martial-arts-skill-development/

Freeman, D. (2021a, May 14). Brazilian Jiu-Jitsu vs Japanese Jiu-Jitsu: The difference you should know. Bjjgireviews.Com. https://bjjgireviews.com/brazilian-Jiu-Jitsu-vs-japanese-Jiu-Jitsu/

Freeman, D. (2021b, May 26). 10 tips to get started in Brazilian Jiu-jitsu (2021). Bjjgireviews.Com. https://bjjgireviews.com/get-started-in-bjj/

Freeman, D. (2021c, June 3). best BJJ Solo Drills you can do at home by yourself (EVERYDAY). Bjjgireviews.Com. https://bjjgireviews.com/bjj-solo-drills

guy. (2019, September 20). 8 Mistakes Typically made by Brazilian Jiu-Jitsu Beginners. Bjjnc.Com. https://www.bjjnc.com/8-mistakes-typically-made-by-brazilian-Jiu-Jitsu-beginners/

How all Brazilian Jiu-Jitsu Submission Holds work. (2020, September 2). Bjj-World.Com. https://bjj-world.com/brazilian-Jiu-Jitsu-submission-holds/

Intermediate bjj: Building submission combinations. (2016, March 31). Jiujitsutimes.Com. https://jiujitsutimes.com/intermediate-bjj-building-submission-combinations/

Jiu Jitsu, L. (2020, April 1). 10 best BJJ drills you can do home alone. Jiujitsulegacy.Com. https://jiujitsulegacy.com/health/strength-conditioning/10-best-bjj-drills-you-can-do-home-alone/

Jiu-jitsu fight energy Management. (2020, January 29). Jiujitsu-News.Com. https://jiujitsu-news.com/Jiu-Jitsu-fight-energy-management/

Kesting, S. (2016, June 18). 37 powerful BJJ submissions for grapplers. Grapplearts.Com. https://www.grapplearts.com/37-powerful-bjj-submissions-for-grapplers/

Kesting, S. (2018, January 16). Japanese Jiujitsu vs BJJ. Grapplearts.Com. https://www.grapplearts.com/japanese-jiujitsu-vs-bjj/

Kesting, S. (2021, March 1). Top 10 throws and takedowns for BJJ. Grapplearts.Com. https://www.grapplearts.com/top-10-throws-and-takedowns-for-bjj/

leticiamedeiros. (2018, November 26). Takedowns for Jiu-jitsu - Gracie Barra. Graciebarra.Com. https://graciebarra.com/gb-learning/takedowns-for-Jiu-Jitsu/

Marlin, S. (2018, December 14). The Difference Between jiu jitsu vs bjj. Martialboss.Com. https://martialboss.com/Jiu-Jitsu-vs-bjj

Martial arts grappling techniques (beginner & advanced). (2018, September 7). Blackbeltwiki.Com. https://blackbeltwiki.com/grappling

Open guard vs closed guard BJJ explained. (2021, January 27). Jiujitsu-News.Com. https://jiujitsu-news.com/open-guard-vs-closed-guard/

Ruiz, B. (2020, May 11). 23 effective bjj takedowns. Mma-Today.Com. https://www.mma-today.com/bjj-takedowns-judo-throws/

Scandinavia, B. J. J. (2016, October 13). All guards in Brazilian Jiu Jitsu (with videos) - BJJ Scandinavia. Bjjscandinavia.Com. http://www.bjjscandinavia.com/2016/13/all-guards-in-brazilian-Jiu-Jitsu-with-videos/

Skoczylas, N. (2020a, October 19). Japanese Jiu-jitsu vs. Brazilian Jiu-jitsu. Projectbjj.Com. https://projectbjj.com/japanese-Jiu-Jitsu-vs-brazilian-Jiu-Jitsu/

Skoczylas, N. (2020b, October 28). What are the fundamentals in Brazilian Jiu-Jitsu? Projectbjj.Com. https://projectbjj.com/what-are-the-fundamentals-in-brazilian-Jiu-Jitsu/

Smith, A. (2017, November 11). Combinations in BJJ. HowTheyPlay. https://howtheyplay.com/individual-sports/Combinations-in-BJJ

Spot, B. (2017, November 20). 6 common BJJ mistakes you should avoid. Bjj-Spot.Com. https://www.bjj-spot.com/common-bjj-mistakes/

Spot, B. (2018a, April 29). Basic BJJ Drills you should do every day. Bjj-Spot.Com. https://www.bjj-spot.com/basic-bjj-drills/

Spot, B. (2018b, September 27). Guard retention – important moves and principles. Bjj-Spot.Com. https://www.bjj-spot.com/guard-retention/

The 17 time-tested benefits of Brazilian Jiu Jitsu. (2020, February 11). Bjjsuccess.Com. https://www.bjjsuccess.com/benefits-of-brazilian-Jiu-Jitsu/

The Benefits of Taking a Grappling Class. (n.d.). Nymaa.Com. from https://www.nymaa.com/martial-arts-blog/The-Benefits-of-Taking-a-Grappling-Class_AE92.html

The best modern BJJ stretching routine for improved grappling. (2020, April 27). Bjjsuccess.Com. https://www.bjjsuccess.com/stretching-for-bjj/

The fundamental BJJ submissions. (2020, November 4). Youjiujitsu.Com. https://youjiujitsu.com/the-fundamental-bjj-submissions/

The pressure game in Jiu-Jitsu. (2015, March 23). Jiujitsutimes.Com. https://jiujitsutimes.com/the-pressure-game-in-Jiu-Jitsu/

The top 4 bjj self defence techniques you should know. (2016, March 10). Jiujitsutimes.Com. https://jiujitsutimes.com/the-top-4-bjj-self-defence-techniques-you-should-know/

The true history of Brazilian Jiu jitsu. (2020, April 9). Bjjsuccess.Com. https://www.bjjsuccess.com/history-of-brazilian-Jiu-Jitsu/

The ULTIMATE analysis of "PRESSURE." (2016, June 19). Jiujitsutimes.Com. https://jiujitsutimes.com/ultimate-analysis-pressure/

The ultimate Brazilian Jiu jitsu guide for beginners. (2020, January 4). Middleeasy.Com. https://middleeasy.com/guides/Jiu-Jitsu-guide/

(N.d.-a). Findyourgi.Com. Retrieved from https://findyourgi.com/what-is-bjj/

(N.d.-b). Letsrollbjj.Com. Retrieved from https://www.letsrollbjj.com/bjj-white-belt-tips/

5 qualities to look for in a Brazilian Jiu-Jitsu instructor. (2016, February 27). Jiujitsutimes.Com. https://jiujitsutimes.com/5-qualities-to-look-for-in-a-brazilian-jiu-jitsu-instructor/

Barra, G. (2015, July 4). The "secret" to getting better at BJJ - Gracie Barra. Graciebarra.Com. https://graciebarra.com/gb-news/the-secret-bjj/

Battle Arts Academy. (2019, December 28). How to get better at Brazilian Jiu-Jitsu: The top tips for beginners. Battleartsacademy.Ca. https://www.battleartsacademy.ca/post/how-to-get-better-at-brazilian-jiu-jitsu-the-top-tips-for-beginners

Park, J. (2014, June 13). 57 Training Tips for Brazilian Jiu Jitsu White Belts. Crazy88mma.Com. https://www.crazy88mma.com/57-training-tips-for-brazilian-jiu-jitsu-white-belts/

10 types of muay Thai kicks. (2019, December 11). Fijimuaythai.com. https://fijimuaythai.com/types-of-muay-thai-kicks/

14 FAV Muay Thai combos for developing RHYTHM & FLOW. (n.d.). Mmashredded.com. https://www.mmashredded.com/blog/muay-thai-combos

5 essential clinching tips. (n.d.). Muay-thai-guy.com. https://www.muay-thai-guy.com/blog/5-essential-clinching-tips

5 essential Muay Thai sparring tips for beginners. (n.d.). 5 Essential Muay Thai Sparring Tips for Beginners. https://www.ubudmuaythai.com/blog/5-essential-muay-thai-sparring-tips-for-beginners

5 essential Muay Thai sweep techniques you must know – evolve university blog. (2023, March 2). Evolve University. https://evolve-university.com/blog/5-essential-muay-thai-sweep-techniques-you-must-know/

A typical Muay Thai workout routine. (n.d.). Muay-Thai-guy.com. https://www.muay-thai-guy.com/blog/muay-thai-workout

Alexis. (2022, August 28). Dutch Kickboxing vs Muay Thai: what are the differences? Mejiro Gym Bali. https://mejirogymbali.com/blog/dutch-kickboxing-vs-muay-thai-differences/

Beginner's GuideTo knee strikes – law of the fist. (2019, June 22). Lawofthefist.com. https://lawofthefist.com/a-beginners-intro-to-the-art-of-knee-strikes/

Best Muay Thai sparring gear. (2019, April 14). Muay Thai Citizen; Kay. https://www.muaythaicitizen.com/best-muay-thai-sparring-gear/

Bryan, A. (2023, January 5). Muay Thai & spirituality. Black Belt Magazine. https://blackbeltmag.com/muay-thai-spirituality

Bryan, A. (n.d.). The ultimate guide to the Muay Thai clinch. Muay-thai-guy.com. https://www.muay-thai-guy.com/blog/clinching-for-muay-thai

Delp, C. (2004). Muay Thai: Traditionen – Grundlagen – Techniken des Thaiboxens (1st ed.). Motorbuch.

Dillon. (2020, May 27). How to practice Muay Thai by yourself: My daily routine. Oneshotmma. https://oneshotmma.com/how-to-practice-muay-thai-by-yourself-my-weekly-routine/

Dunk. (2017, February 15). Common Muay Thai routines when training in Thailand: Part I. Muay Thai; Bokun Wordpress Theme. https://kstmuaythai.com/common-muay-thai-routines-when-training-in-thailand-part-1/

Evolve Vacation. (2018, November 20). How to develop powerful knees in Muay Thai. Evolve Vacation. https://evolve-vacation.com/blog/how-to-develop-powerful-knees-in-muay-thai/

Evolve, M. M. A. (2016, March 23). 7 Muay Thai principles that will make you A better fighter. Evolve Daily. https://evolve-mma.com/blog/7-muay-thai-principles-that-will-make-you-a-better-fighter/

Evolve, M. M. A. (2018, January 15). Muay Thai 101: The roundhouse kick. Evolve Daily. https://evolve-mma.com/blog/muay-thai-101-the-roundhouse-kick/

Evolve, M. M. A. (2020, September 9). The beginner's guide to boxing sparring: 10 things to know. Evolve Daily. https://evolve-mma.com/blog/the-beginners-guide-to-boxing-sparring-10-things-to-know/

Evolve, M. M. A. (2022, February 10). The complete Muay Thai Beginner's Guide. Evolve Daily. https://evolve-mma.com/blog/the-complete-muay-thai-beginners-guide/

Evolve, M. M. A. (2022, June 21). Here's how to utilize sweeps for Muay Thai. Evolve Daily. https://evolve-mma.com/blog/heres-how-to-utilize-sweeps-for-muay-thai/

Evolve, M. M. A. (2022, October 24). Comparing Muay Thai to Dutch kickboxing. Evolve Daily. https://evolve-mma.com/blog/comparing-muay-thai-to-dutch-kickboxing/

Explorer, K. L. (2015, November 24). Muay Thai. Https://www.khaolakexplorer.com/; Khao Lak Explorer. https://www.khaolakexplorer.com/muay-thai/

Hughes, L. (2023, January 26). The Muay Thai workout routine that will get you into shape. Prime Women | An Online Magazine; Prime Women | Online Lifestyle Media for Women over 50. https://primewomen.com/wellness/fitness/muay-thai-workout-routine/

James, K. (2017, January 13). The 8 punches of muay Thai. Fightrr.com. https://fightrr.com/muay-thai/technique/punches

Jones, A. (2023, April 2). Dutch Kickboxing vs. Muay Thai. Fight Falcon – Fight With Style. https://fightfalcon.com/dutch-kickboxing-vs-muay-thai/

Mohan, C. (2020, March 5). Muay Thai training gear you must have in your gym bag. ONE Championship – The Home Of Martial Arts. https://www.onefc.com/lifestyle/muay-thai-training-gear-you-must-have-in-your-gym-bag/

Muay Sok: The Elbow Fighter (June 8th, 2022), Jacob Garner. Muay Sok https://muaythai.com/muay-sok/

Muay Thai – philosophy, techniques, training tips, and more. (n.d.). Ninjaphd.com. https://www.ninjaphd.com/muay-thai/

Muay Thai Guy (2023), 10 Key Muay Thai Defense Techniques Every Fighter Must Know. https://www.muay-thai-guy.com/blog/muay-thai-defense-techniques

Muay Thai history. (2016, March 4). World Thai Boxing Association. https://thaiboxing.com/about/muay-thai-history/

Muay Thai sparring 2023: 10 tips for beginners & more. (2023, March 12). Way of the Fighter. https://wayofthefighter.com/muay-thai-sparring/

Muay Thai Techniques. (n.d.). Blogspot.com. http://muay-thai-techniquess.blogspot.com/2011/06/muay-thai-techniques-clinch-and-neck.html

MuayThaiCitizen, (May 19th, 2022), Kay, Is Muay Thai effective in a Street Fight? https://www.muaythaicitizen.com/is-muay-thai-effective-in-a-street-fight/#:~:text=So%20is%20Muay%20Thai%20effective,of%20controlling%20what%20happens%20next

OneFc (June 30th, 2020), John Wolcott, The 5 Fundamentals Of A Solid Muay Thai Defense. https://www.onefc.com/lifestyle/the-5-fundamentals-of-a-solid-muay-thai-defense/,

Shutts, I. (2018, October 14). Muay Thai boxing and punches. LowKick MMA. https://www.lowkickmma.com/muay-thai-boxing-and-punches

Singpatong-sitnumnoi (December 4th, 2012), Elbow Techniques In Muay Thai http://www.singpatong-sitnumnoi.com/elbow-techniques-in-muay-thai/,

Thailand, M. (2021, February 16). Muay Thai knees. Muay Thailand. https://www.muaythailand.co.uk/blogs/techniques/muay-thai-knees

The 10 best beginner Muay Thai sparring tips. (n.d.). Muay-thai-guy.com. https://www.muay-thai-guy.com/blog/beginner-muay-thai-sparring-tips

The ultimate guide to Muay Thai knees – evolve university blog. (2021, August 14). Evolve University. https://evolve-university.com/blog/the-ultimate-guide-to-muay-thai-knees/

Traditional Muay Thai fighting stances: the Art's bedrock. (n.d.). Muaythai. It. http://www.muaythai.it/traditional-muay-thai-fighting-stances-the-arts-bedrock/

WayOfTheArt (January 18th, 2023), Is Muay Thai Good for Self-Defense? (Street Fight). https://wayofmartialarts.com/is-muay-thai-good-for-self-defense/

Ways Of Martial Arts (January 24, 2023). Muay Thai Elbow Techniques And Combos https://wayofmartialarts.com/muay-thai-elbow-techniques-and-combos/

What is Muay Thai, Muay Thai History of training and fighting. (2008, December 30). Tiger Muay Thai & MMA Training Camp, Phuket, Thailand. https://www.tigermuaythai.com/about-muay-thai/history

Wilmot, A. (2013, July 2). Muay Thai. Awakening Fighters. https://awakeningfighters.com/awakepedia/muay-thai/

Wolcott, J. (2019, October 22). What makes Dutch kickboxing different from other striking arts? ONE Championship – The Home Of Martial Arts. https://www.onefc.com/lifestyle/what-makes-dutch-kickboxing-different-from-other-striking-arts/

Wolcott, J. (2021, July 10). Mastering the Muay Thai stance for beginners. ONE Championship – The Home Of Martial Arts. https://www.onefc.com/lifestyle/muay-thai-stance/

Yip, R. (2022, November 14). 3 common mistakes with your Fighting Stance. Infighting. https://www.infighting.ca/kickboxing/3-common-mistakes-with-your-fighting-stance/

Yokkao (2023), Essential Elbow Techniques In Muay Thai. https://asia.yokkao.com/blogs/news/essential-elbow-techniques-in-muay-thai

Yokkao (February 9th, 2021), How To Improve Muay Thai Skills https://asia.yokkao.com/blogs/news/how-to-improve-muay-thai-skills

(N.d.). Wvmat.com. https://www.wvmat.com/overview.htm

History of wrestling & UWW. (n.d.). United World Wrestling. https://uww.org/organisation/history-wrestling-uww

Overview of wrestling rules. (n.d.). Finalsite.net. https://resources.finalsite.net/images/v1583950707/sacredsf/c1vuicxnw1w5xwmwi7vs/wrestling_packet.pdf

Rookie Road. (2019, December 29). What is wrestling? Rookieroad.com; Rookie Road. https://www.rookieroad.com/wrestling/what-is/

The history of wrestling. (2010, June 10). Athleticscholarships.net. https://www.athleticscholarships.net/history-of-wrestling.htm

What Are the Different Types of Wrestling? (2021, February 18). Fitness Quest. https://www.fitnessquest.com/what-are-the-different-types-of-wrestling/

Wikipedia contributors. (2023, May 29). Wrestling. Wikipedia, The Free Encyclopedia. https://en.wikipedia.org/w/index.php?title=Wrestling&oldid=1157634607

Wild Pages Press. (2017a). Wrestling: Notebook. Createspace Independent Publishing Platform.

Wild Pages Press. (2017b). Wrestling: Notebook. Createspace Independent Publishing Platform.

Wrestling facts. (n.d.). Auburntakedown.com. http://www.auburntakedown.com/parents-corner/wrestling-facts.html

Chen, S. (2021, January 30). 14 basic karate stances help you build a strong base. The karate Blog. https://thekarateblog.com/karate-stances/

Grupp, J. (2003). Shotokan karate Kata: Volume 2 (1st ed.). Meyer & Meyer Sport. https://www.shotokankaratecalgary.com/kata.php

Jutras, M., & The karate Lifestyle. (n.d.). The complete list of basic karate stances. Thekaratelifestyle.com. https://www.thekaratelifestyle.com/list-of-karate-stances/

Karate - Belt Colours & Meaning. (n.d.). Tutorialspoint.com. https://www.tutorialspoint.com/karate/karate_belt_colours_meaning.htm

Karate belts. (2015, June 11). Elite Martial Arts Karate Dojo. https://emadojola.com/karate-belts/

Koch, C. (2023, January 1). karate Kata list of 10 different karate styles [2023]. The karate Blog. https://thekarateblog.com/karate-kata-list/

List of Shotokan katas (with video & written instructions). (2018, September 7). Black Belt Wiki. https://blackbeltwiki.com/shotokan-karate-katas

Shotokan katas. (n.d.). Victoria Shotokan karate and Kobudo Association. https://www.shotokankarate.ca/katas

Vladisavljevic, V. (2022, July 19). Karate belt order: Ranking system explained. Way of Martial Arts. https://wayofmartialarts.com/karate-belts-ranking-system-explained/

14 Basic Taekwondo Kicks (Everyone Should Know!). (2019a, November 29). Wu-Yi Taekwondo. https://www.wuyi-taekwondo.com/taekwondo-kicks

14 Basic Taekwondo Kicks (Everyone Should Know!). (2019b, November 29). Wu-Yi Taekwondo. https://www.wuyi-taekwondo.com/taekwondo-kicks

Basic Moves That Every Student of Taekwondo Should Know. (2010, February 15). Sports Aspire. https://sportsaspire.com/taekwondo-moves

billysmma. (2017, January 4). Basic Taekwondo Stances Explained. Legends MMA. https://legendsmma.net/basic-taekwondo-stances-explained

Blocking (막기 makgi) | Taekwondo Preschool. (n.d.). Taekwondopreschool.com. https://taekwondopreschool.com/blocks.html

Habits of a Taekwondo Martial Artist | Visual.ly. (n.d.). Visual.ly. Retrieved from https://visual.ly/community/Infographics/sports/habits-taekwondo-martial-artist

Josh. (2015, January 16). The 14 Basic Movements of Taekwondo. Martial Methodology. https://martialmethodology.wordpress.com/2015/01/16/the-14-basic-movements-of-taekwondo

Josh. (2017, January 16). How to Get Good at Taekwondo FAST(er). Martial Methodology. https://martialmethodology.wordpress.com/2017/01/15/how-to-get-good-at-taekwondo-fast

List of Taekwondo Kicks (Beginner & Advanced). (n.d.). Black Belt Wiki. https://blackbeltwiki.com/taekwondo-kicks

Murphy, M. F. (2013, February 5). A Beginner's Guide to Taekwondo. Frank Murphy's Masterclass. http://frankmurphysmasterclass.com/2013/02/beginners-guide-taekwondo

Punches and Strikes in TaeKwondo: A Complete List | Tae Kwon Do Nation. (n.d.). TaekwondoNation. https://www.taekwondonation.com/taekwondo-punches

Quality, F. (2016, December 5). A Brief History of Taekwondo. Fight Quality. https://fightquality.com/2016/12/05/a-brief-history-of-taekwondo

Robert. (n.d.). Is Taekwondo Dangerous? Here Is What You Need To Know! Retrieved from https://wayofmartialarts.com/is-taekwondo-dangerous

aekwondo Belt | Dos Taekwondo - Best Taekwondo Academy. (2017, September 26). Dostaekwondo. https://dostaekwondo.com/taekwondo-belt-order-meaning

Taekwondo Belt System | Brisbane Martial Arts. (2009, August 20). Brisbanemartialarts.com.au. https://brisbanemartialarts.com.au/belts-and-stripes

Taekwondo Gradings - JUST KEEP KICKING. (n.d.). Justkeepkicking. Retrieved from http://justkeepkicking.com/taekwondo-gradings

Taekwondo Moves: Powerful Skills and Techniques to Challenge You. (n.d.). Made4Fighters. https://made4fighters.com/blog/taekwondo-moves

Taekwondo Punches & Strikes - Taekwondo Animals.com. (2018). Taekwondo Animals.com. https://taekwondoanimals.com/taekwondo-punches-strikes

The Philosophies Related To Taekwondo. (2017, January 25). Hong Ik Martial Arts. https://hongikmartialarts.com/philosophies-related-taekwondo

Tips for Taekwondo Students. (n.d.). Taekwondo Wiki. Retrieved from https://taekwondo.fandom.com/wiki/Tips_for_Taekwondo_Students

Walking Stance (앞서기 ap-sogi) | Stance (서기 sogi) | Taekwondo Preschool. (n.d.). Taekwondopreschool.com. Retrieved from https://taekwondopreschool.com/tutorialstance2.html

What is Taekwondo? A definition and short history - Master Chong's Tae Kwon Do. (2017). Master Chong's Tae Kwon Do. https://buffalotkd.com/what-is-tae-kwon-do

What You Need To Know Before You Start Taking Taekwondo.... (n.d.). Www.streetdirectory.com. Retrieved from https://www.streetdirectory.com/etoday/-wwjuuw.html

Kung Fu - techniques, kicks, forms (taolu), etc. - black belt wiki. (2018, September 8). Blackbeltwiki.Com. https://blackbeltwiki.com/kung-fu

Li, S. (2019, March 6). The Main Different Kung Fu Styles. China Educational Tours. https://www.chinaeducationaltours.com/guide/culture-chinese-kungfu-styles.htm

Robert. (2020, May 3). Kung Fu styles are explained in detail. Wayofmartialarts.Com. https://wayofmartialarts.com/kung-fu-styles-explained-in-detail

Black Belt Magazine. (2011, March 21). Kung Fu Animal Style #3: Crane. Black Belt Magazine.

https://blackbeltmag.com/the-5-kung-fu-animal-styles-of-the-chinese-martial-arts/kung-fu-animal-style-3-crane

Leonard Lackinger, S. W. W. (n.d.). The Five Animals of Shaolin Kung Fu - Part 1. Shaolin-Wahnam-Wien.At. Retrieved from
https://www.shaolin-wahnam-wien.at/kungfu-5-tiere-1-en.php

martial. (2018, February 13). Kung Fu Animal Styles. Martialtribes.Com.https://www.martialtribes.com/kung-fu-animal-styles

Tai Chi vs. Tae Kwon Do. (2010, December 9). Sportsrec.Com. https://www.sportsrec.com/329232-tai-chi-vs-tae-kwon-do.html

The Five Shaolin Animals. (n.d.). Kungfuforlife.Ca. Retrieved from
https://www.kungfuforlife.ca/the-five-shaolin-animals.html

(N.d.). Laugar-Kungfu.Com. Retrieved from https://www.laugar-kungfu.com/style-5-animals

Shaolin Kung Fu Stances – Spirit Dragon Institute. (n.d.). Spiritdragoninstitute.Com. Retrieved
from http://spiritdragoninstitute.com/kung-fu/shaolin-kung-fu-stances

The Basic kung fu Stances / Horse stance /Taizu kung fu Camp. (2021, January 20). Learnshaolinkungfu.Com. https://www.learnshaolinkungfu.com/kung-fu-stances

5 KUNG FU STANCES (step by step tutorial)

Crane Stance. (n.d.). I-Budo.Com. Retrieved from
http://www.i-budo.com/techniques/basics/stances/crane-stance

Korahais, S. A. (2012, September 26). History of qigong: The 18 Luohan hands. Flowingzen.Com. https://flowingzen.com/4862/18-luohan-hands-qigong

Lohan Qigong 18 hands system and history. (2018, July 27). Taichimontreal.Com.
https://taichimontreal.com/chi-kung/lohan-qigong-system

Shaolin Eighteen Lohan Hands. (n.d.). Shaolin.Org. Retrieved from
https://shaolin.org/chikung/lohan.html

5 tips for finding Zen in the chaos of everyday life. (n.d.). Retrieved from Lovehemp.com
website: https://lovehemp.com/blogs/news/5-tips-for-finding-zen-in-the-chaos-of-everyday-life

8 powerful ancient qigong exercises for cultivating healing energy in the body. (2016, January 19). Retrieved from Consciouslifestylemag.com website:
https://www.consciouslifestylemag.com/qigong-exercises-healing-energy

Bailey, P. (2020, June 29). 10 tips to find zen in the chaos of everyday life. Retrieved from
Mindbodygreen.com website: https://www.mindbodygreen.com/0-21510/10-tips-to-find-zen-in-the-chaos-of-everyday-life.html

Editors of Consumer Guide. (2007, November 19). Taoism and Chi. Retrieved from Howstuffworks.com website: https://people.howstuffworks.com/taoism-and-chi.htm

Find calm amongst the chaos of a stressful life by following these tips to achieve a Zen state of
mind. (2020, March 15). Retrieved from Healthshots.com website:
https://www.healthshots.com/mind/happiness-hacks/find-calm-amongst-the-chaos-of-a-stressful-life-by-following-these-tips-to-achieve-a-zen-state-of-mind

Forms of Qi - vital substances in Chinese medicine. (n.d.). Retrieved from Sacredlotus.com website:

https://www.sacredlotus.com/go/foundations-chinese-medicine/get/forms-of-qi-life-force

HeartMath LLC, C. (2013, August 29). Finding zen: Easy ways to cultivate more inner peace. Retrieved from Huffpost.com website: https://www.huffpost.com/entry/how-to-find-zen_b_3820554

McGinley, K. (2019, December 15). How to find your zen when you're at your breaking point. Retrieved from Chopra.com website: https://chopra.com/articles/how-to-find-your-zen-when-youre-at-your-breaking-point

Naumann, S. (n.d.). A brief history of Shaolin temple. Retrieved from Tripsavvy.com website: https://www.tripsavvy.com/brief-history-shaolin-temple-1495708

O'Brien, B. (n.d.). Zen and Martial Arts. Retrieved from Learnreligions.com website: https://www.learnreligions.com/zen-and-martial-arts-449950

Prickril, B. (2014, January 3). How to harness the power of chi energy. Retrieved from RemedyGrove website: https://remedygrove.com/bodywork/How-to-Harness-Your-Chi-Power

Reninger, E. (n.d.). Qi (chi): The Taoist principle of life force. Retrieved from Learnreligions.com website: https://www.learnreligions.com/what-is-qi-chi-3183052

Retreat, N. Y. K., & View all posts by Nam Yang Kung Fu Retreat. (n.d.). Zen and the Art of Kung Fu. Retrieved from Kungfuretreat.com website: https://kungfuretreat.com/zen-and-the-art-of-kung-fu

Robert. (2020, August 30). What is Zen in martial arts. Retrieved from Wayofmartialarts.com website: https://wayofmartialarts.com/what-is-zen-in-martial-arts

Watts, A. (2000). What is Zen? Novato, CA: New World Library.

Temple, S. (2015, July 23). Shaolin Monk Weapons Shaolin Weapons. Chinashaolintemple.Com. https://www.chinashaolintemple.com/shaolin-monk-weapons-shaolin-weapons

18 Weapons of Shaolin Martial Arts. (n.d.). Shaolinca.Com. Retrieved from http://www.shaolinca.com/18weapons.html

Lama Kung-Fu's 8 Fundamentals. (n.d.). Angelfire.Com. Retrieved from https://www.angelfire.com/ny/sanshou/eights.html

Lama (martial art). (n.d.). Fandom.Com. Retrieved from https://gyaanipedia.fandom.com/wiki/Lama_(martial_art)

Lama Pai. (2018, September 29). Blackbeltwiki.Com. https://blackbeltwiki.com/lama-pai

Lama Pai Kung Fu striking techniques. (2016, April 23). Wordpress.Com. https://nysanda.wordpress.com/2016/04/23/lama-pai-kung-fu-striking-techniques

(N.d.). Geocities.Ws. Retrieved from http://www.geocities.ws/Colosseum/4098/strike.html

Ben Stanley, T.-S. (2016, October 15). Kung Fu kicks. Whitedragonmartialarts.Com. https://www.whitedragonmartialarts.com/kung-fu-kicks

Five Basic Kicks. (n.d.). Shaolin.Org. Retrieved from https://shaolin.org/video-clips-3/intensive2006/kicks/kicks.html

Kongling, M. (2016, June 29). The characteristics of a good kick. 6Dragonskungfu.Com. https://www.6dragonskungfu.com/the-characteristics-of-a-good-kick

Functional Wing Chun. (n.d.). Retrieved from Functionalselfdefense.org website: http://www.functionalselfdefense.org/wing-chun

Wing Chun techniques for beginners – law of the fist. (n.d.). Retrieved from Lawofthefist.com website: https://lawofthefist.com/wing-chun-techniques-for-beginners

Wing Chun techniques: Punch, palm strike, chop, elbow. (n.d.). Retrieved from Wingchunlife.com website: https://www.wingchunlife.com/wing-chun-techniques-strikes.html

Kongling, M. (2019, April 1). 5 wooden dummy drills/exercises ideal for beginners. Retrieved from 6Dragonskungfu.com website: https://www.6dragonskungfu.com/5-wooden-dummy-drills-exercises-ideal-for-beginners

Kriel, F. (2016, October 31). Training at home for beginning students — tiger claw Kung Fu &

Tai chi. Retrieved from Tigerclawmartialarts.com website: https://www.tigerclawmartialarts.com/the-tiger-life/2016/10/31/training-at-home-for-beginning-students

MSISSHINRYU.COM. (n.d.). Retrieved from Msisshinryu.com website: http://www.msisshinryu.com/articles/kano/Judo-contrib.shtml

Waza (Techniques). (n.d.). Retrieved from Judo-ch.jp website: https://www.Judo-ch.jp/english/knowledge/technique/

Goshin Jutsu Kata. (2018, September 21). Blackbeltwiki.Com. https://blackbeltwiki.com/goshin-jutsu-kata

Itsutsu-No Kata. (2018, September 21). Blackbeltwiki.Com. https://blackbeltwiki.com/itsutsu-no-kata

Randori rules. (2013, October 23). Judoinfo.Com. https://Judoinfo.com/randori/

Better ukemi -Judo falling techniques (breakfalls). (2013, October 23). Judoinfo.Com. https://Judoinfo.com/breakfalls/

Glossary of Judo terminology. (n.d.). Judo-Ch.Jp. Retrieved from https://www.Judo-ch.jp/english/dictionary/terms/taisabaki/

Judo basics -beginner's lessons. (2014, April 7). Judoinfo.Com. https://Judoinfo.com/Judo-basics-beginners/

Shizentai: Natural Posture. (n.d.). Kendo-Guide.Com. Retrieved from https://www.kendo-guide.com/shizentai.html

(N.d.). Netdna-Ssl.Com. Retrieved from https://3yryua3n3eu3i4gih2iopzph-wpengine.netdna-ssl.com/wp-content/uploads/2016/07/pdf/posture.pdf

All Judo hand techniques (Te-waza). (2014, April 13). Judoinfo.Com. https://Judoinfo.com/hand-techniques-tewaza/

Glossary of Judo terminology. (n.d.). Judo-Ch.Jp. Retrieved from https://www.Judo-ch.jp/english/dictionary/terms/tewaza/

Judo techniek -Te-waza. (2012, February 21).

Judo Throws -Hand Techniques -black belt wiki. (2018, September 9). Blackbeltwiki.Com. https://blackbeltwiki.com/Judo-throws-hand-techniques

Names of Judo Techniques. (n.d.). KodokanJudoinstitute.Org. Retrieved from http://kodokanJudoinstitute.org/en/waza/list/

Te-waza (手技) Hand throwing techniques | Judo guide. (2016, January 18).

Judo techniek -Koshi-waza. (2012, February 23).

Judo Throws -Hip Techniques -black belt wiki. (2018, September 9). Blackbeltwiki.Com. https://blackbeltwiki.com/Judo-throws-hip-techniques

Koshi waza -Hip techniques. (2016, April 10).

Koshi-waza. (n.d.). Judoenlignes.Com. Retrieved from
https://www.Judoenlignes.com/tachi-waza/nage-waza/koshi-waza/

Koshi-waza (腰技): hip throwing techniques. (n.d.). Akban.Org. Retrieved from
https://www.akban.org/wiki/Category:Koshi-waza_(%E8%85%B0%E6%8A%80):_hip_throwing_techniques

All Judo foot techniques (Ashi-Waza). (2014, April 13). Judoinfo.Com.
https://Judoinfo.com/foot-techniques-ashi-waza/

Ashi-waza -Compilation. (2019, May 16).

Ashi-waza (足技): foot throwing techniques. (n.d.). Akban.Org. Retrieved from
https://www.akban.org/wiki/Category:Ashi-waza_(%E8%B6%B3%E6%8A%80):_foot_throwing_techniques

Fairbrother, N. (2020, May 26). Ashi-waza: 5 best leg throws for beginners.
Kokakids.Co.Uk. https://www.kokakids.co.uk/ashi-waza

Glossary of Judo terminology. (n.d.). Judo-Ch.Jp. Retrieved from https://www.Judo-ch.jp/english/dictionary/terms/asiwaza/

Judo footsweeps in depth. (2020, January 24).

Glossary of Judo terminology. (n.d.). Retrieved from Judo-ch.jp website:
https://www.Judo-ch.jp/english/dictionary/terms/sutemi/

Glossary of Judo waza (techniques) terms. (n.d.). Retrieved from Judo-ch.jp website:
https://www.Judo-ch.jp/english/dictionary/technique/nage/masute/hikikomi/

Judo techniques. (n.d.). Retrieved from Ijf.org website:
https://Judo.ijf.org/techniques/Hane-makikomi

Sacrifice throws. (2016, August 15). Retrieved from Wordpress.com website:
https://lewesmartialarts.wordpress.com/the-techniques/throws/sacrifice-throws/

Sacrifice throws. (n.d.). Retrieved from Dpegan.com website:
https://www.dpegan.com/sacrifice-throws/

Ukemi: A fundamental technique for Judo beginners. (2019, December 30). Retrieved
from Amakella.com website: https://www.amakella.com/ukemi-Judo-breakfalls/

Aikido, G. (2016, September 21). Aikido Osae Waza Control or Pinning Techniques -
Good Aikido -Medium. Medium. https://medium.com/@Aikido/aikido-osae-waza-control-or-pinning-techniques-dd28678b687

Glossary of Judo terminology. (n.d.). Judo-Ch.Jp. Retrieved from https://www.Judo-ch.jp/english/dictionary/terms/osaekomi/

Judo -Pinning Techniques -black belt wiki. (2018, September 9). Blackbeltwiki.Com.
https://blackbeltwiki.com/Judo-pinning-techniques

Westermann, T. (n.d.). Osae komi waza -Pinning techniques. Judotechnik.Eu.
Retrieved from http://www.Judotechnik.eu/Katamewaza/en_osae.php

(N.d.). Quizlet.Com. Retrieved from https://quizlet.com/35724507/yawara-osae-waza-pinning-techniques-flash-cards/

Judo -Choking Techniques -black belt wiki. (2018, September 9). Blackbeltwiki.Com.
https://blackbeltwiki.com/Judo-choking-techniques

Judo Chokes (shimewaza) --choking techniques. (2013, October 23). Judoinfo.Com.
https://Judoinfo.com/chokes/

Shime Waza – Kyushin Ryu Jujitsu. (n.d.). Kyushinryujujitsu.Com. Retrieved from
http://www.kyushinryujujitsu.com/resources/techniques/shime-waza/

Strangles/Chokes (Shime-Waza). (n.d.). CirenJudo.Co.Uk. Retrieved from
https://www.cirenJudo.co.uk/strangles-chokes-shime-waza

Waza (Techniques). (n.d.). Judo-Ch.Jp. Retrieved from https://www.Judo-ch.jp/english/knowledge/technique/

Judo joint locks – kansetsu waza. (2018, June 3).

Kansetsu waza – Launceston Judo club -university of Tasmania Judo. (2020, December 4). LauncestonJudo.Com. https://launcestonJudo.com/kansetsu-waza/

Kansetsu-waza. (n.d.). Judoenlignes.Com. Retrieved from https://www.Judoenlignes.com/ne-waza/kansetsu-waza/

Glossary of Judo waza (techniques) terms. (n.d.). Judo-Ch.Jp. Retrieved from https://www.Judo-ch.jp/english/dictionary/technique/katame/kansetu/udehara/

Goshin Jutsu Kata. (2018, September 21). Blackbeltwiki.Com. https://blackbeltwiki.com/goshin-jutsu-kata

Judo self-defense forms: Goshin jutsu. (2013, October 23). Judoinfo.Com. https://Judoinfo.com/katagosh/

KuSakuraShop. (n.d.). How to choose Judo Kata weapons for the Goshin Jutsu no Kata. Kusakurashop.Com. Retrieved from https://www.kusakurashop.com/pages/Judo-kata-weapons-bokken-jo-tanto-pistol

(N.d.). KodokanJudoinstitute.Org. Retrieved from http://kodokanJudoinstitute.org/en/docs/goshin_jutsu.pdf

Belt Test Syllabus. (2013, July 13). Wordpress.Com. https://ucberkeleyJudo.wordpress.com/resources/belt-test-syllabus/

Judo ranking system and belt colours. (n.d.). Myactivesg.Com. Retrieved from https://www.myactivesg.com/Sports/Judo/How-To-Play/Judo-for-Beginners/Judo-ranking-system-and-belt-colours

Judo: The Japanese art of self-defense. (2013, October 23). Judoinfo.Com. https://Judoinfo.com/kano2/

mtc. (n.d.). Judo Competition Format. Teamscotland.Scot.

WHAT IS JUDO? (n.d.). Com.Au.

51 Judo exercises/drills you can do at home. (2020, March 25).

Davis, N. (2019, September 24). 30 at-home workout moves: 20-minute set, all levels, without equipment. Healthline.Com. https://www.healthline.com/health/fitness-exercise/at-home-workouts

Davis, N. (2020, September 24). 10 best exercises for everyone. Healthline.Com. https://www.healthline.com/health/fitness-exercise/10-best-exercises-everyday

Ellis, M. (2020, March 30). How often should you train Judo? [hint: It depends!]. Craftofcombat.Com. https://craftofcombat.com/how-often-should-you-train-Judo/

Strength training for Judo. (2013, October 23). Judoinfo.Com. https://Judoinfo.com/strengthtraining/

The ultimate guide of Judo exercises. (n.d.). EffectiveJudo.Com. Retrieved from https://effectiveJudo.com/the-ultimate-guide-of-Judo-exercises

7 reasons to learn SAMBO. (n.d.). Retrieved from Sambo.sport website: https://Sambo.sport/en/news/7-prichin-zanyatsya-Sambo

Puncher Staff. (2018, September 26). What is Sambo? The Russian combat martial art explained Retrieved from Punchermedia.com website: https://punchermedia.com/russian-Sambo-explained

Rousseau, R. (n.d.). Russian Sambo: History and Style Guide. Retrieved from Liveabout.com website: https://www.liveabout.com/history-and-style-guide-russian-Sambo-2308279

What is SAMBO? (1483). Retrieved from Insidethegames.biz website:

https://www.insidethegames.biz/articles/1045459/what-is-Sambo

Marc. (2021, May 15). BJJ vs Sambo: Key differences & similarities. Bjjsuccess.Com. https://www.bjjsuccess.com/bjj-vs-Sambo

Robert. (2021, March 15). Sambo vs judo: Differences and effectiveness. Wayofmartialarts.Com. https://wayofmartialarts.com/Sambo-vs-judo

Samhith. (n.d.). Difference between Sambo and wrestling. Differencebetween.Info. Retrieved
from http://www.differencebetween.info/difference-between-Sambo-and-wrestling

Super User. (n.d.). Judo Rules. Rulesofsport.Com. Retrieved from
https://www.rulesofsport.com/sports/judo.html

What martial art is the most effective: Sambo, Judo or BJJ? (n.d.). Quora.Com. Retrieved from https://www.quora.com/What-martial-art-is-the-most-effective-Sambo-Judo-or-BJJ

7 reasons to learn SAMBO. (n.d.). Sambo.Sport. Retrieved from
https://Sambo.sport/en/news/7-prichin-zanyatsya-Sambo

Does Sambo have a ranked belt system? What are the grades of each Sambo belt? (2020,
November 14). Budodragon.Com.
https://budodragon.com/does-Sambo-have-a-ranked-belt-system

Requirements to the Sambo uniform. (n.d.). Sambogear.Com. Retrieved from
https://Sambogear.com/en/pages/requirements-Sambo-uniform

r/Sambo - What does it take to be "Master of the sport" and is there an equivalent in other
combat sports e.g. a 9th degree red belt in BJJ. (n.d.). Reddit.Com. Retrieved from
https://www.reddit.com/r/Sambo/comments/93sy92/what_does_it_take_to_be_master_of_the_sport_and

Sambo – Overview – Physicalguru.com. (n.d.). Physicalguru.Com. Retrieved from
https://physicalguru.com/sports-games/Sambo-overview

Spot, B. (2017, November 23). How effective is the Sambo? Bjj-Spot.Com.
https://www.bjj-spot.com/how-effective-is-the-Sambo

What are the course fees of Mixed Martial Arts training? (n.d.). Quora.Com. Retrieved
from https://www.quora.com/What-are-the-course-fees-of-Mixed-Martial-Arts-training

Fanatics Authors. (n.d.). Top 5 Sambo Fusion Grappling Techniques for BJJ. Bjjfanatics.Com. Retrieved from https://bjjfanatics.com/blogs/news/top-5-Sambo-fusion-grappling-techniques-for-bjj

Kesting, S. (2021, March 1). Top 10 throws and takedowns for BJJ. Grapplearts.Com.
https://www.grapplearts.com/top-10-throws-and-takedowns-for-bjj

lvshaolin. (2019, December 9). 9 judo throws every beginner should learn. Lvshaolin.Com.
https://www.lvshaolin.com/judo-throws

The core concepts of throwing techniques. (2019, November 28). Ymaa.Com.
https://ymaa.com/articles/2019/12/the-core-concepts-of-throwing-techniques

BJJEE. (2020, January 15). How to use the "Georgian grip" to set up throws in BJJ. Bjjee.Com.
https://www.bjjee.com/videos/how-to-use-the-georgian-grip-to-set-up-throws-in-bjj

Five Grips All Grapplers Need to Know. (2021, February 4). Gumacliftonnj.Com.
https://gumacliftonnj.com/five-grips-all-grapplers-need-to-know

Heroes, B. J. J. (2016, October 25). Most common Jiu jitsu hand grips. Bjjheroes.Com. https://www.bjjheroes.com/techniques/most-common-hand-grips-in-jiu-jitsu

5 reasons you should learn self-defence. (2020, February 20). Retrieved from Com.au website: https://shirudoselfdefence.com.au/blog/5-reasons-you-should-learn-self-defence

Barlow, T. (2016, November 23). Three key concepts to defend any submission. Retrieved from Tombarlowonline.com website: https://tombarlowonline.com/three-key-concepts-to-defend-any-submission

Evolve, M. M. A. (2018, May 26). How to break grips in BJJ. Retrieved from Evolve-mma.com website: https://evolve-mma.com/blog/how-to-break-grips-in-bjj

Kongling, M. (2021, February 23). 3 self-defense striking techniques everyone should know. Retrieved from 6Dragonskungfu.com website: https://www.6dragonskungfu.com/3-self-defense-striking-techniques-everyone-should-know

The 5 most effective types of takedown defense. (n.d.). Retrieved from Nymaa.com website: https://www.nymaa.com/announcements/The-5-Most-Effective-Types-of-Takedown-Defense_AE210.html

Vorobiev, M. (2020, July 6). Combat SAMBO for Self-Defense. Retrieved from Firearmsnews.com website: https://www.firearmsnews.com/editorial/combat-Sambo-for-self-defense/378679

Ivanov, D. (2020, February 15). Does Sambo Have Striking Techniques? Mmaclan.Com. https://mmaclan.com/does-Sambo-have-striking-techniques

Ola. (2020, September 30). Striking in BJJ - all you need to know - BJJ spot. Bjj-Spot.Com. https://www.bjj-spot.com/striking-in-bjj-all-you-need-to-know

Marc. (2020, September 7). 40+ Brazilian Jiu-Jitsu submissions you need to know. Bjjsuccess.Com. https://www.bjjsuccess.com/brazilian-jiu-jitsu-submissions

Kesting, S. (2016, June 18). 37 powerful BJJ submissions for grapplers. Grapplearts.Com. https://www.grapplearts.com/37-powerful-bjj-submissions-for-grapplers

MMA Submission Holds - an online guide to mixed martial arts submissions. (2007, February 9). Mma-Training.Com. http://www.mma-training.com/mma-submission-holds

Armbar – BJJ submission explained. (2020, October 16). Lowkickmma.Com. https://www.lowkickmma.com/armbar

MMA Wiki.org Staff. (2014, February 13). Neck Crank. Mmawiki.org. https://www.mmawiki.org/en/neck-crank

Leg locks - positions & submissions - BJJ world. (2018, February 13). Bjj-World.Com. https://bjj-world.com/leg-locks-ultimate-guide-positions-submissions

Downright Nasty Sambo Submissions For BJJ. (2020, July 25). Bjj-World.Com. https://bjj-world.com/Sambo-submissions-for-bjj

Kesting, S. (2016, June 18). 37 powerful BJJ submissions for grapplers. Grapplearts.Com. https://www.grapplearts.com/37-powerful-bjj-submissions-for-grapplers

Kesting, S. (2020, July 24). The ultimate guide to BJJ solo drills. Grapplearts.Com. https://www.grapplearts.com/the-ultimate-guide-to-bjj-solo-drills

List of martial arts stretching techniques. (2018, September 7). Blackbeltwiki.Com. https://blackbeltwiki.com/stretching

No title. (n.d.). Jiujitsutimes.Com. Retrieved from https://www.jiujitsutimes.com/intermediate-bjj-building-submission-combinations

Unsymmetrical grips in judo, sambo and BJJ. https://forums.sherdog.com/threads/unsymmetrical-grips-in-judo-sambo-and-bjj.2823877/

Understanding Sambo https://matcraft.ca/blog/2018/2/13/understanding-sambo

Charles Gracie Jiu-Jitsu academy https://www.charlesgracie.com/tournament-scoring-system/

Murphy, S. (2007, March 17). All you need to know about: capoeira. The Guardian. http://www.theguardian.com/lifeandstyle/2007/mar/17/healthandwellbeing.features4

Rohrig Assuncao, M. (2004). Capoeira: The history of an Afro-Brazilian martial art. Routledge. https://www.discoverahobby.com/Capoeira

The Music and Song of Capoeira - Ginga Capoeira Regional — Ginga Capoeira Regional. (n.d.). Gingacapoeira.Com. Retrieved from http://gingacapoeira.com/music

Robert. (2021, January 3). Capoeira vs taekwondo: Which one is better for you? Wayofmartialarts.Com. https://wayofmartialarts.com/capoeira-vs-taekwondo

PeterSoto. (2021, May 12). What is Capoeira Roda? In Capoeira. Sportsandmartialarts.Com. https://sportsandmartialarts.com/capoeira-roda-capoeira

Roda of capoeira. (2018a, November 8). Decapoeira.Org. https://decapoeira.org/en/roda-de-capoeira

Howcast. (2012, October 15). What Are Capoeira & Jogo de Capoeira? Howcast. https://www.howcast.com/videos/508304-what-are-capoeira-jogo-de-capoeira-capoeira

Capoeira information. (n.d.). Tulane.Edu. Retrieved from http://www.tulane.edu/~capoeira/info.htm

The Capoeira belt system explained by a Capoeira teacher. (2019, October 19). Dendearts.Com. https://dendearts.com/the-capoeira-belt-system-explained-by-a-capoeira-teacher

Rank & Grading System. (n.d.). Capoeirabeiramar.Com. Retrieved from http://capoeirabeiramar.com/classes/rank-grading-system

5 benefits you can get from practicing capoeira. (n.d.). Redbull.Com. Retrieved September 20, 2021, from https://www.redbull.com/pk-en/5-mind-body-soul-benefits-capoeira

Benefits Of Capoeira. (n.d.). Capoeiraoxossilondon.Co.Uk. Retrieved from https://www.capoeiraoxossilondon.co.uk/benefits-of-capoeira

Capoeira's social impact. (n.d.). Lalaue.Com. Retrieved from https://www.lalaue.com/learn-capoeira/capoeiras-social-impact

Health Fitness Revolution. (2015, April 17). Top health benefits of capoeira. Healthfitnessrevolution.Com. https://www.healthfitnessrevolution.com/top-health-benefits-capoeira

Is Capoeira hard to learn? No, and here's why. (2020, May 25). Dendearts.Com. https://dendearts.com/is-capoeira-hard-to-learn-no-and-heres-why

Kingsford-Smith, A. (2013, August 12). Disguised in dance: The secret history of capoeira. Theculturetrip.Com; The Culture Trip. https://theculturetrip.com/south-america/brazil/articles/disguised-in-dance-the-secret-history-of-capoeira

Murphy, S. (2007, March 17). All you need to know about: capoeira. The Guardian. http://www.theguardian.com/lifeandstyle/2007/mar/17/healthandwellbeing.features4

Pelourinho, C. B. (2015, November 14). Top 11 reasons why you must try capoeira. Capoeirabrazilpelo.Com. http://www.capoeirabrazilpelo.com/trycapoeira

da India, S. (n.d.). Capoeira Styles. Capoeira.Online. Retrieved from https://capoeira.online/philosophy/styles

What are the different styles of capoeira? (2011, October 26). Capoeira-Connection.Com. http://capoeira-connection.com/capoeira/2011/10/what-are-the-different-styles-of-capoeira

Wood, J. (2020, July 27). Ginga! 10 Capoeira Movements for Beginners. Retrieved from Soweflow.com website: https://www.soweflow.com/blogs/journal/ginga-10-capoeira-movements-for-beginners

What are capoeira's main philosophies? (2011, October 26). Retrieved from Capoeira-connection.com website: http://capoeira-connection.com/capoeira/2011/10/what-are-capoeiras-main-philosophies

Perninha. (2020, November 13). 11 Basic Capoeira Moves To know, Practice & How to use them.

Capoeira moves, capoeira techniques, and tips for learning! (n.d.). Start-Playing-Capoeira.Com. Retrieved from https://www.start-playing-capoeira.com/capoeira-moves.html

Capoeira Movements. (2013, October 30). Wordpress.Com. https://draculinho.wordpress.com/capoeira-movements

Capoeira Movements. (2013, October 30). Wordpress.Com. https://draculinho.wordpress.com/capoeira-movements

lapinha. (2019, February 9). Is Capoeira the Best Martial Art for self-defense? Papoeira.Com. https://papoeira.com/en/is-capoeira-the-best-martial-art-for-self-defense

Moves. (n.d.). Weebly.Com. Retrieved from https://selfdefense-withcapoeira.weebly.com/moves.html

The complete list of capoeira ground movements/floreios. (2020, June 10). Retrieved from Dendearts.com website: https://dendearts.com/the-complete-list-of-capoeira-ground-movements-floreios

Atabaque · Grinnell college musical instrument collection · Grinnell college libraries. (n.d.). Retrieved from Grinnell.edu website: https://omeka-s.grinnell.edu/s/MusicalInstruments/item/1244

Capoeira and Music. (2018, November 9). Retrieved from Decapoeira.org website: https://decapoeira.org/en/capoeira-and-musica

Capoeira dance in natal: Iconic symbol of Brazilian culture. (2014, April 21). Retrieved from Natalriograndedonorte.com website: https://www.natalriograndedonorte.com/capoeira-dance-natal

Faze Staff. (2014, October 2). Capoeira: Where martial arts meet dance - faze. Retrieved from Faze.ca website: https://faze.ca/capoeira-where-martial-arts-meet-dance

Ganza Musica Brasilis. (n.d.). Retrieved from Musicabrasilis.com website: https://musicabrasilis.com/instruments/ganza

Gorlinski, V. (2018). Berimbau. In Encyclopedia Britannica.

Johnson, C. (2009, August 31). The history of breakdancing... In Capoeira? - GaijinPot InJapan. Retrieved from Gaijinpot.com website: https://injapan.gaijinpot.com/uncategorized/2009/08/31/the-history-of-breakdancing-in-capoeira

Juan Goncalves-Borrega, Smithsonian Center for Folklife and Cultural Heritage. (2017, September 21). How Brazilian capoeira evolved from a martial art to an international dance craze. Retrieved from Smithsonian Magazine website:

https://www.smithsonianmag.com/smithsonian-institution/capoeira-occult-martial-art-international-dance-180964924

Kingsford-Smith, A. (2013, August 12). Disguised in dance: The secret history of capoeira. Retrieved from Theculturetrip.com website: https://theculturetrip.com/south-america/brazil/articles/disguised-in-dance-the-secret-history-of-capoeira

Murphy, S. (2007, March 17). All you need to know about: capoeira. The Guardian. Retrieved from http://www.theguardian.com/lifeandstyle/2007/mar/17/healthandwellbeing.features4

Pandeiro | musical instrument. (n.d.). In Encyclopedia Britannica.

Reco-reco. (2013, July 5). Retrieved from Allaroundthisworld.com website: https://www.allaroundthisworld.com/learn/latin-america/latin-american-instruments/reco-reco

Schmitz, S. (2015, February 5). World Music instrument: The agogô. Retrieved from Centerforworldmusic.org website: https://centerforworldmusic.org/2015/02/world-music-instruments-agogo

Style, B. O., & View my complete profile. (n.d.). Breaking and Capoeira. Retrieved from Breakingandcapoeira.com website: https://www.breakingandcapoeira.com/2019/02/the-influence-of-capoeira-on-breaking.html

The Editors of Encyclopedia Britannica. (2020). Capoeira. In Encyclopedia Britannica.

Capoeira fitness , stay in shape and prevent injuries! (n.d.). Start-Playing-Capoeira.Com. Retrieved from https://www.start-playing-capoeira.com/capoeira-fitness.html

Health Fitness Revolution. (2015, April 17). Top health benefits of capoeira. Healthfitnessrevolution.Com. https://www.healthfitnessrevolution.com/top-health-benefits-capoeira

Kuska, A. M. (2020, March 20). Is capoeira the secret to fitness? Myvetcandy.Com; Vet Candy. https://www.myvetcandy.com/livingblog/2020/3/20/is-capoeira-the-secret-to-fitness

What to expect — capoeira fitness DC. (n.d.). Capoeirafitnessdc.Com. Retrieved from https://www.capoeirafitnessdc.com/new-page

Improving your workouts with Capoeira. (2018, August 15). Brazilianculturalinstitute.Org. https://brazilianculturalinstitute.org/blog/improving-workouts-capoeira

Balacdo, V. A. P. (2017, June 12). 10 tips to be a better student in Capoeira by CM Xara. Cdohawaii.Org. https://cdohawaii.org/2017/06/11/10-tips-to-be-a-better-student-in-capoeira

Imags References

[1] *Antimenes Painter, CC BY 2.5 <https://creativecommons.org/licenses/by/2.5>, via Wikimedia Commons: https://commons.wikimedia.org/wiki/File:Boxers_Panathenaic_Met_06.1021.51.jpg*

[2] *See page for author, CC BY-SA 3.0 NL <https://creativecommons.org/licenses/by-sa/3.0/nl/deed.en>, via Wikimedia Commons https://commons.wikimedia.org/wiki/File:Muhammad_Ali_1966.jpg*

[3] *Brian Birzer http://www.brianbirzer.com, CC BY 2.0 <https://creativecommons.org/licenses/by/2.0>, via Wikimedia Commons https://commons.wikimedia.org/wiki/File:Mike_Tyson_Portrait_lighting_corrected.jpg*

[4] *ian mcwilliams, CC BY 2.0 <https://creativecommons.org/licenses/by/2.0>, via Wikimedia Commons: https://commons.wikimedia.org/wiki/File:Floyd_Mayweather,_Jr._vs._Juan_Manuel_M%C3%A1rquez.jpg*

[5] *https://pxhere.com/en/photo/1044044*

[6] *https://www.pexels.com/photo/boxing-gloves-and-mitts-over-the-grass-5836652/*

[7] *https://www.pexels.com/photo/blurred-sportswoman-demonstrating-technique-of-hand-bandaging-7991696/*

[8] *https://www.pexels.com/photo/smiling-man-wearing-mouth-guard-and-boxing-gloves-7289912/*

[9] *https://unsplash.com/photos/qPhXapAS2Ss?utm_source=unsplash&utm_medium=referral&utm_content=creditShareLink*

[10] *https://www.publicdomainpictures.net/en/view-image.php?image=424842&picture=bicycles-abdominal-workout*

[11] *photographer: Alfred Grohs, CC BY 3.0 <https://creativecommons.org/licenses/by/3.0>, via Wikimedia Commons: https://commons.wikimedia.org/wiki/File:Adolf_Grohs_Boxer_Kurt_Prenzel_Bildseite_(cropped).jpg*

[12] *Alain Delmas (France), CC BY-SA 3.0 <http://creativecommons.org/licenses/by-sa/3.0/>, via Wikimedia Commons: https://commons.wikimedia.org/wiki/File:Slip1.jpg*

[13] *Alain Delmas (France), CC BY-SA 3.0 <http://creativecommons.org/licenses/by-sa/3.0/>, via Wikimedia Commons: https://commons.wikimedia.org/wiki/File:Jab3.jpg*

[14] *Delmas Alain, CC BY-SA 3.0 <https://creativecommons.org/licenses/by-sa/3.0>, via Wikimedia Commons: https://commons.wikimedia.org/wiki/File:Retrait4color.jpg*

[15] *Alain Delmas (France), CC BY-SA 3.0 <http://creativecommons.org/licenses/by-sa/3.0/>, via Wikimedia Commons: https://commons.wikimedia.org/wiki/File:Lecon_crochet.jpg*

[16] *Alain Delmas (France), CC BY-SA 2.5 <https://creativecommons.org/licenses/by-sa/2.5>, via Wikimedia Commons: https://commons.wikimedia.org/wiki/File:Uppercut2.jpg*

[17] *Delmas Alain, CC BY-SA 3.0 <https://creativecommons.org/licenses/by-sa/3.0>, via Wikimedia Commons: https://commons.wikimedia.org/wiki/File:Retrait2color.jpg*

[18] *Alain Delmas (France), CC BY-SA 3.0 <http://creativecommons.org/licenses/by-sa/3.0/>, via Wikimedia Commons: https://commons.wikimedia.org/wiki/File:Drop5.jpg*

[19] *https://unsplash.com/photos/HG1pkXN7SVA?utm_source=unsplash&utm_medium=referral&utm_content=creditShareLink*

[20] *https://unsplash.com/photos/misTB4pmevc?utm_source=unsplash&utm_medium=referral&utm_content=creditShareLink*

[21] *https://unsplash.com/photos/5Ua3axiD0kA?utm_source=unsplash&utm_medium=referral&utm_content=creditShareLink*

[22] https://unsplash.com/photos/8Naac6Zpv28?utm_source=unsplash&utm_medium=referral&utm_content=creditShareLink

[23] Gerrit Phil Baumann, CC BY 3.0 <https://creativecommons.org/licenses/by/3.0>, via Wikimedia Commons: https://commons.wikimedia.org/wiki/File:Muay_Thai_Fight_Us_Vs_Burma_(80668065).jpeg

[24] Alain Delmas (France), CC BY-SA 3.0 <http://creativecommons.org/licenses/by-sa/3.0/>, via Wikimedia Commons: https://commons.wikimedia.org/wiki/File:Jab3.jpg

[25] Delmas Alain, CC BY-SA 3.0 <https://creativecommons.org/licenses/by-sa/3.0>, via Wikimedia Commons: https://commons.wikimedia.org/wiki/File:Retrait4color.jpg

[26] https://www.pexels.com/photo/man-doing-boxing-163403/

[27] https://commons.wikimedia.org/wiki/File:Uppercut_(PSF).png

[28] Delmas Alain, CC BY-SA 3.0 <https://creativecommons.org/licenses/by-sa/3.0>, via Wikimedia Commons: https://commons.wikimedia.org/wiki/File:Drop4color.jpg

[29] Alain Delmas France), CC BY-SA 3.0 <https://creativecommons.org/licenses/by-sa/3.0>, via Wikimedia Commons: https://commons.wikimedia.org/wiki/File:Drop1color.jpg

[30] Delmas Alain, CC BY-SA 3.0 <https://creativecommons.org/licenses/by-sa/3.0>, via Wikimedia Commons: https://commons.wikimedia.org/wiki/File:Spin-back-fist.jpg

[31] Delmas Alain, CC BY-SA 3.0 <https://creativecommons.org/licenses/by-sa/3.0>, via Wikimedia Commons: https://commons.wikimedia.org/wiki/File:Flying-punch.jpg

[32] Krystof Gauthier (France), CC BY-SA 3.0 <https://creativecommons.org/licenses/by-sa/3.0>, via Wikimedia Commons: https://commons.wikimedia.org/wiki/File:Lethwei-Hight-kick.jpg

[33] https://unsplash.com/photos/1jaXXVuPRDc?utm_source=unsplash&utm_medium=referral&utm_content=creditShareLink

[34] https://commons.wikimedia.org/wiki/File:USMC-081025-M-0884D-005.jpg

[35] https://commons.wikimedia.org/wiki/File:USMC-120215-M-SR181-138.jpg

[36] Claus Michelfelder, CC BY-SA 4.0 <https://creativecommons.org/licenses/by-sa/4.0>, via Wikimedia Commons: https://commons.wikimedia.org/wiki/File:WKA_World_Championship_2012_Munich_444.JPG

[37] https://unsplash.com/photos/WX7FSaiYxK8?utm_source=unsplash&utm_medium=referral&utm_content=creditShareLink

[38] https://unsplash.com/photos/o6h-CuvAypE?utm_source=unsplash&utm_medium=referral&utm_content=creditShareLink

[39] https://www.pexels.com/photo/plus-size-woman-standing-on-scale-6551401/

[40] https://www.pexels.com/photo/young-determined-man-training-alone-on-street-sports-ground-in-sunny-day-3768901/

[41] https://www.pexels.com/photo/woman-in-green-sports-bra-and-black-leggings-doing-leg-lunges-999257/

[42] https://commons.wikimedia.org/wiki/File:Submission_wrestling.jpg

[43] daysofthundr46, CC BY-SA 2.0 <https://creativecommons.org/licenses/by-sa/2.0>, via Wikimedia Commons: https://commons.wikimedia.org/wiki/File:Antonio_Thomas_with_armbar.jpg

[44] https://commons.wikimedia.org/wiki/File:DF-SD-01-06921.jpg

[45] https://www.pexels.com/photo/man-in-black-t-shirt-and-black-shorts-standing-on-brown-wooden-floor-4753985/

[46] https://www.pexels.com/photo/people-workout-using-resistance-bands-6516206/

[47] https://unsplash.com/photos/DCqXIFXoqr0?utm_source=unsplash&utm_medium=referral&utm_content=creditShareLink

[48] *Gage Skidmore from Peoria, AZ, United States of America, CC BY-SA 2.0 <https://creativecommons.org/licenses/by-sa/2.0>, via Wikimedia Commons: https://commons.wikimedia.org/wiki/File:John_Cena_July_2018.jpg*

[49] https://unsplash.com/photos/UpFy6jbnXS4?utm_source=unsplash&utm_medium=referral&utm_content=creditShareLink

[50] *Martin Rulsch, Wikimedia Commons, CC BY-SA 4.0, CC BY-SA 4.0 <https://creativecommons.org/licenses/by-sa/4.0>, via Wikimedia Commons: https://commons.wikimedia.org/wiki/File:K1PL_Berlin_2018-09-16_Female_Kata_108.jpg*

[51] *Haresh karate, CC BY-SA 4.0 <https://creativecommons.org/licenses/by-sa/4.0>, via Wikimedia Commons: https://commons.wikimedia.org/wiki/File:Karate_Kata_Heian_Nidan.jpg*

[52] *Haresh karate, CC BY-SA 4.0 <https://creativecommons.org/licenses/by-sa/4.0>, via Wikimedia Commons: https://commons.wikimedia.org/wiki/File:Karate_Kata_Heian_Yondan_Pattern.jpg*

[53] *Regine Becker, Copyrighted free use, via Wikimedia Commons: https://commons.wikimedia.org/wiki/File:MaeWashiGeri.jpg*

[54] *User:Evdcoldeportes, CC BY-SA 2.5 CO <https://creativecommons.org/licenses/by-sa/2.5/co/deed.en>, via Wikimedia Commons: https://commons.wikimedia.org/wiki/File:EVD-kumite-119.jpg*

[55] https://www.pexels.com/photo/men-doing-martial-arts-8611418/

[56] https://www.pexels.com/photo/woman-wearing-white-karati-g-under-blue-sky-3023756/

[57] https://www.pexels.com/photo/man-running-on-sand-field-2827392/

[58] https://unsplash.com/de/fotos/mann-in-weissem-hemd-und-schwazer-hose-sitzt-auf-schwarzem-stuhl-auf-grunem-grasfeld-DE2VQvh2_H8

[59] https://pixabay.com/photos/yoga-taoism-zen-meditation-4536546/

[60] https://unsplash.com/fr/photos/personnes-portant-du-karate-ji-Xl-ilWBKJNk

[61] *Photo by Márton Szalai on Unsplash* https://unsplash.com/photos/man-in-crew-neck-t-shirt-standing-on-grass-field-in-grayscale-photography-TrY_YA-xx4o

[62] https://unsplash.com/photos/man-doing-karate-stunts-on-gym-ngd2uo1evZg

[63] https://unsplash.com/photos/man-in-blue-jacket-and-blue-denim-jeans-standing-on-brown-wooden-log-surrounded-by-green-G548PsS5v2I

[64] https://unsplash.com/photos/person-holding-persons-hand-nRW4I8kuvd8

[65] https://pixabay.com/photos/taekwondo-battle-boxing-kick-leg-1866285/

[66] https://pixabay.com/photos/sport-fitness-workout-gym-crossfit-1283791/

[67] https://www.pexels.com/photo/man-doing-karate-on-the-street-5081179/

[68] https://www.pexels.com/photo/men-practicing-taekwondo-7045486/

[69] https://www.pexels.com/photo/hands-striking-the-man-s-forearm-7045470/

[70] https://www.pexels.com/photo/people-woman-girl-dancing-7045643/

[71] https://www.pexels.com/photo/man-love-people-woman-7045627/

[72] https://unsplash.com/photos/person-holding-persons-hand-nRW4I8kuvd8

[73] https://www.publicdomainpictures.net/en/view-image.php?image=288755&picture=kung-fu-master

[74] *Kevin Poh, CC BY 2.0 <https://creativecommons.org/licenses/by/2.0>, via Wikimedia Commons* https://commons.wikimedia.org/wiki/File:Shaolin_Kung_Fu.jpg

[75] *Benjamin Korankye, CC BY-SA 4.0 <https://creativecommons.org/licenses/by-sa/4.0>, via Wikimedia Commons* https://commons.wikimedia.org/wiki/File:Emp_Qorankye.jpg

[76] *Photo by SOON SANTOS on Unsplash https://unsplash.com/photos/men-doing-karate-in-park--XGqShGxO8E*

[77] *Photo by Uriel Soberanes on Unsplash https://unsplash.com/photos/man-doing-karate-stunts-on-gym-ngd2uo1eyZg*

[78] *Photo by Thao LEE on Unsplash https://unsplash.com/photos/man-wearing-karate-gi-standing-on-road-UpFv6jbnXS4*

[79] *Photo by SOON SANTOS on Unsplash https://unsplash.com/photos/two-men-about-to-sparring-sab37qbGmHc*

[80] *Photo by RDNE Stock project https://www.pexels.com/photo/shirtless-man-kicking-a-punching-bag-7187986/*

[81] *https://www.cleanpng.com/png-kodokan-judo-institute-jujutsu-martial-arts-united-2848649/*

[82] *President.az, CC BY 4.0 <https://creativecommons.org/licenses/by/4.0>, via Wikimedia Commons https://commons.wikimedia.org/wiki/File:Sambo_at_the_2015_European_Games.jpg*

[83] *Korea.net / Korean Culture and Information Service (Photographer name), CC BY-SA 2.0 <https://creativecommons.org/licenses/by-sa/2.0>, via Wikimedia Commons https://commons.wikimedia.org/wiki/File:KOCIS_Korea_Judo_Kim_Jaebum_London_36_(769 6361164).jpg*

[84] *CFS SAMBO FRANCE, CC BY-SA 2.0 <https://creativecommons.org/licenses/by-sa/2.0>, via Wikimedia Commons https://commons.wikimedia.org/wiki/File:Grand_Prix_Paris_de_Sambo_IMG_1923_(34152646 253).jpg*

[85] *https://commons.wikimedia.org/wiki/File:0432-SahinThrowsWood.jpg*

[86] *https://pixabay.com/photos/jiu-jitsu-fight-martial-arts-2184597/*

[87] *https://www.pxfuel.com/en/free-photo-jdshl*

[88] *CFS SAMBO FRANCE, CC BY-SA 2.0 <https://creativecommons.org/licenses/by-sa/2.0>, via Wikimedia Commons https://commons.wikimedia.org/wiki/File:Grand_Prix_Paris_de_Sambo_2017_IMG_2953_(341 24379334).jpg*

[89] *Michael Hultström, CC BY-SA 3.0 <https://creativecommons.org/licenses/by-sa/3.0>, via Wikimedia Commons https://commons.wikimedia.org/wiki/File:O-soto-gari.jpg*

[90] *Ricardo André Frantz (User:Tetraktys), CC BY-SA 3.0 <https://creativecommons.org/licenses/by-sa/3.0>, via Wikimedia Commons https://commons.wikimedia.org/wiki/File:Roda_de_capoeira1.jpg*

[91] *Photo by DCL "650" on Unsplash https://unsplash.com/photos/woman-in-white-long-sleeve-shirt-and-black-pants-running-on-beach-shore-during-daytime-DNRijpvOIdg*

[92] *TheTurducken, CC BY 2.0 <https://creativecommons.org/licenses/by/2.0>, via Wikimedia Commons https://commons.wikimedia.org/wiki/File:Capoeira_Angola_Palmares,_Rabo_de_arraia.jpg*

[93] *Photo by Jason Briscoe on Unsplash https://unsplash.com/photos/silhouette-of-person-kicking-on-mid-air-HN_4K2diUWs*

[94] *MartialArtsNomad.com, CC BY 2.0 <https://creativecommons.org/licenses/by/2.0>, via Wikimedia Commons https://commons.wikimedia.org/wiki/File:The_Ginga-Abada_Capoeira.jpg*

[95] *Ferradura, CC BY 3.0 <https://creativecommons.org/licenses/by/3.0>, via Wikimedia Commons https://commons.wikimedia.org/wiki/File:Au_martelo.JPG*

[96] *Secretaria Especial da Cultura do Ministério da Cidadania, CC BY 2.0 <https://creativecommons.org/licenses/by/2.0>, via Wikimedia Commons https://commons.wikimedia.org/wiki/File:Patrim%C3%B4nio_Imaterial_Capoeira_(4918892936 7).jpg*

[97] *TheTurducken, CC BY 2.0 <https://creativecommons.org/licenses/by/2.0>, via Wikimedia Commons https://commons.wikimedia.org/wiki/File:Rabo_de_arraia_%26_negativa.jpg*

Djino, CC BY-SA 3.0 <https://creativecommons.org/licenses/by-sa/3.0>, via Wikimedia Commons https://commons.wikimedia.org/wiki/File:Esquiva_invertida1.jpg

[99] No machine-readable author provided. ST assumed (based on copyright claims)., Attribution, via Wikimedia Commons https://commons.wikimedia.org/wiki/File:CapoeiraMeialuaDeCompasso%26QuedaDeQuatro_ST_05.jpg

[100] Taken by Efrat Gruner, Edited by Ester Inbar (user:ST - he:user:ST), Attribution, via Wikimedia Commons https://commons.wikimedia.org/wiki/File:CapoeiraNegativa_ST_05.jpg

[101] No machine-readable author provided. ST assumed (based on copyright claims)., Attribution, via Wikimedia Commons https://commons.wikimedia.org/wiki/File:CapoeiraBencao_ST_05.jpg

[102] Alper Çuğun, CC BY 2.0 <https://creativecommons.org/licenses/by/2.0>, via Wikimedia Commons https://commons.wikimedia.org/wiki/File:Illustir_-_271675072.jpg

[103] Image by Alper Çuğun https://creativecommons.org/licenses/by/2.0/ https://www.flickr.com/photos/12505664@N00/2093817286

[104] Marie-Lan Nguyen, CC BY 2.5 <https://creativecommons.org/licenses/by/2.5>, via Wikimedia Commons https://commons.wikimedia.org/wiki/File:Capoeira_demonstration_Master_de_fleuret_2013_t22_1419.jpg

[105] Alno, CC BY-SA 3.0 <http://creativecommons.org/licenses/by-sa/3.0/>, via Wikimedia Commons https://commons.wikimedia.org/wiki/File:Pandeiro.JPG

[106] Photo by Alex Shaw on Unsplash https://unsplash.com/photos/woman-in-black-tank-top-and-black-pants-doing-yoga-mSJsiQCm6og

[107] Foto de Alex Shaw en Unsplash https://unsplash.com/es/fotos/chica-con-camiseta-verde-y-pantalones-grises-haciendo-yoga-en-una-alfombra-de-yoga-rosa-3HC9SIS7H_8

[108] Red CreaDeporte, CC BY 2.0 <https://creativecommons.org/licenses/by/2.0>, via Wikimedia Commons https://commons.wikimedia.org/wiki/File:Capoeira_(13597506973).jpg

[109] Foto de kike vega en Unsplash https://unsplash.com/es/fotos/fotografia-de-silueta-de-mujer-haciendo-yoga-F2qh3yjz6Jk

[110] Estela Neto, CC BY-SA 4.0 <https://creativecommons.org/licenses/by-sa/4.0>, via Wikimedia Commons https://commons.wikimedia.org/wiki/File:Roda_de_Capoeira_tradicional_do_Engenho_da_Rainha_3.jpg